D0706807

THE MODERN DEFENSE INDUSTRY

THE MODERN DEFENSE INDUSTRY

Political, Economic, and Technological Issues

RICHARD A. BITZINGER, EDITOR

PRAEGER SECURITY INTERNATIONAL
An Imprint of ABC-CLIO, LLC

A B C CLIO

Santa Barbara, California • Denver, Colorado • Oxford, England

Copyright 2009 by Richard A. Bitzinger

All rights reserved. No part of this publication may be reproduced,
stored in a retrieval system, or transmitted, in any form or by any means,
electronic, mechanical, photocopying, recording, or otherwise, except
for the inclusion of brief quotations in a review, without prior permission
in writing from the publisher.

Library of Congress Cataloging-in-Publication Data

The modern defense industry : political, economic, and technological issues /
Richard A. Bitzinger, editor.
     p. cm.
  Includes bibliographical references and index.
  ISBN 978-0-275-99475-4 (alk. paper) — ISBN 978-1-56720-749-1 (ebook)
 1. Defense industries. 2. Weapons industry. 3. Globalization.
4. Defense industries—International cooperation. 5. Weapons industry—
International cooperation. I. Bitzinger, Richard.
  HD9743.A2M63 2009
  338.4'7355—dc22   2009030408

13 12 11 10 09   1 2 3 4 5

This book is also available on the World Wide Web as an eBook.
Visit www.abc-clio.com for details.

ABC-CLIO, LLC
130 Cremona Drive, P.O. Box 1911
Santa Barbara, California 93116-1911

This book is printed on acid-free paper ∞
Manufactured in the United States of America

To my father,
Howard A. Bitzinger (1926–2009)

CONTENTS

PREFACE AND ACKNOWLEDGMENTS

It is arguable that, before World War II, there was no global arms industry to speak of, and it certainly did not exist on the same scale as it does today. To be sure, there were armories producing rifles and cannon, shipyards constructing warships of all manner and classes, and during the 1920s and 1930s, aircraft companies manufacturing fighter planes and bombers. At the same time, however, arms manufacturing throughout much of history was small beer—a minor business, and a rather sporadic one at that, rising and falling as wars and conflict waxed and waned. This was reflected in the attention, or more precisely, the *lack* of attention that the defense industry generally received from scholars and other observers, especially political scientists and economists. Aside from a few studies done after World War I on such companies as Krupp, Maxim, and Vickers (the "Merchants of Death" school of literature), there was relatively little serious scholarly effort put into studying the world's arms industry before World War II.

This all changed after that war and the subsequent cold war, largely because those two conflicts dramatically impacted the scale, scope, and character of the global arms industry. After 1939, globalized conflict, in one form or another, became more or less permanent, and as a result, the defense industry also became permanent. Continual warfare, or, during the cold war, the ever-present threat of a serious military confrontation between East and West, required a large, stable, and enduring arms industry capable of churning out the latest and most up-to-date machinery of death. Consequently, the United States progressed almost seamlessly from being the "Arsenal of Democracy" to harboring the military-industrial complex. During this same period, defense industries in Western Europe and the Soviet Union (and its successor state, the Russian Federation) also continued to grow, in size, scope, and technological sophistication, and, like a weed, armaments production spread to other parts of the world, particularly China, Israel, India, South Africa, and Brazil.

As the arms industry expanded in terms of national security significance, economic importance, and technological complexity, its profile also increased, and this triggered an explosion of scholarly study of the global defense industry after 1945. Today, the arms industry is as closely and as intently scrutinized as the automobile, electronics, or financial sectors. And yet many of these studies have ultimately been wanting and unsatisfactory, due to the fact that they are too often fixated on examining highly contemporary events and developments. The challenge with analyzing and assessing the arms industry is that is a constantly mutating and evolving sector. It has experienced considerable stresses and faced considerable difficulties, particularly in the post–cold war era, and it is still dealing with these stresses and difficulties. Consequently, most studies addressing the global arms industry tend to be snapshots of a subject undergoing continual change and transformation.

Hence, this book attempts to be more of a reference volume than a mere collection of essays on the contemporary nature of arms manufacturing, and it attempts to address the phenomenon of the global arms industry from a broader and more historical perspective. Hopefully, therefore, it will have a longer-lasting salience and usefulness for readers, provide them with a deeper knowledge of the global arms industry that can outlast even the shelf life of this work, and educate them so that they can apply what they learn in this volume to subsequent developments involving this constantly evolving industry.

This work consists of two sections. The first section is a collection of essays on the broad subject of the modern arms industry. Following a broad introduction to the challenges facing the global arms industry in the 21st century (Bitzinger), the book first addresses a number of contextual issues in the contemporary defense industry, including trends and developments in the global arms market since the end of the cold war (Dunne and the SIPRI Arms Production Staff), the role of what is called the *iron triangle* in defense procurement (Matthews), the existence and impact of hierarchies in global arms manufacturing (Neuman and Finnegan), the globalization process and its effect on the arms industry, and finally the promises and challenges being brought about by the growing applicability of commercial technologies to defense needs.

The second part of this section covers the modern arms industry from several regional perspectives, focusing mainly on key arms-producing countries or regions, including the United States (Dombrowski and Ross), Western Europe (Bitzinger), Russia (Kogan), and China (Boutin). Additionally, the experiences of emerging, aspiring arms manufacturers in the developing world are addressed here (Boutin).

Thirdly, the book deals with the relationship between the defense industry and the global arms trade, including arms export controls and their connection to national defense industries (Cevasco), the role of offsets and other types of international industrial participation in promoting arms transfers (Udis), and finally the current state of play in the global production and trafficking of small arms (Karp).

Finally, the second section of the book (Appendices I, II, and III) contains a lexicon of helpful terms, organizations, legislation, defense firms, and other references commonly used in discussions and explorations of the defense sector.

I am grateful to many people who helped make this work a reality. Of course, I owe a debt of gratitude to the book's many contributors, who gave willingly of their time and effort to this project. I am also particularly grateful to Ken Boutin and Curie Maharani for their assistance and contributions above and beyond the call of duty. Additionally, I would particularly like to thank the S. Rajaratnam School of International Studies (RSIS) in Singapore, and especially Barry Desker, dean of RSIS, and my supervisor, Dr. Bernard F. W. Loo, for their backing and encouragement in the production of this work. Finally and above all, I want to thank my family, especially my daughters Jennifer and Amy, for their love, affection, and support during the often trying times of finishing this book.

Richard A. Bitzinger
Singapore, May 2009

1

Introduction: Challenges Facing the Global Arms Industry in the 21st Century

Richard A. Bitzinger

As stated in the preface, the global arms industry is a dynamic phenomenon, a constantly moving target. It expands and contracts, it undergoes phases of growth and prosperity and phases of crisis and decline, both on a historical and on a regional basis, and often the two are not in sync with each other. This makes sweeping generalizations about the current and future likely state of the global arms industry, and about the process of global armaments production in general, rather difficult. The 1990s, for instance, were a period of relative upheaval and uncertainty, as defense industries around the world faced a new international reality—military, political, and economic—brought about by the collapse of the Soviet Union and the end of the cold war. The subsequent defense drawdown—which was largely global—forced a severe restructuring and retrenchment of defense-industrial bases almost everywhere. In contrast, the first decade of the 21st century appeared to be one of stabilization and growth—even boom times—for the global arms industry, as military spending rebounded or as large, long-anticipated military programs (particularly in Western Europe, e.g., the Eurofighter Typhoon, the Rafale fighter jet, the NH-90 helicopter, all of which had their start in the 1980s or 1990s) finally entered into production.

The question today is: Will the global arms industry over the next decade or so resemble more the 1990s or the 2000s? Will the expansion continue, or is another contraction sure to follow, given the highly cyclical nature of this particular business sector? And in any event, bust or boom, how will the global arms industry evolve and transform, in terms of size, structure, ownership, and so on? Those are the questions that shape and guide the subsequent chapters in this volume.

That said, there are basically five main factors that appear to be affecting the global defense industry today, which in turn may propel future changes and transformations when it comes to the structure, organization, activities, and processes of this industry. These ground truths influencing and shaping the course of the global arms industry are (1) the hierarchical nature of the global process of armaments production; (2) the impact of military spending upon the defense industry; (3) the effect of the international arms trade; (4) the process of defense-industrial globalization; and (5) the emerging information technologies-based revolution in military affairs.

THE HIERARCHICAL NATURE OF THE GLOBAL ARMS INDUSTRY

It has long been accepted that the global arms industry is hierarchical, and this can greatly affect the nature of armaments production in a given nation and its role and relationship within the global defense business.[1] Although there are no generally agreed upon criteria for how arms-producing nations may be compartmentalized, it is customary to divide the global defense industry into three or four tiers. Keith Krause, for example, defines the first tier of arms suppliers as the *critical innovators* at the technological frontier of arms production, and he confines this group to the United States and the former Soviet Union. He places most of Western Europe into a second tier of *adapters and modifiers* of advanced military technologies. Finally, all remaining arms-producing countries he puts into a third-tier of *copiers* and *reproducers* of existing defense technologies.[2] Andrew Ross accepts Krause's definition of the first tier (i.e., the United States and the USSR), but he places China, along with the major arms producers in the industrialized world (specifically France, Germany, Italy, Japan, Sweden, and the United Kingdom) into his category of second-tier producer-states. Ross then puts most other arms-producing countries—i.e., the developing, newly industrialized, and smaller industrialized nations—into a category of third-tier producers (e.g., Brazil, Israel, India, South Korea, and Taiwan). Finally, he also has a fourth tier of countries with only very limited capabilities for arms production (e.g., Mexico and Nigeria).[3] Bitzinger defines the first tier as comprising the United States and the four largest European arms producers (Britain, France, Germany, and Italy). His second tier comprises a catholic group of countries: (1) industrialized countries possessing small and/or bounded but often quite sophisticated defense industries, such as Australia, Canada, the Czech Republic, Norway, Japan, and Sweden; (2) developing or newly industrialized countries containing modest military-industrial complexes, such as Argentina, Brazil, Indonesia, Iran, Israel, Singapore, South Africa, South Korea, Taiwan, and Turkey; and (3) developing states with large, broad-based defense industries but still lacking the independent research and development (R&D) and industrial capacities to develop and produce highly sophisticated conventional arms (i.e., China and India). Third-tier states are defined as those possessing very limited and generally low-tech arms-production capabilities; countries in this group would include Egypt, Mexico, and Nigeria.[4]

In any event, where a nation roughly falls in the hierarchy of arms-producing states will greatly determine how it will be affected by, and how it might respond to, changes and developments in the global defense business. The five or six top arms-producing states (the United States, the United Kingdom, France, Germany, Russia, and Italy) possess the world's largest and most technologically advanced defense industries, and together they account for roughly 85 percent of all of the world's armaments production.[5] Moreover, they dominate— either singularly or *collectively* (particularly in the case of the major West European arms producers, who are increasingly regionalizing their arms production activities)—the global defense R&D process. Consequently, actions taken by these countries regarding their defense sectors will have profound repercussions for the rest of the global arms industry.

Moreover, however much the larger arms-producing states have been pummeled by developments, the long-term viability of these countries' defense industries is probably never in doubt. Western defense firms may contract, merge, or globalize (see below), and governments may be compelled to underwrite their activities (via state ownership or preferred supplier arrangements), but the large arms-producing countries are unlikely to lose their across-the-board arms production capabilities, even on a national scale. The same cannot be said for the lesser, second- or third-tier of arms-producing states, however. For them, the issue is not simply one of dealing with budget uncertainties and supply and demand—increasingly, it is a matter of sheer survival. These countries' defense industries face many existential challenges that will affect their continued economic/technological viability and autarky, such as the rising cost of military R&D and advanced armaments production; difficulties in accessing (either through importation or through indigenous efforts) state-of-the-art military technologies; and a highly competitive international arms market that discriminates against non-Western suppliers. In most cases, second- or third-tier arms-producing countries must deal with a Hobson's choice of either putting considerably greater efforts and resources into retaining autarky (with no guarantee of success), or accepting an integrated but subordinate role in an increasingly globalized and interdependent defense industry.

DEFENSE SPENDING

Perhaps nothing has impacted the global arms industry more than military spending, and the past two decades have been a roller coaster for global defense expenditures. In the early 1990s, the collapse of Communism and the end of the cold war resulted in major cuts in defense spending. Global defense budgets fell by nearly 35 percent from 1989 to 1999. Defense spending as a percentage of global gross national product (GNP) fell by nearly half, from 4.7 percent to 2.4 percent, while worldwide per capita spending on defense dropped from $254 to $142. In addition, the size of the world's armed forces declined from 28.6 million in 1989 to 21.3 million in 1999. In the United States alone, defense expenditures fell 28 percent in real terms during the 1990s. Among the leading European arms-producing states, total defense spending fell 12 percent between 1991 and 2004, from $194 billion to $170 billion, as measured in constant 2003 U.S. dollars, according to data compiled by the Stockholm International Peace Research Institute (SIPRI). French military expenditures fell by 8 percent over this period, Britain's defense budget declined by 12 percent, and German military spending dropped 30 percent.[6]

Other data show an even starker decline since the end of the cold war. Using constant 2000 U.S. dollars, combined defense spending by Europe's big three (Britain, France, and Germany) fell nearly 20 percent between 1989 and 2003. Over that same period, total military expenditures for the then 15 members of the European Union (EU) declined 14 percent overall.[7] Russian spending dropped precipitously after the collapse of the Soviet Union, from an estimated $200 billion in 1989 to $14 billion in 1999.[8]

The impact on the global arms industry was undeniable. The so-called peace dividend left the world with considerably more capacity and capability to develop and produce arms than it either needed or could reasonably afford. This state of affairs, in turn, compelled leading arms producers to engage in major rationalization and consolidation efforts. Among the large advanced arms-producing countries—e.g., the United States, Britain, and France—hundreds of thousands of defense workers were made redundant and untold numbers of communities were adversely affected as military factories cut back production or even closed down. Furthermore, the post–cold war era witnessed an unprecedented restructuring of the arms industry, both on a national and on a global scale. The number of major defense firms contracted dramatically as defense firms either merged or purchased the military assets of other corporations exiting the defense business. Consequently, armaments production became increasingly concentrated in the hands of fewer but larger defense firms. In particular, the 1990s saw the emergence of several mega-defense firms: Lockheed Martin, Northrop Grumman, and Boeing in the United States, for example, and BAE Systems, Thales, and DASA in Europe.

In more recent years, however, and particularly since the turn of the millennium, global defense expenditures have begun to rebound. According to SIPRI, world military spending has grown by nearly 50 percent between 2000 and 2007. In particular, since 2001, the U.S. defense budget has increased by 59 percent in real terms, and U.S. spending on procurement and R&D more than doubled between fiscal year (FY) 2000 and FY2008, from US$116 billion to US$255 billion.

East Asia and South Asia have also witnessed considerable growth in defense spending in recent years. Among leading arms-producing states in the region, China has increased defense spending by double-digit doses *every year* between 1997 and 2005, or 13.7 percent per annum, in *real,* that is, after inflation, terms, according to the Chinese's own statistics.[9] China's official 2009 budget of US$70.2 billion, for example, constituted a 14.9 percent rise over the previous year. Consequently, Chinese military expenditures have more than *quintupled* in real terms since 1997. Other Asian-Pacific nations have not stood still. Indian defense spending rose 37 percent (in real terms) between 2000 and 2007, according to SIPRI data, while South Korean military expenditures—after experiencing a considerable downturn in the late 1990s, as a result of the Asian Financial Crisis—have increased by 35 percent. Singapore's defense budget rose 33 percent, from US$4.6 billion in 2000, to US$6.1 billion in 2007; in 2008, Singapore's military budget totaled US$7.5 billion.[10] Russian defense expenditure also began to rise in the 2000s, approaching US$38 billion in 2009.[11]

On the other hand, defense spending in Western Europe and Japan has remained static for several years. Combined expenditures on defense equipment for the four largest arms-producing states in NATO (Britain, France, Germany, and Italy) only rose 6 percent between 2000 and 2007, according to NATO data. Japanese defense spending is unofficially pegged at one percent of the gross domestic product (GDP), and consequently has barely moved since the early 1990s, given the country's continuing economic doldrums.

In general, rising defense spending in North America and the Asian-Pacific has enabled these regions to expand and greatly upgrade armaments production. The U.S. defense industry, for example, seems to have pulled itself out of its decline (although this may be temporary, as defense spending is projected to decline in the second decade of the 21st Century), while arms-manufacturing ambitions in China, India, and South Korea have grown considerably in recent years, adding new indigenous programs when it comes to fighter aircraft, surface combatants, missiles, and the like. Meanwhile, Western Europe in particular still seems to be struggling to find equilibrium and stability in its regional defense industry.

THE GROWING CRITICALITY OF THE GLOBAL ARMS MARKET

In the post–cold war era, almost every major arms-manufacturing country has come to depend heavily on overseas sales to bulk up business. As domestic arms markets have shrunk, the overseas business sector has correspondingly grown in importance. European defense firms especially have come to be highly dependent upon foreign sales. In 2007, for example, BAE Systems did only 22 percent of its business in the United Kingdom; the rest was overseas. Thales generated roughly 75 percent of its 2008 revenues from outside France, while Dassault exported 70 percent of its output, and Saab, 68 percent. This trend corresponds with experiences of arms-producing countries elsewhere in the world. Israel's defense industry, for example, typically exports more than three-quarters of its output. The Russian defense industry also has a substantial dependence on arms exports; the collapse of the home market for arms sales, following the breakup of the Soviet Union, has resulted in a situation whereby Russian defense companies have come to rely on overseas business for 80 to 90 percent of their total sales.[12]

The U.S defense industry, with its huge captive domestic arms market, has typically not been as dependent upon overseas sales as its foreign competitors. The major U.S. defense companies garner only a small percentage of their revenues—typically around 5 to 15 percent—from non-U.S. markets. Nevertheless, by the turn of the millennium, several major American weapon systems, such as the F-15 and F-16 fighters and the M-1A1 main battle tank, were being produced solely for export. Additionally, one current U.S. weapons program, the F-35 Joint Strike Fighter (JSF), depends heavily upon foreign funding, foreign industrial participation, and anticipated foreign sales.[13]

Overall, therefore, for many defense firms, overseas sales are no longer a supplemental form of income; they are increasingly critical to the health and survival of the defense-industrial base. Jobs, technology bases, and entire production facilities are now on the line. At the same time, the global arms market has become more complex and competitive. The large numbers of motivated sellers in the West created a buyer's market in arms in which nearly every conceivable kind of conventional weapon system was on the table. Additionally, the end of the cold war, division of the world into communist and capitalist camps greatly opened up the global defense market, and arms sales were, for the most part, no longer restricted for ideological reasons. Consequently, supplier restraint has been replaced by a readiness to sell just about every type of conventional weapon system available. Arms manufacturers are increasingly ready to deal, and offering potential buyers incentives, such as industrial participation (called offsets), technology transfers, and foreign direct investments, have increasingly became part of the cost of doing business, even though these activities can pose potential proliferation concerns and even eventually affect the nature and structure of the global arms industry.

THE GLOBALIZATION OF ARMAMENTS PRODUCTION

The globalization of the arms industry entails a major shift away from traditional, single-country patterns of weapons production toward the more transnational development and manufacture of arms. In an era of constrained military budgets, rising R&D costs, and increasingly competitive defense markets, this internationalization of armaments development and production was seen by a growing number of arms-producing states as perhaps the only affordable means to maintain an economically and technologically competitive defense-industrial base.

Beginning in the mid-1980s, the pace and scale of globalization has accelerated dramatically since the end of the cold war, both quantitatively and qualitatively, and it is increasingly characterized by relatively new kinds of industrial linkages (for the defense sector, that is), such as international subcontracting, joint ventures, and even cross-border mergers and acquisitions (M&As). In several instances, in fact, multinational armaments production has increasingly come to supplement or even supplant wholly indigenous or autonomous weapons production.[14] The western European defense-industrial landscape, for example, has been almost totally transformed over the past decade, due to regional, transnational M&As. Defense firms such as BAE Systems, Thales, Finmeccanica, and Saab can hardly be said to be British, French, Italian, or Swedish in terms of their operations, and the creation of the European Aeronautic Defense and Spain Company (EADS) was an unprecedented act. At the same time, most major defense R&D and production today is multinational, including the Eurofighter combat aircraft, the A400M military transport aircraft, the Meteor air-to-air missile, and the FSAF/PAAMS air-defense system. As such, the European defense sector is almost regionalized, and this regionalization of arms production can be viewed as a transnational extension of the overall consolidation process taking place within the defense industry.

Globalization has also spread to various defense sectors around the world. In Australia, Brazil, South Africa, and South Korea, local military enterprises have been snapped up by foreign investors, and it is difficult to determine whether such firms are even domestic anymore. International joint ventures are also increasingly common, even involving the United States when it comes to critical next-generation weapons programs, such as the JSF.

A subset of the globalization process is the increasing reliance of military systems upon dual-use technologies. Commercial-off-the-shelf (COTS) technologies have played an expanding role in armaments production, particularly in the areas of information technologies (see below), space systems, ship design and construction, new materials (e.g., composites and special alloys), and the like. Increasingly, military effectiveness is a direct consequence of how well defense establishments can leverage commercial technologies. Accordingly, the global trade in dual-use and COTS systems and their subsequent *spin on* to military purposes must be seen as another aspect of the global flow of militarily critical technologies.

The emergence of an increasingly globalized defense technology and industrial base is fundamentally affecting the shape and content of much of the global arms market. This process will likely have profound implications for a variety of national security issues, including defense policy and military doctrine, arms control, regional security, and the future of national defense-industrial bases. Globalization raises obvious concerns about national security needs and the future of self-sufficiency in arms production, the military and commercial effects of global technology diffusion, and conventional arms proliferation. In the first place, globalization is a self-evident challenge to the future of autarky in many countries' arms industries, as foreign ownership and participation in joint ventures and international collaborative arms programs dilute the national nature of their domestic defense-industrial bases. Second, globalization raises considerable apprehensions about the unintended diffusion of advanced military technologies and other know-how pertaining to armaments production, and about the consequences for preventing, delaying, or countering the proliferation of conventional arms. Finally, globalization has fundamental national security implications, to the extent that dependencies upon foreign sources for critical defense systems or subsystems could create undesirable vulnerabilities, especially in times of conflict or war. Overall, the globalization process, as it plays out, will have consequences not only for patterns of national armaments production, but for defense policy, domestic economic growth and development, and international relations.

TECHNOLOGY AND THE REVOLUTION IN MILITARY AFFAIRS

To say that technological innovation significantly impacts armaments production and the arms industry is no great revelation. The evolution of warfare is inexorably intertwined with military-technical advances, and it is just as true today as it was 50, 100, or 500 years ago. This argument is particularly apropos, as there are many who contend that we are presently in the midst of a new "Revolution in Military Affairs" (RMA) that promises to dramatically change the way in which war will be fought, managed, and organized. An RMA is interpreted as nothing less than a paradigm shift in the character and conduct of warfare, and is thus seen as a process of discontinuous and disruptive (as opposed to evolutionary and sustaining) change.[15]

The current RMA model has been inexorably linked to the emerging notions of *network-centric warfare* (NCW), sometimes also referred to as *network-enabled capabilities* or *network-based defense.* According to the NCW concepts, it is the revolution in information technologies (IT)—the growth in computing power, advances in communications and microelectronics, miniaturization, and so on—that makes possible the analogous RMA and enables innovation and improvement in the areas of command, control, communications, computers, intelligence, surveillance, and reconnaissance (C4ISR). Network-centric warfare, according to the U.S. Defense Department,

> generates increased combat power by networking sensors, decision makers, and shooters to achieve shared awareness, increased speed of command, high tempo of operations, greater lethality, increased survivability, and a degree of self-synchronization.[16]

Given the apparently sweeping nature of an RMA, one should expect that the current IT-led RMA will significantly affect the global arms industry. What new technologies and systems is the defense industry expected to provide to transformed militaries, and how would it supply these? How will traditional defense industries fare in the brave new world of network-centric warfare? What might be the role of commercial dual-use enterprises—particularly those in the IT sector—in delivering the required technologies to the RMA?

Will new suppliers necessarily arise, while old ones necessarily fall? In other words, will the global military-industrial complex—forged in World War II and set during the cold war—have to transform itself as well, and, if so, can it?

In turn, how might developments in the global defense industry affect the course of the RMA itself? Do national defense sectors, by way of delivering "the art of the possible," limit national RMAs to what these industries can develop and manufacture for their militaries? How might the process of defense industry globalization—or just globalization in general—affect the diffusion of RMA-related technologies and therefore the implementation of the RMA itself? In particular, how and in what ways might some countries, through overseas arms transfers and international defense-industrial collaboration, become *exporters* of the RMA, and what might be the implications of such globalization? In other words, how might these two institutions, the RMA and the global defense industry, interact with and react to each other in the future?

In the essays that follow, each will deal with some or all of these themes in some manner or form. While each chapter stands alone perfectly well, it is hoped that the entirety of this volume will be synergistic, and that it will provide the reader with a clearer idea of not only what the global arms industry is and where it has come from, but what factors will likely affect and guide where it might go in the future and why.

NOTES

1. See Stephanie G. Neuman, "Industrial Stratification and Third World Military Industries," *International Organization* (Winter 1984): 191–97.
2. Keith Krause, *Arms and the State: Patterns of Military Production and Trade* (Cambridge: Cambridge University Press, 1992), 26–33.
3. Andrew L. Ross, "Full Circle: Conventional Proliferation, the International Arms Trade and Third World Arms Exports," in *The Dilemma of Third World Defense Industries,* ed. Kwang-il Baek, Ronald. D. McLaurin, and Chung-in Moon (Boulder, CO: Westview Press, 1989), 1–31.
4. Richard A. Bitzinger, *Towards a Brave New Arms Industry?* Adelphi paper 356 (London: International Institute for Strategic Studies/Oxford University Press, 2003), 6–7.
5. Elisabeth Sköns and Reinhilde Weidacher, "Arms Production," *SIPRI Yearbook 1999* (Oxford: Oxford University Press, 1999), 405–411.
6. Stockholm International Peace Research Institute, "The SIPRI Military Expenditure Database," http://milexdata.sipri.org.
7. Terence R. Guay, *The Transatlantic Defense Industrial Base: Restructuring Scenarios and their Implications* (Carlisle, PA: Strategic Studies Institute, Army War College, 2005), 8.
8. Stockholm International Peace Research Institute (SIPRI), "The SIPRI Military Expenditure Database," http://milexdata.sipri.org.
9. "Defense Expenditure," *China's National Defense in 2006* (Beijing: Information Office of the State Council of the People's Republic of China, 2006).
10. SIPRI, "The SIPRI Military Expenditure Database."
11. International Institute for Strategic Studies (IISS), *The Military Balance 2009* (London: Routledge, 2009).
12. Alex Vatanka and Richard Weitz, "Russian Roulette—Moscow Seeks Influence through Arms Exports," *Jane's Intelligence Review* (December 6, 2006).

13. The JSF program office expects to sell at least 25 percent, or 730 aircraft, of the first batch of F-35s to the nine nations currently participating in the aircraft's development phase; this figure does not include export sales to other countries (particularly Israel, which has already announced its intention of buying around 100 F-35s). U.S. Defense Department, Official Joint Strike Fighter Web site. http://www.jsf.mil/downloads/documents/ANNEX%20A%20Revision_April%202007.pdf.

14. Richard A. Bitzinger, "The Globalization of the Arms Industry: The Next Proliferation Challenge," *International Security* (Fall 1994): 170.

15. Andrew Krepinevich, "From Cavalry to Computer: The Pattern of Military Revolutions," *The National Interest*, Fall 1994, p. 30.

16. U.S. Department of Defense, Office of Defense Transformation, *Network-Centric Warfare: Creating a Decisive Warfighting Advantage* (Washington, DC: U.S. Department of Defense, 2003), 2.

PART I

The Defense Industry in a Global Context

2

Developments in the Global Arms Industry from the End of the Cold War to the mid-2000s

J. Paul Dunne, with the SIPRI Arms Production Program Staff

The cold war arms industry reflected what is now seen to have been a very specific set of international and domestic forces. Post–cold war developments have transformed the global military economy, not least as a result of trends in military expenditure and technology that have reinforced U.S. dominance. Unlike that of most other countries, U.S. military spending has been growing rapidly.[1] The fixed costs of research and development (R&D) for major systems continue to grow, both for platforms and for the infrastructure (e.g., satellites and strategic air assets) and information systems needed to support network-centric warfare. All countries but the United States thus face structural disarmament, in the sense that they cannot afford to produce a comprehensive range of their own weapon systems because of the fixed costs of replacing conventional military capability with modern systems comparable to those of the United States. This is a particular problem for the other powers that aspire to a military capacity of global significance, in particular the other permanent members of the United Nations Security Council: China, France, Russia, and the United Kingdom.

Current developments in the arms industry include the increasing internationalization of production, the increasing importance of IT (information technology) companies within the defense sector, and the privatization of services that were once provided by the military.[2] These have led to important compositional change in the industry. Factors other than arms control—the budget environment, changing technologies, west European integration, changes in military doctrine, and the emergence of new producers[3]—could all be used to discuss the present situation, although the discussion would be rather different.

The Stockholm International Peace Research Institute (SIPRI) has long been engaged in research, analysis, and assessment of trends and developments in the global arms industry. Work on arms production at SIPRI during the 1980s was concerned with the growth in arms production in the developing world, which was a cause for concern for some commentators.[4]

The SIPRI studies concluded, however, that the attempts to establish self-sufficiency in these countries were unlikely to be successful.[5] At the end of the cold war, as domestic demand for military equipment fell, the concern was the risk of increased arms exports and its likely impact on international security. The focus of research thus shifted to the major arms-producing companies in the West.

The SIPRI Arms Production Project was set up in the environment of the end of the cold war: there were political changes in Eastern Europe, negotiations on conventional arms control (in the Conference on Security and Co-operation in Europe and negotiations on the Treaty on Conventional Armed Forces in Europe, the 1990 CFE Treaty), changing technologies, overcapacities, expansion of the number of producers, and the cascade[6] of weapon systems within the North Atlantic Treaty Organization (NATO).[7] Although the Soviet Union still existed in 1990, the analysis in *SIPRI Yearbook 1990* predicted the need for restructuring the international arms industry and the likely difficulties, suggesting that: "On balance, these trends are likely to lead to a reduction in the size of the world industrial arms base. Difficulties are likely to be encountered by private companies (mainly in the United States and Western Europe) as well as by state-owned factories (mainly in the Soviet Union) that are heavily dependent on arms production."[8]

Issues of conversion—the use of military resources for civil purposes—were a focus of attention, with considerable debates on how changes could be achieved.[9] In this context, for example, the purpose of the 1990 SIPRI Yearbook chapter was "to describe the trends affecting the arms industrial base and to present data on the size and characteristics of the arms industry in the East and West."[10] The authors also stated, "Since over-capacities already exist—with additional capacities in the stage of installation in third world countries and Japan—governments in the West should seriously plan for conversion of parts of the arms industry; otherwise corporations may truly consider themselves as 'victims of peace'."[11] Such statements represent an impressive insight into the issue that would dominate the sector over the next decade, although the authors could not know the degree to which changing geopolitical, technological, and social drivers would restructure the industry.

There have been limitations to the coverage of the SIPRI Arms Production Project, caused by the lack of both data availability and reliability. A network of experts with local knowledge assisted the SIPRI team, but there were problems with coverage of the Soviet Union and its allies because of a lack of reporting by governments. While state ownership in Western countries also limited transparency, it was nevertheless easier to get information on member countries of the Organisation for Economic Co-operation and Development (OECD), and these accounted for most of the data in the tables. Consistency has increased over the years. One way of overcoming the lack of comparable information for major producers has been to include special studies by country experts, who could use a wider range of information to evaluate the changes taking place.[12]

THE COLD WAR ARMS INDUSTRY

The defense industry had unique characteristics during the cold war. The high level of military expenditure in the period after World War II encouraged corporate involvement in lucrative defense orders, while the high R&D expenditure influenced the structure and performance of the companies. High R&D expenditure also influenced the trend in costs, making them higher than civil costs, and the nature of production—with short production runs, technologically advanced and concerned with performance rather than cost minimization—limited the potential for economies of scale and learning.[13] While other large companies were similar in structure, the products generated by defense firms and the subsystems they integrated had different technological forms and requirements. Thus, civil and military products and production processes differed, as did the nature of capital equipment, with labor skills and the organization of production becoming increasingly specific to the sector.

The monopsonistic[14] structure of the market and the nature of the product led to an emphasis on the performance of high-technology weaponry rather than on cost; the financial risk was borne by government, which often financed R&D and in some cases provided investment in capital and infrastructure. The characteristics of the industry also led to elaborate rules and regulations on contracts, which were seen as necessary in the absence of a competitive market and to assure public accountability.[15] In addition, military contingency planning for the worst case led to ever-increasing demand to modernize equipment, with cost only a minor concern. In such an environment, close relations developed between contractors, procurement executives, and the military, leading to a revolving door through which military and civil servants moved to defense contractors with which they had dealings and defense contractors moved into the bureaucracy.[16] It was not surprising that the vested interests in military production formed a powerful interest group, the military-industrial complex, which was capable of pushing for increases in expenditure when there was no obvious change in threats to security.[17]

These characteristics tended to favor those firms that specialized in defense work over other potential competitors. They knew their way around the red tape and had the contacts and links within the state. These firms became experts at getting money out of government, rather than being successful in commercial markets. The companies sought involvement in the development programs for technologically advanced weapon systems as the best means of obtaining the subsequent production contracts. In some cases, this led to *buy-ins,* where firms understated risk or cost in order to win initial contracts and made up the losses later. In addition, some programs saw *gold plating,* where the military continually asked for additions or technological improvements over the contract period. This allowed renegotiation of contracts or additional payments, usually to the advantage of the contractor.[18]

As a result of the structure of the market, there were barriers to both entry and exit (market-related, technological, and procedural). This led to the cold war defense-industrial base being remarkably stable in the composition of main contractors. Moreover, unlike most other manufacturing industries, which went multinational, the arms industry remained national. Smaller countries, which could not afford the large fixed costs, imported major weapon systems.[19]

THE POST–COLD WAR ARMS INDUSTRY

Trends in world military spending can be divided into two major periods in the post–cold war period: a marked decline from the cold war peak in 1987, then a bottoming out around

1998 and an increase in 1998–2005. Indeed, world military spending in 2005 exceeded (in real terms) the peak of spending during the cold war. The United States, which became the major superpower, has been the main contributor to the upward trend in world military expenditure. In 2005, the United States accounted for 48 percent of world military expenditure, with the combined expenditure of next five largest spenders—the United Kingdom, France, Japan, China, and Germany—less than half that of the United States. The 26 members of just one military alliance, NATO, accounted for 70 percent of world military expenditure in 2005.[20]

With the fall in demand following the end of the cold war, the ability of even the major powers to maintain a domestic defense-industrial base was called into question.[21] Governments had to decide whether to allow mergers and acquisitions (M&As) that would reduce competition and, in particular, whether to allow M&As that involved foreign partners. In Europe, the United Kingdom led the way to the degree that its government's definition of the national defense-industrial base was concerned only with the location of production and not with the ownership of the firm.[22] Some smaller European producers, such as Belgium and Norway, followed the United Kingdom. In France and Germany, the issue was much more controversial and continues to be so.[23] The change in the security environment made it harder to justify previous levels of support for the industry, and so competitive procurement policies aimed at value for money were introduced in a number of countries.[24]

The end of the cold war produced not just a quantitative change in the number of weapons required, but a qualitative change in the types required. During the cold war, planning was straightforward—it was fairly clear where, how, and with whom war would be fought if it came. After the cold war there was much less certainty. As Western governments considered the new geopolitical environment, it became apparent that the cold war weapons that made up the bulk of the NATO inventory were unlikely to be what was now required.[25]

Given the long lead times and the commitments made by government bodies, research teams, and companies, there are still pressures to continue to produce these weapon systems and to find roles for them. There has, however, been a clear and important qualitative change in the nature of technology as civil technology has become increasingly important for weapon systems.[26] This was a marked change since, from the end of World War II to the 1980s, military technology had tended to be ahead of civil technology. By the 1990s, in many areas, and particularly electronics, military technology lagged behind civil technology, and military technology was often obsolete before it came into service. Whereas in the past the spin-off of military technology to the civil sector tended to be an important argument for the value of military production, the focus is now more on spinning civil technology *into* the military. Many areas of technology that were once the preserve of the military and security services, such as cryptography, now have primarily commercial applications.

In addition, the use of standard commercial components is an increasing feature of the arms industry: many components of major weapon systems are commercial off-the-shelf products, produced by manufacturers that would not consider themselves part of the arms industry. The major contractors have increasingly become systems integrators, retaining the characteristics of defense specialized firms.[27]

In the post–cold war world, the arms industry's size, structure, and trade are still determined by government policy, as the national government is the main customer and regulates exports. However, there have been clear changes in the structure and nature of the industry. The reduction in demand has led to a situation in which, outside the United States, many companies have become national champions, in many cases monopolies or close to it, with a consequent need for cross-border restructuring.[28]

Concentration

The most striking change in industrial policy was in the United States. During the cold war, industrial planning was undertaken through the Department of Defense (DoD), although not explicitly. This changed in 1993: a merger wave was stimulated when the Deputy Secretary of Defense, William J. Perry, addressed a dinner attended by defense industry executives and openly encouraged consolidation—this became known as the last supper.[29] The presence of financiers at this meeting illustrates the increasing role of financial capital in the arms industry.[30] To promote the consolidation, the DoD allowed companies to write off restructuring costs against military contracts, with the expectation of large cost savings that never materialized.[31] The policy ended when the DoD decided it had gone far enough and blocked the merger of contractors Lockheed Martin with Northrop Grumman in early 1997.[32] This left four major U.S. contractors in 1998: Boeing, Lockheed Martin, Northrop Grumman, and Raytheon—these are now four of the top five companies in the SIPRI Top 100 for 2004.[33]

In Europe, the process of post–cold war adjustment was more complicated, since restructuring necessarily involved cross-border mergers, which raised political issues.[34] The major players in Europe also had quite different ownership structures than those in the United States. For example, in France, Italy, Portugal, and Spain, there was a high degree of state ownership of companies at the end of the cold war. This made the kind of financially driven merger boom that took place in the United States more difficult in Europe. Nonetheless, the driving forces in Europe were similar and led to an increase in concentration. There have been recent moves to integrate European defense markets and further consolidate the sector.[35]

There were three waves of activity in the evolution of BAE Systems' defense activities (see Figure 2.1). First was the consolidation in 1977–87 of the British companies that made up British Aerospace. Then came the acquisitions of European defense interests and of Marconi's defense business in the late 1990s. Finally, the focus moved to acquisitions of U.S. companies. In this phase, the change in name to BAE Systems reflected the company's aim of internationalization and its intention to enter the U.S. market. The evolution of Thales reflects the different experience of the European industry, with continued government ownership and, until recently, opposition to cross-European consolidation (see Figure 2.2). There was a short wave of acquisitions in the early 1990s, then a major wave of acquisitions across the world in the late 1990s. The company's name was changed from Thomson CSF to Thales in 2000, following the acquisition of the British company Racal. With this acquisition, Thales became the second largest contractor to the British Ministry of Defence (after BAE Systems).[36] The change in European government attitudes is further reflected in the evolution of EADS (the European Aeronautic Defence and Space Company; see Figure 2.3), which was formed in 2000 from DASA (a subsidiary of Daimler) of Germany, Aérospatiale Matra of France, and CASA of Spain. EADS developed its defense position through acquisitions in the early 2000s.

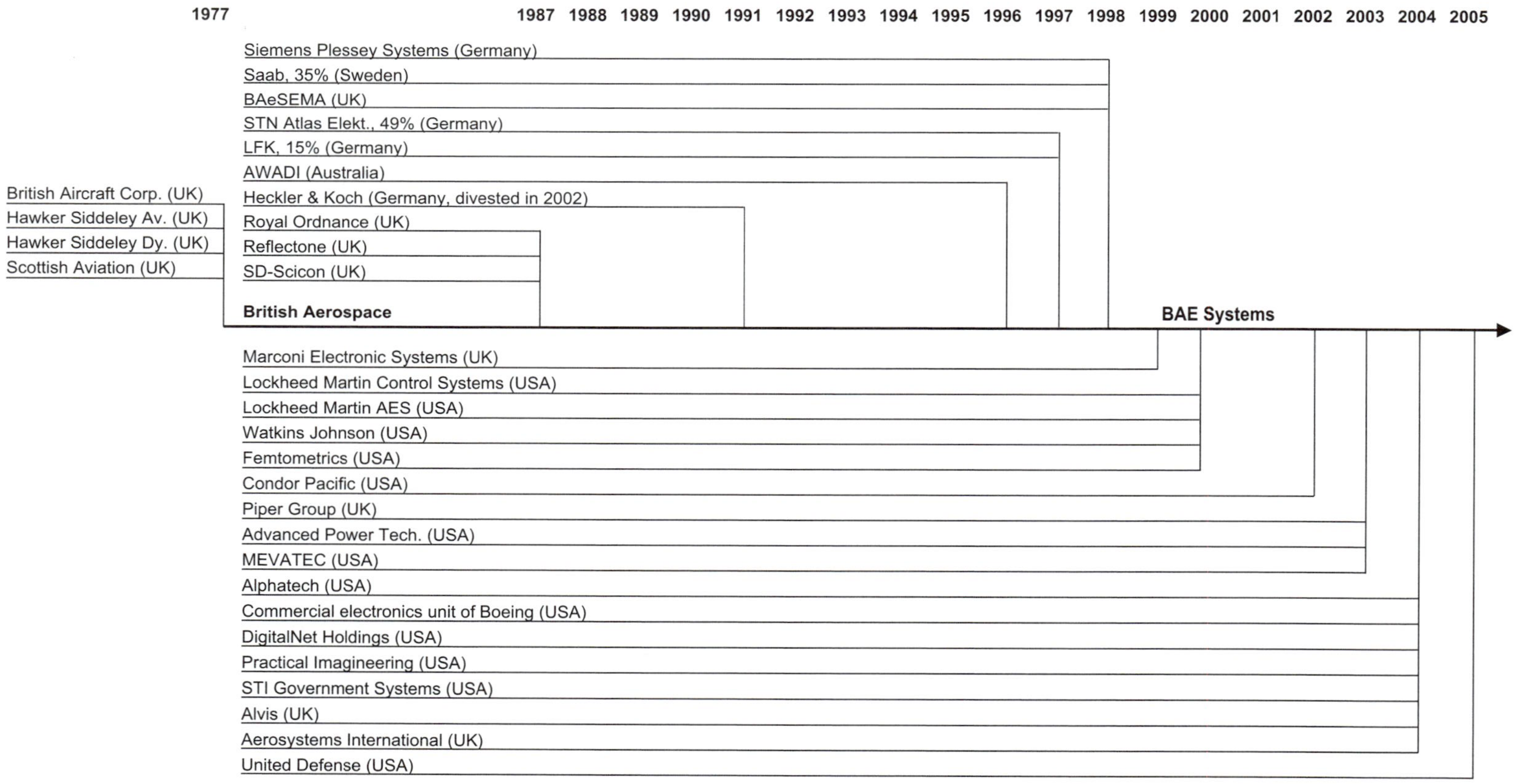

FIGURE 2.1 The formation and major acquisitions of BAE Systems, 1977–2005

Note: This diagram ignores BAE System's civil acquisitions of the 1980s and focuses on its path to defense specialism. The full complexity of these mergers and acquisitions cannot be represented.

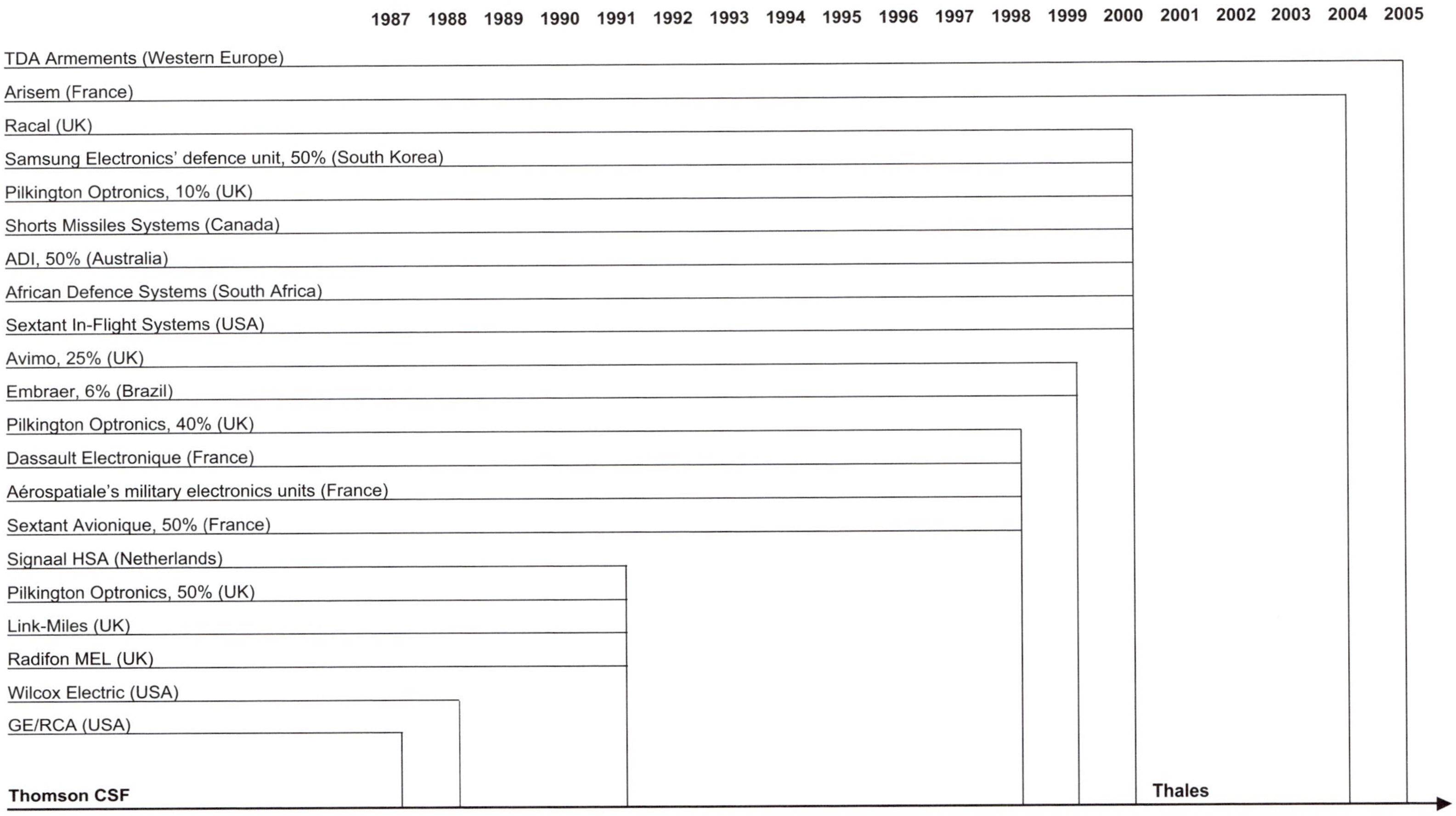

FIGURE 2.2 The formation and major acquisitions of Thales, 1987–2005

Note: The full complexity of these mergers and acquisitions cannot be represented.

19

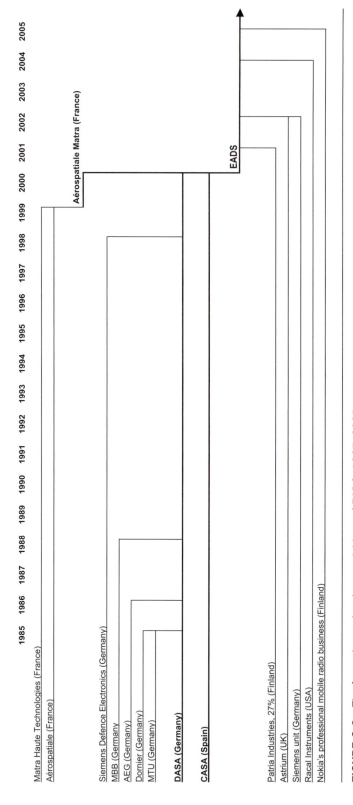

FIGURE 2.3   The formation and major acquisitions of EADS, 1985–2005

Note: The full complexity of these mergers and acquisitions cannot be represented.

Structural Changes

As a result of the merger and acquisition activity since the end of the cold war, there has been a clear change in the structure of the industry. This is shown in Table 2.1, which demonstrates the changes in concentration of the SIPRI Top 100 arms-producing companies in the period 1990–2003. At the end of the cold war, the international arms industry was not very concentrated, with the top 5 companies accounting for 22 percent of the total arms sales of the SIPRI Top 100. It is noticeable that the concentration in total sales was higher than in arms sales, with the top 5 companies accounting for 33 percent of the total sales of the SIPRI Top 100. By 2003, this had changed significantly, with the top 5 firms accounting for 44 percent of total arms sales. This large increase in the share of the top companies is continued further down the list of companies, as shown for the top 10, 15, and 20. In all cases, the big change occurred between 1995 and 2000. Total sales in the period 1990–2003 were also more concentrated in a few companies but, since concentration of total sales was already high in 1990, the increase is not so great. The top 5 companies accounted for 33 percent of the total sales of the SIPRI Top 100 in 1990 and 45 percent in 2003. By 2003, concentration of total sales was quite similar to that of arms sales. This may reflect increasing specialization on defense sales by the major players.[37]

Although by 2003 the 5 largest arms-producing firms accounted for 44 percent of the total arms sales of the SIPRI Top 100, this is still a very low degree of concentration compared to other high-technology markets. The market for major weapon systems would probably have become more highly concentrated, like those for civil airliners or pharmaceuticals, if national governments had not inhibited the growth of multinational firms to protect their defense-industrial base.[38] The international arms market has been dominated by U.S. companies. BAE Systems is the only European company to have consistently been in the top 5 of the SIPRI Top 100, having made a successful push for sales in the U.S. market and gaining special status in bidding for U.S. contracts.[39] European companies are important, however, with Thales, EADS, and Finmeccanica in the top 10. Nearly all arms-producing companies have shown a rise in arms sales between 1998 and 2003 and, apart from the rise of Halliburton, the top 20 companies are relatively stable.

Table 2.1

Concentration of the arms industry, 1990–2003

	Share of total arms sales				Share of total sales			
	1990	1995	2000	2003	1990	1995	2000	2003
Top 5	22	28	41	44	33	34	43	45
Top 10	37	42	57	61	51	52	61	61
Top 15	48	53	65	69	61	64	71	72
Top 20	57	61	70	74	69	72	79	80

Source: SIPRI Arms Industry Database

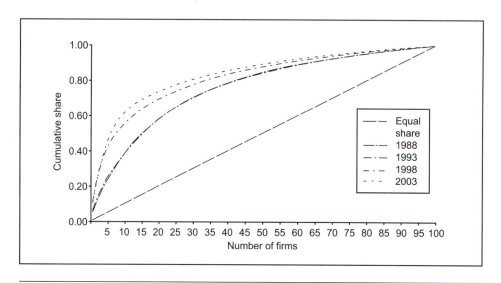

FIGURE 2.4 Size distribution of the SIPRI Top 100 arms-producing companies in 1988, 1993, 1998 and 2003

Note: Each curve shows the cumulative share of the total arms sales of the SIPRI Top 100: the first point on each curve is the share of the largest company; the second point is the total share of the top 2; the third point the total share of the top 3, and so on. If all companies in the Top 100 had an equal share of the total, then the line would be straight; the further the curve deviates from the straight line, the greater the concentration.

The process of significant concentration in the arms industry since the end of the cold war evolved in phases. The most intensive period of concentration was between 1993 and 1998. The process has continued, but slowed down, since then. This is clearly illustrated by Figure 2.4, which shows the cumulative shares of the total sales of the SIPRI Top 100 companies in 1988, 1993, 1998, and 2003. The curves for 1988 and 1993 almost overlap, showing almost no change in the size distribution, but there is a clear increase in concentration between 1993 and 1998, and a further, although smaller, increase between 1998 and 2003.

Corporate Strategies

Faced with the reduction in demand for arms after the cold war, a number of strategic options were open to companies. They could convert their plants to civil production, diversify to produce additional civil products or other military products, divest from military production, cooperate with other companies, or increase military specialization. They also had the option of increasing their exports, whether through new sales and marketing strategies or by finding new markets. However, their choices were constrained by government policy towards their national defense-industrial base and by the nature of the financial systems within which they operated. In principle, the conversion of plants producing military products to producing civil products was an option, but there are very few examples of a successful conversion strategy in this narrow sense in this period. There were more examples of attempts to convert at the company, rather than the plant, level, and of diversification into civil production, but these also had limited success. Some argue that this was a result of firms' internal political battles being won by the advocates of downsizing and focusing or diversifying further into defense over the advocates of convert and diversify into civil, rather than a failure of conversion per se.[40]

The experience of the companies certainly varied as they developed their policies to counter the reduction in the demand for arms.[41] Diversification involved developing new commercial activities either through the organic growth of new businesses or by acquiring existing businesses. It had more chance of success where the firm could build synergies between the military and civil parts of the business, which was more likely to occur in firms with relatively low shares of arms sales. Probably the most impressive diversification was that of the British defense company Racal, which built, and then spun off, the Vodafone mobile phone business. The remaining defense components of Racal were ultimately sold to Thomson CSF of France to form the multinational Thales. There are more examples of unsuccessful diversification. British Aerospace bought a construction company, a property company, and an automobile company. There were plausible tactical justifications for each acquisition, but they did not work. British Aerospace divested each of them and became more focused as a defense company.[42] Some companies, for example, Daimler-Benz, made acquisitions of smaller companies to develop the conglomerate into a broad-based technology company and so reduced their dependency on arms production.[43] For a time, there was also a widespread belief that synergies were possible between automobiles and aerospace, particularly defense aerospace, something on which Saab had based its advertising. The automobile companies Ford, General Motors, and Daimler had all acquired defense units. Ford and General Motors subsequently sold them and Daimler spun off its defense unit, DASA, into the merger with Aérospatiale Matra and CASA to form the multinational EADS.[44]

After the consolidation that followed the 1993 last supper, the remaining U.S. arms producers no longer based their business plans on a broad-based and diversified product range, but rather on specialization in defense products. This was reinforced by Wall Street transactions, which encouraged companies to concentrate on what the stock market called *pure play* and *core competences*.[45] Where competition regulations made it possible, selling defense divisions to competitors was an attractive proposition in a number of cases, since they were worth more to the competitor, who gained increased monopoly power. In the United States, General Dynamics was an early exponent of this strategy and shrank itself rapidly and profitably. In the United Kingdom, the General Electric Company (GEC) sold its defense divisions to British Aerospace in 1999 and turned itself into a purely commercial company, renamed Marconi, which proved to be a disaster.[46]

Cooperation has always been common among aerospace and defense companies. They can use collaboration, joint ventures, and strategic alliances to cut costs—by sharing high R&D and other overhead costs and pooling orders to increase production runs—without losing independence.[47] Joint ventures are partnerships or conglomerates, often formed to share risk or expertise, where two or more businesses agree to share profit, loss, and control in a specific enterprise. They are seen as a good way for companies to combine without having to merge. However, joint ventures can be difficult to manage, and companies generally prefer direct control when they can get it. One of the success stories in military aerospace is the longstanding link between the partly state-owned French aero-engine company Snecma and General Electric of the United States.[48] Strategic alliances are arrangements between companies that pool, exchange, or integrate selected business resources for mutual benefit, while remaining separate entities. These are less complicated than joint ventures. They take many forms and have become more sophisticated and flexible over the past few years. Companies may choose an alliance that involves simple market exchanges or cross-licensing agreements, or they may form a more complicated partnership that includes cooperative manufacturing arrangements or joint-equity ventures. All of these variants have been adopted by arms companies over the past two decades.[49]

The specializing companies, which acquired the defense divisions others divested and often shed civil activities, have also tended to diversify into other weapon systems so that they can market a full product range. Such companies realized the need to internationalize and acted on it. Even before the current wave of restructuring, companies were expanding supply chains internationally, building international joint ventures, and taking strategic shares in foreign companies as an alternative to ownership. This trend has clearly accelerated with the support of governments and has led to marked changes in ownership structures. BAE Systems now sells more to the U.S. DoD than to the British Ministry of Defence (MoD), and the French company Thales is the second largest defense contractor in the United Kingdom.[50]

Another means of replacing domestic demand was through increased exports. Governments, mindful of the need to keep costs down by maintaining or increasing the scale of production of domestic arms producers, supported and encouraged the search for orders abroad. Arms exports became heavily subsidized, both directly and indirectly, through diplomatic pressure, aid, insurance provision, assistance with offset arrangements, and so on.[51] This led to increased competition among arms producers but failed to prevent the inevitable consolidation within the industry.

The different strategies adopted can be identified by considering company data.[52] The companies can be classified as: (a) *winners,* with increased arms sales and increased civil sales; (b) *diversifiers,* with decreased arms sales and increased civil sales; (c) *rearmers,* with increased arms sales and decreased civil sales; and (d) *losers,* with decreased arms sales and decreased civil sales. Diversifiers could have converted plants or diversified through organic growth, acquisitions, or divestment. In Table 2.2, the civil production of the sample—the SIPRI Top 100 arms-producing companies for 1990—was estimated and the frequency distribution for these four categories was considered for both those companies with increasing arms shares and those with decreasing arms shares.

Of the 53 companies that still existed in 2003, the largest group is the winners, about half of whom had a decreased share of their total sales represented by arms sales, meaning that arms sales became less important to the company. While the results for the period 1990–2003 are interesting, they cover a relatively long time period. Since there could have been changes over the period in the strategies and success of companies, it is useful to consider the results over a shorter period, 1990–98. In 1998, there was a similar number of survivors, but a much smaller proportion of these had increased their arms sales (as would be expected in the short term), and there were fewer winners and more diversifiers. While these figures show a high

Table 2.2

Company strategies and analysis of arms-producing companies that survived in the periods 1990–2003 and 1990–98

Fate of the 1990 SIPRI Top 100 arms-producing companies	
Had exited by 2003	18
Had merged or been acquired by 2003	25
No data for 2003	4
Survivors in 2003	53

Analysis of companies in 2003[a]	Arms sales an increased or constant share of total sales	Arms sales a decreased share of total sales	Total
Winners	12	13	25
Diversifiers	2[b]	13	15
Rearmers	7	0	7
Losers	4	2	6
Total survivors	**25**	**28**	**53**

Analysis of companies in 1998[a]	Arms sales an increased or constant share of total sales	Arms sales a decreased share of total sales	Total
Winners	2	9	11
Diversifiers	0	33	33
Rearmers	6	0	6
Losers	4	3	7
Total survivors	**12**	**45**	**57**

[a]*Winners* are companies that increased arms sales and increased civil sales; *diversifiers* are those that decreased arms sales and increased civil sales; *rearmers* are those that increased arms sales and decreased civil sales; and *losers* are those that decreased arms sales and decreased civil sales.

[b]For these two companies, arms sales as a share of total sales remained constant.

Source: SIPRI Arms Industry Database

degree of diversification, they tend to understate the degree of conversion overall, as companies that successfully moved out of arms production became less visible—they leave the SIPRI Top 100 and so do not count as survivors—and gradual policy changes may not make headlines. In addition, according to the Bonn International Center for Conversion (BICC), it is possible that the less visible small- and medium-sized companies have been more successful diversifiers than the large companies among the SIPRI Top 100.[53]

Looking at the changes in the regional distribution of the SIPRI Top 100 arms-producing companies (see Table 2.3), the dominance of U.S.-listed companies is consistent: they made up 60 percent of arms sales in 1990 and 63 percent in 2003. The share for European companies

Table 2.3
Regional distribution of the SIPRI Top 100 arms-producing companies,
1990 and 2003

Region/country[a]	Share of total arms sales (%)		Number of companies	
	1990	*2003*	1990	2003
North America	**60.8**	**63.2**	**49**	**39**
U.S.	60.2	63.0	47	38
Canada	0.6	0.2	2	1
Western Europe	**33.1**	**29.2**	**40**	**36**
U.K.	10.4	11.4	13	12
France	12.0	7.5	11	9
FRG/Germany	5.0	2.2	8	5
Italy	3.4	2.7	3	3
Switzerland	1.1	0.3	2	1
Sweden	0.3	0.9	2	2
Spain	0.9	0.6	1	2
Norway	–	0.2	–	1
Trans-European	–	3.4	–	1
Other OECD	**3.2**	**3.3**	**5**	**10**
Japan	3.2	2.6	5	7
South Korea	–	0.5	–	2
Australia		0.2	–	1
Other non-OECD	**3.0**	**4.6**	**6**	**15**
Israel	1.2	1.5	3	4
India	1.1	1.0	2	3
Singapore	–	0.4	–	1
South Africa	0.7	0.2	1	1
Russia	–	1.5	–	6

[a]This table refers only to parent companies: the arms sales of foreign subsidiaries are included in the sales of the parent company, not in the country where the production actually takes place. The SIPRI Top 100 for 1990 covered only OECD member states and developing countries (excluding inter alia China and Russia). By 2003, the SIPRI Top 100 covered most of the world, but still excluded China.

Sources: I. Anthony, P. Claesson, E. Sköns, and S. T. Wezeman, "Arms Production and Arms Trade," *SIPRI Yearbook 1993: World Armaments and Disarmament* (Oxford University Press: Oxford, 1993), table 10.3, p. 428; and E. Sköns and E. Surry, "Arms Production," *SIPRI Yearbook 2005: Armaments, Disarmament and International Security* (Oxford University Press: Oxford, 2005), table 9.1, p. 384.

FRG = Federal Republic of Germany; OECD = Organisation for Economic Co-operation and Development.

declined from 33 percent to 29 percent over the same period. Interestingly, the United States saw a decline in the number of firms in the SIPRI Top 100 from 49 to 39, while for Europe the decline was only from 40 to 36, reflecting the very different nature of the industry and the restructuring experience in the United States as compared to Europe.[54]

Increasing internationalization of the supply chains is changing the organization of production. Apart from cross-country purchases of finished goods, companies are also changing their supply chain, an example being BAE Systems' purchases in South Africa.[55] The growth of offsets deals has encouraged this development and given importing countries the opportunity to develop niche markets by being part of the supply chain of a major international producer.[56] Arms-producing companies are determining preferred suppliers from a wider range of companies.[57] While the companies rely on domestic support through procurement and support for exports, and so are not truly transnational, they have internationalized. Governments are increasingly willing to recognize that the costs of high-technology defense R&D and smaller national production runs mean that economies of scale need to be met through international collaboration and industrial restructuring. This is very different from a few decades ago, when governments aimed to maintain a comprehensive national defense-industrial base. Major non-U.S. defense companies are also buying defense contractors in the United States as a means of entering the U.S. market, as discussed above.

Acquisitions activity in the arms industry in 1988–89 and in 2005 can be compared by considering the tables of acquisitions in *SIPRI Yearbook 2006* and *SIPRI Yearbook 1990*.[58] There is much less activity in the earlier period, with 18 transactions noted for 1988–89 and 54 for 2005. This may possibly be attributed to better data collection for 2005, but the change in the level of activity and the range of countries involved as acquirer and acquired are striking. The attempt by European firms to move into the U.S. market is very clear, with seven transatlantic acquisitions of U.S. companies in 2005.[59]

The period covered by the SIPRI Arms Industry Database has been one of considerable change and restructuring in the arms industry. While the concentration of major arms producers seems to have stopped in the United States in 1997, it is still continuing at the level of the smaller companies and in the supply chain. Unlike earlier consolidation, which was driven by the need to survive in a declining market, the recent activity seems to be driven more by the need to acquire technology than by the desire for growth.[60] While there has been some activity in Europe, there is still some way to go in terms of restructuring and increasing concentration. A major driver of restructuring is the growing transatlantic nature of the industry, in terms of both the European companies' aspirations to become major players in the U.S. market and the U.S. acceptance that "interoperability requirements, the benefits of cooperative defense programs, and an increasingly global industrial infrastructure require that the [U.S. DoD] be prepared to accept the benefits offered by access to the most innovative, efficient, and competitive suppliers worldwide."[61]

THE CHANGING NATURE OF THE ARMS INDUSTRY

There have been marked changes in the structure of the international arms industry since 1990 and there are likely to be changes in the future. Future prospects for the industry are shaped by a range of factors, including the following.

1. *The changing nature of warfare.* It seems unlikely that the United States and Europe (that is, NATO) will face an enemy that can provide a symmetric response; asymmetric conflict is most likely. This can change the nature of warfare and lead to more informal, guerrilla-type conflicts with implications for the weapon systems required.[62]

2. *The rate of obsolescence of some major weapon systems, such as fighter aircraft.* Recent commentators have suggested that many fighter aircraft are coming to the end of their life and will need to be replaced.[63]

3. *The new security environment and its demands for new types of military missions.* There is likely to be an increasing role for NATO and EU troops in crisis management and peacekeeping roles around the world.[64] This changes both the nature and structure of the required armed forces and the type of weapon systems they need.

4. *The new technologies introduced as a result of the war on terrorism.* The global war on terrorism, which confronts an uncertain enemy, and U.S. homeland security have stimulated the demand for communication and surveillance technologies. Where companies do not have these technologies, they are acquiring them.[65]

5. *The degree of outsourcing of services from the military sector (armed forces and defense ministries).* Defense ministries (particularly the U.S. DoD) are increasingly using private companies to undertake tasks that would have been done by the military in the past.

On the other hand, long lead times and large capital investment in major weapon systems result in considerable inertia. Indeed, the military has always been relatively conservative, fighting battles with the weapons of the last war, leading to a fair amount of STET inertia in procurement and planning. There are still weapon systems coming into service that were designed for the cold war, for example, the Eurofighter Typhoon.[66]

An important remaining question is how much the nature of the industry has changed. It is still greatly influenced by political pressures, both domestic and international. Governments dominate the demand for the products of the sector, and their spending and direct influence inevitably determine industrial structure: governments still decide where to buy, how to buy, and what to buy, although they may now make different decisions than they would have in the past. They can still influence the size and structure of the industry, entry to and exit from the industry, efficiency and ownership, and the level of technology and exports, although they now have less control over prices and profits. In most countries, the state still provides infrastructure. However, pressure groups and lobbyists are increasingly important in the governance of the industry, with Europe following in the footsteps of the United States as European state ownership and control are reduced.[67] In Europe, the increased privatization of defense companies, the reduced barriers to foreign ownership, and greater nondomestic procurements all continue to influence the industry.

The major defense contractors, or at least their defense sections, still differ from civil companies. While less risk is now borne by government and there is less emphasis on performance at the expense of cost, defense contractors still face elaborate rules and regulations in procurement, and government's close links with procurers have been replaced by less formal but not necessarily less effective mechanisms (e.g., lobbying). Non–defense specialists continue to face considerable barriers to entering and exiting the market—marketing, procedural, or technological. However, the technological barriers remain high only for specialists in particular areas.

While companies have been internationalized in terms of markets and their supply chains, they seem loyal to their home base. Incumbents are still favored by the way in which contracts are set up and the major contractors remain expert at getting money out of governments. Governments have overhauled their procurement practices to try to deal with the gold plating, as well as the cost and time overruns, of the cold war industry. As a consequence, they involve companies earlier in the development of equipment to meet particular security needs. The European Defence Agency (EDA) was established to help EU member states develop their defense capabilities for crisis-management operations under the European Security and Defence Policy. The EDA is intended to encourage EU governments to spend their defense budgets on meeting future challenges, rather than past (cold war) threats, and to help identify common needs and promote collaboration.

As defense budgets declined, companies and governments made greater efforts to export weapons, particularly to developing countries. More recently, importing countries have used offsets to justify arms purchases, and arms-exporting countries and companies have thereby become involved in a process of questionable value that could potentially increase the number of producers and exacerbate the problems of overcapacity in certain areas.[68]

It would seem, therefore, that many of the characteristics of the old defense-industrial base remain in spite of the extent of changes in the industry's structure. However, the clear internationalization of production, the changes in ownership, the *spin-in* of civil technologies (such as IT and communications technology), and the increased number of civil companies in the supply chains all make this look like a very different industry. It is also one that is less easy to define and much more difficult to research, meaning that there is some concern as to how transparent the processes of procurement and production will be in the future.

With the growth of privatization across Europe, it is likely that the financial sector will become increasingly important in the arms industry, as it has in the United Kingdom and the United States. The differences between the financial and corporate governance systems in most European countries and those in the United Kingdom and the United States have influenced the ways in which the respective industries have restructured. The last supper in the United States involved financiers as well as companies, and Wall Street played an important role in the restructuring that followed.[69] Similarly, in the United Kingdom, the financial sector and shareholders aided restructuring through their influence on company policies. In Europe, the greater government ownership and the hands-on involvement of institutional shareholders and bankers in company policy through their positions on boards of directors reduced the degree and speed of restructuring. The involvement of banks, investment firms, and holding companies in the restructuring currently taking place in the European arms industry suggests that the process will speed up in Europe.[70] While most of the British defense industry was privatized in the past two decades, in much of the rest of Europe the state still owns a lot of the defense-industrial base, although this is changing. Privatization of the major contractors is increasingly taking place in Europe and, together with the increase in foreign ownership and nondomestic procurements, is likely to have a major influence on the European industry.[71] In addition, there are previously civil companies involved in communications and IT that are feeding off demand from the revolution in military affairs and the war on terrorism and expanding the international defense-industrial base.

The privatization of defense services and support is a further important trend. This has been made apparent in Iraq, with companies taking on support roles that the armed forces would have undertaken in the past, even in areas of conflict. A big growth area is the provision of security—guarding people and buildings. There is a new periphery of private security companies with government contracts and homeland security business, and a new group of civil companies that are becoming involved in defense production.[72] The traditional arms producers have discovered this new market and are buying up some of the start-up companies, the so-called *private military firms*.[73] The changing security environment is likely to have a further impact on this wider security industry, but there is at present little available information on the development of the relevant companies. The increasing privatization of defense and post-conflict reconstruction services could be producing a group of influential, profit-chasing companies that have a vested interest in conflict. This could lead to pressures on governments to extend conflicts or initiate new ones. In the past, the arms-producing companies had a vested interest in the production of weapons and in increasing demand for them, but they did not necessarily benefit from actual conflict. As Herbert Wulf argues, there is a need for an international governance structure to deal with the erosion of the state monopoly of force.[74]

The Developing World

While these changes were taking place in the developed world, adjustments were also taking place in the developing world. Research at SIPRI in the 1980s had correctly assessed that the observed fast growth in arms production capacity in developing countries would be inadequate to permit self-sufficiency or create competition for the developed world.[75] The end of the cold war and the superpower confrontation removed much of the pressure and support for the maintenance of high military burdens in the developing world. The lack of superpower involvement generally reduced tensions, military and military-related aid, and the scale of conflicts (although the number of conflicts increased).

While the large arms industries in China and India are to a great extent insulated from external competition, some other relatively more advanced arms-producing countries in the developing world have also sustained their arms production, for domestic procurement as well as for exports. During the five-year period 2000–2004, there were 7 developing countries among the 30 largest exporters of major weapons: China, Israel, South Korea, Brazil, Indonesia, South Africa, and North Korea.[76] India comes further down on the list in spite of its large arms industry. It has a strong import dependency and its rate of self-reliance in arms procurement is only 30 percent.[77]

Among the remaining developing countries, by the late 1990s, 20–30 were engaged in some form of arms production and arms exports or re-exports.[78] Indigenous arms production efforts are often justified on economic grounds, providing spill-over or spin-off effects on civil industry and foreign exchange earnings through exports, although there is no convincing economic argument or evidence that such economic benefits exist.[79] Offset arrangements and licensed production have often been seen as a means of promoting domestic production and improving the technological level of the systems produced, although some countries now seek the technical know-how to be an intelligent customer rather than aiming to become a producer.[80] Producing small arms and relatively unsophisticated weapon systems is an achievable goal for most developing economies with some industrial base, but developing an arms industry capable of producing large advanced weapon systems is no longer feasible.[81]

These trends were reflected in the SIPRI Top 100 arms-producing companies: although a number of companies based in developing countries have shown some potential to become international players, none has made it so far. Indeed, the changing nature of arms production and the restructuring of the market have reduced the opportunities for less-established companies to become more than links in the supply chains of the major international players.

CONCLUSIONS

The United States continues to dominate the global arms industry. There was some important merger and acquisition activity in recent years, but at a slower pace than before. Further consolidation and restructuring are likely, particularly in Europe, and the industry is likely to continue to expand its supply chain, across both industries and countries. Governments will focus more on capability than on production. Non-U.S. companies will continue to attempt to access the U.S. market and the industry is likely to continue to internationalize. There have been marked changes in the international arms industry since the end of the cold war and further change can be expected. The arms market continues to have a set of unique characteristics, such as the considerable barriers to entry and exit. Some companies have survived from the traditional cold war arms market, while others have managed to exit or enter the new market. A noteworthy trend has been the privatization of defense services and support, which has expanded the security services industry as a periphery around the core arms industry. This could have implications in terms of accountability and transparency.

ACKNOWLEDGMENT

This chapter is a reproduction, with some alteration, of section III of J. P. Dunne and E. Surry, "Arms Production," *SIPRI Yearbook 2006: Armaments, Disarmament and International Security* (Oxford University Press: Oxford, 2006), with the permission of SIPRI and the authors.

NOTES

1. U.S. military expenditure increased by 50 percent in real terms in 1996–2005. China and Russia have also increased their military expenditure tremendously in recent years (by 165% and 49%, respectively, in 1996–2005).
2. E. Sköns, S. Bauer, and E. Surry, "Arms Production," *SIPRI Yearbook 2004: Armaments, Disarmament and International Security* (Oxford University Press: Oxford, 2004), 389.

3. I. Anthony et al., "Arms Production," *SIPRI Yearbook 1990: World Armaments and Disarmament* (Oxford University Press: Oxford, 1990), 319–21.

4. For example, a 1981 RAND report predicted that: "If borne out in future research, one would predict arms production in growing numbers of countries in an economically developing world." A. J. Alexander, W. P. Butz, and M. Mihalka, "Modeling the Production and International Trade of Arms: An Economic Framework for Analyzing Policy Alternatives," (Santa Monica, CA: RAND Note, RAND Corporation, 1981), 17.

5. M. Brzoska and T. Ohlson, *Arms Production in the Third World* (London: Taylor & Francis, 1986); H. Wulf, "Developing Countries," in *The Structure of the Defense Industry: An International Survey,* ed. N. Ball and M. Leitenberg (London: Croom Helm, 1983); and Anthony et al., "Arms Production."

6. In the early 1990s, NATO planned a large internal arms transfer program to compensate for the removal of equipment under the terms of a possible CFE agreement. Secondhand equipment from the more developed member countries would be transferred to the less developed members, who would then destroy equipment that was already planned for replacement.

7. Anthony et al., "Arms Production." See also I. Anthony, A. C. Allebeck, and H. Wulf, *West European Arms Production* (Oxford University Press: Oxford, 1990); M. Brzoska and P. Lock, eds., *Restructuring of Arms Production in Western Europe* (Oxford University Press: Oxford, 1992); and H. Wulf, ed., *Arms Industry Limited* (Oxford University Press: Oxford, 1993).

8. Anthony et al., "Arms Production," 317.

9. For example, M. Brzoska, "Success and Failure in Defense Conversion in the 'Long Decade of Disarmament'," in *Handbook of Defense Economics,* vol. 2, ed. K. Hartley and T. Sandler, (Amsterdam: Amsterdam, 2007); P. Southwood, *Disarming Military Industries* (London: Macmillan, 1991); A. Markusen and J. Yudken, *Dismantling the Cold War Economy* (New York: Basic Books, 1992); K. Hartley, *Economic Aspects of Disarmament: Disarmament as an Investment Process* (Geneva: UNIDIR, 1993); L. J. Dumas, ed., *The Socioeconomics of Conversion from War to Peace* (New York: ME Sharpe, 1995); J. S. Gansler, *Defence Conversion: Transforming the Arsenal of Democracy* (Cambridge, MA: MIT Press, 1995); and P. Dunne, "Conversion in Europe: Challenges and Experiences," in *Defensive Doctrines and Conversion,* ed. B. Moller and L. Voronkov (Aldershot, UK: Dartmouth Publishing Co., 1996), 56–62.

10. Anthony et al., "Arms Production," 317.

11. Anthony et al., "Arms Production," 368.

12. The Soviet Union and Russia have had such treatment. See J. Cooper, "Russian Military Expenditure and Arms Production," *SIPRI Yearbook 2001: Armaments, Disarmament and International Security* (Oxford University Press: Oxford, 2001), 313–22; and J. Cooper, "Developments in the Russian Arms Industry," *SIPRI Yearbook 2006: Armaments, Disarmament and International Security* (Oxford University Press: Oxford, 2006), 431–48.

13. N. Ball and M. Leitenberg, *The Structure of the Defense Industry: An International Survey* (London: Croom Helm, 1983); S. Melman, *The Permanent War Economy* (New York: Simon and Schuster, 1985); P. Dunne, "The Political Economy of Military Expenditure: An Introduction," *Cambridge Journal of Economics* 14, no. 4 (1990): 395–404; and J. Lovering, "Military Expenditure and the Restructuring of Capitalism: The Military Industry in Britain," *Cambridge Journal of Economics* 14, no. 4 (1990): 453–68.

14. In a monopoly situation there are many customers but only one supplier; in a monopsony there are many suppliers (in this case, national arms producers) but only one customer (the national government).

15. J. P. Dunne, "The Defence Industrial Base," in *Handbook of Defense Economics,* vol. 1, ed. K. Hartley and T. Sandler (Amsterdam: Elsevier, 1995), 592–623.

16. G. Adams, *The Iron Triangle: The Politics of Defense Contracting* (New York: Council on Economic Priorities, 1981); and R. Higgs, ed., *Arms Politics and the Economy: Historical and Contemporary Perspectives* (New York: Holmes and Meier, 1990).

17. J. P. Dunne, "The Changing Military Industrial Complex in the UK," *Defence Economics* 4, no. 2 (1993): 91–112; and J. Lovering, "Restructuring the British Defence Industrial Base after the Cold War: Institutional and Geographical Perspectives," *Defence Economics* 4, no. 2 (1993): 123–39.

18. Dunne, "The Defence Industrial Base."

19. Dunne, "The Defence Industrial Base"; and M. Renner, *Economic Adjustment after the Cold War: Strategies for Conversion* (Aldershot, UK: Dartmouth Publishing Co., 1992).

20. A further issue of increasing importance is the hidden defense spending that appears in national accounts under headings other than defense. For example, major actions are paid for from contingency funds; in the new environment of the war against terrorism, what was once defense expenditure appears elsewhere; and there is increased use of civil companies to undertake what would have been the work of the armed forces, but not necessarily recognized as defense, such as post-conflict reconstruction in Iraq. J. Brauer, "United States Military Expenditure," (manuscript, College of Business, Augusta State University, 2005), http://www.aug.edu/˜sbajmb/paper-US_milex.pdf.

21. J. P. Dunne, M. Garcia-Alonso, P. Levine, and R. Smith, "Concentration in the International Arms Industry," Discussion Paper 03/01, School of Economics, University of the West of England, Bristol, 2003, http://carecon.org.uk/DPs/; A. R. Markusen and S. S. Costigan, "The Military Industrial Challenge," in *Arming the Future: A Defense Industry for the 21st Century,* ed. A. R. Markusen and S. S. Costigan (New York: Council on Foreign Relations Press, 1999), 3–34.

22. The first clear and explicit statement of the change in British policy was made in British Ministry of Defence, "Defence Industrial Policy," Ministry of Defence Policy Paper 5, 2002, 9, http://www.mod.uk/DefenceInternet/AboutDefence/CorporatePublications/PolicyStrategy/.

23. C. Serfati et al., eds., *The Restructuring of the European Defence Industry: Dynamics of Change,* European Commission, Directorate General for Research, COST Action A10 (Luxembourg: Office for Official Publications of the European Communities, 2001), in particular L. Mampaey, "Ownership and Regulation of the Defence Industrial Base: The French Case," 123–144; and "Germany Tightens Rules on Foreign Ownership," *Defense News,* September 19, 2005, 20. For a discussion of the "strong influence of the French Government on the French defence industry," see M. Lundmark, "To Be or Not To Be: The Integration and the Non-integration of the French Defence Industry," Base data report FOI-R-1291-SE, Swedish Defence Research Agency (FOI), Stockholm, 2004, 16–17, http://www.foi.se/FOI/templates/PublicationPage____171.aspx; D. Mussington, *Arms Unbound: the Globalization of Defense Production* (Washington, DC: Brassey's, 1994); and E. B. Kapstein, ed., *Global Arms Production: Policy Dilemmas for the 1990s* (Cambridge, MA: Harvard University Press, 1992).

24. On the United Kingdom see J. P. Dunne and G. Macdonald, "Procurement in the Post Cold War World: A Case Study of the UK," in *The Restructuring of the European Defence Industry: Dynamics of Change,* ed. Serfati et al., European Commission, Directorate General for Research, COST Action A10 (Luxembourg: Office for Official Publications of the European Communities, 2001), 101–22.

25. A.J.K. Bailes, O. Melnyk, and I. Anthony, *Relics of Cold War: Europe's Challenge, Ukraine's Experience,* SIPRI Policy Paper 6 (SIPRI: Stockholm, 2003), http://www.sipri.org/.

26. L. M. Branscomb et al., *Beyond Spinoff: Military and Commercial Technologies in a Changing World* (Cambridge, MA: Harvard Business School Press, 1992).

27. J. P. Dunne, M. Garcia-Alonso, P. Levine, and R. P. Smith, "The Evolution of the International Arms Industry," (manuscript, School of Economics, University of the West of England, Bristol,

2005), http://carecon.org.uk/Armsproduction/Evolution2forWolfram.pdf; and A. R. Markusen, "The Post–Cold War Persistence of Defense Specialized Firms," in *The Defense Industry in the Post Cold War Era,* ed. G. I. Susman and S. O'Keefe (Oxford: Elsevier, 1998), 121–46.

28. The situation also meant that any introduction of competition would need to be from foreign firms. This can be implicit rather than explicit, by creating contestable markets with potential competition from abroad, although there may be problems of making incumbents believe that these external competitors would enter the market. Dunne, "The Defence Industrial Base."

29. Perry is reported to have said that he hoped several aircraft firms, three of the five satellite firms, and one of the three missile companies, would disappear through mergers. Markusen, "The Post–Cold War Persistence," 138. A description of the meeting is found in J. A. Turpak, "The Distillation of the Defence Industry," *Airforce Magazine* 81, no. 7 (1998), http://www.afa.org/magazine/July1998/.

30. E. Sköns and E. Surry, "Arms Production," *SIPRI Yearbook 2005: Armaments, Disarmament and International Security* (Oxford: Oxford University Press, 2005), 387. For an analysis of the role of Wall Street in the restructuring of the U.S. arms industry during the 1990s, see Markusen, "The Post–Cold War Persistence."

31. E. Sköns and R. Weidacher, "Arms Production," *SIPRI Yearbook 1999: Armaments, Disarmament and International Security* (Oxford: Oxford University Press, 1999), 397.

32. Markusen and Costigan, "The Military Industrial Challenge," 4.

33. Sköns and Weidacher, "Arms Production," 394–98, in particular figure 10.1. The British company BAE Systems is 4th in the SIPRI Top 100. The 6th, General Dynamics, adopted the strategy of spinning off defense divisions that specialized in areas in which it was not dominant and concentrating on those where it was, becoming a smaller firm in the process. Markusen, "The Post–Cold War Persistence."

34. T. Ripley, "Western European Industry Ownership Jigsaw," *Defence Systems Daily,* May 31, 2005, http://defence-data.com/ripley/pagerip1.htm. The current structure of the European defense industry is described as a spaghetti bowl in K. Vlachos-Dengler, *Off Track?: The Future of the European Defense Industry* (Santa Monica, CA: RAND, 2004).

35. T. Valasek, "EU Wants More Defense Competition, Lower Costs," *ISN Security Watch,* December 1, 2005, http://www.isn.ethz.ch/news/sw/details.cfm?id=13686.

36. Defence Manufacturers Association, "Thales UK PLC," Member listings, http://www.the-dma.org.uk/Secure/Groups/NonMemberDets.asp?ID=817.

37. Computing the coefficient of variation of the SIPRI Top 100 for the same years shows an increasing spread of the size distribution for arms and total sales, with arms sales having a lower spread than total sales in 1988 but increasing more. The results also show that the spread of arms shares across the companies was constant until 1998 and then declined in 1998–2003.

38. Until the 1970s, government procurement rules in many countries restricted the purchase of telecommunications equipment from foreign suppliers and determined the number of firms. The easing of procurement rules that followed the liberalization of the telecommunications market led to very rapid concentration in the world telecommunications industry. This is what might be expected to happen if governments ceased to interfere in the market structure of the arms industry. J. Sutton, *Technology and Market Structure* (Cambridge, MA: MIT Press, 1998).

39. The special status of BAE Systems Inc., as the U.S. unit is known, dates from the later years of the administration of U.S. President Bill Clinton, when the company became the only subsidiary of a foreign defense contractor to win a blanket national interest determination from the DoD, giving it streamlined handling of approvals to work on classified contracts. The parent company does not enjoy the same level of trust. The special security status and track record of Rockville, a BAE

Systems subsidiary, allows it to compete on contracts and buy companies more easily than other foreign units. *Business Week*, "Hands—And Arms—Across the Sea," November 14, 2005, http://www.businessweek.com/magazine/content/05_46/b3959161.htm.

40. Markusen, "The Post–Cold War Persistence."

41. Dunne et al., "The Evolution of the International Arms Industry"; R. Smith and D. Smith, "Corporate Strategy, Corporate Culture and Conversion; Adjustment in the Defence Industry," *Business Strategy Review* 3, no. 2 (1992): 45–58. See also note 9.

42. Some argue that British Aerospace Enterprises, the company's venture capital arm, had potential for success that was never achieved because of the change in corporate strategy. J. Feldman, "The Rise and Fall of British Aerospace Enterprises," Mimeo, National Institute for Working Life, Stockholm, 2000. That process of change is described in R. Evans and C. Price, *Vertical Take-off* (London: Nicolas Brealey Publishing, 1999).

43. M. Stephan, "An Evolutionary Perspective on Corporate Diversification," Paper prepared for the Workshop on Evolutionary Economics, Buchenbach, May 14–17, 2003, http://www.infokom.tudresden.de/papiere buchenbach 2003/CorporateDiversificationPatternsVersion2April2003.pdf; and Renner, *Adjustment After the Cold War*.

44. A. D. James, "Comparing European Responses to Defense Industry Globalization," *Defence & Security Analysis* 18, no. 2 (2002): 123–43. See also *Automotive News*, "Big 3 No Longer Major Players in U.S. Defense," March 31, 2003, http://www.autonews.com/apps/pbcs.dll/article?AID=/20030331/FREE/303310763.

45. Markusen (note 27); Dunne et al., "The Evolution of the International Arms Industry"; M. Oden, "Cashing In, Cashing Out, and Converting: Restructuring of the Defense Industrial Base in the 1990s," in *Arming the Future: A Defense Industry for the 21st Century*, ed. A. R. Markusen and S. S. Costigan (New York: Council on Foreign Relations Press, 1999), 74–105.

46. Marconi was hit by the end of the high-tech boom and ended up effectively bankrupt. *BBC News Online*, "Q&A: Marconi refinancing deal," August 29, 2002, http://news.bbc.co.uk/2/2219039.stm.

47. K. Hartley, "Aerospace: The Political Economy of an Industry," in *The Structure of European Industry*, 2nd ed., ed. H. W. de Jong, (Dordrecht: Kluwer, 1988), 329–54.

48. P. C. Wood and D. S. Sorenson, eds., *International Military Aerospace Collaboration* (Aldershot, UK: Ashgate Publishing, 2000). In May 2005, Snecma merged with Sagem to form SAFRAN.

49. P. Dussage and B. Garrette, "Industrial Alliances in Aerospace and Defence: An Empirical Study of Strategic and Organizational Patterns," *Defence Economics* 4, no. 1 (1992): 45–62.

50. James, "Comparing European Responses to Defense Industry Globalization," The United States now accounts for 40 percent of BAE Systems' annual sales. *Business Week*, "Hands—And Arms—Across the Sea." Thales employs 12,000 people at 70 locations in the United Kingdom. Armed Forces, *Defence Suppliers Directory*, "Thales UK," 2006, http://www.armedforces.co.uk/companies/raq400d01d167144.

51. N. Cooper, *The Business of Death* (London: Taurus Academic Studies, 1997); B. Jackson, *Gunrunners' Gold* (London: World Development Movement, 1995); and P. Ingram and I. Davis, *The Subsidy Trap: British Government Financial Support for Arms Exports and the Defence Industry* (Oxford: Oxford Research Group, 2001).

52. M. Brzoska, P. Wilke, and H. Wulf, "The Changing Civil Military Production Mix in Western Europe," in *Arming the Future: A Defense Industry for the 21st Century*, ed. A. R. Markusen and S. S. Costigan (New York: Council on Foreign Relations Press, 1999), 371–405.

53. This is argued in Bonn International Center for Conversion, *Conversion Survey 1998: Global Disarmament, Defense Industry Consolidation and Conversion* (Oxford: Oxford University Press, 1998), 232.

54. Note that the U.S.-based subsidiaries of European companies have their arms sales registered in the table as those of the European parent company.

55. J. P. Dunne and G. Lamb, "Defence Industrial Participation: The Experience of South Africa," in *Arms Trade and Economic Development: Theory, Policy and Cases in Arms Trade Offsets*, ed. J. Brauer and J. P. Dunne (London: Routledge, 2004), 284–298; and J. P. Dunne, "The Making of Arms in South Africa," *Economics of Peace and Security Journal* 1, no. 1 (2006): 40–48, http://www.epsjournal.org.uk/Vol1/No1/issue.php.

56. There is concern over the cost and sustainability of such policies. Dunne "The Making of Arms in South Africa,"; and J. Brauer, "Arms Trade, Arms Industries and Developing Countries," in *Handbook of Defense Economics*, vol. 2, ed. K. Hartley and T. Sandler, (Amsterdam: Amsterdam, 2007).

57. K. Hartley, P. Dowdall, and D. Braddon, "Defence Industry Supply Chain Literature and Research Review," Department of Trade and Industry, London, 2000; D. Braddon, "The Matrix Reloaded: What Future for the Defence Firm?" *Defence and Peace Economics* 15, no. 6 (2004): 499–507; and P. Dowdall, "Chains Networks and Shifting Paradigms: The UK Defence Industry Supply System," *Defence and Peace Economics* 15, no. 6 (2004): 535–50.

58. See E. Surry, 'Table of Acquisitions', *SIPRI Yearbook 2006: Armaments, Disarmament and International Security* (Oxford University Press: Oxford, 2006), 428–30 and Anthony et al. "Arms Production," Table 8.7, 336.

59. This is also discussed in S. G. Jones, "The Rise of Europe's Defense Industry," US–Europe Analysis Series, Brookings Institution, Washington, DC, 2005, http://www.brookings.edu/fp/cuse/analysis/.

60. Sköns, Bauer, and Surry, "Arms production."

61. U.S. Department of Defense (DoD), "Annual Arms Industrial Capability Report to Congress," Washington, DC, 2004, http://www.acq.osd.mil/ip/ip_products.html, ii.

62. P. Dunay and L. Lachowski, "Euro-Atlantic Security and Institutions," *SIPRI Yearbook 2005* (Oxford: Oxford University Press, 2005), 5.

63. According to one report, "by 2011, the [global fighter aircraft] market will reach a new post-cold war peak, with deliveries reaching $16 billion." Report by the Teal Group (a U.S. consulting firm) reproduced in M. Fabey, "U.S. JSF Casts Long Shadow on Fighter Market," *Defense News*, June 6, 2005, 18. See also Frost & Sullivan, "Future Fighter Aircraft Requirements in Emerging Economies," press release, March 30, 2005, http://www.prnewswire.co.uk/cgi/news/release?id=142913. There is also an increased use of unmanned air vehicles (UAVs) and the establishment of a network-centric warfare environment. D. Jensen, "Avionics Outlook 2006: Rising Expectations," *Avionics Magazine*, January 2006, http://www.defensedaily.com/cgi/av/show_mag.cgi?pub=av&mon=0106.

64. Dunay and Lachowski, "Euro-Atlantic Security and Institutions," 6.

65. Sköns and Surry, "Arms Production," 387.

66. The delays are outlined and the experience of other fighters discussed in B. Dane, "Bumpy Road for Fighters," *Aviation Week & Space Technology*, January 17, 2005, 20–24, http://www.aviationnow.com/media/pdf/sb05_fighters.pdf. See also R. Forsberg, ed., *The Arms Production Dilemma* (Cambridge, MA: MIT Press, 1994).

67. See for example, F. Slijper, "The Emerging EU Military–Industrial Complex: Arms Industry Lobbying in Brussels," Transnational Institute Briefing Series 2005/1, Amsterdam, 2005, http://www.tni.org/pubs-docs/briefings.htm.

68. Brauer and Dunne, eds., *Arms Trade and Economic Development* (London: Routledge, 2004).

69. Markusen, "The Post–Cold War Persistence."

70. See Sköns and Surry, "Arms Production," 387. Financial companies involved include the Carlyle Group, TCG Financial Partners, and Veritas Capital.

71. Under the British Government's Private Finance Initiative (or public–private partnerships STET), the public sector contracts to purchase services on a long-term basis in order to take advantage of private sector management skills, while it is private finance that is at risk. These services include concessions and franchises, where a private sector firm takes on the responsibility for providing a public service, including maintaining, enhancing or constructing the necessary infrastructure. This initiative is having an important impact on state–industry relations in the United Kingdom, and is influencing government policy abroad. It could also lead to new entrants into the defense market.

72. For an analysis of the new developments, see H. Wulf, *Internationalizing and Privatizing War and Peace* (Basingstoke: Palgrave Macmillan, 2005). Wulf distinguishes between private military companies—companies supplying consulting and planning, logistics and support, technical services and repairs, training, peacekeeping, and humanitarian assistance—and private security companies—companies supplying property protection, crime prevention, and correctional services (43–47). There are no detailed estimates of the size or value of these sectors, only rough approximations of their general magnitude. Peter Singer has estimated the annual revenues of the private military industry at approximately $100 billion. P. W. Singer, *Corporate Warriors: The Rise of the Privatized Military Industry* (Ithaca, NY: Cornell University Press, 2003). The OECD has similarly made a rough estimate of the annual turnover of the private security sector, at $100–120 billion. Organisation for Economic Co—operation and Development (OECD), *The Security Economy* (Paris: OECD, 2004), 8, http://www.oecdbookshop.org/oecd/display.asp?SF1=DI&ST1=5LMQCR2JFHKB. If these estimates are accurate, then these two types of companies would have combined annual sales of about $200 billion. See also C. Holmqvist, *Private Security Companies: The Case for Regulation,* SIPRI Policy Paper 9 (SIPRI: Stockholm, 2005), http://www.sipri.org/; and J. Brauer, "An Economic Perspective on Mercenaries, Military Companies, and the Privatisation of Force," *Cambridge Review of International Affairs* 13, no. 1 (2000): 130–46.

73. Wulf, *Internationalizing and Privatizing War and Peace*, 194.

74. Wulf, *Internationalizing and Privatizing War and Peace*, 207. See also Holmqvist, *Private Security Companies: The Case for Regulation.*

75. Brzoska and Ohlson, *Arms Production in the Third World.*

76. S. T. Wezeman and M. Bromley, "The Volume of Transfers of Major Conventional Weapons: By Recipients and Suppliers, 2000–2004," *SIPRI Yearbook 2005* (Oxford: Oxford University Press, 2005), Table 10A.2, 453–54.

77. A. R. Markusen, S. DiGiovanni, and M. C. Leary, eds., *From Defense to Development: International Perspectives on Realizing the Peace Dividend* (London: Routledge, 2003), 191.

78. J. Brauer, "The Arms Industry in Developing Nations: History and Post–Cold War Assessment," in *Arming the South: The Economics of Military Expenditures, Arms Production and Trade in Developing Countries,* ed. J. Brauer and J. P. Dunne (Hampshire: Palgrave, 2002).

79. Brauer, "The Arms Industry in developing nations"; and Brzoska and Ohlson *Arms Production in the Third World.* Brauer argues that the evidence suggests that the arms industries in developing countries depended crucially on established civil capacities, and there in no evidence that arms exports provided net foreign exchange.

80. J. Brauer and J. P. Dunne, "Arms Trade Offsets and Development," *Africanus* 35, no. 1 (2005): 14–24.

81. Markusen et al., eds., *From Defense to Development.*

3

The Defense Iron Triangle Revisited

Ron Matthews and Curie Maharani

The purpose of this chapter is to revisit Gordon Adam's 1982 concept of a defense-related *iron triangle*.[1] A revised interpretation of its contemporary relevance is offered, arguing that the real cause of high and rising defense expenditure is not so much the profit motive of defense contractors and the linked interests of military and government stakeholders, but rather the cost acceleration of next-generation military systems. In the present milieu, defense acquisition has become exceedingly expensive, leading to what the U.S. defense economist, Thomas Callaghan Jr., has described as structural disarmament.[2] Under such conditions, military expenditure rises, but by less than the rapidly inflating costs of acquiring sophisticated weapons, thus degrading affordability for large volume production.[3] This confluence of acquisition challenges has transformed the rigid triangulation of defense-industrial, congressional, and Department of Defense (DoD) forces from a positive set of relationships, seeking value-for-money, to a socially negative condition, perpetuating unjustifiably high levels of defense expenditure.

In this revised view of the iron triangle, the chapter begins by profiling the original sense of the concept, by attempting to balance the putative costs of the military-industrial complex with the realized or potential benefits. Discussion then moves to examine the evolving defense acquisition policies since the 1980s, from a confrontational era in which dialogue between the armed forces, government, congressional committees, and defense industry was seen as collusion, to the present period where cooperation among the three elements of the triangle is actively promoted. Finally, the transformational management policies of the contemporary period are then explored. The dominant theme in this modern era is partnership and cooperation, with the spectrum of initiatives focusing on the promotion of, for instance, smart acquisition, lean logistics, public-private partnerships (particularly private finance initiatives), technology clusters, value chains, outsourcing, foreign direct investment (FDI), and investment offsets. A consequence of these policies is that the management of defense is now more susceptible to beneficial synergies arising from cooperative endeavor than to political lobbying through some notional iron triangle.

OF POWER ELITES, MILITARY-INDUSTRIAL COMPLEXES, AND IRON TRIANGLES . . .

The idea of an incestuous relationship embracing some or all of the key defense stakeholders, such as the DoD, Congressional Committees, local defense contractors and, indeed, the armed forces, arguably has its roots in the writings of Wright Mills in his examination of power elites.[4] The putative relationship between government and other elitist public sector agencies, broadly defined to include the military, took on greater significance when U.S. president Dwight Eisenhower uttered the now immortalized words, "Military-Industrial Complex," in his 1961 farewell address to the nation:

> The conjunction of an immense military establishment and a huge arms industry is new in the American experience. The total influence—economic, political and even spiritual—is felt in every city, every state house and every office of the federal government. . . . In the councils of government, we must guard against the acquisition of unwarranted influence, whether sought or unsought, by the *military industrial complex.*[5]

Subsequent observers, by and large, have adopted Eisenhower's interpretation of the term, the military-industrial complex, as a potentially dangerous and harmful force: a force representing a trinity of powerful interest groups, viewing the perpetuation of defense expenditure and arms acquisition as supporting the parochial goals of these stakeholders. However, the ambiguity of the military-industrial complex terminology has engendered an array of papers in the broad field of the political economy of defense.[6]

Transitioning from the concept of a military-industrial complex to that of an iron triangle makes explicit the trilateral nature of the institutional and bureaucratic relationships within the complex. Of some considerable significance in this regard is that the U.S. defense industry is almost entirely in private sector hands. This raises the specter of monolithic defense contractors instinctively seeking the rewards of profit maximization, irrespective of the impact on society or international security. The prevailing view, then, is that the iron triangle, and before it, the military industrial complex, reflects the greed and avarice of commercial enterprise.[7] The U.S. military-industrial complex is in actuality a private military-industrial complex, comprising the defense contracting behemoths, such as Lockheed Martin, Boeing, BAE Systems, and EADS (European Aeronautic Defence and Space Company).

The U.S. and several other advanced country defense-industrial contexts are different from that of the industrializing states. The immature defense-industrial sectors of the developing world are principally located in the public sector, and thus escape the collusive dangers alluded to by President Eisenhower. Three major reasons, embracing strategic, political, and military considerations, are proffered to explain why developing countries prefer public ownership of defense production facilities.

Strategic Imperative

Emerging states are mostly newly independent, having been released from the yoke of their colonial masters in the years following World War II. For these countries, defense immediately became a priority: development had to be defended. Moreover, for these countries to enjoy meaningful independence, they also had to enjoy self-sustaining development. Increasingly, it was recognized that this can only be secured with the assistance of foreign capital, particularly foreign direct investment; and for this to occur, confidence in the long-term stability of the economy was necessary. Thus, a virtuous cycle of self-reliance, security, and sustainability was sought, inevitably leading to enhanced stability, so reinforcing the development cycle, and, ultimately, achieving greater sovereignty (see Figure 3.1).

Sovereignty went hand-in-glove with independence, not just in the politico-economic domain, but in the defense economic arena, as well. To this day, defense-industrial sovereignty remains a principal goal of developing states, not least because they are located in regions of high tension, but also because they are subject to the threat of conflict and possible arms embargoes.[8] Both India and Pakistan, for instance, have suffered arms embargoes from the United States and European Union when the latter sought an end to hostilities on the Indian Subcontinent. South Africa was also at the receiving end of a United Nations arms embargo following the Sharpeville Massacre of March 21, 1960. In the Far East, China's 1989 Tiananmen Square incident provoked the imposition of a North American and European arms embargo, continuing to be enforced to this day. Finally, Indonesia incurred the wrath of the U.S. following Jakarta's 1999 military action in Timor Leste. The U.S. response was to impose an arms embargo on the TNI (Indonesian armed forces), severely curtailing the operational availability of U.S.-supplied weapon systems.[9] The U.S. embargo taught Indonesia a painful strategic lesson, subsequently leading Jakarta to diversify its sources of military equipment away from the United States. However, while the preponderance

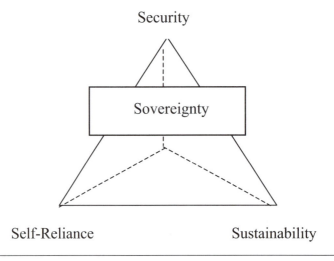

FIGURE 3.1 The iron-triangle of national sovereignty

of Indonesian foreign arms purchases now come from Russia, the danger is that Jakarta has simply exchanged dependence on the United States with that on Russia.[10] Malaysia has faced similar problems of arms dependency, and in an attempt to overcome such vulnerability, the country has pursued a strategy of multiple-sourcing. As a consequence, Malaysia's combat aircraft inventory presently comprises Russian Mig-29 and SU-30 aircraft, U.S. F/A-18 fighters, and British Hawk trainer/fighter aircraft.[11] This degree of weapon systems diversification obviously reduces overall dependency, but does little to diminish strategic vulnerability on the supply of spares and new equipment for particular systems. Moreover, such diversity adds immeasurably to the complexity and cost of logistical resupply.

Politico-Diplomatic Status

In the developing world, and increasingly also in the advanced countries, such as Russia, France, and even the United Kingdom, there is an emerging view that the defense sector needs to be (re-)nationalized to ensure that local sovereignty is maintained. This is particularly the case for newly-independent states. Here, the conventional view is that investment to support military capability is a natural response to nationalist sentiment in post-colonial states. The possession of a strong military establishment symbolizes national power and thus enhances a country's international profile, and, by extension, the status of its government. Military power also carries with it diplomatic clout. It is perhaps no coincidence that all member countries of the UN Security Council possess powerful conventional military forces as well as nuclear weapons capability. Such countries form the mainstay of international peacemaking interventions, and subsequently, are often involved in the peacekeeping and peace-support operations.[12] Thus, those countries possessing a strong military establishment have the potential to influence the global security environment, enhancing their diplomatic status in the world community.

DEFENSE AS AN ECONOMIC DRIVER

Adam Smith argued that defense is the ultimate public good, too important to be left in the hands of the business community. Smith's insistence on public ownership of defense has a twofold justification:

- Firstly, that defense represents one of the best examples of Paretian optimality, that is, where all citizens benefit from the provision of a good, without the danger of free-riding.[13]
- Secondly, policy should be geared towards public ownership of defense undertakings, as only public ownership will ensure that sovereignty of supply remains the overarching stakeholder priority.

Numerous powerful modern defense economies reflect Smith's view that defense should remain firmly in the public domain, not least because it facilitates progress towards the policy goal of defense-industrial self-sufficiency. Russia, India, Pakistan, and China provide good examples of countries that fall into this category. As highlighted previously, there is a strong strategic rationale that underpins self-sufficiency, but economic motives are also pervasive.

The economic basis for promoting local defense industrialization rests on the argument that defense enjoys a positive relationship with economic growth. However, this is a controversial field of inquiry, sparked by the writings of the Belgian defense economist, Emile Benoit, in the 1970s.[14] His particular focus was on the economic impact of increased Indian defense expenditure at the time of the 1962–63 Sino-Indian war. Radically, Benoit posited that increased defense spending led to an increase in national income; that is, there was a positive causal relationship between defense expenditure and economic growth, moving from the former to the latter. Whilst Benoit recognized the existence of *crowding-out costs* associated with raised defense expenditure, he concluded that growth benefits outweighed defense costs.[15] Benoit identified numerous economic benefits stemming from a vibrant defense economy, the principal of which are identified and discussed below:

Employment: an expansive defense economy, including both the armed forces and defense industry, is traditionally a labor-intensive operation. Although this argument is less valid today, given an increasing emphasis on transformational warfare, the idea that defense employs relatively high numbers people probably still finds resonance in the developing world.

Skill generation: arms production is associated with high-technology activities, such as research and development (R&D), precision engineering, and systems integration. These activities demand highly skilled workers engaged in high value-added operations. However, these value activities will only benefit the local economy if arms production is undertaken domestically.[16]

Civil-military integration: the conventional defense-industrial paradigm is that defense contractors operate in technological isolation from the broader commercial economy, but if this isolationist condition can be removed, then there is the potential for exploiting the benefits of high civil-military integration.[17] The contemporary revolution in transformational warfare emphasizes procurement from the high-technology commercial sectors, with consequential benefits to both the defense community and the broader commercial economy. A characteristic of this broader defense economy is that civil subcontractors enjoy higher capacity utilization and thus lower cost, benefiting defense and civil customers alike. Equally, given that subcontractors tend to be small, specialized, and highly skilled, they are therefore also arguably the most innovative actors in this integrated defense economy. The strategically important subcontractors have the potential to act as transmission mechanisms for innovation, irrespective of whether technology moves from the civil economy to defense (technology spin-ons) or from defense to the civil sector (technology spin-offs).

Infrastructural Development: the benefit of defense-induced infrastructural investment continues to have resonance in developing states, such as India, Pakistan, China, and some countries in Africa. As a deliberate government decision, perhaps primarily for strategic reasons, military establishments, including defense factories, are often sited distant from urban industrial conurbations. Defense-industrial isolation from major population centers means that defense establishments necessarily must invest in the development of local infrastructure. These investments will include such strategic development requirements as roads, associated transportation links (such as railways and airports), hospitals, schools, military farms, shops, and an array of basic and sometimes advanced defense-industrial manufacturing and testing facilities.

DEFENSE AS A CENTRIFUGAL FORCE FOR GROWTH

Defense production may act as growth pole within the local economy. Michael Porter was one of the first academics to highlight the importance of *horizontal* and *vertical* industrial relationships among businesses in the same industry and between that industry and supplier industries.[18] The argument is that learning and innovational synergies are likely to arise from geographical proximity, where there are horizontal and vertical concentrations of, respectively, competitor companies and subcontractors; the latter cross-supply rival enterprises in the final goods market, thus transmitting product innovation and/or process efficiency.

There are thus likely to be economic benefits as opposed to political downsides from an iron triangle of military-government-defense-industrial forces. Even from a political standpoint, however, the concept was probably overdone. The collusive nature of the concept was probably a child of its time, in the sense that there was much less scrutiny of acquisition decision-making in the sixties and seventies, and much less independent and governmental auditing and oversight of defense acquisition practices than at the present time. This is not to deny that in economies where defense production is a capitalist endeavor, contractors are motivated to lobby decision makers, seeking to raise the profile of their weapon systems in the tendering and procurement process.[19] This lobbying process, however, is post, rather than prior, to the official commencement of a new weapons program. New capability requirements will be identified in Delphi and similar brainstorming sessions involving diverse strategic, military, government, academic, and industrial experts. Views will solidify over long periods of introspection, reflection, and debate, against specified, but secret Ministry of Defense (MoD) strategic scenarios. The iron triangle participants are involved in the identification of new military capabilities, but their contribution to the debate is far removed from Gordon Adam's original, negative conceptualization of the concept as a consortium of interests perpetuating the production and sale of armaments.

PERTURBATIONS IN DEFENSE ECONOMIC RELATIONS: FROM CONFRONTATION TO COOPERATION

The two decades following the early 1960s, when Eisenhower coined the term, the *military-industrial complex,* can be characterized as a period of unremitting increases in defense spending. The period coincided with the height of the cold war and mutual deterrence between the two capitalist and communist ideological blocks. Massed inventories of platforms, whether for land, air, or sea warfare, reflected a psychosis that military strength is reflected solely through numerical superiority. Military expenditure inexorably rose because of an identifiable omnipresent threat and arms sales hence came easy. Contractors showed scant regard for even the most rudimentary marketing planning; there was no need, given that defense spending was certain and seemingly on a permanently rising trend. This applied to both the national context, where host governments provided assured and ongoing levels of demand, and to the international arms market, also exhibiting predictable and stable growth in arms sales. The big Western defense companies enjoyed limited competition from within a tightly knit international oligopolistic market structure. It was a sellers' market, comprising a small number of dominant defense manufacturers servicing the needs of the so-called third world countries gripped in an ideological vice between capitalism and communism.

Rising Western defense expenditure left the Soviets with little choice but to respond and accelerate the Soviet Union's headlong dash towards economic bankruptcy. However, the West's insatiable appetite for advanced military equipment fuelled strong defense inflationary forces, sowing the seeds of budgetary stress. Consequently, in the 1990s the demand for arms began to falter.

Acquisition of RMA (revolution in military affairs) sophisticated weapon systems was held to be a principal cause of cost escalation along with inefficient procurement practices, and thus a major plank of the policy assault against bloated defense spending was to pare down and restructure acquisition spending. In the United Kingdom, Peter Levine was appointed to spearhead MoD's push to eradicate what had come to be known as *gold plating*; that is, the phenomenon of excessive over-engineering of military equipment resulting in exceedingly high acquisition costs. In tackling this problem, Levine sought to commercialize defense, an approach that threaded neatly into the broad policy fabric of the Thatcher government's economic liberalization crusade in the 1980s.[20] Levine's major policy instrument was competitive tendering, employed to address the problem of high-cost acquisition, engendered by *cost-plus* contracting. Belatedly, the cost-plus option was viewed as antediluvian, save for high-risk, first-of-a-series weapons programs. It had finally been recognized that if margins are calculated as a percentage of cost, then this incentivizes contractors to operate inefficiently. The resultant impact of applying a constant margin on an increasing cost base is higher profit: the *plus* in the cost-plus relation.

Cost containment policies were also beginning to have other wider impacts on the defense economy. Significantly, there was a growing sense among European NATO nations that defense-industrial sovereignty was no longer financially viable, particularly when translated as a comprehensive research, development, and production capability across the broad spectrum of weapon systems. This recognition of constrained national defense resources led increasingly to regional collaborative acquisition initiatives, such as the three-nation Tornado fighter program (Germany, Italy, and the United Kingdom), the Jaguar fighter program (Anglo-French), and the Alpha-jet project (Franco-German). Promotion of the seemingly contradictory acquisition policies of competition *and* cooperation became more pronounced after the sudden and dramatic ending of the cold war, the 1989 implosion of the Soviet Union, and the rapid demise of Communism. The onset of the 1990s heralded the search for elusive peace dividends through defense expenditure contraction in the new benign international strategic environment.[21] The logic of the iron triangle, as originally articulated, was sorely tested during this decade as national and global military expenditure fell precipitously; this revived only in the first decade of the present millennium, particularly post-9/11.

The defense economic turbulence of the 1990s created a breeding ground for the partnering concepts that today have matured into full-blown tried and tested policies. At the national level, cooperative policies began to emerge, such as the United Kingdom's science and technology initiative called Progress through Partnership.[22] This was aimed at reinforcing the partnership between the defense/aerospace industries and the government in an attempt to assuage the progressive erosion of Britain's market share in the global aerospace market. Similarly, at the transnational regional level, there was a concerted European push for defense-industrial integration. Overcapacity and production duplication were the maladies facing Europe in the development of a single European defense market. It was the U.S. government, however, that led the way in defense rationalization. The decisive event occurred in 1992 when the U.S. defense secretary, William Perry, at a meeting now enshrined in defense folklore as the last supper, issued an ultimatum to some 11 major defense contractors: reduce your numbers or go out of business.[23]

The radical shake-out of America's military supply base acted as a reference point for European politicians to demand that similar restructuring policies be enacted in Europe. The build-up of pressure for change culminated in the issuance of the 1998 letter of intent. This represented a framework for European defense-industrial integration and was signed by the heads of state of France, Germany, Italy Spain, Sweden, and the United Kingdom. This signaled a strong intent by all signatory nations to work together on defense matters, seeking procurement harmonization in the short-run, and eradicating wasteful development and production duplication between European nations in the long-run. However, while the intent was genuine, reality has yielded little in the way of tangible defense-industrial integration.

Although only limited progress has been achieved in harmonizing European arms acquisition, there has been some movement towards the institutionalization of European defense. Through a growing sense of intra-European partnership, a common goal of progressively moving towards a European Technological and Industrial Defense base has been agreed upon. In parallel, two important Europe-wide agencies have been established. In the acquisition area, the Organization for Joint Armament Cooperation (OCCAR) was created to manage large European defense programs collectively.[24] These have included the A400m (tactical heavy-lift aircraft), BOXER (multi-role armor vehicles), and FREMM (multi-mission frigates). However, OCCAR has not been an unqualified success. While undoubtedly, governments, armed forces, and defense contractors have worked together in a spirit of regional partnership, frictions over national work-share have constrained high levels of integration. OCCAR's mechanism for determining program work-share is based on what is termed *juste retour* (fair return). From an equity perspective, the notion of a fair return is incontestable, but its economic logic is less than clear. As applied in other major European defense programs, such as the Tornado and Eurofighter, *juste retour* is calculated on the basis that a participating country's work-share (or program input) is linked to its off-take volume (or program output).[25] This is an eminently just or fair allocation mechanism, but one that fails the efficiency test. In the case of the Eurofighter Typhoon Programme, for instance, Spain was one of four country participants in what is, still today, Europe's biggest procurement program. Yet, Spain has had no history, capacity, or indeed, capability in the development and manufacture of advanced combat aircraft.[26] Spain's learning curve was without doubt, steep, and thus costly for the Typhoon program, overall. Through continuation of national defense-industrial priorities, *juste retour* blocks movement towards an international division of labor in the European defense industry. In an attempt to overcome the inherent inefficiency of the *juste retour* allocatory apparatus, an approach was adopted to spread country work-share across several arms programs rather than calibrating work to any one program. Due to limited research on the operational performance of OCCAR, however, it is challenging to reach an informed judgment of the success of this Europe-wide procurement agency. The continued conspicuous absence of laudatory statements evidencing OCCAR's achievements strongly hints that movement towards an integrated European acquisition approach has made only tortuous progress.

A recent important entrant to Europe's defense policy fora is the European Defense Agency (EDA), but its remit is wider than simply procurement.[27] The EDA has proved to be higher profile than OCCAR, focusing on aggressively pushing through an agenda of reform, including the eradication of defense offsets between participating member states and the adoption of a robust position on the consolidation of Europe's defense R&D program. The EDA has adopted strident policy stances on promoting greater European defense integration, and, as a consequence, has gained the respect of government and industry as a prominent actor within the European defense sector. Yet, as with OCCAR, its measurable success has been limited, not only by member states' persistence on prioritizing national sovereignty considerations, but also because the EDA has been hamstrung by a miserly budget of 32 million euros and a policymaking regime in which member states' compliance is voluntary rather than obligatory.[28]

The EDA is a microcosm of a broader thrust towards regional defense cooperation, driven principally by the search for cost reduction. This process of pursuing competitiveness through regional cooperation mirrors parallel developments at the global level. Through the process of defense globalization, military and politico-economic drivers have forged an array of relationships. Different dimensions of partnering have come to be expressed through offshore outsourcing, civil and military offsets, transnational mergers and acquisitions, international strategic alliances, foreign direct investment, and global defense-industrial consortiums. This latter form of partnering provides, arguably, the best example of defense globalization. It symbolizes the development and production of major weapon systems through a multi-country, truly global model of international partnership. Thus, the principal global venture to date, the F-35 Joint Strike Fighter (JSF), represents a positive cross-threading of government, armed forces, and defense-industrial interests across nations.[29] Moreover, as per Europe's regional defense-industrial collaborative programs, the goal has been to capture maximum cost reduction through scale, pursued through, firstly, the establishment of country work-shares, determined via competitive bidding rather than *juste retour* or *offsets,* and, secondly, through the employment of innovative manufacturing and integration techniques. Operationally, however, the consortium's lofty cost-effectiveness ambitions for the F-35 project have failed to live up to expectations. Firstly, the planned cost efficiencies have yet to materialize. A recent effort to measure the progress of JSF has found that its procurement cost had increased by 37 percent compared to the 2001 budget plan.[30] This cost increase has been due to a number of factors, but principally delays in proving the design specification. Secondly, the JSF consortium model has suffered heavy criticism on the high concentration of work allocated to just two partners, the United States and the United Kingdom.[31] The latter country is a full (1st-tier) partner, having invested US$2 billion into the JSF project. Although this represents just 6 percent of the value of the JSF program, the actual contractual value of work enjoyed by the United Kingdom amounts to around 24 percent. Add to this the 73 percent contract value enjoyed by the dominant U.S. partner, then little remains for the other seven, mostly small, participating defense economies. A third serious weakness exposed in the JSF partnership is the

United States' reluctance to release intellectual property rights (IPR) to other participatory states. The tensions came to a head in 2005 when the United States refused to release the software codes to the British to enable the latter to enjoy autonomy in mid-life upgrades, technology insertion, and weapon systems integration.

INTO THE 21ST CENTURY: COOPERATION, NOT CONFRONTATION

The new millennium has witnessed an expansion in defense-related cooperative endeavor. The movement away from confrontational behavior between the MoD and industry has become entrenched in both policy and practice. Partnering across all elements of the triangle, and particularly between the MoD and industry, has become the norm. To provide an appreciation of this partnering revolution, it will be instructive to evaluate a selection of the more significant policy initiatives that have occurred.

Smart Acquisition

The launch of the U.K. smart acquisition policy in 1998 represented a major *demarche* from the *us versus them* defense contracting mentality. A raft of new and somewhat radical policy thrusts were introduced, representing an advance on the McKinsey-inspired procurement model launched earlier in the United States. First and foremost was the promotion of Integrated Project Teams (IPTs). These comprise representation from all three elements (MoD, armed forces, and defense industry) in a cooperative rather than confrontational or collusive iron triangle. A central tenet of the IPT was that its life should run parallel to the life-cycle of the military equipment for which the IPT was formed. The IPT would have management responsibility, including oversight and planning authority, for the defense project throughout all stages of what has come to be termed the CADMID cycle. From Figure 3.2, the sequential stages are detailed as Concept, Assessment, Development, Manufacture, In-service, and Disposal.

The CADMID cycle is a revised version of the earlier Downey model. This newer version of the acquisition cycle incorporates facets that move in sync with the MoD mantra of "faster, cheaper and better procurement."[32] For instance, the number of procurement decision-points (known as gateways) authorizing project progression was reduced from

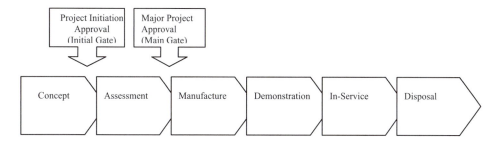

FIGURE 3.2   The U.K. defense acquisition CADMID cycle

Source: http://dasa.mod.uk/natstats/ukds/2007/pdf/c1/Chap1Table117.pdf

four to two: an early gate pre-assessment stage and the principal gate prior to manufacture. Moreover, at the very early concept phase, the plan was to encourage defense contractors to work together, exchanging information and ideas, in joint development of a new military system designed to address emerging threats identified in the MoD's future scenario threat analysis. There was also a requirement that 15 percent of the program funding should be spent early in the procurement cycle to ensure that the concept and systems are thoroughly evaluated, reducing the possibility of later operational problems and delays.[33]

As the acquisition program matures and proceeds through the CADMID cycle, management responsibility migrates from a conceptual and R&D focus to production, in-service logistics, maintenance, repair and overhaul activities, and finally, disposal; the last element of the CADMID cycle represents recognition by the authorities that disposal of certain categories of weapon system, such as nuclear-powered submarines, poses significant environmental, safety, and cost challenges.

A further novel feature of the smart acquisition model was the appointment of a *customer* that industry could identify, and to which it could report. The customer would be organizationally interchangeable, dependent upon the point in the CADMID cycle that the project had reached. Thus, during the early concept, assessment, and development phases, the concept of 'customer 1' (Directors of Equipment Capability) would mean that project responsibility would be firmly located within the MoD. However, as the project moves through the subsequent life-cycle stages, the notion of 'customer 2' comes to the fore, and in-service responsibility moves to a senior manager of the armed forces.

The smart acquisition policy has been reviewed and modified continuously, in harmony with implementation learning in the field. A principal policy adaptation occurred during the early part of this decade when the smart acquisition policy aim of "faster, cheaper and better" was extended to embrace 'and more effectively integrated" leading directly to introduction of the *Lines-of-Development* concept.[34] Lines-of-development was an acknowledgement that IPTs, comprising MoD acquisition and logistics civil servants, military personnel, and defense contractor management, undertake their planning on a stovepipe basis, with limited assessment of a project's interrelationship with other important activities impacting on military effectiveness. The lines-of-development capture important defense activities covering training, equipment, personnel, information, concepts and doctrine, organization, infrastructure, and logistics, all of which interconnect as a system of systems. The IPT's requirement to integrate and coordinate their policies via the relevant lines-of-development was introduced following serious problems encountered on two major acquisition programs. The first was the staggering discovery that if an early design of the Royal Navy's two new 65,000 ton aircraft carriers had been implemented, then the carrier would have been too big to access any of the United Kingdom's naval port facilities. The second problem was linked to a Private Finance Initiative (PFI)–sponsored pilot training program required for the 2005 delivery of 65 U.K. license-produced Apache gunship helicopters. The separate helicopter manufacture and pilot training management teams did not communicate, and thus failed to coordinate the completion of pilot training with helicopter delivery.[35] As a result, there was a serious disconnect between the operational readiness of the helicopters and the availability of pilots to fly them. Apache helicopters had to be stored for up to two years, at a cost of £6 million (approximately US$10 million), waiting for the arrival of trained pilots.

Private Finance Initiatives (PFIs)

The appearance of PFIs in the 1990s launched the phenomenon of public-private partnerships in the U.K. public sector, generally, and particularly in the context of defense investments.[36] PFIs symbolize the middle ground between the ideological extremes of socialism and capitalism. The rationale of PFIs is that they act as financial vehicles aimed at exploiting management synergies stemming from partnering, including, importantly, the sharing, if not total transfer, of program risk.

By mid-2008, over 60 defense PFIs had been established in the United Kingdom, including military housing projects, simulator training equipment, communications and intelligence systems, future vehicles, and future strategic tanker aircraft project.[37] The majority of PFIs are located at the support end of military activity, not least because these are the easiest PFI projects to implement. All stakeholders in the PFI partnership are held to benefit from the arrangement: the consortium of commercial investors, including, often, construction companies, asset management businesses, financial institutions, and technical stakeholders, gain from a project's anticipated positive net present value over an economic life typically spanning 25–30 years; the MoD gains, because, firstly, most projects are off-balance sheet, thus reducing substantial upfront capital expenditure, and, secondly, because prior to authorizing a PFI, rather than an in-house (MoD) investment, the MoD will assure itself that the former option is less costly than the latter, thus saving taxpayers' money; and, finally, the armed forces are happy because they enjoy an enhanced service of higher quality than the previously administered in-house service/facility.[38]

The logic of PFI therefore appears incontestable, with benefits enjoyed by all partners. The financial mechanism for the arrangement is akin to leasing. The private sector consortium will incur the initial heavy cost of construction and service provision, often through subcontracting the services to specialized organizations. Once in place, the new improved service/facility will then be leased to the MoD, with the latter paying a mutually agreed leasing payment. Within the associated Public Service Agreement (PSA) that forms a linked part of the lease agreement, there is a detailed set of performance criteria to which the service providers must adhere.

Failure of the leasor to comply with the agreed standards confers the sanction of non-payment of the agreed fee. This tight and binding lease arrangement ensures that the PFI mechanism works efficiently and effectively for all parties in a ministry-military-industry trilateral relationship.

There are challenges, however, to the PFI concept, both actual and potential; the major ones may be summarized as follows:

- Firstly, once a PFI agreement is established and operates for upwards of 30 years, there is the question as to what happens to the service/facility at the end of its lease-life. Ownership, of course, reverts to the MoD, but at that point will it want to assume formal ownership and management of the service, invest in a replacement build via another PFI, or discontinue with the service. There is thus uncertainty at the expiry of the PFI project's economic life.
- Secondly, there is a real concern that during the life-time of the PFI project, the service or technology provision will become redundant or suffer from technological

obsolescence. Given that typical PFI project lives extend decades into the future, there is a danger in the fast-moving, high-technology defense environment that the facility or service may no longer be viable, having been superseded by other forms of provision. The inherent risks of PFIs are therefore high, particularly when the costly nature of some mega-PFI contracts is taken into account. For instance, the U.K. JSCSC (Staff College), a 30-year PFI project, carries a reported value of £500 million (US$800million) over its projected contractual life.

- Thirdly, PFIs are held to be important innovational developments for public sector-management, because they allow policymakers to focus on policy and exploit commercial competence and efficiency, reaping benefits for taxpayers through risk transfer and enhanced value-for-money. This is fine in theory, but in practice, events have shown that big commercial asset management companies responsible for managing major PFIs, along with the attendant risks, may, like all other private sector operations, suffer financial failure and insolvency. Someone has to pick up the tab, and inevitably, it falls on government to be the ultimate guarantor of PFI project sustainability.

- Fourthly, the cumulative value of PFI projects that have been implemented in the U.K. defense sector is valued at £8,321 million (1987–2007; approximately US$13 billion), reflecting an enormous fixed cost currently recorded off-balance sheet.[39] This is both good and bad; it is good because the present value of defense investment shown on the defense balance sheet is appreciably lower, thus raising the capital productivity of Britain's armed forces, but it is bad because the servicing charge of all MoD PFI projects has now reached 3.7 percent of the overall MoD budget.[40] Dependent on the value and structure of future MoD budgets, this proportionately high PFI servicing cost represents a heavy financial burden, imposing significant opportunity costs on the future defense community.

- Finally, PFIs have until recently been targeting the relatively straightforward and risk-free support projects in, for instance, infrastructure and training. PFI projects focused on the operational teeth-end activities are altogether a more complex and challenging proposition. The United States and United Kingdom's foray into PFIs for air-to-air refueling tankers taxes the credibility of the PFI concept.[41] These air-tanker projects are mega-expensive programs, entailing huge financial, technological, and operational risks. However, the pilots are likely to be military reservists, introducing greater flexibility into the usage of the tanker aircraft. The priority of the tankers will, of course, be for deployment on operational duties, as and when, but otherwise the internal fuel tanks can be stripped out and the aircraft used for commercial tasks.

Technological Partnerships

Strategic partnerships can occur at a multiplicity of personal, corporate, governmental, and institutional levels, and the spatial dimensions may be national, regional, and global. Moreover, in the defense technology field, trilateral relationships are typical, comprising the MoD, defense industry, and armed forces. In the United Kingdom, as has been discussed earlier, an important technology management policy milestone, epitomizing trilateral defense relationships, emerged via the 1987 Smart Acquisition policy.[42] The IPTs represent a challenging fusion of differing ministry-military-industrial cultures and goals. Aside from the fact that IPT members will bring to the proceedings a diverse assortment of organizational and procedural bags and baggage, there is also the distinct likelihood that goal congruence among IPT members will be absent. An immediate source of tension is that for government, defense acquisition will be driven by the need to secure value-for-money. The armed forces' imperative, by contrast, will be to obtain the most effective kit. Somehow these conflicting requirements must be reconciled. A possible solution is outsourcing. For the MoD and defense companies, the rationale for global outsourcing is to reduce procurement and production cost, respectively. However, this is only one side of the efficiency equation. Modern defense management policies are not solely premised on input cost, but also on output effectiveness, that is, battle-winning capability. This input-output relation highlights the importance of the cost-effectiveness trade-off in defense acquisition.[43] Government and contractors increasingly search for cost reduction through defense globalization and open defense trade, with the armed forces prioritizing the need to capture leading-edge military capability. Securing goal congruence for all stakeholders, therefore, often means purchasing defense equipment off shore.

Goal congruence through partnering requires compromise, and the ability to cut through an amalgam of conflicting stakeholder objectives. Although issues such as scale and affordability will influence the character of the relations, the essential need is for all parties to subscribe to the common goal of technology access. This is the principal challenge for all countries, rich or poor, big or small.[44] Often, states will suffer from a small-scale defense requirement, precluding local production. Moreover, although big countries will enjoy the cost benefits of higher procurement volume, they may face barriers in accessing the next generation technology. National solutions for securing defense-related technology are increasingly becoming economically nonviable. The R&D components of transformational weapon systems are incurring costs that are accelerating exponentially. Thus, even the richest country in the world, the United States, cannot justify national capacity in all aspects of defense production.[45] Partnering is promoted as a partial panacea to overcoming the high costs of developing local innovational capability in defense technology. The form that technology partnering can take may be either national or international, though increasingly it is a hybrid of both.

In a bid to generate innovational opportunity, governments often foster institutional R&D cooperation. The United Kingdom, for instance, has established the *towers of excellence* concept, encouraging partnering between government defense institutes, such as Defence Science and Technology Laboratory (DSTL), defense companies, and university departments.[46] The towers represent focused areas of defense capability, with stakeholders targeting expertise and capital in a bid to nurture specific defense systems, such as missiles. In a spirit of international partnership, national towers are now being complemented by international towers of excellence.[47] It is perhaps too early to draw definitive judgments on the success of such models, but the intent is clear: to secure innovational synergies through tightly bounded technological partnering. The towers of excellence concept reflects a policy emphasis on delivering defense innovation through a technology-push process. The policy alternative is to promote innovation via a technology-pull strategy; that is, to create an industrial and technological environment conducive to market-induced technology development. Determining the factors that lie behind effective technology-push strategies is difficult, but market structure is central to the debate. Porter's *diamond* methodology highlighted market structure as a critical factor in the identification of successful economies.[48] He attributed economic vitality and creativity not only to competitiveness deriving from horizontal industrial structures, but also on the extent of vertical industrial relationships. Porter sensed, correctly, that the robust development of vertical industrial structures required spatial proximity as an essential ingredient for technological development.[49] The linked nature of vertical industrial structures and spatial proximity needs further elucidation, not least because the possession of such market characteristics distinguishes the mature and innovative rich countries from those that remain technologically dependent.

Vertical industrial relationships pertain to the quality of what has come to be called the supply or value chain. Such chains typically comprise a myriad of small specialized subcontractors that have invariably evolved over long periods of time, and represent repositories of accumulated intellectual and physical capital. They form part of structured industrial networks reflecting a refined division of labor in supplying the needs of their primary customers: the suppliers focus on innovation, whilst the ultimate customer focuses on scale. Japan's industrial development model provides a good example of this technological dualism. An added dimension in the Japanese case is that the ultimate customer actively seeks to forge close relations with constituent firms in the supply chain, with investment aimed at raising the quality of subcontractor processes. Equally, customers and suppliers are likely to engage in problem-solving cooperation to overcome technological bottlenecks at both the process and product level. The customer or prime contractor is often conscious of the innovation, but it is only the specialist supplier that can translate the idea into a practical reality.

However, for mutual innovational benefit to emerge from supply chain relationships, spatial proximity is essential. Effective problem-solving requires regular contact with design staff, engineers, and technicians. Factory visits and prototype development are also part of the mix. Thus, whilst outsourcing across global supply chains is likely to secure cost reduction, it is unlikely to engender major technological breakthroughs. This is because problem-solving innovation is a daunting exercise in the absence of spatial proximity, given that the prime and subcontractors may be separated by many thousands of miles.

Transformation of national defense contractors into monolithic multinational defense companies, such as BAeS and Lockheed Martin, has heralded the evolution of prime contractors committed to the creation of high–value added activities, including research, design, development, project management, and systems integration. The focus of in-company effort is on core competences, with lower value activities outsourced. Cost reduction is the principal enabler for inclusion of a supplier into a prime contractor's supply chain, but technological capability will be the key decision-making discriminator.

For innovational synergies to be reaped, there must be industrial proximity, not only nationally and intranationally, but also at the regional level. Thus, across all high-technology sectors, particularly defense and aerospace, governments are increasingly seeking to nurture technology clusters. These industrial agglomerations have the aim of promoting innovational opportunities through geographical proximity and enhanced cooperation between prime contractors and supplier industries. Clusters constitute centers of expertise, including both hard engineering capability and soft design and development skills.[50] A region will accumulate talented personnel, and specialize in focused research and production activities. Regions are likely to play host to competing primes, all seeking similar skills, infrastructure, material requirements, and technical facilities. Cost, technical, and innovational synergies will emerge from this regional confluence of competing, complementary, and cooperating prime and subcontractors.

An excellent contemporary example of a modern industrial cluster has regard to the French defense and aerospace (D&A) sector, where, mainly located around Toulouse, there exists a high concentration of defense and high-technology aerospace plants.[51] Significantly, Toulouse is at the epicenter of the European Airbus operations, but located nearby are numerous other major D&A manufacturers, including ATR, a major producer of regional aircraft; Safron, France's micro-turbo engine business, producing missile engines and aircraft power systems; a diverse array of enterprises producing Arianne rockets and communications satellite systems; and, finally, an assortment of component and subassembly firms manufacturing electronic, avionic, and related systems.

Toulouse is situated at the edge of the Garonne River, which extends some 124.2 miles into the Bordeaux region. The area represents France's aerospace valley, perceived as the D&A equivalent of America's Silicon Valley. Located in this Bordeaux cluster is Dassault, the World War II plane and now executive jet producer; there is also EADS, producing high-technology space systems; and a further player is Turbomeca, a major manufacturer of helicopter engines. France's aerospace valley is home to a staggering 1,300 aerospace companies, employing almost 100,000 people.[52] This concentration of highly skilled D&A workers represents more than 60 percent of Germany's total aerospace employment and greater than the total of all Spain's aerospace jobs.[53] The conjoined Toulouse-Bordeaux valley complex extends further, however, linking with another two D&A clusters situated at Marseille and Paris; the former is the home of Eurocopter, the world's biggest producer of helicopters, and the latter is the location of AStech and a multitude of similar aircraft design bureaus. This strategic triangle of related D&A design and manufacturing capacities enjoys the conventional benefit of spatial proximity, but also the modern age advantages of computer-aided design and computer-aided manufacturing (CAD/CAM), with all elements of the triangle virtually connected via instant data transmission.

France's industrial iron triangle possesses three significant attributes:

- **Convergence through collaboration**—to avoid the duplication and fragmentation of effort, the French government has encouraged firms in the three linked clusters to collaborate, and indeed, converge, given the complementarity of related high-technology sectors in fields such as avionics and electronics.
- **Regional partnering**—high-technology primes and small- and medium-sized enterprises (SMEs), operating in the three distinct clusters, benefit from both central and local government funding. On average, national and local government contributes 38 percent of the cost of R&D projects.[54] The projects range from air safety to the development of next-generation onboard systems, and participation from SMEs is actively encouraged.
- **Trilateral R&D relationships**—by March 2007, the Toulouse industrial cluster had attracted 155 million euros in R&D assistance from the central and local

authorities.[55] Aside from these financial sources, a range of other science and technology stakeholders contribute in various ways to the respective cluster's R&D impact. For example, the D&A valley cooperates with training institutes, research bodies, and universities, employing in total around 8,500 public and private research staff.[56]

France is not the only country promoting industrial technological partnerships through high-tech clusters. In recent times, clusters have become a permanent feature of Japan's industrial landscape. Since 2001, around 17 regional industrial cluster projects have been established in Japan.[57] A characteristic of Japan's strategy is that it has sought regional differentiation in the specialist focus of respective clusters. An additional novel feature of Japan's cluster model is that while historically FDI has been deliberately marginalized as a vehicle of technology transfer in Japan, the contemporary cluster strategy has aggressively encouraged foreign investors to participate in cluster development. This is part of an overall government strategy to double FDI as a percentage of national income by 2010.

The Nagoya Region, for instance, houses the world's second largest automotive industrial hub. The region is the home of Toyota, other major car producers, and countless parts suppliers. Also, the U.S. industrial giant, Dupont, recently opened a $10 million research centre to exploit technological synergies from the industrial agglomeration evolving in this region. Northern Kyushu is yet another region hosting an automobile hub that produces 1–1.2 million automobiles annually.[58] Reportedly, over 300 foreign automobile and related companies have been attracted to this burgeoning industrial cluster in recent years.

Japan's evident success in the development of industrial clusters is attributable to a number of factors, not dissimilar from those accounting for the success of France's model. These factors include: economic and currency stability; stringent IPR laws, supportive of an emerging, vibrant, and research-driven culture; generous investment provision from local and central government; attractive business environmental conditions outside the Tokyo metropolitan area, including high productivity and skill-content, combined with low cost structures; and, finally, locational hubs appropriately situated as launching pads for exports to Seoul, Taipei, Shanghai, Hong Kong, and the wider East Asian market.

Industrial clusters are a phenomenon pursued across advanced and developing nations alike. In the D&A sector, there is an obvious focus on cultivating high-end technological innovation. This goal, moreover, is increasingly sought via corporate and institutional policies aimed at exploiting the potential for civil-military integration, facilitated by both technology spin-offs and spin-ons through dual-use industrialization. Singapore's knowledge-led economy provides a good example of this approach, as does Malaysia's Lamut-based Marine cluster, albeit at a lower level of technological sophistication.[59] Common to the concept of industrial clusters is the notion of partnering. This is reflected in the simultaneous overlay of trilateral partnering relationships between technologically complementary and convergent clusters between primes and subprimes and specialist R&D institutes and university departments; their spatial context being both intra- and trans-state.

The final dimension to international cooperative relationships pertains to the increasingly prevalent partnering alliances being forged at the global level. Activated by the search for scale, scope, and innovational benefits, defense multinational companies have entered into international strategic alliances. These alliances often derive from the opportunities thrown up by FDI, including defense globalization via the vehicle of technology offsets and international industrial consortiums. The imperative is for advanced country contractors to access defense markets where demand is strong and growing. Examples of such international tie-ups include the French company, Thales, partnering in the design of U.K. aircraft carriers and also in defense electronics with the South Korean high-tech enterprise, Samsung. Also noteworthy is Rolls-Royce's 2008 decision to join forces with Singapore Aero Engine Service Ltd., in the local assembly of the British company's Trent engine.[60] Boeing, moreover, has linked up with Thales in India for work on the U.S. aerospace company's 787 Dreamliner aircraft.[61] The European company, EADS, has also succumbed to the commercial attractiveness of the growing Indian market, creating an engineering training centre in the Subcontinent, paralleling the existing training centre located near Beijing airport, China.[62] The chronicle of global industrial partnerships is long and growing longer, providing a diverse and interconnected network of industrial and technological relationships.

CONCLUSIONS

This chapter has sought to revisit the notion of an iron triangle in defense relations. This was originally conceptualized as an unholy trinity of MoD, congressional, and defense-industrial interests, intent on the perpetuation of defense sales even against the backdrop of a benign international environment. The essence of this chapter's evaluation is that the pernicious effects of the defense iron triangle are probably not so severe, applicable only to predominantly commercial defense-industrial bases, such as that of the United States. Thus, arguably, the notion of a defense iron triangle is simply a child of its time.

In the 21st century, it is more helpful to focus debate on the positive aspects of cooperation rather than collusion in the broad field of defense economy, especially acquisition. Governments seek to promote goal congruence through the development of constructive relationships with all defense stakeholders; here, the thrust is to capture both public sector affordability and acceptable corporate profitability. The contemporary defense iron triangle represents more of a fusion of stakeholder interests across the defense management spectrum, including acquisition strategy, public-private financial partnering initiatives, value chains, regional industrial cluster policies, and global technology alliances. Thus, with the passage of time, the iron triangle appears to have become malleable, reshaping itself into a force for good rather than evil.

NOTES

1. Gordon Adams, *Iron Triangle, the Politics of Defense Contracting,* (New Brunswick, NJ: Transaction Publishers, 1982).
2. Thomas A. Callaghan, Jr., "The Structural Disarmament of NATO," *NATO Review* 32, no. 3 (1984), 1–6.
3. David Kirkpatrick and Philip Pugh, "Towards the Starship Enterprise—Are the Current Trends in Defense Unit Costs Inexorable?" *Aerospace* 10 (May 1983), 16–22.
4. Wright Mills, *The Power Elite* (New York: Oxford University Press, 1956).
5. www.MilitaryIndustrialComplex.com has been collecting publicly reported U.S. Department of Defense contract information since October 30, 2006. This Web site is a continued culmination of

that collection and seeks to keep the general populace informed about their government's military spending practices when concerning tax payer contributions to the defense of the nation. See http://www.militaryindustrialcomplex.com/eisenhower_farewell_address.asp.

6. For recent analysis of the military-industrial complex, see Frank Slijper, "The Emerging EU Military-Industrial Complex, Arms Lobbying in Brussels," TNI briefing series 2005/1 (Transnational Institute 2005). A critical study on the military-industrial complex in the United States can be found in William D. Hartung, "Military Industrial Complex Revisited: How Weapon Makers Are Shaping US Foreign and Military Policies," World Policy Institute, http://www.fpif.org/papers/micr/companies_body.html. For earlier readings and a comparison to Israel, see Alex Mintz, "The Military-Industrial Complex, American Concept and Israeli Realities," *Journal of Conflict Resolution* 29, no. 4 (1985), 623–639. A theoretical discussion on the military-industrial complex can also be found in Adrian Kuah, "Re-conceptualizing the Military-Industrial Approach: A General System Theory Approach," working paper 96, 2005).

7. See Thomas Hartung, "Gold-plating the Pentagon," *The Nation,* March 1, 1999. Further information can be found at http://www.worldpolicy.org/ and http://www.transparency.org/. www.worldpolicy.org is the official Web site of the World Policy Institute, a non-partisan source of progressive policy analysis and thought leadership for more than four decades, which focuses on complex global challenges that demand cooperative policy solutions to achieve in an interdependent world: an inclusive and sustainable global market economy, engaged global civic participation and effective governance, and collaborative approaches to national and global security.

8. Some countries, like South Africa, Israel, and Sweden, built their own defense industries after they experienced military embargoes from arms suppliers. See Richard Bitzinger, "Towards a Brave New Defense Industries," Adelphi Paper 356 (London: International Institute for Strategic Studies [IISS]/Oxford University Press, 2003).

9. The United States was the biggest weapons supplier to Indonesia in 2000, accounting for 34 percent of total Indonesian weapons imports. The embargo (1999–2005) prevented Indonesia from maintaining and upgrading its aged weapons, resulting in low levels of readiness (30–80%) in 2000. See Andi Widjajanto and Makmur Keliat, in *Indonesia's Defense Economy Reform,* research report (Jakarta: INFID and Pacivis, 2005); and Indria Samego, ed., *Anatomi Kekuatan TNI Sebagai Alat Pertahanan Negara* (Jakarta: Pusat Penelitian Politik [P2P] LIPI, 2002).

10. The share of Russian arms exports to Indonesia jumped to 32 percent in the period 2000–2006, and this trend is likely to continue after Russian and Indonesian governments inked a US$1 billion arms transfer to Indonesia in 2007, using an export credit facility from Russia. See Ron Matthews and Curie Maharani, "Remoulding Indonesian Defense Capability," *RSIS Commentaries,* April 29, 2008, www.rsis.edu.sg/publications/Perspective/RSIS0552008.pdf.

11. Ron Matthews and Kogila Balakrishnan, "Malaysian Defense Industrialisation through Offsets," *Asia Pacific Defense Reporter* (July/August 2006).

12. Michael W. Chinworth and Ron Matthews, "Defense Industrialization through Offsets: The Case of Japan," in *The Economics of Offsets: Defense Procurement Options for the 1990s,* ed. S. Martin (Netherlands: Harwood Press, 1996).

13. Vilfredo Pareto (1848–1923) suggested a criterion for decision making in which each person's needs be met as much as possible without any loss to another person. This has come to be known as Paretian Optimality. The problem with defense is that in the absence of it being treated as a public good, certain segments of the population might opt out from paying the premium, thus reducing security to the broad mass of the population. See T. Cowan, ed., *Public Goods and Market Failures: A Critical Examination,* (New Brunswick, NJ: Transaction Publishers, 1992), 14.

14. Emile Benoit, Max F. Millikan, and Everett E. Hagen, "Effects of Defense on Developing Economies," report ACDA/E-136 (Cambridge, MA: MIT, Center for International Studies, 1971). Benoit's

thesis was also subsequently published in book form: Emile Benoit, *Defense and Economic Growth in Developing Countries* (Lexington, MA: Lexington Books, 1973).

15. Steve Chan, 'The Impact of Defense Spending on Economic Performance: A Survey of Evidence and Problems," *Orbis* 29, no. 2 (1985), 403–34.

16. See Ron Matthews and M. Pardesi, "India's Tortuous Road to Defense Industrial Self-reliance," *Journal Defense and Security Analysis* (December 2007), 419–38.

17. See Ron Matthews and Nellie Zhang, "Small Country 'Total Defense': A Case Study of Singapore," *Journal of Defense Studies* 7, no. 3 (2007), 419–38. See also, Ron Matthews and Michael Chinworth, "Defense Industrialisation through Offsets: The Case of Japan," in *The Economics of Offsets: Defense Procurement and Countertrade,* ed. S. Martin (Netherlands: Harwood Academic Press, 1996),.

18. Michael Porter, "Clusters and Competition, New Agenda for Companies, Government and In-stitutions," in *On Competition,* ed. M.E. Porter (Harvard Business School Press: Boston, MA: 1998).

19. Professor David Kirkpatrick points out that "service chiefs and defense manufacturers argue for higher than optimal levels of defense spending, but it is unclear whether or not they succeed . . . lots of advertising and special pleading but no obvious corruption in general," private correspon-dence, April 13, 2008.

20. Steven Schofield, "Levene Reforms: An Evaluation," *Defense Analysis* 11, no. 2 (1995), 147–74.

21. Derek Braddon, *Exploding the Myth? The Peace Dividend, Regions and Market Adjustment* (Lon-don: Routledge, 2000).

22. U.K. Office of Science and Technology, *Progress through Partnership: Report from the Steering Group of the Technology Foresight Programme 1995* (London: Office of Science and Technology, HMSO, 1995).

23. See Jaques Gansler, *Defense Conversion: Transforming the Arsenal of Democracy* (Cambridge, MA: MIT Press, 1996).

24. For further information on OCCAR, see http://www.occar-ea.org. www.occar-ea.org is the official Web site Organisation Conjointe de Coopération en matière d'Armement. The organization was established to provide more effective and efficient arrangements for the management of certain existing and future collaborative armament programs between the United Kingdom, France, Ger-many, and Italy. The Web site contains the background history, organizational structure, program, corporate document, and business opportunities provided by OCCAR.

25. Ron Matthews, "International Arms Collaboration: The Case of Eurofighter," *International Journal of Aerospace Management* 1, no. 1 (2001), 73–79.

26. See Jordi Molas-Gallart, "Military Production and Innovation in Spain," *Studies in Defense Eco-nomics* 2 (January 1992).

27. See http://www.eda.europa.eu. www.eda.europa.eu is the official Web site of the European De-fence Agency. It contains background history, and activities, including defense procurement op-portunities provided by EDA.

28. See Nick Witney (chief executive of EDA), "The EDA's Goals: Strengthening Europe's Capabili-ties and Defense Industrial Base," speech, the European Institute's Translantic Roundtable on Defense and Security, Washington, DC, February 14, 2007. The EDA budget for 2008 was around 32 million euros, see http://www.defenseindustrydaily.com/eda-gets-budget-boost-as-europeans make-pledges-04269/. www.defenceindustrydaily.com is a prominent Web site containing a well-updated news on defense procurement around the world, divided into several categories, for example aircraft, electronic and industry.

29. See http://www.jsf.mil. www.jsf.mil is the official Web site of the Joint Strike Fighter (JSF) Program, formerly the Joint Advanced Strike Technology (JAST) Program. It is the U.S. Department of De-fense's focal point for defining affordable next generation strike aircraft weapon systems for the

Navy, Air Force, Marines, and allies. The Web site provides historical background, description of program, international collaboration as well as news update on the progress of JSF development.

30. See Andrew Davies, "JSF Cost: Taking Off or Leveling Out," *RUSI Defense System,* June 2008.

31. The Joint Strike Fighter (JSF) international partnership program consists of eight countries, investing$4.375 billion over 10 years in the $25 billion Joint Strike Fighter program. The United Kingdom is the only Level I partner in the program. Other countries, such as Italy and the Netherlands, are Level II partners, and Canada, Denmark, Norway, and Turkey are Level III partners. These partnership levels are determined by the financial contributions countries make to the program.

32. *The Acquisition Handbook,* U.K. MoD (annual editions).

33. Professor David Kirkpatrick argues that the Smart Acquisition policy has not been an unqualified success. One of the problems highlighted was the lack of implementation of smart imperatives. He noted "there is no single reason for non-implementation of the diverse array of smart initiatives, except perhaps that implementation was not considered until after the initiatives had been settled," private correspondence, April 16, 2008.

34. *The Acquisition Handbook.*

35. Ministry of Defense, "Building an Air Manoeuvre Capability: The Introduction of the Apache Helicopter," report, HC 1246 session 2001–2002, October 31, 2002, see http://www.nao.org.uk/publications/nao_reports/01-02/01021246.pdf.

36. Irfan Ansari, "Defense PFIs: Burden or Benefit?" *Accounting and Business,* May 2007, 34–7.

37. "IFSL Research: PFIs in the UK and PPP in Europe 2008," see www.ifsl.org.uk/uploads/PB_PFI2007.pdf. www.ifsl.org.uk is the official Web site of International Finance Service London (IFSL). It is an independent organization representing the whole U.K. financial services industry, to provide analysis and statistics of U.K.-based financial services. The Web site provides information on activities and events.

38. See www.publicprivatefinance.com. www.publicprivatefinance.com is Web site that keeps update of public private partnership program in United Kingdom and around the world.

39. In 1987–2007, there have been 62 PFI defense projects, with an average contractual value of £134 million. Defense PFI projects during this period represented 11.6 percent of total U.K. government PFI projects. See www.ifsl.org.uk/uploads/PB_PFI2007.pdf.

40. See http://www.publications.parliament.uk/pa/cm200607/cmhansrd/cm070309/text/70309w0012.htm. www.parliament.uk is the official Web site of British Parliament. The Web site provides the historical background of Parliament, its activities, as well as Hansard (writing report) of proceedings of the two Houses of Parliament.

41. The Future Strategic Tanker Aircraft (FSTA) is by far the biggest PFI in the world, valued at around US$20 billion, with a contract length of 27 years. The contract was signed between the U.K. MoD and AirTanker as the prime contractor, and its shareholders (Cobham, EADS, Rolls-Royce, Thales U.K., and VT Group), to provide 14 Airbus A330-200 Air-to-Air refueling and air transport aircraft for the United Kingdom, United States, and its partners, to be deployed all over the world. For more information, see http://www.airtanker.co.uk. www.airtanker.co.uk is the official Web site of Airtanker, a U.K. company that was created to provide the Future Strategic Tanker Aircraft (FSTA) service, under a 27-year Private Finance Initiative contract.

42. *The Acquisition Handbook.*

43. David Kirkpatrick, "A UK Perspective on Defense Equipment Acquisition," working paper 41 (Institute for Defense and Security Studies, 2004).

44. Ron Matthews and Curie Maharani, "Beyond the RMA: Survival Strategy for Small Defense Economies," *Connections Journal* 7, no. 2 (2008).

45. *Final Report of the Defense and Science Board Task Force on Globalization and Security* (Washington, DC: Office of the Undersecretary of Defense for Acquisition and Technology, 1999).

46. "Defense Industrial Policy," *U.K. Ministry of Defense Policy Paper,* paper 5, 2002.

47. For Europe, there is now a concerted effort to promote the European Research and Technology Co-operation. See *Framework for a European Defense Research and Technology Strategy,* (EDA, 2007).

48. Michael Porter, *Competitive Advantage of Nations* (New York: The Free Press, 1990).

49. Michael Porter, "Clusters and Competition, New Agenda for Companies, Government and Institutions," in *On Competition,* ed. M. E. Porter (Boston: Harvard Business School Press, 1998).

50. Michael Porter, "Clusters and the New Economics of Competition," *Harvard Business Review,* November-December, 1998. See also Michael Porter, "Innovation: Location Matters," *Sloan Management Review* 42, no. 4 (2001), 28–36.

51. http://www.aerospace-valley.com/docs/site/plaquette-aerospace-an-23–05.pdf, see also http://www.invest-in-france.org/international/en/aerospace-valley-cluster.html. The www.aerospace-valley.com web site is the official web site of the Aerospace Valley association. The organization was created on July 13, 2005, for the national, European, and international development of the Midi-Pyrenees and Aquitaine Aeronautics, Space and Embedded Systems Competitiveness Cluster and received the "Global Cluster" seal of approval from the French government on July 12, 2005. It is formed by the companies, research centers, education and training centers, and authorities involved in the sector from the two regions. The web site contains information on the cluster, the association, and the project.

52. http://www.aerospace-valley.com/docs/site/plaquette-aerospace-an-23–05.pdf, see also http://www.invest-in-france.org/international/en/aerospace-valley-cluster.html.

53. http://www.hanse-aerospace.net/index.php?&L=0. www.hanse-aerospace.net is the official Web site of HANSE-AEROSPACE e. V. It is Germany's largest association of small- and medium-sized aviation and space companies.

54. See R. Tieman, "Valley Where Business Grow Wings," *Financial Times,* October 3, 2007.

55. Tieman, "Valley Where Business Grow Wings."

56. See http://www.aerospace-valley.com/en/the-cluster/research.html.

57. For information on Japan's industrial cluster, see the official Web site on http://www.cluster.gr.jp/en/about/index.html. www.cluster.gr.jp is the official Web site of Japan's industrial cluster. The project, promoted by Ministry of Economy, Trade and Industry (METI) since FY2001, works to form industrial clusters for bringing about a stream of innovation and venture companies in regions. Presently, there are18 projects nationwide, with the joint cooperation of regional Bureaus of Economy, Trade, and Industry and promotion organizations of the private sector; the projects build close cooperative relations with about 10,700 regional SMEs, taking on the challenge of new businesses and more than 290 universities (including industrial colleges).

58. It is estimated that eight automobile manufacturers located in Northern Kyushu and neighboring regions have the capacity to produce four million cars annually. See http://www.kyuden.co.jp/en_investq_industries_car.html. www.kyuden.co.jp is the official Web site of Kyushu Electrin Power Company of Japan. In addition to provide information on investor relations and other company's activities, the Web site also provides information on investing in Kyushu.

59. Ron Matthews, "The Defense Iron Triangle," paper presented at the Malaysia 2008 DSA Conference, Kuala Lumpur, April 2008.

60. "Singapore Airlines Powers Ahead with Latest Rolls-Royce Trent," see http://www.rolls-royce.com/singapore/businesses/default.htm.

61. "Boeing, Thales Sign First 787 Dreamliner Wireless IFE Agreement," see http://www.boeing.com/commercial/787family/news/2005/q3/nr_050930g.html.

62. "EADS Sets up Sourcing Centres in India," *Economic Times,* 2 November 2, 2007, http://indianaviationnews.net/careers/2007/11/eads-sets-up-sourcing-centres-in-india.html.

4

Power, Influence, and Hierarchy: Defense Industries in a Unipolar World

Stephanie G. Neuman

The question "What is power?" has fascinated mankind for centuries. Intellectuals and scholars, popular commentators and laymen have all addressed it. Yet, despite the abundant attention, as Joseph Nye facetiously observed: "Power, like love, is easier to experience than to define or measure."[1]

For the purposes of this chapter, *state power* is defined as the ability of state A to persuade other states to behave in ways consistent with state A's goals and interests. *Influence,* a closely linked concept, is here defined as the instrument used to persuade. Therefore, the more capabilities a state has at its disposal to reward compliance or punish noncooperation, the greater its power and ability to influence. But how successfully a state's capabilities translate into an effective policy tool is contingent on the vulnerability of other states. Thus it is not the physical size, wealth, or military strength of a state that determines its ability to persuade, but its capacity to capitalize on the preferences or liabilities of other states. Although state A may possess more resources than state B, state B must need, want, or fear state A's capabilities in order to be vulnerable to its influence attempts. The success or failure of these attempts may also be highly context-dependent, so that governments will be less vulnerable to external pressure when alternative sources of assistance are available. When no alternative source exists, and the cost of noncooperation is high, governments are prone to comply with the policy demands of a stronger state.[2]

These, then, are the assumptions about state power and influence that guide this discussion. It is posited here that the global defense-industrial sector is a remarkably accurate indicator of the stratification of power in the post–cold war international system. As in the overall system, the United States plays the dominant role in the defense sector as well. It is a comparative advantage used by U.S. policymakers to influence the foreign policy behavior of other states. Curiously, as a policy tool, the defense-industrial sector has hitherto received relatively little scrutiny, even though it not only reflects the international order but often provides the

United States with considerable leverage in it. The defense-industrial sector is, it is argued here, a powerful, if less recognized, diplomatic tool in the United States' political arsenal.

THE RESTRUCTURING OF THE WORLD'S DEFENSE-INDUSTRIAL SECTOR

Contraction and Globalization of Defense Industries

As the perceived conventional threat diminished with the end of the cold war, defense budgets were reduced and major weapons programs slowed down in the main arms-producing countries. In many countries, Western and third world alike,[3] military industrial production was drastically cut and some production lines shut down. Since the mid-1990s, through a process of mergers and acquisitions (M&As), the world's defense-industrial sector has become increasingly concentrated, particularly in the United States, where the number of independent prime contractors fell from 20 to 4.[4] These changes have been accompanied by a rapid globalization of the defense export sector and the emergence of transnational defense companies, especially at the subcontractor level, in the West.[5]

But if mergers and acquisitions are a measure of defense industrial globalization there is considerable variability in its character and extent. The Stockholm International Peace Research Institute (SIPRI) contends that the U.S. defense-industrial sector has opted for certain kinds of global and transnational initiatives while avoiding others. Whereas the United States is eager to exploit foreign sources of technology, it simultaneously seeks to protect itself from becoming too dependent upon foreign suppliers. In fact, studies conducted by the U.S. Department of Defense (DoD) found that dependence upon foreign weapons sources is limited and that what is imported has a negligible impact on the readiness of the military or the U.S. defense-industrial base. In fiscal year (FY) 2006, only about 2.4 percent ($1.9 billion) of Pentagon contracts for defense items and components were awarded foreign suppliers, or less than one percent of all Pentagon contracts.[6]

There are few signs that this will change in the future. Since 9/11, U.S. military spending has emphasized information technology, surveillance, communications, and related systems, many of which require "high levels of security."[7] On these grounds alone, according to some observers, the U.S. government is now less inclined to purchase much military equipment from abroad, and is also reluctant to have U.S. firms collaborate with foreign partners in the development of major weapon systems.[8] As a result, foreign firms—with the possible exception of British firms[9]—find themselves at a competitive disadvantage for Pentagon and Homeland Security contracts. The decision by the U.S. Air Force in 2008 to award a $35 billion contract to Northrop Grumman and the European Aeronautic Defense Space Company (EADS) to build aerial refueling tankers, for example, caused a storm of criticism from some U.S. Congressmen and military analysts who expressed concern that the new aircraft would be designed and built in Europe.[10] As of this writing, the U.S. DoD has reopened the contest for the tanker contract and a final decision has yet to be made. In the United States it is, as SIPRI contends, a policy of moving both towards and away from defense-industrial globalization.

The term *globalization* as applied to Europe's defense industries is equally problematic. Within Europe, transnational activity has not been vigorous, and self-sufficiency/

autonomy/security concerns remain an apparently insurmountable issue. In the late 1990s, given the consolidation of the U.S. defense industry, European defense firms were under pressure to follow suit. While the bulk of Europe's aerospace and defense electronics sectors did consolidate into transnational companies, such as BAE Systems, EADS, Thales, and Finmeccanica, other sectors, such as land vehicles, naval shipyards, and aircraft engines did not. Today, for example, Europe has 20 naval shipbuilders and 23 naval yards, in contrast to the United States, which has only two companies producing warships and six naval yards.[11]

Moreover, little progress has been made toward coordinating procurements or achieving successful collaborative arms projects. As Javier Solana, head of the European Defence Agency (EDA), observed, there is great fragmentation in both supply and demand, little international cooperation between member states, and less than 5 percent of Europe's research and development (R&D) budget is spent collaboratively. Solana cites the 23 separate national programs for armored fighting vehicles running or about to start, with almost no cooperation among European Union (EU) members.[12] Despite the creation of the European Defence Agency in 2004[13] and the political rhetoric of current European leaders, to date, hopes for a common defense-industrial base and the rationalization of European procurement requirements remain unfulfilled. Between July 2006-July 2008, cross-border activity accounted for less than one in four of the contracts awarded through the EDA's Electronic Bulletin Board, the online portal established to foster defense trade within the European Union.[14] As one EU parliamentarian observed: "Foreign suppliers get only 13 percent of the 91 billion euros (about $126.6 billion) spent on defense goods by EU members."[15] Most of Europe's governments are reluctant to see domestic defense companies acquired by foreign firms, and there is little indication that they are willing to stop protecting their domestic defense industries in the interest of military industrial rationalization and integration.[16]

Less is known about the activities of third world defense industries, suggesting that, with few exceptions, they are even less involved in the defense-industrial globalization process. For most third world governments, like their counterparts in the West, autonomy/security concerns dampen their enthusiasm for either foreign ownership of their arms industries or transnational defense-industrial M&As.[17] For most third world countries establishing or sustaining a fledgling national defense-industrial base is a first priority.

The defense industry's perception of future export markets, however, has indisputably been globalized. As armies continue to downsize and domestic military markets shrink, arms producers worldwide are looking abroad to achieve economies of scale for their products and to earn foreign exchange to support their industries.[18] With the possible exception of the United States, in the coming years, domestic defense industries may consider their own military as less important customers than foreign markets. This may have already occurred in some countries. Russian military industries met only 10–15 percent of their armed forces needs in 2004, and exports made up 70–90 percent of production volume and revenues earned by major Russian defense industries. In spite of the growth of domestic procurement, export orders have continued to account for about 60 percent of sales for the leading Russian defense companies. These sales and the revenues they earn are considered so important that some R&D and production programs are tailored specifically for foreign customers rather than the Russian military itself. Victor Litovkin, editor in chief of the "Independent Military Review" supplement to the *Nezavisimaya Gazeta* daily writes that in recent years more than 700 T-90C tanks were delivered to India while the Russian army received only 90. China, Algeria, Venezuela, Indonesia, and others received Sukhoi fighter planes; the Russian Air Force received none. The same, he notes, is true for helicopters, artillery systems, diesel submarines, and surface ships.[19]

In France and Israel, too, export revenues are far higher than domestic sales. The French military has expressed concern that export demand, rather than the needs of the armed forces, drives domestic arms production. In Israel, the military has already become a secondary customer for almost all Israeli defense industries, with exports accounting for between 70–80 percent of their revenues—the reverse of the U.S. market.[20]

Military Transformation

Another factor contributing to defense-industrial restructuring is the transformation of the U.S. defense doctrine. In response to perceived new security threats and burgeoning technological innovations, the new "transformation" doctrine is designed to enable a down-sized U.S. armed forces better address small, complex, non-traditional contingencies. It aims to expand communication among military units and to achieve greater real-time target acquisition, longer-range projection capabilities, increased unit mobility, and improved weapon accuracy and lethality. Central to the goal of transformation is the concept of network-centric warfare whereby sensors, communication systems, and weapon systems are linked into an interconnected grid that provides an integrated picture of the battlefield to all levels of command and control down to the individual soldier.[21]

This concept of full connectivity depends on a host of sophisticated electronic and information technologies, as well as specialized services and technical support that have generated a sizable demand from both the civil defense and military sectors. As the line between traditional defense and internal security grows increasingly blurred in the United States, demand by Homeland Security and military forces for many of the same systems has increased the domestic market for these new dual-use technologies.[22]

Economic pressures combined with a changing, more complex threat environment, have led other governments to downsize and modernize their militaries and defense industries. They, too, seek similar dual-use systems to bolster their armies and domestic defense forces. But given the sophistication and complex manufacturing techniques involved, few defense industries are capable of producing them. In East Asia, for example, Japan, South Korea, Singapore, Taiwan, and China to a lesser extent, have integrated advanced computers, communications equipment, and sensors with precision-guided weapons in an effort to transform their militaries. East Asian defense industries are also in the process of consolidating, privatizing, and internationalizing. But despite their efforts to become less dependent on foreign suppliers, East Asia still finds itself reliant on the West, particularly the U.S., for its most advanced technologies.[23]

Rising Costs

Rising prices across successive generations of weapons present yet another challenge to most governments. Since the end of World War II, the rate of increase has remained relatively stable, with the unit production cost of military weapons rising by an average 5 to 10 percent per year.[24] However, compared to the price of mature systems, such as rifles and machine guns, which increase more slowly, the rate of growth for new technologies is much faster.[25] This is due not only to rising manufacturing costs, but also to the military's requirement for more extensive R&D and more complicated operating and maintenance procedures that require more highly trained personnel and more expensive spare parts. Despite the use of less expensive, off-the-shelf commercial components instead of those designed specifically for the military, the cost of new weapons and military technologies continues to increase. As the price of sophisticated weapons has escalated and defense budgets have fallen, few countries other than the U.S. can afford the many new platforms and technologies associated with network-centric warfare.[26]

The economics of transformation, then, is a major dilemma for defense planners, who recognize that the number of weapon systems in inventory is no longer a reliable indicator of military power or effectiveness. Today, an electronic network of sensors and communications systems is estimated to multiply the utility of individual weapon systems tenfold, by providing broader coverage of the battlefield, allowing a more efficient allocation of forces, enhancing the timing of their operations, and reducing fratricide.[27] But the cost of building and maintaining such a network is substantial, and, with smaller defense budgets, few countries can afford it.

Commercialization/Privatization

In the past, there were dramatic differences between technologies used in commercial and military systems; that, too, is now changing. As the pace of scientific innovation in the civilian economy has increased, military organizations in most major arms-producing countries[28] have turned to the commercial sector, domestic and foreign, for dual-use technologies and breakthrough scientific discoveries. Doing so is also a response to post–cold war political pressure to economize by lowering military expenditures. Jacques Gansler, then U.S. under secretary of defense for acquisition, technology, and logistics, made this point at a 2000 conference promoting the DoD's Dual-Use Science and Technology (S&T) Program.[29] He emphasized that the U.S. military needs to take advantage of the efficiencies, innovation, reduced cycle time and lower cost technologies in the commercial world in order to create economies of scale that can have important cost cutting benefits. Other countries, such as the United Kingdom, have introduced similar incentives to encourage cooperation between the military and the private sector. The U.K. Ministry of Defense (MoD) takes the position that "while the defense industry may continue to lead in some selective military applications . . . most future technological innovations will originate in the commercial sector."[30]

New entities are now also being created to satisfy the military's demand for outsourcing to private firms for other kinds of goods and services. A wide range of military services formerly performed by uniformed or defense department personnel are now delegated to private military companies. This trend is most evident in the United States and the United Kingdom, but it is emerging in other countries as well.[31] In the United States, many traditional defense contractors have, through acquisitions or partnerships, gained a foothold in this market, although large numbers of other commercial companies are also actively participating. The services offered by private firms generally range widely from providing equipment support, training, maintenance, logistical management, and armed security in war zones to administrative assistance for defense departments and ministries.

Two factors driving the U.S. military's growing reliance on private companies, particularly for services, are the Pentagon's belief that it is less expensive to use civilian rather than uniformed personnel and the armed forces' insufficient human resources. Downsizing, which began in the 1990s, has produced a military that often does not have enough uniformed manpower to carry out all of its assigned missions, much less enough personnel trained to operate and maintain leading-edge commercially designed technology. Private companies are now needed to provide a multitude of skills to fill these gaps, particularly in combat zones. Since 2003, the number of private contractors supporting the U.S. military has seen unprecedented growth. During the 1991 Gulf War, approximately 9,000 civilian contractors serviced a military force of 500,000 uniformed personnel, which amounted to approximately one contractor for every 55 soldiers. By 2007, the number of U.S.-paid private contractors in Iraq reportedly exceeded the 160,000 American combat troops stationed there.[32]

The integration of private companies into Europe's military sector is proceeding slowly and unevenly. In the United Kingdom, the role of private contractors as service providers to the military is steadily increasing. By 2006, British private security companies held contracts in Iraq and Afghanistan alone amounting to $1.9 billion (£1 billion) and employed 21,000 personnel in both countries. Other European countries have lagged behind in outsourcing military functions, although Germany, following the example of the United States and the United Kingdom, is now trying to bring in the private sector.[33]

Among third world countries, the pace of integration is even slower and more disparate. Little, if anything, is known about the use of private contractors by third world militaries, and public ownership of defense companies remains the norm. In India, for example, despite the government's good intentions, the private defense sector only receives about nine percent per year of the country's procurement budget. India's nine major defense companies are all state-owned.[34] In Russia, all but one (Irkut) of the major arms-producing companies are government-owned, and close to 500 defense industries have been decreed ineligible for privatization.[35] For Israel, with 65 percent of its defense industry currently state-owned, privatization decisions have proven to be especially difficult. Most private sector executives, along with Israel's MoD, agree that the best way to slim down Israel's bloated defense-industrial base is to privatize and allow Israeli defense firms to compete in the open market. The government, however, has been reluctant to do so, citing security concerns.[36] Even so, privately owned companies comprise approximately a third of the Israeli defense industry base, and a process of industry consolidation through M&As is now underway.[37] Although the integration of private firms into the military sector is proceeding more slowly in some countries than in others, it is gathering momentum. More governments are attempting to integrate private companies into the defense industrial sector. And as armies continue to shrink and the demand for military personnel in war zones rises, it is expected that governments will increasingly turn to contractors to fill the void at home and abroad. According to analyst P. W. Singer, total revenue for the world's private military and security companies is about $100 billion per year and growing rapidly.[38]

The entry of new commercial firms into national defense sectors raises hard questions about what differentiates defense industries from their commercial counterparts. How is military technology to be defined in today's diversified market? How can governments guarantee their own source of military equipment and services during times of crisis? Is it possible for governments to control the proliferation of commercial technologies that have military applications? These questions have important implications not only for defense-industrial production and procurement, but also for arms-control regimes and for military effectiveness and readiness in the future. To date, governments have provided few answers to these questions.[39]

Arms Exports

Since the end of the cold war, falling defense budgets have created a significantly smaller, more concentrated global arms market. The total value of arms deliveries worldwide declined by 17 percent between 1999–2002 and 2003–6. During this period the United States accounted for over 40 percent of the total during this period. The second and third largest arms exporters, Russia and the United Kingdom, delivered 15 percent and 14 percent, respectively. In 2006, the United States alone exported over half ($14 billion) of the world's military equipment and services (see Table 4.1.).[40]

U.S. arms exports since 2006 have continued to rise. Seeking to rearm Iraq and Afghanistan, contain North Korea and Iran, cement relations with former Soviet allies, and sustain a war on terrorism, the U.S. reportedly agreed in 2008 to sell about $32 billion in weapons and military equipment to governments in most parts of the world: the Middle East, North Africa, Asia, Latin America, Europe, and Canada. In addition, the number of countries relying on the U.S. as a primary source of major weapons systems grew with Argentina, Azerbaijan, Brazil, Georgia, India, Iraq, Morocco and Pakistan among the recent additions.[41] If one can speak of a more globalized arms trade, it is U.S. arms that have become most globalized.

A Unipolar Global Defense-Industrial Sector

Collectively these trends underscore the dominance of the United States in the world's defense-industrial sector. U.S. defense spending ($536 billion) in 2006 was five to eight times that of its nearest competitors, and dwarfed that of the rest of the world.[42] With the world's largest defense budget, the United States has also become its largest military market. Total defense expenditure for the five major EU countries (the United Kingdom, France, Germany, Italy, and Spain) in 2006 amounted to about one-third that of the United States (see Table 4.2.) The United States spent $126.3 billion on the purchase of defense equipment and services in 2007. The 25 EU, countries, in contrast, allocated only a third of that. Together, the United Kingdom, France, Germany, Sweden, Spain, and Italy spent an aggregate sum of $36.27 billion for that year.[43]

The comparative size and capabilities of the U.S. defense industry are equally overwhelming. In 2006, 41 U.S. companies accounted for 63 percent of the total arms sales of the world's 100 largest defense industries (see Table 4.3). Not only does the United States produce an

Table 4.1
Arms deliveries to the world, 1999–2006: Leading suppliers compared (in millions of constant 2006 U.S. dollars)

Supplier	Arms Deliveries $ Value 1999–2002	% of World Deliveries 1999–2002	Arms Deliveries $ Value 2003–2006	% of World Deliveries 2003–2006	% Change from 1999–2002 to 2003–2006	Arms Deliveries $ Value 1999–2006	% of World Deliveries 1999–2006	Arms Deliveries $ Value 2006	% of World Deliveries 2006
United States	57,640	39.80%	50,032	41.47%	−13.20%	107,672	40.56%	14,008	51.87%
United Kingdom	21,813	15.06%	14,103	11.69%	−35.35%	35,916	13.53%	3,300	12.22%
Russia	19,041	13.15%	19,713	16.34%	3.53%	38,754	14.60%	5,800	21.48%
France	11,744	8.11%	11,053	9.16%	−5.88%	22,797	8.59%	400	1.48%
Germany	5,969	4.12%	5,780	4.79%	−3.17%	11,749	4.43%	1,000	3.70%
China	3,767	2.60%	3,381	2.80%	−10.25%	7,148	2.69%	700	2.59%
Italy	2,254	1.56%	1,071	0.89%	−52.48%	3,325	1.25%	100	0.37%
All Other European	14,217	9.82%	9,219	7.64%	−35.16%	23,436	8.83%	1,200	4.44%
All Other Countries	8,377	5.78%	6,303	5.22%	−24.76%	14,680	5.53%	500	1.85%
Total	144,822	100.00%	120,655	100.00%	−16.69%	265,477	100.00%	27,008	100.00%

Source: Richard F. Grimmett, *Conventional Arms Transfers to Developing Nations, 1999–2006*, CRS report for Congress, September 26, 2007, Figure 2, 40, and Table 9A, 86. Note that this report does not include U.S. commercially licensed arms export delivery values so the real dollar value of U.S. exports is higher than reflected here.

Table 4.2

States (17) with defense expenditures in excess of $10 billion in 2006 (current U.S. $ billion) list in rank order

Country	$ billions	% of US	% of Sub-Total	% of World Total
United States*	535.9	100.00%	48.3%	41.29%
China[1]	121.9	22.75%	11.0%	9.39%
Russia	70.0	13.06%	6.3%	5.39%
United Kingdom	55.4	10.35%	5.0%	4.27%
France[2]	54.0	10.08%	4.9%	4.16%
Japan*	41.1	7.68%	3.7%	3.17%
Germany[2]	37.8	7.05%	3.4%	2.91%
Italy[2]	30.6	5.72%	2.8%	2.36%
Saudi Arabia[3]	29.5	5.51%	2.7%	2.28%
Korea, South**	24.6	4.59%	2.2%	1.90%
India	22.4	4.18%	2.0%	1.73%
Australia	17.2	3.21%	1.6%	1.33%
Brazil**	16.2	3.02%	1.5%	1.25%
Canada	15.0	2.79%	1.3%	1.15%
Spain***	14.4	2.69%	1.3%	1.11%
Turkey	11.6	2.17%	1.0%	0.90%
Israel	11.0	2.06%	1.0%	0.85%
Top 17 Total	**1108.7**		**100.0%**	**85.43%**
World Total	**1297.8**			**100.00%**

[1]China's defense expenditures are not transparent and therefore subject to varying estimates. China's official defense budget for 2006 of $35 billion does not include large categories of expenditure, including expenses for strategic forces, foreign acquisitions, military-related research and development, and China's paramilitary forces. The figure above is the International Institute for Strategic Studies (IISS) estimate of real defense expenditures for 2006.

[2]Includes military pensions.

[3]Defense budget (including defense and security budget).

*U.S. defense expenditure figures differ somewhat from source to source. In SIPRI's military expenditure database, for example, the figure is $546 billion (current 2006 US$) (accessed June 3, 2008).

**Defense budget

***Includes military pensions plus extra-budgetary expenditure.

Source: International Institute for Strategic Studies (IISS), *The Military Balance 2008* (London:, 2008), Table 37, "International Comparisons of Defense Expenditure and Military Manpower, 2004–2006," 443–48.

across-the-board array of defense systems, but it is the world leader in advanced systems integration and leading-edge technologies. U.S. military R&D expenditures in 2002 were more than three times those of Europe's. A French MoD report on the growing disparity complained that it was now "tantamount to technological disarmament for Europe, with already perceptible consequences." Since then, the gap has grown even wider. By 2006, U.S. military R&D spending ($72 billion) was five times that of all Europe($14.6 billion; see Table 4.4).[44]

What is more, as the world's largest exporter of military equipment, the United States is less dependent on foreign exports to sustain its defense sector than almost all other major arms-producing countries. Using the dollar value of military imports as a percent of military exports as a crude indicator of a country's defense industrial dependency, we find that U.S. arms imports amount to 7.2 percent of the dollar value of its arms exports. Thus, other than France and Russia U.S. dependency on foreign defense imports is less than other major

Table 4.3
The 100 Largest Arms-Producing Companies Ranked by Country of Location and Total Arms Sales 2006 (U.S. dollars current billion)

Country/Region**	Number of Companies	Arms Sales 2006 U.S. current $ bn.***	Percent Arms Production of Total
USA	**41**	**200.2**	**63.4**
Western Europe	**34**	**92.3**	**29.3**
United Kingdom	*11*	*37.3*	*11.8*
France	*6*	*19.5*	*6.2*
Trans-European (EADS)	*1*	*12.6*	*4.0*
Italy	*5*	*11.0*	*3.5*
Germany	*5*	*6.1*	*1.9*
Other W. Europe	*6*	*5.8*	*1.8*
Russia	**8**	**6.1**	**1.9**
Japan	**4**	**5.2**	**1.7**
Israel	**4**	**4.6**	**1.5**
India	**3**	**3.5**	**1.0**
Canada	**1**	**0.5**	**0.2**
Others	**5**	**3.2**	**1.0**
TOTAL	**100**	**315.6**	

*Source: SIPRI Arms Production Database: Top 100 arms-producing companies. http://www.sipri.org/contents/milap/milex/aprod/sipridata.html. (accessed 1/17/09)

**China is excluded from SIPRI's 100 arms producing companies because of lack of reliable data. However, as SIPRI observes, "Chinese arms-producing enterprises would almost certainly be included in the SIPRI Top 100 were data available."

***SIPRI uses the data for arms sales as an approximation of the annual value of arms production. See "Sources and Methods" in SIPRI's Arms Production Database.

Table 4.4

Worldwide military R&D spending, 2001–6 (in constant 2006 U.S. $ billion)

Country	2001	2002	2003	2004	2005	2006
US	46.86*	54.56*	63.07*	68.81*	70.23*	72.04*
UK	4.128	5.409	5.152	4.910	4.667	4.898
Russia	–	1.22**	–	4.28***	–	–
Germany	1.649	1.234	1.546	1.335	1.315	1.450
France	4.704	4.861	4.670	4.467	4.342	5.006
Sweden	0.410	0.661	0.646	0.533	0.559	0.550
Italy	0.482	–	–	0.428***	0.425	0.153
Spain	2.496	2.044	1.925	1.727	1.665	2.074
Norway	0.134	0.138	0.141	0.152	0.162	0.157
Netherlands	0.088	0.830	0.882	0.614	0.101	0.104
Cyprus	–	–	–	–	–	–
Czech Rep.	–	0.019	0.021	0.019	0.018	0.022
Estonia	–	–	–	–	–	–
Hungary	–	–	–	–	0.000	–
Latvia	–	–	–	–	–	–
Lithuania	–	–	–	–	–	–
Malta	–	–	–	–	–	–
Poland	–	–	–	0.019	0.012	0.009
Slovakia	–	0.014	0.011	0.008	0.012	0.010
Slovenia	–	–	0.000	0.007	0.006	–
Austria	0.000	0.000	0.000	0.001	0.000	–
Belgium	0.005	0.007	0.007	0.009	0.007	0.007
Denmark	0.009	0.009	0.022	0.024	0.013	0.014
Finland	0.028	0.029	0.051	0.043	0.064	0.055
Greece	0.005	0.004	0.004	0.004	0.004	0.005
Ireland	0.000	0.000	0.000	0.000	0.000	0.000
Luxembourg	–	–	–	–	0.000	0.000
Portugal	0.023	0.024	0.022	0.009	0.009	0.008
Albania	–	–	–	–	–	–
Bosnia-Herzegovina	–	–	–	–	–	–
Bulgaria	–	–	–	–	–	0.005
Croatia	–	–	0.000	0.002	0.003	0.004
Macedonia	–	–	–	–	–	–

(*Continued*)

Table 4.4

Worldwide military R&D spending, 2001–6 (in constant 2006 U.S. $ billion) (*Continued*)

Country	2001	2002	2003	2004	2005	2006
Moldova	–	–	–	–	–	–
Romania	–	–	–	–	–	–
Serbia & Montenegro	–	–	–	0.004	0.005	0.006
Switzerland	–	0.012	–	0.011	–	0.016
Turkey	–	–	–	–	–	–
European Year Totals	**14.16**	**16.51**	**15.10**	**18.61**	**13.39**	**14.55**
European Year Total as % of US Year Total	**30.22%**	**30.27%**	**23.94%**	**27.04%**	**19.07%**	**20.20%**
China	–	–	–	5.35***	–	–
S. Korea	–	–	–	.856***	–	–
India	.81**	.73**	–	–	–	–
Japan	–	–	–	1.07***	–	–

Source: Wan-Jung Chao, Gregory Sanders, Guy Ben-Ari, Trends in European Defense Spending, 2001-2006, CSIS Center for Strategic and International Studies, April 2008, Table 9, "Defense R&D Expenditure in U.S. Dollars at Constant 2006 Year Prices", p. 17.

*Source: Office of Management and Budget, Department of Defense.

For 2001 see: www.whitehouse.gov/omb/budget/fy2005/defense.html.

For 2002 see: www.whitehouse.gov/omb/budget/fy2004/defense.html.

For 2003 see: www.whitehouse.gov/omb/budget/fy2005/defense.html.

For 2004 see: www.whitehouse.gov/omb/budget/fy2006/defense.html.

For 2005 see: www.whitehouse.gov/omb/budget/fy2007/defense.html.

For 2006 see: www.whitehouse.gov/omb/budget/fy2008/defense.html.

**Source: Frank Killelea "Defense Economics", National Security Analysis Department, Johns Hopkins University Applied Physics Laboratory, March 2005, p. 32.

***Source: Michael Brzoska "Trends in Global Military and Civilian Research and Development (R&D) and their Changing Interface", presented in a workshop organized by the Manchester Institute of Innovation Research for the research network on Policies for Research and Innovation in the Move towards the European Research Area, entitled "Re-evaluating defence R&D and innovative dynamics" on April 2-3, 2007, Figure 1, p. 5.

All figures in italics are estimates.

(−) Indicates data unavailable.

The U.S. Department of Labor Statistics inflation calculator was used to convert current $ into constant 2006 $ US. See: http://data.bls.gov/cgi-bin/cpicalc.pl.

Table 4.5

Ratio of Arms Imports to Arms Exports for the 20 Largest Arms Producing Countries* 2006–2007 (1990 constant U.S. millions)

Country	Arms Imports	Arms Exports	Arms Imports / Arms Exports 2006–2007
USA	1101	15,275	0.07
United Kingdom	1030	2,128	0.48
France	184	4,276	0.04
Italy	878	1,257	0.70
Germany	645	6,286	0.10
Russia	4	11,051	0.0004
Japan	996	n.a.	—
Israel	1994	484	4.12
India	2772	14	198.00
Canada	743	553	1.34
[China**	5,143	917	5.61]
Sweden	211	850	0.25
South Korea	3,334	294	11.34
Spain	923	1,354	0.68
Singapore	754	n.a.	—
Switzerland	196	420	0.47
Australia	1,450	5	290.00
Norway	940	14	67.14
Netherlands	300	2,930	0.10
Finland	239	121	2.0

Sources: SIPRI YEARBOOK 2008, Table 6A. "The SIPRI Top 100 arms-producing companies, 2006." One or more of the world's Top 100 arms producing companies are located in these 20 countries.

SIPRI ARMS TRANSFER DATABASE, http://www.sipri.org/contents/armstrad/at_db.html

SIPRI data on arms transfers is not comparable with other arms transfer data because it does not refer to actual deliveries of major conventional weapons. "Data on arms transfers are presented in the form of SIPRI Trend Indicator Values (TIVs). TIVs are expressed in US$ m. at constant (1990) prices. However, although figures are expressed in US$, TIVs do not represent the financial value of goods transferred. Instead, TIVs are an indication of the volume of arms transferred. Hence, TIVs can be used to measure trends in international arms transfers . . . or to measure a particular country's share of the overall import or export market or the rate of increase or decline in its imports or exports." However, since TIVs do not represent the financial value of the goods transferred, they are not comparable to other arms export/import figures.

*The countries listed are the locations of one or more of the SIPRI Top 100 arms producing companies.

**China is excluded from SIPRI's list of the Top 100 arms producing companies because of lack of reliable data. However, as SIPRI observes, "Chinese arms-producing enterprises would almost certainly be included in the SIPRI Top 100 were data available."

n.a. - data not available

arms producing countries. (see Table 4.5).[45] This combination of factors—the relative autonomy, larger size, and greater strength of its defense-industrial sector—gives the United States a substantial comparative economic and technological advantage but poses thorny dependency issues for other countries.[46]

Economic, Political, and Military Dependency

For smaller arms producers there are few ways to avoid their increasing economic, military, and political dependence upon the United States. The escalating costs of defense technologies alone present military planners everywhere with the dilemma of choosing between greater military effectiveness and necessary budgetary constraint. As the price of weapons continues to rise faster than defense budgets, those governments unwilling to equip forces with older or less capable weapons are choosing to downsize the military, buy the most advanced weapon systems they can afford in fewer numbers, and forego some classes of weapons altogether.

Europe

The problem is no less acute in the major industrialized countries of Europe. The United Kingdom, for example, has made clear that it cannot realistically pursue the wholesale transformation of its forces. As the CEO of the United Kingdom's national trade association observed: "It's impossible as a nation of our size to maintain capability across the board, so we are being forced into making hard choices about what genuinely is needed and where we spend our research money."[47] Instead, Britain has adopted a policy of network-enabled capability[48] that selectively and incrementally transforms the capabilities of its military in those areas "most likely to improve the effectiveness of British armed forces in a context of coalition warfare."[49] France is pursuing a similar policy.

The dark side of this decision is greater military and industrial dependency. As some analysts warn, foregoing the production of one or more classes of weapons means that the military can no longer initiate a full range of military operations except as part of an alliance or coalition. It also means that defense-industrial self-sufficiency will become equally elusive. Maintaining an industry that designs and produces only small numbers of weapons for a downsized military will yield products that are so prohibitive in cost, the government will be unable to afford them. The U.K. government has concluded that the design, development, and production of network-centric technologies "will inevitably be led by the U.S."[50]

Trade figures support this assessment. Although most European arms-producing countries were net exporters in 2006–2007, all but France imported more defense equipment as a percentage of their exports than the United States. The Scandinavian countries, Norway and Finland, were net importers of military-related goods (see Table 4.5). In the future, European dependency on defense imports is likely to grow. As armies continue to downsize, economies of scale considerations will mean that most arms producers will need more export sales to support their own defense-industrial and military needs. But in a contracted market, the prospects for exports are poor. Inevitably, for these governments, the large U.S. military market will be the most attractive target. The problem will be finding a niche for their products within it.

For European arms producers, then, entrance into the U.S. military market for sales and collaborative programs is critical for both the economic viability of their defense industries and the technological sophistication of their armed forces. However, this entails a Hobson's choice: accepting U.S. technology transfer constraints. Unwilling to lose control over the destination and use of its exported technologies, services, and technical data, the United States requires that even close allies agree to retransfer/end-user restrictions and conform to key U.S. export controls. From the perspective of other governments, the cost of entry to the U.S. market is increased dependence for them and greater political leverage for the United States.

Third World Countries

Statistics on arms production for most countries are generally unavailable and what is published is usually unreliable. Most governments provide little information about the manufacture of their military equipment, and those that do use different, often idiosyncratic, definitions of arms production. As SIPRI observes, any comparative analysis of the value and number of arms produced has to rely on rough estimates.[51] This is particularly true for third world countries.

But even inexact estimates of comparative arms production capabilities indicate the extent of concentration in the global arms-production system. For most third world countries, dependency on foreign inputs is even greater than Europe's, with few countries approaching Europe's manufacturing capabilities or production levels, and then only in some categories. Some third world countries can assemble or disassemble military systems but are unable to design and produce their own. Others are advanced at producing platforms, such as armored vehicles, aircraft, or naval vessels, but remain dependent upon imports for their weapons, subunits, and electronic components. A few are proficient in producing some but not all of the advanced components and subcomponents.[52] India, Israel, and South Korea, for example, have developed extensive manufacturing capabilities in a number of areas. None, however, is completely self-reliant, and they remain heavily dependent upon foreign defense imports.

In 2006–2007, for example, all three countries—India, Israel, and South Korea—imported many times more defense items than they exported. The same is true for other third world arms producers. None are net exporters of weapons. (see Table 4.5).

Russia is another exception. Traditionally, the Soviet Union, now Russia, has exported rather than imported military systems, but that may be changing. In the mid-1980s, Russia (then the Soviet Union) was one of the world's largest arms producers. Like the United States it accounted for approximately one-third of the world's arms production. By1996, however, Russia's share had dropped to four percent[53] and its military industries were in disarray. Even soaring oil prices (2000–2008) were of little help. Because of inflationary problems, defense spending growth faltered in real terms and hindered the government's ability to invest in its flagging defense-industrial base.[54] According to the Russian News and Information Service 2009 report, only 36 percent of Russia's strategic defense companies are solvent—and many of these survive only due to export orders—while about another 30 percent are on the verge of bankruptcy.[55]

Although there has been some consolidation in the defense sector and manufacturing output has increased, low R&D expenditure since the breakup of the Soviet Union has meant that Russia's high-technology sectors have fallen behind. In 2008, optimistic estimates placed Russia's share of global high-technology sales at 0.5 percent. To date, Russia's defense industries have been dependent on export orders, largely from China and India; during the post–cold war period, these accounted for 80 percent of Russia's export trade. By 2007, however, China and India's share had declined to 49 percent, since both countries now seek more sophisticated technologies elsewhere.[56]

In 2008 Russia may have reached the maximum possible level of arms exports. Customers were complaining about the poor quality of Russian military products, inordinate production delays, and unrealized contract agreements. A Russian company, *Sevmash*, for example failed to complete a contract with a Norwegian firm for building tankers, and in 2007 Russia announced it was unable to honor a contract concluded with China in 2005 for 34 IL-76 military transport aircraft. Algeria is returning 15 Russian MiG-29 aircraft because the components and assemblies were found to be of unacceptable quality, and India has refused delivery of 7 of 5 anti-submarine IL-38 aircraft and the modernized Soviet submarine "Sinduvijai" on similar grounds.[57]

Moreover competition, not only from high tech Western producers but from countries formerly within the Soviet orbit, has become a major problem. Poland and Ukraine have become arms exporters in their own right, producing less expensive versions of Russian military equipment. China, too, is now making lower cost copies of Russian advanced fighters (SU-27) with sizeable potential sales in the third world.[58]

Russia recognizes that to sustain its export market and modernize its military, it will have to resuscitate its defense-industrial base. To do so, Western and Russian analysts agree, will involve substantial Western technological input. As one Russian observer predicted, it will be the end of the "Soviet industrial paradigm in which every weapon component— from bullet to a ballistic missile—had to be Russian designed and produced."[59]

In 2005, Putin declared that "no country has the whole spectrum of modern technologies necessary for the creation of complicated science-intensive armaments." Russia, he observed, should participate in the "global integration process" through collaboration.[60] By 2007, the total value of "military technical cooperation" between Russia and Europe was reported to have reached $120 million—an increase in trade attributed to Russia's imports of high-technology equipment.[61] Barring a major schism between Russia and the West, Russia, too, is expected to become more dependent on Western defense technology imports in the future.

In contrast to other arms producers, in 1996 the United States accounted for approximately 46–49 percent of the world's arms production. The closest competitors were the United Kingdom and France, with about 9–10 percent each (see Table 4.6). The hierarchy has not changed since then, although the U.S. share of world production apparently has increased further. In 2006, 41 U.S. defense firms accounted for 63.4 percent of the annual dollar value of arms produced by the 100 largest defense firms in the world. The U.K. (11.8%) and France (6.2%) were again the closest competitors. (See Table 4.3).

Faced with shrinking defense budgets and downsized militaries, the long-term viability of many national industries is now in doubt. With the exception of the United States, none

Table 4.6
The 10 largest arms-producing countries ranked by share of world total arms production,[1] 1996

Country	Arms Production as Share of World Total 1996*
USA	**46–49%**
United Kingdom	10%
France	9–10%
Japan	4–5%
Germany	4%
Russia	3–4%
Italy	2%
Canada	2%
South Korea	2%
Israel	2%
	Subtotal 85–90% [c.$170–$180billion]
Other (25)**	**10–15%** [c.$20.5–30.5 billion]
	TOTAL 100% [c.$200 billion current prices]***

*Because exact data on the dollar value of national arms production is unavailable, SIPRI estimates are reported as percent ranges.

**In the "Other" category, 10 countries have annual arms production valued at $1 billion or more but less than $3 billion. [China, Australia, India, The Netherlands, South Africa, Spain, Sweden, Switzerland, Taiwan, Turkey.]

Fifteen countries have annual arms production ranging from $200-999 million. [Austria, Belgium, Denmark, Finland, Greece, Norway, Portugal, Czech Republic, Poland, North Korea, Pakistan, Singapore, Egypt, Iran, Brazil.]

SIPRI's rough estimate of the dollar value of China's arms production in 1996 is $2.25-4.50 billion.

***Total world arms production in 1996 is estimated to be about $200 billion (current prices) with a possible range of $195–205 billion. (P. 409).

Source: Derived from SIPRI Yearbook, 1999, pp. 408–409.

of the major Western arms producers—France, Germany, Italy, or the United Kingdom—has been able to reduce its reliance on foreign imports. Even these advanced industrial economies suffer from insufficient defense R&D, and an inadequate scientific and technical infrastructure,[62] which augur a growing dependency on imported systems. As the pace of technological innovation continues to increase and the gap between the United States and other countries widens, analysts predict that the ability of most defense industries to keep up will diminish. Unless the disparity in R&D and production capabilities between the United States and other arms producers narrows, it will soon be reflected in a widening gap between the quality of their weapon systems and those of the United States, further deepening their reliance on U.S. military resources.

THE EMERGING DEFENSE-INDUSTRIAL SYSTEM: OPTIONS AND STRATEGIES

The emerging global defense-industrial sector, then, is a complex and interconnected system, its shape resembling less the traditional hierarchical pyramid than what Bitzinger calls a *hub and spoke system*.[63] In it, the distinctions between former tiers of arms production capability are eroding as defense industries in Europe and elsewhere begin to forego earlier competencies and depend more on foreign inputs. In this environment the United States is the hub and the rest of the world's defense industries the spokes, as even major arms producers out of economic necessity choose to adopt subordinating survival strategies in a U.S.-dominated system.

Dropping Out and Scaling Back

Economic and political pressures are forcing some states to abandon some, if not all, of their military industries. Brazil and Argentina, for example, have dramatically cut back their defense production and are opting to buy foreign military equipment off the shelf instead.[64] By late 1994, Brazil's military industries were in disarray. Of Brazil's three major arms manufacturers, Avibrs was trying to convert its production to civilian products, Engesa had been dismembered, and Embraer, an aircraft manufacturer in deep financial difficulty, had been privatized. After cancelling its ambitious Program X fighter program in early 2005, Brazil began negotiating with U.S. companies to purchase used aircraft for interim fighter. Other programs have also been delayed or cancelled as the government trains its sights on joint ventures, which it hopes will lead to technology transfers and increased local production. Argentina, too, had cancelled all of its defense production programs by the mid-1990s, and leased its state-owned aerospace company, Area Material Cordoba, to a U.S. firm. The Argentine military has now shifted to purchasing most military equipment and training from the United States.[65]

Indonesia is another example. In the early 1990s, the country possessed numerous defense industries that produced a wide range of military equipment—from light aircraft, helicopters, and transport aircraft to landing craft, patrol boats, ammunition, and small arms. The economic downturn of 1997–98, however, hit the defense industries particularly hard. Many companies went bankrupt or were significantly downsized. As a result, Indonesia's defense industries today are unable to meet the needs of the Indonesian military. Although the government has expressed the desire to end the country's dependency on foreign arms suppliers, Rear Admiral Amirullah Amin observed that Indonesia still "need[s] their technology."[66]

The Israeli case is particularly interesting. Israel's defense industries were established in the 1970s and 1980s in an effort to achieve self-sufficiency and relative autonomy in a difficult political environment. But the end of the cold war and Israel's economic downturn in the early 1990s delivered major blows to the country's defense industries. Strapped for funds, the Israeli Defense Forces (IDF) opted to buy U.S. equipment paid for by the U.S. Foreign Military Financing (FMF) program. Buying off the U.S. shelf, however, has increased Israel's dependence on the United States to finance the purchase of new air and naval platforms, and has undercut domestic arms production. Some 25 percent of Israel's FMF funding is spent on equipment from Israeli suppliers, although each purchase is subject to U.S. consent. Since 1999, the IDF has diverted an ever increasing amount of its domestic spending—including low-tech products like footwear, uniforms, and rations—to equipment made in the United States because it can be paid for by U.S. funds. Industry executives warn that the Israeli industrial base will be dangerously compromised if the government continues to circumvent local industry because of its need to buy U.S. products with U.S. aid.[67]

Although dropping out and scaling back are options of last resort for most arms-producing countries, it may become necessary for many in the future. Germany's industry, for example, is struggling to sustain its technological edge in the face of deep cuts in defense spending and the downsizing of Germany's armed forces. Its defense expenditure as a percentage of the gross domestic product (GDP) is expected to drop below 1 percent, the lowest in NATO. As one German industry official gloomily predicted, "If there is no change, companies will slowly either get out of defense, as Siemens did, or out of Germany." Sweden's defense spending cuts and the shrinking of its military are having an equally negative impact on Swedish defense industries, where the threat of the postponement or abandonment of important programs is real.[68]

A Common Market

Europeans have advanced the idea of constructing a consolidated defense equipment market through cooperation in defense spending and procurement. It is conceived as a common defense market large and powerful enough to compete with that of the United States. To date, attempts to create a unified market and to end costly industrial duplication have foundered on concerns about national sovereignty, the security of supply, and the conflicting strategic interests of Europe's small and large countries. It is, nevertheless, a goal to which many of Europe's governments still aspire.

In November 2005, after a year's deliberation, the EU's European Defence Agency completed development of a new code of conduct. The goal is to create a single, competitive defense market among the EU countries, transforming the procurement of military equipment into a more transparent process by curbing the use of Article 296 of the EU treaty. Article 296 allows governments to invoke national security to shield defense procurements from foreign bidders, and it has been regularly used since 1957 when the European Economic Community was first created. As a result, redundant defense products are manufactured throughout Europe, and much of countries' defense procurement takes place outside EU internal market rules.

Because the new code is voluntary and nonbinding, and includes no mechanism for punishing nonobservant members, it cannot prevent a government from invoking Article 296. Moreover, certain items, such as nuclear weapons and propulsion systems, cryptographic equipment, and chemical, bacteriological, and radiological goods are exempted completely. For those EU countries that look to the U.S. defense sector for sales and profit, a common defense market that excludes the United States will be very costly. François Lureau, chief executive of the Délégation Générale pour l'Armament, commented that the new code "does not intend to close the European defense market. It is open to non-European companies. . . .

Today, France is buying three to four times more armaments from the United States than the other way around." As of this writing, the Code's goal of creating a common defense industry and market remains a hope rather than a plan. As Denis Ranque, chairman and CEO of Thales, commented: "I'm surprised sometimes by the lack of thought of some leaders; continuing to imagine that there could be a single defense industry in Europe seems to me like turkeys voting for Christmas."[69]

Preserving Core Competencies

An increasing number of governments and industries are pursuing a third option—namely, a core competency strategy. Facing the prospect of long-term stagnant domestic growth, arms producers are seeking a niche position in the global defense market by promoting their main comparative strengths—manufacturing skills, lower-cost labor, investment funds, or extended defense markets—as a means of retaining some of their production capabilities and increasing their exports abroad. For many, this means serving as suppliers of specialized items to the U.S. military or as sub-suppliers to U.S. industry-led projects through teaming arrangements, joint ventures, and foreign direct investment (FDI). As an official of the Swedish Defense Materiel Administration (FMV) concluded, "We all want to develop European capabilities, but you cannot neglect the main technology drivers in the field of defense—the U.S. armed forces and U.S. industry. FMV is not in favor of building the 'fortress Europe.'" Saab CEO Ake Svensson confirmed this strategy: "We're not going to be a big systems integrator like Lockheed Martin, Northrop Grumman, or EADS . . . [but] Saab could provide the US with some of its advanced niche products, including those for the radar or aircraft training markets."[70]

The American Option: Subcontracting, Joint Ventures, Acquisitions, and Offsets

Many foreign defense companies, therefore, have been pursuing the American option. The weakness of the dollar has provided added impetus, so that finding business opportunities in the United States is now an even more urgent priority, especially for Europe's leading defense firms. This is reflected in the flow of M&As. In both 2006 and 2007, the worldwide value of M&As in the aerospace and defense sectors was strongly centered on the United States. Of the approximately $29 billion spent in each year, 68 percent was invested the United States in 2006 and 73 percent in 2007.[71] With few exceptions, European defense industries engaged in the United States are buying smaller, largely second-tier companies, establishing subsidiaries, or teaming with American firms to acquire new markets and fortify core strengths.[72]

EADS, the largest defense company in Europe, has aggressively moved to enter the U.S. defense market. In 2004, it formed an American subsidiary, Eurocopter USA, which opened a large new factory in Columbus, Mississippi, and found a partner in the Northrop Grumman Corporation to strengthen its bid to supply aerial refueling planes to the Pentagon. In 2008, EADS announced its long term strategy of increasing its U.S. presence.[73] Similarly, Anglo-Italian helicopter manufacturer AgustaWestland established new headquarters in Virginia as part of its contract to build a fleet of presidential helicopters. Thales Communication (TCI), a subsidiary of the French-based electronics company Thales, makes military communications equipment at its plant in Maryland, including radios for U.S. troops in Iraq and Afghanistan. The U.S. subsidiary of the German company, Heckler & Koch, constructed a $20 million plant in Columbus, Georgia, so that its lightweight assault rifle could have a better chance of winning the bid to replace the U.S. Army's M-16 rifle.[74]

In 2008, Italy's Finmeccanica purchased the New Jersey defense electronics firm, DRS, the first major acquisition a non-U.K. European company has made in the U.S. Finmeccanica's sales in North America are expected to rise from 11 to 23 percent of its total revenues as a result of the buy.[75]

Acquisitions in the United States, however, have been essentially dominated by United Kingdom firms. They accounted for 15 of the 17 acquisitions by foreign companies in 2007 and 14 of the 18 foreign defense-industrial deals in 2008. Following its purchase of the U.S. company, United Defense, in 2005, BAE Systems (U.K.) became the sixth largest supplier to the U.S. DoD, with about 25,000 U.S. employees on its payroll. By 2006 BAE employed more people in the United States (38,000) than in the United Kingdom (32,000) and by 2008 BAE Systems had risen to become the fifth largest supplier of defense material to DoD. Smiths Group, PLC, of London acquired five U.S. defense-related companies and now receives 57 percent of its revenues from the United States. Another British defense firm, QinetiQ, has purchased 11 U.S. companies. In 2006, 36 percent of its income came from the United States. U.K. owned firms, then, have fared comparatively well in the U.S., securing 86 percent of all contracts awarded to foreign defense contractors in 2007 and 90 percent in 2008.[76]

U.S. companies have actively sought investment opportunities abroad, too, but the number of their acquisitions has been comparatively small. In 2005, U.S. companies announced 12 transnational acquisitions, which together cost about $600 million; about 70 percent of that was spent on one Swiss, three Canadian, and three British companies. In comparison, the reported aggregate value of U.S. businesses sold to non-U.S. buyers was roughly 10 times the value of foreign companies bought by U.S. companies. By 2008, the weak dollar had all but halted U.S. buy-outs of European firms. In the first half of 2008, only one U.S. acquisition in Europe was announced. Some analysts believe that if the current economic situation continues, "European deals are likely to remain economically challenging for U.S. buyers, while the draw of the world's largest defense market (and the need to reduce costs by entering the dollar zone) is likely to continue to pull Europeans towards the U.S."[77]

European defense industries may consider these transatlantic transactions a strategy for survival, but the questions of national security and political autonomy have become sensitive issues for many governments. Britain's defense industries may be prospering; in 2007 the revenue generated by U.K. defense companies was about the size of the total U.K. defense budget. To some, however, this is because it is hardly a U.K. industry any more, since so many of Britain's larger companies employ as many (or more) workers in the United States as they do in the United Kingdom.[78] A report by a British union of skilled workers and engineers has pointed to the potential dangers for the U.K. defense-industrial base if the trend continues. It warns that the Ministry of Defense will be reliant on military systems designed and built abroad, and in the future will be unable to buy necessary equipment within the United Kingdom.[79]

Javier Solana sounds a similar alarm for the rest of Europe. Europe's defense industry, he warns, is running the risk of becoming niche producers and subcontractors for U.S. prime contractors: "Unless something is done, the trends point towards a steady contraction of the European defense industry into niche producers working increasingly for U.S. primes."[80]

For most third world arms producers, this is not an issue since only a few have the resources to invest in the U.S. defense-industrial sector. Brazil and Israel are exceptions. Brazil's Embraer teamed with Lockheed Martin and won a contract to provide the U.S. Army with a jet surveillance plane. The plane will be assembled in a plant that Embraer constructed in Jacksonville, Florida.[81] Major Israeli firms, too, such as Israel Aircraft Industries (IAI), Elbit Systems, Electro-Optics Industries (El-Op), and ITL Optronics have purchased controlling stakes in U.S. companies and formed new subsidiaries.

But the majority of third world arms producers, however, have opted for domestic offset programs to help modernize their domestic industrial base. India, for example, requires overseas companies to provide at least 30 percent of the value of defense contracts over $75 million to be offset to local industry. India's defense minister stated: "We would like to have fruitful defense cooperation with countries [that] are prepared to transfer technology and are interested in co-designing, co-development and co-production of defense products."[82]

For many of the world's arms producers, not just those in the third world, industrial offsets are seen as a means of gaining access to advanced military equipment, especially U.S. military technologies. Between 1993 and 2005, Europe, not the third world, accounted for 46.9 percent of the value of U.S. defense export contracts and 65 percent of the value of offset agreements. Asia ranked second in both categories.[83]

Loyal Ally

Establishing a close political/military relationship with the United States is a fifth and closely related policy option. U.S. friends and allies have come to hope and expect that political cooperation will be rewarded with economic and technological benefits, particularly in the defense sector.

Italian defense companies, for example, argue that Italy has supported America in Afghanistan and had more troops in Iraq than any other country except Britain and the United States. As Finmeccanica's chief executive, Pier Francesco Guarguanglini, asserted, "As allies we collaborate, but we must also be considered allies when it comes to accessing the U.S. market." The Italian government has aggressively supported these claims, calling for greater technology transfers from the United States.[84] The 2008 purchase of DRS by Finmeccanica tested the potency of Italy's "loyal ally" strategy.

Britain, too, has lobbied to have the United States waive licensing requirements on military technology transfers to the United Kingdom. Frustrated by the reluctance of U.S. Congress to do so, Britain's Defense Committee Chairman Bruce Georges said, "It seems to me truly absurd for a country like the United Kingdom, which has proved itself to be by far and away the most loyal ally to the United States, to be in the position of almost grovelling to the United States and saying, 'Please will you give us the [technical] information we require.'"[85]

Poland is another example. Dissatisfied with the terms of the agreement for a missile base on its territory, Defense Minister Bogdan Klich declared: "Poland is becoming as important to the United States in this region as Pakistan or Egypt in the Middle East. We expect similar treatment." Polish sources complained that they felt taken for granted by the Bush administration, even though Warsaw has contributed thousands of troops to the U.S.-led military coalitions in Iraq and Afghanistan. "People expected here that there would be some gains and that we'd receive something tangible in exchange," observed the director of the Polish Institute of International Affairs. According to media reports, in exchange for signing the missile shield agreement on August 20, 2008, Poland requested—in addition to security guarantees—assistance in modernizing its armed forces and air defense system, technology transfers, subcontracting opportunities, simplification of U.S. military purchasing procedures, and increased military aid.[86]

For the U.S., however, the "loyal ally" strategy raises difficult security. To pursue its foreign policy agenda, the United States needs the cooperation of allies and friends. But there is a growing gap between what foreign governments hope to receive in compensation for cooperation and how much the United States is willing to share its industrial know-how and technology. It is a delicate issue the U.S. is deciding cautiously on a case by case basis.

The five policy choices described above are, of course, not mutually exclusive. Different combinations are often pursued simultaneously, depending on the players involved and their objectives. Governments may declare a chosen strategy but, in practice, there is often variety in the options they choose. Even France, a vocal advocate of creating a competing European defense market as a means of avoiding dependence on the United States, is now also in favor of more defense-industrial collaboration with the United States. A recent French government study calls for increased transatlantic partnerships and urges French government officials to "overcome the past to work more closely with the U.S."[87]

POLITICAL IMPLICATIONS: AN INSTRUMENT OF LEVERAGE

The radical concentration of the world's defense-industrial sector described above allows the United States a powerful role within the larger international system. During the cold war, U.S. influence was constrained by the bipolar structure of the system. Within the Western alliance, major collaborative programs that helped European arms industries recover from World War II were successfully completed. The two-way street policy of arms cooperation between Europe and the United States. was introduced later in order to reduce duplication in defense research and development. Its stated goals were not very different from those of today: greater standardization and interoperability, the improved defense posture of the NATO alliance, and savings in defense spending. Over time, however, differences arose over the purpose and extent of technology transfers. From the European perspective, access to U.S. technologies and markets was seen in terms of the economic benefits that would accrue to Europe's national defense industries. But the United States, focused on the cold war, insisted upon strict technology transfer restrictions to control the diffusion of American military technology to its enemies[88]—policies that became a contentious issue in U.S. bilateral relations with its allies.

By the late 1980s, however, new opportunities emerged for the United States to revise and reinforce its foreign policy strategies. Foreign governments struggling with heightened economic and strategic insecurities—even those governments once hostile to the United States—were now more receptive and vulnerable to U.S. initiatives. The United States could now wield its comparative military and industrial advantage more freely as an instrument of persuasion. The sheer size and sophistication of the U.S. defense production sector provided U.S. policymakers with a variety of policy options from which to choose. Gradually, a broad and overlapping range of incentives, rewards, and sanctions evolved that the U.S. government now uses to encourage cooperative behavior from other states.

Incentives and Rewards

The broad array of incentives and rewards the United States has to offer for cooperation includes the offer of military credits, offset arrangements, technology transfers, loans, economic aid, joint ventures, different forms of military assistance, and the removal of penalties—whether they are arms embargoes, technology transfer restrictions, onerous export regulations, or high transaction costs. Given the potential rewards, access to the U.S. defense industrial sector has become a strong incentive for political cooperation in the current international system.

As early as 1987, the idea of creating a category of major non-NATO ally (MNNA) had taken hold in U.S. government circles. Conceived as an incentive and reward for cooperation, MNNA status afforded non-NATO countries many of the collaborative and technology transfer advantages provided to full NATO members. MNNA partners in the U.S.-led war on terrorism, for example, receive antiterrorism financial assistance and the Department of State (DoS) has introduced special procedures to expedite military exports to U.S. partners in Afghanistan and Iraq. In addition, the Bush administration made it clear that the $87 billion in reconstruction work for Iraq would go only to those countries with troops in Iraq.[89]

Avoiding prospective penalties is also frequently the incentive for cooperation, moderation, or compromise. The U.S.-EU controversy over EU government subsidies for the Airbus A350 is one example. In May 2005, the United States filed suit in the World Trade Organization (WTO), charging that risk-free EU loans to Airbus for new start aircraft violate global trade rules. The EU countersued, contending that Boeing receives similar loans. In response, the United States maintains that Boeing's loans are commercial loans that must be repaid, and therefore fall within WTO rules. To encourage the EU to end these subsidies, the United States shaped a policy strategy that included both incentives and disincentives. According to Richard Aboulafia, an American aerospace analyst, the incentive is continued access to the U.S. defense market at a time when European companies increasingly "tie their growth to U.S. revenues." The disincentive is the potential for the WTO to rule in favor of the United States or issue findings that worsen transatlantic trade relations.

Since the controversy over subsidies erupted, EADS, in partnership with Northrop Grumman, won a $35 billion DoD contract to supply and maintain 179 tanker planes over two decades. While the EU-U.S. dispute remains before the WTO and the U.S. Air Force tanker competition has been reopened and is still undecided, defense analysts predict that for EU policymakers, the prospect of losing future U.S. defense revenues will, in the long run, be the deciding factor on this issue.[90]

Threats and Sanctions

U.S. policymakers also have invoked a host of embargoes, restrictions, denials, threats, and penalties to encourage other states to comply on various issues. In recent years, for example, the question of military exports to China became a key irritant in U.S.-Israeli and U.S.-European relations, and a litmus test of U.S. influence.

Israel and China. Israel, which receives about $3 billion annually in U.S. foreign aid and actively collaborates in U.S. defense-industrial projects, has followed a strategy of close political/military alliance with the United States. But Israeli-U.S. differences over Israel's exports to China have periodically soured that relationship. In 2005, Israel's reported secret sales of upgrades for the Harpy radar-killing drones to China elicited a strong response and severe sanctions from the United States. These included halting Israeli-U.S. collaborative programs (including the Joint Strike Fighter), ending Israel's role in upgrades to the Joint Direct Attack Munitions Initiative, banning Israeli contributions to the U.S. Army's Future Combat Systems, freezing exchanges of information on the development of an attack drone, and stopping the sale of U.S. night-vision equipment to Israel.[91] Moreover, U.S. suppliers of materials and components to Israel experienced inordinate delays in what were once routine U.S. State Department license approvals. Reportedly, the standard review process that used to take at most two months began dragging out to eight months or more. The head of the Defense Security Cooperation Agency, which manages the Pentagon's foreign sales, declared that the U.S. government would not consider any new defense sales to Israel until the dispute over Israel's sales to China was resolved.[92]

In an effort to end the costly dispute, Israel initiated several policy changes and agreed to others. It prohibited local firms from visiting, discussing, or in any way generating new business with China without written permission from the defense ministry. The prohibition extends not only to defense sales, but also to dual-use items that the United States might perceive as benefiting the Chinese military. Israel's foreign minister publicly apologized for having "damaged U.S. interests," and the director-general of the Israeli MoD resigned under U.S. pressure. Israel also agreed to restructure its agencies regulating defense exports and, it is rumored, acceded to a U.S. demand to report not just exports to China but from Israel to other countries as well. As one senior Israeli defense source observed, "If the United States, which provides Israel with $2 billion in annual military aid, demands that we will not sell anything to China—then we won't. If the Americans decide we should not be selling arms to other countries as well—Israel will have no choice but to comply."[93]

Europe and China. Exports to China have also disrupted U.S.-European relations. In early 2005, the EU considered lifting its 16-year-old arms embargo on China, which had been imposed in 1989 because of the Chinese government's violent suppression of the Tiananmen Square protest. The United States requested that the arms embargo not be lifted and issued a series of public statements to emphasize its request. In March 2005, a Senate resolution declared that lifting the embargo "would potentially adversely affect transatlantic defense cooperation, including future transfers of United States military technology, services, and equipment to European Union countries." Some days later, a senior U.S. official warned, "If the EU does lift its arms embargo against China, it is going to have a significant negative impact on transatlantic defense cooperation."[94]

The incentives for selling to China are very high for Europe. It is China's ongoing military modernization efforts and huge civilian market that beckon. According to one report, by 2040, China's annual demand for military hardware will reach about $295 billion in current dollars. It estimates that the United States will remain the largest defense market ($101 trillion in 2040, accounting for 36 percent of global demand), but China will be the fastest-growing single country in the world.[95]

In spite of the great incentive to export military technology to China, however, antagonizing the United States may be seen as too great a risk. According to defense analyst Loren Thompson, most of the European defense and aerospace companies that do business with the Pentagon stand to lose more than they gain from selling to China. "America is where we're looking for growth," a BAE company spokesman said. "If that becomes mutually exclusive with doing business in China, then we will go with the United States."[96] In April 2005, the European Parliament voted 431–85, with 31 abstentions, in favor of urging the EU not to end the embargo. By April 2006, the vote rose to 618–16 in favor of not ending the embargo. To date, the EU has postponed a final decision.[97]

CONCLUSION

It has been hypothesized in international relations theory that the structure of the international system is a major determinant of a state's foreign policy. Evidence drawn from the global defense sector supports that hypothesis. Carlos Escudé, using Argentina's decision to abandon the development and production of the Condor II missile as a case study, argues that there are three types of functionally differentiated states in the international system: states that command; states that obey (the majority of the interstate community); and rebel states—a small number of third-world regimes that challenge the right of great powers to dominate. States, in his view, can only challenge dominant powers by sacrificing the interests of their citizens. Most states, therefore, have little choice but to accept the existing international hierarchy if they want to develop or foster their own political and economic systems. Although a state can resist if it can tolerate the price of doing so, in the present world order the costs are so high that most states will not risk bearing them.[98]

The United States is well on its way to becoming the sole producer of the world's most advanced conventional weapons. It is argued here that the dominance of the United States in the global defense-industrial system imposes major constraints on the policy choices of most states. Other arms-producing countries, regardless of their former position in the defense-industrial hierarchy, have become increasingly dependent upon the United States for sales, markets, technological innovation, and the advanced technologies needed to modernize their own militaries and defense industries. The same is true for other countries attempting to increase their defense capabilities. This growing dependency has granted the

United States considerable direct and indirect political leverage. From the perspective of most governments, the price of entrance to the U.S. defense market is increasing U.S. influence over the direction of their technological development, the stability of their military industries, and the autonomy of their foreign policy decisions.

This is not to say that the United States has full control over the global military industrial system or the shaping and reshaping of the national industries within it. Nor is the United States engaged on every and all policy issues. Clearly, the political impact of the United States is variable, both in intensity and in content, depending on the policy issues at stake and the degree of U.S. interest involved. By the same token, however, the U.S. defense sector provides American policymakers with a potent foreign policy tool with which to penalize uncooperative behavior, reward cooperation, promote stability, and pursue U.S. foreign policy interests. Given the current structure of the global military industrial sector, most governments have few options other than to accommodate U.S. policy preferences.

ACKNOWLEDGMENT

This chapter also appears in the journal *Defence and Peace Economics,* December 2009 (vol. 20, no. 6).

NOTES

1. Joseph S. Nye, *Bound to Lead: The Changing Nature of American Power* (New York: Basic Books, 1990), 25.
2. On this point, see Thad Dunning, "Conditioning the Effects of Aid: Cold War Politics, Donor Credibility, and Democracy in Africa," *International Organization* 58 (Spring 2004): 409–23; Steven Levitsky and Lucan A. Way, "International Linkage and Democratization," *Journal of Democracy* 16, no. 3 (2005): 21–22. Discussing the prospects of democratization in Africa in the post–cold war world, and the credibility of threats to withdraw foreign aid for noncompliance, Dunning observes "the disappearance of the geostrategic threat from the Soviet Union may have made threats from Western donors to withdraw aid much more credible" (Dunning, "Conditioning the Effects of Aid," 422).
3. During the cold war period, the terms developing countries, less developed countries, underdeveloped countries, third world, and global south generally referred to Africa, the Middle East, Latin America, and Asia (minus Australia and New Zealand)—regions of the world considered economically underdeveloped. Since the disintegration of the Soviet Union, these terms have come to mean different things to different people. Academics argue over the appropriateness of each term, and each has its detractors. This chapter uses *third world* to refer to the above regions of the world (minus Australia and New Zealand), plus the former Soviet Union.
4. David Kirkpatrick, "Trends in the Costs of Weapon Systems and the Consequences," *Defence and Peace Economics* 15, no. 3 (June 2004): 271.
5. The term *globalization* is defined by scholars and analysts in many ways. In this discussion, *globalization* refers to the increasing integration of the defense sector through trade, financial flows, transnational mergers and acquisitions, and the movement of knowledge and technology across international borders. For other definitions, see: International Monetary Fund Staff, "Globalization: Threat or Opportunity?" April 12, 2000 (corrected January 2002) http://www.imf.org/external/

np/exr/ib/2000/041200to.htm#I; Sheila L. Croucher, *Globalization and Belonging: The Politics of Identity in a Changing World* (Oxford: Rowman & Littlefield, 2004); Jagdish Bhagwati, *In Defense of Globalization* (Oxford, New York: Oxford University Press, 2004).

6. U.S. DoD, Office of the Under Secretary of Defense Acquisition, Technology, and Logistics Industrial Policy, "Annual Industrial Capabilities Report to Congress" (U.S. DoD, 2008), 11, http://www.acq.osd.mil/ip/docs/annual_ind_cap_rpt_to_congress-2008.pdf (accessed July 2008). Business groups in the United States have challenged this figure. One spokesman argues that the DoD "does not put much effort into tracking [U.S.] foreign dependency or the consequences of industrial integration." He points out that the Government Accounting Office (GAO) found that the " 'DoD does not consider purchases from a company that is incorporated in the United States but owned by a foreign parent company to be foreign.' Yet such companies are very likely to source foreign components through their parent firm," William R. Hawkins (senior fellow, U.S. Business and Industry Council), testimony, *U.S.-China Commission Hearing on China's Proliferation and the Impact of Trade Policy on Defense Industries in the United States and China,* July 13, 2007, http://www.uscc.gov/hearings/2007hearings/transcripts/july_12_13/williamhawkins.pdf (accessed August 2008).

7. Terrence R. Guay, *Globalization and Its Implications for the Defense Industrial Base* (Carlisle, PA: Strategic Studies Institute, U.S. Army War College, 2007) 9.

8. David W. Thornton, "Consolidating the Defense-Industrial Base in the Post-Cold War Era: Budgetary Priorities and Procurement Policies in the U.S. and Western Europe," *Public Finance and Management* 7, no. 3 (2007): 297.

9. U.S.–U.K. defense trade reflects the preferential treatment the U.S. has accorded its "loyal ally," see p. 135, below. According to the GAO, of the 1,960 U.S. International Traffice in Arms Regulations (ITAR) Exemption certificates issued between 2004 and 2006, 900 were to the United Kingdom. U.S. Government Accountability Office. Report to the Chairman, Committee on Foreign Affaairs, House of Representatives. *Defense Trade: Clarification and More Comprehensive Oversight of Export Exemptions Certified by DOD are Needed.* GAO-07-1103, September 2007, 12.

10. Leslie Wayne, "US-Europe Team Beats Out Boeing on Bit Contract," *New York Times,* March 1, 2008; Dov S. Zakheim and Ronald T. Kadish, "One-Stop Defense Shopping," *Washington Post,* April 28, 2008.

11. Guay, 13.

12. Elizabeth Sköns, Sibylle Bauer, and Eamon Surry, "Arms Production," *SIPRI Yearbook 2004* (Oxford: Oxford University Press, 2004), 405–10; James Murphy, "EU Calls for Closer Coordination of Defense Projects," *Jane's Defence Weekly,* June 1, 2005. See also Keith Hartley, "Collaboration and European Defense Industrial Policy," *Defence and Peace Economics* 19, no. 4 (2008): 303–315ff.

13. The European Defense Agency was created to develop defense capabilities, promote defense research and technology (R&T) and armaments cooperation; strengthen the European industrial base and create a competitive European defense equipment market. As of 2009 there were 26 members. *2005-2009 European Defense Agency Information Site,* [http://www.eda.europa.eu].

14. Gerrard Cowan, "EDA reveals cross-border deal details," *Jane's Defence Industry*, January 22, 2009.

15. Julian Hale, "EU Parliament to Vote on Opening Market," *Defence News,* October 3, 2008.

16. Sam Perlo-Freeman and Elizabeth Sköns, "Arms Production," *SIPRI Yearbook 2008* (Oxford: Oxford University Press, 2008), 271–75; "Ever Closer Union? The Future," *Jane's World Defence Industry,* January 17, 2008.

17. The Indian government, for example, limits foreign direct investment (FDI) in India's defense industries to 26 percent. Jon Grevatt, "Indian Industry Repeats Call for Lower FDI Limit," *Jane's Defence Industry,* May 2, 2008.

18. Between 1980-2000 NATO countries reduced the size of their armies about 30 percent on average. See, Philippe Manigart, "Restructuring the Armed Forces" and "Table 19.4: Force Reduction among NATO Countries (1980-2000), in *Handbook of the Sociology of the Military*, ed. Giuseppe Caforio (New York: Kluwer Academic/Plenum Publishers, 2003), 331-332. Downsizing has become a worldwide trend, as governments seek the economic benefits and military advantages of a smaller, more flexible, leaner and meaner armed forces.

19. Victor Litovkin, "The Achilles Heel of the Defense Industry, Special to *Russia Profile,*" July 1, 2008, http://www.russiaprofile.org. See also: Stephen J. Blank, "Rosoboroneksport: Arms Sales and the Structure of Russian Defense Industry," (Carlisle, PA: Strategic Studies Institute, U.S. Army War College, 2007), 35, 64.; "Moscow Defense Brief," November 2008, http://mdb.cast.ru/mdb/2-2006/item2/item2/; International Institute for Strategic Studies (IISS), "Russia's Defense Industry," *Strategic Comments* 13, no. 8 (2007).

20. Keith Hayward, "'I Have Seen the Future and It Works': The U.S. Defense Industry Transformation: Lessons for the UK Defense Industrial Base," *Defence and Peace Economics* 16, no. 2 (April 2005), 127; Sharon Sadeh, "Israel's Defense Industry in the 21st Century: Challenges and Opportunities," *Strategic Assessment,* December 2004; Barbara Opall-Rome, "Israeli Exporters Hedge Against Declining Dollar," *Defense News,* August 4, 2008; Pierre Tran, "Fewer Rafales? France Plans to Trim Order, Put Money into Plane's Export Appeal," *Defense News,* January 23, 2006.

21. Nancy J. Wesensten, Gregory Belenky, and Thomas J. Balkin, "Cognitive Readiness in Network-Centric Operations," *Parameters,* Spring 2005, 94; Lawrence Freedman, "The Revolution in Strategic Affairs," Adelphi paper 318 (Oxford: Oxford University Press 1998), 110.

22. For example, a number of traditional defense companies are offering missile protection suites for military and civil airlines. See David Mulholland, "Homeland Defense Market Grows," *Jane's Defence Weekly,* August 25, 2004.

23. Susan Willett, "East Asia's Changing Defense Industry," *Survival,* Autumn 1997. Richard A. Bitzinger, "China's Military-Industrial Complex: Is It (Finally) Turning a Corner?" *RSIS Commentaries*, November 21, 2008.

24. David Kirkpatrick, Trends in the Cost of Weapon Systems, And the Consequences, a paper presented at the conference Budgets and Expenditure Choices in the Post-Cold War, sponsored by the George C. Marshall European Center for Security Studies and NATO Economics Directorate, September 15–18, 2003, cited in Controlling Costs in Tactical Aircraft Programs: CDI Congressional Testimony on the FA-22, 6. Prepared Testimony of Christopher Hellmann, for the House Government Reform Committee, Subcommittee on National Security, Emerging Threats and International Relations Hearing on (Controlling Costs in Tactical Aircraft Programs, April 11, 2003, http://www.cdi.org/mrp/fa22.cfm; see also Kirkpatrick, Trends in the Costs of Weapon Systems, *Defence and Peace Economics,* 267.

25. Kirkpatrick suggests that the cost "increased by about three orders of magnitude between the general purpose 'dumb' bomb and the stand-off air-to-ground guided missile." Kirkpatrick, "Trends in the Costs of Weapons Systems," 263.

26. The fighter aircraft industry is but one example. The U.S. F-35 and F-22 are stealth fighter aircraft designed to operate in a network-centric environment. Packed with the latest radars, sensors, and avionics, these fifth-generation fighters are said to provide a first-look, first-shot, first-kill capability. For most governments, however, the development costs are beyond reach. The estimated total cost of the engineering, manufacturing and development phase of the F-22 program, for example, is $69.7 billion. Total estimated development costs for the F-35 are estimated at about $45 billion. One analyst observed: "if you look today, thereare seven fight-jet

manufacturers in the world. My view is that in the next three to five years, there is probably only going to be five." Andrew Chuter, "Brazil, India Hold Fate of Gripen, Other Jets," *Defense News*, June 01, 2009. See also, Tony Capaccio, "GAO Says Joint Strike Fighter Cost is Rising," *Washington Post*, March 12, 2008; "F-22 Raptor Cost," *Global Security.org*, last modified January 21, 2008.

27. Kirkpatrick, "Trends in the Costs of Weapons Systems," 268.

28. According to SIPRI, the overwhelming share of defense industrial production (dollar value) takes place in China, Europe, Russia, and the United States. See Sköns Bauer, and Surry, *SIPRI Yearbook 2004,* 389.

29. The Dual-Use S&T Program provides incentives to encourage commercial contractors to cooperate with the military services and integrate their requirements into a commercial product. Each project is funded by the Pentagon (25%), the services (25%), and the commercial participants (50%). See DoD, news release, "Defense Science and Technology Seminar on Emerging Technologies, Dual-Use Technology," Arlington, VA, March 10, 2000.

30. Hayward, "I Have Seen the Future and It Works," 138.

31. Sam Perlo-Freeman and Elisabeth Sköns, "Arms Production," *SIPRI Yearbook 2008: Armaments, Disarmament and International Security* (Oxford: Oxford University Press, 2008), 263.

32. Estimates vary on the number of contractors in Iraq. According to a *Los Angeles Times* survey, civilian contractors in Iraq numbered 180,000 in 2007—21,000 Americans, 43,000 foreign contractors, and about 118,000 Iraqis. T. Christian Miller, "Contractors Outnumber Troops in Iraq," *Los Angeles Times,* July 4, 2007. See also Nathan Hodge, "High Risk, High Return? Private Security Contractors," *Jane's Defence Weekly,* July 7, 2008.

33. Andrew Chuter, "UK MoD Turns Increasingly to Partnerships," *Defense News,* April 12, 2004; David Mulholland, "Briefing—German Industry—Feeling the Squeeze," *Jane's Defence Weekly,* March 30, 2005; Richard Norton-Taylor, "Fears over Huge Growth in Iraq's Unregulated Private Armies," *The Guardian,* October 31, 2006.

34. *Jane's Special Report,* "Indian Defence and Security—Industry-Forces and Future Trends," July 14, 2000; *Jane's World Defence Industry,* "India—Defense Industry," June 5, 2008.

35. Elizabeth Sköns and Eamon Surry, "Arms Production," *SIPRI Yearbook 2005,* (Oxford: Oxford University Press, 2005, 401; *Integrum,* "Facts and Information on the Defense Industry of Russia," April 30, 2008 http://www.integrum.com (accessed June 20, 2008).

36. Barbara Opall-Rome, "Israeli Moves Pit Private Against State-Owned Firms," *Defense News,* January 3, 2005; Alon Ben-David, "Interview: Ilan Biran, Chairman of Rafael Advanced Defense Systems," *Jane's Defence Weekly,* May 23, 2008.

37. Sadeh, "Israel's Defense Industry in the 21st Century."

38. P. W. Singer, "The Dogs of War Go Corporate," *London News Review,* March 19, 2004; and "Private Military Firms," *Encarta Online Encyclopedia 2008,* http://encarta,msn.com (accessed June 21, 2008).

39. The United States is struggling with these questions. The stringent implementation arrangements contained in the U.K. and Australian trade treaties that were designed to eliminate most licensing requirements to an "approved community" of government and private companies sharply demonstrate the security concerns of American policymakers. For example, one of the provisions in the Australian-U.S. treaty requires Australian companies and individuals to have classified clearances to be eligible for the treaty's licensing exemptions. Australians will also have to undergo background checks for indicators of significant links to people from countries listed as undesirable in the U.S. International Traffic in Arms Regulations. The Australian defense trade treaty is similar to the one signed by the United States and Britain in 2007. William Matthews,

"Australia-U.S. Trade Pact is Full of Restrictions," *Defense News,* March 31, 2008. Although both treaties were signed in 2007, to date neither has been ratified by the U.S. Senate. The Senate Foreign Relations Committee in September 2008 deferred approval of the treaties because of "too many unresolved questions." The fate of the treaties, however, remains unclear. The former Foreign Relations Committee Chairman, Joseph Biden (now U.S. Vice President) and the ranking Committee minority member, Senator Richard Lugar, continue to support the treaties, and so American commentators have expressed optimism about their chances for approval in 2009. "Editorial, ITAR Treaties Keep Moving," *Defense News,* September 22, 2008. Greater concern has been expressed in the UK. A spokesman for the Society of British Aerospace Companies (SBAC) referring to the Obama Administration's "Buy America" policy said: "The concern is that if there is a trend is [sic] towards protectionism . . . would this affect negotiations on the treaty?" Keri Wagstaff-Smith, " 'Buy America' plan raises fears for trade treaty," *Jane's Defence Industry,* February 5, 2009.

40. Richard F. Grimmett, *Conventional Arms Transfers to Developing Nations, 1999–2006,* research service report for Congress, September 26, 2007, Figure 2, 40. Note that this report does not include U.S. commercially licensed arms export delivery values, so that the dollar value of U.S. exports is significantly higher than reflected here.

41. Eric Lipton, "With White House Push, U.S. Arms Sales Jump," *New York Times,* September 14, 2008.

42. Because China's defense spending is not transparent, it is difficult to compare it to that of other countries. Estimates of the real dollar value of China's defense spending have generated much controversy each year. Figures for 2006 range from $35 billion in the official Chinese White Paper, *China's National Defense in 2006* (Information Office of the State Council of the People's Republic of China, 2006), to the IISS figure of $122 billion (See Table 4.2.) In 2007, the debate over China's military expenditures continued. The U.S. DoD stated that, rather than China's published 2007 figures of $46.21 billion, the People's Liberation Army (PLA) actually enjoyed between $97 billion and $139 billion in funding that year. These figures include activities that China does not declare as military expenditures, such as foreign acquisitions, China's nuclear program, defense industry subsidies, and other provincial contributions to the PLA. *Jane's Defence Weekly,* "Power to the People: China's Military Modernization, Part One," June 21, 2008.

43. *Jane's Defence Weekly,* "Reflecting Change: 2007 Annual Defense," December 26, 2007. U.S. budget estimate for 2008. Department of Defense, *Budget of the United States 2008,* http://www.whitehouse. gov/omb/budget/fy2008/defense.html; Keri Smith, "Solana Warns Europe on Niche Status," *Jane's Defence Weekly,* February 7, 2007.

44. J.A.C. Lewis, "France: Europe Faces R&D Crisis," *Jane's Defence Weekly,* April 23, 2003; Table 11A.2. "Expenditures on military equipment and military R&D in Western Europe and the USA, 1991–2002," *SIPRI Yearbook 2003* (Oxford: Oxford University Press, 2003), 405; European Defense Agency (EDA), "European-United States Defense Expenditure in 2006," http://www.eda. Europa.eu; Guy Anderson, "Looking for Growth: Defense Mergers and Acquisitions," *Jane's Defence Weekly,* March 5, 2008.

45. For a discussion of the current state of Russia's defense industries see, below, pp. 125–127.

46. Even the economic downturn in 2008, which buffeted the defense economies of other countries, left the U.S. defense-industrial sector comparatively unscathed. Antonie Boessenkool, "Tough Economic Year Not Too Bad for Defense Firms," *Defense News,* December 15, 2008.

47. Andrew Chuter, "Ian Godden (CEO, Society of British Aerospace Companies) interview, *Defense News,* July 21, 2008.

48. Min (DP) Lord Willy Bach "Network Enabled Capability," speech, Intellect Defense Briefing Group Christmas Lunch, December 15, 2003, see also, U.K. Ministry of Defense, "Network En-

abled Capability, JSP 777 Edn 1," also at www.ams.mod.uk; and Andrew Chuter, "UK White Paper Will Describe Policy, Not Cuts," *Defense News,* December 1, 2003.

49. Andrew D. James, "European Military Capability, the Defense Industry and the Future Shape of Armaments Cooperation," *Defense and Security Analysis,* March 2005.

50. James, "European Military Capabilities," 11.

51. Elizabeth Sköns and Reinhilde Weidacher, 'Arms Production', *SIPRI Yearbook 1999* (Oxford: Oxford University Press, 1999), 407.

52. Jurgen Brauer, "The Arms Industry in Developing Nations" (paper presented at the conference on Military Expenditures in Developing and Emerging Nations, Middlesex University, London, March 13, 1998), 4.

53. Elizabeth Sköns and Reinhilde Weidacher, "Arms Production," *SIPRI Yearbook 1999,* Oxford: Oxford University Press, 411.

54. For an analysis of the effects of inflation on Russia's defense-industrial base, see *Jane's Defence Industry,* "Analysis: Russia's Defense Spending and Defense Industrial Base," August 11, 2008; *Jane's Defence Industry,* "Analysis: Russian Budget Suffers Corrosive Effects of Inflation," August 8, 2008.

55. Vladimir Petrov, "Moscow acts to bolster failing defence industries," *Jane's Defence Weekly*, March 3, 2009. Nikita Petrov, "Russian Defense Industry Still Faces Problems," RIA Novosti (Russian news and information service), January 9, 2008, http:/en.rian.ru/analysis/20080109/95840754.html (accessed June 4, 2008); *Jane's Defence Industry,* "Analysis: Russian Budget Suffers Corrosive Effects of Inflation." The problem is exacerbated by a significant brain drain from Russia. In total, *Pravda* estimates that half the Russian population of scientists and industrial specialists have either moved abroad or into other types of employment. *Jane's Defence Industry,* "Analysis: Russia's Defense Spending and Defense Industrial Base," August 11, 2008. *Jane's Defence Industry,* "Analysis: Russia's defense spending and defense industrial base"; Litovkin, "The Achilles Heel of the Defense Industry."

56. IISS, "Russia's Defense Industry"; Gerrard Cowan, "China's Arms Spending Continues to Soar," *Jane's Defence Weekly,* July 28, 2008.

57. Pavel Felgengauer, "Rejects-making contract," *Novayagazeta,* No. 14, February 28, 2008. http://en.novayagazeta.ru/data/2008/14/02.html.

58. Colin Koh and Ron Matthews, "Russian Arms Sales: The Other Story Behind Somalia's Piracy," *RSIS Commentaries*, October 17, 2008, 2; Dimitri Sudakov, "Russia infuriated with Chinese export copies of SU-27 jet fighters," *Pravda, RU,* April 22, 2008; http://english.pravda.ru/russia/economics/22-04-2008/104975-Russia_China.

59. Nabi Abdullaev, "Thales Scores 1st in Russia," *Defense News,* July 21, 2008.

60. Nikolai Novichkov, "Russian Industry Hits High-Tech Low," *Jane's Defence Weekly,* January 23, 2008.

61. Gerrard Cowan, "Russian-European Military Technical Cooperation Hits $120million," *Jane's Defence Industry,* June 26, 2008.

62. See Richard Bitzinger, "Problems and Prospects Facing Second-Tier Arms-Producing States in the Post-Cold War Era: A Comparative Assessment," (paper delivered to the Council on Foreign Relations Study Group on the Arms Trade and the Transnationalization of the Defense Industry: Economic Versus Security Drivers, 2000), 1.

63. Bitzinger, "Problems and Prospects," 3.

64. This is, generally, the military's favored procurement option. Most military organizations prefer to purchase the most advanced systems they can operate and afford, which in most cases means foreign imports rather than domestic products. South Korea's military, for example, argues that, given its vulnerable security situation, it requires the most sophisticated weapon systems that incorporate the latest technology. It views foreign purchases as more reliable and up-to-date than

locally produced systems. See *Jane's Sentinel Security Assessment,* "China and Northeast Asia: Defense Production and R&D, Korea, South," April 19, 2005. The Israeli armed forces, too, have always preferred to buy off the shelf foreign equipment and have objected to the costly investment in domestic weapons programs funded by the defense budget which, in their view, are dated by the time they arrive from production.

65. Christopher P. Cavas, "Lack of Strategy Plagues Brazil's Industry," *Defense News,* April 25, 2005; Bitzinger, "Problems and Prospects"; Michael Day, "Country Briefing—Brazil: On a Shoestring," *Jane's Defence Weekly,* April 20, 2005; GlobalSecurity.org, "Military Industry [Brazil] "and "Argentine Defense Industry," April 27, 2005, http://www.globalsecurity.org/military/world/argentina/industry.htm.

66. *Jane's Sentinel Security Assessment,* "Southeast Asia: Defense Production and R&D," April 5, 2005; *Jakarta Post,* "PT Dirgantara Reports Buoyant Sales," February 10, 2006; Indahnesia.com, "PT Dirgantara Indonesia Claims Production of 484 Planes," January 3, 2006; *Jane's World Defence Industry,* "Indonesia—Defense Industry," August 8, 2008; *Jakarta Post,* "TNI Says Can't Rely on Local Arms," July 12, 2008.

67. Robin Hughes and Ilan Ostfeld, "Israeli Defense Industry: In the Lion's Den," *Jane's Defence Weekly,* February 26, 2003.

68. David Mulholland, "German Industry: Export Drive," *Jane's Defence Weekly,* October 29, 2003; Joris Janssen Lok, "Swedish Defense Industry Warms to Exports as Domestic Markets Cool," *International Defense Review,* May 1, 2005; Gerard O'Dwyer, "Nordic Countries Want Cooperation," *Defense News,* March 17, 2008.

69. See: European Defence Agency (EDA), "The Code of Conduct on Defence Procurement" November 21, 2005, www.eda.eu.int. See also Brooks Tigner, "EU Tears Down Protectionist Walls, But New Rules Only Help European Companies," *Defense News,* November 21, 2005. Quotation in Pierre Tran, "Paris Works to Calm US Export Fears," *Defense News,* November 14, 2005; *Jane's World Defence Industry,* "The Trans-Atlantic Gap," executive overview, February 13, 2007; Denish Ranque, "Interview: Denis Ranque, Chairman and CEO, Thales," *Defense News,* September 10, 2007.

70. Lok, "Swedish Defense Industry Warms to Exports"; Keri Wagstaff-Smith, "Saab CEO Confirms US Acquisition Strategy," *Jane's Defence Industry,* July 4, 2008.

71. Guy Anderson, "The Drive for Growth: Mergers and Acquisitions Activity in the Aerospace and Defence Sector," *Jane's Defence Industry,* March 1, 2008.

72. Perlo-Freeman and Sköns, "Arms Production," 266–267.

73. Matthias Blamont, "EADS's U.S. Acquisition Hopes Seen Taking Time," *Reuters,* May 21, 2008.

74. Jonathan Karp and Andy Pastor, "Northrop, EADS to Link Up for Bid," *Wall Street Journal,* June 8, 2005; William Matthews, "Who Wins When Foreign Firms Build Factories?" *Defense News,* January 10, 2005; William Hawkins, "Preserve American Defense Production," *Defense News,* September 22, 2003; Joshua Kucera, "Mark Ronald—BAE Systems North America Chief Executive Officer," *Jane's Defence Weekly,* July 6, 2005; Matthew Swibel, "UK: Cutting a Larger Slice of the Sticky US Defense Pie," *CorpWatch,* April 29, 2005; Jerry Grossman, "Market Watch: International Transactions Fuel Rise in M&A Volume," *Washington Technology,* October 8, 2005.

75. William R. Hawkins, "U.S. Defense Industry Succumbs to Outsourcing National Security," *American Economic Alert,* December 27, 2006; David Gow, "Think Italian, act global," May 14, 2008 http://www.guardian.co.uk; "Finmeccanica outlines benefits of DRS merger," *Jane's Defence Weekly,* August 1, 2008; Gerrard Cowan, "Finmeccanica Buys DRS Technologies," *Jane's Defence Weekly,* October 24, 2008; Guy Anderson, "The drive for growth: mergers and acquisitions activity in the aerospace and defense sector," *Jane's Defence Industry,* March 1, 2008.

76. Parmy Olson, "BAE Marches into the U.S. with Armor," *Forbes*, July 5, 2007; Hoovers Online, "BAE Systems Inc. Overview," http://www.hoovers.com/bae-systems-inc./—ID109919—/free-co-factsheet.xhtml (accessed June 2, 2008); Guy Anderson, "BAE Systems moves into top five of US DoD suppliers for 2008," *Jane's Defence Industry*, February 11, 2009; *Jane's Defence Industry*, "European drift west turns to stampede in 2008," Industry Briefing, March 9, 2008.

77. See Grossman, "Market Watch"; Guy Anderson and Matthew Smith "Analysis: 2008 Sees Subdued M&A Activity," *Jane's Defence Industry*, August 11, 2008.

78. Gerrard Cowan, "Branching Out to Gain Momentum: UK Market Health Check," *Jane's Defence Weekly*, August 11, 2008.

79. Amicus, "Maintaining a Critical Mass for UK Defense," June 19, 2005, www.amicustheunion.org.

80. Gerrard Cowan and Keri Smith, "Solana Warns Europe on Niche Status," *Jane's Defence Weekly*, February 7, 2008. Academic analysts, such as Keith Hartley, observe that the U.S. model of international collaboration typically involves sharing production work only. The United States retains leadership "of design work with production sharing of U.S. designs through licensed production, co-production and offsets." Keith Hartley, "Collaboration and European Defense Industrial Policy," *Defence and Peace Economics*, 19, no. 4, (2008), 308.

81. Egan Scully, Christopher Cavas, and Gopal Ratnam, "Brazil Breaks into US Market," *Defense News*, August 9, 2004; Matthews, "Who Wins."

82. Jon Grevatt, "India Declares an End to 'Procurement Alone' Policy," *Jane's Defence Weekly*, May 30, 2008.

83. U.S. Department of Commerce's Bureau of Industry and Security Office of Strategic Industries and Economic Security, "Offsets in Defense Trade Eleventh Report to Congress, January 2007," *DISAM Journal of International Security Assistance Management* 29, no. 3 (2007), 56.

84. Tom Kington and Gopal Ratnam, "Italy Turns War Support into US Work," *Defense News*, November 8, 2004.

85. Tony Skinner, "UK Steps up Arms Accord Pressure on US," *Jane's Defence Weekly*, February 23, 2005. The Defense Trade Cooperation Treaty, designed to deal with Britain's complaints, is now before the U.S. Congress. It has met with considerable resistance from U.S. senators on security grounds. See *Hearing of the Senate Foreign Relations Committee: Treaty Doc. 110–10, Treaty Between the Governments of the United States of America and the United Kingdom Concerning Defense Trade Cooperation*, U.S. Senate Committee on Foreign Relations, Dirksen Senate Office Building, Washington, DC 20510-6225, May 21, 2008.

86. John McCaslin, "U.S. Defense Sector in Poland: Lead Nation at the International Defense Industry Exhibition in Kielce," *American Investor*, September 2007; *Washington Post*, "New Team in Poland Cool to U.S. Shield: Premier Conditions Support on More Aid," January 19, 2008; Reuben F. Johnson, "Maintaining A Base: Trouble in Poland's Defense Industry," *Weekly Standard*, January 17, 2008; "US, Poland Sign Strategic Cooperation Declaration," text of report in English by Polish national independent news agency PAP, BBC Worldwide Monitoring, August 20, 2008.

87. Tigner, "EU Threatens to Build Own Defense Market." *Defense News*, January 24, 2005.

88. See Wilfred Von Zastrow, *The Two-Way Street: US/European Armaments Cooperation Within NATO* (Washington, DC: National War College Strategic Studies Project, 1985).

89. As of 2009, 14 countries have been granted MNNA status: Argentina (1998), Australia (1989), Bahrain (2002), Egypt (1989), Israel (1989), Japan (1989), Jordan (1996), Kuwait (2004), Morocco (2004), New Zealand (1997), Pakistan (2004), Philippines (2003), Thailand (2003), Republic of Korea (1989). "American Service members' Protection Act (ASPA), Security Assistance Team, U.S. Department of State, July 22, 2009, http://www.state.gov/t/pm/ppa/sat;,See also, U.S. Department of State, "Department of State to Expedite Export Licenses for Iraq Coalition Partners," media note, March 26,

2003; and Joshua Kucera, "U.S. Extends Training of Georgian Armed Forces," *Jane's Defence Weekly,* April 13, 2005.

90. Paul Meller and Elizabeth Decker, "Europe Strikes Back in Plane Dispute," *New York Times,* June 1, 2005; Michael Sirak, "EU Faces Tough Choice over Aircraft Subsidies," *Jane's Defence Weekly,* June 8, 2005.

91. Zeev Schiff, "US to Israel: Tighten Arms Export Supervision," *Haaretz,* June 12, 2005.

92. Opall-Rome, "Israel Restricts Firms' Contact with China" and "New Technology Transfers to China On Hold, Pentagon Official Confirms," *Defense Daily,* June 16, 2005.

93. The average annual $3 billion in U.S. foreign assistance to Israel is now only military aid. U.S. economic aid to Israel ended in 2008. Steven Erlanger "Israel to Get $30 Billion in Military Aid from U.S." *New York Times,* August 17, 2007; Barbara Opall-Rome, "Israeli Moves Pit Private Against State-Owned Firms"; *Defense News,* January 3, 2005; Barbara Opall-Rome, "Israeli FM Regrets China Arms Sale Could Have Damaged US Interests," Defense News, June 20, 2005; Alon Ben-David, "Israel-US Crisis Eases," *Jane's Defence Weekly,* June 2, 2005, and *Jane's Defence Weekly,* "Israeli Contractors Concerned over US Export Request," June 22, 2005; *Jane's Sentinel Security Assessment,* "Israel, External Affairs," May 19, 2005.

94. Mulholland, "Briefing-German Industry."

95. Gopal Ratnam, "For Defense Market Success, Go East: Goldman Sachs Sees High Demand in Asia for Next 3 Decades," *Defense News,* October 3, 2005.

96. Mark Lauder, "Europe Wants China Sales But Not Just of Weapons," *New York Times,* February 24, 2005.

97. *EU Business,* "EU should maintain arms embargo on China, say Euro-MPs," April 23, 2008, http://www.eubusiness.com/news-eu.

98. Carlos Escudé, "An Introduction to Peripheral Realism and Its Implications for the Interstate System: Argentina and the Condor II Missile Project," in *International Relations Theory and the Third World,* ed. Stephanie G. Neuman (New York, St. Martin's Press, 1995), 55–75.

5

The Evolution of International Defense Hierarchies

Philip Finnegan

The worldwide defense industry is engaged in a tug of war between globalization and traditional national hierarchies. The trend is towards the development of international defense hierarchies based on international supply chains. The evolution of these international defense hierarchies has implications in areas ranging from the costs of defense procurement to the political process of setting defense equipment priorities to the freedom of defense trade. Trends towards globalization in other sectors of the economy that are creating economic hierarchies are being adopted in defense as well. Since defense is based on the government spending of national procurement dollars, the process is slower and more difficult that in other sectors of the economy that rely on freer trade terms.

The process is not a smooth one. National defense hierarchies play a critical role in military cooperation between nations and in setting defense priorities. Particularly in the United States, hierarchies headed by prime contractors have tended to promote military industrial cooperation. In other cases, they have served to block that cooperation, resisting change. Increasingly the global defense hierarchy is dominated by U.S. and U.S.-based defense companies. These companies have access to the research, development, and procurement funding that is essential for the development of new products and the large production runs that provide economies of scale. There are dangers posed by the development of these powerful international hierarchies. They do have a role in limiting competition by concentrating technology and marketing power in a limited number of companies. Depending on whether they are dominant in the market or not, they may serve as a powerful force in either opening or closing an individual national market.

At times, their power and that of their political allies encourages spending on unneeded military systems, keeping production lines open even when the Pentagon or European defense agencies would rather stop a procurement. As such, they can be a source of lethargy in military requirements. The development of these hierarchies and the dependency that can stem from them also has important implications in international defense policy that go beyond domestic defense procurement and international defense trade. The position of the United States at the head of the worldwide defense-industrial hierarchy provides it with another policy lever that can be used to counter other companies' or countries' defense trade with undesirable countries or to promote particular U.S. defense priorities.

These hierarchies may be subject to disruption. Changing technologies could undermine existing companies and enable new companies to achieve preeminent positions. Unmanned aerial vehicles (UAVs), in particular, are a potentially disruptive technology in which smaller companies and the industry of smaller nations appears to be successfully challenging the traditional defense leaders. Not only could technology reshape these hierarchies; policy shifts could have even more profound effects. The need for competition in the United States is creating pressure to either reverse some of the concentration in the defense industry or open the U.S. market to international competition.

THE NATURE OF THE DEFENSE HIERARCHY

Hierarchy in the worldwide defense industry is based upon technological capabilities and access to defense budgetary support. As a result there are both national and international hierarchies that are continuing to evolve. The defense industry in general is dominated by companies that act as prime contractors, designing and integrating weapon systems such as fighters or tanks. They design the weapon systems and then contract with subcontractors for various electronic sensors, engines, and weapons. The prime contractors then are responsible for the final assembly and testing of the weapon systems. These hierarchies are becoming increasingly narrow at the top as consolidation of the worldwide defense industry continues. While there were 11 prime contractors in fixed-wing military aircraft in the United States in 1960, that number has now been cut to 3 (Lockheed Martin, Boeing, and Northrop Grumman).[1] That same process has been occurring in European countries. There were 19 U.K. military fixed-wing and rotor aircraft manufacturers in 1945. By 1960, that number had dwindled to 11. It currently stands at only two, only one of which is still U.K.-owned (BAE Systems). Westland, a helicopter manufacturer, is now part of AgustaWestland, a unit of Italy's Finmeccanica.[2]

The hierarchy is characterized not only by the size of the companies but also by their capabilities. Large U.S. prime contractors have a broad array of technological capabilities. For example, Lockheed Martin, the largest U.S. defense manufacturer, is a market leader in fighter aircraft, transport aircraft, satellites, space launch vehicles, missiles, airborne radar, ground radar, electro-optics, avionics, electronic warfare, sonar and anti-submarine equipment, undersea weapons, air defense systems, command, control, and communications. Even the largest continental European competitors do not have nearly such breadth as their American competitors. European Aeronautic Defense and Space (EADS), Netherlands, the largest continental defense manufacturer, has capabilities in fighter aircraft, transport aircraft, space launch vehicles, and missiles (through a joint venture). Its capabilities in defense electronics are much more limited. Finmeccanica, the largest Italian defense company, is a world leader in helicopters and aircraft, and also does some limited defense electronics.

In addition to the hierarchy based upon their role in weapons production, there are international hierarchies. With the lack of free trade in defense goods, the size and capabilities of national defense companies correlates closely to the amount nations spend on defense. Of the world's 10 largest defense companies in 2007, 7 were American (Lockheed Martin, Boeing, Northrop Grumman, Raytheon, General Dynamics, L-3 Communications, and United Technologies). An 8th (BAE Systems) derives almost half of its sales from U.S. subsidiaries it has acquired.[3] Lockheed Martin, the largest U.S. defense company, had almost three times the defense sales of the largest continental European manufacturer, EADS.

The size and technological sophistication of U.S. and European prime contractors mean that they will frequently take on subcontractors in other countries as well as their own. This enables them to meet domestic requirements for local content in national defense procurements. It also integrates companies in the developing world into the worldwide defense-industrial hierarchy. This process of creating a more sophisticated, rigid defense hierarchy has been driven by several factors. The worldwide decline of defense spending in the post–cold war era has led many countries and companies to recognize that consolidation was essential. Shortly after Bill Clinton became president, Defense Secretary Les Aspen warned major U.S. senior defense industry executives that only half of the current companies were needed and that the Pentagon was unwilling to pay for unneeded defense capacity. As a result, a wave of mergers followed that created five mega–defense companies, including Lockheed Martin, Boeing, Northrop Grumman, General Dynamics, and Raytheon. As defense spending experienced a strong increase in the post-9/11 era, these companies were in a position to dominate the defense hierarchy.

Technological trends have also favored the concentration of power in a small number of extremely capable firms. Network-centric warfare, which now dominates U.S. military strategy, dictates that advantage comes from having a force that is networked as much as possible. This facilitates the easy flow of information from intelligence assets to the battlefield and between the various military services. The result is a much faster response time to any threat and the possibility to bring quickly as much capability as needed to the battle.

Developing advanced network-centric systems requires a broad array of capabilities including considerable software expertise as well as the traditional skills of designing aircraft, tanks, or ships. This requires extremely capable prime contractors capable of managing extremely complex projects. This trend creates large networks of subcontractors reporting to the prime contractors. For example, the Future Combat Systems, the U.S. Army's largest program, which is intended to create the network centric army of the future, includes some 550 subcontractors, all of which ultimately report to the prime contractor team of Boeing and Science Applications International Corporation. As part of the project, the Boeing-SAIC team oversees everything from unmanned armored vehicles to communications to unmanned aerial vehicles. The complexity of weapon systems also dictates that fewer can be afforded, meaning that fewer prime contractors can produce systems. Norm Augustine's famous law about the rise in the cost of aircraft suggested that by 2054 the entire U.S. defense budget would be devoted to purchasing one aircraft. That rise in cost has been a prime motivation for the U.S. government in its effort to support consolidation in the defense industry, particularly in the early 1990s.

THE EVOLUTION OF DEFENSE HIERARCHIES

After the destruction of the continental European arms industry in World War II, the U.S. defense industry was dominant. As countries rearmed, they purchased weapons from the United States and European countries conducted licensed production of those weapon systems. Gradually the European companies involved in this licensed production developed their ability to produce components and carry out local final assembly. This culminated in the development of indigenous research and development capabilities in major European countries. Companies gained the ability to be prime contractors and compete with major American companies in the export of weapon systems. As the defense industry grew in Western Europe there was a new impetus towards cooperative production with in the United States. In the early 1970s, this meant that the United States offered 12 weapon systems for dual production both in Europe and the United States. In the 1980s, cooperation evolved again into the Foreign Cooperative Test program, which searched for foreign non-developmental items that could meet U.S. military requirements.[4] Also, a number of cooperative programs began in an attempt to further this industrial cooperation on a government-to-government led level.[5]

In addition to this thrust in the 1980s towards military industrial cooperation with the United States in individual programs, a strong trend developed of greater intra-European cooperation. Increasingly, European governments and industry recognized that they could no longer fund major development programs on a national basis. The costs were simply too great and potential production runs too small. The Tornado supersonic ground attack bomber—a Franco-German-Italian fighter—was followed by the Eurofighter Typhoon, which also brought Spain into the aircraft production program. Other programs, such as the A400M tactical airlifter (France, Germany, Italy, Spain, the United Kingdom, Turkey, Belgium, and Luxembourg), the NH-90 helicopter (Germany, Italy, France, and the Netherlands), the EH-101 helicopter (United Kingdom, Italy), and the Storm Shadow missile (France, United Kingdom) followed. Each of these programs is based on the concept that work-share depends on the amount invested in the program by each country. Each country's industry will get contracts based on the percentage of aircraft to be purchased by their military.

As the impetus towards greater cooperation within Europe and in trying to penetrate the U.S. market has grown among European firms, they have also been engaged in consolidation to build firms more capable of cooperating with their U.S. counterparts. In the late 1990s, BAE Systems merged with GEC Marconi's defense business to create the United Kingdom's national champion. In 2000, the EADS, the first transnational European firm, was created with the merger of French, German, and Spanish companies. The 2001 creation of the MBDA missile consortium, which combines French, German, Italian, and British missile businesses, formed a missile company that rivals the size of its leading U.S. competitors.

The evolution of U.S. and European defense companies to create companies better able to play within a global defense market has been mirrored by dramatic changes in defense companies in developing countries. South Africa, Chile, Indonesia, and Brazil all tried to develop indigenous capabilities that could conduct major exports of domestic weapon systems in the 1970s and 1980s. With the development of a globalized arms system and the influence of democratic change, each of those countries has been forced to give up these aspirations. Insofar as those countries remain involved in aerospace, they have tended to be integrated into the global defense economy. Chile and Brazil, which were major exporters of weapons during the Iraq-Iran war, have both receded from the defense market. Brazil's Embraer has tended to focus on its regional jet business rather than defense. Indonesia's aircraft ambitions ended with austerity programs that cut the industry subsidies that kept it alive. South Africa has been working to integrate its defense industry into the globalized economy as a subcontractor to Western firms. Denel, South Africa's largest defense firm, has been in the process of finding Western partners to take stakes in the company's individual businesses, including its gas turbine engine business and its optronics business. A major portion of the company's work as subcontractors to companies providing armaments to South Africa has created offsets to keep some of the work in the country.

Generally, this is the current role of arms industries in developing countries. They can provide localized production that meets requirements that arms exporters put business into the developing country making the arms purchase. That gives the emerging country manufacturer a position as a preferred subcontractor. Alternatively, they may have comparative advantages in areas such as labor costs that enable them to play a niche role in the product even without offset requirements. However, all pretensions of being a prime contractor able to compete with U.S. and European prime contractors is generally ending as second-tier arms producing countries and industries become integrated in the worldwide defense hierarchy.[6]

THE SHIFT IN FAVOR OF THE UNITED STATES

The end of the cold war has seen a growing gap between the defense budgets of European nations and that of the United States that favors the growing concentration of products, technology, and marketing power within the U.S. defense industry. Of the $1.2 trillion spent on defense globally in 2005, the United States spent $495 billion or 41 percent, according to the International Institute for Strategic Studies (IISS). By comparison, all NATO countries other than the United States spent $259 billion, only about 52 percent of the total spent by the United States.[7] The gap in spending is more pronounced when spending for individual countries is considered. Combined, the six major European arms producing nations (France, Germany, Italy, Spain, Sweden, and the United Kingdom) spent $38.9 billion on modernization funding (the combination of procurement and research and development [R&D] dollars) in 2006.[8] In the 2006 budget for the Department of Defense (DoD), the U.S. government spent $86.1 billion on defense procurement (excluding supplementals). Another $71 billion was spent on R&D. That combined modernization spending of $157.1 billion represented 34 percent of Pentagon spending that year. By comparison, the only major European arms-producing country to beat that level was Sweden, with 43.6 percent of its budget spent on modernization. France spent 23.2 percent. The United Kingdom spent 21.2 percent. Italy, which also has major industry, spent only 7.2 percent.[9] Yet in terms of magnitude, major European countries' budgets pale in comparison with that of the United

States. The U.K. modernization budget totaled $12.6 billion in 2006. The French investment budget totaled $12.7 billion for the same year.[10] Each of those was not even a 10th of the U.S. budget.

The predominant importance of the U.S. defense budget for procurement and R&D dollars has led European companies to seek to be integrated into the U.S. hierarchy, either as subcontractors or as prime contractors. In cases in which European companies have chosen the subcontractor model, they act as a subcontractor to a U.S. company that then is able to make the sale to the Pentagon. Increasingly, European companies are seeking to integrate themselves directly into the U.S. hierarchy by acquiring U.S. defense businesses.

DEFENSE TRADE AND PRODUCTION LINE IMPLICATIONS OF HIERARCHICAL INDUSTRY TRENDS

U.S. and European hierarchies have an increasingly important role to play in international defense cooperation and in setting defense requirements. In international cooperation, in recent years U.S. companies have served as a force to open international markets, particularly in areas in which there are multiple large companies. Lockheed Martin teamed with AgustaWestland to bring a version of the EH-101 helicopter to the United States as the new presidential helicopter, beating Sikorsky Aircraft. Northrop Grumman teamed with EADS to win the $40 billion U.S. Air Force tanker competition, beating heavily favored Boeing. In these cases, U.S. companies, which had no capability in a particular area, worked to broaden their business base by working with a major European company to beat U.S. competitors. Lockheed Martin had no helicopter capability. Northrop Grumman had no tanker capability. Major U.S. companies have also argued forcefully against many Buy America rules with their industry association, the Aerospace Industries Association, in the forefront of lobbying Congress against such laws. Their interest is in performing systems integration themselves and being able to outsource subsystems and components to hold down costs and fulfill offset requirements for foreign customers. They seek to use globalization to reinforce their role at the top of the hierarchy in systems integration rather than trying to create an autonomous capability within the United States.

In Europe, the hierarchy often tends to work in favor of a more restrictive trade policy. The existence of individual national champions rather than multiple national champions, as in the United States, means that the individual national champions often are interested in reinforcing barriers to international trade to increase their own business base. For example, BAE Systems, which worked aggressively to open the U.S. market, has argued forcefully with the British Ministry of Defence (MoD) that there was a need to curb competition to protect the U.K. industrial base.[11] Its thinking was rewarded with a new U.K. industrial strategy that is more concerned with maintaining capabilities in the country.

To limit the damage in the United States created by excessive power in single companies, the U.S. government has repeatedly stepped in to stop mergers that it though would be anticompetitive. Most notably, it blocked the merger of Lockheed Martin and Northrop Grumman in 1997. Mergers of the top four U.S. defense companies among themselves are now considered unlikely, as the government continues to maintain limited competition among leading prime contractors. The power wielded by these hierarchies means that they are frequently able to influence defense policy in prioritizing weapons purchases. The Pentagon has repeatedly proposed canceling weapon systems, including the F-14 fighter, the V-22 Osprey tilt-rotor aircraft, the C-130 tactical transport, and the C-17 strategic transport, but Congressional supporters concerned about job impacts have successfully delayed or avoided cancelation in each of these cases. The contractors for each of these systems were able to mobilize not just their own company to support continued procurement, but also their subcontractors. To kill the F-14 fighter, the Pentagon was forced by a 1989 congressional agreement to buy an additional 18 jets worth $1.6 billion in exchange for promising that the tooling would be destroyed to prevent further lobbying in future years to keep the production line open.

EUROPEAN RESPONSES

The evolution of hierarchy in the defense industry is moving towards a strong predominance of U.S. government and U.S. industry. European governments and industry have responded in three ways to the U.S. dominance in the defense industry, including greater intra-European cooperation, fitting into a global supply chain dominated by U.S. industry, and becoming part of the U.S. defense-industrial base.

The first response has been to consolidate European industry and create European programs to counter the dominance of U.S. defense companies and programs in international markets. As noted earlier, this has resulted in the creation of EADS, the world's second largest aerospace company, and MBDA, a unified missile company that is as large as its U.S. competitors in sales. This response threatens to culminate in a closing of European defense markets to defend these companies' dominant position in their home markets. There is also that danger that a European preference could be introduced within the European Union. This would make it more difficult for the more open markets such as the United Kingdom or the non-arms-producing countries in Eastern Europe to purchase U.S. weaponry. However, if the United States continues its trend towards greater purchase of European systems, an outright European preference is unlikely to make much headway.

The second European response to the U.S. dominance in the defense industry has been to fit into the global supply chain dominated by U.S. industry. Globalization in commercial aerospace has been driven by the need to find the best value regardless of national origin. This involves finding the best subcontractors, regardless of their country. Globalization in defense faces serious constraints from national governments wanting to ensure that money they invest in defense is spent heavily within their own countries. Despite this, the F-35 Joint Strike Fighter (JSF) is a clear example of the trends towards a new form of globalization in the defense industry. The JSF is a next-generation U.S. fighter program that has achieved unprecedented support and participation in its development from U.S. allies. The philosophy departs from the fixed work-share percentages of past programs in favor of best value. A more affordable fighter aircraft is to be generated by taking advantage of a global supply chain that recognizes the different comparative advantages of different international companies. Eight countries (United Kingdom, Italy, Netherlands,

Turkey, Canada, Australia, Denmark, and Norway) signed up to invest in the aircraft's development at various levels of financial commitment. In return, those countries' industries received the right to compete for contracts to be awarded based on best value. As a result, the United Kingdom's BAE Systems was named a major subcontractor in the program. Italian companies will have the following roles: Avio, turbine components; Microtechnica, engine anti-icing systems; and Piaggio Aero Industries, engine parts. The Netherlands' Stork Aerospace will fabricate all flight moveable door and wing parts for initial low-rate production aircraft. Turkey's Tusas Aerospace Industries is responsible for subassemblies and some engine parts.

With the U.S. government acting as the driving force behind the program and the major investor in development, it should be expected that this will become a model for the subordination of other national industries within a U.S. hierarchy headed by U.S. prime contractor, the Lockheed Martin Corporation. The program is potentially worth more than $40 billion for only the United States and United Kingdom's military requirements. This is a marked departure from the fair return (*juste retour*) required in joint European programs. Programs that include Eurofighter and A400M require that participants receive a percentage of work equivalent to their own investment in the program. Obviously, the JSF is a departure from past joint programs in favor of the globalization and specialization that is sweeping through the commercial aerospace market. In focusing on best value, it promises to make the JSF as competitive as possible in world markets by keeping its cost down. This will put serious pressure on products created in the old system, which focuses on national origin. Clearly, the nature of globalization combined with the heavy defense spending in the United States gives U.S. industry a place at the pinnacle of the defense hierarchy.

The last response of European industry has been to seek to become part of the U.S. defense industry. This has been a particularly important part of the U.K. industry's response, but it is also catching on in continental European industry as well. Increasingly, European companies are seeking to develop their own relationship as a prime contractor with the Pentagon. To do this, they are making large numbers of acquisitions of defense properties in the United States. From 2000 to 2006, European companies purchased $13.7 billion in U.S. defense and aerospace businesses, of which 75 percent were purchased by U.K. companies. Those acquisitions were heavily concentrated in ground systems, which represented 35 percent of the total, and defense electronics, which represented 34 percent.[12] By comparison, U.S. defense companies have purchased extremely few European defense businesses. There is little need for U.S. companies to invest in smaller, stagnant markets with relatively little research funding. This drive to get into the U.S. market has made a number of U.K. firms heavily dependent on the U.S. defense market. BAE Systems, the largest defense contractor in the United Kingdom, has made a string of acquisitions that have positioned it to carry out 40 percent of its defense sales in the United States. Smaller companies have made acquisitions that have made them even more dependent on the U.S. market. GKN Aerospace, an aerostructures manufacturer, derives 65 percent of its sales from North America and its largest defense program is the F-35 Joint Strike Fighter. Meggitt Defense Systems, which does precision mechanical systems for combat vehicles, performs two-thirds of its work in the United States. Similarly, Cobham, a UK defense electronics company, makes almost two-thirds of its defense sales to the United States. Ultra Electronics, a defense electronics manufacturer, makes 42 percent of its sales to the United States, the same percentage as it sells to the United Kingdom.

TECHNOLOGIES THAT ARE POTENTIALLY DISRUPTIVE TO THE HIERARCHY

Clearly, the continuing evolution of technology could have a serious impact on the existing hierarchy of defense firms. New technologies could undercut the dominant position of leading manufacturers now and make new firms competitive outside of the existing hierarchy. Unmanned aerial vehicles (UAVs) are a clear example of such a revolutionary technology. Israel has been a leader in the development of tactical and mini-UAVs, giving its companies a role envied by larger U.S. and European companies. In tactical UAVs, Israel developed the Scout and Mastiff programs of the early 1980s. This created the basis for the expertise that now characterizes Israeli UAV programs, ranging from Israel Aircraft Industries' (IAI's) long-endurance Heron to Elbit's Hermes UAV family. The extent to which Israeli UAV programs have been successful in creating a viable new first rank competitor for significantly larger U.S. and European firms is exemplified by Israeli successes in European markets. The U.K.'s tactical UAV Watchkeeper program was won by Elbit Systems, a leading Israeli defense electronics company. It beat Lockheed Martin and Northrop Grumman, two of the largest U.S. defense companies, as well as BAE Systems, the U.K. national champion. France based its Eagle I program on IAI's Heron program and its planned Eagle 2 system on another Israeli Aircraft Industries UAV. Israeli companies also have stronger potential for export than their American counterparts. Traditionally, Israel has been willing to export technologies to countries that U.S. companies would not be allowed to serve.

This phenomenon has also been noticeable in U.S. domestic markets. In the tactical and small UAV markets, smaller companies and start-ups play an extremely important role. United Industrial, a small company recently acquired by Textron, positioned itself as the primary provider of tactical UAVs to the U.S. Army. AeroVironment, a small start-up, has established itself as the dominant provider of small UAVs to the U.S. military. General Atomics has been a dominant player through its development of the popular Predator UAV, used extensively in Iraq and Afghanistan.

Tactical UAVs have several distinctive characteristics that make it possible to upset the traditional hierarchies within the national and international defense industries. Generally, UAVs are produced on a smaller scale than the large assembly line production that gives advantages to U.S. and European manufacturers. While a rapid-growth market, they still lack the size of a market such as that of fighter aircraft or combat vehicles, meaning that larger companies are less aggressive in pursuing the market. As a revolutionary technology, early innovators have the clear advantage. In this case, this favors Israeli manufacturers.

Still, despite their ability to disrupt traditional hierarchies in the short run, the hierarchies are ultimately likely to reassert themselves. The three largest U.S. defense companies— Lockheed Martin, Northrop Grumman, and Boeing—are all investing company funds in research and development. Also, Boeing and Northrop Grumman have both acquired small UAV companies to bolster their own expertise.

MARKET AND POLICY FORCES THAT ARE POTENTIALLY DISRUPTIVE TO THE HIERARCHY

A potential threat to existing hierarchies could come from a change in Pentagon policy that pushes the need for greater competition. Cost growth and delays are becoming routine for U.S. defense programs. The General Accountability Office found that there were 95 major defense acquisition programs, valued at $1.6 trillion. Those programs had increased their R&D costs by 40 percent on average, and acquisition costs by 26 percent. These programs had an average delay of 21 months.[13] Such serious problems in the U.S. defense-industrial base are fueling calls to reestablish the competitive diversity that existed during the cold war.[14] Exactly how that would occur is still unclear, although it would certainly disrupt the existing defense hierarchy and some of the power of the mega–defense companies.

There is the possibility that current defense hierarchies will change based on shifts in U.S. and European policy that permits a freer market. This is another option to improve competition. A shift towards more open defense markets would create a major change in industry hierarchies. In commercial aerospace, globalization is creating a hierarchy based upon specialization. Prime contractors such as Boeing or Airbus focus on the high-end integration of aircraft while increasing their outsourcing of other processes to major subcontractors.

Boeing, with its new 787 Dreamliner commercial airliner, is leading the trend towards maintaining a production hierarchy while fundamentally changing its work processes. Boeing is outsourcing 70 percent of the new airliner, more than it has ever outsourced on any previous airliner. The goal is to build closer relationships with risk-sharing partners who are able to take on greater roles than past subcontractors. In this case, this has meant that Mitsubishi Heavy Industries in Japan is manufacturing the composite wings for the 787. Boeing has never before outsourced a new airplane wing design and assembly.

The U.S. DoD has been reluctant to allow the adoption of such a global supply chain on an international basis in defense. In an examination of 12 major programs in 2004, the U.S. DoD found that foreign subcontracts represented only ten percent of the total contract value, $96.5 million out of $986 million spent on the systems.[15] That model is now shifting in favor of a greater commitment to globalization, even within defense. In recent years, the Pentagon has shown increased openness to the process of purchasing weapon systems from foreign companies. EADS won the $2 billion Light Utility Helicopter program. In conjunction with Northrop Grumman, it also won the $40 billion military tanker program. Finmeccanica, working with L-3 Communications, won the Joint Cargo Aircraft program.

These victories by foreign companies in the U.S. market are a major departure from the past, reflecting another stage of the gradual globalization of the defense industry. While they give foreign companies an unprecedented role in making large sales to the United States, they also serve to integrate them into the U.S. defense system and into alliances with U.S. defense companies, who may act as prime contractors leading their team in the competition.

The impetus now for international cooperation comes from industry itself, teaming to compete on cross-border programs. Since defense programs by their very nature are not based on free trade, hierarchical relationships form on the basis of national origin. Companies based in a state involved in a defense acquisition have a natural advantage and are able to create teams that include prime contractors from other countries that have already built a system. For example, EADS, the largest European aerospace company, is providing a derivative of Global Hawk, a strategic UAV, to meet a German defense requirement. L-3 Communications is offering an Italian aircraft, the C-27J, to meet the needs of the U.S. Army-Air Force Joint Cargo Aircraft program.

POLICY IMPLICATIONS

Clearly, the European industry's need to be integrated into the U.S. defense-industrial base has policy implications for the U.S. government. It presents the U.S. government with an increased array of policy weapons with which to influence European and other states' behavior.

This has clearly come to the fore in discussions on China. After Israeli officials misled U.S. officials about an upgrade of Harpy anti-radar missiles, the U.S. government responded by imposing a number of retaliatory measures, including stopping military cooperation on the JSF and stopping Israeli industry contributions to the U.S. Army's Future Combat Systems, the Army's largest program.[16] Ultimately, Israel agreed to put rigid new restrictions on exports to China.

In 2005, when the European Union was considering lifting its arms embargo against China, U.S. officials warned that doing so could adversely affect the prospects of European companies seeking U.S. contracts. Deputy Secretary of State Bob Zellnick noted that the U.S. DoD was increasing its procurement of foreign defense systems, but lifting the embargo would "increase the chance that Congress will cut off a number of these activities."[17]

Missile cooperation has also been an area in which the United States considered offering a carrot to European allies to generate support, although the initiative was not fully implemented. The United States offered to involve the European defense industry in the International Kinetic Energy Interceptor. The plan was to develop an alternative interceptor using European technology at the same time as the main one was being developed in the United States by U.S. industry. The initiative had the potential to develop European defense industry support for the controversial U.S. missile defense effort. In the end, funding for the plan was cut and it was never implemented.

Obviously, the policy tools available to the United States go beyond cooperation in various programs such as missile defense or the JSF. They also include willingness to allow European companies to continue to purchase U.S. defense firms. This is particularly critical to European firms as they seek to penetrate the U.S. defense market. The Committee on Foreign Investment in the United States, an interagency U.S. government group headed by the secretary of the treasury, examines deals with possible national security implications. Its reviews are generally cursory, and it is extremely rare that they challenge any transaction. That review process has the potential to be tightened. In addition, the Pentagon's increased willingness to buy foreign weapon systems offers a powerful incentive to foreign firms to avoid antagonizing the world's largest arms purchaser. The DoD's newfound willingness to buy foreign military systems is always subject to a reversal of policy.

NOTES

1. John Birkler, Anthony G. Bower, Jeffrey Drezner, Gordon Lee, Mark Lorell, Giles Smith, Fred Timson et al., *Competition and Innovation in the U.S. Fixed Wing Military Aircraft Industry* (Santa Monica, CA: Rand National Defense Research Institute, 2003), 2.
2. Adapted from Martin J. Bollinger and John R. Harbison, *Consolidation in Aerospace/Defense: What's Next?* (Los Angeles: Booz Allen & Hamilton, 1992), 4.
3. *Defense News,* "Top 100 List," July 16, 2007, 12.
4. CSIS, *Final Report of the CSIS Commission on Transatlantic Security and Industrial Cooperation in the Twenty-First Century* (Washington, DC: CSIS, 2003), 36–38.
5. CSIS, *Final Report,* 36–38.
6. Richard A. Bitzinger, *Towards a Brave New Arms Industry?* (London: International Institute for Strategic Studies, 2003), 62–79.
7. International Institute for Strategic Studies (IISS), *The Military Balance 2007* (London: Routledge, 2007).
8. CSIS Defense-Industrial Initiatives Group, *Trends in European Defense Spending, 2001–2006* (Washington, DC: CSIS, 2008), 12.
9. CSIS Defense-Industrial Initiatives Group, *Trends in European Defense Spending,* 14.
10. CSIS Defense-Industrial Initiatives Group, *Trends in European Defense Spending,* 12.
11. Douglas Barrie, "BAE Urges U.K. to Curb Defense Competition," *Aviation Week and Space Technology,* July 15, 2002 (http://defense-archive.teldan.com/Article/BAE_Urges_UK_to_Curb_Defense_Competition.aspx?sID=350827).
12. Philip Finnegan, "International Defense and Homeland Security Markets," presentation at the AIAA Aerospace Markets—The Decade Ahead conference, March 6, 2007.
13. Michael J. Sullivan (director of acquisition and sourcing management, U.S. General Accountability Office), statement before the Committee on Oversight and Government Reform and the Subcommittee on National Security and Foreign Affairs, House of Representatives, 4.
14. Dov S. Zakheim and Ronald T. Kadish, "One-Stop Defense Shopping," *Washington Post,* April 28, 2008.
15. U.S. Department of Defense (DoD), "Study on Impact of Foreign Sourcing of Systems," January 2004, Washington, DC, iv.
16. Stephanie G. Neuman, "Defense Industries and Global Dependency," *Orbis,* Summer 2006, 449.
17. James G. Neuger, "U.S. Wins EU Allies in Bid to Keep Chinese Arms Ban," April 5, 2005, Bloomberg.com (http://www.bloomberg.com/apps/news?pid=10000087&sid=a2hXTb90yKFE&refer=top_world_news).

6

The Globalization of Defense Industries

Keith Hayward

At the end of the cold war, superficially at least, the world defense industry changed with remarkable rapidity. In the United States, the process of rationalization, partly inspired by the so called last supper speech by the defense secretary, occurred quickly, leaving a small group of mega-primes and semi-primes dominating the U.S. defense industrial base. European defense firms, albeit at a slower pace, followed suit. These essentially domestic changes then began to assume a more explicit international dimension, a process that can be described at least in part as the globalization of defense industrial activity.

The process and direction of globalization is the subject of considerable academic debate.[1] There are those who would question the concept fundamentally—seeing it as no more than the continued development of a process of internationalization that began in the 19th century or even earlier. Others see contemporary globalization as presaging a qualitative transformation in world society. This view asserts the arrival or the imminent arrival of a truly world economy in which distinct national economies and, therefore, domestic strategies of national economic management, are increasingly irrelevant. Nation states are seen to have ceased to be effective economic managers. In effect, they have been relegated to the status of municipalities within the global economic system. Their job is to provide the infrastructure and public goods that business needs at the lowest possible cost. In the most optimistic views, the economic interdependence resulting from globalization will dramatically reduce the likelihood of armed conflict, with a commensurate effect on the need for conventional security systems and defense capabilities, thus making the current defense industrial system redundant.[2]

However it is defined, for most of the last century, the defense sector remained largely immune from globalization, with clearly delineated national defense companies supported by national governments. Defense production and weapons procurement was keyed directly into national political and bureaucratic processes. In some cases, the state owned the facilities and the design centers associated with defense development and production. It certainly funded most, if not all of the critical research that underpinned increasingly high-tech weaponry. As national security was directly linked to industrial and technological capabilities, defense production was subject to political control, affecting inward investment, relations with foreign companies, and the export of goods and the transfer of technology.

EUROPEAN DEFENSE INDUSTRIAL COLLABORATION— GOVERNMENT-LED INTERNATIONALIZATION

Moving into the 21st century, the state as promoter and end customer of weapons development and manufacturing remains the predominant model in the defense sector. But the purity of the national model of the defense industrial base had already been affected by changes in the structure of procurement, particularly in Europe where cost and market pressures had forced its leading powers into assuming closer and, in some cases, interdependent relationships in defense equipment and production. This process had begun in the 1960s, largely in military aerospace. By the end of the 20th century, collaboration had extended to most other sectors, and as we will consider shortly, and had encouraged the emergence of transnational defense firms.

For the most part, the first 40 years or so of European collaboration were essentially based on government-to-government deals. Governments chose their national champions, and the work was divided on a fair return (*juste retour*) basis; resources invested, order take-up determined industrial outputs. The process was highly politicized and resulted in increased overheads and, in some cases, additional delay and uncertainty. But once started, collaborative programs were better protected against national budget cuts and participants were guaranteed equal access to the technology developed for the program. By the 1990s, European defense equipment collaboration had produced a complicated network of alliances and programs, but these were rarely developed under the same managerial umbrella.

Elsewhere, with very few exceptions, the United States could afford to stand aside from the collaborative impulse. In any event, Europeans especially felt that working with the United States left them as junior partners, less able to access technology and dependent on the vagaries of U.S. procurement politics. But even the United States was not immune to the increasing role of global supply chains and other less obvious forms of internationalization. Indeed, by the 21st century, as much for political as economic reasons, the United States had also launched one of the most extensive and expensive international programs, the JSF (Joint Strike Fighter). Other parts of the defense world had also gone down the partnership route, license-build having an even longer history than European-style collaboration. Ostensibly, national platforms would have systems and equipment bought-in. Sales of defense equipment would often be associated with offset deals, keeping the customer's defense companies in business.

However, this form of internationalization was still clearly based on distinctly nationally owned and operated companies. Links in the case of prime and large equipment systems were usually negotiated on an ad hoc basis. The role of genuinely multinational companies managing and integrating operations across several frontiers was limited. Foreign direct investment (FDI) in national defense firms was equally confined to a few historic examples, often associated with ex-imperial connections (the United Kingdom), geographic proximity (United States-Canada), or again the result of offset agreements.

INVESTMENT-LED DEFENSE INDUSTRIAL GLOBALIZATION

This pattern has begun to change. The last 10 years have seen signs of a more comprehensive form of globalization in defense production associated with the emergence of transnational defense companies and the growth of FDI in national defense industrial bases. These developments do have the potential to change the nature of defense supply radically; but the theme of this chapter is to show that, for the moment at least, the scope and location of globalization is much narrower than might be imagined. Moreover, its long-term impact is most likely to be negatively felt in Europe. In short, investment-led defense industrial globalization is largely transatlantic and dominated by Anglo-American companies; continued expansion could severely undermine European efforts to maintain a reasonably comprehensive regional defense industrial capability.

Defense industry globalization resembles an iceberg, with much more significant activity below the surface. Further down the supply chain, the need to insert leading-edge commercial technology into defense systems has stimulated the globalization process. So has an interest in capturing the assumed cost savings of commercial off-the-shelf procurement and reducing the development time of major weapons systems.[3] To take one widely cited example, the embedded software in many weapon systems could come from anywhere in a global industry. National defense customers are increasingly dependent on global suppliers who have little incentive to conform to the political or bureaucratic requirements of specialized defense contracting. Much of this process is largely hidden from view and is outside formal political regulation.

The rapid globalization of supply chains and the use of commercially developed technology are obscuring the national origins of many defense components and subsystems. Cash-strapped governments have mixed reactions to these developments. They want to increase the efficiency of defense contracting, perhaps through encouraging international competition, but they are also apprehensive about the implications of losing control over key industrial assets and core technologies.[4] But if much of the globalization process is occurring below the radar screen of government concern or even visibility, then governments will have only limited ability to regulate the process, control the flow of defense technologies, or maintain a role in defense-industrial policy.

This issue has become even more problematic with the emergence of investment-led globalization at a prime or at least semi-prime/original equipment manufacturer (OEM) level. It is in some respects linked to the perceived need on the part of governments to maintain competition in national markets by soliciting bids for key contracts from international suppliers. This has been exacerbated by the process of national rationalization and concentration, both in the United States and in Europe, especially in the United Kingdom. The changing technological base of much of modern weapons has also encouraged this process, where there is a need to access technology often developed by existing multinational companies. But the former is much more important than the latter, primarily as at the highest level, the ability to invest in national defense markets remains subject to government control (either formally or residually). Matters are more fluid and porous lower down the supply chain, but governments, especially the United States, are increasingly keen to identify and if necessary protect key niche suppliers from foreign ownership, or at least to vet mergers and acquisitions (M&As).

Because of the essentially politicized nature of the process, the extent of genuine globalization at the prime-contractor level has so far been limited. The formation of European Aeronautic Defense and Space Company (EADS) and BAE Systems in Europe created two transnational defense primes; but only BAE Systems can claim to be a global mega-prime with a significant presence in both the U.S. and European defense markets, and even its prime-contractor status is still largely based on its U.K. market position and its central place in government-negotiated European programs. The U.S. primes still have very few overseas assets or, by European standards, extensive networks of collaborative activity. There are, however, increasing flows of FDI in the defense-aerospace industries, especially among supplier companies. Much of this investment is directed at the U.S. market, motivated by the need to get round U.S. barriers to the purchase of foreign weapons and to access U.S. technology.

However, continuing concerns for national security and economic advantage may encourage governments to focus even more clearly on what they can see, and in areas they can do something about. There will be continued regulation—certainly in the United States—of M&As at the prime and high-level subsystems-supplier echelon.[5] But while the process of defense-industry globalization might be delayed, it cannot be stopped. The key question is how far the process can go without requiring a fundamental change in the relationship between governments and defense companies whereby firms are allowed to operate more freely in world markets, but can expect less direct support for research and development (R&D) and fewer political advantages in national markets.

Under these conditions, globalized defense firms are likely to behave like other transnational companies National-security considerations would continue to impose some constraints on their freedom to transfer technology, core manufacturing assets, and, especially, systems-integration skills. In most other respects, however, globalized companies would make investment decisions on the basis of market access and industry efficiency. Consolidated defense-aerospace prime contractors would be even more motivated to source from an international supply base offering a cost-effective mix of world-class technology, best price, and delivery times. In many instances, subcontractors would be linked to the primes in preferred-supplier agreements, trading long-term assured custom and participation in the design and development process for commitments to reduce cost progressively. At all points in the manufacturing system, companies would be searching globally for added value in both products and processes.

The domestic consolidation process has been driven by a belief that big is better and biggest is better still. Scale is important in building capacity to bear the financial and technical risks of being a prime contractor. It also increases the political critical mass—the better to manage customer relations and to influence the political process through mobilizing the political and economic power of a large corporation. Horizontal integration provides the potential to capture a wider range of defense contracts, exploiting managerial skills transferable between different platforms. In some cases, the defense prime also has the potential to exploit vertical integration, winning profitable subcontracts and, with lifecycle contracting increasingly popular, to take a large share of support and through-life business.

European defense-industrial rationalization has also been driven by the perceived need to build an alternative centre of production to the United States. Motives have been a mixture of industrial and technological policy and genuine concern to maintain independent sources of supply. As in the United States, much of this has been based on national rationalization and mergers. This has led to even higher levels of national concentration, often creating monopoly national champions. Collaboration between national companies has emerged as the strategy of choice for most European countries (France being something of an exception). While ad hoc collaboration has helped to keep industrial capacity in existence (particularly in aerospace), the process has often increased the cost of procurement. The European defense market, despite recent moves under the auspices of the European Commission to create a more open and coherent structure, remains largely a matter of national choice. A similar position obtains for investment in long-term R&D.

From the late 1990s, European defense companies have begun to assume a more transnational character. In this respect, the United Kingdom has been a market leader both in terms of encouraging and allowing inward investment in the domestic defense-industrial base and seeking overseas opportunities, especially in the United States. This, as we will see, has helped to define defense industrial globalization largely in terms of an Anglo-Saxon process. BAE Systems has emerged as a key individual player in this process. Outside of the United Kingdom, EADS has consolidated a large section of French, German, and Spanish defense aerospace capacity. The French firm Thales has created a number of linked national centers and, recently, the Italian Finmeccanica has been aggressive in acquiring foreign assets, particularly in the United Kingdom. All of the European majors have sought, and some have succeeded, in following the United Kingdom into investment in the United States.

However, the problem of national fragmentation and political intervention remains a limiting issue in Europe. The weaknesses of EADS's multinational management system and its continuing links with three national governments have been exposed by recent crises in its civil operation. National strategies for defense-industrial and technological development still dominate, despite attempts by pan-European institutions (such as the European Defense Agency) to coordinate future planning. The dominant role of the United Kingdom, France, Germany, and Italy in European defense also tends to create conflicts of interest between the big four and the rest of Europe. But most importantly, the different direction taken by the United Kingdom, with a strong industrial and military commitment to the transatlantic link, poses the most profound challenge to the creation of a more integrated European defense-industrial base. Combined with a continuing reluctance to spend money on defense, this implies continuing decline in the region's independent capabilities.

NATIONAL DEFENSE INDUSTRIES OUTSIDE THE NORTH ATLANTIC REGION

Defense industrial globalization centers on the operations of largely American and west European companies. There are only a handful of non-European and non-American defense companies in the world's top 100 defense firms. But many countries have a basic defense-industrial capability, and several are linked to the global defense-industrial core through collaboration, partnership agreements, and other ad hoc networks. Some of course, primarily Russia and China, are outside of this relationship.

Russia

Russia, despite years of neglect in the immediate years following the end of the cold war, has still retained sufficient capability to remain a major if declining arms-exporting country. The Russian government is backing its aerospace and defense industries in a bid to catch up with Western manufacturers. Military strategic interests and commercial goals drive this modernization program. A revitalized Russia wants the means to project both regional and global power, as well as to prevent further Western inroads into its civil market.

Since the end of the Soviet Union, Russian defense industries, especially aerospace has suffered from under investment in R&D and defense procurement, although in some areas export sales have remained buoyant, especially to countries that cannot afford Western equipment, are denied access to U.S. or European products, or simply want to avoid dependence on Western suppliers.

The Russian government has announced ambitious plans to rebuild Russian aerospace and to modernize the armed forces. At $32 billion a year, Russian defense spending is only just above U.K. levels and is dwarfed by U.S. spending. The government has promised a $200 billion revamp up to 2015. A considerable proportion will have to be spent on R&D to close the quality gap with the United States, as well as to improve conditions for personnel. But there are plans for a new generation of fighters comparable to the F-22 and the JSF, as well as UAS development. New bombers and strategic missiles may also be developed over the next decade.

On the supply side, the Russian government has rationalized the industry, focusing development on larger groups of companies. Fixed-wing development will centre on the Russian Aircraft Corporation (OAK) or the United Aircraft Corporation. Based around Sukhoi, OAK has an asset value of around $4 billion, and shares are likely to be floated in 2009 or early 2010. The Russian helicopter sector is also being rationalized in a move designed to improve its ability to compete with European and U.S. rivals. As a result, Helicopters of Russia (Vertolyety Rossii), also known as Helicopter Holding, now has control over a dozen design houses and production plants, with strong vertical control ensured through majority government stakes in all of the absorbed companies. There are some prospects for cooperation with Western companies, but concerns about Russia's future defense and foreign policy may limit this to civil programs or relatively low-threat dual technology sectors.

China

China has raised its defense budget by 17.6 percent to $59 billion, citing the need to increase salaries, cope with the high cost of oil, and modernize its military. Further details have not been revealed, but the move follows Beijing's typical defense spending growth of more than 15 percent annually over the past few years. The U.S. Department of Defense (DoD) also contends that China's actual defense spending is routinely double that which is officially admitted. China has ambitions to be a regional superpower and is committed to forcing modernization centering on the RMA/military transformation process. However, its existing indigenous capabilities are modest and dependent on links with Russia and some Western companies, including Israel. However, Western companies are constrained by national and regional embargoes, or indirectly by the threat of U.S. sanction, from cooperating with China. This has extended to some dual technologies, especially in the space sector. China does have a growing competence in space, including overtly military programs.

India

India has one of the highest levels of defense spending in the developing world. India's budget grew by 10 percent to 1.05 trillion rupees ($26.5 billion)—just under 2 percent of its gross domestic product (GDP)—although further funds are available for procurements if needed. Just under half of this total is for procurement, with 25 percent allocated to the air force. Like China, India is experiencing a period of explosive economic growth. For the most part, this is driven by private capital, although the Indian state sector remains a significant player in a number of strategic industries, especially aerospace. Indian companies are also active overseas investors, and Indian multinationals are emerging as important actors in the world economy. India is also noted as a major centre for IT and software development, and a center for global outsourcing, particularly in services. Indian IT capabilities, already employed by the global aerospace industry, are likely to be an important factor in India's future role in the sector.

Indian defense acquisition policy has been shaped by a determination to develop its indigenous defense industry base.[6] This has required license production and local assembly wherever possible. Until recently, India has bought its weapons from European states, Israel, and, most importantly, from the Soviet Union/Russia. Russia is still India's main source of defense equipment—some 70 percent of current inventory. With limited success, India has also sought to develop indigenous designs. The LCA fighter has been in development since the 1980s and has still to enter service.

Indian procurement has been heavily affected by bureaucratic paralysis that has made it very difficult to conclude contracts. Procurement decision making has also been affected by a series of corruption scandals. Reforms designed to improve and expedite the process were introduced in 2005. Earlier, in 2001, India moved to open up its defense industry to inward investment. Bureaucratic problems have frequently forced the Ministry of Defence (MoD) to return parts of the annual budget due to decision-making delay. India may well turn to Western suppliers for some of its future advanced weaponry. This will again require substantial offset investment in the Indian defense industry. But its future as part of a globalized defense industry will remain limited. Despite continuing ambitions to create a modern aerospace and defense-industrial base, state engagement and bureaucratic issues will hinder both indigenous development and prospects for effective partnership with overseas suppliers.

Japan

Japan is perhaps the most important non-U.S.-European player in the globalized defense industry. In terms of published data (which tends to underestimate the size of the Russian and Chinese defense industries) it is the world's fourth or fifth defense-industrial base, and has one of the largest procurement budgets. While its defense budget is set at about 1 percent of the GDP, the sheer size of the Japanese economy ensures that Japan is the world's second-ranked military power in terms of expenditure. However, due to high personnel costs, procurement accounts for only around 19 percent of the total defense budget.[7]

Historically, Japan has been closely linked to the United States and, for political reasons as well as industrial benefit, has had a strong preference for buying American equipment. As part of a well-defined industry policy, much of this has been license-built and produced onshore. From time to time, Japan has been tempted to launch indigenous programs, most notably the FSX of the 1970s. At the time, this was much vaunted as a precursor not only to an expanded native defense-industrial capability, but also as a potential springboard to an independent civil aerospace industry. As such, American cooperation with its design and systems development was much criticized in the United States. In reality, the eventual product was an expensive modest update of the F-16. Indeed, in general, the outcome of Japanese defense-industrial activity has been disappointing and costly to the Japanese defense budget. Japanese industry, however, seems to have derived more than useful technological returns from exploiting spin-off opportunities through the vertical integration of enterprises.

Industrial and technology policy interests have played a major (often decisive) role in procurement policy. Japan's determination to support its relatively small defense-industrial base has led to higher unit costs. There are still strict restrictions on the export of Japanese weapon systems, which also add to procurement costs. Finally, the absence of genuine collaborative relations with overseas companies has further limited Japanese ability to acquire technology and to defray development and procurement costs.

The Japanese military, though subject to tight civil control, is in favor of a more active security role. While constrained defense budgets have led to cuts in equipment numbers, the Japanese military has continued to focus on quality, with an emphasis on high technology and firepower. Japan is committed to forcing modernization through network-centric concepts and to further extend the range of its power projection capabilities, including more advanced airborne weapons. This is also driven by the need to remain interoperable with the United States. Japan may be moving to develop a STOVL-capable carrier force. There is growing pressure to end the restrictions on arms exporting and to seek more equitable and beneficial forms of industrial cooperation, primarily aimed at deepening relations with the United States. However, Japan has still to make up its mind about its next generation fighter, and may have lost an opportunity to become a key player in the JSF program. There are also signs that the Japanese military is becoming more influential in defense procurement, and that pure defense-industrial interests will play a diminishing role in the future.

Other National Capabilities

Outside the big players, there are a number of significant defense industrial players. In particular, Israel has a very impressive defense industrial base, supported by highly innovative technologies, especially in unmanned platforms and electronics. As a result, Israeli companies have become key suppliers to a number of other national defense industries, and a small but significant investor in the United States. South Korea and Taiwan, for obvious geo-political reasons, have sought to maintain a high level of national capability. Several Latin American countries have some capability, but are primarily concerned with license production and offset led production. South Africa, thanks to its Apartheid isolation, has inherited a relatively large defense industrial base—by far the largest in Africa. It is linked to several Western companies, especially BAE Systems. Similarly, Australia has identified aerospace, both civil and military, as a strategic investment, and is an important member of the JSF coalition. The size of the Australian industry, as well as the likely level of government and private investment, will limit the future scope for expansion. Australia will continue to hold attractions as an effective and competitive partner and subcontractor in foreign-led programs. This is underlined by the pattern of inward investment in the industry. Along with the United Kingdom, Australia is viewed positively by the U.S. government as a safe and reliable recipient of American technology. This has been underlined by the signing of a U.S.-Australian treaty on defense trade currently before the U.S. Senate for ratification.

National motives for developing indigenous defense-industrial complexes have ranged from security autarky to stimulating economic development. At a minimum, states have sought to offset the cost of defense equipment procurement with some degree of domestic production. In some cases, states have deliberately targeted the defense sector as a source of technological innovation, often with mixed results and usually at much greater cost than off-the-shelf purchases. Several companies from beyond the Atlantic world are aggressive players in niche defense-export markets, especially in the case of less-developed states or where U.S. or European embargoes and political sensitivities have blocked sales. In recent years, the technical difficulties inherent in developing and producing more complex equipment and wider economic problems have led some states to curb their ambitions to develop autonomous defense-industrial capabilities. The result has often been domestic rationalization and an increased interest in attracting foreign investment in indigenous companies.

In most cases, however, the primary relationship between core manufacturers and the rest of the world has been through direct offset sales, that is, sales involving some domestic production or the sourcing of components from the purchasing country, or other joint-venture activity. In some cases, this has involved investment in process and product capabilities to bring the partner company up to world standards, but there is also an increasing interest in using such partnerships to extend a company's product range and to exploit specialized technological capabilities, as well as to lower labor and manufacturing costs.

The emerging new defense-industrial base may afford more opportunities for new entrants, as Israel is already demonstrating. The growing role of commercially derived technology, especially in the IT area, may enable some states to achieve a much more advanced military capability. However, the ability of countries to take advantage of these opportunities varies considerably. The more advanced technological and industrial systems of Japan, Korea, Singapore, and Australia are clearly well-placed to build on a broader dual civil-military technology base. The integration of commercially developed software into defense systems would, for example, afford opportunities for the Indian software industry indirectly to become part of the world defense-industrial system. However, even the Japanese have found it hard to make the leap from advanced defense manufacturer to the level of systems integrator.

Israel is an especially interesting case. With a history of developing basic platforms through the selective insertion of indigenous technology, Israeli defense companies have acquired an impressive range of advanced capabilities, including Unmanned Aerial Vehicles (UAVs) and in intelligence and surveillance systems. Israeli companies have strong and often-privileged links with U.S. defense companies, and are involved in a number of cooperative ventures with European firms. Israel has courted controversy, and the opposition of the U.S. government in proposing force modernization programs for China, including airborne early-warning technology. Israel is clearly a key candidate for closer incorporation into the global core of U.S. and European defense industries. However, much would depend upon the evolution of international relations in the Middle East. European firms would be reluctant to risk their commercial relationship with Arab states through too close a relationship with Israeli industry.

REGULATING THE DEFENSE TRANSNATIONAL

Other chapters have described regulatory regimes (especially those of the United States), but the emergence of a globalised defense industry should pose a significant challenge to such controls. As Anne Markusen suggested in the 1990s, "a global defense industry will mean a few, large transnational contractors facing a wider array of buyers. Market power will shift from governments to the private sector."[8] As the U.S. Defense Science Board noted in 1999, it is possible to envisage controls and concerns narrowing to a much more focused group of technologies and largely managerial skills centering on the integration of complex systems, or systems of systems.[9] This would still imply a radical shift in the relationship between the defense industries and the state. Markusen predicted that governments will have to work together to "regulate their defense industries and co-ordinate arms export policies or face slowed innovation, inflated prices, and accelerated arms proliferation."[10]

However, so far national restraints are proving resilient and robust against the forces for change. Transnational defense firms, like their equivalents in other sectors, have found ad hoc ways of working around some of the national restrictions on the export of certain defense products and on collaboration with overseas-based firms. But there are still significant barriers to achieving optimal industrial and commercial arrangements for the internal transfer of technology personnel and the formulation and implementation of corporate strategy. Governments will still want to ensure that the globalization of defense-industrial production will not compromise national security, and that the national economy will continue to benefit from defense equipment development and procurement. In particular, national governments will want to retain some control over vital defense technologies and their diffusion into the wider international system. National military establishments will retain an interest in the formulation of defense equipment specifications, defense R&D, and the cost-effective procurement of military products. These concerns are to a degree evident in other sectors, but they are felt most acutely in the defense sector where public money and security are directly involved.

The experience to date has also shown that intergovernmental cooperation to control or to facilitate defense-industrial globalization has been slow to materialize. In the 1990s, the six leading European defense nations signed a letter of intent (LOI) with a view to negotiating a more effective defense trading relationship. In part, this was explicitly designed to help the emerging European defense transnationals by establishing an agreement framework governing, inter alia, export controls, security of supply, and personnel clearances. In practice, although some aspects of the LOI process have been delivered, it produced few direct benefits for defense industries. At a different level, progress toward a more integrated EU defense market and procurement system has been equally slow, affected as often as not by continuing differences between EU governments about the direction and depth of the process. Either national strategies (for example, the United Kingdom's succession of Defense Industry Policy, Defense Industry Strategy, and Defense Technology Strategy papers) or bilateral initiatives (notably Anglo-French links) have continued to prevail. And as we have noted earlier, domestic political interests have exacerbated EADS's problems.

Since much of the globalization of defense industrial activity is more implicit than explicit, either through the supply chain or as defense equipment and systems companies, even more to rely on civil technology offered by established global companies, the ability of governments anywhere, even in the United States, to control or to regulate the process will be limited. It may be sufficient to focus on those parts of the supply chain where governments are still gatekeepers controlling access to key technologies and capabilities, and determining the general outline of national defense-industrial structures. However, as commercial technology becomes ever more important to the functioning of complex weapon systems or systems of systems, and if better-established globalized enterprises are drawn into defense production, governments may lose much of their bargaining power and leverage.

DEFENSE INDUSTRIAL GLOBALIZATION—THE U.S.-U.K. AXIS

For all the emergence of a global defense supply chain and the wider dissemination of key defense-relevant technologies, the operation of a global defense market, supplied by defense transnationals, is something of an illusion. In terms of absolute size, the available defense market is dominated by the U.S.-European axis; and the former hugely outweighs the latter in terms of scale and scope. As we have noted above, Europe has seen the emergence of transnational defense companies such as EADS, Finmeccanica, MBDA, Thales, Rolls-Royce, and BAE Systems. In some cases—and EADS is the most notable example—these have grown out of an increasingly dense network of ad hoc collaboration. This has proven a mixed blessing, with EADS inheriting a complex and debilitating multinational managerial system reflecting its Franco-German (and Spanish) origins. Equally, attempts to reformulate the mix involving Thales and other companies were heavily influenced by national (primarily French) concerns about the future of national defense-industrial assets.

In practice, U.S. and especially British firms have been the most aggressive and successful innovators as transnational defense firms. In this respect, BAE Systems has emerged as the most significant player; but all of the leading U.K. defense companies have acquired a U.S. footprint. Several American companies have reciprocated, taking advantage of the United Kingdom's remarkably liberal attitude toward inward investment and a relatively open approach to procurement. Significantly, a number of European companies—notably Finmeccanica and Thales—have also acquired U.K. assets not only to compete for British contracts, but also to take advantage of an acquired company's U.S. located assets. These, in turn, have helped to provide a springboard of political acceptability for further U.S. expansion.

The motivation for this activity is simple to identify—"follow the money." The U.S. defense market is the world's largest and most valuable. Access is strictly controlled and subject to implicit but none the less strict 100 percent offset requirement for major purchases of foreign equipment. A U.S. partner is essential and must show clear employment and other advantages to succeed in competitions. More indirectly, and perhaps more crucially, investing in the United States gives access to U.S. R&D funding, even black budgets—as long as the investor is prepared to accept restrictions on managerial control and direction, especially over technological assets. Conversely, the European market, although having fewer restrictions on technology transfers, has been increasingly problematic, less promising in terms of new programs, and very much less attractive in terms of technology generation.

The British presence is partly a product of historical accident. The high level of government-to-government cooperation, including in intelligence and nuclear weapons, has helped U.K. business to prove its acceptability and good faith as a protector of U.S. technological interests. These links have been reinforced by the close military ties between the two armed forces, and the concern of the United Kingdom to maintain interoperability with the American military. The United Kingdom has been more willing than most of the other leading European states to procure weapons from the United States. In some important instances, particularly the JSF, this has led to substantive industrial collaboration. Finally, as we have noted already, the United Kingdom has been fully open to inward investment in its relatively buoyant defense market to U.S. companies. It should also be noted that many U.K. companies have chosen to attack the U.S. market because they have been excluded from, or restricted from, bidding in European programs by the application of *juste retour* and other political barriers. By the same token, investing in many European countries to circumvent these restrictions is similarly obstructed. In short, for many U.K. firms, the United States is a relatively better, easier, and freer place in which to conduct defense business than is Europe.

Other European, and some other national firms—notably Israeli, have followed, or have aspired to follow the U.K. path. The Italian company Finmeccanica has been especially successful in forging links inside the U.S. defense-industrial base, with the French Thales also well-regarded as a U.S.-based supplier. In both cases, much of their initial U.S. footprint has followed acquisitions of U.K. companies with existing U.S. assets. Finmeccanica has begun to expand on this beachhead, supported by two important sales to the DoD. EADS has expressed similar interest in developing a comparable presence, and sees its success in selling the Airbus A330 as a solution to the U.S. Air Force's tanker requirement as a possible breakthrough. However, with the exception of Finmeccanica, none have replicated the British presence. Equally importantly, to date there are few examples of U.S. investment in the French or Italian defense industries. While it is debatable whether U.S. firms would find either to be an attractive target, the reality is that government controls would obstruct the kind of two-way interaction that has linked the U.S.-U.S. defense industries.

TOWARD A TRANSATLANTIC (AND TRANSPACIFIC) DEFENSE MARKET

As other chapters have described, attempts to improve the regulatory framework governing U.S.-U.K. cooperation in defense trade have a long history. Despite much high-level good will and some attempts by the British to lever their stalwart support for coalition operations into a better regime for defense trade, little had been achieved by 2007. Clearly, failure to move very far in respect of ITAR (International Traffic in Arms Regulations) reform did not prevent the continued development of closer ties between U.K. and U.S. defense companies. Similarly, although dogged by several disputes over technology transfer, the United Kingdom has maintained its strong position on the F-35 JSF program.

In 2007, in an attempt to bypass opposition to reform in the House of Representatives, the U.K. and U.S. governments signed a Defense Trade Treaty. This was shortly followed by a similar agreement with Australia. Both required Senate approval, but the Senate in general has been more favorably inclined toward reform. The path to ratification has not been easy, and by the summer of 2008, it was still being examined in detail by the Senate Foreign Relations Committee. The key issues were exactly which items would or would not be excluded from the treaty and the exact composition of which U.K. defense companies would be allowed into a defined community. The status of foreign-owned, U.K.-located companies was evidently of particular concern to the Senate. Ratification may yet be blocked by the start of the 2008 political season. If so, the treaty will fall, and the United Kingdom and Australia will have to face a new administration and a new senate in 2009.

Critically for the companies designated by the U.K. and Australian governments, they would effectively be inside the ITAR framework, or at least spared some of the restrictions that currently impede cooperation between companies on both sides of the Atlantic and Pacific. Reform would also enable transnational companies to operate and to organize internal transfers of information and personnel more effectively and efficiently. The implications for U.K.-located defense companies could be profound. In the case of the U.K. treaty, the U.S. MoD will be expected to approve and to vouch for companies allowed to operate within the terms of the treaty. Once within the approved community, the treaty would allow companies a much freer exchange of technology, information, and cleared personnel. Any transfer from the United Kingdom to a third party would continue to require U.S. ITAR approval.

The treaty would reinforce the already strong transatlantic axis in the U.K. defense-industrial base. The treaty may not make it harder to cooperate with Europe, but given the relative size of the markets, the availability of R&D money, and a more straightforward political context, U.K. defense companies would inevitably be tempted to do more business with the Americans. It would create an assured defense-industrial and technological community on both sides of the Atlantic where the prospects cooperation could be more easily explored that would increase the momentum favoring transatlantic programs.[11]

Assuming that the treaty placed before the Senate does broadly satisfy all concerned, ratification would significantly improve relations between the defense communities on both sides of the Atlantic and Pacific. At a governmental level, it would further deepen the already close relationship that links the U.S. and U.K. defense science establishments. The treaties would further improve the interoperability of U.S., U.K., and Australian armed forces by removing most of the restrictions on the transfer of information and technology for use in time sensitive contexts. Overall, it should fulfill most of the requirements demanded by the U.K. MoD to ensure operational sovereignty of U.S.-sourced equipment and technology. The Australia-U.S. relationship would similarly move to a different level, and this would no doubt have positive implications for three-way industrial cooperation.

More optimistically, the treaty might set a precedent for other European nations, thus opening up the prospect of a genuine transatlantic defense market. But as this is likely to require individual treaties, political sensitivities might prove too much, even though some of the wounds caused by the 2003 Iraq War have begun to heal.

Whatever happens to these treaties, the need for national technology transfer regimes to reflect industrial realities will not go away. No country has a monopoly on security relevant science and technology. Global defense companies are now the norm. International cooperation to develop expensive weaponry is vital, even for the United States. The aim must be to prevent the proliferation of the most sensitive materials through more sophisticated, selectively applied measures, not outmoded crude procedures that only hurt allies and one's own industry and armed forces.

CONCLUSION

Globalization is unquestionably changing the environment within which national defense industries operate. The number of transnational defense enterprises is increasing and globalized supply chains are becoming the norm, even for core national programs. However, defense is still different from other industries. State involvement is still regarded as appropriate but when there is growing reluctance on the part of the taxpayer to pay the price of even limited independence in defense production, for example, in Europe, it is harder for nationally based defense firms to survive, at least at the prime-contractor level. National subsystems manufacturers are still viable, if they achieve the financial and technical mass capable of matching the world (that is, U.S.) standards; however, with reduced or non-existent government support, they will need to expand their overseas operations in order to remain profitable and competitive.

Generally, the small and the weak do not inherit the defense world, and that is how, with a few exceptions, individual Western European defense companies appear when compared to U.S. companies and their potential to dominate the globalised defense industry. This is even truer for the rest of the world. However, if the underlying trend toward a more globalized and open technological environment continue, there will be more opportunities for companies outside the defense arena to take a leading role in defense equipment and systems supply.

Unless there is a rapid movement toward a collective European research effort and an integrated defense market, European defense industrial capability will drift further behind the United States. The gap between Europe and the rest of the world will narrow. The most successful European firms may migrate or merge with U.S. primes to become integral parts of a more globalized U.S. industry serving world markets. In this respect, European hopes of maintaining and certainly expanding an indigenous defense-industrial base look increasingly dubious. The decline will not be immediate; the momentum of existing programs will ensure sufficient work to keep European factories busy for a generation. European governments will continue to support local industry for social as well as security reasons. But without rapid and more fundamental reform to both the supply and demand side of procurement, Europe's defense industry will lose its competitive edge and still further ability to match the technological competence of U.S., or U.S.-centered, companies.

This will put the United States in an even more dominant defense-industrial position, although the U.S. government and its military establishment will have to accept greater dependence on external supply. However, while it will be difficult, if not impossible, to control defense technology, sufficient core capabilities and skills will remain in the United States to ensure that the U.S. government will have proportionately more control over the flow and direction of defense developments than any other political entity. In this respect, it is still difficult to see an end to U.S. military technological hegemony. The extent to which this hegemony will be unassailable may, however, depend upon how quickly and how successfully its leading defense-industrial players respond to the demands of new security requirements and assume more flexible and adaptive corporate structures.

ACKNOWLEDGMENT

This chapter had its inspiration in Keith Hayward, "The Globalization of Defense Industries," *Survival* 42, no. 2 (2000), 115–32.

NOTES

1. See, for example, P. Hirst and G. Thomson, *Globalization in Question* (Cambridge: Polity Press, 1996); R. J. Barry Jones, *The World Turned Upside Down?* (Manchester: Manchester University Press, 2000).
2. See Allen Hammond, *Which World—Scenarios for the 21st Century* (London: Earthscan, 1998) and U.S. National Intelligence Board, *Global Trends 2015,* NIB 2000–2002(National Intelligence Board: Washington, DC, 2000). Two of Hammond's scenarios imply a much-reduced threat perspective, even if the world's ecological problems grow more intense. However, his other two are much less optimistic. The NIB view, unsurprisingly perhaps, is very much less sanguine about the likely reduction in international tension over the next two decades.
3. COTS may not always be the cheaper option for the defense customer; its procedures and time scales are not in synch with the commercial world. The commercial provider will not keep open obsolete lines or maintain old software protocols to meet a military lead time of 10 years or more.
4. As the 1999 U.S. Defense Science Board (DSB) report on Defense Industry Globalization observed, "the concept of foreign direct investment in the US defense sector is antithetical to traditional defense industrial base concepts." Defense Science Board, *Globalization and Security* (Washington, DC: DSB, 1999), 11.
5. The U.S. and European governments are committed to improving the conditions of trade for defense transnationals, most notably in the areas of technology transfer and export controls, personnel clearances, and intellectual property rights.
6. Richard A. Bitzinger, "India's Once and Future Defense Industry," *RSIS Commentaries,* October 8, 2007.
7. See, C. W. Hughes, *Japan's Re-emergence as a 'Normal' Military Power,* Adelphi paper 368–69 (London: IISS, 2004).
8. Anne Markusen, "The Rise of World Weapons," *Foreign Affairs,* Spring 1999, 41.

9. See the recommendations of the DSB, *Globalization and Security.*

10. Markusen, "The Rise of World Weapons."

11. There is an issue about the status of the treaty in relation to EU law and draft proposals on the EU defense market. If EU firms in the United Kingdom are outside the approved list, they might have a case under EU competition law. Even non-U.K.-located companies might have a case. A bilateral treaty is commonly subordinate to EU law. The crux will be whether the article 296 national security exemptions to EU law would apply.

7

The Role, Promise, and Challenges of Dual-Use Technologies in National Defense

Kathleen A. Walsh

What do a club wielded by an angry Neanderthal and a modern electronic video game have in common? Both are dual-use technologies. That is, both a primitive club and the technology that powers modern video games can be used for different or dual purposes, whether peaceful and benign or for more malign intent.

In the technological realm, the term *dual use* means that a technology can be employed for either or both commercial (peaceful) and defense (military or security) purposes.[1] This common definition of dual use, in fact, is deceptively simple. In the first instance, such a broad definition could theoretically encompass almost any tool or technology as having inherently dual uses. Thus, the club wielded by Stanley Kubrick's ape (actually a bone) in the opening scene of the movie *2001: A Space Odyssey* could be used to hunt animals for food or to club an opponent to death.[2] The same holds true for more modern technologies. For example, Sony's popular PlayStation 2 video gaming console uses microchip technology that can also be used to enhance cruise missile targeting.[3]

This common and very broad definition of dual-use technology suggests that the technology itself is the independent variable, and the intent of the user the dependent or decisive factor. But this would be misleading, for dual-use technologies are today increasingly developed in order to serve both purposes, commercial and defense—to be used toward both peaceful and military purposes.[4] This is a key distinction: it means that the technology itself as well as the users and their purpose(s) matter in determining how valuable or potentially worrisome the technology might or might not be. Hence, the term *dual-use technology,* when applied in a contemporary context, introduces an inherently very complex set of issues (including capability and intent, motive, opportunity, opportunity costs, and more) that must be considered by industry leaders, defense officials, and policymakers alike. This chapter explores the evolution of dual-use technology as a now-essential element in modern defense industrialization and some of the complex policy issues and strategic challenges that have accompanied its growing application through the past half century.

THE EVOLUTION OF DUAL-USE IN THE MODERN AGE: FROM WEST TO EAST

The history of dual-use technology in the, modern defense-industrial sector dates back primarily to the World War II era. The United States emerged from the ashes of the Second World War as a fast-growing and major world power, in both military and economic terms. This lead position expanded during the bipolar contest that characterized the nearly half-century cold war contest with the Soviet Union. In these and subsequent military contests, the United States has pioneered the development of dual-use technologies and the revolutionary strategies to incorporate them into the defense sector in order to enhance military advantage. It is for this reason that an examination of the importance of dual-use technology in modern defense-industrial development starts with a look at its evolution as it emerged in the U.S. context. This evolutionary path would similarly take hold elsewhere—including in Europe and Asia, as discussed below—as its advantages became increasingly obvious and more easily exploitable in other contexts.

The evolving importance of dual-use technologies as a critical foundation for modern defense-industrial development in the United States can be separated into four distinct phases. The first phase, from about the 1940s to the end of World War II, represents the initial realization of the need for a permanent dual economy, able to serve commercial industry during peacetime and to be mobilized during times of war. The second phase includes the immediate post–World War II years through the height of the cold war era, the success of which in the United States rested upon the critical decision made after World War II to maintain even in peacetime a close defense-commercial industrial relationship in order to promote technological spin-offs from government-funded defense projects to the commercial economy. The third phase took hold in the period after the end of the cold war and is commonly referred to in the defense realm as an era dominated by a revolution in military affairs (RMA) and in the commercial realm as economic globalization. Finally, the fourth distinct phase of an evolving dual-use-oriented economy and defense-industrial sector is the one we are in today, which is characterized by efforts to transform bureaucratic and industrial institutions and processes so as to (among other things) enhance dual-use defense-industrial development. What follows is a brief discussion of each phase in this evolution as well as a few ideas on what the next phase might bring.

Phase I—Forged by War: Lessons Learned in Science, Technology and Defense-industrial Mobilization

In the United States, as in much of the West, the strategic employment of dual-use technologies for defense-industrial development dates back to World War II. In anticipation of U.S. entry into the war as well as during the war, scientific inventions and technological innovations from whatever their source were promoted and employed as a necessary ingredient for winning the war. While most of the key inventions and innovations of the time emerged from the defense sector, this was due in no small part to the tremendous influx of civilian engineers, scientists, mathematicians, academics, and others into government-sponsored programs as part of the war effort. With these experts came ideas, practices, and processes from the private sector that, when provided with ample government support, were generally more easily and quickly realized than probably would have occurred in the commercial realm alone. The Manhattan Project in the United States to develop the first atomic weapon and Britain's earlier breakthroughs on radar technology are just two examples of defense programs that effectively leveraged existing, commercial, or otherwise publicly available (if nascent) technologies, scientific findings, and other ideas in the service of defense purposes.

While a similar pattern of employing private-sector know-how toward defense purposes occurred during World War I, this joint activity was then viewed as a necessary diversion of resources, and the practice (and requisite trade restrictions) by and large did not persist during the interwar years.[5] But among the key lessons learned by U.S. policymakers during World War II was the fact that mobilizing the economy to a full war footing once again had proven far harder and time-consuming than expected. In what is now recognized as a critical paradigm shift in how the U.S. scientific and industrial communities interact with government in a continuous public-private sector scientific and technological cooperative, a key advisor to President Franklin Roosevelt recommended that the close scientific and technological cooperation established among the government, academic, and industrial sectors during the war should continue into the postwar years and receive substantial public financing to sustain it. In the landmark 1945 study entitled *Science: The Endless Frontier,* Vannevar Bush, Roosevelt's Director of the Office of Scientific Research and Development, outlined the rationale behind sustaining both a strong science and technology (S&T) workforce and its connections to the government after the war as a means of ensuring future U.S. national security via maintaining a dominant global position in scientific and technological fields:

> We cannot again rely on our allies to hold off the enemy while we struggle to catch up. There must be more—and more adequate—military research in peacetime. It is essential that the civilian scientists continue in peacetime some portion of those contributions to national security which they have made so effectively during the war. This can best be done through a civilian-controlled organization with close liaison with the Army and Navy, but with funds direct from Congress, and the clear power to initiate military research which will supplement and strengthen that carried on directly under the control of the Army and Navy.[6]

Thus was born within the next few years the National Science Foundation (NSF), an independent federal agency whose mandate remains "to promote the progress of science; to advance the national health, prosperity, and welfare; [and] to secure the national defense."[7] Underlying Bush's report and recommendation to the president to establish an NSF-like agency was, in fact, a dual-purpose rationale: to insure national security needs would be met continuously as well as to serve the general welfare:

> Science can be effective in the national welfare only as a member of a team, whether the conditions be peace or war. But without scientific progress no amount of achievement in

other directions can insure our health, prosperity, and security as a nation in the modern world.[8]

Consequently, public-private sector collaboration on science and technology development and the employment of potential dual-use technologies as a foundation for modern defense-industrial development became viewed as both a necessary and an increasingly attractive strategy. Yet, at the same time, there was growing concern in the scientific community and elsewhere regarding the potential for military exploitation of future scientific study and findings. The Manhattan Project and its rival programs in Germany and soon the Soviet Union provided fresh examples of the inherent dual purposes to which such advanced science and technology could be put.

Hence, it was during this period when dual-use and other strategically important technologies became a pronounced and regular international security concern, and a specific focus, of modern government policy:

> Before 1940 the United States had no legal mechanism for controlling peacetime exports of militarily significant products or information to potential enemies. Consequently, despite the growing military threat posed by fascism and militarism in the late 1930s, there were no legal constraints on exports, and U.S. firms were free to sell almost anything to Germany, Italy, or Japan virtually until the outbreak of hostilities. Japan's military industry in particular seems to have benefitted to a considerable degree from free access to technology, strategic materials, and capitol from the United States.[9]

Although much of the U.S. scientific, technological, and defense advances that emerged during this era stemmed from interdisciplinary collaboration among an international array of experts (Einstein, Fermi, Szilard, and others), the lesson learned from the war years was that the knowledge, expertise, and transference of such knowledge across borders (along with the potential for changing political allegiances) could provide a potentially definitive strategic advantage to one party over another. New U.S. policies for export control were instituted to try to prevent potential global adversaries from acquiring and similarly exploiting advanced science and technologies for military purposes.[10] As a result, dual use export controls—statutory and regulatory constraints on the trade of certain strategically important goods and technologies—would become a new norm in international affairs affecting both the defense-industrial and commercial sectors.

U.S. law was fundamentally changed in 1940 with passage of the Export Control Act, which allowed restrictions to be placed on exports of military equipment, munitions, materials, components, supplies, servicing, and more to certain countries. This law would be renewed every few years throughout the war and ultimately replaced with the basic statutory and executive framework that still underpins U.S. dual-use export controls today.[11] The emerging cold war with the Soviet Union and its communist allies after World War II would also lead the United States and its NATO allies to establish in 1949 an informal (non-treaty), multilateral agreement to try to starve, or at least stall, Soviet and Warsaw Pact defense-industrial development by withholding access to dual-use and other Western defense-related technologies.[12] The mechanism established for this purpose was a joint working group: the Coordinating Committee on Multilateral Export Controls (CoCom); it would survive through the end of the cold war and witness the demise of the Soviet Union before the arrangement was disbanded. But the concept of trying to forestall another state (or non-state) actor's efforts to exploit S&T for dual purposes would remain a core foreign and security policy objective and continues to be applied today, as demonstrated in recent years by efforts to constrain nuclear weapons development in Iran and North Korea.

Phase 2—Post–World War II and the Cold War: The Era of Defense Conversion and Technology Spin-offs

As the post–World War II era transitioned into what would become the cold war, the role played by dual-use technologies would shift emphasis and mainly take the form of defense spin-offs. The term *spin-off* refers to technology developed in the defense sector and adapted (or spun off) to the commercial marketplace. Prime examples of spin-off technology from this period include computer hardware, software, and electronics, automotive, and space advances, jet engines, and nuclear power.

During this second phase, spanning roughly the 1950s through the 1980s, government-funded research and development (R&D) would play a dominant role in determining what scientific and technological advances would be pursued and for what purpose(s). Greater government involvement translated into new and expanded institutions backed by expansive public funding. The early years in this period witnessed the emergence of several government agencies established to develop specific, strategic areas of S&T, primarily for defense purposes. These included the National Aeronautics and Space Administration (NASA) established in 1958 in response to the Soviet's launch of the Sputnik satellite; the Defense Advanced Research Projects Agency (DARPA, originally just ARPA), set up the same year to compete head-to-head with emerging Soviet scientific advances such as those demonstrated by the surprise Sputnik launch; and the Atomic Energy Commission, which took over from the Manhattan Project to focus on both military and civilian nuclear projects, and with particular urgency following the Soviet Union's own inaugural atomic blast in 1949.[13] These institutions and large-scale research programs were mission-driven research efforts and, given the importance of the missions assigned them, guaranteed strong and continuous government support.

It is, in fact a post–World War II tendency for the United States to direct tremendous S&T assets and funds toward developing technological solutions when spurred on by perceived external threats to national security interests. The already mentioned Sputnik launch would be followed by more examples of high-level government support of S&T, as during the initial stages of the Vietnam War; the first and latter halves of the cold war; in response to the rise of Japan's industrial manufacturing capabilities; the post-9/11 period; and today's admonitions for greater S&T investment by the U.S. government to ensure it maintains a competitive edge vis-à-vis China and other rapidly emerging economies.[14]

During the cold war period, however, large-scale, mission-oriented government S&T programs and institutions focused primarily on pursuing basic (i.e., theoretical or experimental) scientific research. Much of the resulting applications research was also mainly oriented toward defense purposes; commercial or technological development efforts at this time were considered a lesser priority, though they remained an anticipated by-product or spin-off from the primary, defense research activities (as a potential means of realizing some return on investment or profiting through a separate, subsidiary venture).[15] For example, NASA's space research led to the development of advanced rocket launchers, space capsules, satellites, lasers, and other potentially dual-use technologies. Many of these were eventually spun off into commercial products, services, and technologies that would become increasingly available for public, even global, consumption over the following decades (e.g., weather forecasting, satellite launching, navigation systems, etc.).[16] Similarly, DARPA's initial research into computer networking to link communications across the defense establishment would eventually serve as the backbone for the initial version of the Internet.[17] The network of national research laboratories spawned from the earlier war effort would likewise translate research derived from nuclear and related sciences into commercial technologies used by the public today and employed in medical and other advances and industrial applications.

Although a deliberate and expected derivative of the original government funding, this type of technology transfer from the military realm to commercial uses was considered a decidedly secondary priority. Yet, over time and with greater commercial successes came greater public awareness of the potential for commercial-industrial advances as a result of defense spending and growing anticipation of continued spin-off technologies as a result of federal R&D funding. In time and with the rise in competition for resources as the cold war wore on, this public-private sector competition for funding would spark a heated public policy debate as to the proper balance of defense and/or commercial benefit from government R&D funding and whether enough spin-off was occurring for all the defense dollars being spent. This debate continues today.

A key part of the debate over the balance of public- and private-sector R&D funding revolves around defining—particularly when under fiscal constraints—what is in the nation's best interest when it comes to funding S&T research. The questions are simple: how much to fund, whom to fund, and with what expected benefits for national security, the economy, and society? From the 1950s, rising markedly in the 1960s, and lasting up until 1980, the federal government expended more on R&D funding than did industry or the academic research community.[18] This trend coincides with the defense conversion strategy of employing federal R&D primarily for defense purposes with the expectation of eventual spin-off opportunities for the commercial sector and academic community. Yet, as this public-private practice of S&T collaboration grew in size, scope, and duration over these three decades, it became increasingly clear that there was more to this relationship than was captured by the defense conversion model. In fact, it became apparent that a critical part of the success of the defense-to-commercial or spin-off model was the emergence of what is now commonly referred to as a national innovation system (NIS).

The specific makeup of an NIS is unique to each nation-state but generally involves interaction between and among three core communities: (1) corporate and industrial enterprises; (2) the academic, research, and scientific communities; and (3) government agencies with money to expend. In the United States, an NIS model had begun to develop across these three broad communities such that over time identifiable centers (or clusters) of scientific, technological, and industrial development had emerged. This systemic model of innovation is exemplified by California's Silicon Valley and mirrored in other regional centers as well, such as the high-tech corridor outside Boston and North Carolina's Research Triangle area.[19] The key to the initial success of Silicon Valley and other high-tech innovation clusters is now understood to have been due to the multidisciplinary convergence, intermingling, and market-oriented system of scientists, engineers, academics, and corporate entrepreneurs supported by funds from private financiers and government R&D programs. In other words, what emerged was a multidirectional, multipurpose, and multifunded system of innovation that served well the interests of all three communities: government, industry, and academia. Thus, the environment began to shift toward a system that rewarded defense conversion spin-off while also providing emerging opportunities for the opposite: commercial-to-defense technology spin-ons.

Given the growing bounty of government funding available during this period, it is not surprising that a more expansive U.S. defense industry began to emerge. In its early years, the defense industry comprised mainly commercial enterprises funded under contract to the government as well as research laboratories scattered across the land and similarly engaged in government-sponsored research projects. These institutions would combine to play an increasingly vital role between defense-oriented research and the broader commercial realm to which technologies could eventually be spun-off. Many of today's recognized leaders in the defense sector (e.g., Lockheed Martin, Boeing, Raytheon) became prominent industry leaders during this period when government funding was flush and market opportunities were increasingly abundant.

Nonetheless, commercial spin-offs from defense contracted research during this era were at times an afterthought. One oft-repeated example of this is Boeing's 747 commercial airliner. Only having lost an initial bid to build the next-generation transport plane to rival Lockheed did Boeing executives decide to apply the technology and know-how they had developed as part of the defense contract bidding process to commercial use.[20] The result was the Boeing 747 airframe, which remains in service today.

Over time and with precedents such as Boeing's commercial success as incentive, some U.S. defense firms began to combine defense research and defense-conversion efforts into a single business, with designed-in dual-use development opportunities included as a simultaneous or sequential part of the production process. This led to firms or research laboratories establishing dual-tiered structures with government-contracted research on one side of the business and private-sector, industry- and profit-oriented research conducted as a separate branch of the business. Firms or labs adopting this division of labor and organizational structure often did so due to research and product specifications that were (and are) frequently required as part of defense research projects, not to mention the need to maintain program secrecy as part of many defense projects.[21] This dual-structured approach served to provide a necessary firewall between research conducted in order to serve national security interests (and Pentagon-mandated secrecy) and technologies developed mainly for the marketplace.

Such a bifurcated corporate model, however, also tended to slow defense conversion and profit-making endeavors. Large firms were generally better able to maintain this dual structure (and its inherent costs), while smaller-size enterprises often faced a choice between devoting personnel, product lines, and priority to one (defense) or the other (commercial) venture. Due to the rapid rise in federally funded R&D during the early cold war years, many such enterprises gave priority to defense R&D. Yet this trend would begin to shift over time as industry began to finance more commerce-oriented R&D through successful defense conversion efforts and via the emergence of venture capitalists as a Silicon Valley fixture. The growth in commercial opportunities and funds, in turn, helped foster the emergence of component and subcomponent manufacturers able to supply parts and services to either or both defense and private industry clients. Consequently, this expanding marketplace of defense and commercial industry enterprises, research facilities (including labs, federally funded R&D centers, and university-based research programs), and smaller, subcontracting enterprises developed into a formidable, dual-purpose defense technology industrial base (DTIB).

In his farewell address, President Eisenhower would warn the country of the dangers inherent in a growing military-industrial complex, raising concerns about this sector's growing power and influence across the economic and political spheres, as well as highlighting the potential for upsetting the proper, dual-purpose balance between government's interest in pursuing science and technology for defense purposes and S&T advances as necessary to enhance general welfare and human understanding.[22] The American DTIB would continue to grow nevertheless and to serve as an essential base for U.S. economic growth and national security for decades to come.

The American public, in fact, grew to believe in and to support the basic tradeoff that the DTIB model promoted: that massive government spending on R&D for defense would eventually be converted into advances in the commercial realm. NASA's tremendous advances during the late 1960s and 1970s, in particular stemming from the Apollo missions, epitomized this optimistic point of view. Ask anyone of the baby boom generation or their offspring what spin-off technologies NASA generated during this era, and one is likely to hear in response: Teflon, Velcro, and Tang. Subsequent studies have pointed out that these commercial products were not NASA spin-offs at all; each was developed prior to the Apollo missions. Nevertheless, these products were indeed used by NASA astronauts and then sold with the NASA imprint to consumers. Selling the advantages of defense conversion to the public—including to the media and Congress—was part of NASA's organizational mandate as well as a deliberate strategy to help maintain public support for continued high-level government funding. The many scientific and technological benefits derived from NASA's science and engineering have been compiled, in fact, into an annual document along with other advertising materials. For over 30 years NASA's *Spinoff* publication—and, today, website—has tracked NASA's innovative technological contributions as a demonstration of the value afforded the public from continued high-level government investment in NASA's scientific and technological endeavors.[23]

By the latter stages of the cold war era, however, critiques of the defense conversion model had begun to grow in frequency and volume. Analysts increasingly pointed out that the promised payoff from defense industry to commercial spin-off was not as easy, inherent, or cost-effective as had often been presumed. In part this was a problem stemming from success. As the DTIB grew, military production became increasingly advanced and more specialized. Yet as federally funded S&T and R&D adjusted to meet the demands of greater military specifications, this in turn created a growing divergence between technologies employed in the defense and the commercial sphere, making dual-use technologies less—not more—viable. As explained in a classic text examining defense conversion's unexpected challenges:

> Since World War II . . . much military hardware has diverged from its nearest civilian analogs . . . When it comes to tanks, aircraft, and electronic command and control systems, similarities remain at component and subsystem levels. But whereas early World War I tanks were built from farm tractors, today few parallels can be found at the system level between the Army's M-1 tank and civilian trucks, tractors, or off-road construction equipment.[24]

By the 1980s, this technological, dual-use divide had evolved into a growing national security, scientific, and economic competitiveness concern. U.S. defense technology had advanced substantially in qualitative terms, but fears persisted that the Soviets and their Warsaw Pact allies remained quantitatively superior and could benefit from being technology followers (i.e., advancing more quickly technologically by following along a similar scientific, technological, or industrial path already laid out by U.S. or allied scientists and engineers). These concerns grew as cold war clashes increased during the late Carter and two-term Reagan years, particularly in the face of growing criticisms of CoCom's effectiveness in controlling Soviet access to allied military technologies.[25]

During this era, too, the scientific community had grown divided over the need either to control better or to loosen government restrictions governing scientific exchanges. Many in the academic and research communities argued the case for expanding national and international scientific exchanges to ensure open access to exploratory sciences and basic R&D. Meanwhile government officials and others were growing more concerned about the potential for military exploitation via such exchanges of ideas; government-funded researchers found themselves awkwardly in between. The Reagan administration's concerns about the potential for Soviet gains vis-à-vis U.S. defense technology capabilities led to an expansion and reinforcement of U.S. and allied export control policies, including the standing up of a new Defense Department suborganization: the Defense Technology Security Administration (DTSA). The DTSA was "created with the sole bureaucratic purpose to block the export of any questionable item to the Soviets or their allies."[26] This mandate included dual-use technologies, and DTSA was viewed as quite forceful in pressing its security concerns in interagency meetings.[27] However, this perspective and resulting expanded control policies, in turn, exacerbated already tense relations between the government and some in the academic community, a divide stemming from the Vietnam War era. The gulf between the two expanded as scientists pressed against government-imposed restrictions on travel, publishing, and other means of scientific exchange. The growing rift was bridged only when President Reagan signed a National Security Decision Directive (NSDD 189) in 1985, guaranteeing that basic scientific research would remain free of government restriction beyond that requiring government classification. In other words, basic science and research conducted by the scientific community for the sake of enhancing human knowledge of the universe would not be controlled by the government so as to ensure that unfettered scientific advances could carry on and continue to serve broad U.S. national interests, including national security.[28] This principle and directive still underpin relations between the public and private sectors involved in S&T development today.

At the same time, federal R&D spending, which had peaked in the mid-to-late 1960s, hit what would be a decade-long plateau. As a result, government R&D slowly but decidedly gave way to industry R&D spending. Commercial R&D expenditures outpaced government R&D funding for the first time in 1980 and marked a new trend that has since continued and, in fact, expanded. At the same time, new technological rivals had begun to emerge on the horizon as Europe and Japan became more industrially competitive with U.S. manufacturing in the automotive, aerospace, electronics, and other strategic sectors. Similar to the scientific realm, trends in the commercial sector increasingly pointed to the need to trade and invest internationally in order to take advantage of newly emerging overseas market opportunities.

National budgetary constraints stemming from the oil crisis and other political events of the 1970s and '80s also pressed policymakers and industry leaders to question the value of public-private sector collaboration on advanced technological endeavors. These concerns arose due to studies that began to show that defense conversion was not resulting in as many commercial technology breakthroughs as originally envisioned, nor was it as easy or profitable to conduct as in the past given rising military specifications in defense programs. Consequently, analysts began to argue that a new approach was needed to meet a more broadly defined notion of U.S. national interests—one that addressed changing dynamics in the national and international defense, industrial, and scientific communities. What emerged from this diverse set of converging trends was a fundamental shift in the country's strategic approach to, and objective of, S&T development. This paradigm shift would come to be called a revolution in military affairs (RMA).

Phase III—A Revolution in Military Affairs in a New Era
of Globalization: The Age of Information Technology

U.S. defense strategy had been, since the dawn of the cold war, not to outspend or to match exactly Soviet defenses (both were seen as unlikely to succeed given the Soviet's advantage in quantitative terms), but to outmatch them in technological terms. In sum, if the Soviets sent a man into space, the United States would send a man to the moon. Thus was born a form of technological arms race. A key difference in winning this race, as it would turn out, would be the evolving NIS and the dual-use precept that has underlain the U.S. marketplace since World War II. This foundation helped to diffuse technological advances across the defense and commercial domains, which created a benign development cycle, thereby fostering even more advanced defense and commercial technological development. The same dynamics, however, posed tremendous new challenges to U.S. policymakers also charged with preventing the spread of dual-use technologies that could be used to either make toys or be converted into developing advanced weapons.

This was the context in which the RMA was born. It was the Soviets, in fact, who are credited with first identifying the notion of realizing a fundamental shift in defense capabilities based upon effective exploitation of new technologies (the Soviet's term being military technology revolution, or MTR). The Soviets' main concern in this regard was the United States. The Pentagon's Office of Net Assessment (ONA) and acquisitions department also picked up on this notion and helped develop it into a new U.S. defense-industrial strategy, the shorthand for which became RMA. Both terms—MTR and RMA—presume the incorporation and exploitation of dual-use technologies as a core part of the strategy.[29]

The seeds of a future RMA were sown decades before the actual demonstration of RMA weaponry, which happened most dramatically during the 1991 Gulf War. Defense planners in the 1970s and 1980s, faced with a quantitatively superior adversary and fluctuating defense budgets at home, sought to exploit newly emerging technologies as a means of keeping ahead of, or at least keeping at bay, Soviet technological advances. These efforts, of course, were aided by the technology sanction regime that CoCom enforced and in which U.S. allies were partners, as well as by unilateral U.S. export control policies. The U.S. defense-industrial strategy that arose in this context was termed the offset strategy, the idea being to offset Soviet advantages with technological (today we might say asymmetric) capabilities. This strategy was developed in the late 1970s under the aegis of the first scientist to become secretary of defense—Harold Brown—and an under secretary for research and engineering who himself would years later become defense secretary, William Perry.[30] As Perry testified decades later, the Offset Strategy had three main pillars:

> Developing greatly improved **sensors** so that we could locate enemy tanks, [and] vehicles anywhere on the battlefield at any time.
>
> The second came to be called **Smart Weapons**, [which] was developing precision-guide munitions. Once we located an enemy unit a smart weapon could destroy it with one attempt, which is a dramatic difference from the firing accuracy, which had existed at that time and had been relevant in all earlier wars.
>
> The third part of the Offset Strategy was to develop what came to be called **Stealth**, so that our vehicles, our airplanes, and our ships, and so on, would not be subject to the same kind of precision attack that we were inflicting on others.[31] What all three of these capabilities had in common was that each rested upon significant advances made in information technology (IT). As Perry explained in 2005: "I elected to use information technology as the primary tool for doing that because we had then, as we have now, a commanding lead in that field."[32]

But the creative center of gravity for information technology had shifted during the previous era from the public to the private sector. In the 1960s, DARPA (then called ARPA) had begun developing the underlying networking concepts, technological know-how, and technical capabilities needed to implement the ARPANET (i.e., what would later become the Internet) with the aid of leading universities.[33] However, it was consumer networks and products developed and sold by private computer, telecom, and electronics firms such as IBM, AT&T, Microsoft, Sun Microsystems, and Intel that would later spark the dramatic IT capabilities revolution that we are still experiencing today and that has transformed the Internet into a global phenomenon. It is doubtful that such a fundamental, fast, and now worldwide change in IT would have occurred solely under DARPA's mandate; nor would the private firms involved have had the wherewithal to achieve their technological break-throughs or dominant market positions without substantial government support. This support typically took the form of capital investments, protective import tariffs, tax incentives, technology transfer contracts with federal research labs and executive agencies, favorable immigration laws and visa regulations, and so on. Consequently, the RMA as it evolved from the 1970s through to the 1990s would come to rest upon a dual spin-off and spin-on defense-industrial model. This dynamic, in turn, resulted in an even stronger and more integrated DTIB. As outlined in a 1988 study by the Office of Technology Assessment (OTA): "As the civilian industries move increasingly to the cutting edge of technology, the defense technology base becomes embedded in—and largely inseparable from—the national technology base."[34]

In particular, a new focus on spin-on technology, made possible by increased levels of R&D spending by industry, helped instigate the RMA. As the innovative center of gravity in IT shifted toward the private sector, it also impacted Department of Defense (DoD) strategies on future development and acquisition of defense technologies. The DoD sought increasingly to take advantage of commercially developed technologies that could be adapted, often at less cost, to defense purposes than if singularly developed within the lengthy and often costly defense procurement process. This approach became an even more attractive strategy once the end of the cold war turned the country's attention to a potential peace dividend and the subsequent draw-down began in defense spending. Changes in the political and commercial environments had a significant impact on the defense sector and U.S. strategy toward building the next military. As explained by a prominent observer of both defense and industry trends at the time:

> there has been a significant reversal of the post-WWII model for military technology development. Since the early 1970s, a growing fraction of the new technology required for the next generation of military systems has been derived from or closely related to commercial (i.e., civilian) development efforts, rather than programs strictly and separately supported by the military. Moreover, following the philosophy of "spin on," largely pioneered by the Japanese, companies in the West are now actively looking for opportunities to apply commercially-developed technology to military systems, rather than the other way around, as in earlier days.[35]

This development model led to an emphasis on employing commercial off-the-shelf (COTS) technologies as a larger part of defense programs. The COTS approach rests on the ability to take a technology off the shelf of a commercial enterprise (think Home Depot) and insert it effectively (with modest, if any modifications) into a defense platform. The COTS paradigm works particularly well for smaller, more simply designed components that can be used for a multitude of (or dual) purposes and is most cost-effective when used in standard configurations. Consequently, the COTS strategy has helped promote a trend toward a disaggregation of product or platform technologies into more discrete components that can be applied in a modular fashion to any number of purposes, either commercial or defense-oriented. (In this sense, the technology itself is dual-use regardless of a user's intent.) In turn, high-tech industries, particularly the IT sector, have become increasingly disaggregated, with once giant-size, autonomous firms that contained the entire vertical production chain within their corporate structure (from concept and production through marketing and shipping) transforming into new, more horizontally integrated (i.e., connected across industry) and specialized enterprises that focus on one key part (or select parts) of the production chain. The latter approach applies the notion of technological competitive advantage while leveraging that of other firms throughout the production chain, a business model that in an age of globalization works well on both a national and global scale.

In the defense sector, the post–cold war decline in defense spending paired with growing incentives apparent in the COTS business paradigm led some defense firms to leave the defense sector in favor of more commercial endeavors. These decisions were aided by a strong push from DoD leaders who, in the early 1990s, were interested in paring down the troubled defense industry. Among those that remained, a new emphasis was placed on systems integration: the ability to integrate many different technologies (of commercial and/or defense origin) into a new, more advanced defense system. This shift toward more horizontal, modular, and dual-use defense-industrial development would serve as rationale for both commercial and defense industry firms to expand investments around the globe, in allied countries and beyond. The more commerce-oriented, global business model absent a cold war–like adversary also prompted an easing of export controls governing such dual-use trade, particularly in the IT sector.

Information technology would not be the only industry or technology sector to play a key part in the RMA, but it would be the main driving force. IT advances have served as the foundation underlying an evolution of defense strategies, doctrine, and operational concepts ranging from network-centered warfare to full-spectrum dominance, and effects-based operations to cyber-warfare and more.[36] The idea underlying each of these techno-strategic concepts is that improvements in information technology, its strategic integration, and operational application to the battlefield will provide a revolutionary advantage to U.S. and allied forces. The Department of Defense also has pursued RMA-style advances in other areas such as the aerospace sector—including the use of unmanned aerial vehicles (UAVs) and in satellite-related technologies—as well as naval networking systems (used in both closed and open or international networks such as for the prevention and management of natural disasters), and increasingly in biotechnology advances such as biometrics (the use of physical or behavioral traits as identification markers). This RMA-oriented approach to modern military strategy and operations is only possible, of course, because of similarly revolutionary changes to the global marketplace, which the defense sector and the dual-use concept both promote and rely upon for continued advances in defense-industrial development.

It is IT's inherent fungibility that has made it an ideal platform for RMA and for expanding interactions across conventional boundaries: IT is fast, ever-declining in size and cost, and employs a near-universal language of 1's and 0's. The current wave of globalization wherein the international exchange of ideas, people, goods, and knowledge is fast-paced, low-cost, and increasingly ubiquitous across cultures is, in fact, largely due to advances in IT and its relatively easy dissemination and exploitation for different purposes.

As demonstrated under the offset strategy pursued in the 1970s and '80s, the DoD has been a consistent supporter of exploiting IT and instituting a more dual-use defense-industrial system. In fact, the DoD's reliance upon the commercial sector has markedly expanded since then. The practice of employing leading scientists, engineers, and other private-sector experts during World War II remains similar to practices employed by the DoD and other parts of the government today. Cooperation among the government, industry, and academic communities was further elevated under a Clinton-Gore technology development initiative announced in 1993 that specifically set out a plan to enhance the federal government's role (including the DoD, particularly DARPA) in supporting commercial technology innovation as well as seeking to reorient the Department of Defense toward "developing a strategy to improve the integration of defense and commercial technology development."[37] Further, in 1999, the Defense Science Board (DSB) published a landmark study outlining the DoD's inherent interest in pursuing and exploiting further dual-use defense-industrial opportunities in a global as well as U.S. economic environment despite the inherent risks.[38] The basic strategy recommended in the DSB report was not unlike that employed during the cold war: fully explore and exploit technological advances in both defense-industrial and commercial realms in order to stay technologically ahead of any and all potential adversaries. The main difference in the 1999 report was the global scope of this proposed effort. Because so much of commercial industry had expanded offshore to take advantage of new opportunities afforded by globalization—including many of the commercial and defense industry suppliers, subcomponent manufacturers, and contractors to the DoD—the DSB deemed it imperative to U.S. national security that these trends be more strategically integrated, exploited, and expanded upon, and as quickly as possible. Defense Department leaders have maintained this basic strategic and dual-use construct into the 21st century, with DoD officials acknowledging the military and defense-industrial sphere's inherent and growing dependency on the U.S. and global marketplace for science, technology, and research as well as for logistics operations and supply of critical materials, minerals, components, and more.

The same phenomenon, however, that has powered the RMA and lead to Tom Friedman's famously characterized flat world—wherein, with the aid of Google and other IT technologies, those born in Beijing or Bangalore can satisfy their curiosity and learn almost anything as well as someone born in Britain or Boston—also presents tremendous new challenges to the task of preventing access by potential adversaries to strategically critical, dual-use technology and know-how. Prime among these concerns today is nuclear science, which can be employed for peaceful nuclear energy purposes and/or to develop nuclear weapons. And, as the A. Q. Khan scenario of a former Pakistani nuclear scientist-turned-nuclear arms dealer makes clear, an individual with a passport, an email account, and some nuclear expertise (whether an individually acquired understanding of nuclear scientific concepts or merely acquired designs or other documents) can proliferate weapons of mass destruction (WMD) technology far easier today than ever before. Due to such concerns, even before the attacks of 9/11 (though accelerated since then), the scientific community and defense officials have worked more closely together to find new ways to cooperate in helping to prevent WMD proliferation while also preserving the important principle of open scientific inquiry and exploration as well as commercial enterprise.

These growing concerns over the spread of not only weapons, goods, and technologies in a globalized world economy, but also the intangible or tacit knowledge resident in experts' minds, led the United States and some international partners to adopt new export control innovations in the 1990s.[39] One of these, the *deemed* export regime adopted in 1994, seeks to monitor, license, and thus mitigate the risks inherent in sharing information across porous borders. As explained by the Department of Commerce, which regulates dual-use exports via licensing processes:

An export of technology or source code (except encryption source code) is "deemed" to take place when it is released to a foreign national [or foreign corporation] within the United States ... Technology is "released" for export when it is available to foreign nationals for visual inspection (such as reading technical specifications, plans, blueprints, etc.); when technology is exchanged orally; or when technology is made available by practice or application under the guidance of persons with knowledge of the technology.[40]

There are, of course, some exceptions to this general rule, including a provision excepting fundamental scientific research.[41] Yet the attempt to even try to regulate such interpersonal interactions, particularly given the difficulties of accomplishing this effectively in an increasingly globalized economic system, is indicative of how essential U.S. policymakers continue to view dual-use technology (and know-how) to ensuring U.S. national security interests. The deemed export policy complemented efforts under other export control regimes including the Wassenaar Arrangement on Export Controls for Conventional Arms and Dual-Use Goods and Technologies, established in 1996, and three other multilateral, conventional arms and WMD nonproliferation export control regimes (i.e., the Australia Group governing chemical and biological weapons–related technologies, the Nuclear Suppliers Group, and the Missile Technology Control Regime or MTCR). These and related regimes focus on controlling both the technology itself and the users' likely or suspicious intent in determining whether an export is considered worrisome and requires monitoring, licensing, or a denied sale.

Whether the deemed export and other dual-use export control goals are achievable, sufficient, worth the effort and cost (including opportunity costs), or even counterproductive to U.S. national security objectives and interests remains a matter of much public policy debate. What all agree on, however, is the continued importance of dual-use technologies and a dual, public-private sector approach to advancing U.S. technological innovation as an essential part of maintaining both a healthy defense-industrial and commercial public sector. At the same time, proliferation concerns continue to grow in a post-9/11 security environment and an age of rising global terrorism. In other words, the dual-use dilemma will be with us for some time to come.

Phase 4: The Post–Cold War World and Beyond

Once the cold war ended, defense planners were faced with the dilemma of how to ensure national security interests devoid of any clearly identifiable foe. The construct eventually arrived at was termed "capabilities-based planning" vice *threat*-based planning. That is, U.S. defense strategy would shift from focusing on the threat posed by a specific adversary as the main measure of determining what types of forces (and the technologies that underpin them) and force posture would be needed to a strategy based upon developing a wide range of capabilities that could be applied across a variety of circumstances, scenarios, and future adversaries. This approach fit a period of time characterized by declining defense budgets and when no clear threat had appeared on the near-term horizon, at least not until the al Qaeda attacks in 2001. This capabilities-based planning (CBP) approach, even more than the past threat-oriented strategies, hinges on U.S. ability to explore, exploit, and enhance technologies in the commercial and defense realms, within national boundaries as well as across the globe. As such, it is arguably an even more dual-use-oriented approach than its traditional threat-based predecessor.

In order to implement the CBP regime and to expand further upon RMA concepts of development, the Pentagon needed to transform fundamentally the way it planned, budgeted, operated. The demonstration of RMA concepts during the 1991 Gulf War proved both heartening and troubling to U.S. defense planners. Although the application of IT, stealth, and precision-guided munitions (PGMs) to the battlefield had been largely effective and impressive, numerous trouble spots had also appeared. Thus, while the RMA construct remained an important driver of defense-industrial development, the focus within the Department of Defense shifted toward transformation of the defense enterprise: transforming the Pentagon's own processes to enable better exploitation of the RMA and development of a range of new capabilities designed for future conflicts and warfighters.

Defense Secretary Donald Rumsfeld is perhaps most closely associated with the idea of defense transformation, but he was in many ways more the implementer of an idea that had been developing some years earlier. According to one observer, development of the concepts underlying CBP was already "well underway" in practice among the military services, if not via the formal defense resourcing processes, as early as 1994.[42] Nonetheless, Secretary Rumsfeld took the opportunity upon coming back into office in 2001 to implement a fundamentally new approach to defense acquisition that would transform the way the DoD thought about and would procure future weapon systems. As outlined in the 2001 Quadrennial Defense Review, the fourth pillar of transformation rested on "Developing transformational capabilities through increased and wide-ranging science and technology, selective increases in procurement, and innovations in DoD processes."[43] As such, transformation went far beyond the scientific and technological realms to reach into the organizational, procedural, and operational arenas. These efforts are still underway.

Among the most relevant techno-organizational changes wrought by transformation is the pursuit of enhanced interoperability of defense systems and the deliberate conception of potential intangible solutions to defense needs. Not only are COTS solutions to achieving lower-cost, standardized component designs, products, and services possible, but so are GOTS—or government off-the-shelf solutions—sought after as potential sources for solutions to future challenges. As employed in DoD parlance, "GOTS systems are those in current use by government agencies, and may include NASA, the Department of Homeland Security, and other entities."[44]

Moreover, the notion of interoperability has been expanded within the defense resourcing process to promote more cross-Service and even international technology solutions. No longer do Services or combatant commanders request ships, planes, or tanks, but rather capabilities that can be employed by—and across—a joint force. A description of the Joint Tactical Radio System (JTRS) outlines this novel approach to CBP and transformational technology development well:

By developing and implementing an open architecture of cutting-edge radio waveform technology, multiple radio types (e.g., handheld, ground-mobile, airborne, maritime) are now allowed to communicate with one another. The ultimate goal is to produce a family of interoperable, modular, software-defined radios that operate as nodes in a network to endure secure wireless communication and networking services for mobile and fixed forces. These goals extend to U.S. Allies, joint and coalition partners, and in time, disaster response personnel.[45]

The JTRS is being developed by a wide array of commercial and defense firms in the United States and abroad. While the system will remain a military and highly classified system, COTS input and spin-offs are an expected part of the development process.[46]

Bureaucratic processes established under Rumsfeld and since expanded under Secretary Robert Gates require such dual-use considerations and the approval of several layers of senior officials seeking to identify cross-service efficiencies. A key part of this process involves *functional capabilities boards* in which a broad-section of the defense community is involved in determining the capabilities that are or will be required by the military in the future. This also includes defense industry representatives when invited. The basic idea underlying the CBP approach is that, as much as possible, future defense platforms will be what is commonly termed born joint as early in the development and procurement processes as possible (rather than being integrated at the end of the process, which can be more difficult among diverse systems, not to mention more costly). Another consideration by these boards is whether some defense needs might be addressed by intangible solutions (i.e., by a change in doctrine, organization, training, or other nonmaterial response), or in other words, by knowledge. Where this is the case, it again raises the dual-use question of whether such knowledge could be used to threaten as well as to benefit U.S. interests if placed in the wrong hands. Each of these examples of enhanced defense-industrial development raises new potential dilemmas for policymakers trying to gain as much as possible from dual-use development concepts while simultaneously mitigating the inherent risks in a globalized world system.

CONCLUSION: WHAT'S AHEAD FOR DUAL-USE TECHNOLOGIES IN THE DEFENSE-INDUSTRIAL DOMAIN?

From the evolution of the role of dual-use technology and its increasingly vital role in the defense sector as outlined in this chapter, it is clear that over time there has been an additive importance to preserving, promoting, and expanding the dual-use defense-industrial model. More than half a century after Vannevar Bush's initial call to maintain high-level government support for basic R&D for the sake of both defense and public interests, this conceptual approach remains largely intact (if marginally and monetarily different) today. This same basic idea is what underpins numerous recent studies concerned with current and future U.S. technological competitiveness, most of which call for maintaining and/or increasing levels of government funding for S&T and R&D for much the same reasons as first enunciated in Franklin Roosevelt's day: that government funding for experimental research serves U.S. defense *and* consumer interests.[47]

The defense conversion or spin-off concept is also inherent in these assessments and resulting policy recommendations that advocate increased government R&D investment.

One stark example of this is continued congressional and public support for agencies like NASA in the belief that the type of experimental research employed, driven, and discovered by NASA projects will dually serve defense needs and industry, consumers, and humanity's knowledge of the universe. There are also initiatives currently under review for expanding upon the earlier NASA, DARPA, and similar defense conversion models of development. This includes the recent ARPA-E initiative, which harkens back to the early days of [D]ARPA and calls for a new infusion of federal funding toward *energy* technology research (thus the name, ARPA-E) in the interest of both defense and industrial technological advances, for the efficiencies and cost savings it could provide both sectors.[48]

Similarly, the notion of supporting RMA and the global economic trends that both feed and promote it have come to be widely accepted not only in the United States but in government and industry circles worldwide, from Beijing to Brussels to Bangor. Allied and other militaries are attempting their own RMAs and seeking to enhance development of their own NIS in order to better leverage globalization dynamics.[49] Of course, the same can be said of those seeking to exploit these same trends to fashion new and disruptive, asymmetric, terrorist, or mass destruction weapons. Consequently, officials at the Department of Homeland Security and elsewhere are employing dual-use approaches to developing new technologies designed to help thwart threats such as these against U.S. national security and economic interests.

Finally, defense transformation efforts continue apace with added emphasis being placed on enhancing dual-use development processes. As concluded in a recent Defense Science Board study on the defense-industrial structure for transformation, the next steps are to "Articulate a National Security Industrial Vision; adopt government policies to implement the Vision; structure incentives for industry to achieve the Vision; and monitor ongoing industrial dynamics to ensure its realization."[50] Integral to achieving this vision, according to the DoD taskforce, is a focus on competition, innovation, lowering costs, IT, the government-industry relationship and a "relentless search for superior technology, manufacturing, and logistics coupled with a willingness to look beyond the traditional defense industry to commercial suppliers, including companies located outside the U.S. with militarily-relevant capabilities."[51]

Building upon such a foundation, what will the future hold for dual-use as a developmental construct for the U.S. defense-industrial development model? Barring a fundamental, long-term disruption in the current global economic system (beyond what the present financial crisis suggests), it seems reasonable to conclude that the pattern of continued, cumulative, and conceptually dual-use approach to defense and industrial development that we have witnessed over the last half century will continue to evolve over the foreseeable future. Many point to the dynamic prospects of nanotechnology and new science and technology innovations in energy security as the next revolutionary dual-use fields of inquiry. Interestingly, these and other key strategic technology fields are the same identified in Washington as in Beijing and other major global power centers. Yet, this suggests a critical fork in the road lies ahead. If the evolutionary path of dual-use-inspired defense and industrial development is to continue along similar lines across the globe, it follows that the United States and China (see appendix on China's adoption of a dual-use defense-industrial model)—or states similar to China in military and industrial strength and similarly ideologically at odds—must choose to: (1) integrate the other's role in the system;

(2) develop separate systems (in a CoCom-like fashion); or (3) fundamentally change or reverse course and revert to a more nationalistic or even mercantilist development model. The latter two options would represent a radical departure from the current path; the United States and others already appear some way down the first. Nevertheless, whichever choice is made, the dual-use dilemmas inherent in the modern defense-industrial domain will remain.

NOTES

The views expressed in this chapter are the author's and do not reflect official U.S. government policy. Any and all errors are the author's alone.

1. Of course, this definition begs the question of what constitutes a technology. There is no universal consensus on what exactly defines *technology*, in part because different societies view technology in distinct ways, some as simply a tangible instrument, tool, or product, others as an intangible understanding of the science or engineering underlying a product, design, or technique. Moreover, our view of technology has changed over time and will probably continue to do so. This chapter employs this full range of definitions as it outlines the evolution of dual-use technology's role in defense-industrial development.

2. Arthur C. Clarke and Stanley Kubrick, 2001: A Space Odyssey, screenplay, 1968. The author is grateful to Tom Beall for inspiring this example as a useful way of exploring the nature of technology.

3. Richard Re, "From Playstation to Detonation: The Potential Threat of Dual-Use Technology," Harvard International Review 23, no. 1 (2001), 30–33.

4. The terms *science and technology* (S&T) and *research and development* (R&D) are used more or less interchangeably in this chapter. While there are technical distinctions between the two terms and the fields of endeavor they encompass, the terms are used here in accordance with the term defense S&T as defined in Department of Defense funding programs as comprising: basic research (6.1) or scientific/exploratory research; applied research (6.2); and advanced technology development (6.3). As outlined in *Department of Defense Financial Management Regulations,* vol 2B chapter 5, section 50201 (July 2008) available online at http://www.defenselink.mil/comptroller/fmr/02b/02b_05.pdf.

5. There were, of course, some exceptions, including the establishment in 1916 of the National Research Council in the United States and the Porton Down facility in the United Kingdom. U.K. Ministry of Defence Web site, http://www.mod.uk/DefenceInternet/AboutDefence/WhatWeDo/HealthandSafety/PortonDownVolunteers/.

6. Vannevar Bush, Science: The Endless Frontier (Washington, DC: National Science Foundation, 1945), http://www.nsf.gov/od/lpa/nsf50/vbush1945.htm.

7. It took several years for the idea to work through Washington's many political hurdles, but the NSF (National Science Foundation) was formally established five years later, in 1950. National Science Foundation Web site, http://www.nsf.gov/about/glance.jsp.

8. Bush, *Science.*

9. Panel on the Impact of National Security Controls on International Technology Transfer, Committee on Science, Engineering, and Public Policy of the National Academy of Science, National Academy of Engineering, and Institute of Medicine, Balancing the National Interest: U.S. National Security Export Controls and Global Economic Competition (Washington, DC: National Academy Press, 1987), 71.

10. Judith Reppy, "Managing Dual-Use Technology in an Age of Uncertainty," The Forum 4, no. 1, Article 2 (2006): 1.

11. While the 1940 ECA did not mark the first time the U.S. government had instituted dual-use export controls, a practice that dates back to the late 18th and early 19th centuries in America (and much earlier in other societies), it was the first time in the modern era that U.S. dual-use export controls were instituted as a regular (i.e., during peacetime as well as conflict or national emergency) and an enduring national security policy instrument. Since 1940, the United States has continuously instituted some form of dual-use exports controls whether through legislation or ad hoc regulation. In 1949, Congress passed another Export Control Act, which would subsequently give way to the 1979 Export Administration Act. The latter was "substantially unchanged" from the 1949 act and remains the main statutory authority today for U.S. dual-use export controls, as amended, and (since the EAA's expiration in 1994) as authorized and extended by Executive Order. Reppy, "Managing Dual-Use Technology"; National Academy of Science, National Academy of Engineering, and Institute of Medicine, Balancing the National Interest, 71–73; and for a comprehensive history of US dual-use export controls, see Richard T. Cupitt, *Reluctant Champions: Truman, Eisenhower, Bush, and Clinton–U.S. Presidential Policy and Strategic Export Controls* (New York: Routledge, 2000), particularly Chapters 2 and 3, 31-50 and 51-83, respectively.

12. National Academy of Science, National Academy of Engineering, and Institute of Medicine, Balancing the National Interest, 71–73.

13. Deborah D. Stine, "The Manhattan Project, the Apollo Program, and Federal Energy Technology R&D Programs: A Comparative Analysis," Congressional Research Service report RL34645 (Washington, DC: Library of Congress, 2009). For an historic overview of DARPA over its 50-year history, see Graham Warwick and Guy Norris, "DARPA at 50," special issue, Aviation Week and Space Technology, August 18–25, 2008, 1–20.

14. Kathleen Walsh, "Soaring Eagle, Flying Dragon: Industrial R&D and Innovation in the United States and China," Proceedings of the China-US Forum on Science and Technology Policy (Arlington, VA: George Mason University, 2006), 220, http://www.law.gmu.edu/nctl/stpp/STPolicy_Forum.php.

15. The terms used here and throughout the chapter adhere to the definitions of research as basic, applied, and technology development, as outlined by the National Science Foundation. See National Science Board (NSB), Science and Engineering Indicators 2006 (Arlington, VA: National Science Foundation, 2006), 4–8.

16. National Aeronautics and Space Administration, "About NASA: What Does NASA Do?" (2008), Web site: http://www.nasa.gov/about/highlights/what_does_nasa_do.html.

17. Mitch Waldrop, "DARPA and the Internet Revolution," 50 Years of Bridging the Gap, 78–85, http://www.darpa.mil/Docs/Internet_Development_200807180909255.pdf.

18. National Science Foundation, Division of Science Resources Statistics, "New Estimates of National Research and Development Expenditures Show 5.8% Growth in 2007," Figure 3NSF 08–317 (Arlington, VA: NSF, 2008).

19. AnnaLee Saxenian, Regional Advantage: Culture and Competition in Silicon Valley and Route 128 (Cambridge, MA: Harvard University Press, 1994); Richard Nelson, National Innovation Systems: A Comparative Analysis (New York: Oxford University Press, 1993).

20. The Boeing example is cited by Lewis Branscomb as a classic case of spin-off in Sandra Hackman and Robert Howard, "Rethinking the Military's Role in the Economy," Technology Review 92, no. 6 (1989): 56.

21. There were, of course, some exceptions to this general rule. Hughes Aircraft is cited as an example of an enterprise engaged in both defense and commercial research and whose engineers worked on both sides of the business simultaneously. Yet, this was generally the exception to the rule of separate defense and commercial elements of large defense industry enterprises. Hackman and Howard, "Rethinking the Military's Role," 57.

22. President Dwight D. Eisenhower, "Farewell Radio and Television Address to the American People," (January 17, 1961), transcript available online care of the Dwight D. Eisenhower Presidential Library and Museum, Abiline, KS at http://www.eisenhower.archives.gov/All_About_Ike/Speeches/Farewell_Address.pdf.

23. Alic, John A., Lewis M. Branscomb, Harvey Brooks, Ashton B. Carter, and Gerald Epstein. *Beyond Spinoff: Military and Commercial Technologies in a Changing World.* (Boston: Harvard Business School Press, April 1992) 55-57.

24. Alic, et al., 37.

25. Dov S. Zakheim, "Export Controls and Military Planning," working paper 7, Study Group on Enhancing Multilateral Export Controls (Washington, DC: Henry L. Stimson Center, 2000).

26. Zakheim, "Export Controls and Military Planning," iv.

27. National Academy of Science, National Academy of Engineering, and Institute of Medicine, Balancing the National Interest, 93–96.

28. For a historical overview of NSDD 189, see John C. Crowley, "Science and Secrecy: NSDD 189—Prologue to a New Dialogue?" presented at the American Association for the Advancement of Science R&D Colloquium, April 10, 2003.

29. Bjorn Moller, "The Revolution in Military Affairs: Myth or Reality?" working paper, 11, http://www.copri.dk/publications/Wp/WP%202002/15–2002.doc; Ronald O'Rourke, "Defense Transformation: Background and Oversight Issues for Congress," Congressional Research Report RL 32238 (Washington, DC: Library of Congress, 2007), 4. O'Rourke, 4.

30. "Harold Brown," Secretary of Defense Biographies, http://www.defenselink.mil/specials/secdef_histories/bios/brown.htm; Ashton B. Carter and William J. Perry, Preventive Defense: A New Security Strategy for America (Washington, DC: The Brookings Institution, 1999), 175–180.

31. William S. Perry, testimony Before the US-China Economic and Security Review Commission, April 2005, 6, http://www.uscc.gov/hearings/2005hearings/transcripts/05_04_21_22.pdf.

32. Perry, 6.

33. Mitch Waldrop, "DARPA and the Internet Revolution," *DARPA: 50 Years of Bridging the Gap.*" (2008), 78-85.

34. U.S. Congress, Office of Technology Assessment, *The Defense Technology Base: Introduction and Overview–A Special Report*, OTA-ISC-374 (Washington, DC: U.S. Government Printing Office, 1988), 5.

35. Mitch Wallerstein, "Conceptual Approaches to the Problem of Dual-Use Technology," in Dual-Use Technologies and Export Control in the Post-Cold War Era, Office of International Affairs, National Research Council (Washington, DC: National Academies Press, 2004), 111, http://www.nap.edu/openbook.php?record_id=2270&page=111.

36. These and other RMA concepts were promoted in defense strategic planning documents such as the Joint Vision 2010 and its follow-on Joint Vision 2020, among others, http://www.dtic.mil/jv2010/jv2010.pdf.

37. President William J. Clinton and Vice President Albert Gore Jr., "Technology for America's Economic Growth, A New Direction to Build Economic Strength" (February 22, 1993).

38. Office of the Under Secretary for Acquisition and Technology, Final Report of the Defense Science Board Task Force on Globalization and Security (Washington, DC: Department of Defense, December 1999).

39. Other globalization-era export control policy innovations include the *catch-all rule* (in which exports not otherwise licensed but suspected of possible diversion to noncommercial or unlicensed use must be reported to authorities) and provisions to monitor (vice license) exported encryption technology as well as enhanced regulations and enforcement of transshipped goods that transit numerous international ports of entry.

40. U.S. Department of Commerce, "Deemed Exports: Questions and Answers," http://www.bis.doc.gov/deemedexports/deemedexportsfaqs.html#.

41. This includes "basic and applied research in science and engineering where the resulting information is ordinarily published and shared broadly within the scientific community," as outlined by the Department of Commerce, which oversees the US dual-use export regime, http://www.bis.doc.gov/deemedexports/deemedexportsfaqs.html.

42. Raoul Henri Alcala, "Guiding Principles for Revolution, Evolution, and Continuity in Military Affairs," fn 10, in Whither the RMA: Two Perspectives on Tomorrow's Army, Paul Bracken and Raoul Henri Alcala (Carlisle, PA: Strategic Studies Institute, U.S. Army War College, 1994).

43. Donald Rumsfeld, Quadrennial Defense Review Report, September 30, 2001, www.defenselink.mil/pubs/pdfs/qdr2001.pdf.

44. Defense Science Board, Buying Commercial: Gaining the Cost/Schedule Benefits for Defense Systems—Report of the Defense Science Board Task Force on Integrating Commercial Systems into the DOD, Effectively and Efficiently (Washington, DC: Office of the Under Secretary of Acquisition, Technology and Logistics, February 2009), 2.

45. Taken from JTRS promotional material; JTRS, *Connecting the Tactical Edge,* 2009, http://jpeojtrs.mil.

46. See, for instance, David B. Cotton, "SDR and JTRS Starting to Get in Tune, COTS Journal (January 2007).

47. Many public and private sector organizations have published studies in recent years advocating the need to spend more money on S&T and R&D in pursuit of enhanced national security, as well as economic and societal interests. The most prominent among these is the Committee on Prospering in the Global Economy in the 21st Century, Rising above the Gathering Storm: Energizing and Employing America for a Brighter Economic Future (Washington, DC: National Academies Press, 2007).

48. Stine, "The Manhattan Project."

49. Richard A. Bitzinger, "Come the Revolution: Transforming the Asia-Pacific's Militaries," *Naval War College Review 58*, no. 4 (2005)[0].

50. Defense Science Board, Creating an Effective National Security Industrial Base for the 21st Century: An Action Plan to Address the Coming Crisis, 7, 2008, http://www.acq.osd.mil/dsb/reports/2008–07.

51. Defense Science Board, Creating an Effective National Security Industrial Base for the 21st Century.

52. There is not space available here to provide a thorough treatment of China's dual-use and RMA-style policies, perspectives, or prospects. For more in-depth assessments of the dual-use paradigm and evolving RMA in China, see Jorn Brommelhorster and John Frankenstein, eds., Mixed Motives, Uncertain Outcomes: Defense Conversion in China (Boulder, CO: Lynne Reinner, 1997); Kathleen A. Walsh, Foreign High-tech R&D in China: Risks, Rewards, and Implications for US-China Relations (Washington, DC: Stimson Center, 2003); Richard A. Bitzinger, "Come the Revolution: Transforming the Asia-Pacific's Militaries," Naval War College Review 58, no. 4 (2005), 39–60; Andrew S. Erickson and Kathleen A. Walsh, "National Security Challenges and Competition: Defense and Space R&D in the Chinese Strategic Context," in William A. Blaniped, J. Thomas Ratchford, and Rodney W. Nichols, eds., Technology in Society (Netherlands: Elsevier Ltd., 2008); David M. Lampton, *The Three Faces of Chinese Power: Might, Monday, and Minds* (Berkeley: University of California, 2008); Tai Ming Cheung, Fortifying China: The Struggle to Build a Modern Defense Economy (Ithaca, NY: Cornell University Press, 2009), among other recent texts.

53. An oft-noted U.S.-China defense collaboration begun in the mid-1980s involved U.S. assistance in developing avionics technologies for the F-8 jet fighter. The Peace Pearl program was terminated

due to the sanctions levied against China post-Tiananmen. See Shirley Kan, "US-China Military Contacts: Issues for Congress," CRS report for Congress RL32496 (updated February 1, 2008)

54. Cheung provides a useful and detailed assessment of each line and how it has been interpreted differently over time. See Cheung, *Fortifying China,* 7–9.

55. Walsh, Foreign High-tech R&D in China.

56. Bates Gill and Lonnie Henley, China and the Revolution in Military Affairs (Carlisle, PA: U.S. Army War College, 1996).

57. Nan Li, "New Developments in the PLA's Operational Doctrine and Strategies," in China's Evolving Military Doctrine," Issues and Insights 6, no. 20, Nan Li, Eric McVadon, and Qinghong Wang, eds. (Honolulu: Pacific Forum, 2006), 5-12.

58. Cheung, *Fortifying China,* 103.

59. Information Office of the State Council of the People's Republic of China, *China's National Defense in 2008,* defense white paper (Beijing: PRC, 2009).

60. Erickson & Walsh, 7.

Appendix: The RMA and Dual-Use Paradigm Abroad: China Adopts a Dual-Use Economy with Chinese Characteristics

Following the 1991 Gulf War defeat of Iraq, the leadership in Beijing came to a startling realization: their existing military doctrine of *People's War*—wherein any enemy would be drawn into the Chinese hinterland and there be defeated by force of the Chinese populace—was woefully outmatched by what they saw on television. This doctrinal approach was no match for over-the-horizon, stealth, and precision-guided munitions, and more, as fielded by the U.S. military in Operation Desert Storm. It would set China off on its own revolution in military affairs, one that was uniquely Chinese but bears notable similarities to the U.S. RMA and transformational efforts.[52]

The People's Republic of China (PRC) has developed a unique techno-military series of doctrines since the defeat by Mao Zedong of the Communists' rivals in the 1949 civil war, the Kuomintang, whose political descendants now rule Taiwan. The aforementioned People's War doctrine dominated during the post–civil war Mao years (1949–76) and influenced both China's dependence on Soviet military technologies and assistance (up until the Sino-Soviet split in the late 1950s), as well as China's massive government-funded research campaigns that would underpin the PRC's first atomic bomb and ballistic missile capabilities. While the latter state-run S&T programs were intended primarily to achieve their strategic missions, commercial spin-off products were ostensibly considered a potential side-benefit as well.

Following the transition from Mao to Deng Xiaoping's rule (1978–97), the concept of defense conversion became a formal strategy. In this period, economic reform via Deng's famous "Open Door" policy was Beijing's prime focus; military advances were expected to support industrial capabilities and vice versa. Deng's policy, outlined in a famous 16-character mandate (see Table 7.1), outlined a spin-on and spin-off paradigm for China's military modernization. Nevertheless, in practice, this policy emphasized more the spin-off aspect as a means of supplementing China's military budget and reducing an oversized defense-industrial sector; actual spin-on from the commercial-to-defense sector occurred only rarely and typically under the aegis of state-run programs such as the 863 basic research program. The limited progress was due to the vagaries of the Chinese Communist system at this time as well as a military force posture that deliberately separated Chinese defense industry resources in the country's central provinces (i.e., far away from the more vulnerable coastal or border areas where Beijing feared potential adversaries would likely strike) and, thus, apart from the main commercial industrial centers. Even as China's security environment improved and Beijing welcomed international defense-industrial cooperation with the United States and other partners, the events at Tiananmen Square in 1989 brought this collaboration to a halt.[53] Thus, while a dual-use concept was apparent in the PRC's early defense-industrial designs, in reality the spin-off approach dominated, and these efforts ultimately produced disappointing results.[54]

It was under Jiang Zemin's leadership (1993–2003) that the PRC would adopt what looked more familiar from a Western perspective in terms of establishing a more synchronous defense-industrial base connected to reformed, more profit-oriented commercial enterprises, and supported by ambitious, dual-use scientific and technological development programs as well as an economy increasingly open to foreign investment and the global marketplace. Innovation became a watch-word in both the defense and commercial sectors under Jiang, who sought to advance China's modernization through science and education (adopting a policy of *Ke Jiao Xing Guo* or "strengthening the country through science and education"). It was during this era, too, that the notion of China's rise took dramatic hold of the world as we witnessed not only unprecedented rapid growth in China's economy but also an impressive shift in global investment, resources, and even commercial R&D being outsourced to the Chinese mainland.[55] China also began to develop its own NIS at this time, adopting many of the motifs and lessons learned in the United States and elsewhere in developing a uniquely Chinese innovation system. Accompanying this broad economic

Table 7.1
Deng Xiaoping's 16-Character Slogan: Then and Now

Deng Era		21st century version	
Junmin Jiehe	Combines military and civil	*Junmin Jiehe*	Combining civil and military needs
Pingzhan Jiehe	Combines peace and war	*Yujin Yumin*	Locating military potential in civilian capabilities
Junpin youxian	Gives priority to military products	*Dali Xietong*	Vigorously promoting coordination and cooperation
Yimin yangjun	Lets the civil support the military	*Zizhu Chuangxin*	Conducting independent innovation

Note: Cheung provides a useful and detailed assessment of each line and how it has been interpreted differently over time. See Tai Ming Cheung, Fortifying China: The Struggle to Build a Modern Defense Economy (Ithaca, NY: Cornell University Press, 2009) 7–9.

development strategy was a similarly bold change in China's military modernization efforts. By the mid-1990s, it was clear that Beijing had adopted a broad-based, mainly spin-on-oriented economic development model in pursuit of its own RMA, though one with distinct Chinese characteristics.[56]

While China's foreign and defense policy would be geared toward preparing for "local wars under modern [and later 'high-tech'] conditions" at this time, the defense-industrial domain would be shifted toward development under the policy called Military Strategic Guidelines for the New Period.[57] As Cheung describes it, "The operational dimensions of this strategy pointed to the need for China to develop critical military capabilities such as air power, electronic and information warfare, and long-range precision weapons supplied by a technological and industrial base able to mobilize for a fast-paced and high-intensity conflict."[58] The key aspect of this approach was an emerging commercial and defense-industrial sector that, through many decades of troubled reforms and aided by a tremendous influx of foreign investment and dual-use technologies, particularly IT, had begun to emerge as a more solid, stable, and dependable part of China's economy.

President Hu Jintao (2003–present), in turn, has built upon Jiang's legacy by adopting a scientific concept of development (*Kexue Fazhan Guan*). Under this strategy, China arguably has embarked upon its own version of defense transformation with a policy that emphasizes an updated version of Deng's original *Junmin Jiehe* strategy (see Table 7.1) via the pursuit of *informatization* (i.e., employing information technology to develop new, dual-use products, designs, techniques, civil-military organizational strategies, and so on). In other words, China's economy is now fully geared toward leveraging a dual spin-on and spin-off approach to economic and defense-industrial development. This strategy—which underlies China's modernization goals to at least the year 2020—relies upon continued globalization in the world economy, consistently high levels of foreign investment and increasingly advanced dual-use technologies and know-how flowing into China's economy, as well as a rising capacity for indigenous innovation.

The latter strategy appears to have already resulted in some surprising advances. Chinese spending on R&D is rising fast among both the state and industry sectors. Chinese high-tech commercial firms have increased investments overseas (and are being pressed by the Chinese Central Government to do so), become increasingly competitive against domestic and foreign competitors alike in certain high-tech fields, and begun to show nascent signs of independent innovation. Moreover, China's commercial and defense-industrial sectors are forming a more cohesive system on which China's military is better able to rely. As outlined in China's latest Defense White Paper under the heading Science, Technology and Industry for National Defense, the strategy is outlined as follows:

> China is accelerating reform and innovation in its defense-related science, technology and industry, promoting strategic and specialization-oriented restructuring of defense industry enterprises, enhancing the capabilities of independent innovation in the R&D of weaponry and equipment, and striving to establish a new system of defense-related science, technology and industry which caters to both military and civilian needs, and channels military potential to civilian use.[59]

Subsequently, China's technological progress in both commercial and defense-industrial sectors has generated new debates in the West over just how far China has come in recent years, and how quickly—and the level it could reach in coming years—as new (and even some surprising) commercial and defense capabilities have emerged. Recent defense achievements include a dramatically demonstrated antisatellite capability, the appearance in rapid fashion of new series of submarines in production, and the PRC's rapid space advances.

The United States and China appear therefore to be pursuing an increasingly similar, dual-use approach to defense-industrial development.

"Both US and PRC defense R&D strategies seek to promote dual-use technologies developed largely by private enterprises conducting business around the globe. Both countries, moreover, are blessed with the ability to attract the world's leading high-tech investors and researchers to their shores, thereby enhancing potential overall R&D capacity. Both also continue to supplement commercial R&D efforts with government-funded programs designed to strategically guide national R&D efforts and prioritize strategically important sectors."[60]

In short, the two countries are more similar today in these respects than they are different, and are increasingly interdependent in both commercial and defense realms.

PART II

The Defense Industry: Regional Perspectives

8

The Revolution in Military Affairs, Transformation, and the U.S. Defense Industry

Peter Dombrowski and Andrew L. Ross

The world's militaries are said to be in the throes of a revolution that may fundamentally and profoundly alter the future conduct of war. Characterized variously as a military technological revolution (MTR), a revolution in military affairs (RMA), and transformation, the spur to this ongoing military revolution is the broader information revolution.[1] In what has become known as the IT-RMA—information technology revolution in military affairs—military establishments are transitioning from the industrial age to the information age. As in the past, military change is a response to more far-reaching societal change. Technological, organizational, and doctrinal change are again in the offing. Far-reaching military innovation is the order of the day.

The post–cold war U.S. defense establishment has been in the vanguard of military transformation. Despite its stark military advantage over foes and friends alike, U.S. leaders intend to not merely maintain but increase U.S. military dominance. The message to military competitors is clear: challenging the United States is futile.[2]

Military change diffuses, however, whether slowly or rapidly. Innovators such as the United States do not long maintain their competitive advantage. Allies, competitors, and even potential adversaries will emulate, adapt, improve upon, and counter their innovations.[3] The spread of recent U.S. innovations to Asia, Europe, and the Middle East is already evident. China, for example, currently pursues defense modernization under the rubric of informatization, a process that sounds quite similar to U.S. transformation, with its emphasis on information-intensive warfare. As Richard Bitzinger has observed, the Chinese version of transformation relies on "short-duration, high-intensity conflicts characterized by mobility, speed and long-range attack, employing joint operations fought simultaneously throughout the entire air, land, sea, space and electromagnetic battlespace, and relying heavily upon extremely lethal high-technology weapons."[4]

Since the concept of military transformation entered the national security lexicon, analysts have sought to determine how the revolution in military affairs will affect the multibillion dollar defense-industrial sector both in the United States and across the globe. The answer lies in the evolving nature of military transformation and ongoing changes in the defense sector. Our assessment here focuses on (1) the current state of military transformation in the United States; and (2) the implications of current trends in military transformation for the global defense industry.

THE RMA/TRANSFORMATION ENTERPRISE

Recognition of an apparently emerging RMA and the subsequent call for transformation predated the administration of George W. Bush by more than a decade.[5] During the waning years of the cold war, Soviet observers of U.S. military doctrine and capabilities diagnosed a military technological revolution in the making. Early MTR/RMA stirrings in the United States yielded Andrew Krepinevich's Office of Net Assessment (ONA) 1992 report, called *The Military-Technical Revolution: A Preliminary Assessment.*[6] During the Clinton administration's first term, ONA director Andrew W. Marshall emerged as the central intellectual and organizational/bureaucratic advocate for an RMA within the Office of the Secretary of Defense (OSD). In a 1993 memorandum entitled Some Thoughts on Military Revolutions, Marshall speculated about "the *emerging* military revolution, or the *potential* military revolution" and "periods of revolution where the character of warfare itself changes" and foreshadowed what was to come: "There may not be any new platforms (e.g., carriers) for innovators to rally round and commit themselves to. . . . The technologies (information, computational, communication) that seem central suffuse everything."[7]

Following the display of U.S. military prowess during the 1991 Gulf War, the (RMA) became a central preoccupation of the American national security and defense community. The subsequent RMA campaign evolved into the transformation enterprise during the course of the 1990s. Transformation transitioned from a rather diffuse set of ideas and concepts loosely supported by historical scholarship to an enterprise—a complex, risky political-economic undertaking in which the U.S. government sought to enhance its military capabilities and the private defense-industrial sector sought to reap renewed profits from defense sales at home and abroad.

Transformation has proved to be a nebulous concept, often employed to justify—or sell—programs whether they fit the profile of transformation or were distinctly nontransformational.[8] For some, apparently, this was a virtue. According to E. C. "Pete" Aldridge, Jr., a former under secretary of defense for acquisition, technology, and logistics (AT&L), "transformation is a loose concept and we are the better for it."[9] This loose approach may have served the purposes of the visionaries and defense firms simply interested in increasing sales, but it did not provide clear guidelines for the defense planners charged with the task of implementing transformation. The 2001 *Quadrennial Defense Review Report* imbued transformation with greater specificity:

Transformation results from *the exploitation of new approaches to operational concepts and capabilities,* the use of old and new technologies, and *new forms of organization* that more effectively anticipate new or still emerging strategic and operational challenges and opportunities and that *render previous methods of conducting war obsolete or subordinate*. Transformation can involve *fundamental change in the form of military operations,* as well as a potential change in their scale. It can encompass the *displacement of one form of war with another,* such as *fundamental change in the ways war is waged* in the air, on land and at sea. It can also involve the *emergence of new kinds of war,* such as armed conflict in *new dimensions of the battlespace.*[10]

Later, the 2003 *Transformation Planning Guidance* characterized transformation as

a process that shapes the changing nature of military competition and cooperation through *new combinations of concepts, capabilities, people and organizations* that exploit our nation's advantages and protect against our asymmetric vulnerabilities to sustain our strategic position.[11]

This process entails "redefining standards for military success by accomplishing military missions that were previously unimaginable or impossible" and calls for "new operating concepts that employ new organizational constructs, capabilities, and doctrine."[12] Proponents believe the process will eventually realize the strategic and operational promise of the revolution in military affairs.

RMA concepts and language appeared in early post–cold war service documents such as the army's Force XXI, the navy's ". . . From the Sea" and "Forward . . . From the Sea," the Marine Corps' "Operational Maneuver . . . From the Sea," and the air force's "Global Reach, Global Power." Paul Bracken's 1993 article on the military after next help inspire research into the army, navy, and air force after next.[13] Military champions such as Admiral William A. Owens and Vice Admiral Arthur K. Cebrowski supported transformation and revolution. Admiral Owens argued that the RMA required the creation of a system of systems that consisted of battlespace awareness, advanced command, control, communications, computing, and intelligence (C4I), and precision force systems.[14] During Owens's tenure as vice chairman of the Joint Chiefs of Staff, the 1996 *Joint Vision 2010* (*JV 2010*), which emphasized the massing of effects rather than forces, information superiority, technological innovation, and the emerging operational concepts of dominant maneuver, precision engagement, focused logistics, and full-dimensional protection, was developed. Admiral Cebrowski, who upon his retirement from the U.S. Navy, became the first director of OSD's Office of Force Transformation, relentlessly promoted the concept of network-centric warfare that now pervades joint and service RMA/transformation plans and programs.[15]

From the perspective of RMA and transformation advocates, initial post–cold war defense posture reviews were rather stolid undertakings.[16] Revolutionary and transformational considerations were notably absent in the rationale provided for the Base Force in 1992.[17] The Bottom-Up Review of 1993 was virtually devoid of any real recognition of the need to remake the U.S. military.[18] Even the 1997 quadrennial defense review (QDR), which more prominently featured transformation issues, was more about modernization and reform than revolution.[19]

The National Defense Panel's (NDP's) December 1997 report, *Transforming Defense: National Security in the 21st Century,* was a tipping point for the RMA/transformation enterprise.[20] Having been mandated by Congress to provide an independent assessment of the Clinton administration's 1997 QDR and to fundamentally rethink the U.S. defense posture, the NDP obliged. The RMA and transformation were unequivocally embraced. "The United States," the panel declared, "needs to launch a transformation strategy *now*"[21] and ensure that the Department of Defense (DoD) and the services "accord the highest priority to executing" it.[22] It asserted that the future is more important than the present, that the capabilities the military needs for the future were not those it possessed at the time, that the utility of legacy systems must be reexamined, and that the commitment to jointness must be serious. The panel challenged many verities, including the need for balance as endorsed by Clinton Secretary of Defense William Cohen. It supported exploiting "rapid advances in information and information-related technologies" as emphasized in *Joint Vision 2010*.[23] Critical future capabilities identified by the NDP included information systems architectures, information operations, and infrastructure protection, automation, mobility, stealth, speed, depth, and precision strike.[24] As Steven Metz has noted, subsequent Clinton administration national security and defense planning documents supported transformation.[25]

Transformation's technological, doctrinal, and organizational components, and the multidimensional, synergistic relationships among them, are evident in both the 2001 QDR and the Transformation Planning Guidance (TPG).[26] Transformation requires both hardware (technology, weapons, and platforms) innovation and software (organizational and doctrinal) innovation. Planning documents emphasize new rather than improved, discontinuous rather than incremental change, and disruptive, even revolutionary, rather than sustaining, evolutionary innovation. The military must leap ahead by skipping generations of technology. Transformation is more than routine modernization. Creativity, innovation, and experimentation, even risk taking, are to be front and center. To achieve the IT-RMA, the military services, OSD, and the defense industry must abandon business as usual.

Transformation and the Bush Administration

Transformation came to be closely associated with the Bush administration, particularly with former Secretary of Defense Donald Rumsfeld. In January 2001, the administration of George W. Bush assumed office determined to institutionalize military transformation. The new president's commitment to transformation had been markedly evident on the campaign trail. In a September 23, 1999 speech at The Citadel, the then governor Bush spoke of "creating the military of the next century" and "a revolution in the technology of war." He declared that the U.S. military "must be agile, lethal, readily deployable, and require a minimum of logistical support." "The real goal," he emphasized, "is to move beyond marginal improvements . . . to skip a generation of technology." He proclaimed the need for "a new spirit of innovation" that would result in the lighter land forces, stealthy naval vessels, and long-range, precision-strike airpower (unmanned as well as manned) required for the future.[27]

The Bush administration's support for transformation was formalized in the September 2001 *Quadrennial Defense Review Report*:

> A fundamental challenge confronting DoD is ensuring that U.S. forces have the capabilities they need to carry out the new defense strategy and meet the demands of the

21st century. Toward that end, *it is imperative that the United States invests and transforms its forces and capabilities.*[28]

Seeking to reinvigorate and institutionalize the enterprise, a multitude of transformation visions, guidance, and roadmaps were added to the Joint Staff's foundation document of *Joint Vision 2020* (*JV 2020*). Within the Pentagon and across the functional and geographic commands and the services, the language of transformation became ubiquitous.

The 2006 *Quadrennial Defense Review Report*[29] reaffirmed the Bush administration's commitment to transformation even as it fought the war on terrorism in addition to wars in Afghanistan and Iraq. With the flurry of OSD, Joint Staff, and service transformation visions, guidance, and roadmaps—and the multitude of operational concepts, goals, pillars, elements, and capabilities generated by *JV 2010* and *JV 2020*—the primary features of a transformed military have become more readily apparent. They include:

- Networked nodes—platforms, weapons, sensors, and, particularly, command, control, communications, computing, intelligence, surveillance, and reconnaissance (C4ISR) assets;
- Distributed forces and capabilities;
- Speed (of command, deployment, and employment);
- Light, agile, nimble forces able to operate simultaneously in geographically and environmentally distinct theaters;
- Expeditionary forces;
- Precision engagement (i.e., global precision strike capabilities);
- Shared situational awareness (networked ubiquitous sensors are to provide a common operational picture that facilitates collaboration and self-synchronization);
- Flexible/adaptable/modular forces;
- Stealth (low observable forces);
- Joint (interdependent and integrated)/interoperable forces;
- Sustainable forces.

Transformation proponents envision a vast array of new and emerging technologies and capabilities. Unmanned systems will saturate the battlespace from space to under the oceans. Sensors will be ubiquitous. Smaller, faster, lighter ships sporting new hull forms will ply the seas. Forces will be based at sea. Hypersonic craft will blur the distinction between the atmosphere and space. New forms of kinetic energy will be deployed. Nanotechnologies will be pervasive. Biotechnology will erode the distinction between human and machine. Nonlethal technologies will be employed to disable enemy combatants and may well rival lethal technologies.

But information technologies (IT) lie at the center of the transformation enterprise.[30] As Alberts, Garstka, and Stein put it, "Information Technology is the DNA of the Information Age."[31] Information technology's privileged position has long been acknowledged.[32] *Joint Vision 2020*, like *Joint Vision 2010*, singled out information superiority as a key enabler of transformation. Information and knowledge superiority are to be the source of the future joint force's full spectrum dominance and promise dominant maneuver, precision engagement, focused logistics, and full dimensional protection. IT makes possible the critical characteristic of a transformed information age force: networked nodes. Networking allows for distributing forces and capabilities; speed of command, deployment, and employment; lighter, agile, nimble, modular, more expeditionary forces; real-time precision strike; the collaboration and self-synchronization provided by shared situational awareness; and integrated, interdependent, sustainable joint operations.

If transformation succeeds, future military operations will be network-centric rather than platform-centric. Networked capabilities and forces will be distributed rather than massed; fires rather than forces will be massed. Information operations and cyber operations will rival conventional operations. Platforms will be tailored to the network, not the network to platforms. Traditional hardware will no longer have pride of place. IT software will be the new hardware. Information architecture is already at the heart of new systems. Lancaster's equations are giving way to Moore's Law and Metcalfe's Law. C4ISR will rule. The competition among warfighters for more bits and bytes will be fiercer than the competition for bullets and bombs. Demand for bandwidth will outstrip demand for throw weight.[33] Processing power will displace explosive yield. The collection, processing, fusion, and dissemination of data will be the new logistics.

The Status of Military Transformation

With the Bush administration's tenure having come to an end, it is possible to take stock of the progress made toward military transformation. Although then secretary of defense Rumsfeld had moved rapidly to implement his president's campaign rhetoric in support of an RMA in 2001, the success of this effort was in doubt after the first nine months of the new administration. Rumsfeld, it was claimed, was not up to the task of overcoming resistance within the military to many tenets of the RMA; some officers and experts argued that the benefits of transformation were illusory; others argued that so-called legacy programs were still valuable in the post–cold war security environment. With 9/11, the Bush administration was reenergized, not only to hunt down al Qaeda and state supporters of terrorism, but also to push forward with rebuilding U.S. military forces.

What was labeled the *long war*[34]—roughly the campaigns in Afghanistan and Iraq plus an alleged global war on terror—affected both the pace and extent of transformation. The perception of heightened external threat levels after 9/11 and renewed support for higher military spending provided opportunities for transformation advocates and industry alike. Military spending increased rapidly and the Afghan and Iraq campaigns further tested, on a much grander scale, weapons and systems that first appeared with the Persian Gulf War and in the Balkans during the 1990s. Some accounts attribute the operational successes in the Persian Gulf War to military transformation.[35] This certainly was the position taken by its advocates, including those in the Office of Force Transformation.

Broad-based transformation goals may have suffered as the operational challenges of ongoing campaigns served to focus &D resources on technologies and systems barely on the radar screen of early transformation advocates. Two programs illustrate this dynamic: the search for solutions to the tactical problems posed by improvised explosive devices (IEDs) and accelerated programs to develop mine resistant ambush protected vehicles (MRAPs). Both programs, however necessary for warfighters, have been costly in terms of research dollars and the attention of the research and acquisition communities.

The costs of the ongoing wars, both material and intellectual, have slowed transformation and diverted attention from long-term objectives. Already, some of the more truly transformational programs launched during the Bush administration, including the navy's littoral combat vessel and the Army's ambitious Future Combat Systems (FCS) program, have been cut back or delayed. The effects of Iraq and Afghanistan will linger, perhaps long after the wars are brought to conclusion. Resetting the force, especially for the U.S. Army and Marine Corps, will be extremely expensive. Although the army has already received $38 billion to reset more than 300,000 pieces of major equipment, the Congressional Budget Office estimated that it will require roughly "$13 billion annually for such purposes for as long as the war in Iraq continues at its current level and for at least two years after U.S. forces are withdrawn."[36] How long Iraq operations will last is unclear; Senator John McCain, the Republican presidential nominee in 2008, backed off his startling, off-the-cuff assertion that the United States may remain in Iraq for 100 years. In May 2008, he estimated 2013 as a likely pull-out date.[37] This would require approximately $91 billion in reset monies for the army, and presumably significantly more for U.S. Marine Corps and Air Force units directly engaged in combat operations.

Beyond spending patterns for research, development, testing, and evaluation (RDT&E) and procurement, the reduced attention to transformation has also manifested itself in terms of rhetoric and organizational emphases. While the former secretary of defense Rumsfeld continued to focus on transformation goals even as it became increasingly clear that Iraq was consuming virtually all of the energy and resources of the U.S. military, his successor, Robert Gates, has been much more circumspect, as was evident during the course of both his December 2006 Senate confirmation hearing and his swearing-in ceremony remarks.[38]

Organizationally the fate of the Office of Force Transformation (OFT) is instructive. With the untimely death of its initial director, retired vice admiral Arthur Cebrowski, OFT was quickly sidetracked into science experiments. Shortly thereafter it was downgraded and then disestablished. Yet while Cebrowski's departure as director of OFT and the subsequent demise of the office had given rise to concerns, the establishment of a deputy assistant secretary for forces transformation in the Office of the Under Secretary of Defense for Policy may be interpreted as evidence of the continuing institutionalization of transformation within the DoD. That institutionalization is evident as well in the deputy security of defense's August 9, 2007, memorandum on DoD transformation priorities and the Combined Joint Chiefs of Staff (CJCS) guidance for 2007–8, which features RMA and transformation language in its call for a "commitment to change," "effects-based thinking," "different kinds of warfighters, mission systems and strategies," a military that is "smarter, lighter, more agile, and more lethal," and "increased precision, speed and agility," and for "push[ing] new boundaries, seek[ing] new opportunities and challenge[ing] existing assumptions."[39]

Ironically, however, the institutionalization of transformation within OSD and the military services by its champions in the Bush administration may well have rendered it mundane. After all, it is the rhetoric rather than the reality of transformation that has been institutionalized. True transformation, clearly, requires more than the standard issue evolutionary technological, doctrinal, or organizational advances that amount only to business as usual. It entails not incremental, evolutionary change but discontinuous, disruptive innovation. However, the U.S. transformation enterprise thus far falls short. Joint and service plans and programs have yet to match up to transformation visions. While the visions promise discontinuity and disruption, plans and programs support only incremental, sustaining advances. Technological generation-skipping is nowhere to be found. Doctrine development is more linear than nonlinear. Organizational change features evolution and adaptation rather than re-creation or, even, restructuring. Unless the gap between visions and plans and programs can be bridged, transformation is fated to be little more than routine modernization. At best, it will amount to modernization plus.[40]

Thus the proffered new order has been absorbed by the old order, the new rule set subsumed by the old rule set. Its institutionalization appears to have made transformation nonthreatening, toothless, and even benign. Instead of disguising disruptive innovation as sustaining innovation in an effort to protect it, overcome inertia and resistance, and disarm opponents,[41] champions of the contemporary transformation enterprise have been reduced to disguising sustaining innovation as disruptive innovation.

THE TRANSFORMATION ENTERPRISE AND INDUSTRY

In a market economy, the demand for the technological innovations required to bring about military transformation must, for the most part,[42] be met by private industry. The ability of private sector defense firms to support the transformation enterprise is thus critical to its success.[43] If these firms cannot produce the innovations deemed necessary to fulfill the promise of transformation and do so at a reasonable cost, the entire enterprise will be endangered. Moreover, the overall health of the defense market in the United States and across the globe will affect the ability of firms, no matter how attentive to the military's demands for innovation and how well run, to meet transformation requirements effectively.

The Post–Cold War Defense Sector [44]

As the transformation enterprise gained traction within the national security community and the military services, the U.S. defense industry was undergoing a major shake out. First, and most important, declining defense budgets decreased demand, especially for major new weapon systems. With too many defense firms chasing too few dollars, the American defense industry began a period of consolidation, looking for new ways to remain healthy and profitable. Some firms closed or sold off defense product lines, while others took the reverse position of trimming nondefense work in order to protect core competencies. Second, as economic globalization accelerated in diverse sectors ranging from finance to transportation, some U.S. firms sought overseas sales by either buying into existing markets or seeking relief from U.S. export controls, which made it difficult and expensive for U.S. firms to sell equipment and services abroad. Consolidation, globalization, and commercial-military integration have been highlighted in assessments of the post–cold war U.S. defense industry.

Consolidation.   Defense-industrial consolidation refers to the mergers and acquisitions (M&As) that have transformed the defense-industrial landscape.[45] From the end of the cold war to roughly 9/11, that landscape has been dramatically altered by consolidation.

The number of separate businesses plunged in many sectors of the defense industry during the 1990s. Many of the most famous names in American industry, from General Motors and Ford to Hughes Aircraft and McDonnell Douglas, either left the defense business or exist today only as divisions of larger enterprises. The few remaining big defense firms generally comprise several formerly independent companies or defense-oriented divisions sold by other companies that have themselves left the defense business. Post–cold war consolidation peaked in 1999 and was not surpassed until 2006 when defense and aerospace companies worldwide completed M&A deals worth more than $40 billion in a total of 370 transactions.[46]

With consolidation, the largest defense firms maintain multiple centers of excellence, allowing them to bid on a wide range of platforms and integration programs. Mergers and acquisitions have broadened the defense conglomerates' portfolios of programs. Post-consolidation integration and restructuring at the level of design teams and production facilities is loose at best. At the same time, by adding military businesses and spinning off commercially oriented facilities, the parent companies in the defense industry have typically become even more dependent on military customers than the largest defense firms were in the past.

Even in acquisition programs in which multiple suppliers bid for a development or production contract, political and bureaucratic forces often ensure that competition is stunted. Weapon system competitions are often not winner take all affairs but rather design competitions in which different firms compete only for the selection of their respective approaches. A prime is selected, but the losers share in production. In some cases sharing means that each firm builds entire platforms or systems; in others it means that losing firms become subcontractors to the winning firm or team of firms. Politicians and industrial-base advocates often justify such production sharing by arguing that it helps to maintain firms with core defense-production capacities so that they might bid on future projects. In reality, shared production results also from the concerns of the DoD and Congress about the domestic political impact of closing defense plants—often with little regard for the economic cost. The result is that the salutary effect of competition on prices touted by economic theorists is considerably diluted in the defense industry.

A related criticism of defense industry consolidation—that it may limit the industry's propensity to innovate—is tied directly to the implementation of transformation. When firms invest in innovation, their goal is to create new products and thus potential new sources of revenue. However, firms are especially interested in products that are already programmed into the defense budget; because of the up-front investment required for innovation, defense suppliers are biased toward extending the production of current systems rather than pushing the technological envelope for new products. Many critics of consolidation presume that the key motivation to innovate in the defense sector comes from industry competition—that it is firms not currently selling legacy systems that will be most motivated to develop new products, in the hope of replacing established sellers.

Incentives for innovation in the defense market actually differ somewhat from this traditional economic view, because the military market is a near monopsony, and the military customer demands unique products. Even in sectors in which suppliers face demand from perfectly competitive consumers, the economics literature does not provide a clear picture of the role of competition in promoting innovation.[47] Competition may provide firms with an incentive to innovate, but it reduces their capability to earn returns that recoup up-front investment; firms in competitive industries may accordingly invest less in research and development (R&D). In the defense industry, however, a powerful, single customer pays directly for the initial R&D investment and sets the agenda for innovation. True consolidation of production lines in the defense industry may even free resources that the military could use to support additional R&D.

Consolidation has thus had potentially serious implications for military transformation in terms of price and innovation. Analysts generally believe that less competition among defense contractors will lead to increased prices, decreased responsiveness to the needs of the military, and less innovation. This logic largely tracks with standard economic theory, but it must be applied to the defense sector with care. As we will demonstrate shortly, consolidation may also have important implications for government-industry relations in terms of who performs systems integration functions and under what conditions.

Globalization.   Despite the hype,[48] defense-industrial globalization is more mirage than reality. There are numerous dimensions of economic globalization, including most prominently trade, investment, and technology diffusion. On all three counts, there is reason to doubt that the defense sector will follow other sectors, such as the automobile industry or machine tools, much less service industries like banking and transportation, down the road toward globalization.

There are many impediments to higher levels of cross-border defense-related trade, investment, and technology flows. First, impediments to defense exports, from limited demand to concerns about regional instability and proliferation, are legitimate, however much the defense industry would like a freer hand to peddle its wares overseas. Second, cross-border defense industry investments, with some significant exceptions, often generate security concerns in host-nation governments, including the United States. Even if the worldwide trend toward reducing regulation and privatizing public services continues, most countries will still believe that controlling basic weapons production facilities is prudent. Third, advanced military technologies in the United States and elsewhere are largely the product of public investment; few government officials want to share the public patrimony even with close allies—much less with countries that qualify merely as potential allies or friends. These limits also apply to firms that produce dual-use rather than specifically military technologies.

In addition, defense-industrial globalization is an uneven process. For much of the world, it consists largely of imports and limited licensing agreements to assemble, and perhaps produce, lower-end systems and components; there is no requirement for technology-intensive, transformed forces. For many countries, the potential for globalization is also constrained by the limited resources available for defense.[49]

Commercial-military integration.   Throughout the 1990s and the first years of the 21st century, political leaders and defense industry analysts called for replacing a defense-industrial base separated from commercial industry with a single, integrated industrial base that would serve multiple customers.[50] Some argued that the integrated industrial base would be necessary to give defense customers access to more advanced technology under continuous development for commercial applications.[51] Many transformation advocates argued that a military intent on transforming itself should turn away from traditional suppliers and toward firms at the forefront of the new economy. Others suggested that the transition to commercial military integration had already taken place. That assessment was premature; if anything, as the second decade of the 21st century approaches, many defense firms have shed commercial divisions and product lines while acquiring more defense-related capabilities through mergers and acquisitions. Commercial firms were, and are, for the most part, relatively uninterested in commercial-military integration; for firms like Microsoft, the U.S. military does not represent a large enough market to justify entering into anything other than sales agreements. Commercial-military integration may have some impact on inexpensive, low-end, simplified acquisition threshold products and on subcomponent purchases, but for the primary systems under consideration with respect to military transformation, the military customer need not, cannot, and should not rely on commercial-military integration.

Links between the commercial world and the defense industry have been developed as a result of the DoD's push to integrate commercial off-the-shelf technologies (COTS) into its defense systems as a way to reduce costs, increase capabilities, and shorten weapons-acquisition and development cycles. Incorporating those subsystems into military products can help the military avoid technological obsolescence in the face of nimble overseas competitors, who might be able to cherry-pick the best and most affordable commercial systems for their own limited defense investments. The defense acquisition community needs to develop the organizational capability to scan commercial innovation so that it can choose suitable technologies to integrate into weapon systems. Practically speaking, that scanning function is one of the services that the DoD can and should purchase from technical advisors, systems integrators, and prime contractors. Direct contact between the military customer and commercial suppliers is not necessarily required.

Commercial IT firms that are ready to serve as component suppliers are unlikely to transform the defense industry as a whole, however. The process of civil-military integration has not progressed much beyond strategic teaming arrangements, licensing agreements, and the purchase of COTS subsystems, and the reasons for the limited commercial-military integration are unlikely to change. Other practical difficulties inhibit commercial-military integration as well: Government contracting requires specialized competencies that are not usually found in the commercial IT sector (for example, dealing with the Federal Acquisition Regulations, or FAR).

Defense contractors' organizational cultures and personnel are well suited to keeping the DoD customer happy, while the more informal methods of the IT sector often produce culture shock in the military acquisition system. The necessary concern of the military with secrecy, accuracy, and information assurance—more important than ever in the post-9/11 government-contracting environment—runs contrary to the instincts of many IT firms. Acquisition reform efforts may sometimes make it easier for nontraditional defense suppliers to enter the defense procurement marketplace; time, experience, and the generational shifts that all organizations will encounter in the coming years may help to overcome the informal barriers to cooperation between the commercial IT world and the DoD. But the incentives to surmount the barriers will remain weak, because the entire defense budget for science and technology (S&T), R&D, and procurement represents a relatively small prize for American industry. As a result, defense firms will continue to guard their core competencies at the level of systems contracting, and commercial IT firms are not likely to alter their business practices to try to become systems suppliers.

Defense Industry and Transformation

In the early stages of the U.S. infatuation with transformation, some analysts speculated that the defense industry itself would be transformed in the effort to realize an IT-RMA. After all, in the United States most defense firms rely heavily on government contracts;[52] few have pursued a business strategy of diversification, or what has been called civil-military integration, with sufficient vigor to make them independent.[53] Demand, expressed in government contracts for transformational systems, might force the entire industry to adapt, willingly or not. It now appears that the broader defense sector dynamics brought about by the end of the cold war aside, the government's push for military transformation has affected the defense sector, but not necessarily in the ways experts predicted or in ways that should be judged transformative.

Previously, we argued that the posited transformation of the defense industry depends largely on the weapons, weapon systems, and defense-industrial sector under consideration.[54] In short, there is no one model for defense industry transformation. Dombrowski and Gholz extended this argument still further in concluding that, for the most part, large traditional defense suppliers, the prime contractors or primes, were well-positioned to provide transformational systems.[55] In short, the basic characteristics of the defense sector will not change under the influence of military transformation. Traditional suppliers will supply transformational equipment, however it is defined; nontraditional firms like those from the IT sector will enter the market largely by teaming with existing defense firms, as component suppliers, or through M&As; non-U.S. firms will attempt to enter U.S. markets because that is where the money is, but they will do so largely by acquiring American firms,[56] selling components, licensing technologies, or partnering with American firms.

Although we stand by these arguments, several developments suggest that while most of the macro changes to the defense industry originally envisioned by transformation advocates have not materialized, there are signs of other unanticipated shifts with consequences for the U.S. defense-industrial sector, progress toward military transformation, and the spread of both transformation and defense firms capable of supporting transformation across the globe. One significant shift is the ascendance of systems integration as the key defense-industrial sector and an essential competency of prime contractors. To be effective, the networks demanded by the 2001 and 2006 QDRs and other strategic documents—the systems of linked platforms, weapons, sensors, and, particularly, C4ISR assets—must be designed and built together, most preferably overseen by a single entity.

By definition, the IT-RMA depends upon the more intensive use of a wide range of technologies ranging from computing to communications into both (1) individual weapons and military platforms and (2) the entire complex of weapon systems and supporting technologies used by the military. One problem with this process is that, increasingly, the U.S.

government does not possess the in-house technical knowledge and managerial capabilities necessary to procure transformational systems. This shortfall in know-how is exacerbated by an overly bureaucratic and increasingly antiquated acquisition system that is ill-prepared to cope with new, more complex systems. Modest reforms such as spiral development have not been helpful; indeed, they have worsened existing procurement problems.

Why, then, are prime contractors emerging as the critical systems integrators during this period of military transformation? After all, possible integrators can be the government itself, a private firm such as a prime contractor, or an independent organization.[57] As numerous independent audits suggest, the government as represented by the Department of Defense and the service acquisition communities is far less able to provide "system of systems" integration than in the past; a shrinking workforce,[58] lost expertise, and other institutional factors have reduced government acquisition management capabilities and capacities. Independent organizations such as federally funded research and development centers (FFRDCs) have much to recommend them, at least in theory, but have little support within the overall national security community. MITRE, RAND, JPL and other FFRDCs have limited systems integration capabilities.

By default, then, the task of providing the "system of systems" integration required by a military dead set on transformation or forcing an IT-RMA falls to the private sector—or more properly the prime contractors with the financial, intellectual, and experiential wherewithal to undertake multibillion dollar, multiyear, inherently risky development, engineering, and production programs. Prime contractors do not need to be encouraged by the government; they have plenty of incentives to participate and actively market their competency in systems integration.[59] Thus, we agree with Hartley and Sandler that "The future defense firm will be a global company focusing on prime contracting/systems integration, supplying world markets and buying-in specialist tasks from suppliers throughout the world rather than undertaking work in-house and relying on national suppliers."[60] In fact, the future is now.

Systems integration has thus become one of the core capabilities claimed by defense firms and a key service offered to purchasers of major weapon systems. Two major acquisition programs requiring different levels of systems integration illustrate the difficulties facing both advocates of transformation and the defense industry as systems integration migrates to the private sector:[61] (1) the littoral combat ship of the U.S. Navy, which requires platform integration and (1) the Future Combat System program of the U.S. Army, which requires systems of systems integration. There are, of course, other weapon systems described as transformative that we could have used to illustrate our argument, including, for example, the U.S. Coast Guard's Deepwater program and the multiservice, multirole Joint Strike Fighter (JSF) program. Moreover, any of the systems identified as necessary for developing a network-centric force—from the Global Information Grid (GIG) to the army's Warfighter Information Network (WINT-T) programs—would also have sufficed.[62]

Littoral combat ship (LCS). The LCS is a relatively small, relatively fast, and relatively inexpensive combat ship. It is designed to be modular; the basic sea frame will be outfitted with one of three alternative mission packages—antisubmarine warfare (ASW), mine warfare, or surface warfare. Each mission module includes weapons, vehicles, and sensors, as well as supporting equipment, containers, and software. The navy wants to procure a total of 55 LCSs as well as 64 warfare packages—16 antisubmarine, 24 mine, and 24 surface packages—to outfit the LCSs.[63] This new class of ships represents the backbone of the navy's 30-year shipbuilding program initiated in fiscal year (FY) 09 to reach a force level of 313 ships of all types.[64] As chief of naval operations, Admiral Gary Roughhead has argued, "You can look at the shipbuilding plan and you can see that LCS is the major driver of the number, and it's not just to drive the number higher."[65]

The LCS is part of the navy's new family of ships that includes the U.S. Navy's next-generation destroyer, DDG 1000, and cruiser, CG(X). It complements the capabilities of the DDG 1000 and the CG(X) by focusing on littoral missions and, in particular, asymmetric threats. The family of ships is to be interlinked both by networks and by the insertion of common technologies across classes using spiral development. Further, in the case of the LCS, each vessel will require integration with the various components of its modular mission packages (such as unmanned aerial vehicles [UAVs] and unmanned undersea vehicles [UUVs]) and, if early operational concepts hold, with squadrons of other LCS fighting in concert.

The initial approach to developing the LCS had five teams competing for the opportunity to design the new class of vessels. In 2004, two teams, one headed by Lockheed Martin and the other by General Dynamics, were awarded final design contracts.[66] This account will focus on the Lockheed Martin variant. The LCS project represented a challenge to Lockheed-Martin because it is not a shipbuilder per se. Its experience with naval vessels is largely as a ship system integrator, a role it played most prominently perhaps on the Blue Team that produced one of the designs for the DD-21 in the late-1990s. To build the hull or sea frame, Lockheed Martin contracted with Marinette Marine.[67] Marinette Marine, despite having a long history of building naval and coast guard vessels, was apparently unprepared for the LCS project's complexity and program management and technical challenges.[68] Reports indicate that neither the navy nor Lockheed Martin provided sufficient oversight to catch difficulties with the program or Marinette Marine's activities.[69]

Modularity of various types—principally, construction, configuration, and mission—adds to the importance of systems integration for the LCS. Mission modules are being developed separately and will include initial testing on other classes of ships due to delays in production of the two initial LCS sea frames. Modularity compounds the more general configuration integration problem both because of the extent of mission package modularity required and the complexity of testing without actual sea frames. At an even more basic level, both Marinette Marine and Bollinger, the hull builder for the General Dynamics version, the LCS-2, will employ modular construction techniques such as building portions of the vessel out of sequence and at different sites only to be assembled into the final hull.[70]

Many of the numerous program management problems that have surfaced with the LCS can be linked to the issue of systems integration. Government audits indicate that Marinette Marine, the firm building Freedom (LCS 1) for Lockheed Martin, has experienced major difficulties in managing the program. In response to challenges, Congress and the OSD have periodically threatened LCS funding and imposed restrictions on navy plans. To date, while the entire program remains on track, the fate of the next several LCS to be produced remain in doubt.[71]

Future Combat System (FCS).   According to the U.S. Army, the FCS represents its first major modernization program in four decades; it is intended to implement the army future warfare vision.[72] According to Boeing, the co-lead systems integrator with the Science Applications International Corporation (SAIC) for the FCS, the program is

> an Army modernization initiative designed to link soldiers to a wide range of weapons, sensors, and information systems by means of a mobile ad hoc network architecture that will enable unprecedented levels of joint interoperability, shared situational awareness and the ability to execute highly synchronized mission operations.[73]

Ultimately, a complex, multilevel network of networks (including standards, transport, services, applications, sensors, and platforms) is to link individual soldiers with at least 14 combat systems ranging from manned and unmanned ground vehicles to unmanned aerial vehicles and sensors of many types. The FCS is to be developed in three stages—(1) concept and technology development, (2) system design and demonstration, and (3) production—by 2014.

If the army succeeds with FCS it will outfit nearly one-third of its 70 combat brigades with the FCS for a total cost of perhaps $300 billion. The stakes are huge. By 2015, when the first combat brigade is scheduled to field the FSC, the program is expected to consume fully 40 percent of the entire army procurement budget; it is expected to continue to do so at similar or higher levels until 2025, according to the Congressional Budget Office (CBO).[74]

To date, the FCS has run into three major difficulties: (1) cost increases, (2) timeline slippages, and (3) performance shortfalls. One major explanation for the weaknesses of the FCS is the assignment of Boeing and SAIC as lead systems integrators.[75] Lead systems integrators play a dual role in defense acquisitions; they serve as traditional contractors by providing a product for the customer, and also serve as partners in managing the program itself.[76] As the army's experience with Boeing and SAIC indicate, it is not clear that even the most capable of defense firms is up to the greater than expected systems integration challenges posed by transformation.

The LCS and FCS examples represent two cases where the U.S. government turned to private firms to perform the systems integration role traditionally undertaken by the government itself. In both cases, false starts, delays, cost increases, and increasingly adversarial oversight by Congress and OSD have damaged program credibility in Congress and thus endangered funding in the long run. These are not, of course, the only programs in the history of U.S. military acquisition to experience such troubles. But the ongoing complications are taking place at a point in history when the United States might be facing a window of vulnerability. Senior political and military leaders have promised military transformation, but defense-industrial issues, particularly on-going difficulties with systems integration, remain an impediment.

Systems integration difficulties have been brought to the fore by the major oversight agencies in the U.S. government, including the Government Accountability Office (GAO) and the Congressional Research Service (CRS). With regard to the FCS, GAO analysts argue that "the vast scope of the FCS and the synonymy of the program with the future Army, poses risks for the Army's ability to provide independent oversight in the long term."[77] In brief, the GAO believes that the close relationship between the army, Boeing, and SAIC, the FCS systems integrators, weakens army control over the program. Lead systems integrators (LSI) both develop and manage the programs under contractual conditions that necessarily provide appropriate incentives. The more general CRS analysis argues that the role of lead systems integrators raises numerous oversight issues for Congress, including problems with inadequate transparency, potential conflicts of interest, questions about who certifies that work has been completed, whether it is possible to recompete LSI contracts, and whether performing an LSI function gives a firm unfair advantages in future contract competitions.[78]

The 2008 House defense authorization bill proposed prohibiting the DoD from awarding any new contracts for LSI functions in the procurement of major systems as of October 1, 2011. Although the Senate version of the bill did not specifically mention LSIs, Section 807 of the National Defense Authorization Act for FY2007 imposes limits on contractors acting as lead system integrators in the acquisition of major DoD systems.[79] The DoD issued an interim rule, which took effect on February 10, 2008, amending the Defense Federal Acquisition Regulation Supplement (DFARS) to implement Section 807.

Yet the attention and oversight of auditors and Congress may not be enough to overcome the trend toward the use of major contractors as systems integrators in the long run. The lack of experienced and appropriately trained government personnel, and the ever-increasing pressure to decrease the number of government employees, may ensure that the systems integrator issue will be revisited in the near to medium term.

Global Impact of U.S. Defense Industry Responses to Military Transformation

The implications of current U.S. difficulties executing programs requiring a high degree of systems integration at all levels—from weapons to platform to system—have both domestic and international implications. On the domestic side, cost increases and program delays may hinder the scope and pace of transformation, regardless of whether transformation is or is not in the best interests of the nation. They also have encouraged greater congressional oversight and added impetus to calls for acquisition reform including, approaches like what has been called the revolution in business affairs. Depending on where one sits, these may be positive developments, but certainly they portend more institutional and programmatic turmoil as institutional arrangements and rules continue to be revised and reformed.

The international implications of the movement of large contractors toward systems integration are diverse. Large European firms including BAE Systems, EADS, and Finmeccanica have largely followed, with a slight delay, their North American counterparts. In the post–cold war period, they too went through bouts of consolidation and civil-military integration, not to mention a long-term infatuation with globalization. Globalization, in particular, encouraged European firms as they sought to break down barriers to the North American market and link when possible with U.S. and other non-European firms to acquire technologies and entry into markets. More to the point, with U.S. defense budgets shrinking more slowly than their European counterparts during the 1990s and rising more rapidly after 9/11, European firms sought globalization (or perhaps Americanization) to follow the money and hence profits. Today they too are positioning themselves as systems integrators in Europe, when possible in the United States, and globally.

With regard to the relationship between military transformation in other countries aside from North America, Europe, and one or two other countries (like China), the move toward systems integration as a core business capability (even if by necessity) may provide even greater commercial advantages to the 10 or 20 largest defense firms. Countries seeking to purchase transformative military systems and equipment may have to rely even more heavily on nonindigenous producers or risk fielding inferior weapons and systems.

At a more modest level, using prime contractors as integrators allows second- and third-tier producers to enter markets, including that of the United States, as subcomponent suppliers and design agents, for example, with less direct interaction with the military acquisition system. In the case of the LCS, for example, the two sea fames adapted for LCS 1 and 2 came from overseas firms. This may provide opportunities for individual firms, but it may also add to the integration difficulties with systems of systems programs. COTS, especially from offshore vendors, may save costs while increasing management burdens. Moreover, as with all prime contractors, LSIs will continue to be tempted to buy internally. And less than adequate government enforcement of rules and norms favoring greater competition will undermine the entry of new firms, foreign or otherwise, into the U.S. defense market.

CONCLUSION

Defense transformation remains a priority of the U.S. military, but the ability of the OSD and the four military services to deliver on the promise of the IT-RMA is in doubt, at least at the pace and to the extent envisioned by early transformation proponents. The Iraq and Afghanistan campaigns have cost the U.S. military, especially the army and Marine Corps, an enormous amount of equipment that will have to be reset and/or replaced. Whether recapitalization will lead to more innovative systems such as the FCS or less futuristic modernization is as yet unclear. Postwar recapitalization will, in all likelihood, take into account the hard-fought lessons of actual combat in the post-9/11 era; Secretary of Defense Robert Gates has clearly weighed in on the side of worrying more about current conflicts than the next war, much less the war after next.[80] Some assumptions of early transformation proponents have fallen by the wayside. Smaller, faster, and lighter may make sense in theory, but in reality America's enemies have proved resilient and adaptive. Light ground systems have proved vulnerable to increasingly powerful improvised explosive devises (IEDs) and small arms.[81] The perceived need to maintain a naval forward presence, particularly "credible combat power forward,"[82] at a time when the number of ships available to both the U.S. Navy and major U.S. allies such as Great Britain is declining suggests that smaller, less expensive vessels will remain appealing. Yet, rapidly increasing shipbuilding costs may ultimately limit the size of the force, even when large numbers of vessels, like the LCS, are meant to be smaller, cheaper, and tailored to a new international security environment.

The defense industry did adapt to the transformation mandate in the late 1990s and the first years of the 21st century, but events overcame the best of intentions. Industry trends since the demise of the Soviet threat reduced the ability of industry to respond to calls for transformation. In particular, the imperative for systems integration implied by network-centric approaches to warfare has not been always been well served by the large prime contractors that emerged triumphant in the late 1990s. COTS technologies once thought to promise cost savings and innovative, cutting edge technologies for military systems have sometimes proved chimerical. Military purchasers have ceded oversight to private firms working on their own accounts and, perhaps, more willing to misrepresent technological possibilities and challenges.

Globalization also remains a fact of life, with paradoxical affects on American defense firms. The spread of technologies and knowledge continues apace, despite restrictions imposed by the United States and other Western governments. The restrictions on American firms—including buy American provisions, DFAR regulations, export controls, and Exon-Florio restrictions, among others—have prevented them from taking full advantage of potential advantages from partnering and purchasing abroad, and have only slowed the spread of technologies. The need for systems integration to take full advantage of military transformation provides opportunities for American prime contractors, but it may also encourage other government and nongovernment competitors to develop the necessary capabilities. The Chinese military, for example, has managed to leap ahead in some key warfighting areas with help from foreign military purchases and its own society's growing technical sophistication. It may be just a matter of time before demand combined with the diffusion of knowledge undermines the advantages of the U.S. military and its partners in the transformation enterprise.

ACKNOWLEDGMENT

This chapter is adapted from Peter Dombrowski and Andrew L. Ross, "The Revolution in Military Affairs, Transformation, and the U.S. Defense Industry," *Security Challenges* (Vol. 4, No.4, 2008), 13–38. Reprinted with permission.

NOTES

1. Peter Dombrowski and Eugene Gholz, *Selling Military Transformation: Technological Innovation and the Defense Industry* (New York: Columbia University Press, 2006).
2. In making the case for transformation, former secretary Rumsfeld, America's foremost recent civilian champion of transformation, was quite explicit on this point when he declared that "we must develop new assets, the mere possession of which discourages adversaries from competing." Donald H. Rumsfeld, "Transforming the Military," *Foreign Affairs* 81, no. 3 (2002): 27.
3. Emily O. Goldman and Leslie C. Eliason, eds., *The Diffusion of Military Technology and Ideas* (Stanford: Stanford University Press, 2003).
4. Richard Bitzinger, "China Adapts to US Defense Transformation," Institute of Defence and Strategic Studies, Nanyang Technological University (November 10, 2006), http://www.isn.ethz.ch (accessed May 12, 2008).
5. For a useful recent account, and critique, of the development of the U.S. transformation enterprise, see Frederick W. Kagan, *Finding the Target: The Transformation of American Military Policy* (New York: Encounter Books, 2006). Other scholars trace the current period of transformation back more than 30 years, to the Assault Breaker and Joint Air Land Battle innovations of the 1970s and 1980s. See Robert R. Tomes, *US Defense Strategy From Vietnam to Operation Iraqi Freedom: Military Innovation and the New American Way of War, 1973-2003* (London: Routledge, 2007).
6. Andrew F. Krepinevich, Jr., *The Military-Technical Revolution: A Preliminary Assessment* (Washington, DC: Center for Strategic and Budgetary Assessments, 2002.

7. A. W. Marshall, "Some Thoughts on Military Revolutions," memorandum for the record, July 27, 1993; emphasis in the original. A profile of Marshall and ONA is provided by Nicholas Lemann, "Dreaming about War," *New Yorker,* July 16, 2001, 32–38.

8. The meaning of transformation is probed as well by Derrick J. Neal, "Do We Really Understand What is Meant by Transformational Change for Defence?" *Defence Studies* 6, no. 1 (2006): 73–96. The short answer to the question posed by Neal is "no."

9. E. C. "Pete" Aldridge Jr., "Technology and National Defense," address to DARPA Tech, July 30, 2002.

10. Department of Defense (DoD), *Quadrennial Defense Review Report* (Washington, DC: DoD, 2001), 29. Emphasis added.

11. Department of Defense (DoD), *Transformation Planning Guidance* (Washington, DC: Department of Defense, 2003), 3. Emphasis added.

12. DoD, *Transformation Planning Guidance,* 3–4.

13. Paul Bracken, "The Military after Next," *The Washington Quarterly* 16, no. 4 (1993): 157–174.

14. William A. Owens, "The Emerging System of Systems," in *Proceedings of the U.S. Naval Institute,* May 1995, 36–39. After his retirement from active duty service, Owens continued to promote the RMA in work such as *Lifting the Fog of War* (with Ed Offley) (Baltimore: The Johns Hopkins University Press, 2001), and "The Once and Future Revolution in Military Affairs," *Joint Forces Quarterly* 31 (Summer 2002): 55–61.

15. Arthur K. Cebrowski and John J. Garstka, "Network-Centric Warfare: Its Origin and Future," in *Proceedings of the U.S. Naval Institute,* January 1998, 28–35. A central, but near-impenetrable, text on NCW is David S. Alberts, John J. Garstka, and Frederick P. Stein, *Network Centric Warfare: Developing and Leveraging Information Superiority,* 2nd ed. (Washington, DC: C4ISR Cooperative Research Program, 1999). For a more accessible accounts of network-centric warfare, see Peter J. Dombrowski and Andrew L. Ross, "Transforming the Navy: Punching a Featherbed?" *Naval War College Review* 56, no. 3 (2003): 107–131; and Paul T. Mitchell, *Network Centric Warfare: Coalition Operations in the Age of US Military Primacy,* Adelphi paper 385 (London and New York: Routledge, for the International Institute for Strategic Studies, 2006). A penetrating analytical critique of NCW is provided by Darryn J. Reid, Graham Goodman, Wayne Johnson, and Ralph E. Giffin, "All that Glistens: Is Network-Centric Warfare Really Scientific?" *Defense and Security Analysis* 21, no. 4 (2005): 335–367. At OFT, Cebrowski continued to call for "placing a few big bets." See Arthur Cebrowski, "What is Transformation?" Office of Force Transformation, Washington, DC (no date) (http://www.oft.osd.mil/what_is_transformation.cfm.)

16. A valuable assessment of the Base Force, BUR, and 1997 QDR is provided by Eric V. Larson, David T. Orletsky, and Kristen Leuschner, *Defense Planning in a Decade of Change: Lessons from the Base Force, Bottom-Up Review, and Quadrennial Defense Review* (Santa Monica: RAND, 2001).

17. General Colin L. Powell, *National Military Strategy of the United States* (Washington, DC: Joint Chiefs of Staff, 1992).

18. Les Aspin, *Report of the Bottom-Up Review* (Washington, DC: Department of Defense, 1993).

19. William S. Cohen, *Report of the Quadrennial Defense Review* (Washington, DC: Department of Defense, 1997).

20. National Defense Panel, *Transforming Defense: National Security in the 21st Century* (Arlington, VA: National Defense Panel, 1997).

21. National Defense Panel, *Transforming Defense,* i; emphasis added.

22. National Defense Panel, *Transforming Defense,* iv.

23. National Defense Panel, *Transforming Defense,* 43.

24. National Defense Panel, *Transforming Defense,* 43–48.

25. Steven Metz, "America's Defense Transformation: A Conceptual and Political History," *Defence Studies* 6, no. 1 (2006): 1–25.

26. The multidimensional nature of an RMA or transformation is also emphasized in Colin S. Gray, "Technology as a Dynamic of Defence Transformation," *Defence Studies* 6, no. 1 (2006): 26–51.

27. Governor George W. Bush, "A Period of Consequences," speech at The Citadel, September 23, 1999.

28. Department of Defense (DoD), *Quadrennial Defense Review Report* (Washington, DC: Department of Defense, 2001), 40. Emphasis added.

29. DoD, *Quadrennial Defense Review Report,* vi, ix.

30. Note the centrality of IT in the discussions of transformation's technology requirements provided by Bruce Berkowitz, *The New Face of War: How War Will Be Fought in the 21st Century* (New York: The Free Press, 2003); Bill Owens, with Ed Offley, *Lifting the Fog of War* (Baltimore: The Johns Hopkins University Press, 2001), 97–149; and Douglas A. Macgregor, *Transformation Under Fire: Revolutionizing How America Fights* (Westport: Praeger, 2003), 249–283.

31. David S. Alberts, John J. Garstka, and Frederick P. Stein, *Network Centric Warfare,* 15.

32. For an exploration of the implications of the IT revolution for international security see Emily O. Goldman, ed., *National Security in the Information Age* (London: Frank Cass, 2004).

33. On the DoD's enormous bandwidth requirements, see Tim Weiner, "Pentagon Envisioning a Costly Internet for War," *New York Times,* November 13, 2004; and Susan M. Menke, "Pentagon Weighs Satellite Needs," *Washington Post,* November 22, 2004.

34. Rumsfeld's "Long War" speech on February 2, 2006, came on the eve of the Pentagon's release of its 2006 Quadrennial Defense Review (QDR).

35. Max Boot, *War Made New: Technology, Warfare, and the Course of History, 1500 to Today* (New York: Gotham Books: 2006).

36. Congressional Budget Office, *Replacing and Repairing Aging Equipment used in Iraq and Afghanistan: The Army's Reset Program* (Washington, DC: CBO, September 2007), ix.

37. Elisabeth Bumiller, "McCain Sees Troops Coming Home by 2013," *New York Times,* May 15, 2008.

38. Secretary Gates's responses to the advance policy questions posed by the SASC are available at http://armed-services.senate.gov/statemnt/2006/December/Gates%2012–05–06.pdf (accessed March 15, 2007). Robert Gates, swearing-in remarks, The Pentagon, 18 December 2006; http://www.defenselink.mil/speeches/speech.aspx?speechid=1077 (accessed on March 15, 2007).

39. Admiral M. G. Mullen (USN, chairman of the Joint Chiefs of Staff), "CJCS Guidance for 2007–2008," October 1, 2007.

40. For a systematic assessment of the gap between transformation visions and rhetoric and USN plans and programs, see Peter J. Dombrowski and Andrew L. Ross, "Transforming the Navy: Punching a Featherbed?" *Naval War College Review* 56, no. 3 (2003): 107–131.

41. As champions of disruptive innovation have done in the past; see Terry C. Pierce, *Warfighting and Disruptive Technologies: Disguising Innovation* (London and New York: Frank Cass, 2004).

42. Important exceptions to this generalization are the resources controlled by government agencies like the Defense Advanced Research Projects Agency, the Office of Naval Research, and the numerous federal laboratories, among many others, that disburse taxpayer dollars for science and technology and research and development projects. In theory, the military benefits not only from the Office of the Secretary of Defense (OSD) and service-funded projects, but also from civilian programs run by organizations like the National Science Foundation. For an overview of federal spending in these areas, see Michael E. Davey et al., *Federal Research and Development Funding, FY2008* (Washington, DC: Congressional Research Service, 2007).

43. A point recognized by the National Defense Panel's discussion of "Transforming the Industrial Base" in *Transforming Defense*, 74–77.

44. For more details see, among others, Peter J. Dombrowski, Eugene Gholz, and Andrew L. Ross, "Military Transformation and the Defense Industry After Next" Newport paper 18, (Newport, RI: Naval War College Press, 2003), 21–28.

45. The post–cold war era was hardly the first period of defense industry consolidation. For historical perspectives see, for example, Aaron L. Friedberg, *In the Shadow of the Garrison State: America's Anti-statism and its Cold War Strategy* (Princeton: Princeton University Press, 2000), especially chapter 6–7.

46. *PRNewswire*, "Defense Mergers & Acquisitions Tallies $40 Billion in 2006 Deals; 2007 Sizzles With $25 Billion in Deals to Date," April 7, 2007.

47. Linda R. Cohen and Roger Noll, "Government Support for R&D," in *The Technology Pork Barrel*, ed. Linda R. Cohen and Roger Noll (Washington, DC: Brookings Institution, 1991), 25.

48. For example, Ann Markusen, "The Rise of World Weapons," *Foreign Policy* 114 (Spring 1999), 40–51.

49. Some of these themes are further developed in Andrew L. Ross, "Defense Industry Globalization: Contrarian Observations," in *Defense Industry Globalization*, (Washington, DC: The Atlantic Council of the United States, 2002), 35–42.

50. John A. Alic, L. M. Branscomb, A. B. Carter, and G. L. Epstein, *Beyond Spinoff: Military and Commercial Technologies in a Changing World* (Boston: Harvard Business School Press, 1992).

51. For a positive assessment see Michael Oden, "Cashing In, Cashing Out, and Converting: Restructuring the Defense Industrial Base in the 1990s," in *Arming the Future: A Defense Industry for the 21st Century*, ed. Ann R. Markusen and Sean S. Costigan (New York: Council on Foreign Relations Press, 1999), 74–105.

52. As Terrence Guay observes, this is not necessarily the case in other countries and regions. In Europe, for example, a number of large defense contractors are also major players in civilian markets. Terrence R. Guay, *Globalization and its Implications for the Defense Industrial Base* (Carlisle, PA: U.S. Army War College, 2007), http://www.StrategicStudiesInstitute.army.mil.

53. Large defense firms that rely on both military and civilian contracts, like Boeing for example, do so for historical reasons and/or because of the unique characteristics of their sector.

54. Peter J. Dombrowski, Eugene Gholz, and Andrew L. Ross, *Military Transformation and the Defense Industry after Next*, Newport paper 18 (Newport, RI: Naval War College Press, 2003).

55. Peter Dombrowski and Eugene Gholz, *Buying Military Transformation: Technological Innovation and the Defense Industry* (New York: Columbia University Press, 2006).

56. See for example BAE Systems, which bought a number of mid-tier American firms but has been forced by U.S. regulations to firewall its American operations from those in the United Kingdom or elsewhere.

57. Dombrowski and Gholz, *Buying Military Transformation*, 132–135.

58. For one example, on the decreased size of the acquisition workforce and its implications, see Stephen Howard Chadwick, *Defense Acquisition: Overview, Issues, and Options for Congress*, CRS report for Congress (Washington, DC: Congressional Research Service, 2007), 28.

59. Dombrowski and Gholz, *Buying Military Transformation*, 132.

60. Keith Hartley and Todd Sandler, "The Future of the Defense Firm," http://www.york.ac.uk/depts/econ/documents/research/region.pdf (accessed May 20, 2008).

61. On the three levels of systems integration see Dombrowski and Gholz, *Buying Military Transformation*, 112–115.

62. Clay Wilson, *Network Centric Operations: Background and Oversight Issues for Congress* (Washington, DC: Congressional Research Service, 2007), 35–41.

63. Rebekah Gordon, "Littoral Combat Ship Mission Modules to be Tested on Other Vessels," *Inside the Navy,* May 12, 2008.

64. Ron O'Rourke, *Navy Force Structure and Shipbuilding Plans: Background and Issues for Congress* (Washington, DC: Congressional Research Service, 2008), especially 5.

65. Dan Taylor, "Roughhead: Navy Looking For A Ceiling Over The 313-Ship Floor," *Inside the Navy,* February 18, 2008.

66. Scott C. Truver, "Taking Back the Littoral: US Navy Littoral Combat Ship Programme Update . . . And More!" *Naval Forces* 27, no. 3 (2006).

67. Geoff Fein, "Team Effort Leads Lockheed Martin LCS Design," *Defense Daily* 226, no. 22 (2005): 1.

68. The Freedom's hull design was commercial and designers underestimated the difficulty of modify it to make it suitable for naval operations.

69. Christopher J. Castelli, "Audit Exposes Failed Management of Troubled Littoral Warship," *Inside the Navy,* February 4, 2008.

70. On modularity variants in the context of the LCS program, see Robert O. Work, *Naval Transformation and the Littoral Combat Ship* (Washington, DC: Center for Strategic and Budgetary Assessments, 2004), especially 119–121, http://www.csbaonline.

71. Ronald O'Rourke, *Navy Littoral Combat Ship (LCS) Program: Background, Oversight Issues, and Options for Congress* (Washington, DC: Congressional Research Service, 2008).

72. Whether the FCS will actually fulfill this role is unclear.

73. Boeing corporate Web site (http://www.boeing.com/defense-space/ic/fcs/bia/index.html).

74. Congressional Budget Office, *The Army's Future Combat Systems Program and Alternatives* (Washington, DC: Congressional Budget Office, 2006), 40.

75. General Accounting Office (GAO), *Defense Acquisitions: Role of Lead Systems Integrator on Future Combat Systems Programs Poses Oversight Challenges,* GAO-07–380 (Washington, DC: GAO 2007).

76. GAO, *Defense Acquisitions.* Definition adapted from page 1.

77. GAO, *Defense Acquisitions,* 10.

78. Valerie Bailey Grasso, *Defense Acquisition: Use of Lead System Integrators—Background, Oversight, Issues and Options for Congress,* CRS report for Congress (Washington, DC: CRS, 2007), 3–5.

79. Robert Brodsky, Zack Phillips, and Katherine McIntire Peters, "Big Contracts, Big Problems," *Government Executive* 39, no. 14 (2007): 27.

80. Thom Shanker, "Gates Says New Arms Must Play Role Now," *New York Times,* May 14, 2008. Relevant excerpts from the Gates speech at a Heritage Foundation sponsored conference include: "I have noticed too much of a tendency towards what might be called next-war-itis—the propensity of much of the defense establishment to be in favor of what might be needed in a future conflict. . . . Over all, the kinds of capabilities we will most likely need in the years ahead will often resemble the kinds of capabilities we need today."

81. GAO, *Defense Acquisitions,* 63.

82. On the imperatives of the new tri-service maritime strategy, see "A Cooperative Strategy for 21st Century Seapower," presented by the chief of naval operations and the commandants of the U.S. Marine Corps and U.S. Coast Guard at the International Seapower Symposium, Newport, RI, October 17, 2007, http://www.navy.mil/maritime.

9

The European Defense Industry in the 21st Century: Challenges and Responses

Richard A. Bitzinger

The European arms industry has long been under strain. In recent years, however, pressures on the European defense sector have increased as the U.S. defense industry—Europe's largest competitor in this area—has widened the economic and technological gap. This disparity has been further exacerbated by the process of U.S. defense transformation, which threatens to drive this transatlantic wedge even wider. Increasingly, the European defense industry faces a fundamental challenge of maintaining its economic and technological competitiveness.

The early 21st century, therefore, is a time of particular transition and change for the European arms industry. Many issues critical to the future of the European defense-industrial base, long ignored or deferred, are finally being addressed, including:

- How are European defense firms going to square the circle between the growing U.S. economic and technological challenge and static or declining European defense resources?
- What is the optimal structure and form for the European defense industry to ensure its economic and technological competitiveness?
- What future *national* responses regarding defense-industrial policy, requirements, procurement, and production are likely to be the most—and least—effective solutions to these economic and technological challenges?
- What is the role and significance of defense industry internationalization (i.e., regionalization and globalization) in this readjustment process?
- What is the impact of the still quite powerful countervailing forces of nationalistic protectionism and of transnationalism on the process of creating a more Europeanized defense-industrial base?

How Europe deals with these issues and challenges will have obvious implications for the United States, including (1) the U.S. defense industry's continued access to the European arms market (i.e., the emergence of an increasingly protectionist Fortress Europe when it comes to defense research and development (R&D), production, and procurement), (2) the U.S. government's continued access to innovative European technologies and other kinds of defense resources, (3) the future of transatlantic armaments cooperation, (4) the U.S.-European competition over third-party arms markets, and (5) controlling the sale of advanced European defense systems to U.S.-embargoed countries (such as China). How these trends might affect major U.S. defense companies with large holdings or interests in Europe, or, conversely, whether European defense firms with large investments in the United States will be particularly affected by future European actions. Consequently, the next several years promise to be a period of considerable transition and stress for the world's two largest defense industries.

THE U.S. ECONOMIC AND TECHNOLOGICAL CHALLENGE TO THE EUROPEAN DEFENSE INDUSTRY

Two broad developments within the U.S. defense technology and industrial base constitute a growing challenge to the European defense industry. In the first place, the consolidation and rationalization that has taken place within the U.S. defense industry over the past 15 years has resulted in the formation of a handful of very large, highly concentrated—and highly competitive—American arms manufacturers. At the same time, the effort to transform the U.S. armed forces along the lines of the information technologies (IT)-based Revolution in military affairs (RMA) has stimulated new investments in U.S. R&D that, in turn, are widening the technological gap between the U.S. and European defense industries. Both of these developments threaten to leave individual European defense companies weak and marginalized in the global arms business. Therefore, they form the most critical external drivers affecting the regionalization and globalization of the European defense industry.

The U.S. Defense Industry's Challenge to Europe

The consolidation and rationalization of the U.S. defense industry since the end of the cold war has left it much more adept than its European counterparts when it comes to innovating and competing in the global arms marketplace. During the 1990s, the U.S. defense sector downsized considerably, closing down excess production facilities and eliminating hundreds of thousands of positions from the workforce. At the same time, several large-scale mergers and acquisitions (M&As) took place within the U.S. defense-industrial base, resulting in the emergence of five mega–defense companies: Boeing, Lockheed Martin, Northrop Grumman, Raytheon, and General Dynamics. These M&As have greatly reduced competition in the U.S. defense sector and concentrated armaments production in the hands of just a few, very large defense firms. Whereas in the past, most U.S. defense firms were engaged in just one or two areas of armaments production, today's mega–defense companies are active in several different sectors, ranging from aerospace to shipbuilding to land systems. Moreover, each mega-company has expanded its reach into the all-important IT sector and is now as engaged in electronics and software as in military aircraft or armored vehicles or naval shipbuilding.

Consequently, these five mega-firms now control more key U.S. military programs and have access to more U.S. Department of Defense (DoD) R&D funding—this is particularly important as U.S. expenditures for military equipment have increased dramatically since the turn of the millennium; U.S. spending on procurement and R&D more than doubled between fiscal year (FY)2000 and FY2008, from $116 billion to $255 billion in recent years. Whereas in FY1990, the 10 largest U.S. defense contractors accounted for only 28 percent of all prime contracts, in FY2006, *the top five alone* accounted for 28.5 percent—in addition to receiving 56 percent of all DoD funding for research, development, testing, and evaluation (RDT&E).

As a result, just a handful of U.S. defense firms dominate the global arms industry. In 2007, 4 of the world's top 5 defense companies, and 7 of the top 10, were American; only Britain's BAE Systems (which in 2007 ranked number three in the world) is as large in the defense business as these firms (see Figure 9.1). In addition, these U.S. mega–defense companies have emerged as critical lead systems integrators, capable of managing very large, complicated acquisition programs that require amalgamating several disparate pieces of military hardware (and, increasingly, software) into a single functioning system of systems.[1] As such, these firms can offer themselves as one-stop shops for customers seeking solutions to highly complex military requirements.[2]

U.S. arms manufacturers dominate in two of the world's most critical arms markets—at home and in the global arms export business. The U.S. defense market accounts for almost half of all the world's arms purchases, and it is one of the few arms markets that are cur-

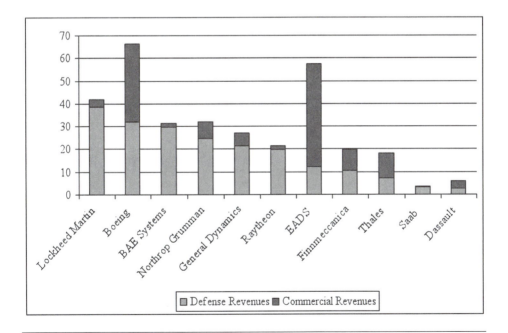

FIGURE 9.1   Major U.S. and European defense firms, 2007 (revenues in billions of U.S. dollars)
Source: Defense News

rently growing. At the same time, U.S. defense firms easily capture more than 90 percent of all defense contracting in the home market. This large—and admittedly highly protected—national market gives U.S. defense firms a solid base of money-spinning procurement contracts and lucrative R&D funding from which to expand into the global arms market.

In addition, the U.S. defense industry dominates the global trade in off-the-shelf arms sales, regularly capturing 40 to 50 percent of a worldwide arms market that was worth around $60 billion in 2007.[3] Despite this predominance, the major U.S. defense firms actually have a low dependency upon on non-U.S. markets for their overall incomes. In 2007, for example, overseas military sales accounted for only 15 percent of Lockheed Martin's total revenues, 9 percent of Boeing's, 10 percent of General Dynamics', and 5.5 percent of Northrop Grumman's.[4]

Ironically, therefore, U.S. firms, almost as a sideline effort, are confronting European arms producers in third-party markets that are essential to their survival. The U.S. defense industry is under much less economic pressure overall to look aggressively for business beyond its borders, and yet it leads the global arms export business. U.S. arms producers have considerable clout when it comes to foreign arms sales. Large domestic production runs permit it to sell systems overseas at very competitive prices. It can also offer very attractive industrial and technological inducements (i.e., offsets and coproduction rights). The U.S. government can use its superpower status to pressure allies to buy American. In addition, the U.S. defense industry's deep pockets—that is, its ability to access considerable R&D funding from the U.S. Defense Department—ensures that it will remain on the technical-industrial cutting-edge, and that it will be able to develop and manufacture military systems that will be very attractive, both technologically and financially, on the international market.

U.S. Defense Transformation and Europe

The ongoing transformation of the U.S. military represents a second technological and industrial challenge to the European defense industry. Defense transformation, centered on the IT-based RMA (IT-RMA), has preoccupied the U.S. DoD for over a decade. For the United States, defense transformation is more than modernization—it is nothing short of a paradigm shift in the character and conduct of warfare. Krepinevich, for example, argues that an RMA occurs when:

> the application of new technologies into a significant number of military systems combines with innovative operational concepts and organizational adaptation in a way that fundamentally alters the character and conduct of a conflict. It does so by producing a dramatic increase . . . in the combat potential and military effectiveness of armed forces.[5]

In a similar vein, RAND defines an RMA as

> a paradigm shift in the nature and conduct of military operations which either renders obsolete or irrelevant one or more core competencies in a dominant player, or creates one or more core competencies in some dimension of warfare, or both.[6]

Consequently, defense transformation is fundamentally a process of discontinuous, disruptive, and revolutionary change, as opposed to incremental, sustaining, and evolutionary change.[7]

The U.S. transformational model is inexorably linked to the information revolution of the past two or three decades and to resultant emerging concepts of *network-centric warfare* (NCW). The information revolution has made possible significant innovation and improvement in the fields of sensors, seekers, data management, computing and communications, automation, range, and precision.[8] NCW, in turn, utilizes these breakthroughs in information technology in order to achieve exponential improvements in battlefield knowledge, connectivity, and response. NCW, according to the U.S. DoD's Office of Defense Transformation

> generates increased combat power by networking sensors, decision makers, and shooters to achieve shared awareness, increased speed of command, high tempo of operations, greater lethality, increased survivability, and a degree of self-synchronization.[9]

The U.S. transformational model does not imply the simple overlay of new technologies and new hardware over existing force structures. It entails fundamentally changing the way a military does its business—doctrinally, organizationally, and institutionally. It also requires advanced systems integration skills to knit disparate military systems into together complex operational networks. Finally, it demands elemental changes in the ways militaries procure critical military equipment, and reform of the national and defense technological and industrial bases that contribute to the development and production of transformational systems. All this, in turn, requires vision and leadership at the top in order to develop the basic concepts of defense transformation, establish the necessary institutional and political momentum for implementing transformation, and allocate the financial resources and human capital required for the task of implementation.[10] For all these reasons, therefore, transformation has major implications for the future course of U.S. defense and security policy.

For most of Europe, however, network-centric warfare is less about *transformation*—that is, disruptive innovation—than about *force modernization*—that is, a process of evolutionary, steady-state, and sustaining innovation.[11] There exists considerably more skepticism in Europe as to whether the nature of NCW is truly transformational and whether the U.S. model is applicable to Europe (in addition to whether it is even affordable). On the whole, European conceptualizations of defense transformation and the IT-RMA are not nearly as ambitious nor as strategic as in the United States. Europe has been slower to adopt transformational technologies or to adopt them in a sufficiently comprehensive and synergistic manner.

In general, most European countries are pursuing a more selective and incremental approach toward applying transformational technologies and systems to their armed forces, utilizing them more as force multipliers.[12] The United Kingdom's Network Enabled Capability (NEC) concept, for instance, is nowhere as far-reaching as the U.S. NCW, and it is intended more to improve the compatibility and interoperability with U.S. forces in joint operations; key elements of the British NEC concept are improved command, control, communications, computing, intelligence, surveillance, reconnaissance (C4ISR) (e.g., the

Bowman tactical radio system, the Skynet 5 communication satellite system), force projection (the C-17 transport aircraft, new air-to-air refueling aircraft, two new aircraft carriers), and precision-strike (the Storm Shadow cruise missile).[13] France is currently engaged in some rather modest demonstrator programs to improve its command and control capabilities, mainly at the tactical level, rather than designing new network concepts for the entire French armed forces.[14] Elements of a future new French C4ISR system include the Syracuse satellite communications system, the Helios II military surveillance satellite, and the MALE (medium-altitude, long-endurance) UAV (unmanned aerial vehicle).[15] For its part, Sweden has been experimenting with network-based defense (NBD) since the late 1990s, based on the concept of a highly networked military organization, thus permitting improved situational awareness, more integrated command, control, and communications, faster decision making, and greater flexibility in responding to threats; at the same time, however, Sweden is not anticipating any major changes in its present force structure, continuing to rely heavily on conscript forces, albeit smaller and more deployable, oriented mainly toward defending the country against armed attacks.[16]

European transformational efforts still appear to be more platform-oriented than capabilities- or effects-based. In fact, defense transformation in Europe still seems both piecemeal and post hoc—that is, designating a preexisting or long-anticipated military hardware to be a transformational system. Germany, for example, is making only modest investments in such areas as force projection (the A400M transport aircraft), precision-strike (the Taurus stand-off weapon), and missile defense (the Medium Extended Air Defense System, or MEADS). British and French force modernization plans continue to emphasize the acquisition of such items as aircraft carriers and combat aircraft, while Sweden places its Gripen fighter jet at the center of its NBD concept, as a prime agent for information gathering and precision engagement. Consequently, *modernization plus,* rather than transformation, would appear to be a more accurate description of current European military programs.

In addition, there does not appear to be any pan-European transformational vision that in turn drives requirements, programs, and interoperability, particularly on a regional basis. National European concepts of network-centric warfare do not emphasize jointness and interoperability with other militaries. In particular, many national C4ISR networks are not designed to share data about threats and engagements with alliance partners.[17] The one possible exception is the United Kingdom, and its NEC model is geared mainly toward improving coalition operations with the United States.[18]

Macroeconomic conditions in Europe's defense sector have only compounded the European disadvantage when it comes to developing transformational technologies and systems. In the first place, Europe simply is not able to keep up with the United States when it comes to dedicating the kind of resources necessary to match U.S. transformational efforts. After the cold war, total defense spending for the six largest arms-producing countries in Europe (the United Kingdom, France, Germany, Italy, Spain, and Sweden) fell 12 percent between 1991 and 2004 (as measured in constant 2003 U.S. dollars). Defense R&D—the seed corn for transformational technologies and systems—was hit particularly hard. According to the Aerospace and Defense Industries Association of Europe (ASD), R&D spending by the European Union (EU) member states on military aerospace fell by 47 percent from 1999 to

2003, from €5.7 billion ($8.1 billion) to €3 billion ($3.9 billion). Since then, defense spending has been mostly static.

The United States greatly outspends Europe when it comes to defense. According to statistics put out by the European Defense Agency (EDA), the EU, as a whole, spent €41.8 billion ($60 billion) on equipment and R&D in 2007. In comparison, U.S. expenditures on equipment and R&D for the same year totaled approximately €154.9 billion ($221 billion). In other words, Washington spent more than *three* times as much on equipment as the entire EU, and almost *six* times as much on R&D. In addition, the share of the U.S. defense budget going to procurement and R&D is nearly two-thirds as large again as Europe's: 34 percent of all military expenditures versus 20.5 percent for the EU.

A fragmented European arms market, combined with the predominance of legacy programs, further rations and restricts the ability of European militaries to make the required investments in transformational technologies and systems. European arms procurement is currently beset with duplicative and competing programs, such as three fighter aircraft (Rafale, Eurofighter, and Gripen), two heavy-lift utility helicopters (the EH-101 and the NH-90), at least three air-defense surface combatants (the Franco-Italian Horizon and the Spanish F-100 frigates, and the British Type-45 destroyer), and countless armored vehicles. This redundancy reduces the overall buying power of European procurement funding even further. Finally, just a few large legacy programs have siphoned off most available funds for R&D and procurement; the Eurofighter, for example, is expected to account for over half of German, Italian, and Spanish equipment spending for the next several years.[19]

In general, current defense transformational models require shifting substantial spending away from traditional platforms and systems in order to meet transformational needs in such areas as surveillance, targeting, command and control, and precision engagement. These requirements in turn are "likely to require difficult decisions related to force structures, the mix of platforms and enabling capabilities and the like."[20] It is a choice that few European countries presently appear willing or able to make.

According to a report put out in the late 1990s by the National Defense University, key U.S. allies in Europe were falling far behind the United States in harnessing the key information-based technologies of the RMA. Not only are these countries' militaries spending too little on RMA-related military R&D, the report argued, but they lacked both a "vibrant information technology market" and defense industries that are "agile enough to buy the best from that market." As a result, "European forces cannot acquire information-age capabilities from industries that are not able consistently to provide them at affordable prices."[21]

Since this report was written, the transatlantic divide has, if anything, worsened. To be sure, the European defense industry possesses considerable nascent skills and know-how when it comes to developing the technologies and systems that would comprise elements of a transformed force.[22] However, the slowness or reluctance on the part of European governments and militaries (both on a national and regional scale) to adopt transformational concepts and to make adequate investments in transformational and next-generation technologies and systems has only widened the technological-industrial gap between the U.S. and European defense industries and put the latter at an even greater disadvantage.

THE EUROPEAN RESPONSE: REGIONALIZATION AND GLOBALIZATION

The growing global technological and economic dominance of the U.S. defense industry is a direct and grave challenge to the future relevance of the European arms industry, its closest rival. This competition, in turn, has been one of the major forces behind the regionalization and internationalization of the European defense industry.

The Inadequacy of National Responses

As in the United States, the European defense industry has undergone considerable consolidation and rationalization. During the 1990s, national champions emerged in several key arms-producing countries in western Europe as the result of privatization efforts and successive M&A activities; these national champions included BAE Systems (United Kingdom), DaimlerChrysler Aerospace (Germany), Aerospatiale Matra (France), Finmeccanica (Italy), and Saab (Sweden). Each one of these firms more or less came to dominate arms manufacturing in their respective countries. In addition, the European defense sector underwent its own radical downsizing, eliminating roughly half of its workforce—approximately 450,000 jobs—during the 1990s; within just the aerospace industry, the number of workers employed in defense production fell from 276,000 in 1990 to 148,000 in 2003.

Such efforts, enacted on a strictly national scale, have been an inadequate solution, however. National markets were still too small to support even a heavily rationalized defense industry. European arms manufacturers, therefore, have had little choice but to think and act globally. For one thing, Europe's defense industry is, in general, much more exposed to and dependent on foreign markets: at present, companies such as BAE Systems, Thales, Dassault, and Finmeccanica earn up to 75 percent of their revenues from foreign sales.

At the same time, the escalating financial and technological demands of state-of-the-art arms production, declining defense spending at home, and stiffening competition from U.S. defense firms have increasingly driven European arms manufacturers to look beyond their own national borders in order to leverage technology breakthroughs, rationalize military R&D and production, increase efficiencies and economies of scale in arms production, and penetrate foreign markets. Internationalizing their operations, therefore, has become more or less a simple matter of economic survival for Europe's defense firms, while European governments and militaries need to collaborate with each other in order to achieve any significant technological synergies or cost efficiencies.

The Regionalization of the European Defense Industry

Consequently, Europe's defense sector is generally pursuing internationalization—both on a regional and, increasingly, on a global scale—as a core corporate strategy.

In the first place, since the end of the cold war, the European defense industry has increasingly engaged in pan-European solutions to pan-European problems of economic and technological competitiveness, *particularly when it comes to critical, next-generation technologies and military systems.* The past decade has seen the European defense industry expand—on a regional, cooperative basis—into program areas that were previously ceded to the U.S. industry, such as:

- **Strategic airlift:** *A400M transport aircraft* (Belgium, France, Germany, Luxembourg, Portugal, Spain, Turkey, United Kingdom)
- **Advanced air-to-air missiles:** *Meteor* (France, Germany, Italy, Spain, Sweden, United Kingdom); *IRIS-T* (Germany, Greece, Italy, Norway, Sweden)
- **Space systems:** *Galileo satellite navigation system* (France, Germany, Italy, Spain, United Kingdom); *Helios II surveillance satellite* (France, Germany); *Skynet 5 satellite communications system* (France, Germany, United Kingdom)
- **Unmanned combat systems:** *Neuron UCAV* (France, Greece, Spain, Sweden, Switzerland)
- **Standoff precision-guided weapons:** *Storm Shadow/Scalp* (France, United Kingdom); *Taurus* (Germany, Sweden)
- **Missile defenses:** *FSAF/PAAMS surface-to-air missile* (France, Italy, United Kingdom)

Accordingly, Europe's leading defense firms have greatly expanded their regional operations through different types of pan-European teaming arrangements, strategic alliances, joint venture companies, and even M&As. In many areas of European armaments production, therefore, multinational collaborative efforts have become the norm and are rooted in transnational enterprises. Important pan-European arms manufacturing operations include:

- **Airbus Military Company,** a consortium operated by Airbus Industries to design and manufacture the A400M transport aircraft; members countries include Belgium, France, Germany, Luxembourg, Portugal, Spain, Turkey, and the United Kingdom.
- **Astrium,** a Franco-German-Spanish satellite joint venture company, which also owns and operates satellite production facilities in the United Kingdom.
- **Eurocopter,** a Franco-German joint venture company that produces, among other things, the Tiger attack helicopter.
- **MBDA,** an Anglo-French-Italian joint venture missile company—that additionally owns minority stakes in two German missile firms, BGT (20 percent) and LFK (30 percent), as well as a 40 percent share in *Empress de Missiles Espanola,* Spain's leading guided weapons company—and that is the lead contractor for the Meteor missile.
- **NH Industries,** a Franco-German-Italian-Dutch consortium building the NH-90 heavy-lift military helicopter.

At the same time, Europe's leading arms industries have increasingly pursued M&A activities beyond their borders, acquiring or making substantial investments in defense firms in other European countries. As such, the regionalization of arms production can be viewed as a transnational extension of the overall consolidation process taking place within the defense industry. For example, BAE Systems is a partner in MBDA and Airbus Industries, and it owns defense subsidiaries in Sweden (Bofors Defense and Hägglunds); it also holds a 20 percent stake in the Swedish military aircraft manufacturer Saab. Thales, a self-described multidomestic company, has acquired wholly owned subsidiaries in both the Netherlands and the United Kingdom, as well as sizable investments in other defense concerns in

Germany, Italy, Portugal, and Spain. Currently, approximately one-third percent of Thales's European workforce is based outside France.

The European Aeronautic Defense and Spain Company (EADS) is perhaps the ultimate result of pan-European defense consolidation. It was created in 2000 through the merger of DaimlerChrysler Aerospace (DASA) of Germany, France's Aerospatiale Matra, and CASA of Spain. EADS is a truly transnational defense firm: the company is headquartered in a neutral country (the Netherlands), and it has two chief executive officers, one French and one German. In addition to controlling 80 percent of Airbus Industries and 47 percent of Dassault, the French combat aircraft manufacturer, EADS owns and or has substantial shareholdings in several pan-European joint ventures, including Eurocopter, MBDA, Astrium, Taurus systems, Inmize (a Spanish missile company), and ATR (a Franco-Italian joint venture building regional transport aircraft). Outside of its three home countries, EADS also has a large industrial footprint in the United Kingdom, with over 12,000 employees, and it also owns a 27 percent stake in Patria Industries, Finland's leading defense firm.

Extra-European Globalization: Embracing the Second-Tier Arms Producers

In addition to regionalizing operations on a pan-European scale, Europe's leading defense firms have increasingly expanded beyond Europe and the transatlantic relationship in order to create a truly global network of ownership arrangements, international joint ventures, and other cooperative approaches. In this regard, European arms manufacturers are much more globalized than are U.S. defense companies, particularly when it comes to the second-tier arms-producing states in Africa, Asia, and Latin America:

- BAE Systems operates several subsidiary or joint venture operations in Australia, Canada, Singapore, and South Africa. For example, BAE Systems acquired a 20 percent stake in South Africa's Advanced Technologies and Engineering (ATE), and it recently gained that country's OMC armored vehicle manufacturing firm when it bought Alvis.
- Thales has operations or holdings in several non-European countries, including Australia, Brazil, South Korea, and South Africa. It owns 100 percent of Australian Defense Industries (now Thales Australia), the country's leading producer of naval vessels, military vehicles, and ordnance, and also operates subsidiaries in Singapore (Avimo) and South Africa (African Defense Systems), as well as joint ventures with South Korea's Samsung Electronics and with Malaysia's Sapura. Altogether, nearly 15 percent of the company's workforce is located outside of Europe.
- EADS has industrial operations and joint ventures in several regions around the world, mainly through the ongoing activities of its national corporate groupings. CASA of Spain, for example, has had a longstanding arrangement with Indonesian Aerospace to jointly manufacture the CN-235 transport aircraft. DASA, meanwhile, already had a sizable industrial presence in South Africa's arms industry prior to the EADS merger. Eurocopter controls Australian Aerospace Resources, and it is currently producing the EC-120 light helicopter in cooperation with Singapore Technologies Aerospace and CATIC of China. Finally, Airbus (which is 80 percent owned by

EADS) recently signed up South Africa as a partner on the A400M transport aircraft project—the program's first non-European industrial participant.

- Several smaller European defense firms have increasingly globalized their operations. Saab recently acquired Grintek, a South African defense electronics firm, while the French jet engine manufacturer Snecma recently acquired Denel Airmotive of South Africa, a maker of small aero-engines. Dassault owns a 5.7 percent share in the Brazil aircraft manufacturer Embraer.

Reaching Out to Russia and China

The European defense industry is also seeking to expand cooperation with Russia and China, albeit slowly and haphazardly. These efforts have tended to revolve around ad hoc collaborative programs rather than joint ventures or foreign direct investment (FDI), as Beijing and Moscow place considerable controls over foreign participation in their defense industries. For example, Eurocopter operated a joint venture company with the Mil and Kazan helicopter companies during the 1990s to develop a larger version of the Mil-38 transport helicopter, but Eurocopter withdrew in 2003 after the Russians passed a law restricting foreign management and intellectual rights. Current Russian-Europe defense projects include a joint arrangement between EADS and Khrunichev to build space launch vehicles, and an export variant of the Kamov Ka-52 attack helicopter, equipped with a French avionic suite integrated by Sextant Avionique of France. In addition, the French companies Thales and Snecma worked with MiG-MAPO to develop the MiG-AT trainer jet, supplying the engines and avionics for the aircraft, while Aermacchi of Italy collaborated with the Yakovlev Aviation Corporation on design and development the Yak-130 trainer aircraft.

In general, however, Russian-European defense-industrial cooperation has been a difficult affair, due mainly to a lack of money or markets. Several German companies, including DASA and BMW Rolls-Royce, cooperated with Russia and Ukraine in the late 1990s on the An-70 transport aircraft, but this joint program was effectively killed when the A400M was initiated. The MiG-AT program has so far failed to secure any orders, while Aermacchi eventually pulled out of the Yak-130 program and began marketing its own version of the aircraft as the M-346 trainer jet.

China has been a largely proscribed market since the 1989 arms embargo imposed by the EU in the wake of the Tiananmen Square massacre. This ban, however, covers only weapons systems and does not apply to the transfer of nonlethal and dual-use equipment to China. In fact, European defense firms have collaborated with the Chinese on a number of dual-use programs, including helicopters, radars, jet engines, and satellite technology. Eurocopter, for example, is coproducing the EC-120 lightweight utility helicopter with China and Singapore. China also license-produces two other Eurocopter helicopters, the AS-365 (designed as the Z-9 by the Chinese), and the AS-350 (Z-11); both are being produced for the Chinese military in attack helicopter variants carrying antitank missiles. Rolls-Royce has a joint venture with Xian Aero Engine Group to produce turbine engine components. Beijing is a risk-sharing partner in the European Galileo satellite navigation project, and China's Tsinghua University is cooperating with Britain's Surrey Satellite Technology company to develop microsatellites.

A particular concern is that Europe might sell components or subsystems that could greatly contribute to the modernization of the Chinese military and fill critical technology gaps. Europe has considerable expertise in many defense niches that would be of great interest to the Chinese, including air-independent propulsion for submarines, airborne command and control, satellites, sensors, helicopters, jet engines, and advanced manufacturing processes. At the same time, China has both the resources—its defense budget has tripled over the past decade—and the motivations—as an aspiring great power in the Asia-Pacific region—to acquire such capabilities. Should the EU arms embargo be lifted, this would certainly ease the possible transfer of such technologies to China and permit European defense firms to expand their cooperation with Chinese arms manufacturers.

REPERCUSSIONS OF EUROPEAN DEFENSE-INDUSTRIAL GLOBALIZATION

As the European defense-industrial base continues to regionalize and internationalize its operations in order to remain globally competitive, there is growing concern that this process will reinforce a Fortress Europe approach to armaments production that, in turn, will be detrimental to the U.S. defense industry. The EDA, for example, in working to strengthen the European defense technology and industrial base, is generally regarded as inwardly focused on Europe's domestic defense-industrial challenges.[23] As one analyst has argued:

> For France, the EDA is a platform to create a European defense manufacturing base, supported by more spending on R&D and with contract preferences for European firms. In a sense, the EDA transfers France's statist approach to business-government relations to the EU level.[24]

In pursuing pan-European solutions, Europe may knock down protectionist barriers within its borders, only to replace these with a *regionalized* system of protection. In other words, a wider, more open defense market *within* Europe could also lead to a more closed market to arms suppliers *outside* its territory—that is, higher barriers and tougher burdens for non-European defense firms trying to penetrate the European arms market or do business within Europe.

Such a move would naturally have an adverse impact on transatlantic armament collaboration. In the first place, intra-European defense-industrial cooperation is increasing, while transatlantic collaboration—a few large programs (such as the Joint Strike Fighter) notwithstanding—appears to be stagnant. Seth Jones, utilizing the DPB Globalization Database, found that since 1990, "European defense firms were almost twice as likely to pursue coproduction and codevelopment projects with each other than with U.S. firms."[25] Moreover, Europe is using regional armaments programs in order to break into new, heretofore *U.S.-dominated* defense sectors, such as strategic airlift, space-based reconnaissance and navigation systems, standoff precision-strike weapons, and active radar-guided air-to-air missiles. At the same time, in order to gain access to the European arms market, outside—and especially U.S.—defense firms would likely come under increased pressure to sweeten the pot by offering more technology transfers, coproduction rights, joint ventures, and codevelopment arrangements.[26]

European defense-industrial globalization activities taking place outside of Europe and North America raise additional concerns for the U.S. defense industry. Utilizing collaborative projects, joint ventures, and especially FDI, European defense firms have made remarkable progress over the past decade in penetrating arms markets around the world, and this local presence could give them an edge in some countries' future procurement decisions. Many countries around the world increasingly make technology transfer and industrial participation a precondition for arms imports; investing in local arms industries is basically an entrance fee into these markets, and in this regard European defense companies could have a leg-up over their American counterparts. Consequently, the U.S. defense industry could begin to find itself shut out of some foreign markets.

Additionally, European defense firms often use local subsidiaries and joint ventures as jumping-off points to penetrate regional arms markets. Thales, for example, is cooperating with Malaysia's Sapura to help manufacture and market military communications equipment throughout Southeast Asia. Thales also operates a joint venture with South Korea's Samsung to produce avionics, radar, electro-optics, combat systems, and tactical communications and information systems, and which intends to become Northeast Asia's leading defense electronics company by 2015.[27]

Consequently, we could be seeing the emergence of a new hub-and-spoke model of globalized armament production, with Europe's leading defense firms at the core and global supply lines extending out to smaller arms firms in Africa, Asia, and Latin America. The European companies would serve as centers of excellence, providing the process of internationalized armament production with its critical design, development, and systems integration inputs, along with the production of more advanced subsystems, such as engines, wings, sensors, information systems, and other electronics. Arms producers in the periphery would mainly be responsible for supplying niche systems, low-tech items, and some final assembly. Again, by not globalizing, U.S. defense firms could find themselves locked out of innovative and cost-effective ways to develop, manufacture, and market next-generation weapon systems.[28]

At the same time, such globalization efforts may be limited in effect. For one thing, investments in other countries' defense industries are no guarantee of arms sales. Despite France's considerable investment in Embraer, for example, Brazil still cancelled its plans to purchase new fighter aircraft. In addition, the U.S. defense industry still has a lot of clout when it comes to overseas arms sales; it recently defeated its European competition in selling F-16 fighters to Chile and Poland, and in selling F-15 fighters to South Korea. And the United States can offer very attractive offsets and industrial/technological enticements when it wants to—for example, the lucrative codevelopment and subcontracting arrangements it offered to foreign firms partnering on the F-35 Joint Strike Fighter (JSF) program.

Finally, despite all the efforts by European defense firms to establish linkages with defense industries in Asia, Africa, the Middle East, and Latin America, they remain, for the most part, minor investments. In general, Europe and North America are the still the world's two largest arms markets, and the United States in particular is still *the* market to break into (see below). Consequently, these two regions still account for the lion's share of revenues for Europe's major defense firms. Only around one-quarter of BAE Systems' sales in 2004, for example, was to areas outside of Europe and North America, and EADS's was around one-third (including Airbus sales). Finmeccanica sold nearly 80 percent of its output to North America and Europe in 2003, with the rest of the world accounting for only 11 percent of revenues. Even Thales, with its multidomestic business strategy, still relies heavily upon sales to Europe and the United States, which accounted for 70 percent of its corporate income in 2004.

Counter-Regionalism #1: Enduring Protectionism and
Parochialism in the European Defense Industry

Despite the prevailing currents driving European defense firms to seek supranational solutions to the challenges of technological and economic competitiveness, the globalization of the European arms industry—indeed, even the *regionalization* of the arms industry—is by no means a predetermined or clear-cut process. In the first place, protectionist and parochial interests still exert very powerful influences on national decision making when it comes to arms procurement and production. Governments continue to give considerable thought to national requirements when it comes to economic benefits (jobs, industrial participation, export potential, keeping public monies from flowing out of the country), security of supply (self-sufficiency, reducing a country's vulnerability to foreign sanctions or embargoes), and technology (maintaining the national defense technology base). Consequently, even in the United Kingdom—perhaps the most open defense procurement market in Europe—there is still a lot of political pressure to protect home industries and home markets first, and to look for international cooperative avenues when economic and technological considerations force them.[29] Even then, most European governments continue to insist on a fair return (*juste retour*) on their investment in collaborative programs, in terms of work-share and technology sharing.

Even within an ostensibly transnational corporation such as EADS, most armaments production is still conducted on a more or less national basis, and firewalls still exist to protect national proprietary technologies. Germany and Spain, for example, still zealously guard their work-shares on the Eurofighter, as do the German and French divisions of Eurocopter when it comes to building the Franco-German Tiger attack helicopter. International collaborative programs undertaken under the auspices of EADS—such as the A400M transport aircraft or the Skynet 5 communications satellite—are still run more as ad hoc consortia than as truly transnational programs based on comparative economic and technological advantage.

Moreover, EADS has so far failed to create a truly transnational corporate culture, and considerable tensions remain between the various French, German, and Spanish agents. There is a growing concern that EADS is becoming essentially a French company—a belief that was only strengthened by rumors in 2004–5 that EADS was planning on acquiring a large piece of Thales, which would have marginalized the German role in the company. This concern was further highlighted by the conflict within EADS a few years ago over the selection of new German and French co-CEOs, when the then-head of Airbus, Frenchman Noel Forgeard, was widely perceived as trying to consolidate control of the company under a single, French chief executive.[30]

At the same time, there is very little that is German in EADS in terms of programs. The French dominate many corporate business areas, including Airbus, missiles (MBDA), Eurocopter, and Space (the Ariane launcher). Most German activity is concentrated in defense work (such as Eurofighter), but this business segment constitutes only around one-quarter of all EADS revenues.[31]

The Spanish element within EADS has voiced similar complaints about the French ascendancy within the company. For example, CASA was supposed to take the lead in the design and manufacture of the pan-European A400M transport aircraft, but the Airbus leadership subsequently decided to shift A400M development to its headquarters in Toulouse, France, leaving CASA with only final assembly. Consequently, some Spanish officials want to increase their nation's stake in EADS from its current 5.5 percent, in order to give the Spanish a larger say in how the company is run.[32]

At the same time, European defense firms tend to mirror the protectionist sentiments of their governments. Most defense companies in Europe still see their countries as captive markets, and they are not above playing the protectionist card when it comes to securing contracts. Germany, for example, recently approved ThyssenKrupp's acquisition of the German submarine builder HDW from its U.S. owners, One Equity Partners, and it furthermore passed legislation greatly curtailing foreign ownership of national strategic industries.[33] In addition, the United Kingdom has sought ways to keep BAE Systems' Hawk trainer jet program alive, France acquired Nexter's new CAESAR artillery system, Spain bought additional frigates from its Navantia shipyards, and Sweden purchased additional Gripen fighter jets to keep Saab's production lines open. According to the European Defense Agency, in 2007, less than 20 percent of all EU defense procurement was procured through European collaboration.[34]

Counter-Regionalism #2: The Continuing Lure of the U.S. Arms Market

Another side to this counter-regionalist momentum is the drive to continue transatlantic defense-industrial connections. Despite strong pressures from France and Germany for a European preference in procurement and production, most other European arms producers—companies and countries alike—remain keen on building bridges to the U.S. defense industry. The United States is easily the world's largest arms buyer, easily accounting for around *half* of all worldwide defense purchases, and no European firm is prepared to write off the U.S. market completely. For many European defense companies, capturing even a small fraction of the U.S. defense business could translate into sizable revenues. In this regard, therefore, these firms are pursuing both pan-European and transatlantic linkages, depending on where they perceive maximum profitability.

Consequently, many of Europe's arms manufacturers have labored hard in recent years to enter the U.S. arms market or to partner with U.S. firms on export-oriented products. BAE Systems, in fact, does more business in North America (£6.4 billion [$10.7 billion] worth of sales in 2007) than in the rest of Europe (£2.6 billion [$4.4 billion]), or, indeed, even the United Kingdom (£3.4 billion [$5.7 billion]); North America has become the company's single largest market, accounting for 41 percent of all corporate income in 2007.[35]

There is speculation that BAE Systems is shifting its emphasis from Europe to the United States, both reducing its involvement in continental defense programs and increasing its activities in North America. BAE Systems has come to conclude that trying to break into other European counties' highly protected national arms markets, or working with other European firms on third-party sales, is no longer worth the effort.[36] In recent years, therefore, the company has dissolved AMS, its avionics and communications joint venture with Finmeccanica, and sold off its share of the business to its former Italian partner. It reduced its stake in Saab, from 35 percent to 20 percent, and returned its 50 percent share in Gripen International, a Swedish-British company to globally market the JAS-39 Gripen fighter jet. BAE Systems divested itself of the German small arms manufacturer Heckler & Koch, and of its stake in the pan-European satellite company, Astrium, and it broke up its joint ownership arrangement with Siemens of the German electronics firm STN Atlas and plans to sell its remaining assets in the company. BAE Systems plans to remain mainly in Europe, where it expects to extract long-term profitability or find large enough markets to support a company of its size, such as in the missile, fighter aircraft, and commercial jetliner sectors; hence, it is preserving its stakes in MBDA, Airbus, and the Eurofighter program.[37]

At the same time, BAE Systems has expanded its North American activities. Since the late 1990s the company has acquired more than a dozen U.S. defense firms, and as such was the 12th largest contractor to the U.S. Defense Department in FY2004. Most recently, it acquired United Defense Limited (UDL), which builds the Bradley infantry fighting vehicle and the Paladin self-propelled howitzer, on the expectation that it will earn significant revenues servicing, maintaining, and upgrading armored vehicles for the U.S. military. Finally, BAE Systems is the only Level One partner in the U.S.-led F-35 Joint Strike Fighter program, which promises considerable long-term revenues—perhaps even more than the Eurofighter Typhoon (particularly when it comes to third-party exports).

Other British firms are also increasingly active in the U.S. defense industry, to the detriment of Europe, including Rolls-Royce, Smiths Industries, Meggitt, and QinetiQ. Overall, Washington has a much higher comfort level with British acquisitions of the U.S. defense businesses than with other potential European investors, and this is reflected in the fact that British firms outnumber their European counterparts in FDI in the U.S. defense sector by a wide margin.[38]

Defense industries in Italy, Spain, and Sweden have been equally comfortable having a foot in both the European and transatlantic camps. Due to their much smaller sizes, companies such as Saab, Finmeccanica, and Navantia have had to be much more flexible and nimble players in the global defense business than their larger European cousins, such as Thales or EADS. Consequently, these companies have increasingly pressed their comparative advantages and core competencies—for example, shipbuilding in Spain, helicopters in Italy, and aerospace and C4ISR in Sweden—to excel at being niche players in the global arms industry, and this has often entailed partnering with U.S. firms. Finmeccanica, for instance, is a member of the JSF team, as well as being a partner with the United States on the C-27 transport aircraft. Navantia is collaborating with Lockheed Martin on the Advanced Frigate Consortium (AFCON), which integrates a smaller version of the Aegis SPY-1 air defense combat system into a frigate-sized naval vessel. Sweden, meanwhile, is currently cooperating with the U.S. Army on the Excalibur precision-guided artillery round, and it has contracted to several U.S. firms, such as Boeing and IBM, on its nascent networked-based defense concept.

Even French companies are not prepared to abandon the potential of the U.S. defense market. Thales operates a joint venture with Raytheon to develop and market radars and command and control systems around the world. The company is currently the 74th largest contractor to the U.S. Defense Department, and it plans to double its sales to the United States over the next decade.

EADS is also eager to expand into the U.S. defense market. North America is EADS's largest market outside of Europe, and nearly as big as the rest of world combined; the company already has more employees in the United States than it has outside Europe. It recently opened a factory in Mississippi to produce helicopters for the U.S. Border Patrol, and a facility in Alabama to manufacture the CN-235 transport aircraft for the U.S. Coast Guard. EADS also set up an Airbus design center in Kansas and is prepared to establish a production plant in the United States to build tanker aircraft for the U.S. Air Force. In late 2004, EADS made its first U.S. acquisition, buying Racal Instruments.[39]

CONCLUSIONS

There are very powerful factors driving both integration and division within the European defense industry. Certainly, the politics of European unionization—for example, the Common Foreign and Security Policy (CSFP) and the European Security and Defense Policy (ESDP)—are very influential in promoting pan-European armaments cooperation and strengthening the shift from a series of national defense-industrial bases to a truly European defense industry. Economics and the emerging technological demands of next-generation warfare (i.e., the RMA and defense transformation) are also instrumental in pressing the integration agenda: the growing global technological and economic dominance of the U.S. defense industry has been one of the major forces behind the regionalization of the European defense industry.

At the same time, as the European arms industry has become more attuned to market forces, individual firms have been both freer and more motivated to seek out comparative advantages in partnerships outside of Europe where they perceive better prospects for long-term revenues and access to innovative technologies. Even a highly integrated European arms market would be too small to support a Fortress Europe, given the continued likelihood of extremely constrained resources for R&D and procurement. In this regard, many European defense firms will continue to find considerable appeal in partnering with U.S. companies—hence the strong interest that many European defense companies have shown in working with the United States on the Joint Strike Fighter.

On the other hand, neither exports, nor consolidation and rationalization, nor global industrial linkages are going to solve the underlying crisis confronting the European defense-industrial base. There are only two solutions: (1) increase defense and R&D spending, which is very unlikely in the short or even medium term, and/or (2) gain greater access to the U.S. defense market, which even EADS and Thales are now realizing is a must.

Consequently, over the next decade or so, one of two possible alternatives could emerge in the restructuring of the European defense industry: (1) a *hybrid* defense-industrial base that is much more integrated on a pan-European scale, but which is still comprised mainly of national defense firms; (2) a *bifurcated* defense-industrial base divided between those pursuing closer involvement in the U.S. arms business, and those seeking to create a truly regionalized competitor to the U.S. defense industry. Both of these alternatives present challenges and opportunities for the U.S. defense industry and U.S. policymakers.

A hybrid European defense-industrial base would be one that is more integrated on a pan-European scale than it is at the present, but also one in which many national defense firms—mainly national champions—still predominate and where national decision making institutions and structures still prevail when it comes national defense requirements and procurement. Current political, economic, and technological drivers almost certainly ensure that there will be increased regional (and especially EU-instigated) collaboration in research and technology, that at least some procurement will be decided and executed on a pan-European basis (e.g., through the EDA, the Organization for Joint Armament Co-operation (OCCAR), or some other institution), and that there will be additional mergers and acquisitions within the European defense-industrial base (particularly within the land armaments and shipbuilding sectors).

At the same time, a unitary European military-industry complex is highly unlikely. Strong national preferences and priorities for defense procurement and production will continue to contend with integrationist trends. Key procurement decision making will continue to occur primarily at the national level, and governments will continue to ensure that defense expenditures are returned to their constituents in terms of jobs, technologies, and other benefits. In addition, there will likely be no single European defense company, as was once anticipated; BAE Systems is unlikely to merge with EADS, and Thales may continue to exist as a distinct corporate entity. Even many smaller defense firms, such as Saab, Finmeccanica, and Dassault, will probably remain independent, nationally incorporated enterprises, albeit much more globalized in terms of activities and ownership. The European defense-industrial base will be more rationalized and more internationalized—both on a regional and a global scale (including, in many cases, strengthened transatlantic linkages)—but it will probably look at lot like it does at present: a mixture of transnational corporations (EADS), globalized national champions (BAE Systems, Thales), and small and medium-sized enterprises serving as niche players in an increasingly globalized arms-producing network (Saab, Patria, Rheinmetall, Stork).

Obviously, a more Europeanized arms market and defense industry could further drive the tendency toward a European preference and raise the bar for U.S. companies seeking to sell their wares to the continent. In the face of increased competition from the U.S. defense industry, many Europeans do believe that there is little alternative to creating a truly pan-European arms industry, as well as a more integrated, and perhaps even insular, defense market. On the other hand, a stronger and more unified European defense technology and industrial base could be a better partner for U.S. industry, and be better able to bring innovative technologies and systems that would enhance transatlantic armaments cooperation to the table; therefore, collaboration could be enhanced by a more efficient European arms industry, especially if these companies are also guided by market forces that encourage them to seek best value for money and comparative advantage in partnering. Overall, a consolidated, restructured, rationalized, and integrated European defense industry would be situated to compete and cooperate better with U.S. industry.

Alternatively, some European firms could increasingly pursue closer linkages with the U.S. defense industry and defense market, thus diluting any pan-European integrationist process. For example, many firms in the United Kingdom—especially BAE Systems, Smiths Industries, and Rolls-Royce—have been eager to access and integrate themselves in the U.S. defense market over the past decade, often at the expense of the European continental defense sector; BAE Systems, in fact, is practically an American company already. Additionally, many smaller European defense firms, while not abandoning their European ties, are increasingly driven by economic necessity to pursue closer connections to the U.S. defense market. As a result, the European defense market could break into two large factions: one led by France—with a not-entirely-happy Germany in tow—that seeks to build a unified European industry and market to counter the United States; and one led by the British defense industry—and most likely including many smaller countries' national champions, such as Saab, Navantia, and Finmeccanica—that becomes increasingly integrated and co-opted by the American defense-industrial base and market. Such an alternative, of course, would greatly weaken the French-led European integration process (which could be further undermined by the ongoing Franco-German friction within EADS).

The United States could stand to benefit from such a schism. In particular, it could use this division to preempt the emergence of more protectionist European defense market, increase competition in the U.S. defense market, and maintain its access to unique European technologies. In this regard, it might behoove the United States to open up its defense market to greater penetration by U.S.-based subsidiaries of and/or joint ventures with the big European companies. The United States might also use access to its market as a means to extract political concessions from European defense firms. In particular, as European companies are increasingly involved in the U.S. defense-industrial base, they appear to be increasingly willing to restrict the sale of arms to China and other countries of concern, so as not to jeopardize their continuing access to the U.S. market. For example, BAE Systems has publicly stated that it will not violate U.S. export prohibitions to China, even if the EU and the British government overturn their respective arms bans. Thus, increased European penetration of the U.S. arms market could not only enhance U.S. domestic competition, and therefore benefit U.S. Defense Department procurement; it may also increase U.S. leverage over European defense export and industrial policies.

NOTES

1. Boeing, for example, is the lead systems integrator for Future Combat Systems, which involves 18 individual systems, including ground vehicles, airborne platforms, and sensors.
2. Gopal Ratnam, "The Rise of the Lead Systems Integrator," *Defense News.*
3. Richard F. Grimmett, *Conventional Arms Transfers to Developing Nations, 2000–2007* (Washington, DC: Congressional Research Service, 2007), 64, 69.
4. Data derived from various company Web sites.
5. Andrew Krepinevich, "From Cavalry to Computer: The Pattern of Military Revolutions," *The National Interest,* Fall 1994, 30.

6. Richard O. Hundley, *Past Revolutions, Future Transformations* (Santa Monica, CA: Rand, 1999), quoted in *Economist,* "Transformed: A Survey of the Defense Industry," July 20, 2002, 7.

7. *Economist,* "Transformed," 7.

8. Center for Strategic and Budgetary Assessments (CSBA), *The Emerging RMA* (Washington, DC: CSBA, n.d.), http://www.csbaonline.org/2Strategic_Studies/2Emerging_RMA/Emerging_RMA.html.

9. U.S. Department of Defense, Office of Defense Transformation, *Network-Centric Warfare: Creating a Decisive Warfighting Advantage* (Washington, DC: U.S. Department of Defense, 2003), 2.

10. CSBA, *Transformation Strategy* (Washington, DC: CSBA, n.d.), http://www.csbaonline.org/2Strategic_Studies/3Transformation_Strategy/Transformation_Strategy.html.

11. Peter J. Dombrowski, Eugene Gholz, and Andrew L. Ross, *Military Transformation and the Defense Industry after Next: The Defense Industrial Implications of Network-Centric Warfare* (Newport, RI: Naval War College Press, 2002), 14–16.

12. Andrew James, "European Military Capabilities, the Defense Industry and the Future Shape of Armaments Co-operation," *Defense & Security Analysis,* March 2005, 8.

13. Andrew James, "The Defense Industry and Transformation: A European Perspective," in *Transatlantic Transformations: Equipping NATO for the 21st Century,* ed. Daniel S. Hamilton (Washington, DC: Center for Transatlantic Relations, Johns Hopkins School of Advanced International Studies, 2004), 168–169.

14. Mattias Axelson and E. Anders Eriksson, *Towards an Industry for Network Based Defense?* (Stockholm: Swedish Defense Research Agency, 2002), 30

15. James, "The Defense Industry and Transformation," 169.

16. Joris Janssen Lok, "Swedish Armed Forces Face Up to the Changing Threat," *International Defense Review,* August 1, 2003.

17. *Economist,* "Defense: Platform Envy," December 12, 1998.

18. Personal interviews.

19. James, "The Defense Industry and Transformation," 168.

20. James, "The Defense Industry and Transformation," 168.

21. David C. Gompert, Richard L. Kugler, and Martin C. Libicki, *Mind the Gap: Promoting a Transatlantic Revolution in Military Affairs* (Washington, DC: National Defense University Press, 1999), 11–12.

22. Gordon Adams, Guy Ben-Ari, John Logsdon, and Ray Williamson, "C4ISR in European Defense Industries," appendix 1 in *Bridging the Gap: European C4ISR Capabilities and Transatlantic Interoperability* (Washington, DC: George Washington University, 2004).

23. Brooks Tigner, "European Defence Agency May Buy UAVs," *Defense News,* April 25, 2005.

24. Terence R. Guay, *The Transatlantic Defense Industrial Base: Restructuring Scenarios and Their Implications* (Carlisle Barracks, PA: U.S. Army War College, Strategic Studies Institute, April 2005), 13.

25. Seth G. Jones, "The European Defense Industry," manuscript, August 2005, 8.

26. Personal interviews.

27. Samsung Thales Web site, http://www.samsungthales.com.

28. For more on the hub-and-spoke concept, see Richard A. Bitzinger, *Towards a Brave New Arms Industry?* (London: International Institute for Strategic Studies/Oxford University Press, 2003).

29. Andrew Chuter, "U.K. To Set Industry Strategy in 2005," *Defense News,* November 11, 2004; U.K. Ministry of Defence, *Defence Industrial Policy,* MoD policy paper 5 (London: Ministry of Defence, October 2002); personal interviews, March 2005.

30. Personal interviews; J.A.C. Lewis, "Germany Fears France is Pushing to Dominate EADS," *Jane's Defense Weekly,* November 24, 2004; David Mulholland, "German Industry—Feeling the Squeeze," *Jane's Defense Weekly,* March 30, 2005.

31. Personal interviews; EADS corporate Web site, http://www.eads-nv.com.

32. Martin Agüera, "Why Spain Wants More of EADS," *Defense News,* April 11, 2005.

33. Mulholland, "German Industry—Feeling the Squeeze."

34. European Defence Agency (EDA), *Defence Data of EDA Participating Member States in 2007* (Brussels: European Defence Agency, 2008), 10, 33.

35. Data derived from the BAE Systems Web site, http://www.baesystems.com.

36. Personal interviews.

37. In addition, GKN sold off its share in AgustaWestland helicopters to Finmeccanica.

38. Guy Anderson, "European Industry's Drift West Becomes a Stampede," *Jane's Defense Weekly,* Mary 13, 2009; David Mulholland, "European Invaders Snap Up U.S. Companies," *Jane's Defense Weekly,* November 3, 2004.

39. Mulholland, "European Invaders Snap Up U.S. Companies."

10

The Russian Defense Industry 1991–2008: From the Collapse of the Former Soviet Union to the Global Financial Crisis

Eugene Kogan

Addressing the issue of the Russian military-industrial complex (MIC, or its Russian acronym VPK) is like listening to a scratched record. The litany of complaints is long and repetitive: an ageing workforce and a problem in recruiting younger workers, lack of investment in basic infrastructure such as new machine tools and equipment, and overcapacities, namely a very large number of enterprises (1,264) that, despite the 18 years of restructuring, still remain in business.

In addition, the open sources are full of concepts, ideas and programs, and statements about restructuring and reform of the MIC. In reading the open sources on the state of the MIC, one needs to read between the lines and see the contradictions between the various reports, which are not immediately obvious. It is therefore reasonable to conclude that little has been done *in practice* to restructure the complex and make it economically viable and efficient, although the Russian officials would dismiss this claim out of hand.

In 1997, the government proposed the idea of creating financial-industrial groups (FIGs). Starting in 2001, the main thrust of the reforms has been and still is bringing all the Russian enterprises into various holding companies (also known as holdings). According to government officials, the number of holdings varies between 20 and 75. Despite both initiatives, they proved to be unsuccessful, although government officials and officials of the Russian MIC would disagree with this assessment.

The Russian government has barely accepted the existence of the private enterprises within the MIC. At the same time, it has consistently pursued its goal of returning the private enterprises that were created in 2004 to the fold of state-owned enterprises. These enterprises were centered on segments of the military aviation sector, including the aero-engine sector. They were restructured and turned into economically viable and financially profitable businesses. However, the state decided to nationalize the sector, effectively killing the goose that laid the golden egg for the state. As a result, the successful pockets of the

MIC ceased to exist in December 2008 and, instead, the Russian government is pursuing the creation of a giant company, the United Aircraft Building Corporation (UABC or, as it known in Russian, Ob'edinennaya Aviastroitel'naya Kompaniya [OAK]). The UABC was supposed to become fully operational in 2007, but as of March 2009 it remained in bureaucratic limbo. The UABC case is the most prominent example of consolidation pursued by the government in the last four years.

It appears that the process of restructuring has reached its limit and the government has fully reasserted its control over the MIC. If that is what the former president and current prime minister, Vladimir Putin, and his team set out to accomplish, then they have certainly achieved their goal. It can be further stated that the era of privately owned enterprises has come to an end.

CONVERSION AND REFORM OF THE DEFENSE INDUSTRY: 1991–1997

Basically, the development and restructuring of the Russian defense industry between 1991 and 2008 can be divided into four phases: conversion and reform (1991–97); the creation of financial-industrial groups (FIGs) and, later on, state-owned holding companies (1997–2002); the consolidation of holding companies (2002–06); and the renationalization of the defense industry (2006–08).

The first phase began in 1991 and reached its nadir in 1997—this period was associated directly with the conversion of the defense industry in Russia, and a huge number of articles, reports, and books were published in Russian, English, and German, The Bonn International Center for Conversion (BICC) was established in 1994 to deal with the issue of defense conversion in general and defense conversion in Russia in particular.[1] As described below, the conversion and reform of the defense industry was accompanied by a sharp fall in the enterprises' output for domestic needs, a deterioration of the industry in general, and a loss of skilled labor.

When the Soviet Union collapsed in 1991, Russia inherited 85 percent of the former Soviet Union's (FSU's) MIC. In 1992 the country possessed 2,160 defense industry enterprises, with 25 percent of the workforce involved in research and development (R&D), while the remaining 75 percent catered for production.[2] After the collapse of the FSU, the Russian president Boris Yeltsin, maintained Mikhail Gorbachev's policy, further cutting the numerical strength of the army and the budget of the defense industry. In the 1990s, when Russian defense orders were low, a considerable number of MIC enterprises survived on export sales to China and India in particular. Export orders were not sufficient to keep the MIC from degradation. In Boris Yeltsin's eight-year presidential term some 70 percent of the skilled workforce left jobs at the plants and design bureaus. As a result, the total number of MIC jobs fell to some two million (of which one million worked in the nuclear industry). It was not just manpower at issue; production tools were also out-of-date. The number of machine tools made more than 10 years ago stands at 85 percent, and 60 percent were made over 20 years ago.[3] Ivan Safranchuk of the Moscow-based Centre for Defense Information (CDI) noted that after the fall of the Soviet Union in 1991, the reforms needed to be carried out within the MIC never took place.[4] What actually happened was an almost total conversion of the defense industry to civilian needs. This conversion has largely failed and, as a result, as early as 1999, 1,489 enterprises were officially counted as belonging to the defense complex, including 724 industrial enterprises and 545 research organizations. Therefore, it can be estimated that the total number of direct defense contractors was reduced by about one-third in the 1990s.[5] By the mid-1990s, about 25 percent of the defense enterprises had gone bankrupt, while the rest of the companies that made a profit were heavily taxed by the state (the tax was between 65% and 90%).[6] Thus, their financial situation remained difficult.

In 1997 when the state funding alone for the defense order was at 21 percent and the skilled workforce was leaving the MIC in large numbers, a federal program was rapidly developed for the restructuring and conversion of the MIC for the years 1998–2000. In 1998 a law concerning the defense conversion of the Russian Federation was issued. According to experts from Nezavisimoye Voennoye Obozreniye (NVO), both the federal program and the law "failed because of the strategic errors made by planning and in executing them." As a result, the MIC declined further, its scientific-technical potential decreased sharply, and basic research suffered from a severe lack of funding.[7] Kseniya Gonchar was more specific in naming the problems that the defense industry encountered. She stated that the ideology behind the restructuring programs has been challenged by budget constraints and has conflicted with the interests of the many actors involved, as well as necessitating high social costs. Moreover, by mid-2000, Russia had its fifth government in two years. Unfortunately for defense restructuring reform, the reaction to administrative changes has always been to slow down and delay matters and reshape the interest group that had reached consensus under the previous government.[8]

To conclude, the first phase of the reforms sent the defense industry into financial ruin and led to the loss of a considerable number of skilled workers.

FROM FIGS TO HOLDINGS: 1997–2002

The second phase began in 1997 and ended in 2002. At that time the government accepted the federal program mentioned above, but this has not yet been implemented.[9] The result was that noted by Gonchar, namely that as of early 1999, military output decreased by almost 80 percent and civilian output by 60 percent. She also noted that duplication of weapon systems and double-sourcing contributed to overcapacities. An additional reason for the cuts was the coexistence of both modern and technically outdated enterprises, leading to the simultaneous production of several generations of weaponry. The military authorities wanted to rid themselves of the responsibility of keeping the obsolete entities running and insisted that they close down, rather than restructuring or merging them.[10] However, the Russian government at that time, immediately after the financial crisis of July 1998, was not ready to follow such a drastic course. In 1999, President Vladimir Putin, acting at that time as prime minister, declared arms manufacturing for domestic requirements to be a priority, thus replacing the previous focus on conversion and arms exports.[11] As of the late 1990s, two-thirds of the military output was exported and only one-third was purchased by the Russian military.[12] Thus, acting Prime Minister Putin's decision at that time highlighted his goal of focusing on domestic procurement, which until then was in low demand. Gonchar noted that the domestic arms procurement resulted in low utilization of capacities, low economics of scale, high production costs and prices, and, in general, led to the poor economic and financial standing of the majority of defense enterprises.[13]

During this period, the issue of defense industry conversion evaporated and the idea that emerged from this was the creation of the FIGs, a Russian system similar to the of South Korean chaebol conglomerate. Even prior to 1997, Russian officials travelled to South Korea to learn about the chaebol, the business group structure that dominated South Korea during the 1990s. It had become clear that the introduction of FIGs did not help in the restructure of the complex because tough measures such as the closure of enterprises and bankruptcies were avoided. This avoidance of tough measures can be seen as a consistent pattern in the Russian reforms.

In an interview in 2008 with Alexander Rybas, director-general of the Tula-based KB Priborostroeniye (KBP) Instrument Design Bureau, he stated that the eight years of Vladimir Putin's presidency, which began in 2000, were a period in which the country and the defense industry were climbing out of the post-Soviet crisis.[14] It can be said that the defense industry's climb was long and hard. However, the basic reforms within the MIC, such as restructuring, mergers, and the downsizing of the industry that Russian officials debated at length were either pursued at a very slow pace or abandoned altogether and, as a result, reforms achieved very little.

"THE HOLDINGS ARE DEAD! LONG LIVE THE HOLDINGS": 2002–2006

The third phase began in 2002 and was accompanied by a federal program to reform and develop the MIC between 2002 and 2006, which was accepted by the government in October 2001. The program was prepared by Deputy Prime Minister Ilya Klebanov, and foresaw the creation of 74 holding companies. In 2002, however, the number of foreseen holding companies decreased to 42. By late November 2003, only 3 holding companies had been established. Prime Minister Mikhail Kasyanov was angry with the results of the program. As a result, Boris Alyoshin, deputy prime minister, who replaced Ilya Klebanov, was given the task of developing a revised version of the federal program.[15] It can be said that governmental programs in Russia have largely turned out to be failures.

Vitaly Shlykov, former deputy minister of defense and a member of the private Council on Foreign and Defense Policy (SVOP), said clearly that the creation of the holding companies could be compared to a "still-born child." He added that "The MIC represents a huge financial flow and today we speak about redistribution of control over that flow and not about increasing the efficiency of the complex." On the other hand, Alexei Arbatov asserted that holding companies are the real way out of the crisis for the MIC.[16] According to Sergei Vasil'yev, an aviation engineer, "Structural restructuring does not allow one to perform better. The aero-engine companies are no longer competing for a quality product but just for the 'window dressing'. As a result, I am doubtful whether the newly created holdings are capable of manufacturing equipment better then the defense enterprises of the past."[17]

It can certainly be stated that the formation of holdings to alleviate the ills of the defense industry proved unsuccessful.[18] The October 2004 issue of *NVO* noted that it appeared although the holding companies that were talked about in 2001 would no longer be remembered.[19] Apparently, this statement about the holding companies has proved to be completely off the mark, and the government has slowly but surely pursued the task of creating holdings, although as previously stated, using holdings as a panacea proved to be unsuccessful.

Between 2003 and 2004, the Russian government issued a register of VPK enterprises that included 1,264 entries. Of these 691 were unitary state enterprises and 573 were joint stock companies. At that time, the government announced plans for the creation of between 60 and 70 integrated structures (or holdings) within the MIC/VPK, which would then merge into 20.[20] This was the first post-Soviet era register of VPK enterprises, and it showed that almost 1,000 defense enterprises had left the MIC altogether.

In October 2004, Prime Minister Mikhail Fradkov asked the Ministry for Industry and Energy to prepare an outline of the federal state program for the development of the MIC for the years 2006–10. It was assumed that the new program was to allow the Russian MIC to be fully restored and developed in the future. Some within the MIC were afraid that the government officials were going to suggest their own scheme for reforming the MIC. As a result, the flourishing enterprises and design bureaus were to come under the officials' control; a new division of the complex was not to be in the interests of national defense.[21]

In late July 2005, *NVO* reported that the MIC department within the Ministry for Industry and Energy, headed by Yuri Koptev, had prepared an analytical report concerning the development strategy of the complex. The report analyzed the implementation of the federal program for the years 2002–06. Experts from the department flatly rejected all of the government officials' statements that the MIC was being reborn. They concluded that one-third of the enterprises were bankrupt; in fact, the state of the MIC had not changed for several years. The same figure, namely one-third, was cited by Givi Djandjgava, vice president of the League of Assistance to Defense Enterprises, in 2003. Djandjgava emphasized that, for several years, no investment had been made in the defense enterprises and, as a result, they had no funds. He added that financial investment into R&D in Russia was ten-times less than that of developed countries; investment into the main funds was five-times less, allocation for training the workforce was five-times less and labour efficiency was between five- and ten-times less." Experts added that, in the current state of the MIC, they could see no improvements. According to experts, a new federal program for the years 2006–10 would provide an incentive to the 1,265 defense enterprises. However, they were also obliged to state that this program could be implemented only if the defense order was implemented 100 percent, if the necessary investment was allocated, and the program of structural reshaping of the complex was completed.[22] There were too many *ifs* attached to the new program, and in the Russian reality, ifs mean no.

In early August 2005, in an interview, Konstantin Makienko, deputy director of the Centre for Analysis of Strategies and Technologies (CAST), noted that the "Government has neither labor policy nor any other policy regarding the MIC. The complex has been relegated to the margins of the government's attention. The MIC has few managers who are well-acquainted with business processes and technology production and are also honest managers. There is a shortage of skilled labor; the complex lost the mid-level layer of engineers and designers. In order to fill the lost positions the state should have shown the nation and the entrepreneurs that the defense industry is an important and interesting sector of the industry."[23] As it turned out, the state did not demonstrate the importance of the sector, although there was some rhetoric.

To sum up, the third phase was accompanied by statements that did not match the reality on the ground. The statements made by experts under the leadership of Yuri Koptev, by Givi Djandjgava, and by Konstantin Makienko, exposed the sobering reality of the state of the defense complex.

FULL SPEED TO NATIONALIZATION OF THE DEFENSE INDUSTRY: 2006–2008

The fourth phase was directly associated with Sergei Ivanov, minister of defense who, in May 2007, was promoted to the post of first deputy prime minister and given the task "to give the Russian economy a more innovative character" in both the civilian and military-industrial sector. But after 15 years of deterioration, innovation was hardly the hallmark of Russian industry. In the words of Peter Westin, chief economist at the Moscow-based MDM Bank, Ivanov's task of bringing the defense industry into the modern age could "work in the long run, but it is going to be very difficult." What was required, Westin said, was partnership between the civilian and military sectors—which was being obstructed by the closed, secretive nature of the defense industry. Westin added that "Right now you have a tendency where the state is the commander and that is what you do not want to see."[24] Westin's views are not shared by the Russian government. Furthermore, the Russian government's reassertion of fully controlling the defense complex contradicts Westin's remarks.

The other crucial problem that was underlined by Yuri Eliseyev, director-general of the Russian jet engine manufacturer MMPP Salyut, was an acute shortage of skilled young workers. The average age of the workforce in the MIC is between 45 and 50 years. The older experienced workers are gradually retiring and their replacement by a new young prospective skilled labor force is very slow.[25]

Sergei Ivanov noted in an article published in 2006 that despite the fact that the general state of the MIC is not bad, this does not mean that there are no problems. The most important problem is that the defense enterprises are not sufficiently engaged in the production of high-tech civilian goods. The quality of weapon systems is not always up to the mark, and there are certain problems in maintaining the mobilization readiness of the enterprises. The defense industry also needs financial restructuring. Some enterprises are bankrupt, while others are pseudo-bankrupt; still other industrial groups may be merely seeking to size the territory and facilities for subsequent reprofiling of production.[26] In January 2006, a report assessing the state of the Russian aviation industry was published online. It stated clearly that less than or about one-third of the total enterprises in the aviation industry, or between 80 and 100, were actually operational.[27]

Alexander Brindikov, the president of the League of Assistance to Defense Enterprises, claimed on March 16, 2007, that the country's defense companies require $5.3 billion annually for modernization and retooling. In 2006, the federal budget accounted for 29.9 percent of the total. Credit accounted for a further 23.4 percent, while the remainder came from the accumulated equity of the individual enterprises. Although the Russian state has become an increasingly significant stakeholder in the industrial enterprises in recent years, according to Brindikov it has not provided sufficient funds for the reforms. On March 14, 2007, Sergei Ivanov said that he expects Russia's defense companies—which have returned an average production growth of 7 percent per annum over the last five years—to be profitable from 2010 onwards.[28] This is certainly not going to happen—this is the result of the global financial crisis and its belated impact on Russia, the defense industry credit crunch, and a 15 percent cut from the current defense budget, which might be not be the last cut in 2009. These issues are discussed in detail below. At the same time, according to Boris Alyoshin of the Federal Agency on Industry, defense enterprises use the financial means allocated for their needs ineffectively—including both the finance from the state budget and their own—and, as a result, modernization of the weapon systems is proceeding very slowly. Alyoshin added that "The structure of the defense industry should be drastically changed." He continued, "Today our defense enterprises are unable to compete with foreign companies. Often state contracts are given to foreign companies."[29] Alyoshin did not elaborate further on either of these two statements.

In an interview, Mikhail Babich, deputy chairman of the State Duma Defense Committee, noted that the current trend in the MIC is very worrisome. He clearly stated that a newly created company, Russian Technologies (Rossiiskiye Tekhnologii), arguing that one-third of the MIC enterprises are bankrupt and that another third is close to bankruptcy, and that only the final third is in good condition. In addition, enterprises need to stop lagging behind in technological terms and state enterprises should be modernized. Babich added that "We practically do not invest financial means in the retooling of enterprises. As a result, we are lagging behind our foreign competitors in various directions in between five- and fifteen fold. Therefore, we turn out to be not only uncompetitive but we also use the financial means allocated from the state budget ineffectively."[30]

A total of 2.5 million people are currently employed in the MIC. That is about half million more than in 1999. In fact, the MIC over the last ten years has recruited half a million new workers, but this figure is not high enough to maintain the MIC operations. According to Sergei Ivanov, the problems of the workforce within the MIC is well-known. The problem is mainly related to age. Even within the scientific institutes and design bureaus about 50 percent of the workforce is in the retirement age group while, on the manufacturing side, this number is about 30 percent. Therefore, there is a real danger of losing skills and knowledge transfer from the older to a younger generation.[31] In addition, there are the problems noted at the beginning of the article, namely that the machine tools are old and in need of modernization (this has not been addressed over the last 18 years, incidentally). The ammunition sector is in a worse shape than the other sectors of the defense industry as a result of the ageing equipment and the loss of the skilled labor, wherein many workers have left the sector altogether.[32]

CONCLUSION

What is the solution that the government is proposing to remedy the state of the defense industry? In Russia, the government calls it consolidation or the bringing together of the various sectors' defense enterprises into holdings. This shows that the Russian government never gave up the idea of creating the holdings that the October 2004 issue of *NVO* thought were passé.

It can be stated that the earlier round of industry consolidation began with consolidation of the United Aircraft Building Corporation (UABC). On February 22, 2005, President Vladimir Putin ordered the establishment of the UABC. This is how consolidation proceeds in Russia, by order, without taking the industrial rationale into consideration. The private companies in the aviation sector in particular were merged with the state companies, and the state retained a stake of over 75 percent in the nationalized company. But as recently as March 2009, this company had not yet been established.[33]

In March 2007, President Putin ordered the creation of the United Shipbuilding Corporation, which was to include all fully or partially state-owned naval enterprises. Putin's decree gave the government four months to do all the paperwork and conduct an evaluation of the companies that would go into holding.[34] So far, very little has happened to implement this.

In addition, on August 11, 2007, Putin issued a decree to integrate aero-engine manufacturers.[35] According to Sergei Ivanov, four aero-engine groups should have been formed by the end of 2007.[36] In late July 2008, *Defense News* reported that the Kremlin-driven consolidation of the Russian defense industry had run into problems in the aero-engine sector, as two privately owned companies both rebelled over coming under government control. Ufa Engine-Building Industrial Association (UMPO) and the Yaroslav-based NPO Saturn Company, which are in the process of merging, are resisting being consolidated into an engine-building holding controlled by state-owned Oboronprom.[37] It took the global financial crisis and personal intervention by Prime Minister Putin to force Russia's last major independent aero-engine manufacturers to submit to government control.[38] To put it mildly, the above described consolidation can be called consolidation *à la russe,* namely, breaking elbows but at least keeping necks intact.

In July 2008, the Russian government decided to embark on a further round of industry consolidation, with far-reaching consequences for the defense sector. Russia's president, Dmitry Medvedev, issued a decree allowing the handover of the state's stake in over 400 companies to Russian Technologies. According to Russian Technologies management, nearly 80 percent of these companies are active in the defense sector. Sergei Chemezov, the head of Russian Technologies, says that the 400 companies will be brought together into around 30 holdings.

The creation of Russian Technologies would create a second focus for defense and aerospace alongside the United Aircraft Building Corporation. Many of the UABC's avionics and aircraft systems suppliers will become part of Russian Technologies. More importantly, the latter company will also control Russia's aero-engine manufacturers through the creation of the United Engine Manufacturing Corporation.

The Russian government has been trying to reestablish control over key industrial sectors, including defense and aerospace. Supporters of the conglomerate suggest that one of the objectives of the creation of Russian Technologies was to avoid the risk of defense suppliers being acquired by private capital, and having their efforts redirected to the development and production of commercial goods. Another aim was to create several vertically integrated holding companies, pulling together businesses in weapons design, development, and production. Some state-owned research institutes are also involved in the consolidation.[39]

Some senior Russian scientists at the Siberian Aeronautical Research Institute (SibNIA) in Novosibirsk told *Jane's* in early 2008 that there was a fatal flaw in the formation of Russian

Technologies: the basic research and development centers are not part of this massive real-location of state resources or the formation of large conglomerates such as UABC and the Almaz-Antei Air-Defense Consortium. One scientist said that "At present we receive from the state only about 10 percent of the funding we need to keep our institute functioning and the rest we have to go begging for."[40] It also appears that the same amount of funding or even less will be allocated in the not too distant future, since the Russian government, despite the constant promises, constantly cuts the budget.

Alexander Rybas, director-general of KBP Instrument Design Bureau, noted in September 2008 that "Russia is currently moving into the development period and Russia needs different managers for the industry and new technologies, including management technologies. Today, most Russian defense enterprises are run by the former Soviet directors. A new type of manager is emerging very slowly—those who understand what the market economy with the strong participation of the state is—inside the Russian defense industry. This happens a little faster in the aviation and shipbuilding industries because they have a stronger market orientation.

For a qualitative leap, the defense industry as well as the decision-making part of the government needs to accumulate a critical number of such people, which I believe will happen in seven or eight years."[41] Questions that are still to be answered have to do with what will happen to the MIC up to this point. Will it continue to muddle through as it has done over the last 18 years? What will be the ultimate cost of this? Will there be another federal program with no real substance and the same problems that accompanied the complex over the last 18 years? Or will there be something else that perhaps the government of Russia is not yet ready to undertake? Perhaps these are the reforms that Rybas implies might take place in the not too distant future.

According to Rybas, "The demand for Russian arms has grown way beyond our production capacities. We may face a situation when foreign customers will start turning away because of the delays between the signing of the contract and the actual shipments . . . And only then, the government will be forced to actually set off reforms, changing management models and bringing in new people."[42] There is an additional problem, namely that the currently established holdings have a monopoly over state defense order, and they set the cost of the contract and deliver fewer quality goods to the customer.[43]

The fourth phase is also directly related to the global financial crisis that occurred in the first half of 2008. The repercussions of this latest crisis reached Russia in the summer of 2008 and hit the defense complex in late 2008. According to Konstantin Makienko, deputy director of CAST, in the summer of 2008 the defense complex encountered worsening credit conditions. A large number of the MIC enterprises were obliged to take credit in order to fulfill their export and state defense order contracts because allocation of funds from the Ministry of Defense (MoD) reaches them either sporadically or belatedly.[44]

Russia's deputy prime minister and former minister of defense, Sergei Ivanov, warned on the November 11, 2008, that the country's defense industries have been ' "crippled" by the global financial crisis, adding during a televised address that they are facing "dire cash shortages." He called on state banks to provide additional funding to alleviate a "situation [that] could become quite painful for the industry."

The cost of developing Russia's defense-industrial base (DIB) has been estimated at $19.25 billion, with industry expected to pick up 40 percent of the total bill. The modernization of the DIB and the wider modernization of Russia's military are unlikely to be derailed entirely by current financial crisis problems; both are viewed as too high a priority. This suggests that greater government involvement in an already heavily state-controlled and subsidized sector will be the only course of action open to Moscow in the short to medium term.

Despite Ivanov's call on state banks, the current investment climate is clearly not conducive to new market listings. Furthermore, commercial banks are unlikely to look favorably on loans to Russia's heavily subsidized—and largely loss-making—defense ventures in a time of poor liquidity and a general risk aversion. This puts the burden of easing the pressures on the industry onto the government. Overall, a greater influx of government money seems inevitable; this investment is likely to be both inflationary and eroded by inflation.[45]

FIGURE 10.1   Cartoons by Lance Sucharov. Used with permission.

Russia is reported to have put together a $5.4 billion package of measures aimed at relieving the "dire cash shortage" of its defense-industrial base and to keep the reform of its military sector on track despite the effects of the global financial crisis. RIA Novosti news agency said that state-controlled defense conglomerates Russian Technologies and UABC are likely to be the principle beneficiaries. Whether the $5.4 billion support package will be followed (or will need to be followed) by additional measures remains to be seen. It should also be asked whether such measures will go some way toward helping industry face its underlying problems, such as dated management practices and a culture that discourages an entrepreneurial approach. It can be said that these factors may not be helped by greater government control.[46]

To conclude, it can be said that the Russian defense industry has reached an impasse and has not created an economically viable and competitive defense industry over the last 18 years. The military aviation segment of the industry, which was competitive and profitable until December 2008, was nationalized by the government and its post-nationalization story may not repeat its pre-nationalization success story. The rest of the defense industry was neither viable nor competitive, although officials of the Russian defense industry would claim otherwise. It can be also said that after 18 years of constant delays and no real implementation of a restructuring process, the government has created national champions that will hinder competition and will need to be constantly subsidized. If that is what the former president and current prime minister Vladimir Putin and his team have set out to accomplish then they have certainly accomplished their mission. The cartoons above portray the present situation of the national champions.[47]

NOTES

1. Kseniya Gonchar, Yevgeny Kuznetsov, and Alexander Ozhegov, *Conversion of the Post-Soviet Defense Industry: Implications for Russian Economic Development,* brief 1 (Bonn: Bonn International Center for Conversion [BICC], 1995); Nicola Mögel, Thomas Sachse, and Hans-Henning Schröder, *Chancen und Probleme der Rüstungskonversion in der Gemeinschaft Unabhängiger Staaten* [*Opportunities and Problems of the Defense Conversion in the Commonwealth of Independent States*], report 2 (Bonn: BICC, 1995); Joseph DiChiaro III, ed., "Conversion of the Defense Industry in Russia and Eastern Europe," *Proceedings of the BICC/CISAC Workshop on Conversion,* August 10–13, 1994, report 3 (Bonn: BICC, 1995); Petra Opitz, *Krisenmanagement in der russischen Rüstungsindustrie. Regionale und unternehmensbezogene Konversionsstrategien* [*Crisis Management in the Defense Industry. Regional and Enterprise Drawn Conversion Strategies*], report 6 (Bonn: BICC, 1995); Yevgeny Kuznetsov (editor), Igor Musienko and Alexander Vorobyev, *Learning to Restructure: Studies of Transformation in the Russian Defense Sector,* paper 3 (Bonn: BICC, 1996), http://www.bicc.de/uploads/pdf/publications/papers/paper03/paper03.pdf; Kseniya Gonchar, *Research and Development (R&D) Conversion in Russia,* report 10 (Bonn: BICC, 1997); Kseniya Gonchar, *Conversion within the Context of Economic Reform: The Case of Nizhniy Novgorod Oblast,* paper 14 (Bonn: BICC, 1998), http://www.bicc.de/uploads/pdf/publications/papers/paper14/paper14.pdf.
2. *Jane's Defence Weekly,* January 10, 2007, 24.
3. *Jane's Defence Weekly,* January 10, 2007, 25. For an earlier article on the issue of departure of the skilled workforce, see Alexander Babakin, "Gryadet ocherednoye reformirovaniye oboronnoi promyshlennosti" ("Another Restructuring of the Defence Industry is Taking Place"), http://nvo.ng.ru/forces/2004-10-01/1_reform.html.

4. Agence France-Presse, Moscow. "Russian Arms Industry Reform Will Be Long Haul: Analysts." http://www.defensenews.com/story.php?F=2565768&C=europe (accessed February 19, 2007). According to Nikolai Mikhailov, military expert for the Moscow-based Council for Foreign and Defense Policy (or Sovet po Vneshnei i Oboronnoi Politike—SVOP), no real measures had been taken over the last fifteen years to deter a further crisis within the MIC. For the complete article, see Vladimir Ivanov, "Mrak v kontse tunnelya" ("Darkness At the End of the Tunnel.") http://nvo.ng.ru/armament/2004-04-16/6_mrak.html.

5. Kseniya Gonchar, *Russia's Defense Industry at the Turn of the Century*, brief 17 (Bonn: BICC, 2000), 23, http://www.bicc.de/uploads/pdf/publications/brief/brief17/brief17.pdf.

6. V. Burenok, G. Babkin, and A. Kosenko, "Oboronno-promyshlennyi kompleks: sostoyaniye i perspektivy razvitiya" [Military-industrial Complex: The State and the Prospects for Development], *Voennaya Mysl* 6 (2005): 37.

7. http://nvo.ng.ru/forces/2004-10-01/1_reform.html.

8. Gonchar, *Russia's Defense Industry,* 21.

9. Alexander Babakin, "Otechestvennaya oboronka proizvodit massovyi brak" ("National Defence Complex Manufacture Massive Damaged Goods"), http://nvo.ng.ru/armament/2004-07-02/1_abroad.html.

10. Gonchar, *Russia's Defense Industry,* 23–24.

11. Gonchar, *Russia's Defense Industry,* 17.

12. Gonchar, *Russia's Defense Industry,* 38.

13. Gonchar, *Russia's Defense Industry,* 40.

14. *Defense News,* September 15, 2008, 34.

15. For a complete article, see Konstantin Lantratov, "Pravitel'stvo peresmotrit programmu reformirovaniya oboronnogo kompleksa" ("Government Will Review Reform Program Of the Defence Complex"), http://www.kommersant.ru/archive/archive-material.html?docId=427814 (accessed November 14, 2003). See also Viktor Myasnikov, "My lyubim planov svoikh gromad'yev" ("We Like Our Great Plans"), http://nvo.ng.ru//concepts/2003-11-21/1_opk; http://nvo.ng.ru/armament/2004-07-02/1_abroad.html. Ilya Klebanov's program foresees the existence of both structures: state-owned and private, while Boris Alyoshin's program foresees the existence of a single state-owned corporation. For an analysis of both approaches, of Klebanov and of Alyoshin, see Ruslan Pukhov, "Vyzhivaet sil'neishii. Gosudarstvennoi politiki v oboronke bol'she net" ("The Stronger Survives. There Is No More State Policy Regarding the Defence Complex"), http://www.cast.ru/comments/?form=print&id=135 (accessed June 29, 2004).

16. http://nvo.ng.ru/armament/2004-04-16/6_mrak.html. For the redistribution of the control, see note 39. Mikhail Kasyanov, the then prime minister, signed a decree over the control of Holding Sukhoi, the Antei-Almaz Corporation, the Tactical Missiles Corporation, the Russian Electronics Joint-Stock Company (JSC), and the Russian Chemical Defense (or Roskhimzashchita) Corporation. According to the source, the decree issued by Kasyanov had little to do with the improved efficieny of the enterprises but much to do with the government officials' redistribution of the state property. Vladimir Ivanov, "Pravitel'stvo pomyalo tsvet oboronki" ("Government Took Control Over the Best Of the Best Of the Defence Complex."), see http://nvo.ng.ru/armament/2004-01-30/6_oboronka.html. A very similar notion was on elaborated by Konstantin Makienko in an interview with Nikolai Poroskov online. http://www.cast.ru/comments/?form=print&id=191 (accessed August 9, 2005). For further information, see note 39.

17. For a complete article, see Natalia Melikova and Vladimir Gundarov, "Aviakholdingi na nizkom starte" ("The Aviation Holdings Are on a Low Start"), http://www.ng.ru/index1/ (accessed August 13, 2007).

18. See, for instance, Viktor Myasnikov, "Eshche 365 tyazhelykh dnei dlya voenproma" ("Further 365 Difficult Days for the Defence Industry"), http://nvo.ng.ru (and not eu!)/armament/2006-12-29/1_voenprom.html. For the confirmation of the author's statement that formation of holding companies has failed, see Viktor Myasnikov, "Oruzhie prodavat', predpriyatiya pokupat'" ("Arms Sale, Enterprises Buy"), http://nvo.ng.ru/printed/7184 (accessed March 16, 2007). For the creation of the holdings, see "Russia's Defense Industry. Phoenix from the Ashes?" *International Institute for Strategic Studies (IISS)* 13, no. 8 (2007): 2.

19. See note 3; http://nvo.ng.ru/forces/2004-10-01/1_reform.html.

20. *Jane's Defence Weekly,* January 10, 2007, 24. In 2006 there were 656 unitary state enterprises and 609 joint stock companies. *Oboronno-promyshlennyi kompleks Rossiiskoi Federatsii 2005–2006* [*Military-Industrial Complex of the Russian Federation, 2005–2006*] (Moscow: Novosti, 2006), 25.

21. See note 3; http://nvo.ng.ru/forces/2004-10-01/1_reform.html.

22. For a complete article, see Vadim Solov'yev and Vladimir Ivanov, "Gosprogramma vooruzhenii na 2002-2006 gody provalena" ("The Federal Armaments Program for the Years 2002-2006 Has Failed"), http://nvo.ng.ru/wars/2005-07-29/1_gosprogramma.html. For a comment that by the mid-1990s, about 25 percent of the defense industry had become bankrupt, see Burenok, Babkin, and Kosenko, "Oboronno-promyshlennyi kompleks.'" Almost 10 years of restructuring have in no way produced a clean bill for the industry.

23. http://www.cast.ru/comments/?form=print&id=191 accessed on August 9, 2005. For further details, see Konstantin Makienko in an interview, note 16).

24. For a complete article, see Agence France-Presse, Moscow. "Russian Arms Industry Reform Will Be Long Haul: Analyst"), http://www.defensenews.com/story.php?F=2565768&C=europe February 19, 2007. The same source also noted that Safranchuk added: "Many factories are in ruin, you need a lot of investment after fifteen years of negligence." This report sharply contradicts the assessment presented in *Russia's Defense Industry: Phoenix from the Ashes?* 1.

25. For a complete article, see Yuri Eliseyev in an interview with Olga Pospelova online. See also Andrei Bondarenko, "Aviatsionno-obrazovatel'nyi piar" ("The Aviation Educational Public Relations"), http://www.redstar.ru/2007/03/15_03/1_02.html. See also http://www.ng.ru/printed/76976 (accessed April 4, 2007); http://www.ng.ru/ideas/2008-06-16/1_opk.html?mthree=4; and Tomasz Szulc and Eugene Kogan, "Russian Military Helicopters: Technologies and Markets," *Military Technology* 5 (2008): 76. As long ago as November 2003, Yuri Solomonov, director-general of the Moscow Institute of Thermal Technology (MITT), said that the average age of the workforce in the military-industrial complex (MIC) was 50 years. Andrei Garavskii, "Oboronka v glukhoi oborone" ("The Defence Complex in a Deep Crisis,") http://www.redstar.ru/2003/11/01_11/n.html.

26. Sergei Ivanov, "General State of Military-Industrial Complex is Not Bad," *Military Parade* (May 2006), 6. The same notion that "the defense enterprises are not sufficiently engaged" was underlined in an article published in *NVO* online, http://nvo.ng.eu/armament/2006-12-29/1_voenprom.html.

27. "The State of the Russian Aviation Industry and Export Opportunities," *Conflict Studies Research Centre,* Russian series 06/04 (January 2006), http://www.da.mod.uk/colleges/arag/documentlistings/russian/. See in particular: Key Points, 1–3.

28. *Jane's Defence Weekly,* March 21, 2007, 20.

29. Mikhail Lukanin, "Oboronka zadirayet tseny" ("The Defence Industry Charges Extra Money"), http://nvo.ng.ru/printed/7251(accessed April 6, 2007). Alyoshin did not, however, elaborate further on his statement. See also *Jane's Defence Weekly,* November 19, 2008, 21. As long ago as November 2003, Yuri Solomonov said that over the last years, the MIC had lost about 200 advanced technologies. http://www.redstar.ru/2003/11/01_11/n.html.

30. http://www.ng.ru/ideas/2008-06-16/1_opk.html?mthree=4. For earlier reports highlighting the state of the machinery in the defense industry, see http://nvo.ng.ru/armament/2004-07-02/1_abroad.html; http://nvo.ng.ru/wars/2005-07-29/1_gosprogramma.html; Burenok, Babkin, and Kosenko, "Oboronno-promyshlennyi kompleks," 41. For the state of defense enterprises, see Burenok, Babkin, and Kosenko, "Oboronno-promyshlennyi kompleks," and note 22. For the ineffective use of finances, see note 29. On November 25, 2007, President Vladimir Putin promoted the director-general of Rosoboronexport Sergei Chemezov to head the new corporation called Russian Technologies, Reuters, Moscow. "Putin Appoints Weapons Export Chief to Head Russian Technologies." http://www.defensenews.com/story.php?F=3208372&C=europe (accessed November 26, 2007). For a very favorable reaction to the creation of Russian Technologies, see *Jane's Defence Weekly,* February 27, 2007, 22; the correspondent's views can be contradicted in asserting that the last 18 years have shown that the defense industry reforms imposed by the government and/or forced consolidation of the enterprises, as discussed further below, have not transformed the industry and made it a competitive force at home and/or abroad. As for the second assertion, that the Russian government may allow foreign companies to acquire a stake in Russian Technologies and the previously inaccessible Rosoboronexport, it may do this on its own terms but with strings attached. Certainly the stakes will be on or about less than 25 percent if the government sees the foreign organizations as potentially conducive to Russian interests.

31. For a complete article and in particular for the measures undertaken to alleviate the shortage of labor within the MIC, see http://www.redstar.ru/2008/11/21_11/2_04.html. See also http://www.ng.ru/economics/2009-01-16/1_rockets.html. For an earlier report, see http://nvo.ng.ru/wars/2005-07-29/1_gosprogramma.html. For the acute shortage of engineers in the aviation, shipbuilding and electronics sectors of the industry, see an earlier article online http://www.ng.ru/politics/2008-03-07/4_chemezov.html. For Konstantin Makienko in an interview, see note 16 and Yuri Eliseyev in an interview, see note 25.

32. Leonid Orlenko, "Den'gi dlya organizatsii proizvodstva i armii" ("Funds for Organization of Production and Army"), http://nvo.ng.ru/forces/2008-11-21/6_modernisation.html. For an earlier article on the state of the ammunition industry, see Burenok, Babkin, and Kosenko, "Oboronno-promyshlennyi kompleks," 41; http://nvo.ng.eu/armament/2006-12-29/1_voenprom.html. According to Makienko, the ammunition sector of the defense industry should be supported by the state. http://www.cast.ru/comments/?form=print&id=191(accessed August 9, 2005).

33. For an earlier report concerning the establishment of the UABC, see http://www.cast.ru/comments/?form=print&id=191 (accessed August 9, 2005). See also Eugene Kogan, "Under the Cloak of the OAK" *Military Technology* 6 (2007): 61–65; Tomasz Szulc, "Russian Aerospace. Consolidation Progresses," *Military Technology* 6 (2007): 66–78. For details about the protracted consolidation of the UABC, which is running behind schedule, see *Aviation Week and Space Technology,* January 26, 2009, 306. For the possible date of the UABC Initial Public Offering (IPO), see Oksana Novozhenina, "OAK pereschitala samolety" ("OAK Recounted Aircraft"), http://www.gazeta.ru/business/2009/02/13/2941835.shtml.

34. Nabi Abdullaev, "Russian Consolidation Fails to Speed Orders," http://www.defensenews.com/story.php?F=2678110&C=europe (accessed April 23, 2007).

35. For complete articles, see Vladimir Alexandrov, "Pretendenty na serdtse aviaproma" ("Contenders for the Heart of the Aviation Industry"), http://nvo.ng.ru/armament/2007-08-17/1_engine.html; *Aviation Week and Space Technology,* August 20 and 27, 2007, 41.

36. *Flight International,* August 21–27, 2007, 12. According to *Defense News,* July 28, 2008, 18, Oboronprom was tasked with consolidating the country's aero-engine manufacturers in 15 months. The consolidation, however, had neither occurred by the end of 2007 nor in 15 months. In December

2008 major independent aero-engine manufacturers submitted themselves to government control. For the crash of the last independent aero-engine manufacturers, see note 38.

37. For the complete article, see *Defense News,* July 28, 2008, 18. It should be remembered that Oboronprom is 100 percent controlled by Rosoboronexport, the state-arms export monopoly, which in turn is consolidated into Russian Technologies, a state-owned corporation headed by Sergei Chemezov. On Russian Technologies, see note 30.

38. For a complete article, see *Defense News,* January 5, 2009, 4, 6. As for the personal intervention of Prime Minister Vladimir Putin, see http://www.vesti.ru/doc.html?id=229325&cid=5 (accessed December 2, 2008). See also Konstantin Makienko, "Finansovyi krizis i VPK: Problemy i perspektivy" ("Financial Crisis and the Military-Industrial Complex: Problems and Prospects"), http://www.cast.ru/comments/?form=print&id=330 (accessed December 8, 2008).

39. For an earlier notion that the main reform mechanism favored by President Vladimir Putin and the first deputy prime minister Sergei Ivanov was to increase government ownership over the defense complex, see "Russia's Defense Industry: Phoenix from the Ashes?,"; *Aviation Week and Space Technology,* July 28, 2008, 50. See also *Jane's Defence Weekly,* August 6, 2008, 20. Apparently, in January 2004, Mikhail Kasyanov, the then prime minister, signed a decree over the control of Holding Sukhoi, the Antei-Almaz Corporation, the Tactical Missiles Corporation, the Russian Electronics Joint-Stock Company (JSC), and the Russian Chemical Defense (or *Roskhimzashchita*) Corporation. According to the source, the decree issued by Kasyanov had little to do with the improved efficiency of the enterprises but much to do with the government officials' redistribution of the state property. A very similar notion was on elaborated by Konstantin Makienko in an interview online, (accessed August 9, 2005). See also note 16. For the Russian Technologies appraisal of the MIC, see note 30. For the widespread embezzlement and misuse of state funds by defense companies and the government policy of increasing state control over the strategic sectors of the economy, which include the defense industry, see *Defense News,* October 6, 2008, 62. During a meeting between Prime Minister Vladimir Putin and Deputy Prime Minister Sergei Ivanov, the former demanded that the latter report how and where the allocated budget funds for the MIC are used. Apparently, Ivanov did not have full clarity regarding the questions. Igor Naumov, "Pushki vmesto masla" ("Cannons Instead of Butter"), http://www.ng.ru/economics/2008-09-15/6_army. html. Interestingly enough *Krasnaya Zvezda* claimed in 2006 that the state control over the expenditure allocated to the MIC had hardened. Andrei Garavskii, "Oboronka-briz peremen" ("Tee Defence Industry—Wind of Change"), http://www.redstar.ru/2006/11/22_11/1_02.html. Apparently the measure was insufficient, although officials within the Russian MIC would claim the opposite.

40. For a complete article, see *Jane's Defence Weekly,* August 6, 2008, 20.

41. *Defense News,* September 15, 2008, 34.

42. *Defense News,* September 15, 2008, 34. A very similar statement, namely that "A growth in the number of government orders and export contracts has overloaded defense enterprises, whose productivity has not changed" was also expressed by Sergei Chemezov, director-general of Russian Technologies. See Chemezov: "Moshchnosti Rossiiskogo VPK podoshli k predelu svoikh vozmozhnostei" (Chemezov: "The Capacity of the Russian Military-Industrial Complex Has Reached Its Ceiling"), http://www.gazeta.ru/news/business/2008/07/16/n_1244102.shtml and *Jane's Defence Weekly,* August 6, 2008, 20.

43. For a complete article, see Viktor Myasnikov and Mikhail Sergeyev, "Oboronka skatilas' v monpol'ku" ("The Military-Industrial Complex has Turn Into Monopoly"), http://www.ng.ru/index1/ (accessed April 20, 2007).

44. For a complete article, see http://www.cast.ru/comments/?form=print&id=330 (accessed December 8, 2008). See also "Rossiiskaya oboronka derzhitsya na chestnom slove Putina" (The Rus-

sian Defence Industry is Relying on the Thruthfulness of Putin"), http://www.izvestia.ru/news/news198694(accessed February 25, 2009).

45. For a complete article, see *Jane's Defence Weekly,* November 19, 2008, 21.

46. *Jane's Defence Weekly,* December 17, 2008, 19. In addition, as was reported earlier, the predominantly stated owned nature of the defense industry hampers Russia's ability to become more productive and efficient as the foreign private investment available to other sectors of the economy cannot flow into defense enterprises. *Jane's Defence Weekly,* August 20, 2008, 20.

47. The cartoons in this article were envisaged by the author and drawn by Lance Sucharov. I am very grateful to Lance Sucharov for them.

11

Arms and Autonomy: The Limits of China's Defense-Industrial Transformation

J. D. Kenneth Boutin

China's defense-industrial base is being transformed by the changing industrial landscape and by government efforts to enhance the capacity of industry to satisfy the ambitious armaments requirements of the People's Liberation Army (PLA). China is an archetypical techno-nationalist state, but has charted its own course in the pursuit of defense-industrial self-sufficiency. The sensitivity of the issue of dependence is reflected in China's defense-industrial development. For much of the history of the People's Republic, China's defense industry was effectively isolated from external market influences, and remains far less globalized than elsewhere, despite the progressive marketization of research and development (R&D) and production as the importance of commercial considerations in state-owned enterprises (SOEs) increases and authorities seek to harness emerging private-sector industrial capacities to the requirements of defense. The internal contradictions of China's defense-industrial model pose a major policy dilemma due to the difficulties inherent in attempting to exploit the opportunities provided by transnational processes of technological development and application without undermining defense-industrial autonomy. The nature of its defense-industrial transformation has major implications for China: while commercialization is helping to narrow the qualitative capability gap with other major industrialized states, restrictions on the transnational integration of defense firms constitute a significant obstacle to sustained capacity development.

This chapter examines the structural transformation of China's defense-industrial base and its evolving defense-industrial strategy as authorities strive to address the requirements stemming from the PLA's ongoing modernization while minimizing the exposure of defense firms to market fluctuations and politically-driven arms embargoes. It begins by considering the influences on China's defense-industrial strategy, before examining China's post-1978 defense-industrial revolution and the implications stemming from its approach to its complex and demanding policy requirements.

DEFENSE-INDUSTRIAL AUTONOMY IN CHINA

China was unique among developing states in that it succeeded in attaining genuine defense-industrial autonomy. While highly prized, this objective has proven very elusive in practice due to the necessity of sustained political support and commitment of resources. That China was able to accomplish this demonstrates the depth of commitment on the part of its leaders and the impact of difficult relationships with its arms suppliers in the past.

Defense-industrial autonomy is a long-established policy objective in China. Defense industrialization has constituted a key pillar of the national security agenda since China was subjected to the attentions of aggressive foreign powers fielding military forces equipped to a standard far surpassing those of China in the 19th century. The development of an indigenous capacity to produce modern arms was central to the Self-Strengthening Movement of the late imperial period. As one Chinese official wrote in 1864, "We must imitate the steamers [i.e. warships] in order to deprive the foreigners of the superiority through the very weapon they depend upon."[1] A number of arsenals were established in an effort to free China from the need to import arms from the very states that threatened its security. Defense industrialization remained an important policy objective during the tumultuous 1916–28 so-called "Warlord Period" and was pursued by the government of the Republic of China during World War II.[2] Despite determined efforts, China remained dependent on arms imports and often experienced difficulties securing adequate supplies in the face of financial constraints and politically driven arms embargoes.[3]

The importance attached to defense-industrial development did not abate with the restoration of effective central government when the People's Republic of China was established in 1949. China's new leaders moved quickly to reconstitute and develop the national defense-industrial base, and emphasized the importance of defense-related technological development in the Common Program of 1950, which served as the initial de facto constitution.[4] China registered impressive progress, and by 1960 it was self-sufficient in many categories of arms. The domestic orientation of China's defense industries was such that they were considered part of the logistical infrastructure of the PLA.[5] While it would be inaccurate to assume complete unity of purpose on the part of China's leaders since 1949, there has been general consensus on the necessity of maintaining comprehensive national defense-industrial capabilities.

China's post-1949 defense-industrial structure was geared toward the objective of autonomy. The government restored existing facilities and expanded its production capabilities using the Soviet Union's defense-industrial model as a template.[6] The salient features of China's defense-industrial model included a highly centralized and bureaucratic structure.[7] There was a state monopoly on defense-industrial R&D and production, with SOEs responsible for all production, and R&D the product of state research institutes and state-supported academic institutions.[8] Defense-related R&D and production was closely managed by relevant government ministries.

The security considerations underlying China's defense industrialization had an impact that extended well beyond the structure of industry. The focus on supporting China's defense establishment meant that the issue of economic viability did not figure significantly in defense-industrial considerations, though the size of the internal market provided by the

PLA certainly generated substantial economies of scale in many cases.[9] The subordination of economic to strategic considerations was further demonstrated by the extent to which China was prepared to go to preserve its defense-industrial capabilities in the event of a conflict. The "Third Front" initiative, which was pursued from the late 1960s through to the late 1970s, saw the geographical dispersal of defense-related production and R&D facilities to remote areas of central China at great cost in the interest of reducing their vulnerability to attack.[10]

The need to develop autonomous defense-industrial capabilities while recovering from the effects of a century of conflict and civil war discouraged ambitious R&D and production programs. Unlike many developing states, China's leaders were prepared to forego attempting to develop and produce arms approximating—or even approaching—the technological frontiers marked out by the advanced industrial states. A risk-averse nature was a feature of China's defense-industrial strategy that distinguished it from that of the Soviet Union.[11] China's defense-industrial program focused on evolutionary developments of existing arms designs at the expense of pursuing potentially promising but untried developmental paths. China did conform to the classical model of defense industrialization outlined in the preceding chapter of this volume, in the sense that it progressed to more advanced designs entailing progressively higher degrees of local responsibility. In terms of combat aircraft, for example, China began by producing the Soviet MiG-15 under license, and stepped up to reverse engineering Soviet designs such as the MiG-21, before producing derivatives of foreign designs and ultimately developing advanced indigenous designs such as the J-10. The technological bar has been notably lower than in the Soviet Union and other major states, however, with China's sights set on relatively modest objectives. It is noteworthy that, even now, efforts are being made to exploit what little potential remains in the design of the MiG-21 alongside the development of designs such as the J-10.

While Chinese authorities are not alone in valuing defense-industrial autonomy, the extent and vigor with which it has been pursued sets China apart. This has been a constant feature of its defense-industrial strategy that has survived administrative reorganizations and fluctuating funding levels. In most developing states, efforts to promote autonomous defense-industrial capabilities focus on the national production capability, and even this often is limited to coproduction or even the local assembly of foreign designs. In the case of China, this was coupled with interest in developing comprehensive R&D capabilities, albeit of a less advanced nature than those of other major states.

The strength of this objective in the case of China is also reflected in the relative isolation of its defense-industrial base. While Chinese authorities were prepared to accept foreign assistance, including in the form of technological inputs, they were wary of arrangements that had the potential to place China in a dependent relationship. China eschewed long-term defense-industrial relationships after 1960 in favor of the opportunistic exploitation of offshore resources through reverse engineering foreign designs and other forms of illicit technology transfer. The technical missions dispatched abroad by China after 1978 with the ostensible purpose of procuring arms were soon recognized as attempts to garner technological insights.[12] It was similarly recognized that there was little scope for exporting to China without contributing to its long-term defense-industrial development through technology transfer.[13]

The prioritization of defense-industrial autonomy is a direct consequence of China's treatment by foreign powers during the so-called "Century of Shame" that only ended with the establishment of the People's Republic, and of its experience with the international arms market. Official concern over the scope for meeting the material requirements of the PLA internationally without incurring a high political cost was reinforced by developments such as the Western arms embargo applied between the early 1950s and 1980s; the abrupt loss of access to Soviet arms and defense-industrial assistance after the Sino-Soviet split in 1960, which led to the abandonment of hundreds of Soviet-supported industrial projects and left China with a woefully inadequate capacity for the conduct of R&D;[14] and by the partial Western arms embargo reimposed following the suppression of demonstrations at Tiananmen Square in Beijing in 1989.[15]

China's emphasis on defense-industrial autonomy was more than a matter of making a virtue out of necessity. Bitter experience has driven home the importance of maintaining an independent national capacity for the development and production of arms. China's established defense-industrial model is consistent with its general emphasis on self-reliance (*zili gengsheng*), which has been considered an "indispensable component" of its security.[16] The speed with which China moved to reconstitute and expand its defense-industrial capabilities after 1949, despite the availability of Soviet arms, was noteworthy. While the secondary importance of technological progress can be attributed in part to China's relatively underdeveloped industrial capacity following a century of civil war and conflict, this testifies to the impact of concern over the political implications of defense-industrial dependence, as developing an advanced defense-related R&D capacity in the circumstances China was in at that point would have required a far more extensive foreign role than its leaders were prepared to accept.

China's defense-industrial strategy provided it with a strong capacity for the large-scale manufacture of a comprehensive range of relatively unsophisticated arms, but with little scope for matching, let alone surpassing, the qualitative capabilities demonstrated by other major states. China's defense-industrial autonomy thus came at a high qualitative cost. China has tended to produce arms that are obsolescent, if not obsolete, and has introduced new generations of equipment long after other major states. Its defense industries proved unable even to maintain their relative position in more sophisticated categories of arms. In the area of fighter aircraft, for example, China experienced absolute progress but relative decline in that it produced the early 1950s–vintage technology J-6 fighter in the 1960s, but by the 1980s only had progressed to producing the J-7, which was based on the Soviet MiG-21 design dating from the late 1950s. This has had major implications for China in terms of the potential utility of the PLA as a policy instrument, and determined China's niche as a supplier of low-cost, low-capability arms in the international market.

CHINA'S MODERN INDUSTRIAL REVOLUTION

China's defense-industrial model only came under threat when the changing strategic environment generated arms requirements that were beyond its capacity to deliver. Its established approach was adequate as long as People's War, with its emphasis on drawing invaders deep into China where they could be defeated by numerically superior Chinese forces, was regarded as a viable strategic doctrine. China's defense-industrial strategy was not considered adequate in the policy watershed that followed the death of Mao Zedong in 1976 and the subsequent reconsideration of the threat environment, which generated a force modernization agenda that national industry was ill-prepared to support. By the early 1980s, it was acknowledged that the PLA would be relying more on technology.[17] The subsequent formal abandonment of the People's War doctrine and the lackluster performance of Chinese arms in the Gulf War of 1990–91 have meant that technological obsolescence is no longer an option for the PLA, and its arms requirements continue to expand in concert with its ongoing doctrinal development.[18] The revolution in military affairs (RMA) has reached China, with the PLA now seeking to field high-technology forces.[19]

The defense-industrial impact of China's heightened emphasis on advanced arms has been softened by the organizational difficulties and resource requirements involved in transforming the PLA to meet its new doctrinal requirements. The sheer size of the PLA and the extent of the changes required mean that, despite increased defense expenditures and the fact that its reorganization has been underway for some time, this still has far to go. The introduction of modern capabilities is an ongoing process, which has enabled Chinese authorities to focus on meeting the material requirements of a relatively small section of the PLA. Demands on the defense-industrial base will increase, however, as the military reform process deepens.

Concern over the technological competence of China's defense industries has been accompanied by attention to the issue of their efficiency. China's defense-industrial base was characterized by outdated production facilities, overcapacity, unprofitability, and weak accountability.[20] These features are recognized as obstacles to its capacity to respond to the changing requirements of its primary customer, particularly given the budgetary pressures facing the government, which mean that defense-industrial development must compete for resources with other pressing requirements. The prioritization of accelerated economic development from the late 1970s onward demanded resources that otherwise would have been available for defense-industrial development. While the government has been in a position to devote substantial resources to defense-related R&D and production, this evidently has not kept pace with the requirements of force modernization. This deficit has encouraged attention to the issue of the efficiency of the SOEs constituting the defense-industrial base and promoted efforts to more effectively harness the capacity of those that were primarily engaged in meeting the requirements of the civil sector. By the early 1980s, there were renewed calls for "integrating military and civil production."[21]

China's integrated approach to industrial development constitutes a key feature of its current defense-industrial strategy.[22] Chinese authorities have sought to exploit the excess capacity of defense firms to help meet civil requirements, including through technology transfer.[23] Alongside this, the government has recognized the scope for the civil SOE sector to demonstrate useful practices to defense SOEs, as well as providing more direct assistance. Civil SOEs potentially offer invaluable opportunities for accessing militarily relevant dual-use technologies and commercial off-the-shelf (COTS) products through commercial channels. This capacity has grown as civil SOEs have developed their R&D capabilities and have become more active participants in the global economy, and as technological requirements in the civil and defense sectors have converged.

The importance of civil industry in China's defense-industrial strategy means that recent trends must be examined in the context of its overall economic development. The importance of this has increased as the developmental paths of China's civil and defense industries have diverged. The pattern of development in China's civil SOE sector has involved the deepening integration of firms in globalized, transnational processes of R&D and production. This has not been mirrored in the defense SOE sector, where security-driven concern over dependence has limited the scope for this. The civil sector thus serves as a means of accessing globalized industrial processes without incurring the political costs that would result from allowing the defense industry to engage at this level. China's defense-industrial development is being pursued in tandem with its general economic development as a result of its efforts to exploit the opportunities provided by globalization in this manner.

The changed political environment that resulted from the death of Mao provided space for both economic reforms and for the development of private sector industrial capabilities, which have proven mutually supporting. Heightened attention to economic development has seen considerable emphasis on technological progress and on greater participation in the global economy.[24] This paved the way for the progressive introduction of what is termed *market socialism*. Rather than involving any definite long-term strategy, this developed gradually from the initial approval for the establishment of operations in a select number of special economic zones (SEZs) by foreign firms, including those active in high-technology product areas.[25] In many cases, Chinese subsidiaries of foreign firms developed into more substantive production facilities and, in some cases, even progressed to undertaking R&D on behalf of the parent firm. Chinese SOEs, meanwhile, were also developing their capacities to participate in the global economy and began to forge ties with foreign partners. There has been increasing Chinese participation in transnational structures for technological development, application, and diffusion as its economy has developed. This has taken the form of project-specific joint ventures and longer-term strategic partnerships, and there is growing interest in the codevelopment of products for the global market. Chinese-based multinational corporations such as Lenovo have emerged in recent years and are helping to drive this trend.

It is noteworthy that Chinese authorities have permitted these trends to develop in crucial high-technology industrial sectors such as aerospace and information technology (IT). In fact, the development of innovative functional relationships with foreign capability partners has been supported by the Chinese government. It has encouraged collaboration with foreign firms, and in 2001 adopted the "going out" strategy, which encouraged offshore investment by Chinese firms.[26] In the aerospace sector, Chinese SOEs now participate as risk-sharing partners in multilateral R&D programs, such as that for the EC 120 Colibri light helicopter and the Airbus A350 airliner.[27] This is a significant trend due to the importance attached to high-technology industry in terms of China's overall economic development and its efforts to modernize its defense-industrial base, and demonstrates the perceived value to Chinese policy requirements of extensive engagement of offshore high-technology industry.

These trends have been accompanied by the transformation of the domestic environment for R&D and production. There has been a progressive commercialization of R&D and production as officials and managers have learnt through their collaboration with offshore industry. This has involved the introduction of measures designed to enhance efficiency and profitability, and efforts have been made since the mid-1990s to develop a more market-oriented R&D system, including through transforming state research institutes into independent enterprises.[28] In 2001, Minister of Science and Technology Xu Guanhua emphasized that research institutes "should make their own ends meet."[29] The Chinese industrial landscape now encompasses what has been termed the quasi-state or quasi-market sector. This refers to the growing number of semi-autonomous firms established by state bodies under what is sometimes regarded as a form of limited privatization.[30] This is not true privatization in that it reflects efforts to draw on the market for capital by allowing enterprises to offer shares rather than any interest in allowing the market to shape these enterprises, but nonetheless represents a significant shift for Chinese economic policy.

These trends, however pale in comparison to the reemergence of the private sector as a significant factor in the Chinese economy. This includes in terms of defense-industrial activities, as noted below. This constitutes a major policy departure for China given its political and economic background and official socialist ideology. This trend and the deepening commercialization of SOEs have been made possible by the success of market socialism as a developmental approach. This has facilitated official openness to the erosion of the boundaries separating domestic from foreign industry. Deng Xiaoping, for example, praised the SEZs as "windows of technology" for China.[31]

These trends, if allowed to progress in the manner they have elsewhere, threaten to undermine the autonomy of China's defense-industrial base. That their impact has been rather less up to this point is evidence of the continued salience of official concern over the political implications of defense-industrial dependence. This is leading Chinese authorities to seek to set the terms in which industry engages the global economy. These terms are intended to preserve the autonomy of its defense-industrial base.

ENDURING CONCERNS AND NEW REQUIREMENTS

The difficult task facing Chinese authorities is how to manage defense-industrial development that meets the arms requirements of the PLA in such a manner that it does not jeopardize the autonomy of the defense-industrial base. Defense-industrial transformation is not being pursued with the intention of relinquishing the central role of the state, nor does it involve a shift away from the traditional emphasis on import substitution.[32] The qualitative arms requirements resulting from interest in developing the capabilities of the PLA compel authorities to relax the standards of defense-industrial autonomy, but this objective has by no means been abandoned. Recognition of the necessity of revising the defense-industrial strategy has been evident since the early 1980s. In 1983, for example, Defense Minister Zhang Aiping conceded that it was necessary for China to access foreign technologies while reaffirming the importance of defense-industrial self-reliance.[33] Support within the PLA for defense-industrial transformation has been evident for some time.[34]

China's defense-industrial transformation has been gradual. This has involved a succession of incremental policy changes, rather than a systematic long-term strategy. National defense was one of the "Four Modernizations" announced in 1975, but market-oriented economic reforms have only gradually and partially extended to the defense-industrial sector. Early transformative efforts focused on organizational restructuring and managerial changes in order to enhance the efficiency and productivity of defense SOEs. These efforts continue, and have been joined by interest in promoting both greater competition in the defense-industrial sector and collaboration between compatible SOEs. Commercialization is now well established in the defense-industrial base. Restructuring efforts have seen the establishment of semi-autonomous enterprises such as the China North Industries Corporation (NORINCO), as well as significant decentralization.[35] This has been accompanied by some rationalization of industrial capabilities, which mirrors the consolidation trends found in other countries as industry struggled with the contracted post–cold war defense market.

Tension between the imperatives of security and modernization has been manifest in the initially very tentative and still gradual nature of China's defense-industrial "opening up" to the world, which continues to lag far behind that of its economy in general. Despite the similarity of the concerns underlying efforts to revise industrial strategies in the civil and defense SOE sectors, the globalization in the defense-industrial sector remains quite limited. The globalization of China's defense-industrial sector began with efforts to supplement national resources through substantive but still very selective purchases from other states.[36] In some cases, this support was illicit, but China's improving political relationships with Western states enabled it to draw openly on the resources of an expanding range of defense firms. This itself posed no real threat to China's defense-industrial autonomy, but laid the basis for engaging foreign industry at a more basic level in terms of drawing on foreign firms for technical assistance, which was evident by the early 1980s.[37] To this end, the China National Aero Technology Import and Export Corporation (CATIC) established offices in the United States and the United Kingdom by 1982 and SOEs began to send representatives to international arms exhibitions.[38]

The transition from what was basically a Soviet-type defense-industrial base is continuing, but does not correspond to developmental patterns evident elsewhere, despite common concern over spiraling operational and resource requirements.[39] Chinese authorities are resisting globalization in limiting the extent and nature of collaboration with foreign industry and by ensuring that control of key industries remains in Chinese hands. While Chinese officials invited foreign investment in the defense-industrial sector in the early 1990s,[40] the "shareholding reforms" announced by the Commission of Science, Technology, and Industry for National Defense (COSTIND) in 2007 permit this only under certain conditions.[41] Globalization involving the Chinese defense-industrial base is effectively one-way, with approval and support for defense enterprises' efforts to exploit the opportunities this presents abroad, but not for any loss of control or capacity at home. As a result, China's developing defense-industrial capabilities are much more dependent on general economic reforms and the general development of industry than is usual. The principal features of China's present defense-industrial model are outlined in the section that follows.

THE CHINESE DEFENSE-INDUSTRIAL MODEL

Rather than the straightforward and static division of labor that formerly characterized the Chinese defense-industrial base, it now features competition between defense SOEs. Recent years have seen the emergence of an intensely competitive domestic defense-industrial environment, with different enterprises developing competing designs to vie for PLA orders. Chinese authorities support the development of competing arms designs as a means of encouraging efficiency and competitiveness, and are no longer necessarily committed to the preservation of the production or R&D capabilities of a particular SOE.[42] This approach is paying dividends in driving defense SOEs to develop the advanced arms required by the PLA. Unlike the situation elsewhere, however, this is not encouraging them to globalize their operations, other than in the limited sense of acquiring or otherwise gaining access to the resources of foreign high-technology firms. The consequences of this are explored below.

This commercialization of the Chinese defense-industrial base has had unintended—though not entirely negative—effects in encouraging firms to seek to maintain themselves through exports. The increasing importance of commercial considerations of profitability is encouraging defense SOEs to export their products. China first exhibited defense-related products in the West in the early 1980s,[43] and it soon emerged as a major supplier to the Middle East. Recent years have seen increasing interest in exports, with more attention to developing products for the export market and more active marketing by firms such as NORINCO and the Poly Technologies Corporation.

China's role as an arms supplier has evolved in concert with its industrial development and the increasing importance of exports to Chinese firms. Chinese arms transfers are now more economically than politically driven, and there has been a notable transition of China as an exporter of the arms designs that were fielded by the PLA to an exporter of a wider range of arms and a provider of an extensive array of arms-related technologies and services. This reflects both the evolving capabilities of Chinese industry and the crowded nature of that section of the international arms market occupied by states in a position to supply low-cost, low-capability arms. The proliferation of arms developed by defense SOEs with the export market in mind has largely comprised designs offering reasonably advanced capabilities at relatively low cost. China's profile as an arms supplier has come to include supplying components and technologies in support of offshore arms R&D and production programs.[44] These activities have official support due to the obvious benefits that arms exports provide for China.

The growing role of the private sector is an important aspect of the commercialization of China's defense-industrial base. A growing number of privately owned high-technology firms are contributing to state-led defense programs.[45] Though the private sector is not extensively developed at present, current trends suggest that it will continue to expand with the encouragement and support of the government. The government has issued guidelines for private sector defense firms, and it announced in 2006 that it was prepared to subsidize the manufacture of arms by the private sector.[46] The 863 Plan is but one of a number of programs developed for the general support of industry that have considerable scope for contributing to the capacity of private industry to support defense-industrial requirements.

Chinese authorities remain intent on maintaining close control over key activities in order to ensure that the defense-industrial base continues to meet the requirements of the PLA. This is evident at both the domestic and international levels. Successive organizational restructurings have not seen the elimination of supervisory mechanisms in the defense-industrial sector, and a tight rein is maintained on those international activities that have the potential to affect China's defense-industrial autonomy. Interest in ensuring the continued capacity of defense SOEs to meet the requirements of the PLA is manifest in efforts to maintain their focus on defense-related activities in an environment of potentially lucrative development and production for the civil market.[47]

The nature of China's interstate defense-industrial relationships is also noteworthy. These largely involve states that are far less developed than China in defense-industrial terms, with China assuming the leading role, and are often project-specific. Most programs are limited to the production or even assembly of Chinese arms abroad. Examples include the assistance provided Pakistan to enable it to produce the Chinese-designed JF-17 fighter aircraft. Where defense-industrial collaboration does involve R&D, this is concerned with relatively unsophisticated arms and China clearly is the dominant partner, such as with the K-8 trainer aircraft, which also involves Pakistan. China has entered into a number of project-specific defense-industrial cooperation agreements in the past few years. In most cases, China constitutes the lead nation, partnering with states such as Indonesia and Pakistan.[48] China may be involved on a more equitable level with Russia, however.[49] The Chinese government is most open to substantial collaboration on R&D where this involves designs that are not intended for fielding by the PLA. Framework agreements for general defense-industrial collaboration are much less in evidence, but include an agreement signed with Chile in 1993 and one reached with Indonesia in 2000.[50]

The Chinese government is notably eclectic in its choice of defense-industrial partners and arms sources. It is prepared to draw on the products and services of the defense industries of a broad range of states, including Israel, with which it has not traditionally enjoyed close political relations. This approach is a common feature of concern over the political implications of dependence on arms suppliers, and serves to lessen the potential influence of any single supplier.

China continues to support the PLA's modernization efforts though reverse engineering foreign arms designs and looking to offshore industry for an indication of potentially useful technological approaches. The continuing use of these tactics does much to sustain China's image as a copier of foreign arms, despite the technological competency demonstrated by its industry. Interest in maintaining defense-industrial autonomy has also not stood in the way of procuring arms where this is seen as justified by the capability enhancements that it may provide the PLA.[51]

AUTONOMY AND THE LIMITS OF CHANGE

China's distinct policy requirements will encourage it to continue on its present course. The globalization of the civil industrial sector is crucial given the government's approach to both economic and defense-industrial development. Chinese authorities cannot be unaware that a more dynamic and globally connected industrial base is better positioned to provide advanced technologies relevant to the requirements of the PLA, including through leveraging commercial ties with offshore industry. As Feigenbaum notes, "Chinese technology planners now understand defense requirements are thoroughly derivative of commercial developments."[52] At the same time, however, the dictates of security will continue to exert a restraining influence on this approach.

China's defense-industrial model provides an improved basis for meeting its requirements. It can be expected that China will see a reduction in its traditionally protracted developmental cycles for major arms. An accelerated pace of technological innovation will help to narrow the qualitative gap with the other major industrialized states, but is unlikely to provide the basis for any substantial bypassing of product generations. It is likely that China will improve is reputation as a source of arms that are competitive in qualitative as well as price terms. China has made impressive progress in this direction already with its growing success in exporting arms to what are, for it, nontraditional markets in Latin America, Europe, and sub-Saharan Africa.

While the structural transformation of China's defense-industrial landscape is providing it with more capable and more efficient capabilities, its strategy prevents it from realizing the full potential of its market-oriented economic reform efforts. The continuing requirement for a high level of autonomy encompassing both R&D and production will result in SOEs retaining their central role as the cornerstone of the defense-industrial base for the foreseeable future, for example. This defense-industrial model will require the continuing commitment of far more substantial resources to defense SOEs by the Chinese government than would be the case if it were prepared to be less political in its approach to their operations. Effectively balancing the requirements of the civil- and defense-industrial sectors will require skilful management. The progressive development of the Chinese economy will generate pressures in the private and state sectors of industry that will be difficult to reconcile with the demands of defense-industrial autonomy over the long term.

The most serious implications resulting from China's defense-industrial strategy derive from the nature of its engagement with processes of globalization. The intermediate position of the Chinese government with respect to globalization where the defense-industrial sector is concerned is having an impact on its potential for benefiting from participation in processes of globalization. China's essentially exploitative approach to dealing with offshore industry discourages the development and deepening of collaborative arrangements, and will continue to generate and sustain political opposition to offshore operations of Chinese high-technology industry. While there is openness to Chinese investment in the defense-industrial sector in a number of states, this generally does not extend to the developed industrial states that have the most to offer China.[53] Chinese-owned enterprises are regarded in many cases as front companies for illicit technology transfer in these states. This is generating significant concern on the part of a number of foreign governments on security grounds.

Concern is most evident on the part of the United States, where the issues raised in the Cox Report of 1999 remain salient. The extent to which China's defense-industrial progress has benefited from the activities of the civil sector are recognized in the United States.[54] As a result, China constitutes the major object of attention of the comprehensive regime designed to maintain the defense-industrial advantage of the United States. It has developed extensive regulatory requirements concerning mergers and acquisitions involving American firms by foreign firms that are state-owned where this potentially affects its national security. The Exon-Florio provision of the Omnibus Trade and Competitiveness Act of 1988 enables the U.S. government to block mergers or acquisitions of firms where there is "credible evidence" that this would have a detrimental impact on national security.[55]

The Committee on Foreign Investment in the United States (CFIUS) pays particular attention to Chinese firms as a result of concern over the defense-industrial implications of the American activities of Chinese firms, and potentially considers all Chinese enterprises to be state-owned due to the difficulties inherent in distinguishing between its state and private sectors.[56] Similar scrutiny is exercised over collaborative arrangements involving Chinese industry, with a negative impact on China's industrial development.

Recognition of the impact of its current approach on its long-term defense-industrial development may prompt reconsideration of this approach, but the price in terms of autonomy will likely prove too high to allow for any significant change. Chinese authorities will continue to face the "autarky-efficiency dilemma" described by Andrew Moravcsik: "the inescapable fact that greater autonomy can be bought only at the price of reduced efficiency in armament production."[57] There is greater potential for concern over the long-term implications of the integration of Chinese high-technology industry in transnational R&D and production processes to encourage a policy shift, if integration reaches the point where China is regarded as too vulnerable to external political and market influences.[58]

CONCLUSION

China is likely to maintain its position as the state that has succeeded in developing comprehensive national defense-industrial capabilities from a very basic starting point, albeit at a high cost in qualitative terms. China's interest in technological progress is unlikely to abate, but defense-industrial autonomy will remain a key policy objective. China's interest in bypassing complete generations of arms is unlikely to be realized as long as it pursues its present approach, though it may well register impressive progress in particular sectors, such as has already occurred in a number of areas like antiship missiles and antisatellite weapons.

The Chinese government has demonstrated that it is prepared to consider major policy shifts in its defense-industrial strategy, and Chinese industry has proven its adaptability to changing government requirements. This suggests that there is considerable scope for China's defense-industrial policy to evolve further as requirements and structural conditions demand.

NOTES

1. Quoted in John L. Rawlinson, *China's Struggle for Naval Development 1839–1895* (Cambridge, MA: Harvard University Press, 1967), 38.
2. For the Warlord Period, see Anthony B. Chan, *Arming the Chinese: The Western Armaments Trade in Warlord China, 1920–1928* (Vancouver: University of British Columbia Press, 1982), 110–15; for World War II, see William C. Kirby, "The Chinese War Economy," in *China's Bitter Victory: The War with Japan 1937–1945,* ed. James C. Hsiung and Steven I. Levine (Armonk, NY: M.E. Sharpe, 1992), 193–96.
3. See, for example: Chan, *Arming the Chinese,* 59.
4. Yeu-Farn Wang, *China's Science and Technology Policy: 1949–1989* (Aldershot: Avebury, 1993), 37. See David Shambaugh, *Modernizing China's Military: Progress, Problems, and Prospects* (Berkeley, CA: University of California Press, 2002), 226; and Yitzhak Shichor, "Conversion and Diversion: The Politics of China's Military Industry after Mao," in *The Politics and Economics of Defence*

Industries, ed. Efraim Inbar and Benzion Zilberfarb (London: Frank Cass, 1998), 137, for an indication of the extent of early efforts to develop the defense-industrial base under the People's Republic.

5. James Mulvenon, *Soldiers of Fortune: The Rise and Fall of the Chinese Military-Business Complex, 1978–1999,* paper 15 (Bonn: Bonn International Center for Conversion [BICC], 1999), 7. See also Paul Humes Folta, *From Swords to Plowshares? Defense Industry Reform in the PRC* (Boulder, CO: Westview Press, 1992), 5.

6. It is important to note, however, that some of its key features predate the People's Republic by a long time. See Peter A. Lorge, *The Asian Military Revolution: From Gunpowder to the Bomb* (Cambridge: Cambridge University Press, 2008), 71.

7. Richard A. Bitzinger, "Reforming China's Defense Industry: Progress in Spite of Itself?" *The Korean Journal of Defense Analysis* 19, no. 3 (2007): 106.

8. The exception to this was the limited tolerance of private enterprises until about 1956, but this did not involve large firms. See Wang, *China's Science and Technology Policy 1949–1989,* 43; and Tony Saich, "Reform of China's Science and Technology Organizational System," in *Science and Technology in Post-Mao China,* ed. Denis Fred Simon and Merle Goldman (Cambridge, MA: Harvard University Press, 1989), 73.

9. See, for example, Ron Matthews and Xu Bo, "China's Aerospace Self-Reliance Still Elusive," *Asia-Pacific Defence Reporter* 28, no. 6 (2002): 36.

10. Shambaugh, *Modernizing China's Military,* 227.

11. See Bitzinger, "Reforming China's Defense Industry," 106.

12. Harlan W. Jencks, *From Muskets to Missiles: Politics and Professionalism in the Chinese Army, 1945–1981* (Boulder, CO: Westview Press, 1982), 198. Chinese military and industry personnel continue to exploit the potential of prospective arms purchases to gain technological insights from foreign industry. See Reuben F. Johnson, "Talks Twist and Turn as Chinese Navy Eyes Su-33," *Jane's Defence Weekly* March 18, 2009, 4.

13. *Jane's Defence Weekly,* "Exporting to China Will Mean Technology Transfer," June 29, 1985, 1290.

14. Bates Gill and Taeho Kim, *China's Arms Acquisitions from Abroad: A Quest for "Superb and Secret Weapons,"* SIPRI research report 11 (Oxford: Oxford University Press, 1995), 31; and Iris Chang, *Thread of the Silkworm* (New York: Basic Books, 1995), 208.

15. See Michael Mecham, "U.S. Suspends Military Sales in Wake of Massacre in China," *Aviation Week & Space Technology* June 12, 1989, 69–72.

16. Han S. Park and Kyung A. Park, "Ideology and Security: Self-Reliance in China and North Korea," in *National Security in the Third World: The Management of Internal and External Threats,* ed. Edward E. Azar and Chung-in Moon (Aldershot: Edward Elgar Publishing, 1988), 119.

17. Richard J. Latham, "The People's Republic of China: Profits, Consumerism, and Arms Sales," in *The Implications of Third World Military Industrialization: Sowing the Serpents' Teeth,* ed. James Everett Katz (Lexington, MA: D.C. Heath and Co., 1986), 189.

18. See Paul Beaver, "China Eyes the West to Finance Defence Growth," *Jane's Defence Weekly* July 23, 1997, 21.

19. See Anthony H. Cordesman and Martin Kleiber, *Chinese Military Modernization: Force Development and Strategic Capabilities* (Washington, DC: The CSIS Press, 2007), for an indication of the expanding technological requirements of the PLA.

20. See Bitzinger, "Reforming China's Defense Industry," 105–07.

21. Latham, "The People's Republic of China," 189–90.

22. This has been reaffirmed in China's most recent defense white paper. See Information Office of the State Council of the People's Republic of China, *China's National Defense in 2008* (Beijing: Information Office of the State Council of the People's Republic of China, 2009), 43.

23. See *Jane's Defence Weekly,* "China Declassifies Technologies," November 4, 1989), 953.

24. See Lawrence C. Reardon, *The Reluctant Dragon: Crisis Cycles in Chinese Foreign Economic Policy* (Seattle, WA: The University of Washington Press, 2002), 190–91.

25. See Richard A. Bitzinger, "Dual-Use Technologies, Civil-Military Integration, and China's Defense Industry," in *Chinese Civil-Military Relations: The Transformation of the People's Liberation Army,* ed. Nan Li (London: Routledge, 2006), 181.

26. Edward M. Graham and David M. Marchick, *US National Security and Direct Foreign Investment* (Washington, DC: Institute for International Economics, 2006), 100–101.

27. Lindsey Shanson, "Three Sign Up for P 120 Production," *Jane's Defence Weekly,* February 24, 1990), 367; and Jon Grevatt, "Airbus Inks Two Deals with Chinese Aerospace Industries," *Jane's Defence Weekly* December 5, 2007), 17.

28. Sylvia Schwaag Serger and Magnus Breidne, "China's Fifteen-Year Plan for Science and Technology: An Assessment," *Asia Policy* 4 (2007): 138–40.

29. Xinhua News Agency, "China: Science Minister Calls for Restructuring Research Bodies," April 24, 2001 (BBC Monitoring Global Newsline, 2001).

30. See Bruce Gilley, "Caught in a Double Bind," *Far Eastern Economic Review* 164, no. 11 (2001): 51–54.

31. Lawrence C. Reardon, "The Rise and Decline of China's Export Processing Zones," *Journal of Contemporary China* 5, no. 13 (1996): 295.

32. Tai Ming Cheung, *Fortifying China: The Struggle to Build a Modern Defense Economy* (Ithaca, NY: Cornell University Press, 2009), 238.

33. Gill and Kim, *China's Arms Acquisitions from Abroad,* 35.

34. See Darren Lake, "PLA Urges Reform of Defence Industry," *Jane's Defence Weekly,* September 6, 2000, 25.

35. See Robert Karniol, "China's Bid to Improve R&D Management," *Jane's Defence Weekly,* September 19, 1987, 597; and *Jane's Defence Weekly,* "Industry Embraces Market Forces," December 16, 1998, 28. For a comprehensive overview of recent policy initiatives, see Bitzinger, "Reforming China's Defense Industry," 107–12.

36. See Gill and Kim, *China's Arms Acquisitions from Abroad,* 92–93, for an indication of some of the programs involved.

37. See, for example: Tony Banks, "Racal Signs SWSA Agreement with China," *Jane's Defence Weekly* September 12, 1987, 499; and *Jane's Defence Weekly,* "SNECMA Signs F-7 Engine Contract," October 22, 1988, 1004.

38. *Jane's Defence Review,* "Chinese Aerospace Products," *Jane's Defence Review* 3, no. 1 (1982): 3.

39. See David Mussington, *Arms Unbound: The Globalization of Defense Production,* CSIA Studies in International Security 4 (Washington, DC: CSIA and Brassey's, 1994), for an overviews of general post–cold war defense-industrial trends.

40. Paul Beaver, "China to Liberalize Defence Industry," *Jane's Defence Weekly* October 24, 1992, 11.

41. *Jane's Industry Quarterly,* "Exports and Global Influence," *Jane's Industry Quarterly* 1, no. 1 (2008): 9. For a useful survey of relevant initiatives, see: Evan S. Medeiros, Roger Cliff, Keith Crane, and James C. Mulvenon, et al., *A New Direction for China's Defense Industry* (Santa Monica, CA: Rand Corp., 2005), 39–46.

42. See, for example: Sergio Coniglio, "China Develops Stealth Fighter," *Military Technology* 30, no. 2 (2006): 44.

43. *Jane's Defence Review,* "Chinese Aerospace Products," *Jane's Defence Review* 3, no. 1 (1982): 3.

44. See, for example: Samuel Blythe, "Myanmar Receives Frigate Engines from China," *Jane's Defence Weekly* August 1, 2007), 16; and Robert Hewson, "China, Iran Share Missile Know-how," *Jane's Defence Weekly* December 4, 2002), 15.

45. See, for example, Tai Ming Cheung, *Fortifying China*, 215–21.

46. Jon Grevatt, "China Outlines Guidelines for Private Investors," *Jane's Defence Weekly* August 15, 2007), 20; and Ben Vogel, "China to Subsidise Private Sector Defence Activities," *Jane's Defence Weekly* August 16, 2006, 18.

47. *Jane's Defence Weekly*, "Industry Overhaul Continues," July 11, 2001, 26.

48. See, for example: Jon Grevatt, "Pakistan and India Consider Further Industry Co-operation," *Jane's Defence Weekly*, April 23, 2008, 26.

49. See Tomasz Szulc, "A Brief History of 'Thunders': The Development of Chinese Air-to-Air Missiles," *Military Technology* 27, no. 11 (2003): 35. Another possible exception is collaboration with Iran in the area of missile development. Considerable uncertainty surrounds the nature and extent of collaboration with Iran, however. See Eric Arnett, "Chinese Blow Cold on East Wind Missile Plan," *Jane's Defence Weekly*, December 4, 1996), 3; and Robert Hewson, "China Rolls Out Z-9 Helo Naval Variant with Anti-Ship Missile," *Jane's Defence Weekly*, August 6, 2008, 8.

50. *Military Technology*, "Chile and China Sign Cooperation Agreement," *Military Technology* 17, no. 6 (1993): 78; and John Haseman, "Indonesia, China Expand Co-operation," *Jane's Defence Weekly*, May 24, 2000, 4.

51. See Nikolai Novichkov, "China's Russian Kilo Buy May Put Song Submarine Future in Doubt," *Jane's Defence Weekly*, June 12, 2002, 3.

52. Evan A. Feigenbaum, *China's Techno-warriors: National Security and Strategic Competition from the Nuclear to the Information Age* (Stanford, CA: Stanford University Press, 2003), 219.

53. See, for example: Jon Grevatt, "Indonesia, China Agree Equipment Development Deal," *Jane's Defence Weekly* January 23, 2008, 16.

54. Grevatt, "Airbus Inks Two Deals with Chinese Aerospace Industries," 17.

55. James K. Jackson, *The Exon-Florio National Security Test for Foreign Investment* (Washington, DC: Congressional Research Service, 2008), 3.

56. Graham and Marchick, *US National Security and Direct Foreign Investment*, 104–105.

57. Andrew Moravcsik, "Arms and Autonomy in Modern European History," *Daedalus* 120, no. 4 (1991): 23.

58. J. D. Kenneth Boutin, *Reconceptualizing Asia-Pacific Defence Industrialization: The New Political Economy of Security*, CANCAPS paper 35 (Toronto: Canadian Consortium on Asia Pacific Security, 2004), 12–13.

12

Emerging Defense Industries: Prospects and Implications

J. D. Kenneth Boutin

Defense industrialization in less developed areas is hardly a new phenomenon, but only became widespread following World War II. The contemporary defense-industrial landscape features a substantial body of emerging producers alongside the established producers of the developed industrial states. The ranks of the defense-industrial producers expanded greatly following World War II as political authorities in newly independent states sought to develop local capabilities for the production and development of armaments, while authorities in states that were already independent sought to enhance existing defense industries. Despite results that were are often disappointing, defense industrialization remains an important policy objective throughout the developing world.

Perspectives on the emergence of new or significantly more capable defense-industrial producers vary greatly. While defense industrialization is supported by some as a means of overcoming the dependency inherent in relying on other states for crucial arms supplies, thereby enhancing national sovereignty, or as an important vehicle for economic development, others are concerned about its contribution to the potentially destabilizing proliferation of advanced military capabilities, the eroding effectiveness of arms trade controls, or the potentially negative socioeconomic effects of defense industrialization. The complexity of the issues involved and the politico-military implications of defense industrialization in developing states ensure that this will continue to be the subject of intense scholarly and policy debate.

This chapter analyses the prospects and implications of defense industrialization in developing states. It considers the objectives underlying efforts to develop indigenous defense-industrial capabilities, the benefits this has for the states concerned, and the politico-military implications of defense industrialization. While resource and structural obstacles limit the development of extensive national capabilities in many cases, defense industrialization still contributes to important national objectives, and policy interest in this remains strong as a result. The most impressive defense-industrial strides are being made in the emerging industrial states, but even here this is not producing defense-industrial autonomy. The distinct nature of defense industrialization in these states, where this is integral to general processes of industrial and technological development involving extensive transnational integration, highlights the need to reconsider some of the assumptions that have guided analyses of developing state defense industrialization.

IMPORTING THE EUROPEAN ARSENAL?

Defense industrialization in developing states is generally examined through a conceptual lens informed by the example of the developed industrial states. It is commonly accepted that political authorities in developing states aspire to defense-industrial capabilities similar to those that supposedly characterize European, North American, and select Asian states such as Japan, and that they will develop these capabilities incrementally. These expectations provide a useful starting point for analyzing relevant trends and developments, but must be qualified in respect to the developing states. While political authorities in many developing states appear intent on emulating the defense industries commonly identified with the developed industrial states, more complex policy requirements, structural impediments, and the increasingly demanding developmental and production requirements of advanced arms may result in defense industrialization that differs significantly from that in the developed states.

The classical model of defense industrialization that is informed by expectations deriving from the developed industrial states involves the progressive development of increasingly sophisticated and autonomous indigenous capabilities for arms-related production and research and development (R&D). This model assumes that political authorities are interested in establishing an independent capability to meet the full range of their arms requirements, and that the route by which they do so will be linear. The logic inherent in the gradual development of national capabilities that is manifest in this understanding of defense industrialization contributes to its continuing currency in scholarly and policy circles.

The conventional wisdom regarding defense industrialization is reflected in efforts to categorize developing states' defense industries in terms of distinct capability tiers, and in the development of templates identifying sequential developmental stages in defense industrialization.[1] These constitute useful descriptive devices and offer general guides for considering potential defense-industrial trajectories in developing states. Both must be used with caution, however. There are major difficulties inherent in attempting to categorize defense-industrial activities, which are compounded in the case of the emerging industrial states by the crucial role of foreign industrial and technological assets, while efforts to develop suitable templates are complicated by often-significant intersectoral differences and the sporadic nature of defense-industrial development in many developing states. Despite this, defense-industrial programs in developing states are commonly assessed against the standard of the developed industrial states.

The classical model of defense industrialization is relevant to the developing states. Political authorities in many cases are interested in following the defense-industrial lead of the developed industrial states, both in terms of objectives and the course by which they are attained. It is also often the case that defense-industrial capabilities develop very gradually. As noted below, however, defense-industrial programs do not necessarily conform to official statements, and the protracted nature of defense industrialization does not necessarily reflect a methodical developmental approach. It is important to move beyond a focus on policy declarations and to consider the factors underlying the nature of defense industrialization in developing states in analyzing its prospects and implications.

Defense-industrial objectives and developmental patterns in the developing states are examined below. This indicates the extent to which defense industrialization in developing states differs from the classical model. While, generally, developing state defense industrialization falls well short of providing sustainable comprehensive national capabilities, it still offers important politico-military and other benefits to the states concerned.

The Objectives of Defense Industrialization

National security concerns are generally assumed to drive defense industrialization. National security constitutes an issue of great importance—if not the primary focus—of authorities in many states, and it is not coincidental that fluctuating interest in defense industrialization often corresponds to changes in the national security environment. An increased emphasis on defense industrialization characterizes periods of international tension or conflict, such as that leading up to World War II and during the cold war.[2] It is noteworthy that the more ambitious defense-industrial programs in the developing world tend to be found in states with strong national security concerns, such as India, Iran, Pakistan, and South Africa.

The political implications of dependence on foreign arms suppliers underpin the importance of defense industrialization to national security. The arms supply environment can be unpredictable and unreliable, particularly during periods of heightened international tension, and there is considerable scope for arms suppliers to exploit the political leverage they have with developing state customers. There are numerous cases of developing states being embargoed or otherwise encountering major difficulties in securing adequate arms supplies during times of conflict. Iran, for example, suffered considerable material losses during the early stages of its war with Iraq as a result of the U.S. arms embargo imposed after the overthrow of the shah.[3]

Concerns stemming from the vagaries of the international arms market encourage the development of national capabilities to meet the material requirements of local defense establishments. Developing a defense-industrial base capable of independently developing and producing the full range of arms required is necessary if states are to escape their dependence on external suppliers and maximize their political freedom of action. Some analysts argue that this objective is so crucial that political authorities in developing states are prepared to subordinate economic development to the requirements of defense industrialization.[4] The particular types of arms that national defense industries need to be able to supply and support vary considerably between states. It is generally the case, however, that this involves advanced, high-technology arms as well as more low technology arms, given the nature of contemporary warfare. Qualitative considerations are crucial given the implications of being unable at least to match the military capabilities of potential international rivals. This encourages efforts to develop and maintain substantial technological leads in crucial arms categories, which depends on a sustained national capacity for arms-related R&D as well as production.

The development of autonomous capabilities is also crucial to defense industrialization's contribution to national security, as a reliance on external sources of technology, components, production equipment, and even design cues can involve dependence no less than the import of complete arms.[5] At any rate, relying on external resources is not necessarily as straightforward as it first appears, as this may still require considerable adaptation or indigenization to meet local requirements. Autonomy demands a defense-industrial base that is organized along territorial lines, with key activities located within and under the effective control of the state in question. The specific requirements of autonomy vary from case to case based on the perceived nature of the military threat, but in general, the greater the capacity of a state's defense-industrial base to provide and support arms independently, the more it enhances national security.

While security is clearly important to authorities in the developing states, understandings of security and the nature of security threats may differ considerably from those of the developed states. The security agendas of developing states may reflect a primary focus on internal security issues, or approach national security in the context of a regional environment where potential rivals pose little threat because of their underdeveloped military capabilities. It may even be the case that security concerns of a nontraditional nature, which do not focus on the state at all, constitute the primary focus of concern. This has major implications for the defense-industrial agendas of developing states.

Political authorities in many developing states regard a defense-industrial base as crucial in national security terms, and indicate their intention of developing a national capacity for the development and production of a comprehensive range of arms. The postwar record of defense industrialization is mixed, however. Authorities may formulate very ambitious defense-industrial agendas, which often extend to developing autonomous national production and R&D capabilities for the full range of arms required. In many cases, defense industrialization is pursued regardless of its economic viability, with states seeking to develop and produce arms that could be imported easily and affordably. The common practice of basing defense industries around a state armaments sector results from recognition of the fact that ensuring that they are state owned or administered maximizes national autonomy. Political authorities may go to extraordinary lengths to maintain this. Defense-industrial protectionism such as restrictions on foreign ownership is quite common, for example, as authorities seek to shelter crucial industries from potentially detrimental market forces. Political authorities may even accept qualitative sacrifices in the interest of supporting local firms. These features demonstrate the importance attached to defense industrialization in many developing states for reasons of national security.

This must be balanced against the fact that, in many developing states, no attempt is made to autonomously develop and produce a comprehensive range of arms. Political authorities tend to be very selective in deciding which defense-industrial capabilities to develop. While an import-substitution focus is a common feature of defense industrialization in developing states, national objectives are often quite modest. Authorities generally focus on developing particular strategic defense-industrial capabilities, and are often prepared to accept a high level of foreign input in what they do develop and produce. Only rarely do states attempt to develop a completely autonomous capacity for the development, production, and support of arms. It may be the case, for example, that efforts are made to develop extensive national capabilities in a limited range of arms, while continuing to rely on foreign support in others. Political authorities often choose the path of least resistance in choosing to develop local capabilities for low-risk, low-technology arms such as small arms, while accepting crucial ongoing foreign support for more advanced arms such as combat aircraft and armored vehicles.

Security does not necessarily constitute the sole determinant of defense industrialization in developing states. Even where the requirements of national security are paramount, economic and political considerations may play an important role. Economic objectives are particularly prominent in developing states. As well as providing employment opportunities, defense industrialization is often approached as an important vehicle for industrial and technological progress. Authorities in developing states frequently expect that successful defense-industrial development will constitute a catalyst for national development.[6] Defense industrialization's efficacy in this respect derives from its potential effect in spurring local industry to enhance its technological capacity and managerial skills, and through the industrial offsets—particularly technology transfers—that commonly accompany arms transfers. Arms transfers are sometimes closely linked to national development efforts in developing states and, as a result. The issue of the anticipated economic benefits can be decisive in the awarding of contracts.[7]

A further set of potential objectives involves political stature and prestige. Political authorities in some states consider the development and production of advanced arms to be indicative of the level of national development.[8] This perspective encourages a focus on high-profile arms such as combat aircraft, armored vehicles, and missile systems. These have considerable symbolic value, but such a focus may not be sustainable and may produce irregular patterns of defense industrialization, unless this is pursued in conjunction with more conventional defense-industrial objectives.

It should be noted that the varied defense-industrial objectives of developing states are not entirely mutually incompatible. Defense industrialization in many cases is distinguished by multiple objectives. This can have as great an impact on patterns of defense industrialization as the resource and structural obstacles facing developing states.

Patterns of Defense Industrialization

Patterns of defense industrialization in the developing world often do not conform to the classical model, although certain features of this model are found in a number of developing states. This includes the efforts made to use current capabilities as a basis for further progress and the interest in developing defense-industrial capabilities gradually, by progressing from relatively simple activities such as the assembly of foreign arms under license to co-production of foreign designs, and from there on to increasingly independent production and R&D. These features are by no means universal, however.

The development of defense-industrial capabilities in developing states is often neither linear nor systematic. In many cases, defense industrialization appears more opportunistic

than deliberate. Particular defense-industrial capabilities may emerge as a result of opportunities that arise through political ties or the offsets accompanying arms purchases. It may
also be the case that perceived structural and resource limitations exert a strong influence
on defense-industrial trajectories by affecting the choice of projects or the nature and extent
of local participation.[9] While this may be wise in cases where it results in defense industrialization being well-grounded in local industrial capabilities, it may limit future developmental options.

Another important factor is the potential effect of overly optimistic plans and expectations. This may affect the degree of local content, the technological sophistication of arms,
or the time frame involved in their development and production. Overambitious defense-
industrial programs often result where impatience with a more gradual approach leads
political authorities to attempt to leap ahead by ordering arms into production whose designs are still immature. Egypt, for example, initiated an abortive national ballistic missile
program in the 1960s, despite its underdeveloped industrial base.[10] Political authorities in
many developing states have discovered that unrealistic initiatives are difficult to bring to
fruition.

These factors help to account for the apparent illogic of defense industrialization in many
developing states. Often, defense industrialization does not involve a linear progression in
the development of capabilities, and may even involve very intermittent efforts, with the
result that particular national capabilities may stagnate or even lapse. It also often fails to
conform to best practice as this is understood in the developed states. There may be major
intersectoral differences in development patterns as authorities focus on the development
of particular niche capabilities. While sustained interest in defense industrialization across
the developing world demonstrates the importance that is attached to it, patterns of defense
industrialization highlight the problematic nature of conventional understandings of defense industrialization in many cases.

The Emerging Industrial States

The difficulties involved in attempting to reconcile developing state defense industrialization with conventional expectations are greatest with respect to those developing states that
can be classified as *emerging industrial states*. The members of this select group of states are
distinguished by their impressive industrial and technological strides. Though these states,
which include Singapore, South Korea, and Taiwan, are often still considered developing,
they have developed well past most of the developing states. It is important to differentiate
between the emerging industrial states and the other developing states in defense-industrial
terms, as the former are demonstrating a growing capacity to close the defense-industrial
gap with the developed industrial states. The emerging industrial states are making good
progress in overcoming resource and structural obstacles and are developing extensive
defense-industrial capabilities. Political authorities in these states have formulated very
ambitious defense-industrial agendas, to which they appear very committed over the long
term.

The emerging industrial states are distinguished by more than their defense-industrial
successes. It also is the case that patterns of defense industrialization in these states differ

greatly both from the other developing states and from the classical model of defense in-dustrialization. The success of their developmental approach has the potential to encourage other developing states to follow suit, though in most cases they lack the capacity to do so effectively at the present time.

The defense-industrial programs of the emerging industrial states are based on global-ization. Processes of globalization affecting the defense-industrial landscape emerged in the 1980s and continue to deepen, driven by commercial pressures and a degree of politi-cal acquiescence in cases where authorities recognize its necessity. These processes did not originate in the defense field, but similar pressures are making themselves felt here as well.[11] This structural transformation is impacting on defense industries in an increasing number of states. It is serving to integrate the defense industries of developing states into trans-national industrial networks, and provides considerable potential for the development of niche capabilities on the part of developing states.[12]

Their impressive developmental and defense-industrial progress testifies to the prospects for states to exploit the opportunities stemming from the ongoing structural transformation of the technological environment. This transformation involves increasingly transnational processes of technological development, application, and diffusion. This deepening tech-nological globalization provides increasing opportunities for states that are in a position to participate in these processes. The export-oriented economies of the emerging industrial states are highly integrated into transnational industrial networks, enabling them to engage foreign firms in advanced R&D and production through interfirm alliances and partner-ships. This is providing firms in emerging industrial states with a growing capacity to draw on foreign industrial and technological resources as they contribute to foreign-based R&D and production programs, enabling them to narrow—if not close—technological gaps.[13]

This is having a major impact in defense-industrial terms. The extensive industrial ties with foreign firms, many of which are based in the developed industrial states, are provid-ing increasing opportunities to undertake the development and production of advanced arms, and they are well-positioned to draw on foreign technological assets on a sustained basis.[14] The defense-industrial programs of the emerging industrial states stand to benefit enormously from enhanced access to defense-related technologies. This can include shar-ing developmental and production costs and reducing the risks involved, increasing access to foreign technological sources and R&D facilities, promoting economies of scale, and facilitating access to export markets. Advanced arms such as Taiwan's Ching-Kuo fighter and South Korea's Golden Eagle trainer have benefited from such ties.

This model differs from the efforts made by some developing states to supplement in-digenous defense-industrial capabilities with foreign inputs by its long-term nature and the extent to which this is being pursued in concert with general national industrial and technological development. This goes well beyond the practice of most developing states, which continue to rely on foreign support, such as dual-use technologies and components, but which see this as a temporary expedient. Technological globalization enables emerg-ing industrial state firms to enter high-technology product areas at a higher point on the learning curve, increases the potential for local firms to assimilate advanced technologies, and sustains their progress through continued access to technology that is at or near the state of the art. This includes enhanced potential to access offshore R&D and production facilities in a manner similar to Germany during the interwar period, when access to foreign research facilities and factories in the Soviet Union and elsewhere enabled it to pursue arms programs prohibited under the Versailles Treaty.[15]

The impact of the general industrial trends involved in technological globalization is being enhanced by the growing importance of the private sector in arms-related R&D and production in the emerging industrial states. In some cases, this involves the privatization of state-owned defense firms, and in others a major attitude shift in accepting that non-state actors are able to contribute to the development of the national defense-industrial base.[16] The growing defense-industrial role of the private sector in these states is facilitating the development of increasingly extensive transnational interfirm linkages. The fact that defense industrialization is so well grounded in the general industrial environment of the state increases the prospects that the emerging industrial states will exhibit increasingly impressive defense-industrial capabilities.

The impact of this trend is readily apparent. Very impressive defense-industrial progress has been registered by the emerging industrial states, which are demonstrating a growing capacity to develop and produce a broad range of sophisticated arms, including aircraft, armored vehicles, and missile systems. A number of these states, such as South Korea and Singapore, are even emerging as important arms exporters in their own right. Even more significant is the growing involvement of emerging industrial state–based firms in defense-industrial programs in the developed industrial states, such as the American-led Joint Strike Fighter (JSF) program.[17]

While the emerging industrial states are closing the defense-industrial capability gap with the developed industrial states, this is not validating the classical model of defense industrialization. The pattern of defense industrialization in these states is contrary to what is expected, as the ongoing role of foreign industrial and technological assets in defense industrialization in these states is incompatible with the objective of national autonomy. The emerging industrial states are sacrificing defense-industrial self-reliance in the interest of providing a basis for sustainable long-term progress, though the fact that this is based on interfirm collaboration, which is more difficult for authorities in other states to control, lessens the degree of vulnerability involved.

THE PROSPECTS OF DEFENSE INDUSTRIALIZATION

While even the developed industrial states face major obstacles in developing and maintaining defense-industrial capabilities, those confronting developing states are far more daunting. The particular difficulties involved in developing defense industries in states that are less well endowed with industrial capabilities and natural resources have been noted since the 1930s, when a scholarly body of literature on the subject began to emerge.[18]

The defense-industrial programs of many developing states have been beset by problems as authorities have struggled to acquire, master, and apply complex advanced technologies. Political authorities face daunting challenges of a structural nature, resource challenges, and in some cases attitudinal challenges, which continue to limit the scope for defense-industrial progress in many cases. The structural obstacles they face stem from their relatively restricted access to crucial technologies and production equipment, resulting from the fact that, in most cases, these originate in the developed industrial states, and may be subject to supply-side controls. Resource obstacles potentially include the domestic financial, technological, industrial, and testing infrastructure resources needed to develop and produce arms. The financial requirements of both R&D and production have soared as technological frontiers advance. Attitudinal obstacles are evident in a number of cases where political authorities in developing states have proven reluctant to consider locally developed and produced arms as good as those that are available from more established suppliers.[19] To this must be added the negative impact on the long-term development of defense-industrial capabilities of the tendency, in some cases, to undertake the development and production of arms that involve too many technical risks given established local capabilities.

The postwar record of many developing states, particularly in terms of advanced arms, testifies to the enduring difficulties they face. This has been manifest in program delays, escalating costs, technological compromises, and the abortive nature of many projects. Many developing states have failed to rise above very basic levels of defense-industrial competency, and in few cases has the development of defense-industrial capabilities in developing states kept pace with expanding technological frontiers. While the developmental and production barriers involved in low-technology arms such as small arms and light weapons are easily surmounted by all but the most underdeveloped of states, those involved in high-technology arms have risen steadily and continue to rise. This has major implications for the long-term prospects of defense industrialization in most developing states, including in terms of both autonomy and sustainability.

Defense-industrial autonomy is very difficult to achieve, even for the developed industrial states. The scope for developing a truly independent defense-industrial base is limited, except in cases where political authorities are in a position and prepared to devote the necessary resources. Establishing a genuinely autonomous defense-industrial base requires major resources unless local arms requirements are limited to unsophisticated arms such as small arms, light weapons, and motor transport vehicles; this is rarely the case. As Stephanie Neuman points out, defense-industrial self-reliance has not even been achieved by most of the developed industrial states.[20] The difficulties faced by developing states are much greater due to their difficulties in mustering the required resources, including in terms of financial, technological, and infrastructure resources. Most developing states cannot sustain the high levels of investment necessary to develop an infrastructure of advanced testing facilities such as wind tunnels, for example.

For most developing industrial states, defense-industrial autonomy remains an elusive goal. India's Tejas light combat aircraft (LCA), which has been under development since 1983, has experienced major delays, and now is not scheduled to be fielded until 2010, for example. Even this timeframe will only be attainable due to the Indian government's willingness to compromise its requirement of autonomy. Instead of being completely indigenously designed and produced as was intended, the Tejas will incorporate significant foreign components and design inputs.[21]

Similarly, achieving defense-industrial sustainability has proven to be difficult for most developing states. The difficulties involved in developing sustainable defense-industrial capabilities are more acute for developing states, which often lack extensive commercial industrial bases upon which to establish such activity. In many cases, defense industrialization efforts result in the development of "enclave" industries that are relatively isolated from the civil sector, which complicates efforts to sustain them and requires greater state resources. Most developing states are poorly positioned to bear this burden. Not only do they face major difficulties in providing the ongoing financial support that this generally requires, but they also often experience difficulties in providing sufficient industrial and technological resources and the necessary infrastructure for R&D.[22]

For most developing states, defense-industrial autonomy and sustainability are practical only in terms of unsophisticated arms. Most developing states will continue to require on-going foreign assistance for anything more than this. In many cases, arms transfers, the off-sets that accompany them, and dual-use technologies will continue to be crucial to defense industrialization. The extent to which this involves continued relationships of dependence, with all that this entails for developing states, may be mitigated by technological globaliza-tion, even for those developing states that are not extensively integrated into the global economy. Deepening technological globalization complicates efforts by states to control outward technological diffusion, increasing the chances for developing states to circum-vent political barriers to the diffusion of arms-related technologies. The long-term defense-industrial prospects for the emerging industrial states are relatively positive, but only because their particular developmental model effectively foregoes autonomy. Defense industrializa-tion in these states is being pursued in concert with general industrial and technological progress in the context of participation in the global economy.

The changing supply-side dynamic resulting from the emergence of new arms suppliers also stands to benefit defense industrialization in developing states. A number of develop-ing states, of which the emerging industrial states are most prominent, are enhancing their capabilities to supply arm-related components, technologies, and production equipment, and to provide testing facilities. The increasing range of potential suppliers for many items provides developing states with greater choices and reduces the potential for individual suppliers to use arms transfer relationships as instruments of political leverage.

The Benefits of Limited Defense Industrialization

Defense industrialization in developing states often fails to produce national capabilities sufficiently comprehensive and autonomous to free these states from their dependence on foreign suppliers. Nonetheless, defense industrialization is often considered valuable. It continues to be supported, as it helps to insulate states from some of the more immediate effects of restrictions on access to arms supplies. Even the production of basic small arms and artillery ammunition can provide a state with some capacity to engage in combat with-out immediate resupply, and relatively simple measures such as a local capacity to supply small arms and to undertake vehicle maintenance can significantly enhance this. The more sophisticated the local defense industry and the less dependent it is on foreign components, production equipment, and expertise, the greater the scope for autonomous action for po-litical authorities.

Limited defense industrialization has the added benefit of helping to reduce the costs of supporting the local defense establishment while also supporting domestic in-dustry. In some cases, such as in Brazil during the 1970s and 1980s, limited defense industrialization has provided the basis for profitable exports.[23] Some states are prepared to accept less autonomous defense-industrial capabilities to develop while developing significant export capabilities as a result. The actual contribution of defense industrialization to economic development varies greatly. It may be quite limited where defense and civil industries are effectively isolated, where defense industrialization is inappropriate in commercial terms, or where states lack the capacity to exploit the opportunities provided, but significant spillover to local industry may result.[24]

THE IMPLICATIONS OF DEFENSE INDUSTRIALIZATION

As outlined above, there is little apparent threat to the established hierarchy of defense-industrial producers. With few exceptions, the defense industries of developing states are still emerging despite some determined efforts to narrow, if not close, the defense-industrial capability gap with the developed industrial states. The exceptions are the emerging industrial states, but in these cases the distinct nature of defense industrialization ensures that local capabilities will remain closely linked to those of more established defense-industrial producers.

Defense industrialization entails major politico-military implications for the developing states where this is being pursued and for the states that deal with them. The implications of defense industrialization vary considerably from case to case. This is due in large part to the very uneven record of defense industrialization in developing states and the differing positions of developed industrial states.

The issue of the impact of defense industrialization on the world military order has been debated for some time. Many observers note the potential for this to enable developing and emerging industrial states to overcome the established center/periphery distinction in military capabilities.[25] The politico-military implications of defense industrialization depend in large part upon local progress. In most developing states, defense-industrial progress has been very modest, with states restricted to providing basic supplies, such as small arms ammunition, and a limited maintenance capacity, or a capacity to assemble or coproduce a limited range of equipment. Depot-level maintenance, production, and R&D of sophisticated arms remain beyond the scope of most developing states. In these cases, defense industrialization poses no threat to the hierarchy of military powers.

Defense industrialization is contributing to the development of more advanced military capabilities in some developing states. A number of developing states are enhancing their capacity to provide or support crucial types of arms, and some states are developing sustained defense-industrial capabilities in particular areas as a result of their capacity for R&D as well as production. The capacity to draw on indigenous industrial infrastructure can greatly enhance the political utility of the defense establishment. This stems from the importance of being able to maintain crucial arms during times of tension or crisis, and to replace any equipment losses.

The issue of the implications of defense industrialization for the political independence of developing states is quite complex. This is complicated by the declining scope for political leverage resulting from the increasingly transnational nature of arms-related R&D and production. The scope for political influence via arms transfers varies between cases.

Dependence on an arms supplier does not necessarily translate into political leverage on its part, but the scope for leverage is greatest in cases where the recipients are dependent on particular arms suppliers.[26] The changing nature of the arms supply environment resulting from the rise of nontraditional emerging industrial state suppliers is broadening the options for arms importers, potentially providing political authorities in developing states with greater scope to avoid such situations. As a result, the failure of developing states to develop autonomous comprehensive defense-industrial capabilities does not necessarily involve as high a political cost as once was the case.

Defense industrialization has major implications in terms of the capacity of established defense-industrial producers to develop and implement effective arms embargoes. The increasing number of suppliers that must be included in order to ensure the effectiveness of arms embargoes complicates such efforts. It was noted as far back as the 1980s that the emergence of significant defense industries in newly industrialized states such as Brazil, Israel, and South Africa was enabling them to supply arms to states that were unable to secure arms from their traditional suppliers due to their political positions or human rights records.[27] At the same time, however, the central importance in developing state defense industries of arms-related R&D and production processes that are based elsewhere provides considerable scope for political influence, should political authorities in supplier states be prepared to go to the lengths necessary to restrict access in the current environment. As a result, the influence of a state with the resources of the United States is not necessarily diminished by "defense globalization."[28]

In addition, it is more difficult to secure state support for controls on arms-related components, production equipment, and technology than complete arms. Defense industrialization in developing states is not nearly as controversial as the issue of arms transfers to developing states, and so tends to generate less public demands on policy communities to intervene to prevent it. As a result, processes contributing to defense industrialization in developing states can be expected to remain less subject to external controls than arms transfers themselves.

This issue is somewhat academic in that most of the developed industrial states that are in a position to do so do not seek to employ arms transfers as instruments of influence except in isolated cases. This generally occurs when developing states are considered to be acting beyond the pale in terms of human rights. In these cases, defense industrialization in the developing states might have a particularly significant impact, providing the potential for political authorities to pursue important national objectives without regard for the norms and wishes of the international community. This may provide them with considerable scope to deny basic civil liberties and violate human rights.

CONCLUDING REMARKS

The importance attached to defense industrialization in the developing states is unlikely to abate, given its potential advantages in both politico-military and economic terms. The scope for most of these states to become self-reliant in defense-industrial terms is very limited, however, and will remain so.

There is an important group of developing states where defense-industrial development is likely to prove more significant over the long term. Defense industrialization in the emerging industrial states does not correspond to the expectations of many observers, but their development of increasingly sophisticated general industrial capabilities across a broad range of product areas is providing them with a basis for sustained defense-industrial development. The overlapping nature of their commercial and military sectors and their extensive integration into transnational industrial processes means that their defense-industrial bases will not be autonomous, but it also means that they will have much readier access to external defense-industrial resources, and that they will constitute increasingly important contributors to defense-related R&D and production in other states.

The politico-military implications of the development of defense-industrial capabilities of the emerging industrial states are considerable. Not only does it have the potential to render these states increasingly resistant to efforts to employ access to arms as an instrument of influence, but it also is providing them with an increasing capacity to supplement, if not supplant, established suppliers of arms to developing states. This will continue to erode the effectiveness of supply-side arms and technology controls.

The nature of defense industrialization in the emerging industrial states highlights the inadequacy of established understandings of developing state defense industrialization. The chosen path of defense industrialization in the emerging industrial states demonstrates the importance of reconsidering how we regard defense industrialization in developing states, and our understanding of the role and importance of non-state actors and industrial processes.

NOTES

1. See, for example Janne E. Nolan, *Military Industry in Taiwan and South Korea* (Houndmills: Mac-Millan Press, 1986), 46; and James Everett Katz, "Understanding Arms Production in Developing Countries," in *Arms Production in Developing Countries: An Analysis of Decision Making,* ed. James Everett Katz (Lexington, MA: D.C. Heath and Co., 1984), 8. The framework provided by Barry Buzan and Eric Herring in *The Arms Dynamic in World Politics* (Boulder, CO: Lynne Rienner Publishers, 1998), 42–46, is distinguished by its capacity to accommodate different approaches to the development of defense-industrial capabilities.

2. See Michael Brzoska and Thomas Ohlson, "Arms Production in the Third World: An Overview," in *Arms Production in the Third World,* ed. Michael Brzoska and Thomas Ohlson (London: Taylor & Francis, 1986), 7–10.

3. Anthony H. Cordesman and Abraham R. Wagner, *The Lessons of Modern War,* vol. 2, *The Iran-Iraq War* (Boulder, CO: Westview Press, 1990), 453.

4. See Rodney W. Jones and Steven A. Hildreth, *Modern Weapons and Third World Powers* (Boulder, CO: Westview Press, 1984), 63.

5. Andrew L. Ross, "World Order and Arms Production in the Third World," in *The Implications of Third World Military Industrialization: Sowing the Serpents' Teeth,* ed. James Everett Katz, ed. (Lexington, MA: D.C. Heath and Co., 1986), 278.

6. Gautam Sen, *The Military Origins of Industrialisation and International Trade Rivalry* (New York, NY: St. Martin's Press, 1984), 7. See also Robert Karniol, "Linking Defence with Economic Progress," *Jane's Defence Weekly* November 25, 1995, 40.

7. See, for example Rahul Bedi, "India Releases Delayed RfP for MRCA Purchase," *Jane's Defence Weekly,* September 5, 2007, 20.

8. See, for example James Elliot and Ezio Bonsignore, "Asia's 'New' Aerospace Industry: At the Turning Point?" *Military Technology* 22, no. 2 (1998): 24.

9. See, for example the statement of the Malaysian defense minister in *Jane's Defence Weekly,* "Malaysia May Produce Own Defence Equipment," March 12, 1988, 445.

10. Wyn Q. Bowen, *The Politics of Ballistic Missile Nonproliferation* (Houndmills, UK: Macmillan Press, 2000), 21.

11. Jacques S. Gansler, "The Future of the Defence Firm: Integrating Civil and Military Technologies," in *The Future of the Defence Firm: New Challenges, New Directions,* ed. Andrew Latham and Nicholas Hooper (Dordrecht, The Netherlands: Kluwer Academic Publishers, 1995), 89–91. See Keith Hayward, "The Globalisation of Defence Industries," *Survival* 43, no. 2 (2001): 115–32, for a useful discussion of globalizing trends and their impact on defense industries.

12. Richard A. Bitzinger, *Towards a Brave New Arms Industry?* Adelphi paper 356 (London: International Institute for Strategic Studies, 2003), 74–75.

13. J. D. Kenneth Boutin, *Reconceptualizing Asia-Pacific Defence Industrialization: The New Political Economy of Security,* CANCAPS paper 35 (Toronto: Canadian Consortium on Asia Pacific Security, 2004), 4–7.

14. See J. D. Kenneth Boutin, *Technological Globalisation and Regional Security in East Asia,* IDSS working paper 65 (Singapore: Institute of Defence and Strategic Studies, 2004), 5–12.

15. See Edward Hallett Carr, *German-Soviet Relations Between the Two World Wars, 1919–1939* (New York: Harper & Row, 1951), 60–61.

16. See, for example Jon Grevatt, "AIDC Finally Set for Privatisation," *Jane's Defence Weekly,* February 27, 2008), 15.

17. See Sharon Hobson, Joris Janssen Lok, Lale Sariibrahimoglu, and David Mulholland, et al., "Not All JSF Partners are Reaping Contract Awards," *Jane's Defence Weekly,* May 26, 2004), 21.

18. See H.C. Engelbrecht and F.C. Hanighen, *Merchants of Death: A Study of the International Armament Industry* (New York: Dodd, Mead & Co., 1934), 263.

19. See Riad Kahwaji, "Making Headway," *Defense News,* May 26, 2003, 19.

20. Stephanie G. Neuman, "Defense Industries and Global Dependency," *Orbis* 50, no. 3 (2006): 440.

21. Rahul Bedi, "Tejas Moves Slowly towards IOC," *Jane's Defence Weekly,* February 20, 2008, 17.

22. James Everett Katz, "Factors Affecting Military Scientific Research in the Third World," in *The Implications of Third World Military Industrialization: Sowing the Serpents' Teeth,* ed. James Everett Katz (Lexington, MA: D.C. Heath and Co., 1986), 296–97.

23. Ken Conca, "Third World Military Industrialization and the Evolving Security System," in *The Highest Stakes: The Economic Foundations of the Next Security System,* Wayne Sandholtz, Michael Borrus, John Zysman, Ken Conca, Jay Stowsky, Steven Vogel, and Steve Weber et al. (New York: Oxford University Press, 1992), 151–52.

24. For a useful discussion of some of the issues involved in offsets and their potential contribution to local industrial progress, see D. S. Leonidis-Plessas, "Aspects and Trends of International Offset Co-production Projects," *Military Technology* 7, no. 7 (1983): 12–25.

25. See Edward J. Laurance, *The International Arms Trade* (New York: Lexington Books, 1992), 158.

26. See Stephanie Neuman, *Defense Industries and Dependency: Current and Future Trends in the Global Defense Sector* (Zurich: Swiss Federal Institute of Technology, 2006), 23.

27. Bruce E. Arlinghaus, "Social Versus Military Development: Positive and Normative Dimensions," in *Arms Production in Developing Countries: An Analysis of Decision Making,* ed. James Everett Katz (Lexington, MA: D.C. Heath and Co., 1984), 45.

28. Jonathan D. Caverley, "United States Hegemony and the New Economics of Defense," *Security Studies* 16, no. 4 (2007): 611–14.

PART III

The Defense Industry and the Arms Trade

13

Export Controls and Their Relationship to National Defense Industries

Francis Cevasco

This chapter will examine export control as practiced by governments domestically and multinationally. It will then examine political, economic, and national security dimensions of exports, the differing perspectives of suppliers and recipients, and tensions between governments and industry over export policy and practice. Finally, it will consider current issues and future challenges for the global arms industry.

WHY EXPORT CONTROL?

The foundation upon which nations build their global political influence, and the military strength that further buttresses that influence, may be characterized in a variety of ways; a strong, integrated domestic economy, a capable domestic commercial and defense technology base, and an efficient and effective domestic commercial and defense industry. All three of the foundation's components are closely interrelated. A strong private sector economy generates the capital and talent for the domestic technology and industry base; and a capable advanced technology and industrial base correlates with economic growth rates that are a multiple of the rates associated with less technologically advanced industrial sectors.[1] Centrally planned economies are an exception to the previous points—the state may have sufficient power to draw resources from throughout the economy and apply them to its military establishment, but such approaches are often to the detriment of economic growth, which in turn reduces the resources available, negatively affecting national security.

Global Influence in Practice

The actual degree of global influence available in practice is dependent upon the magnitude of the three-component foundation relative to that of the corresponding foundation in other nations. Any action that erodes, or even threatens to erode, one or more of the three components of the foundation will cause a diminution of the nation's influence. In that context, export control becomes an essential element of every nation's national security and foreign policy, as it safeguards a nation's intellectual property. Most economically successful nations with diversified industrial sectors invest significant resources into the creation of new intellectual property—what this chapter refers to as technology. The term *technology,* as used in this chapter, is applied broadly to encompass defense-relevant technical data, military equipment, some commercial products, and the know-how to produce them.

Nations remain ahead of their economic competitors and potential adversaries by creating new technology, applying that technology to create new products and increase military capabilities, doing so at a more rapid rate than others, and protecting the technology. It is the fourth element that drives nations to exercise control of technologies and equipment that could otherwise be used to advantage by a commercial competitor, potential adversary, or current adversary.

Companies and countries remain ahead of the competition by both running faster (to create new technology and apply it in useful ways) and by slowing the inevitable leakage that erodes their market share or political influence. And the operative word is *slow* rather than *prevent* leakage, as eliminating leakage in today's highly interconnected world is not possible and probably not even desirable. Industry manages the inevitability of technology leakage, and the fact that technology has what might be called a shelf life, by funding future development and innovation through the timely sales abroad of products and technology no longer on the cutting edge.

Unlike in the 1970s and earlier, when the United States was dominant in military technology, today technology is much more widely dispersed throughout the developed and developing countries. The military and its suppliers draw increasingly on commercial technology,[2] and technologists communicate and collaborate regularly with their foreign counterparts. Moreover, it is the open communication of ideas and consequent collaboration that stimulates new technology and innovation.

And not all technology exports warrant equal protection. Sale of equipment conveys less sensitive technology and risk than does the transfer of production technology. Similarly, sale conveys substantially less than co-development.

DOMESTIC EXPORT CONTROLS

Exports are regulated by government export control organizations. The export control approach practiced by governments varies by country, but is generally based on a combination of law, regulations, and policies.

While this chapter will not attempt a comprehensive examination of national export controls, it will briefly examine the approaches taken in Japan, the United States, and the United Kingdom. It should be recognized, however, that other capitals structure and manage export control in their own distinctive manner to accommodate cultural differences and domestic and foreign policy considerations. Nonetheless, the key guiding principle in all cases is national self-interest.

The approaches adopted by governments may be aggregated under several broad motivations: political, economic, and those of national security. Usually, one finds a combination of all three at work.

Japan

Japan's approach to export control is based on its *three principles* policy, adopted in 1967. The policy prohibited arms exports to: nations in the Communist bloc, nations under UN sanctions, and nations in areas of tension. Unique among developed nations is Japan's expansive interpretation of its policy, as announced by the Japanese government in 1976, which effectively precludes all arms transfers, including military technology. Implementation is the responsibility of the Japanese Ministry of Economy, Trade and Industry (METI). The transfer of Japanese military technology and ballistic missile defense–related equipment to the United States remains the only explicitly acknowledged exception to Japan's strict policy.

United States

U.S. defense export control policy is based on a 1975 law[3] implemented by the Department of State (DoS) in consultation with the Department of Defense (DoD), through the International Traffic in Arms Regulations (ITAR) governing export of defense articles. However, some commercial U.S. technology and equipment are categorized as dual-use items (i.e., they can have direct military application). Such items are subject to controls under a different set of laws, regulations, and policies, implemented by the U.S. Department of Commerce (DoC).

The underlying U.S. law is based on three objectives. Firstly, the United States can benefit from sharing military technology with allied and friendly governments. This benefit derives from helping to increase the capability of other nations to accomplish objectives in consonance with U.S. political and national security goals. These include: protecting their homeland; functioning as capable members of defense alliances to deter aggression, as was the case with NATO during the cold war; and acquiring the capability to function either alone or as part of a coalition deployed to regional trouble spots for peacekeeping, peace-enforcement, or peacemaking.

Secondly, the law asserts that the U.S. government may withhold exports when an export could potentially damage U.S. interests either directly or indirectly. U.S. political, economic, and security interests all come strongly into play in this regard. Some U.S. technologies have been developed at great expense and may be, and have been, withheld from even the closest of allies due to concerns about the technologies being diverted or retransferred into the wrong hands. If sophisticated military technology is compromised, this might enable others to reduce or impair the effectiveness of U.S. weapon systems. This objective compels the export control community to identify risks to U.S. interests and collaborate with technologists and operational forces to manage those risks.

Thirdly, the law asserts the need to limit proliferation of weapons due to concern that the introduction or accumulation of weapons in some regions could exacerbate existing or potential instabilities. Concerns over weapons proliferation in such instances includes both lesser, but nonetheless lethal, weapons such as small arms, and sophisticated weapons like fighter aircraft, aerial refueling capabilities, man-portable air defense systems, and others that would empower terrorists and facilitate aggression. One benchmark for implementing this objective is to avoid introducing new military capabilities into a region where such introduction could contribute to regional instability.

United Kingdom

The U.K. export control system is operated by a single Export Licensing Community. This community comprises five government departments: the Department of Trade and Industry, the Foreign and Commonwealth Office, the Ministry of Defence, the Department for International Development, and Her Majesty's Revenue and Customs. The community's mission statement calls for "Promoting global security through strategic export controls, facilitating responsible exports." In practice, the U.K. export control system is designed to "ensure sensitive goods and technology are kept out of the wrong hands [and] . . . facilitate responsible defence exports, as these depend on a sound regime of controls." The export control system is also designed to "administer the licensing system efficiently so that we keep the compliance burden on U.K. exporters to the minimum."[4]

While the Japanese export control system is focused primarily on political motivation, the U.S. and U.K. systems represent a mix of all three motivations: political, economic, and national security interests.

MULTINATIONAL EXPORT CONTROLS

There are four multilateral export control regimes that have been established by countries that share common concerns about the potential dangers posed by unregulated foreign transfers of certain classes of technologies and equipment. These are the Australia Group, the Nuclear Suppliers Group, the Wassenaar Arrangement, and the Missile Technology Control Regime.

The Australia Group (AG) dates from 1985. Its member countries have committed to minimizing "the risk of assisting chemical and biological weapon proliferation." Actual controls are administered by individual member countries, informed by the exchange of insights and concerns expressed at the AG's annual meetings. The members agree that their export licensing measures should be formulated in a way that is "effective in impeding the production of chemical and biological weapons, practical, and reasonably easy to implement, and [does] not impede the normal trade of materials and equipment used for legitimate purposes." Membership has grown from the initial 15 member countries to 40 countries plus the European Union (EU) organization.[5] Australia is the permanent chair and secretariat. The AG produces an export control list and best practice export control guidelines.

The Nuclear Suppliers Group (NSG) was founded in 1975 due to the concerns of several governments about the Indian nuclear test held the previous year. The countries were worried about the threat of further nuclear weapon proliferation and set about to control "the export and re-transfer of materials that may be applicable to nuclear weapon development and by improving safeguards and protection on existing materials." Membership has grown from the initial 7 member countries to 45.[6]

The Missile Technology Control Regime (MTCR) was founded in 1987 by countries interested in restricting proliferation of unmanned systems (and related technology) capable of delivering weapons of mass destruction (i.e., propelling a 227 pound warhead at least186 miles. The systems of specific interest to MTCR members include: ballistic missiles, space launch vehicles and sounding rockets, unmanned aerial vehicles (UAVs), cruise missiles, drones, and remotely piloted vehicles. Membership grew from the initial 7 members to 34. The MTCR has no secretariat. Distribution of the regime's working papers is carried out through a point of contact, the functions of which are performed by the Ministry of Foreign Affairs of France.[7]

The **Wassenaar Arrangement (WA)** replaced the cold war–era Coordinating Committee for Multilateral Export Controls (CoCom), which was established in 1947 to embargo Western exports to Eastern Bloc countries. CoCom had 17 member countries (15 NATO members, Australia, and Japan). Its members agreed at their November 1993 meeting to phase out the organization because the Soviet Union had disintegrated. They also agreed to replace it with a new organization concerned with reducing proliferation rather then restraining the Soviet Union's economy. The negotiation process produced agreement in 1995 on a basic framework termed the Wassenaar Arrangement. The WA became operational in 1996 with the adoption of initial elements. Membership grew from the initial 33 to 40 member countries, and is administered by a secretariat located in Vienna, Austria.[8]

As with the AG, all actual implementation of agreed collective positions and actions in the NSG, the MTCR, and the WA are executed by individual nations and under their national export control systems.

POLITICAL, ECONOMIC, AND NATIONAL SECURITY IMPLICATIONS

Export sale and transfer of weapon systems and other defense articles can be, and in the case of the United States have long been, a major element of foreign and national security policy. Existing allies can be supported and strengthened, friendly governments rewarded, and wavering or less than friendly governments punished or rewarded as the situation dictates. The timely approval of an export license can smooth the path in difficult negotiations with other governments or sow good will for such things as military overflight requests, basing rights and facilities, and political considerations in other areas.

Advantages

In the cold war era, the United States purposefully authorized exports of critical technologies and weapons to key NATO allies. The exports helped NATO forces to maintain technological superiority over Warsaw Pact forces, offsetting the numerical advantage of those forces. Elsewhere, as in NATO, governments with largely aligned world views are natural export partners. The supplier demonstrates a certain trust by approving the export and the recipient feels differentiated from other states by becoming a valued member of the supplier's circle. Through major system exports, suppliers and recipients tend be linked politically and industrially for several decades. A major export can also include substantial military-military engagement in the form of training on the new equipment and associated subsequent military exercises.

Stronger allies and friendly nations reduce the likelihood of the United States and other major military powers being called upon for help, except in very dire circumstances. In addition, the availability of a coterie of strong and competent allies capable of collective action to address potential problems in distant regions can lessen the burden on the United States and contribute to international order and stability—a core U.S. foreign policy goal. Common exercises establish a joint capability that can be exploited in deployments as a coalition, all facilitated by the interoperability gained by using the same or similar equipment. Such deployments may be sent to regional trouble spots and demonstrate important political agreement as well as military capability.

Disadvantages

However, the exercise of effective export controls can produce negative effects as well as positive ones. Among close allies, as well as friendly governments, export licensing issues can cause frustration, disappointment, and even adverse consequences across the spectrum of political, economic, and security relationships—this is especially true as increasingly sensitive technologies are involved. Even when controversial licensing issues are resolved positively, the process of reaching accord can frequently produce lingering tensions and irritation that tend to build rather than dissipate over time. Although the need to assess carefully the potential negative implications of a decision to deny export is well recognized by some (even many) in government and industry, others are deaf to such concerns. One reason the forces supporting tighter controls (usually the same parties resisting the reform of existing controls) often prevail is that it is easier to argue in favor of reducing risk to national security (by disapproving exports) than it is to argue in favor of strengthening allies who underinvest in their defense.

Economics

National governments and defense industries can reap substantial economic benefits from exporting military systems. Exports provide a mechanism for governments and industry to recover some of the initial investment in developing and producing military systems and equipment. Such investments may amount to anywhere from hundreds of millions to tens of billions of dollars. Some export recipients pay government-imposed recoupment charges for nonrecurring research and development (R&D) investments based on a pro rata share of the production runs. Recipients often become partners sharing the cost of future system upgrades. This reduces the costs for the producing nation and creates more sales for industry. Unit prices decline as production runs grow and economies of scale take effect, benefiting both the exporting and the purchasing governments. In cases where the recipient draws on the supplier's logistic system, costs of the supporting infrastructure are shared among all the users, as well as the economies of scale derived from a broader customer base. The arrangements are not all one-sided favoring only the supplier. The purchasing government avoids the risk inherent in developing a new military system, knowing that many new programs falter and are cancelled, and the investment lost. The purchasing government also obtains a proven system from an active production line at a fixed unit price that benefits from production learning curve effects.

The stability of a defense program, in terms of continued funding, may increase when both domestic forces and allied forces acquire a system. Stability benefits the governments and the companies involved in the production; and, with the offset arrangements that accompany major weapon system sales, industry in the recipient country also benefits. In addition, foreign partnerships, with their infusions of outside capital, can tip the balance in decisions by nations as to whether to fund new start programs, thereby discounting, or in some cases appearing to discount, national costs. Industry benefits by having the long odds against new start programs significantly and sometime decisively shortened.

EXPORT CONTROL DECISIONS: THEIR BASIS AND HOW THEY ARE MADE AND RECEIVED

Export controls were initially designed to prevent the flow of military technology and equipment to hostile or otherwise undesirable states. Most, but not all, arms exporting countries consciously avoid transferring military technology and equipment to the most egregious of the problematic states. However, even otherwise like-minded governments sometimes differ when deciding which states are really dangerous or which military technology or dual-use commercial technology transfers are prudent and which are not. Several agencies within governments may play a role in determining what may be exported, to whom it may be exported, and under what conditions it may be exported. Foreign policy and national security policy are collectively in play as exports released to hostile, failed, or otherwise unstable states could be used to directly threaten national interests. Thus, export decisions cannot be taken lightly.

Export control decisions can also be a powerful instrument for creating goodwill and the potential for influence, a prime ingredient of future relationships. They can lead to increased alignments of national interests and possibly even alliances. But national export decisions also have the potential to erode existing goodwill and undermine the solidarity of existing alliances.

There is no globally accepted right for governments to demand that other governments authorize exports of whatever technology is requested. The eligibility of countries, and their domestic companies, to receive military technology and equipment is determined by the exporting government. The mechanisms employed in assessing eligibility vary widely from one exporting country to the other, as can the results. These are national decisions, and nations may well reach different conclusions even when dealing with like circumstances. Export decisions can trouble third parties and cause the governments to enter into discussions where the relevant facts are made known and the issues considered. However, the exporting government makes the final decision.

Friendly governments are sometimes offended when their expressions of interest in acquiring specific equipment are either denied outright or precipitate a review process whose outcome is unpredictable and may extend for months and even years. Perception of overly rigorous reviews by an exporting government can result in turning allies and friends away and into the hands of competitors. Some countries start the process by letting their interests be known quietly; they then await a reaction from the exporting government. These nations may issue a specific request only after they establish that the exporting government will respond positively, thus avoiding embarrassment or ill will.

As modern weapons and technology have become ever more sophisticated, some exporting governments are in a position to offer a broad spectrum of system capabilities in a given weapon system, and have used this fact to help mitigate the negative political and economic effects of outright license denial. A cannon is a cannon is a cannon, and cannon export decisions tend to be rather binary. Even in such a simple case, however, a supplier can either offer or withhold sophisticated ammunition; and sophisticated ammunition could magnify the combat effectiveness of the cannon. In contrast, a modern software driven airborne radar system offers a multiplicity of opportunities to tailor export decisions not only to individual customers needs, but also to the perceived friendliness, reliability, and even utility of that customer.

Through such means, the exporting nation can usually retain all the political, economic, and security benefits associated with a major sale while avoiding or minimizing the real or perceived risks associated with the export. Nations and their defense industries that are capable of fine-tuning their export products in such a fashion enjoy a distinct advantage in the international arms marketplace. Nonetheless, such stratagems are not without certain attendant risks. Recipient countries do not welcome learning that neighboring states have acquired more capability for like purchases. Such realizations can seriously erode the less tangible benefits of an export sale. For this reason, exporting nations tend to closely guard the details of their fine-tuning.

Also, in cases where a given major sale is intensely competitive, the recipient country has been known to play the offerings of one competitor off those of the other. When this occurs, the technology ante tends to go up; industry presses the exporting government for greater technology transfer and the tensions rise, especially when industry perceives its national export authority to be less than forthcoming. Inevitably, these situations produce a proliferation of advanced technology and set the stage for the next round of competition on the international stage.

Export of the most sophisticated, capable, and current technology may be reserved for only the closest, most trusted of allies. But some systems and technologies may be viewed as so sensitive that they are not shared with any others. Of the sophisticated systems or technologies deemed suitable for export to close allies, export approval may be accompanied by numerous conditions or provisos because compromising the technology embedded in such systems would carry with it the greatest threat to the exporting government.

Should such a system or technology fall into the wrong hands, a hostile party could determine its strengths, but also, more importantly, determine its weaknesses, and develop countermeasures that could neutralize its future value to both the exporter and recipient. Close allies tend to view as onerous and resent significant and highly limiting conditions on their purchases, especially those that are perceived to infringe on their sovereignty. Some categories of restriction cause particular displeasure, especially: those limiting or prohibiting third-party transfers; those prohibiting sale of production know-how; and those prohibiting the transfer of data that enable design characteristics to be altered. Serious disagreements in each of these areas have caused the denial of licenses and/or loss of sales. Naturally, when export control decisions are perceived to be based on arbitrary or unreasonable conditions, resentments occur, both on the part of the would-be recipient and the industries on each side of the transaction.

Less close allies and other friendly nations will be eligible for less sophisticated, less capable, and older technology. Less sophisticated systems may well be more than adequate for the purposes of countries concerned only with discouraging adventurism by their neighbors. This may or may not temper their interest in the more sophisticated items on offer in the marketplace. But states regarded as less reliable by exporting governments are viewed as more likely to compromise technology, intentionally or through lack of adequate preventive measures, than would closer allies. Yet, the risk of compromise may not be a determinative concern of the exporting government if it and its closest allies already have more advanced next-generation systems or superior countermeasures in the hands of its military forces.

Some supplier states begin with a presumption of denial that may be reversed only after lengthy internal reviews and deliberations. And even then, export may come, as previously mentioned, with numerous conditions. Release decisions become increasingly murky when supplier governments are approached by would-be recipients that are viewed as further and further from their national interests.

Other supplier states may begin with a presumption of approval unless there is some clear reason to deny the license. One such objective could be interest in securing support of recipients for initiatives advanced in an international forum, for example, a planned United Nations vote on an initiative sponsored by the supplier government. Another objective is economic, to improve the competitive position of domestic arms producers in the international marketplace; a supplier may consciously accept some security risk in exchange for the revenues and jobs earned by exports.

GROUPINGS OF COUNTRIES

Countries view their defense technology and industrial bases through a prism shaped by national factors—scale, security strategy, and economics. Within that context, a domestic defense industry can become as large, capable, and as dominant in the export marketplace as its government facilitates by funding R&D and production of military technology and systems and allowing (perhaps even actively supporting) military systems exports. Though each country is different, these various possibilities and considerations manifest themselves in the form of several major groups of countries.

Large Countries with Large GDPs and Global Aspirations

The largest countries will often have large defense establishments structured to advance their aspirations on the global stage. The United States, China, and Russia fall easily into this category with 2008 gross domestic products (GDPs) of $14.2 trillion, $3.9 trillion, and $1.6 trillion, respectively.[9] But each places a different emphasis on export sales; each has a different approach to export control; and each services a different customer base. The United States has a large defense industry, but also has large domestic requirements for what its industry produces. Thus, U.S. defense companies view exports as highly desirable but hardly essential for their survival—U.S. defense exports comprise less than one-fifth of total U.S. arms production. Exports are desirable for U.S. industry because they add to the bottom line and allow companies to help sustain large staffs of talented scientists, engineers, and key production workers. Exports are also desirable for the U.S. government because of foreign policy and national security reasons, and because, economically, they reduce unit costs of defense equipment and extend production lines after U.S. needs are initially satisfied. But in practice, U.S. government export decisions are more effective in reducing the risk of technology compromise than boosting export revenues and the U.S. jobs they produce.

As China has been significantly increasing defense expenditures, its industry is heavily engaged in producing many of the systems needed to equip its military forces. In those cases where it seeks systems beyond the level of sophistication available from its domestic defense companies, it acquires from others—primarily Russia. China, in turn supplies military systems to countries considered unstable by the United States and many other Western suppliers—China shares those customers with a few other states that have a similarly liberal approach to arms exports. Today, Russia depends largely on export sales to sustain its defense industry until such time as the Russian economy provides sufficient resources for its own defense modernization. As in the case of China, Russia is relatively liberal by Western standards about who its customers are and draws largely, but not exclusively, from a base of countries viewed as untrustworthy by the Western powers.

Large Countries with Large GDPs and Mainly Domestic Aspirations

Japan may be the sole member of this group. Its 2008 ($4.9 trillion) GDP ranked second in the world; only the U.S. GDP was larger. Japan has a capable but modest-scale defense industry and depends on the United States to supply what domestic industry cannot. Japan has concerns about others in its region and is committed to a strong self-defense capability. However, as Japan's export policy effectively precludes arms exports, Japanese defense companies occupy a very tenuous position. They depend on government largess to remain economically viable, denying industry the traditional benefits of economies of scale in production and creating an environment inconsistent with innovation and cost consciousness.

Small Countries with Global Aspirations and Large GDPs

The smaller states have substantially less flexibility than the United States, China, and Russia. Among these states are several that have global aspirations (e.g., France and the United Kingdom, each with 2008 GDPs of over $2 trillion) and are convinced they need a competent national defense industry. The domestic defense market is significant (the two have the highest defense investment levels in Europe) but insufficient to sustain a world-class defense industry. Therefore, these counties assign a high priority to defense exports whose magnitude may be a modest multiple of the domestic demand. Achieving that level of exports annually requires active marketing campaigns by industry aided by the direct engagement of senior government officials, including the head of state in the case of the largest sales. Success also requires a domestic export control regime that reaches decisions informed by facts, not political rhetoric, about which countries are eligible as export customers.

Small Countries with Modest Global Aspirations and Significant GDPs

Smaller states with a more inward looking set of objectives (e.g., defense of national territory and populations) may also assign high priority to sustaining a domestic defense-industrial base. Germany and Italy with 2008 GDPs of $3.7 trillion and $2.3 trillion, respectively, expect their companies to survive on their own merits, selling to the domestic and export markets. However, both are advantaged because German and Italian defense investment levels are among the highest in Europe, exceeded only by France and the United Kingdom. German export rules are relatively strict despite the negative impact on German companies, while Italian export rules are largely consistent with those of other Western powers.

Large Countries with Modest GDPs and Regional Aspirations

Several countries come to mind to populate this group; among them are Australia, Brazil, India, and Korea—with 2008 GDPs in the $0.9–$1.6 trillion range. Each has a domestic defense industry, each seeks (in differing degrees) to expand that industry and understands that exports are an important component of the revenues needed to achieve the goal. Each has an export control regime that has evolved over time and is under pressure from domestic industry but largely aligned with the Western powers.

Small Pariah Countries Seeking Revenue

North Korea is a special case. It is a poor country with very limited resources and the exploitation of what resources it has is constrained by its government. The country has used arms exports as one of several means to generate revenue. It has done so clandestinely by marketing weapon systems (e.g., ballistic missiles) to countries like Iraq and Syria. Revenue generation clearly trumps traditional export control considerations.

INHERENT TENSIONS AND INDUSTRY IMPLICATIONS

Export controls can have a substantial influence on a domestic defense industry and advanced technology industries. Therefore, it is inevitable that frictions between governments and their domestic industries will occasionally emerge. These will be most in evidence in countries where government export policies are ambiguous and export licensing practices are both inefficient and less than transparent. This is especially true when licensing decisions are protracted and the outcome is unpredictable.

Unlike in the 1970s, defense technology and defense companies in the 21st century are broadly distributed geographically. The largest concentrations of defense technologists and defense production facilities remain in the United States and western Europe, but capable developers and producers exist elsewhere.

Some developing countries, concerned about the political and economic implications of dependency on the major suppliers, have declared a national strategic goal to achieve at least a modest position in the global aerospace and defense industry. The addition of new capacity at a time when excess capacity still remains from the cold war–era is not especially wise from an economic perspective, but such decisions may be driven by strategic considerations such as a desire to become more self-sufficient. Other considerations may also prevail, including a goal to utilize national defense investments to become somewhat competitive and enter the world market, as well as providing future domestic employment, especially in the fields of electronics and aerospace. New entrants into the business are initially disadvantaged by their lack of a defense technology and production base, lack of experience in the global arms market, and lack of credibility with potential customers and industrial partners. Such nations will often attempt to leverage defense purchases from more industrialized suppliers to achieve these goals. Offset arrangements, as well as licensed production and coproduction agreements, are commonly used vehicles in this process.

Offset arrangements, as well as licensed production and coproduction agreements, are viewed by supplier governments and the defense industry alike with some misgivings. The dynamic of selling the older and less capable technology, licensing its production, and, in effect, facilitating some future competition can produce stronger sales, additional income, and perhaps the opportunity for useful joint ventures. The dynamic described does not create either a military or technology threat to the supplier. However, over time, it can also erode sales and disperse future business opportunities. Thus, the global overcapacity is currently being worsened by the emergence of new entrants from the developing world. Tensions are a natural consequence, as supplier states are providing the wherewithal willingly as international competition proceeds apace. Supplier governments have additional concerns. Export control systems are not designed to deal with terrorists and other nonstate actors, but nonetheless must take into account the possibility of diversions and unauthorized retransfers to them. The more widely defense production capacity is dispersed, the more difficult the problems of proliferation become, and the greater the likelihood that defense articles will reach unacceptable end users. These concerns are somewhat independent of the sophistication of the end product. Consequently, and as a further complicating and tension-inducing factor, governments, as is their wont, often apply broad-brush restrictions and conditions to licenses, especially coproduction and technical assistance licenses. These may well be inappropriate to the majority of the cases and with most recipients. Therefore, such items require all parties to the license to expend time and effort to address them. This frequently becomes stressful to all.

In practice, the export control community in some countries may act in a very conservative manner to minimize risk to its members. Conservatism may provide solace for export license examiners but it may also frustrate allies, friends, and exporters for any of a number of reasons. Control lists may have a cold war flavor to them and reflect a time when a country was preeminent both in terms of its military technology and the military systems it developed and produced. However, much of the formerly preeminent technology is more of a commodity than a critical exception today. Rejecting the proposed exporting of such technology then becomes more a display of principle than any expectation that the technology will be denied to a prospective customer—as there may be several other qualified sources elsewhere. Perhaps most frustrating to responsible companies is when export control staffs assign great significance to technology that the developer knows is one or more generations old. Another such situation occurs when some in the export control community display the attitude that industry is so greedy that it will sell anything to anybody or that industry executives are fundamentally dishonest. Sometimes forgotten is that intellectual property is industry's future; industry will protect that intellectual property at least as diligently as governments protect their secrets.

CURRENT ISSUES AND FUTURE CHALLENGES

While tensions are, to some degree, an inevitable function of the defense export control process itself, and despite laudable efforts in some nations, most notably the United States, to attempt improvements in the efficiency of defense export licensing, it is hard to see that tensions between the government export control systems and defense industry will diminish any time soon. Indeed, they are likely to increase. As we have seen, there is an enduring overcapacity in the global defense industry. This capacity has been sustained and even extended in large part by industry itself. Increasing competition in the global defense market will tend to make each sale more important, each license denial more critical, every failure more significant, and thus each future sales opportunity will grow in importance.

Governments are also conflicted. As international terrorism becomes increasingly alarming, strong defense forces, systems, and capabilities are viewed as ever more essential. Yet, the proliferation of lethal weapons and technology engenders grave concern among supplier states. National defense budgets are flat in most supplier states, with the United States and China, at least for the moment, being the major exceptions. Nondefense demands against national budgets are growing, putting pressure on defense establishments to subsidize costs through the various benefits of foreign defense sales.

Further complicating the picture are the remarkable technological advances in defense and dual-use areas, as well as in the commercial sector, coupled with effects of globalization that have raised serious concerns about the efficacy of almost any control system at all.

The most sensitive defense technologies produce hugely difficult problems for national defense establishments. Stealth and counter-stealth technologies have provided warfighters with unbelievable advantages, albeit at colossal cost. Such investments have been deemed necessary by the most advanced supplier states, and any potential diminishment of the military value of such investments is seen as a catastrophe. Consider, for example, the fact that a multibillion dollar investment can be effectively countered by the expenditure of a trivial number of millions, if the correct information falls into the wrong hands. Governments are understandably reluctant to share such technology when the consequences are so dire. This raises unique and extremely difficult issues for governments and industry to resolve. This situation is particularly fraught given that stealth and counter-stealth are being applied to an ever growing number of combat systems. Similar situations and concerns exist for anti-tamper technologies, among others. Even less sophisticated weapons warrant careful consideration by exporting countries. National leaders do not want to find themselves explaining to an angry public why their boys are being killed by rifles supplied by their own government.

NOTES

1. United States National Science Board, Science and Engineering Indicators 2008, 6–17. The average annual growth of high-technology manufacturing in 1986–2005 "was 6%, more than double the rate for other manufacturing industries." High-technology manufacturing consists of five sectors: aircraft and spacecraft; pharmaceuticals; office, accounting, and computing machinery; radio, television, and communications equipment; and medical, precision, and optical instruments.

2. One example is information technology, which underpinned the revolution in military affairs that evolved into network centricity. Another example is microelectronics—which for a time the military sought to control, but discovered that they could not do so and learned with dismay that even when they were partially successful, they could not afford to acquire and utilize the product without leveraging the vast investments and economies of scale provided by the commercial sector.

3. Arms Export Control Act of 1975, subchapter I, Foreign and National Security Policy Objectives and Restraints, section 2751.

4. Foreign and Commonwealth Office Web site.www.fco.gov.uk.

5. Australia Group Web site.www.australiagroup.net.

6. Nuclear Suppliers Group Web site.www.nuclearsuppliersgroup.org.

7. Missile Technology Control Regime Web site.www.mtcr.info.

8. Wassenaar Arrangement Web site.www.wassenaar.org.

9. *World Development Indicators Database,* World Bank, July 1, 2009. http://siteresources.worldbank.org/DATASTATISTICS/Resources/wdi09introch4.pdf.

14

Offsets and International Industrial Participation

Bernard Udis

OFFSETS: DEFINITION, GOALS, AND THEORY

Offsets in international defense trade became ubiquitous in sales of technologically advanced equipment beginning in the late 1960s and early 1970s. The most common offset agreement commits the selling firm to perform some nonmarket requirement as a necessary condition for the sale. Such requirements vary widely, ranging from an agreement by the seller to purchase products and/or services from the buying country that are essentially unrelated to the equipment sale being negotiated, to the explicit transfer of technology, investment, and various coproduction arrangements. Commitments involving work by industry of the buying country on the product whose sale is being negotiated are described as direct offsets, while other unrelated arrangements are known as indirect offsets.

Some observers have likened offsets to barter, but this view is misleading. In the view of a careful student of the offset phenomenon:

> it is the concept of added reciprocity which is central to the practice. This is the notion that the transaction should create some economic activity over and above that which would occur if it were only a cash transaction. That is, the purpose of counter-trade [offsets] is not to avoid the use of cash for an exchange of goods or services; rather, it is to have some added impact or effect beyond the exchange of goods per se.[1]

Since such transactions occur outside conventional market operations, many economic theorists stamp them as trade diverting and, hence, welfare reducing. This position has been repeatedly uttered and has almost assumed a mantra-like quality. *Diversion* refers to the forceful twisting away of the terms of a transaction from those likely to have evolved optimally in a competitive market, usually as a result of the exercise of monopoly influence. The applicability of the familiar efficiency argument for a simple market exchange is based upon the assumption of a competitive market structure. The imperfectly competitive nature of the aerospace industry opens the likelihood of oligopolistic market distortions resulting in resource misallocation under free trade. In such circumstances, trade or industrial policy may be introduced to counter such distortions in what may reasonably be described as a second-best case.

In the defense case, the buyer is a government agency, again suggesting that the assumptions of market competition may be misapplied. Additionally, economists have usually concentrated on a single goal in identifying an optimal policy with limited, if any, attention focused on other goals in the social calculus of public decision making. Multiple policy objectives that characterize real-world decision making by government officials convert a theoretically optimal policy for the attainment of a single goal into a mutually contradictory mélange.

The reality faced by policymakers most often requires them to adopt a broad approach to the selection of programs that simultaneously advance several objectives in a somewhat consistent way while steering around the political and economic constraints that narrow the range of available alternatives. In such an environment, offsets may appear to offer a relatively safe route through a dangerous minefield, or, in technical terms, an efficient contract. Such multidimensional contracts challenge the popular theoretical view that all dimensions can be translated into money at a common and objectively determined rate in a competitive market. Thus, the emergence of a lower price for the buyer may not automatically prove to be the optimal solution.

In an international market for advanced technology products, participants face uncertain product quality, imperfect competition, and a complex contract-enforcement climate. In such an environment, with substantial inhibitions to the unfettered use of price variations to adjust to changing conditions of supply and demand, bargaining is a natural development.

Several distinguished economists have recognized these developments and a sample of their views may prove instructive. Williamson has commented on the tendency of orthodox economists to see nontraditional modes of organization and contracting as proof of attempts to monopolize rather than simply to economize on transaction costs.[2] Recent growth of trade in arms, information technology, and various forms of training has led Intriligator to suggest that analysis may have to proceed beyond traditional classical theories that evolved in a world of trade in basic commodities.[3]

Goals of Offsets

Since offsets are usually demanded by the buyer, focus on goals will be limited here to the perspective of the buyer. Historically, a wide array of goals has been reflected in offset negotiations. A study of offset terms reveals such objectives as economizing in the use of what may have appeared to be scarce foreign exchange; providing jobs and production for domestic labor and industry (and, simultaneously, a defense against attacks from domestic political foes for enriching foreigners at the expense of citizens); acquiring valuable technology and training that will advance the competitiveness of local industry, and perhaps spread from the defense industry to the broader economy; and a means to circumvent foreign buy-national requirements and thus enhance the export potential of domestic industry. The popularity of these goals have changed over time and space, varying with such factors as foreign exchange rates, perception of national security environment, level of industrial development, level of economic growth, offset experience, and so on. The diversity of such goals and the factors influencing them make any effort to evaluate their results and impact in the aggregate most difficult. However, given the widespread appearance of technology acquisition in offset history, it may be useful to examine the theory of technology transfer to understand why offsets appear to be a convenient avenue for its attainment.

Critics of offsets often ask why such a desire to acquire advanced technology is not addressed more directly through purchase of the technology in the market rather than through the more circuitous route of participating in an offset arrangement. In an important article, Teece has criticized the portrayal of the firm by traditional microeconomic theory as an abstract bundle of productive transformations characterized by a production function regarded as a datum. He objects to this conceptualization since it implies that a firm's behavior is stored in symbolic form in "a book of blueprints."[4]

Teece challenges this book of blueprints metaphor, stressing the tacit nature of much individual knowledge that can be articulated only with difficulty. He observes, "in the exercise of individual skill, many actions are taken that are not the result of considered choices but rather are automatic responses that constitute aspects of skill."[5] When transferring this concept from the individual to the routine operations of a business organization, "much that could in principle be deliberated is instead done automatically in response to signals arising from the organization or its environment."[6] Thus, organizational memory exists and it is based on routines. Members of the organization must be able to receive and interpret information arising from within the organization and its environment in order to trigger an appropriate response from their repertoire. Since technology transfer between firms involves a shift across organizational boundaries, the transmission of an individual's knowledge of a routine separated from its context may be unsuccessful.

Even if one assumes that both parties are aware of the opportunity to gain via exchange and buyers acknowledge the existence of valuable information for which they are willing to pay, much more than a simple market exchange is usually necessary. As already noted, the exchange of technology has powerful tacit and learning-by-doing characteristics that often require that individual and organizational knowledge and experience accompany the transfer of purely technical information and data. Open reciprocal information is necessary both to identify and disclose opportunities that may exist for the exchange of information and aid the actual transfer to take place. The parties in such a situation are linked in what Williamson has labeled a "small numbers trading relation"; this carries risks for both parties arising out of the strategic manipulation of information or misrepresentation of intentions.[7] Specific examples include a "seller exposed to hazards such as the possibility that the buyer will employ the knowledge in subtle ways not covered by the contract, or the buyer [leapfrogging] the licensor's technology and [becoming] an unexpected competitive threat." Alternatively, "the buyer is exposed to hazards such as the seller asserting that the technology has better performance or cost reducing characteristics than is actually the case, or the seller might render promised transfer assistance in a perfunctory fashion."[8] After raising the possibility of bonding or performance guarantees as possible ways to reduce risk, Teece notes that so long as the measurement of the performance of the technology is ambiguous, "costly haggling" might still ensue.

Williamson sees the answer to this vexing problem in what he calls "relational contracting,"[9] and one such example bears a strong resemblance to the direct offset structure where a form of bilateral governance emerges under which the autonomy of the parties is maintained. Here, independent firms engage in trade with both parties committed to the maintenance of a friendly and cooperative relationship as a goal of greater value than possible short-term gains available through opportunistic behavior. A carefully designed offset arrangement may also rely upon reputation effects and principal-agent relations to furnish powerful incentives for the provider of technology to ensure a completely successful transfer.

Reputation effects are more likely to be effective in the case of a product that is well known, especially when the seller's product name is familiar. Thus, in the first 15 years or so of its life, most informed stories in the press referred not to the F-16 but to the "General Dynamics F-16." This helped motivate General Dynamics (GD) to ensure that transfers of technology to partner states were successfully conducted to minimize the risk of a high accident rate besmirching the GD name. In the case of the Joint Strike Fighter (JSF), Lockheed Martin is similarly vulnerable.[10]

Reputation effects are also an element in many principal-agent cases where the challenge is to devise systems that minimize the potential conflict between groups that may not necessarily share the same goals. Such a case may be found in the relations between owners and hired managers; managers and employees; or even physicians and patients. In the last case, one is reminded of the implicit contracts that exist to control the tendency of doctors to prescribe more medical care than their patients might prefer. The preference of surgeons for a surgical option and of radiologists for their specialty is well known. Fortunately, there are many factors in the physician-patient relationship that serve to bring the differing interests closer together. Patients are not obliged to accept their doctor's recommendation for treatment, and they may seek a second opinion. In extreme cases, physician behavior may be influenced by the existence of peer review boards, which certainly can affect reputations.[11]

In the international trade in defense environment, as well, the challenge for the buyer is to formulate a system that provides an incentive for the seller to seriously accept the buyer's objective as his own.[12]

To have explained why several offset arrangements appear attractive does not constitute an endorsement of the offset route as the optimal one. However, it does suggest why, in many cases, buyers have selected that route to achieve their objectives. Policymakers who, for whatever reason, object to the offset option will likely be more successful if they can suggest alternative policies to buying states that can better help them to attain their goals. Understanding the objectives of buying states is essential to that recommendation.

U.S. OFFSET DATA: COLLECTION AND FINDINGS

Section 309 of the 1986 amendments to the Defense Production Act (DPA) dealt with the topic of offsets in defense trade. It mandated that the president submit an annual report to Congress on the impact of offsets on the U.S. defense-industrial base. The Office of Management and Budget was assigned to coordinate an interagency committee consisting of representatives from the departments of commerce, defense, labor, treasury, and the Office of the U.S. Trade Representative. A series of annual reports was prepared and issued by this committee between 1986 and 1990. They included relevant statistics on offsets and valuable case studies of U.S. military aircraft and missile sales to other countries: F-16s to Belgium, the Netherlands, Denmark, Norway, and Greece; Patriot missiles to West Germany and the Netherlands; AWACS aircraft to the United Kingdom and France; and F-18s to Canada, Australia, and Spain.

When the DPA expired in October1990, so did the reporting requirement. Several interludes of revival and expiration followed, with the act finally revised on October 29, 1992, retroactive to March 1, 1992. While factors other than offsets were apparently more important elements in explaining this strange sequence of actions, the return of the DPA also restored the offset-reporting requirement—but with some interesting differences. Henceforth, the secretary of commerce was to be responsible for the preparation of the reports and was designated to function as the executive agent of the president in administering the requirements of section 309 of the DPA. It should be noted that the Office of Management and Budget was removed from membership in the interagency committee as well as from its former leadership role in the work of the committee. The prevailing opinion at the time saw this change as a reflection of the ire of some congressional critics at the former committee's reports, which had concluded that the impact of offsets on the U.S. economy and defense technology base were relatively minor. The reports also provided a fairly sophisticated analysis of proposed congressional protectionist actions.[13]

The most recent publication in the series *Offsets in Defense Trade* bears the date of December 2007 and contains data current through 2006. This document (pp. iv-v, 2–1 to 2–7, 2–9, 2–11, 2–13, 4–5 to 4–7, 4–9 to 4–10, 5–17) is the source of the data that follow below, unless otherwise indicated. In examining offset data, it is necessary to distinguish between two different concepts: the number and value of new offset agreements between the U.S. defense sector and foreign governments, growing out of a U.S. defense-related export sale; and actual transactions in furtherance of the terms of preexisting offset agreements.

Twelve prime U.S. defense contractors reported that they entered into 44 new offset agreements with 20 countries in 2006. The number of such agreements and their estimated value were higher than in 2005, the year with the minimum number of agreements over the 1993–2006 period. The 2006 value of such offsets equaled $3.4 billion out of a defense export value base of $4.8 billion, or 70.9 percent. Some interesting differences emerge when the figures are disaggregated by geographic region. European nations received an average of 85.5 percent of the contract value of defense exports as offsets. The non-European states averaged offset requirements of 42.3 percent, a significant decline from their 93.2 percent in 2004.

The December 2007 offset report presents comparable figures for the 1993–2006 period. Over this 14-year interval, U.S. firms entered into 582 offset agreements with 42 countries, valued at $60.0 billion, or 71.2 percent of the export contract sales value of $84.3 billion. Aerospace defense system sales accounted for slightly over four-fifths of those export contracts. During this longer period, European states represented 65.9 percent of the total value of offset agreements, but this was only 48.0 percent of the value of related export contracts. The size of the European offset demands averaged 97.7 percent of export contract values during the 1993–2006 period. Offset agreements valued at 100 percent or more of contract value accounted for 74.4 percent of European agreements. These percentages peaked at 153.3 percent in 2003. In 2006, the European average increased to 85.5 percent, from 83.7 percent in 2005. The lowest European average was 63.9 percent (of export contract value) in 2004.

The offset average for non-European states was 46.7 percent of contract value over the 1993–2006 period. In general, Middle Eastern and Asian countries demanded lower offset levels than did the Europeans. Of the 269 offset agreements with non-European countries, 68.4 percent required offset percentages of 50 percent or less. Only 31.6 percent demanded percentages greater than 50 percent, and just 10 of the non-European offset agreements provided for offset requirements of over 100 percent.

During the 14 year period, Austria led all other countries with offset percentages equal to 172.2 percent of the value of defense exports. The next five countries and their percentages were Poland (167.7 percent), the Netherlands (117.3 percent), South Africa (116.0 percent), Greece (114.2 percent), and Sweden (103.9 percent).

The authors of the commerce department report also calculated a moving weighted average to smooth out yearly fluctuations in both defense sales and offsets. The weighted world trend of offset percentage values rose from 49.3 percent to 102.9 percent between 1993 and 2005, and then decreased to 76.7 percent in 2004–6. During that period, the European percentage figure rose from 87.1 to 133.9, but then fell to 81.2 from 2004 to 2006. The required percentage for the rest of the world increased from 27.6 to 73.0 over the full 14-year period.

As noted above, another important part of the offset phenomenon consists of transactions initiated to satisfy obligations in furtherance of the terms of earlier offset agreements. U.S. companies reported the total value of such offset transactions in 2006 at $4.7 billion. Indirect offset transactions constituted 63.6 percent of that figure, while direct offsets amounted to 36 percent.

During the 1993–2006 period, U.S. companies reported a total of 8,660 offset transactions covering 45 countries. The total value of such transactions equaled $42 billion, of which indirect offsets accounted for 59.5 percent while direct offsets constituted 39.86 percent. The tiny unaccounted balance represented offsets of unspecified types. The majority of offset transactions (77.4 percent) during this span of time were found in the categories of purchases, subcontracts, and technology transfers. Their respective shares of the total category were 38.2 percent, 22.2 percent, and 16.5 percent.

With respect to industrial sectors, the majority of offset transactions fell into a small number of major industries involved in defense production. The largest group by far was transportation equipment (SIC [Standard Industrial Classification] 37), which accounted for 53.2 percent of the total value of offset transactions in the 1993–2006 period. Second was the electronics/electrical sector (SIC 36), representing only 12.9 percent of total value.

Over the past 30 years, many changes have occurred in the use of offsets in defense trade. Such variables as the magnitude and value of offset demands, the relative importance of direct versus indirect offsets, the use of brokers to facilitate the indirect variety, the length of the period allowed in which to complete offset requirements, and the methods of enforcement have all shifted.

The comparison period may be lengthened by utilizing data for the bulk of the 1980s and the pre-1980 years from a document from the earlier reporting series assembled under the auspices of the Office of Management and Budget (OMB).[14] The data may not be completely comparable with the later series, but may still be useful in suggesting broad changes. This document reports *value of implementation* in millions of current dollars. For the pre-1980 years, $312.1 million was recorded, in contrast with $10.786 million in the 1980–1987 period (p. 137). Data classified as *actual value of transactions* in the December 2007 report of the current series (p. vi) were recorded as $42.0 billion for the 1993–2006 period. During the three time periods reported, direct offsets amounted to 26.2 percent, 30.9 percent, and 39.6 percent, while indirect offsets registered 69.9 percent, 61.4 percent, and 59.5 percent, respectively. In any single period, the percentages do not equal 100 percent due to the inclusion in the total of offsets unspecified by type. It appears that offset demanders' preference for economic activity closely related to the product of the transaction has gradually been realized, while prime contractors' desire to protect the original production layout has been slowly sacrificed.

In the past, brokers were often utilized to assist major defense contractors to convert physical quantities of items acquired under indirect offset contracts into cash. Typically, brokers' fees were considered relatively small and saved, say, aerospace firms from determining how to dispose of items as diverse as hams and tourist trips. Commodity brokers, financial departments of banks, and specialized trading companies were utilized for such tasks.

In more recent years, a new type of broker has appeared—one that specializes in commercializing new technologies developed in university or independent research laboratories. Typically, such organizations are staffed with highly qualified scientists and engineers who have little talent for marketing their discoveries. The new generation of brokers, often staffed with technically oriented personnel, concentrates on bringing such developments to the attention of major defense firms with significant technology transfer obligations to foreign governments. Such obligations often focus on environmental and/or health improvements. For a fee, such brokers offer to act as matchmakers, as it were, bringing new and promising technology forward for the principal contractor to offer in furtherance of meeting such responsibilities. At the moment, reliable data to quantify such functions appear to be unavailable.

Another consideration is the length of the time period over which the offset commitments may be fulfilled. The longer the period, the more difficult it is to attribute subsequent purchases by the prime contractor to the offset requirements. During the 1980–87 time interval, the average term was 11 years in offset deals entered into by U.S. firms.[15] This period has been declining, as foreign demanders of offsets have become both more sophisticated and more exacting. Thus, in the 1993–2006 timeframe, the average period had fallen to just below 7 years.[16] The length of the period appears to have stabilized at this level more recently. Other considerations appear to have played a role, particularly the phenomenon of offset credit banking, under which a principal contractor with unexpired offset credits may, as it were, bank them for future use—at least for some specified period of time.

Of further interest is the method of enforcement of offset terms. During the earlier 1980–87 period, a commitment to best efforts was reported in some 68 percent of cases studied, while the remaining 32 percent specified liquidated damages or some other form of financial penalty for failure to meet contractual obligations.[17] Thus, two-thirds of the cases relied upon a figurative handshake to ensure that contract terms would be met. By 1993–97, a best efforts commitment had dropped to about 50 percent, and while such information is no longer reported in the current annual report series, an educated guess by a commerce department official put the figure at no more than 33 percent. Thus, it would again appear that offset demanders have become less willing to tolerate an informal and undemanding approach to enforcement of contract terms.

A LOOK AHEAD: OFFSETS OR PRODUCTION CONSORTIA?

Any effort to evaluate the effect of offsets on both receivers and givers must begin by recognizing the complexities inherent in the phenomenon. As noted above, countries demanding offsets differ widely in their goals and in the relative success or failure of the attempt. There has been a shortage of objective and careful work in the area. The attempt to lump together such a diverse group of policies resembles the famous legend of several blind men attempting to describe an elephant after each has performed a physical examination of different parts of the animal.

The foregoing sections have presented several theoretical and real-world considerations that suggest the need for caution before wholeheartedly endorsing the view of offsets as trade diverting and welfare reducing. A high-ranking executive of a major U.S. aerospace firm recently observed that "Many supplier relationships of today are built on offset relationships of two decades ago. We have now learned how to work together without offsets."[18] What is particularly intriguing here is that over a decade ago, a Swiss executive described a principal goal of his country's offset policy to be bringing the high quality of Swiss industry to the attention of foreign (U.S.) industrialists.[19] This anecdote provides some support for a point made in the conclusions of a paper on offsets published some years ago:

> If their principal effect is to pressure the principal design contractor to broaden its horizons in the search for subcontractors, offsets may actually lead to a more efficient pattern of production linkages and a welfare-enhancing arrangement. Here, an alliance between liberal trade theorists and anti-offset interests may be perverse."[20]

The authors of the above paper concluded that while some offsets may be efficiency and welfare enhancing, others may contribute to structural inefficiencies in the global economy. Thus, they recommended a serious attempt to identify criteria to differentiate between the two prior to any effort at international control.[21] The need still exists.

BEYOND OFFSETS

Over the years, the heavy attention paid to offsets has tended to veil the fact that offsets, per se, are not a stand-alone phenomenon, but rather represent a stage in the evolving dynamic of international trade in defense items. The post–World War II period began with the transfer by the U.S. military of surplus armaments to newly liberated countries. Gradually, this evolved into widespread production under license of American weapons and aircraft, with liberal terms to ease the dollar shortage of the period. In states with a historic aircraft tradition, indigenous design and production began to appear, followed in the 1970s by a growing use of offset programs.

While little attention has been paid to the principal reasons for the success and/or failure of such programs, it is clear that in many cases, significant technological progress was acquired by the industries of participating buyer states. For example, in a paper that is generally critical of the offset experience of Spanish industry in the F-18 offset program, Molas-Gallart notes that "there were, in fact, cases of Spanish firms building areas of expertise which they would use on new programs and would become part of their technological portfolio." He cites one of the best-known cases as that of the Spanish electronics firm CE-SELSA in its work on simulators, which has contributed to its work in other international programs and the development of its own systems.[22] It should also be noted that the Spanish aerospace firm CASA is currently a junior partner in the European aerospace conglomerate EADS (European Aeronautic Defence and Space Company), which produces both military aircraft (the European fighter aircraft known as Typhoon) and civilian passenger aircraft (the Airbus family). Some years ago in private interviews, Spanish government officials expressed such developments as goals of CASA's participation in the F-18 program.

In fact, the evolution of Spanish offset policy provides a microcosmic example of what may be happening more generally in the offset area.[23] When the Spanish offset agreement was negotiated in the early 1980s, indirect offsets were much more important than the direct variety. This resulted in a large number of companies involved in generally small offset activities. A significant effort was required to administer these offset operations, as McDonnell Douglas submitted these projects for approval individually and each had to be approved by the Spanish Offset Management Office. Soon, the office was inundated with paperwork. During the 10-year program, thousands of projects and project applications were processed. The relatively small share of defense-related offsets (28 percent of total program value) was a disappointment, as was the even smaller share representing technology transfer.

Following the expiration of the formal contract period, a three year grace period was negotiated, which incorporated substantial changes, reflecting the experiences of the first decade. In retrospect, from the Spanish perspective, the original program was structured in a way that generated high overhead and transaction costs due to an excessive number of projects with inadequate strategic focus. The emphasis shifted dramatically from indirect to direct offsets, which were closely associated with the F-18 aircraft. The nature of these offsets had to be agreed upon by the Spanish side in advance, so they were no longer simply reacting to suggestions initiated by McDonnell Douglas.

In the early years of the program, Spanish industry had only a limited capacity to handle direct work on the aircraft. The Spanish defense industry was fragmented, technologically weak, and largely state owned. The principal actors were each associated with one of the three armed forces: CASA (Construcciones Aeronauticas, S. A.); BAZAN for the navy; and ENSB (Empresa Nacional Santa Barbara), which produced land armaments for the army. To correct this situation, the Spanish government began to incorporate local industry into defense research activities. From the mid-1980s to 1991, government support of defense research and development (R&D) had climbed from insignificant levels to nearly 30 percent of the Spanish government's total R&D outlays.

These efforts had repercussions beyond the F-18 program and served to bring the capability of the Spanish industrial base closer to the level of its neighbors. Spain became a player in various European collaborative arms design and production programs, including the European Fighter Aircraft (Typhoon) project, which by the early 1990s was absorbing more then three-fifths of total Spanish defense R&D. It should be noted that the companies receiving the bulk of this investment were largely those that had been most involved in the F-18 direct offset activities.

Thus, Spanish defense acquisition programs had shifted from classical offsets to multinational collaboration, which gave the Spanish partner a voice in terms of system configuration. An interesting example is provided by Spain's purchase of 8 Harriers and updating of 12 Harrier AV-8B's in the early 1990s. The work of developing a new Harrier variant was organized as a joint program with the United States, Italy, and Spain. Though a step up from the role of buyer with offsets, there was some concern that Spain might find itself a junior partner providing unsophisticated parts for a larger, integrated European defense market.

It was hoped that the Spanish defense industrial base could be strengthened through a program of foreign direct investment (FDI). This would not be completely new, as U.S. and French firms had acquired minority holdings in state-owned defense companies during the late 1960s and early 1970s. However, these activities were usually tied to specific procurements, which, at their conclusion, tended to wither away in the absence of follow-up orders.

There was particular concern for the major Spanish prime contractors (CASA, ENSB, and BAZAN—now known as IZAR). What was sought was an ongoing partnership with established foreign firms that would ease Spanish producers into an international supply chain. A series of deals with foreign firms eventually saw CASA entering the new European consortium EADS.

After a series of efforts to attract FDI into ENSB, in an unexpected move, the company was sold to General Dynamics of the United States in the spring of 2000. Although Kraus Maffei (KM) of Germany had been successful in selling its Leopard tanks to Spain (which were being produced in ENSB facilities), GD, a major competitor of KM, now owned ENSB. This required the establishment of a "Chinese Wall" to protect the confidentiality of KM technology and to prevent it from falling into the hands of GD. This will be a challenging task, not unlike that faced by Lockheed Martin in producing two new USAF fighters, the F-22 and F-35, with a different set of partners involved in each project. The Spanish government will also have to determine what its role will be in providing a continuous stream of orders necessary to retain the interest of its foreign partners.

OFFSETS VERSUS INDUSTRIAL PARTICIPATION?

The wording of this subsection title suggests that the structure of the JSF program may foretell the direction of future international collaboration. Respected defense economists have examined the question and given somewhat varying answers. The program's theoretical emphasis on work assignment based on quality rather than politically attractive work-share schemes has naturally appealed to those trained to economize in the use of scarce resources and who view waste as close to sinful. Two British economists have examined the issue. Keith Hartley sees the JSF as providing a model for future multinational collaboration, which would be desirable if it can be attained.[24] Ron Matthews identifies offset policies that might enhance technological development, but doubts the likelihood of their adoption. He concludes, "This is an ambitious agenda, and hanging on the presumption that offsets are here to stay. History has shown this is not to be the case."[25] This would appear to be a rather unequivocal prediction of the demise of offsets. In a later paper, Matthews describes collaborative projects like the Typhoon and consortium ventures like the JSF as demonstrating "the twin attraction of member countries enjoying [lower] R&D costs and higher economies of scale from the unification of markets. The lowest cost-acquisition option is arguably the global consortia model." He goes on to note: "However, although this model carries the benefits of a more refined international division of labor, including lower cost and enhanced product quality, the downside is the erosion of defense-industrial sovereignty caused by increased dependence on offshore vendors. The question, however, is whether this loss of defense-industrial sovereignty any longer matters? Further (transformational) warfare is expected to be a quick and decisive exercise. It will incorporate a coalition doctrinal approach, justifying further cooperation in the development of weapons systems as self-reliance becomes less and less an affordable option."[26]

Matthews perceptive paper also recognizes that the "global consortia model, requiring that work-share be based on the competitiveness of member countries' national industries has meant that the majority of work has been captured by highly efficient US and UK defense contractors, leaving minimal work for smaller country participants."[27] Only time will tell whether this vision will be an accurate picture of the future of, say, the JSF program. However, it appears to support an earlier designation of the modern international defense marketplace as resembling a hub-and-spoke model with

> a few large first-tier firms operating at the centre with lines of outsourced production extending to second-tier states on the periphery. First-tier players would serve as "centers of excellence," providing armaments production with its critical design, development, and systems integration inputs, along with the production of more advanced subsystems, such as engines, wings, sensors, information systems, and other electronics. Second-tier arms-producers would mainly be responsible for supplying niche systems or low-tech items, such as structural components. Final assembly could take place in either country, depending on the end-user. Such cooperative arrangements could be highly formalized, involving a second-tier firm working for only one first-tier producer, presumably as a wholly- or partially-owned subsidiary. It is, however, likely that this process would entail second-tier enterprises being engaged in subcontracts or joint venture partnerships with several first-tier firms at the same time. As such, future armaments production could more closely resemble the modern concept of the "virtual corporation"—independent firms coming together on an as-needed basis in order to design and/or develop and/or manufacture a product, only on a global scale.[28]

OFFSETS AND THE F-35 JOINT STRIKE FIGHTER (JSF)

As noted above, the JSF program was designed to avoid offsets in the relations between the United States and the eight partner states. Theoretically, the partners have agreed that selection of participating producers in their countries would be the responsibility of the overall prime contractor, Lockheed Martin. In reality, there may be some room for negotiating whether this could be interpreted to mean that Lockheed would have the final word in choosing from a list provided by the partner state. Lockheed has already complained that particular partners have attempted to recruit the Joint Program Office to apply pressure to obtain a favorable decision from Lockheed. In any event, this issue is likely to remain a continuing problem and a subject for ongoing negotiation. The heart of the problem is found in the expectation that participation in the F-35 supply chain will be restricted to firms that have a reputation for efficient work. As Markowski and Hall have noted, "There appears to be little scope for pump priming new or untested suppliers" in the project.[29]

Another likely source of difficulty looms in the future as nonmember countries appear to negotiate purchases of the JSF under terms of the Foreign Military Sales (FMS) program. There is a high probability that they will demand direct offset work on their aircraft and the terms of such purchases will be negotiated by the U.S. Department of Defense (DoD), not the Joint Program Office. The potential award of such offsets will clearly not be welcomed by the original partner states that paid an initiation fee, as it were, to join the program. Such a circumstance could also result in the replacement of efficient subcontractors in the supply chain with less efficient producers in the new buying state. The possible waiver of the usual R&D recoupment charge to encourage such sales would also come at the expense of the partner states that were to share in such fees as a benefit of membership.

All things considered, there is not likely to be a clean break from offsets as multinational consortia such as the JSF become more popular. As Molas-Gallart has observed,

> This is not to say that offsets are a thing of the past. Although their relative importance is diminishing, Spain has accumulated important experience in negotiating and managing offset agreements. Because the Spanish administration feels it is learning to extract better offsets then before, the offset option will remain an alternative to consider in almost any offset transaction. Yet with the preference given to other forms of "compensation" like international cooperation, or direct foreign investment in Spanish defense production, offsets will probably be increasingly limited to small transactions. . . . In other words, offsets are here to stay as one element of the Spanish arms purchasing policy.[30]

Spain is unlikely to be the only country to adopt such a policy.

CONCLUSIONS

Globalization leads to greater economic interdependence as a consequence of the seeking out of lower-cost sources of supply wherever they are located. This conflicts with the desire for national defense-industrial self-sufficiency. Direct offsets provide a route to acquiring advanced weapon systems from abroad while preserving and/or advancing some domestic defense industry capabilities, at least in sectors deemed essential. The U.K. defense industrial strategy (DIS) was an explicit effort to identify such capabilities as an important part of the effort to sustain national sovereignty.

Arguments for caution against the blandishments of lower-cost foreign sources have a long history, beginning as far back as Adam Smith's famous national defense exception from his recommended open market endorsements. Among his recommendations as to how the United States could continue on the cutting edge of advanced military technology, Ben Rich, long-time leader of the Lockheed Skunk Works, included a warning against the temptation of a continuous search for lowest-cost sources. In his words:

> Another sound management practice that is gospel at the Skunk Works is to stick with reliable suppliers. Japanese auto manufacturers discovered long ago that periodically switching suppliers and selecting new ones on the basis of lowest bidders proved a costly blunder. New suppliers frequently underbid just to gain a foothold in an industry, then meet their expenses by providing inferior parts and quality that can seriously impair overall performance standards. And even if a new supplier does produce quality parts according to the specifications, his parts will not necessarily match those furnished by the previous supplier: his tooling and calibrations might be different, causing the major manufacturer extra costs to rework other system components.
>
> For these reasons Japanese manufacturers usually form lasting relationships with proven suppliers, and we at the Skunk Works do the same. We believe that trouble-free relationships with old suppliers will ultimately keep the price of our products lower than if we were to periodically put their contracts up for the lowest bid.[31]

In a recent statement, Peter Hintze, Germany's state secretary for aerospace, advised Airbus management against excessive internationalization of its supply chain in the development of its A-350 aircraft. He stated, "We believe it is in Airbus's advantage to keep research, development and industrial production in Europe."

He criticized Airbus for shifting work overseas just because of the weak dollar, noting that structural decisions based on what may be short-term conditions were unwise. In an argument remarkably similar to that of Rich, he stressed that Airbus could obtain the advantage of lower long-term costs by maintaining its relations with traditional suppliers with an earned reputation for quality work.[32]

Analysts should avoid the temptation to dismiss the national defense rationale as a simplistic and unconvincing consideration in the negotiation of offset terms. It should be included in any list of motives for offset demands, whether cloaked in sophisticated terms such as *operational sovereignty* or not. Security of supply remains an important consideration in source selection, and may be seen as outweighing otherwise attractive economic terms of offer.

Another related point that has not received adequate attention is the growing intragovernmental tension between ministries of defense and of economics/finance viewing the benefit-cost ratio of offsets from their differing perspectives. Thus, if the hoped for benefits from such agreements come at a price that elevates the cost of acquiring an aircraft from abroad, but without a corresponding increase in the defense budget, the military properly sees a reduction in its actual number of aircraft received. Here, a clear challenge appears that pits economic advantage against national security. Even within the military, considerations of quantity versus quality may lead to further discord.

It is interesting to note that offsets may deserve double billing both as a partial contribution to globalization and also a reaction to it. In a world of rapid change, it would not be surprising to observe that offsets have also demonstrated such change. As argued here, they should be studied as but one phase in the dynamic evolution of international defense trade relationships.

ACKNOWLEDGMENT

This work was partly funded by the Acquisition Research Program of the U.S. Naval Postgraduate School, and this support is gratefully acknowledged.

NOTES

1. Grant T. Hammond, *Countertrade, Offsets and Barter in International Political Economy* (New York: St. Martin's Press, 1990), 5.

2. Oliver E. Williamson, *The Economic Institutions of Capitalism: Firms, Markets, Relational Contracting* (New York: The Free Press, 1985).

3. Michael D. Intriligator, "Comment," in *U.S. Trade Policies in a Changing World Economy*, ed. Robert Stern (Cambridge: MIT Press, 1987), 364–369.

4. David J. Teece, "Towards an Economic Theory of the Multi-Product Firm," *Journal of Economic Behavior and Organization* 3 (1982): 39–63, especially 43. The original conceptualization is found in Sidney G. Winter, "An Essay on the Theory of Production," in *Economics and the World around It*, ed. S. H. Hymans (Ann Arbor: University of Michigan Press, 1982), 55–91, especially 58.

5. Teece, "Towards an Economic Theory of the Multi-Product Firm," 44.

6. Teece, "Towards an Economic Theory of the Multi-Product Firm," 44

7. Oliver E. Williamson, *Markets and Hierarchies: Analysis and Antitrust Implications* (New York: The Free Press, 1975), 26–28.

8. Teece, "Towards an Economic Theory of the Multi-Product Firm," 52.

9. Williamson, *Markets and Hierarchies*, 250–52.

10. For a recent comprehensive treatment of reputation effects, see W. Bentley MacLeod, "Reputations, Relationships, and Contract Enforcement," *Journal of Economic Literature* 45, no. 3 (2007): 595–628.

11. See Walter Nicholson, *Intermediate Economics and its Applications*, 5th ed. (Chicago: The Dryden Press, 1990), 302.

12. For a recent theoretical treatment of principal agent relationships, see Jean-Jacques Laffont and David Martimort, *The Theory of Incentives: The Principal Agency Model* (Princeton: Princeton University Press, 2002).

13. For a more detailed review of the developments of this period, see Bernard Udis and Keith E. Maskus, "US Offset Policy," in *The Economics of Offsets: Defense Procurement and Countertrade*, ed. Stephen Martin (Amsterdam: Harwood Academic Publishers, 1996), 357–79.

14. Office of Management and Budget (OMB), *Offsets in Military Exports*, (Washington, DC, Author: April 16, 1990).

15. OMB, *Offsets in Military Exports*, 136.

16. U.S. Department of Commerce, *Offsets in Defense Trade*, (Washington, DC: Author December 2007), 4–7.

17. OMB, *Offsets in Military Exports*, 134.

18. Personal interview, 2007.

19. Personal interview, 1992.

20. Bernard Udis and Keith Maskus, "Offsets as Industrial Policy: Lessons from Aerospace," *Defense Economics* 2, no. 6 (1991): 151–164, especially 163. This paper has been republished in Keith Hartley and Todd Sandler, eds., *The Economics of Defense*, International Library of Critical Writings in Economics (Cheltenham, U.K. and Northampton, MA: Elgar Reference Collection, 2001).

21. Udis and Maskus, "Offsets As Industrial Policy."

22. Jordi Molas-Gallart, "Spain: A Shifting Approach to Defense Procurement and Industrial Policy," in *Studies in Defense Procurement,* ed. U. G. Berkok (Kingston, ON: Queen's University, School of Policy Studies, 2006), 95–104, especially 97.

23. Much of the following material is drawn from Jordi Molas-Gallart, "From Offsets to Industrial Cooperation: Spain's Changing Strategies as an Arms Importer," in *The Economics of Offsets: Defense Procurement and Countertrade,* ed. Stephen Martin (Amsterdam: Harwood Academic Publishers, 1996), 299–320.

24. Keith Hartley, "Offsets and the Joint Strike Fighter in the UK and the Netherlands," in *Arms Trade and Economic Development,* ed. J. Brauer and P. Dunne (London: Routledge, 2004), 117–36, especially 133–34.

25. Ron Matthews, "Defense Offsets: Policy versus Pragmatism," in *Arms Trade and Economic Development,* ed. J. Brauer and P. Dunne (London: Routledge, 2004), 89–102, especially 100.

26. Ron Matthews, "Smart Management of Smart Weapons," in *Studies in Defense Procurement,* ed. U. G. Berkok (Kingston, ON: Queen's University, School of Policy Studies, 2006), 75–93, especially 82–83.

27. Ron Matthews, "Smart Management of Smart Weapons," 86.

28. Richard A. Bitzinger, *Toward a Brave New Arms Industry?* Adelphi Paper 356, International Institute for Strategic Studies (New York: Oxford University Press, 2003), 74–75.

29. Stefan Markowski and Peter Hall, "Defense Procurement and Industry Development: Some Lessons from Australia," in *Studies in Defense Procurement,* ed. U. G. Berkok (Kingston, ON: Queen's University, School of Policy Studies, 2006), 9–73, especially 19.

30. Jordi Molas-Gallart, "From Offsets to Industrial Cooperation: Spain's Changing Strategies as an Arms Importer," in *The Economics of Offsets: Defense Procurement and Countertrade,* ed. Stephen Martin (Amsterdam: Harwood Academic Publishers, 1996), 317.

31. Ben R. Rich and Leo Janos, *Skunk Works* (Boston: Little, Brown, 1994), 333.

32. Robert Wall and Jens Flottau, "Difference of Opinion: As Airbus Mulls Future Agenda Governments Signal Concern," *Aviation Week,* June 2, 2008, 34–35.

15

The Global Small Arms Industry: Transformed by War and Society

Aaron Karp

Call it benign neglect. When contemporary studies of arms production and the arms trade took form in the 1960s and 1970s, military-related industries were preoccupied with the weapons of superpower rivalry. It was an era when *major weapons* were understood, intuitively and exclusively, as fundamentally distinct categories. The weapons that mattered most were nuclear weapons, their delivery systems, and major conventional weapons. Everything else was, by definition, something less.

As recently as the interwar years, small arms were a principal subject of armaments policy and study.[1] In the years after, small arms and light weapons (SALW), the weapons that had dominated warfare throughout human history, receded into the background, unable to compete for high-level attention with the aircraft, missiles, ships, and tanks that came to symbolize major power warfare. In the very best studies of weapons diffusion during the superpower years, small arms were acknowledged but otherwise overlooked.[2] They simply did not seem so important.

In the 1990s, though, small arms came back. As the most common and deadly weapons of postmodern war, they became a synonym for instability, ungovernability, and social pathology. The rising salience of small arms is a direct result of the decline of major war and the corresponding elevation of non-state actors. Small arms are the weapons of globalization, the increasingly ubiquitous symbols of the great leveling of peoples the world over.[3] Just as other international hierarchies are being leveled, so it is with weapons. It is in no small part because of the proliferation of small arms that the state's Weberian monopoly on the legitimate use of force is an increasingly archaic memory.[4] The superficial differences between small arms and major weapon systems remain obvious, especially in terms of cost, complexity, and size. But in terms of destructiveness or political effect, the distinctions are much less obvious.

It is no accident that the smallest and least sophisticated weapons have become among the most visible and controversial. But importance does not automatically mean insight. While small arms production is back as a vital element of military-industrial study and policy, the subject remains poorly understood. Despite their elevation to the top of the global arms control and disarmament agenda, small arms remain as enigmatic as ever. Systematic or even reliable data are lacking. The most important places and numbers of their manufacture are often unknown. The output of smaller producers must usually be guessed. Trends in production usually must be estimated. Efforts to identify basic vectors of availability—increasing? decreasing? this region or that?—often elicit sincere shoulder shrugging.

To be sure, frustration can be exaggerated. There is nothing unique about the poverty of small arms production studies. Indeed, small arms industries are heavily publicized compared to the most obscure shadow lands of defense manufacturing, whole industrial sectors like ordnance, fuel and resupply, base construction, systems integration, or simulation and modeling services. Compared to the most impossibly complex fields like cyber conflict or private security services, small arms production almost looks tidy.

This chapter reviews the state of academic research on small arms production, stressing the findings from research of the last decade. During this period, considerable progress has been made. Useful data sources and models have been developed. We now have a sense of the scale of the industry and vital trends. Most major actors are known, as are general production quantities and the prospects for technological innovations.

The elusiveness of small arms production is troublesome, not because we know so little, but because we need to know much more. Above all, we face the complexities created by the way these products are used. Unlike other military goods and services—used largely if not exclusively by states—small arms, light weapons and their ammunition are ideally suited for non-state actors. Whether they are sought by major insurgencies, sectarian militants, criminal gangs, individual criminals, psychopaths, or frightened neighbors, access to small arms is almost never an insurmountable hurdle. The small arms industry matters most, in other words, because it is the most classically liberal of military industries. It is so profoundly democratic that even to brand it a military industry is questionable.

This chapter relies largely on data previously developed for the Small Arms Survey, a research institute in Geneva. The data it emphasizes only support general conclusions, often highly tentative, but also reveal basic trends about small arms production. The trends emphasized here point to a great convergence in the control of weapons technology. The old distinctions between military and civilian firearms—a truism of the 20th century—are gradually disappearing.

The chapter shows that military small arms procurement is declining. Military research and development (R&D) for new generation small arms continues, but it has only led to limited procurement. Military markets are being replaced, both in quantity and quality, by civilian sales. This is clearest in the United States, but also true of many other countries in the third world. This transformation appears to be the strongest force driving future small arms production and sales. This aspect of the weapons industry is undergoing a fundamental transformation, no longer driven so much by military requirements as by the demands of civilian society.

AN INDUSTRY TRANSFORMED BY THE TRANSFORMATION
OF WARFARE

Overlooking small arms, light weapons, and ammunition production was questionable even during the cold war. As the guerrilla successes and near-successes of the Vietnam War, African decolonization, and Central American war revealed, the insurgent plus small arms synergy was as meaningful then as ever. Not technological trends, but socially constructed choices, cast small arms in apparent obscurity. Western military doctrine privileged nuclear and major weapons, making insurgency and small arms seem historically trivial.[5] As militaries everywhere struggle today to release themselves from the blinders of mid-20th century assumptions, counterinsurgency is finally getting full recognition at the top of global military hierarchies.[6] And the weapons of rebellion are also gaining visibility.

The most salient objects of violence, in other words, are a direct manifestation of the shifting nature of war. Nuclear and major conventional weapon systems have lost none of their destructive power, but the forms of warfare they serve are less relevant in global affairs. In the math of postmodern violence, no relationship matters as much as the synergism of men and guns. Since the rise of systematic research on substate conflict in the early 1990s, armed conflict has been structured around this trope, so much so that many of us mistook small arms and armed conflict for synonyms. No serious observer assumed the gun-conflict connection was exclusive—other things kill in war—but it seemed sufficient to explain most postmodern organized violence.

As many observers have rightly noted, non-state actors tend to rely on old-fashioned infantry weapons. The Kalashnikov is the weapon that changed armed conflict more than any other, the universally understood symbol of insurrection and mayhem. Constituting roughly half of all modern military weapons in existence (between 70 and 100 million out of some 124–156 million modern military rifles, and 200 million military small arms) and by far the least carefully controlled, they are a direct force shaping armed violence (Table 15.1).[7] To a surprising degree, it can be argued that the world does not have a gun problem so much as a Kalashnikov problem. The seemingly limitless reservoirs of aging AKs, easy to use and maintain, seem sufficient to plague the planet for a very long time.[8]

But there are limits to Kalashnikov logic. The rise of urban gun crime has no more connection to the proliferation of assault rifles than rural gun suicide. They Both are serious problems, even if they do not dominate the foreground of political contestation. Nor are combatants exclusively bound to guns. Experience in the Middle East and Afghanistan shows that insurgent warriors have lost none of their traditional willingness to innovate. As the offensive force of the future, insurgents control the pace of innovation. When Kalashnikov rifles no longer bring the results they need, warriors will find something else.[9] Their sheer numbers, however, insure that they will litter the background of virtually any violent conflict.

The impact of small arms reaches far beyond battlefields. Most small arms belong to civilians. They are the predominant owners and users. Of the estimated 300,000 gun deaths around the world every year, at least two-thirds are homicides and suicides unrelated to armed conflict or warfare.[10] This aspect of small arms is in some respects even more controversial, relating directly to the delicate issues of balancing conflicting civil rights. Even more

Table 15.1
Production of major modern military rifles (in millions)

Type	Primary supplier	Total (millions)
Kalashnikovs	Russia	70-100
SKS, Type 56	Russia/China	15
M16, M4	United States	14
G3	Germany	7
Type 63	China	6
FAL	Belgium	6
M14	United States	1.4
Stgw 57, 90	Switzerland	1.2
INSAS	India	0.5
F1	France	0.4
L85	United Kingdom	0.4
Other		5
Total (rounded)		*125-155 mn*

Note: Types are represented generically. Kalashnikov, for example, refers to all automatic rifles derived from the original AK-47 design, and produced in dozens of countries.

Source: Adapted from Aaron Karp, "Trickle and Torrent: State Stockpiles," *Small Arms Survey 2006: Unfinished Business* (Oxford: Oxford University Press, 2006), 54–56.

than changes in warfare, it is the rising international salience of armed violence in general that pushes small arms to the forefront of world politics.

TECHNOLOGICAL STASIS

Much of the distinctiveness of the small arms industry derives from the unique vintage and durability of its wares. As technological artifacts, most small arms are exceptionally old. Designs currently in widespread use are based entirely on chemical and mechanical principles that were in use by the 1890s.[11] Fully functional versions of all the types of firearms capable of fully automatic operation, and most types of light weapons currently in use, were available by the 1940s (Table 15.2). The choice of holotypes in this table is open to debate; careful research often reveals even older examples.[12] What is clear is that this is not new technology. Based exclusively on the concepts of the mechanical era, the production of such things is extraordinarily simple by current manufacturing standards. Consequently, barriers to market entry today are few. No scientific originality is necessary, nor is it really worth the bother.

A major research difficulty for analyzing the trajectory of small arms development is tracing the actual patterns of innovation. The countries of origin in Table 15.2 refer to initial mass production; design is invariably more nuanced, as is subsequent licensed (and

Table 15.2
Older than they look: The introduction of major contemporary weapons types

Type	Operational	Example	Source
bolt-action rifle	1890s	Mauser G98	Germany
pistol	1910s	M1911	U.S./Germany/etc.
machine gun	1910s	M1918A2 BAR	France/U.S.
submachine gun	1920s	Bergmann MP18	Italy/Germany
automatic rifle	1940s	Sturmgewehr 44	Germany
rocket-propelled grenade	1940s	RPG-2	USSR/U.K./U.S.

often unlicensed) production. Claims about the origins of contemporary firearms mechanisms and configurations have been strongly *nationalized*. Assertions of unique national characteristics are part and parcel of the weapons business, an industry that emerged to serve the nation-state.[13] All major powers have museums and histories of small arms design stressing a nationalist perspective, telling linear stories of *our* designers and *our* weapons.[14] They indulge nationalist feelings more than they illuminate the convoluted path of actual design and development.

In practice, nationalist tropes conceal the inherent internationalism of military requirement setting, as well as weapons design and development. From the start of the gunpowder revolution in the 14th century, designers belonged to an implicit—sometimes explicit—international intellectual community.[15] The best small arms makers have always been well informed about the work of their rivals and expectations of their clients. No major military power ever isolated its small arms establishment from outside influence. In a process that invites Darwinian metaphor, good ideas were quickly accepted and improved while inferior ones were just as rapidly abandoned. The results are readily seen in most any gun collection; it is no accident that virtually all small arms of a particular class look virtually identical. Only an experienced eye can distinguish the national origins of the many revolvers in production today, or most pistols, shotguns, rifles, and machine guns.

Cosmetics aside, the functional differences are also very slim. Although collectors—the creators of the massive literature comparing firearms—might protest, to the detached observer the differences in performance between the major small arms in production today seem slight. Allowing for differences in cartridge (which determines the amount of explosive powder), caliber (bullet size), and firing mechanism (single shot, gas operated, etc.), the destructive capabilities are remarkably homogeneous. As a result, there are few rewards for producing weapons that introduce eccentricities; it is a better commercial strategy for firms to market reliability rather than radical distinctiveness. Guns not only look alike, they are growing more similar over time.

The technological plateau of small arms design is broad, but not without its limits. As discussed below, significant sums are being spent to transform capabilities by harnessing new design concepts, materials, and electronics. The new generation prototypes certainly look different. Some observers go so far as to predict new generations of weapons, distinguished primarily by much higher rates of fire.[16] But any radically new firearms will almost certainly be very costly, limiting their ability to replace older design in overall production trends. Innovation has been most profound in completely different areas, such as the introduction of man-portable air-defense missiles in the early 1970s, and the far more insidious rise of new insurgent weapons like suicide bombing in the 1980s and improvised explosive devises and rockets in the 2000s.

To be sure, the small arms plateau is not unique. Anyone who has boarded a C-130 or a 50-year-old warship has seen compelling evidence of stable technology. Small arms stand out, rather, because they require little or no updating. One of the most extreme examples is the Browning M2 heavy machine gun. Accepted for military use by the U.S. Army in 1921, it remains in production to this day, almost completely unaltered.[17] The archetypal military rifles, the various versions of the Kalashnikov family, are often simply called AK-47s, denoting the year the holotype was accepted by the Red Army, a title it will take far into the future.[18]

INVITATION FOR DIFFUSION

The effects of technological stasis are readily seen in the extraordinary number of manufacturers of small arms. The proliferation of production would seem to be a relatively straightforward reification of Raymond Vernon's product cycle model. In its classic formulation from 1966, innovation and production start in the largest and most advanced markets.[19] Over time, designs standardize, allowing production to shift to poorer economies in pursuit of factor advantages, especially lower production costs.[20] Only through further innovation can the originators maintain their position, something that globalization increasingly challenges.

The product cycle model has not been easily applied to defense industries. As even Adam Smith observed, national security policy often justifies maintenance of economically inefficient producers.[21] Long assumed to be the basic force behind the global spread of defense industries in the 1970s and '80s, the product cycle failed to anticipate the contraction of regional defense manufacturers in the 1990s. When regional defense industries began to contract, the previous dominance of major powers in arms markets was restored for the most part.

Small arms stand out as an exception to that trend. While regional producers have surrendered most of their dreams about building aircraft, ships, and tanks, they have done quite will in specific sectors, above all small arms. With proven firearms designs from the 1950s readily available to those willing to pay licensing fees, and new enough designs feasible at minimal expense, countries that would wither before the prospect of making major weaponry can easily build small arms. Most regional makers do not produce unique designs. Instead, they concentrate on licensed versions of the Kalashnikov or the German G-3.[22]

The best-known review of the field concluded that, as of 2002, at least 1,134 companies in 98 countries produced small arms or ammunition. Of these, 30 countries are significant producers (with significant export potential). Total global production appears to have averaged roughly 7.5 to 8 million small arms annually, mostly for civilian markets, especially American civilians.[23] The total value of their small arms and ammunition production is approximately $7–8 billion.[24] These figures should be treated delicately; they conflate current and inactive manufacturers, mass producers, specialty firms, and so on. Production has almost certainly increased since then, pushed by the demand from war in Afghanistan and Iraq, and the American public (see below).

As can be seen, the world's armed forces are not the dominant buyers (Tables 15.3 and Figure 15.1). Most of the world's newly produced small arms—approximately seven million out of some eight million manufactured annually—are bought by civilians. The disparity would be even more extreme if secondhand markets were included, since civilian

Table 15.3

Contemporary markets, approximate annual firearms production and purchases, 2006

Buyer	Millions of Guns	Percent
American civilians	5	62
European civilians	1	13
civilians elsewhere	1	13
militaries	0.5–1	12
Total annual production	*7.5–8*	*100*

Note: Includes only factory-made military small arms and civilian firearms. The figure does not include craft production or sales of secondhand weapons. Weapons for law enforcement agencies and private security companies are counted in civilian totals.

Sources: Small Arms Survey 2002, 2003, 2006.

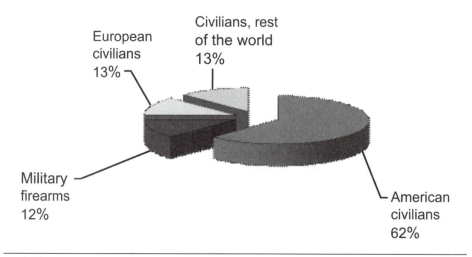

FIGURE 15.1   Who buys newly manufactured firearms?

Sources: Small Arms Survey 2002, 2003, 2006.

firearms are resold in substantial numbers, well over three million annually in the United States alone. To be sure, numbers are not everything; military small arms tend to be much more powerful, with capability for fully automatic fire, something usually lacking in civilian counterparts.

Production and trade in military small arms, moreover, is especially hard to estimate. While many countries release data on new civilian gun imports, exports, and registration, few discuss their military trade with the same transparency. Worst of all are some of the countries suspected of the largest sales: Belgium, China, Egypt, Pakistan, and Russia. In 2002, the Small Arms Survey estimated that military production had fallen since the end of the cold war from an average of about 2 million annually to roughly 800,000.[25] A subsequent reevaluation concluded that total military production is probably closer to 500,000.[26] All such numbers should be treated only as suggestions. Law enforcement agencies are an even smaller market presence, overlooked here.

In addition to factory production, a complete accounting of global small arms production must include *craft production*. Small scale, hand manufacturing in garage workshops is a major source of firearms supply in much of the world. In countries like Chile, Ghana, Pakistan, and the Philippines, it may be the dominant source of new firearms. Craft weapons can be very crude improvisations or persuasive copies of advanced products. Their impact on global statistics is very difficult to estimate.[27] A revealing example of the scale of such production can be found in Ghana, where police estimate there are 75,000 illegal craft guns now circulating, constituting the vast majority of the country's roughly 125,000 unregistered firearms.[28]

THE ELUSIVENESS OF SMALL ARMS PRODUCTION

While outside observers have a reasonable sense of total numbers of nuclear weapons and relatively accurate data about the production of major conventional weapons, the same cannot be said about small arms. Their production has spread around the world so extensively that even identifying the countries in which they are produced is tricky.

Small arms production is among the most obscure aspects in military procurement. Not only is small arms production less understood than most other aspects of arms manufacturing, production is probably the least understood aspect of the small arms procurement cycle. Although precise data is lacking, broad trends in the development, trade, use, and destruction of surplus small arms are relatively accessible. The same cannot be said of production, where systematic data are lacking, insights tend to be weak, and trends are unclear. While analysts know much more than ever before, confidence in the findings has to be tentative.

The only comprehensive data on small arms covers global inventories. Through a combination of data gathering and parametric estimation, it can be said with reasonable certainly (plus or minus ten percent) that there are about 850 million SALW in the world today. These are divided among some 650 million civilian owners, 200 million military, 25 million law enforcement, and fewer than one million among insurgencies and other non–state armed groups (Figure 15.2).[29] These categories can be broken down for 178 countries, all those with a population of at least 250,000 people. Because global ownership is relatively static, changing no more than two percent annually (seven to eight million new firearms,

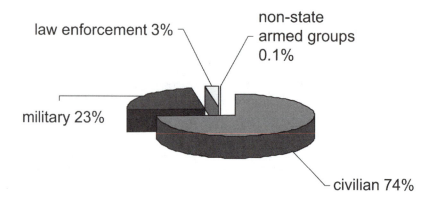

law enforcement 3%

non-state armed groups 0.1%

military 23%

civilian 74%

FIGURE 15.2   Global distribution of small arms

Sources: Aaron Karp, "Trickle and Torrent: State Stockpiles," *Small Arms Survey 2006: Unfinished Business* (Oxford: Oxford University Press, 2006), 37; and Aaron Karp, "Completing the Count: Civilian Firearms," *Small Arms Survey 2007: Guns and the City* (Cambridge: Cambridge University Press, 2007), 39.

and three or four million more secondhand), estimation of inventories is far easier than some other small arms research problems.

The trade in small arms is much harder, representing a much more dynamic problem, with considerable change from year to year. Without official data it is virtually impossible to determine, and even that is rarely complete. The classic sources of arms trade statistics are not helpful. Reporting in the International Institute for Strategic Studies' (IISS's) *Military Balance* and the more detailed Stockholm International Peace Research Institute data set are building block models only useful for major conventional weapons. They do not systematically cover small arms, most light weapons, or ammunition. The most comprehensive source for almost three decades was the U.S. Arms Control and Disarmament Agency's *World Military Expenditures and Arms Transfers.* This too had its limits. It lumped the value of small arms and ammunition transfers together with everything else, from tactical aircraft to military fuel. Still, it was uniquely complete. The last report was published in 1999; the Bush administration showed no interest in the required declassification. Key officials were shifted to other offices and it died quietly.

The most comprehensive source of data on the international small arms trade is the *Comtrade* database, maintained by the UN Statistical Office.[30] Comtrade allows countries to report on all elements of their imports and exports, with a full spectrum of categories to cover military and civilian (sporting) small arms, as well as light weapons and ammunition. The data appear only as then-year dollar amounts. With total reporting averaging at about $1.5 to 2 billion, Comtrade probably captures one-third to one-half of the total international trade, but there is no way to be sure. Exclusive use of dollar amounts, moreover, makes comparisons difficult, more so because some countries define declared values differently. Thus, there is no reliable way to estimate the number of weapons involved. Many countries, typically citing national security, refuse to report small arms for their armed forces or foreign military clients; among these are the largest exporters, including Austria, Belgium, China,

Egypt, Pakistan, Russia, Serbia, and the United States. There are analytical techniques that can be used to identify some missing reports, but never comprehensively. Other weaknesses of the system are the amateurism or exhaustion of the civil servants filling in reports; there are many human errors made.[31]

Originally structured exclusively to report transfers of major conventional weapons platforms, in 2006 the *UN Arms Register* was modified to encourage countries to submit information about their trade in SALW, as well as their national inventories. In 2008, 25 countries used the Arms Register to report exports of nearly 2.1 million small arms. This is a large proportion of the total trade.[32] Although it is impossible to be certain, the report probably accounted for one-fourth to one-fifth of the total global trade, assuming annual sales of 7 to 8 million new guns, and a secondhand market of 4 to 5 million more.

Of those small arms exports reported though the register, over two-thirds, almost 1,550,000, were bought by the United States.[33] This reflects not only the seemingly insatiable U.S. demand for guns, but also the predominance of European and Latin American suppliers among the its leading suppliers, the very countries most willing to report. The United States has not submitted small arms trade reports of its own, presumably because of the 2003 Tiahrt Amendment. This measure, an amendment to the annual Department of Justice appropriations act, forbids the Bureau of Alcohol, Tobacco, Firearms and Explosives (ATF) from revealing information about firearms purchases, ostensibly to protect U.S. gun buyers from political interference. The United States partially compensates through reporting to the U.S. Congress on its military exports (*the 655 reports*), and customs data on civilian imports and exports.

Other major lacunas in the UN Arms Register are the same countries whose reporting to Comtrade is most suspect: Austria, Belgium, China, Egypt, Pakistan, Russia, Serbia, the United States, and so on. The net result is a very useful tool for evaluating specific countries, but little insight where it is wanted most.

Not only is there considerable doubt about the total numbers of small arms manufactured and where they go; there is also the problem of their fate. Weapons have life cycles. They are created and, eventually, retired or scrapped. The number of small arms that disappear from the world's inventories every year can only be guessed. Because guns are very durable, the total proportion could be very low. Unlike major systems, they can survive for centuries with nothing more than proper storage. Even small arms in need of repair can be resuscitated after decades or centuries of disuse. The largest source of attrition may be formal disarmament of state surpluses, which has destroyed an average of 430,000 military small arms annually since 1990.[34] There are no comparable processes for civilian weapons.

Lest scholars and policymakers feel too demoralized, they can take comfort in ironic awareness that there is always something worse. For all the limits of insight into *small arms* production, the state of knowledge about *ammunition* production is greatly inferior. Ammunition supplies, moreover, are often much more important in the actual conduct of war, especially in weak or collapsed states, where the ability of non–state armed groups to acquire ammunition often determines the scale of fighting.[35] Compared to related fields like child soldiers or the international trade in illegal drugs, small arms looks pretty firm.

INDUSTRIAL TRENDS

So little is known about the small arms industry, informed observers struggle to determine whether it is healthy, and expanding or shrinking. The lack of reliable, longitudinal data from governments is a major problem. With many of the most important SALW makers in private hands, moreover—key firms like Beretta, Bushmaster, Colt, Glock, and Taurus are not publically traded—reporting requirements for businesses are few and little information on sales is available.

And procurement can be erratic. With minimal maintenance, guns last a long time and replacement is not routine. Unlike aircraft or tanks, which have relatively well-defined life cycles, firearms can remain in use for decades, and there is often no obvious product replacement cycle. There is certainly no equivalent for flight hours and aircraft or rounds fired for artillery. Consequently, much small arms replacement tends to be spasmodic and somewhat unpredictable.

The most important forces shaping the military small arms market may have nothing to do with the guns and mortars themselves. Above all, the dramatic reduction in military personal following the end of the cold war undercut military requirements and sales opportunities. Military personnel around the world have declined, from their contemporary height (for most countries in 1987–89) of 111,729,000 personnel to their 2007 level of 68,967,000.[36] This decline, 38 percent, is one of the remarkable consequences of the end of the cold war and the reduction in state-to-state warfare. With vast legacy stockpiles left in storage, many countries have been engaged in surplus weapons destruction or exports of secondhand equipment just to clear their inventories.[37] The purchases of the new weapons that have been best publicized are typically for elite troops rather than the rearmament of major units.

The major exceptions to these tendencies were created by the U.S.-led wars in Afghanistan and Iraq. The need to organize, train, and equip security services created a need for hundreds of thousands of small arms. There were 379,250 surplus SALW delivered to Iraq through 2006. Mostly Kalashnikov rifles, these were purchased or donated from Eastern European and Balkan allies. The United States also bought from Austria 138,000 newly manufactured Glock pistols for Iraq.[38] In late 2006, orders were placed for 123,544 newly manufactured M16 rifles for Iraqi security services. When completed, this will bring total U.S.-brokered deliveries to Iraq to 640,794. In Afghanistan, from June 2002 through June 2008, America provided about 375,563 small arms, many donated by eastern European and Balkan governments.[39]

When the world's only superpower goes to war, it dwarfs all other military activity. Combined U.S.-brokered deliveries to the two countries equal a total of 1,016,357 SALW. These are by far the largest known small arms rearmament processes being undertaken anywhere today. Most were secondhand; they are not reflected in Figure 15.2, which covers only new production. By comparison, the highly controversial decision by the Venezuelan president, Hugo Chavez, in 2005 to replace its 60,000 old Belgian FAL rifles, mostly from the 1960s, with new Russian-made Kalashnikovs, initially involved only 100,000 new weapons.[40] The Venezuelan deal was the largest in recent years and deserves careful consideration, but the U.S.-brokered transactions surpass any contemporary military scale.

While China and Russia probably led military small arms export for much of the 20th century, the United States probably regained a leading market position when it began re-arming Afghan and Iraqi security services. Through 2006, they were supplied with familiar Kalashnikovs. U.S. Central Command (CentCom) became the world's largest arms broker-age, buying from eastern Europe—especially the former Yugoslavia—and shipping to its new clients. Later that year, though, CentCom began to reequip these forces with American M16s, shifting out of the brokerage business as it initially ransacked U.S. Army stockpiles of older M16A2s from its principle storage facility in Aniston, Alabama, then began inviting new contracts. The switch has never been formally explained in public, but serves many advantages. Although it is harder to care for and use, the M16 facilitates training in U.S. aimed fire doctrine instead of Kalashnikov bullet hose tactics.

Allowing for the temporary increase in the total military market due to the U.S.-sponsored expansion of Afghan and Iraqi security services, the rest of the market appears likely to continue a trajectory of gradual decline. This is shown in market predictions by Forecast Associates, a U.S. research firm. The source of some of the few longitudinal extrapolations for the industry, they anticipate a general downward pattern (Figure 15.3). Forecast does not offer predictions for all SALW. The examples shown here were chosen for their clear predictions and data. They are far from authoritative, but convey the same sense of impending market contraction.

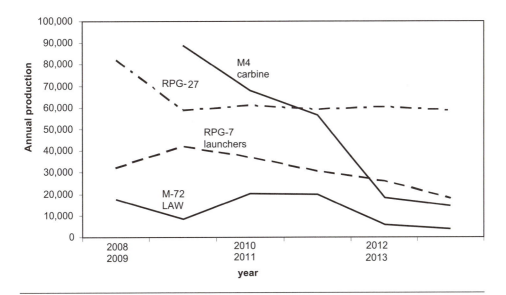

FIGURE 15.3   Predicted production of selected small arms and light weapons

Sources: "Appendix VIII," *Ordnance and Munitions Forecast* (Newtown, Connecticut: Forecast International, 2008, 9. "Military Small Arms" (United States)," *Ordnance and Munitions Forecast* (Newtown, Connecticut: Forecast International), 2009, 26. "RPG-7 and RPG-16," *Ordnance and Munitions Forecast* (Newtown, Connecticut: Forecast International, 2008) 9-10; "RPG-18/RPG-22/RPG-26/RPG-27," *Ordnance and Munitions Forecast* (Newtown, Connecticut: Forecast International, 2008), 8.

WHY IS INNOVATION SO HARD?

It is not obvious why small arms technology has remained so gyroscopically stable. Many critics agree that current versions—including the Kalashnikov and M16 families—have inadequacies and limits that can be remedied through readily imagined innovation. And there is no shortage of ideas for highly improved alternatives. Despite considerable effort, however, no major alternative to the small arms technology of the 1940s has been adapted by any military organization.

The introduction of revolutionary firearms was one of the definitive characteristics of U.S. technology in the 19th and early 20th century. The last show of this inspiration came just in time for World War II, when the U.S. Army adopted the semi-automatic M1 Garand rifle. Since then, it has resisted small arms innovation with a determination that leaves outside observers perplexed or just amazed. The M1 was the world's best military rifle in general use at the start of World War II. But before the war was over, it was dangerously inadequate compared to the fully automatic rifles beginning to equip German soldiers in large numbers. By the middle of the 20th century, army innovativeness was all but lost. It would take the U.S. Army almost 20 years to adopt a suitable alternative to the Kalashnikov; even that weapon was dubious when first introduced. It required two decades of improvements, and never matched key capabilities of its adversary.

The seeming inability of the U.S. Army to lead small arms innovation is a mystery that confounds facile analysis. To some critics, U.S. Army ordnance represents the worst in bureaucratic culture, systematically resisting change out of misplaced, romantic loyalty to the weapons of its past.[41] Other observers look at particular choices that poisoned later decision making. Aaron Friedberg stressed small arms as a prime victim of the end of the arsenal system that dominated U.S. small arms procurement from 1794 through the 1950s. The U.S. Army was comfortable with its own manufacturing base. It took external pressure to force it to relinquish control, through the ideologically driven recommendations of the 1955 Hoover commission report and the Eisenhower reforms to strengthen the Office of the Secretary of Defense in 1958. Despite such pressure, small arms remained one of the last redoubts of army control until the last product of the arsenal system, the Springfield Arsenal–designed M14 rifle, proved manifestly unsuitable.[42] The inadequacies of the M14 led Secretary Robert McNamara to support further privatization on the basis of systemic incompetence, especially compelling when private industry appeared to offer a highly superior product in the Armalite-Colt M16.[43]

Ironically, the arsenal system proved much easier to end in form than in practice. While development and production was successfully shifted to private enterprises, the U.S. Army Ordnance Corps retained enormous control. Escaping the practical effects of the arsenal system proved effectively impossible. In his classic version, James Fallows tells of how army ordnance preferred a dangerously unreliable weapon of its own specifications to an externally created one that actually worked. By modifying the original design (principally the powder of its 5.56 mm cartridge) the army made its first generation M16s extremely vulnerable to jamming. Lauren Holland goes so far as to argue that the army's resistance to the M16 constituted an "attack on democracy."[44] While this sounds exaggerated, it certainly represents one of the monumental case studies of organizational intransigence. Only through congressional oversight were design flaws introduced by the army remedied. Fallows, reflecting the defense reform perspective of the era, lays excessive blame on the army; some of the flaws of the M16 were intrinsic to its design and never remedied. By every analysis, he concludes that the army did itself no favors.[45]

Over time, the U.S. Army became far too jealous of the weapon it originally resisted. Efforts to introduce a replacement that would remedy some of the original flaws of the M16 have been resisted with all the tenacity the army showed when defending its arsenal system. The agent of change was none other than the weapon the M16 was designed to counter, the increasingly ancient Kalashnikov.

By the early 2000s, routine combat against Kalashnikov-armed forces in Afghanistan and Iraq created widespread agreement on the need for American small arms with greater reliability and ease of operation. Several searches were undertaken. Manufacturers produced a large number of alternatives. Some responded to a request for expensive, highly capable weapons combining rifles with electronically fused grenade launchers. Others programs were modestly conceived to elicit more reliable rifles and machine guns. As of mid-2009, none had culminated in successful recommendations for procurement.

Instead of adopting new small arms, many military organizations have pursued incremental changes to their current weaponry. Some have substituted modestly altered rifles, such as the bullpup configuration favored by Austria, Australia, and a few of their clients. But this only rearranges the pieces of earlier automatic rifles for slightly better efficiency; it introduces no new physical principles of operation or significantly different capabilities. Added telescopes, laser target designators, and night vision devices are more popular improvements, increasing capability without altering the rifle itself.

There is an irony here. The same military organizations that advocate transformation through major weapon systems, most strikingly with future combat systems (FCS), vigorously resist efforts to change their small arms. As a response to technological opportunity, this resembles the problems Elting Morison identified in naval gunnery over a century ago.[46] Morison described the U.S. and U.K. navies accepting dramatic change in some areas, adopting turbine engines, oil fuel, or battleships, but resisting it in others. Most dramatic was their extreme resistance to improved gunnery practices. Even in the midst of transformation, Morison found the armed services struggling to preserve the familiar comforts of incrementalism. If this remains true of the U.S. Army and Marine Corps too, widespread adoption of a new generation of small arms could be very distant.

One can exaggerate criticism targeted specifically at U.S. military small arms procurement. The entire U.S. military procurement system is little better. A failure to address the implication of commitments to too many costly projects and further price increases in the 2000s culminated in widespread questioning of America's approach to weapons buying. Many observers argued that the system was ill, unable to buy the equipment it was created to procure.[47] Calls for procurement reform are aimed at all aspects of the military-industrial system.[48] Nor, it should be noted, is any other country doing significantly better. Several countries are buying newer model small arms, but they accomplish this by truncating their technical ambitions. None have been able to leap into the new generation alternatives sought by the U.S. Army. The problems with U.S. military small arms buying are not unique; to the contrary, they may be the oldest and most intractable of its weapons buying problems.

While the U.S. arsenal system was anachronistic in many respects, the evidence that it retarded acquisition of more advanced weapons is ambiguous at best. The weaknesses of the M14 and the regrettable alterations to the M16 can be pinned on arsenal decisions. The same is not true of the resistance to replacements for the M16, which came long after the end of the arsenal system. The latter testifies to more endemic problems within the U.S. Army. Bureaucratic politics were more important, governing choices more adamantly than the specific means of production. But this is hardly a satisfying explanation. The inability to replace weapons that soldiers consistently found disappointing remains an extraordinary enigma. It is hard to escape the conclusion that, in the second half of the 20th century, the United States lost the ability to innovate in military small arms. This did not just occur in the United States; states generally were reacting much more than initiating.

THE NEW DOMINANT ACTOR

Having yielded control over the processes of technical innovation, the world's armed forces increasingly find themselves challenged by more adroit elements of society. The proliferation of small arms benefits non-state actors above all, facilitating secessionism and chaos. Although we associate these developments with regional environments, where weak states face well-armed warlords and narco-insurgencies, similar processes can be seen virtually everywhere. Society, in other words, is moving ahead of the state. In most countries, the process is slow, more worrisome than threatening. In the United States, though, social leadership is much more profound.

The United States is the world's greatest consumer of guns, weapons bought overwhelmingly by its private citizens. So great is American public demand that whole industries elsewhere have been created primarily to satisfy it, including major firms in Austria, Brazil, and Japan. China was poised to swamp the American market in the late 1980s, until stopped cold by an executive order from President George H. W. Bush in 1989.[49] Currently, eastern and southern European manufacturers are adapting most rapidly to American business opportunities.

Through most of the 1990s and 2000s, the American people bought approximately 5 million newly manufactured guns every year. Another 3 million are sold secondhand by commercial dealers.[50] The number sold privately and through gun shows is unknown. This trend has been interrupted dramatically on two occasions. The election of President Clinton in 1992 was soon followed by a sales increase to 8 million new guns in 1993.

Much the same happened after the election of President Obama in 2008. The scale of the sales boom since the November 2008 presidential election cannot be determined with accuracy, but considerable information conveys a sense of scale. News reports after the 2008 election revealed that Brady background checks—when federally licensed dealers clear their clients with the police—had increased by 20 to 42 percent.[51]

Not only are Americans buying more guns, they are also buying much more powerful weapons. The sales boom of 1993–94 was limited by the assault gun ban imposed that year, which blocked sales of newly manufactured assault rifles, specifically semi-automatic versions of military rifles. Without such a prohibition, which President Bush allowed to expire in 2004, the boom market of 2008–9 focused on just such weapons.

There are no overall statistics on American civilian assault weapon buying. Based on a combination of official data and expert estimates, immediately after the 1993 assault gun ban ended in 2004, sales jumped to approximately 350,000 annually (Table 15.4). These are mostly semi-automatic rifles, otherwise mostly identical to military versions capable of fully automatic fire. The total in Table 15.4 probably underestimates total civilian purchasing. Table 15.4 stresses civilian and some law enforcement purchases; it includes previously owned weapons imported into the United States, but it excludes the resale of used guns already in the country, including the retransfer of former U.S. defense department weapons to law enforcement agencies. Although it should be an important part of the overall picture, Table 15.4 also excludes, for lack of data, U.S. exports of civilian- and police-owned semi-automatic weapons, such as illegal sales to Canada and Mexico. Numbers are weak, but the latter probably draws over 10,000 semi-automatic rifles out of the United States annually.

Table 15.4

American civilian and police purchases of new and imported semi-automatic rifles, 2005

Producer/ importer	Type	Manufacturers	total U.S. sales	source
Bushmaster	AR versions	United States	66'000	ATFE 2005
DPMS	AR versions	United States	22'000	ATFE 2006
Various	AR versions	United States	70'000	ATFE 2007
Century Arms	AK/AR/CMETE/ Galil, etc.	Egypt, Romania, others	60'000	estimated
SAIGA/ IZAMSH	AK versions	Russia, Bulgaria	20'000	estimated
FN	FAL/BAR versions	Belgium, Brazil, others	20'000	estimated
HK	G3	Germ, Pak, Portugal, others	15'000	estimated
Sturm, Ruger	Mini-14	United States	15'000	estimated
SIG	550, 556, etc.	Switzerland	5'000	estimated
Remington	7400, 750 etc.	United States	15'000	estimated
Others			*50'000*	estimated
Total			*358'000*	

Notes: AR versions include AR15, M16, M4, and so on. AK versions include all semi-automatic rifle caliber versions of the Kalashnikov family. Total figures here do not include fully automatic weapons, or semi-automatic versions of submachine guns or shotguns.

Sources: ATFE data from Cameron Hopkins, "M4 ranch rifle," *Black Rifles 2009* (New York: Harris Publishing, 2008), 87. Charles Kirsh provided the original source and the ratios on which quantities of other guns are estimated.

Even before the post-2008 election sales boom, in other words, American civilians were buying only somewhat fewer assault rifles than the world's armed forces: at least 350,000 annually for civilians as of 2006, compared to some 500,000 for all militaries. The increase in civilian buying since has been widely observed. The best data on assault gun sales after the 2008 election come from the quarterly reports of two firms—Smith and Wesson, and Sturm, Ruger—the only publicly traded American gun manufacturers. Showing the effects of a rapidly growing market, Sturm, Ruger saw its firearm orders grow from $156 million in 2007 to $234 million in 2008. Smith and Wesson released more detailed information, showing that revolver and pistol sales grew by 45 percent. Demand for tactical rifles (assault rifles) was even stronger, with sales increasing by 111 percent in the first quarter of 2009. Only sales of hunting rifles declined.[52]

It is difficult to extrapolate from specific cases, but the increase in assault rifles sales during the 2008–9 boom market undoubtedly pushed U.S. civilian purchasing beyond previously recorded levels. American civilian buying may well have surpassed 500,000, making it a market as big as or bigger than all global military small arms buying combined. Whether this translates into healthy long-term profits for specific firms is unclear. Before the sudden sales increase, small arms makers appeared to be struggling with excess capacity.[53] The rapid increase is a response to idiosyncratic forces. It does not seem sustainable. The market will probably return to sustained sales closer to its old level rather than inflated heights. But there is no reason to expect the market to collapse.

The effects of these trends on global small arms proportions are striking. The United States Department of Defense owns about 3 million firearms for some 2.4 million active and reserve military personnel. This is about 1.5 percent of the world total of 200 million military small arms.[54] The U.S. military, in other words, has no major small arms surplus and does not stress a large arsenal as a matter of policy. This is not because they are unengaged; low official gun numbers come while two wars are being fought. Instead, the U.S. armed forces rely on JDAMs and allies to achieve many of the jobs that other countries solve with bullets.

But the civilian situation is very, very different. American civilians own roughly 300 million out of some 650 civilian firearms worldwide, or 50 percent the word total. They are the most heavily armed people in the world, followed by the populations of Yemen, Serbia, and Finland.[55] Because of the overwhelming size of the American civilian market, one can reasonably wonder if it makes sense to ask about global trends at all. The reality of the international small arms market is American domestic consumption, with the rest of the world adding another one-third or so.

CONCLUSION

The guns may look the same, but the markets are very dynamic. This review shows above all that the global small arms market is changing fundamentally. Civilian dominance is growing. Although evidence is incomplete, it appears that the U.S. domestic market is the most important force for the future of the global small arms industry. Reversing the familiar clichés of the 19th and 20th centuries, in small arms as in innumerable other fields affected by liberalization and globalization, society increasingly dominates the state. This is most profound in the United States, but also in other societies that permit unregistered civilian sales, such as Iraq, Pakistan, Saudi Arabia, and Yemen.

Major military small arms sectors are in long-term decline. Due to immense stockpiles of cold war era Kalashnikovs, military cutbacks, and the declining relevance of many older infantry weapons like mortars and heavy machine guns, sales of new equipment for armed forces appear to have declined. While some modernization is inevitable, the scale will not match previous rounds of rearmament. Many countries are happy with older generation, cold war and pre–cold war legacy weapons, further reducing opportunities for sales of newer versions. The ubiquity of cheap Kalashnikovs has given it near monopolistic reign in many regions. Markets for staple weapons of the cold war era, like the Belgian FAL and German G3 rifle, appear to have shrunk most. Only those sectors available to U.S. consumers are unambiguously promising.

Another major theme to emerge here is the technological convergence between military and civilian sectors. Despite many efforts to develop and buy new small arms technologies, military guns are not advancing significantly, while civilian buying is. Whether legally or not, civilians are acquiring the weapons previously reserved for the armed forces. Even without the United States, global civilian gun inventories already outnumber military arsenals. Military superiority lies instead in the greater firepower of its weapons. But this advantage also appears to be eroding.

Although their effects are highly uneven, these changes can be seen virtually everywhere. Certainly, no country is immune to the process of convergence, although strong legislation and enforcement can reduce it to a glacial pace. Police everywhere complain bitterly about rising criminal firepower. Much faster change comes in places where these forces are starkest, especially the United States and countries with very weak states. The most important factor governing the global small arms market is not the UN small arms process or regional agreements, although some of these are surprisingly effective. The most powerful single factor, rather, is U.S. policy. U.S. gun control (or gun advocacy) has a more immediate impact on how many guns and what types there are in the world. As officials in Canada, Mexico, and the Caribbean maintain, their gun problems are essentially a subset of those in the United States.[56] Their own national policies are effectively swamped by those of their large neighbor. Given the extraordinary scale of the American civilian market, it is inevitable that other countries will begin to feel similar effects in the years ahead.

This helps to explain the limits of current arms control and disarmament processes as well. Agreements like the 1997 Ottawa convention banning antipersonnel landmines and the 2008 Oslo treaty for the elimination of cluster munitions are not marginal. In the best tradition of Westphalianism, they work because they organize states to deal with the property of states. They establish useful tools for restraining the freedom of states, deepening and broadening the postmodern program of taming the state. Similar mechanisms can help to ameliorate small arms problems, but they cannot solve them. Directed at states, the simply miss the actors most important in the long run.

With power shifting from states to societies, no single treaty can manage small arms issues. There will be no single panacea for small arms proliferation. Many techniques have been applied, including tighter gun trade controls, banning particular types of weaponry, surplus turn-ins and destruction, and disarmament of insurgent factions. All of these approaches have their share of accomplishments and disappointments; all will continue to be applied. But the overwhelming importance of domestic markets, as shown here, points in a particular direction. Of greatest importance for the effective management of global small arms are policy tools that get closest to civilian markets and civilian demand.

NOTES

1. There has been a renaissance in historical studies of small arms trade. See Gábor Ágoston, *Guns for the Sultan: Military Power and the Weapons Industry in the Ottoman Empire* (Cambridge: Cambridge University Press, 2005); Joseph Bradley, *Guns for the Tsar: American Technology and the Small Arms Industry in Nineteenth-Century Russia* (DeKalb, Illinois: Northern Illinois University Press, 1990); and Gerald Howson, *Arms for Spain: The Untold Story of the Spanish Civil War* (New York: St. Martin's Press, 1999).

2. Such as the Stockholm International Peace Research Institute (SIPRI), *Arms Trade with the Third World* (Stockholm: Almqvist & Wiksell, 1971); and Michael Brzoska and Thomas Ohlson, eds., *Arms Production in the Third World* (London: Taylor & Francis, 1986).

3. This perspective on globalization is developed in Jonathan Krishner, "Globalization, American Power, and International Security," *Political Science Quarterly* (Fall 2008): 363–90.

4. See Keith Krause, ed., "Challenging the Weberian State: Armed Groups and Contemporary Conflicts," special issue, *Contemporary Security Policy* 30, no. 2 (2009).

5. The classic interpretation is Barry R. Posen, "The Importance of Military Doctrine," ch. 1 in *The Sources of Military Doctrine* (Ithaca, NY: Cornell University Press, 1984).

6. T. X. Hammes, *The Sling and the Stone: On War in the 21st Century* (Osceola, WI: Zenith Press, 2004); and Aaron Karp, Regina Karp, and Terry Terriff, eds., *Global Insurgency and the Future of Armed Conflict* (London: Routledge, 2007).

7. On Kalashnikov and other production quantities, see Aaron Karp, "Trickle and Torrent: State Stockpiles," *Small Arms Survey 2006: Unfinished Business* (Oxford: Oxford University Press, 2006), 54–56.

8. Larry Kahaner, *AK-47: The Weapon that Changed the Face of War* (New York: Wiley, 2007).

9. Insurgency makes fools of everyone who fails to anticipate constant innovation. I wish my own early work on the small arms revolution at least mentioned IEDs. Karp, "Arming Ethnic Conflict," *Arms Control Today*, September 1993.

10. *Global Burden of Armed Violence* (Geneva: Geneva Declaration, 2008), 9, 67, 69.

11. As illustrated by the life work of the designer John Browning. See the biography by John Browning and Curt Gentry, *John M. Browning, American Gunmaker* (New York: Doubleday, 1964).

12. An example of these debates is Carlo Kopp, "Origins of the Assault Rifle," *Defence Today*, October/November 2007, 74–75.

13. David E. H. Edgerton, "The Contradictions of Techno-Nationalism and Techno-Globalism: A Historical Perspective," *New Global Studies* 1, no. 1 (2007), pp. 1–32.

14. For example, in his mammoth classic *The Gun and Its Development* (1910), W.W. Greener leaves no doubt that the modern firearm is entirely British, until trends force him to acknowledge a burgeoning American role. A recent example of the conflict between nationalist pride and cosmopolitan awareness is Alexander Rose, *American Rifle: A Biography* (New York: Delacorte Press, 2008).

15. Kenneth Chase, *Firearms: A Global History to 1700* (New York: Cambridge University Press, 2003); and Alfred W. Crosby, *Throwing Fire: Projectile Technology Through History* (New York: Cambridge University Press, 2002).

16. Tim Blackmore, "Cyclic Gun-human Evolution," *Bulletin of Science, Technology and Science* 26, no. 5 (2006): 363–69.

17. *Defence-Aerospace,* "General Dynamics Awarded $28 Million for Production of M2 Heavy Barrel Machine Guns," April 15, 2009.

18. Kahaner, *AK-47.*

19. Raymond Vernon, "International Investment and International Trade in the Product Cycle," *Quarterly Journal of Economics* 80, no. 2 (1966): 190–207.

20. The role of the product cycle in globalization is heavily debated. John Cantwell, "The Globalization of Technology: What Remains of the Product Cycle Model?" *Cambridge Journal of Economics* 19, no. 1 (1995): 155–174, challenges some aspects, especially regarding the origins of technology, but accepts the model's assumptions about its dispersion. Edwin Lai finds more consistent evidence in favor of the model in *The International Production Cycle and Globalization of Production,* staff papers 5 (Dallas: Federal Reserve Bank of Dallas, 2008).

21. Edward Mead Earle, "Adam Smith, Alexander Hamilton, Friedrich List: The Economic Foundations of Military Power," in *Makers of Modern Strategy,* ed. Peter Paret (Princeton: Princeton University Press, 1986), especially 2207–30.

22. Pete Abel, "Manufacturing Trends: Globalising the Source," in *Running Guns: The Global Market in Small Arms,* ed. Lora Lumpe (London: Zed Books, 2000), 81–104.

23. *Small Arms Survey 2003: Development Denied* (Oxford: Oxford University Press, 2003), 9.

24. *Small Arms Survey 2002: Counting the Human Cost* (Oxford: Oxford University Press, 2002), 9; *Small Arms Survey 2003,* 9.

25. *Small Arms Survey 2002,* 13.

26. James Bevan, "Military Demand and Supply," ch. 1 in *Small Arms Survey 2006: Unfinished Business* (Oxford: Oxford University Press, 2006).

27. *Small Arms Survey 2003,* ch. 1.

28. Francis Langumba Keili, "Small Arms and Light Weapons Transfer in West Africa," *Disarmament Forum* 4 (2008), 7.

29. Aaron Karp, "Trickle and Torrent," 37; and Karp, "Completing the Count," 39.

30. Nicholas Marsh, *The Methodology Used in Creating a Comtrade Based Dataset of Small Arms Transfers* (Oslo: Peace Research Institute, Oslo, 2005).

31. In 2006, for example, the Small Arms Survey reported a small but surprising value of Swiss guns exported to Sudan, in apparent contravention of the UN Security Council. Subsequent reevaluation supported the conclusion that a Sudanese customs official probably entered the Comtrade reporting abbreviation for the official Latin name of Switzerland (CH, for Confoederatio Helvetica) mistakenly when they meant China (CN).

32. Jeff Abramson, "UN Register Captures Expanded Small Arms Trade," *Arms Control Today,* October 2008.

33. Abramson, "UN Register Captures Expanded Small Arms Trade."

34. Karp, *Inconspicuous Disarmament,* 5.

35. James Bevan, *Conventional Ammunition in Surplus* (Geneva: Small Arms Survey, January 2008).

36. Karp, "A Semi-automatic Process? Identifying and Destroying Military Surplus," ch. 3 in *Small Arms Survey 2008: Risk and Resilience* (Cambridge: Cambridge University Press, 2008), Appendix I. "Highest Contemporary and Current Uniform-wearing Military Personnel, Active and Reserve." Based on data from then-year volumes of the IISS *Military Balance.*

37. Karp, *Inconspicuous Disarmament.*

38. C. J. Chivers, "Black-Market Weapon Prices Surge in Iraq Chaos," *New York Times,* December 10, 2006; and *Stabilizing Iraq: DoD Cannot Ensure That U.S.-Funded Equipment Has Reached Iraqi Security Forces,* GAO-07–711 (Washington, DC: U.S. Government Accountability Office, 2007), 11.

39. *Afghan Security: Lack of Systematic Tracking Raises Significant Accountability Concerns about Weapons Provided to Afghan National Security Force,* GAO-09–267 (Washington, DC: U.S. Government Accountability Office, 2009), i, 6, 34.

40. Greg Morsbach, "Russian Arms Arrive in Venezuela," *BBC News,* June 3, 2006.

41. William H. Hallahan, *Misfire: the History of How America's Small Arms Have Failed Our Military* (New York: Scribners, 1994).

42. Aaron Friedberg, *In the Shadow of the Garrison State: America and its Cold War Grand Strategy* (Princeton: Princeton University Press, 2000), 264–72, 277–80.

43. Thomas L. McNaugher, *Marksmanship, McNamara, and the M16 Rifle: Organizations, Analysis, and Weapons Acquisition* (Santa Monica: Rand Corporation, 1979).

44. Lauren H. Holland, *Weapons Under Fire* (London: Routledge, 1997), 213–4.

45. James Fallows, *National Defense* (New York: Random House, 1981).

46. Elting E. Morison, "Gunfire at Sea: A Case Study of Intervention," ch. 2 in *Men, Machines and Modern Times* (Cambridge, Massachusetts: MIT Press, 1966). A more formal version of the same argument is James Q. Wilson's classic, "Innovation in Organization: Notes towards a Theory," in *Approaches to Organizational Design,* ed. James D. Thompson, and Victor Harold Vroom,(Pittsburgh: University of Pittsburgh Press, 1971), 195–218.

47. Robert N. Charette, "What's Wrong with Weapons Acquisitions?" *IEEE Spectrum,* November 2008; and studies by Anthony H. Cordesman, *America's Self-Destroying Airpower: Becoming Your Own Peer Threat,* and *Abandon Ships: The Costly Illusion of Unaffordable Transformation* (Washington, DC: Center for Strategic and International Studies, 2008).

48. Steve Vogel, "Hill Panel to Begin Review of Defense Acquisition System," *Washington Post,* March 9, 2009.

49. Kirk Johnson, "Gun Import Ban Enriches Small U.S. Arms Makers," *New York Times,* July 14, 1989.

50. *Commerce in Firearms in the United States* (Washington, D.C.: Department of the Treasury, Bureau of Alcohol, Tobacco and Firearms, 2000).

51. Brendan Gibbons, "Gun Sales Increase with Fear of New Policies: The Administration Might Extend the Ban on Weapons that Expired in 2004," *The Maneater* (Columbia, Missouri), March 9, 2009.

52. "Sturm, Ruger and Company, Inc. Reports 2008 Results and Files Annual Report on Form 10-K," *Business Wire,* February 24, 2009; and "Smith & Wesson Holding Corp.," *MarketWatch.com,* March 12, 2009.

53. D. Kahraman, J. Brauer, P. Hall, P. Basciano, and S. Markowski, "Sturm Ruger and Co: Financial Analysis of a Major Firearms Manufacturer," paper presented at the 12th Conference on Economic and Security, Ankara, Turkey, 11–13 June 2008, 16; and Peter Hall, Stefan Markowski, and Jurgen Brauer, "The U.S. Small Arms Industry: Profit, Proliferation and Performance," unpublished paper, June 2007.

54. Karp, "Trickle and Torrent."

55. Karp, "Completing the Count," 45–46.

56. The role of American guns in neighboring states is strongly disputed by American gun advocates. The clearest information is in William Newell (special agent in charge, Phoenix Field Division, Bureau of Alcohol, Tobacco, Firearms and Explosives)," testimony before the U.S. House of Representatives, Committee on Appropriations, Subcommittee on Commerce, Justice, Science and Related Activities, Washington, DC, March 24, 2009.

APPENDIX I

Key Defense-Industrial and Arms Trade–Related Terms

J. D. Kenneth Boutin

ACQUISITION AND CROSS-SERVICING AGREEMENT

This is an agreement signed between the United States and another country that provides for the exchange of military support by their armed forces. Acquisition and cross-servicing agreements can cover the provision of equipment and logistical support. These agreements set out the terms of support, including how this is to be reimbursed by the receiving state. This type of agreement is intended to cover contingencies where requirements cannot be adequately addressed through national means. Acquisition and cross-servicing agreements supplement the out-of-area logistic capabilities of the United States, thereby enabling it to function more effectively in operations abroad, and provide a mechanism for the expeditious supply of arms and provision of logistical support to other countries in times of conflict or heightened tension. This type of agreement is a product of interest in more effectively supporting equipment in emerging operational environments, the requirements of which are proving more difficult with the introduction of each new product generation.

ACQUISITION ROADMAP

Procurement authorities in many states develop what are called roadmaps (keep) to help guide their arms development and procurement efforts. Acquisition roadmaps set out desired future capabilities and equipment requirements in a specific area, such as tactical air defense, and outline a long-term strategy for meeting these requirements. An example of this approach is the American Conventional Engagement Capability Roadmap. Acquisition roadmaps may include an assessment of current capabilities that identifies capability shortfalls and areas of excess capability, as well as setting general targets for future capability acquisition through the development or importation of future generations of equipment. In some cases, acquisition roadmaps are updated on an annual basis. The use of acquisition roadmaps is growing as equipment requirements become more complex and the resources required to meet them increase, which force procurement authorities to consider carefully how they can most efficiently meet their requirements. As well as providing an important planning document for procurement authorities, acquisition roadmaps provide industry with an indication of potential future procurement programs, for which they can then better prepare to bid.

ADVANCED CONCEPT TECHNOLOGY DEMONSTRATION (ACTD)

Advanced Concept Technology Demonstration Is an American program designed to expedite the process of fielding cutting-edge technologies by bypassing the standard acquisition process. ACTDs are near-term activities intended to identify equipment requirements, evaluate mature technologies, and help to determine potentially useful technologies, with the intention of moving the latter quickly to the point where they can be fielded should they prove sufficiently promising. Reducing the costs associated with developing advanced arms is a secondary objective of ACTDs. For this reason, they include assessments of affordability. ACTDs generally run for two to four years, and in many cases are open to participation by other states with similar equipment requirements. They define equipment requirements by procuring prototypes that are then subjected to extensive field testing by military personnel. ACTD programs often lead to the deployment of operational systems, either through the fielding of limited quantities of prototype equipment as an interim measure, or by developing designs to the point where they can enter the standard acquisition process at an appropriate stage, possibly as late as the stage of *low-rate initial production.* ACTDs constitute a significant example of *agile acquisition,* and this is likely to remain an important defense-industrial mechanism in the United States given trends in equipment requirements and the difficulties experienced in meeting these through mainstream procurement channels. ACTDs are distinct from *advanced technology demonstrations* (ATDs), which are intended to prove the feasibility and maturity of specific technologies and reduce the risk associated with their development, though in some cases successful ATDs mature into ACTDs.

AGILE ACQUISITION

This is a general approach that developed in response to the escalating costs and increasingly protracted processes of the development and production of advanced arms. Agile acquisition initiatives are intended to reduce costs and shorten the time required to move promising designs through the development cycle and on to *full-rate production.* Agile acquisition encompasses a range of initiatives, including greater a reliance on *commercial off-the-shelf* components and technologies and support for the development of *dual-use technologies,* but is most notable for developing simplified and expedited procurement processes that serve to erode the distinction between what formerly constituted distinct phases of development and production. Agile acquisition initiatives often feature mechanisms for bridging the gap between developers and operators and generally involve more flexible arrangements with reduced formal reporting requirements. These initiatives are most evident on the part of states with high qualitative equipment requirements, such as the United States and the United Kingdom. The U.K.'s *urgent operational requirement* provision represents an effort to circumvent lengthy procurement processes and quickly field equipment that is regarded as crucial in light of emerging operational requirements. In the United States, this approach is manifest in the *advanced concept technology demonstration* process. While agile acquisition has considerable potential to overcome the limitations of mainstream procurement processes, this comes at the cost of the increased danger that expedited developmental processes may result in the deployment of equipment designs that are insufficiently mature or robust, or that display poor interoperability with other equipment that is in service or under development. It is noteworthy that despite the obvious benefits of this approach, in no country have agile acquisition initiatives entirely replaced established procurement mechanisms.

ARMS EMBARGOES

An arms embargo refers to the prohibition of sale, transfer, lease, provision of financing and/or technical assistance of weaponry, and, in some cases, dual-use goods and their associated technology to a government, group, or individual in a certain country. The aim of putting an arms embargo in place is to signal disapproval of the behavior of the targeted country's government, a group, or an individual; to remain neutral in a conflict; and to lessen a party's capability to engage in conflict, in a way that avoids a great peril to the country's people. An arms embargo is considered as smart, focused kind of embargo to be used alongside travel bans, financial or aviation-related embargoes, and many more.

Although the mechanism to use arms embargoes had existed under chapter 7 of the United Nations' Charter since 1945, since the cold war ended, this political tool has increasingly been in use. During the cold war period, hostility between the USSR and United States, along with their allies, made it difficult to deliver an effective embargo, since the two great powers tended to undermine each other's political efforts. The UN arms embargo of the apartheid regime in South Africa in 1977 was the first embargo imposed on a UN member country. Since 1990, the UN has imposed at least 27 embargoes. Among the countries that have experienced an arms embargo are South Africa, Afghanistan, Iraq, Haiti, Liberia, Libya, Sierra Leone, Somalia, Rwanda, and Yugoslavia. Not only applicable to states, UN also placed embargoes on individuals and groups like Osama bin Laden and al Qaeda due to their terrorism activities. UN arms embargoes, however, have been criticized as merely a last resort, used when the situation is already deteriorating, hence making it difficult to meet the objective of the arms embargo. UN arms embargoes can be either mandatory or voluntary. It is also known that member countries often violate UN arms embargoes even if they are mandatory.

The EU (European Union) also implements the embargoes issued by the UN. Within the framework of the Common Foreign and Security Policy (CFSP), the EU applies restrictive measures in pursuit of the specific CFSP objectives set out in the EU treaty. The EU supports UN embargoes because their implementation essentially relies on the political willingness of the member states to employ their national law to criminalize violators. However, sometimes EU member countries have different interest in the embargo, for example in the case of the arms embargo to China. France and Germany have supported the view that the embargo should be lifted, while the Scandinavian countries persistently use human rights violation as a rationale to maintain the embargo.

The United States, the biggest exporter of arms in the world, also has its own mechanism of arms embargo. Not only following UN arms embargoes, the United States also applies a unilateral arms embargo. This mechanism is regulated under the Arms Export Control Acts (AECA) and International Traffic in Arms Regulation (ITAR). ITAR stated that a nation may lose U.S. foreign military financing (FMF), loans, or the rights to purchase and have sales agreements related to defense articles or services if it commits a "substantial violation," subject to the interpretation of the U.S. authority. At least 26 countries have been banned from receiving U.S. arms, including China, Cuba, Iran, Lebanon, and Venezuela. U.S. arms embargo has been criticized as a worn-out and double-standard policy, with an unclear end result. Indeed, the U.S. arms embargoes used against the United Kingdom, France, and Israel, who attacked Egypt due to its effort to nationalize the Suez Canal, effectively stopped the 1956 Suez War. However, the U.S.'s unilateral arms embargo for Indonesia (1999–2005) simply led Jakarta to seek weapons from Russia.

Even though the effectiveness of the arms embargo is in question, it is still a popular initiative. A study by the Stockholm International Peace Research Institute (SIPRI) on the effectiveness of 27 UN embargoes since 1990 led to the conclusion that only 25 percent of all arms embargoes can be considered effective. Some achieved the desired effect while, others just worsened the situation or were counterproductive. Arms embargoes of Israel, China, and South Africa have led the three countries to build their own defense-industrial base in order to lessen dependency on foreign suppliers and strengthen the self-reliance. Arms embargo during the Yugoslavian war in the 1990s arguably worsened the conflict because it secured the military superiority of the Serbian forces.

AUTARKY

Autarky, derived from Greek word *autarkies,* means self-sufficiency or being economically independent. Every state wants to be self-sufficient in defense for obvious reasons. Autarky, as opposed to dependency, seeks to guarantee full sovereignty of the state in both domestic and foreign policy. Being dependent on foreign suppliers implies a great danger: either this dependency can be used as political leverage to interfere in domestic situation or, worse, a weapons transfer cut-off or embargo may undermine a country's defense capabilities in a critical time. Example of countries that see autarky as inevitable are Sweden, a non-aligned country during the cold war, and Israel, South Korea, India, and Pakistan, which are facing security threats from their neighbors. The need for self-sufficiency is greater in the absence of reliable suppliers. In addition to security and political reasons, the other reason for self sufficiency policy is to enhance one country's position in the regional or international arena because these countries want to be seen as a new power.

Autarky has been used interchangeably with self-reliance. However, these two terms actually have different meanings. While in self-sufficiency there is no room for dependency, self-reliance implies a more rational option. Self-reliance allows the acquisition of technology from foreign countries for a period of time, but with the intention of reducing this dependency through incorporation of the technology into the local industrial base or indigenization. Self-reliance, therefore, is merely a cornerstone to be used in obtaining self-sufficiency.

Defense self-sufficiency is achieved through developing and maintaining a defense-industrial base capable of providing all military capability requirements. The degree of a state's sufficiency can be seen from its minimum dependency on arms imports. Judging from this, it can be said that most countries have failed in their efforts. Big arms producing countries like the United Kingdom, France, Germany, and Russia are still importing great amount of weapons. Others, like India and China, have not been able to reduce their dependency on arms imports, despite the fact that they have had massive defense-industrial programs for years.

Nowadays, autarky is considered elusive, except perhaps for United States. Lots of countries give up self-sufficiency because it is too expensive. It is simply impossible to control the whole supply chain of the defense industry. Downsized militaries, reduced defense budgets, and increased unit production costs of new weapons have forced countries to rethink their strategy, and some have eventually given in to globalization. Countries are now being more selective in controlling only critical weapons technology, and tend to collaborate with other states or accept the private sector's involvement to develop other types of weapons. Even though local defense industries are still maintained, following massive cross-border mergers and acquisitions, collaboration and outsourcing supply chains, defense firms are now conducting more business with other countries than they originally did. For example, BAE Systems, the U.K.'s biggest defense firm, is now conducting more business with the U.S. government.

BATTLE LABORATORY (BATTLE LAB)

Battle laboratories are facilities intended to accelerate innovation and to expedite the fielding of new generations of equipment by demonstrating the capabilities of emerging technologies. They also play an important role in helping to develop operational doctrine for the employment of the equipment items that result from them. A key feature of battle labs is their effort to bridge the divide between equipment developers and users by incorporating service personnel at a much earlier stage of the procurement process than generally is the case, and by involving industry in developing equipment specifications. Battle labs typically involve a mix of military personnel, scientists, and engineers. They may focus on the development of prototypes of totally new equipment types or on modifying designs that have already entered service. Battle labs often sponsor equipment demonstrations and deploy prototype equipment for military exercises as a means of exhibiting the equipment's capabilities in an operational environment. This approach is best developed in the United States, where the first such facility was established in the early 1990s, and which now boasts a number of battle labs, such as the U.S. Air Force's Air Mobility Battlelab. In some cases, these are termed *warfighting laboratories,* such as the Marine Corps Warfighting Laboratory. Some American battle labs are open to participation by foreign industry, and can involve observers from other states with similar equipment requirements. Battle labs also have been established by Australia and the United Kingdom. In the United Kingdom, they are complemented by *brainstorming labs,* which focus on the development of new operational procedures. As with other recent initiatives to develop more efficient and timely procurement processes, battle labs do so at the cost of the increased risk resulting from reduced oversight.

BUYERS GROUP

This is a group of states that collaborate in the procurement of equipment where there is sufficient overlap in their requirements to justify the procurement of a common design. Buyers groups generally include countries that share close political relationships, and have been a feature of the international arms market for some time. The most prominent example is the four-nation group within the North Atlantic Treaty Organization (NATO) that selected the F-16 Fighting Falcon as their next-generation fighter in the 1970s. Buyers groups are useful in that they can potentially negotiate more favorable purchase terms through the economy of scale that they offer, including in terms of offsets, and have better prospects for viable local production or *coproduction* for the same reason. A buyers group also provides a basis for ongoing collaboration in supporting the equipment procured throughout its service life. Despite their many advantages, buyers groups remain more the exception than the norm. It often proves difficult in practice to harmonize requirements sufficiently to provide for a joint procurement, as the disappointing record of collaborative arms development projects by NATO members demonstrates.

CASCADE (OR CASCADING) OF ARMS

Cascading of arms is a process whereby surplus arms are transferred to another state that is less well equipped, where this equipment can replace or supplement its existing fleet. This practice has been around for some time, but the term came into prominence around the end of the cold war, when the changing security environment and equipment cuts mandated by the Conventional Forces in Europe treaty led a number of the members of NATO to reduce their arsenals by passing equipment on to members of the alliance that were not as well equipped, and to offer arms at concessionary rates to non-NATO states. This resulted in further large-scale arms transfers in a number of cases as the recipients transferred older arms to other states in turn. The cascading of arms continues, albeit on a reduced scale, as states seek to support other states and offset the costs associated with the introduction of new equipment.

CENTER OF EXCELLENCE (COE)

A center of excellence is a facility that provides critical expertise for a particular type of equipment or a particular technology. While examples of CoEs can be found in many product areas, they are most common in those that involve advanced technologies. In many cases, CoEs play an important developmental role, and feature prominently in national efforts to develop their defense-industrial capabilities. CoEs are often linked with procurement authorities and with research and development (R&D) facilities as a means of effectively drawing on their expertise on a sustained basis. Centers of excellence may be firms that have been designated as such by the government, or can be government-operated facilities established with this objective in mind. This approach is proving increasingly popular as the pace of technological progress in many equipment areas accelerates and procurement authorities seek to establish a sustained national basis for staying abreast of developmental trends and for supporting the long-term development of the defense-industrial base.

CIVIL-MILITARY INTEGRATION (CMI)

Civil-military integration (CMI) is the process of merging the defense-industrial base and the larger commercial-industrial base; the common technologies, processes, labor, equipment, material, and facilities can be utilized to meet both defense and commercial needs. Although the idea has already existed for several decades, it was after the end of cold war that this concept gained a major spotlight in the United States. In the United States, CMI has been claimed to be the most essential factor for the transformation of defense acquisition practices and the industrial structure. Conflicting interest between reducing defense resources and maintaining a strong defense-industrial base forced the United States to look to other countries like France, China, and Japan in terms of how to integrate its alienated defense-industrial base with that of civilian development.

According to the U.S. Congressional Office of Technology Assessment, CMI includes: cooperation between government and commercial facilities in research and development (R&D), manufacturing, and/or maintenance operations; combined production of similar military and commercial items, including components and subsystems, side by side on a single production line or within a single firm or facility; and direct use of commercial off-the-shelf (COTS) items within military systems. CMI can occur on three levels: facility, firm, and sector. Facilities can share personnel, equipment, and materials, and even manufacture defense and civilian goods side by side. Firm-level integration involves separate production lines but the joint military-civilian use of corporate resources (management, labor, and equipment). Finally, integrated industrial sectors (such as aerospace or shipbuilding) can draw from a common pool of R&D activities, technologies, and production processes.

CMI offers many potential benefits. First, adapting available commercial technologies to meeting military needs can save money, shorten development and production cycles, and reduce risks in weapons development. CMI can also improve the quality of military equipment and contribute to the more efficient production and acquisition of military systems. Above all, CMI permits arms industries and militaries to leverage critical technological advances in sectors where the civilian side has clearly taken the lead in innovation, particularly in information technologies (IT) such as communications, computing, and microelectronics. However, CMI requires massive changes in the way the government conducts business; the Department of Defense (DoD) is now forced to perceive industry as a partner rather than keeping the commercial sector at arm's length.

There are many factors that favor CMI. First, trends in technology are blurring the differences between commercial and defense technology. Second, overlapping product technology at the lower tiers like composite materials, pumps, valves, and so on can readily serve the military as well as civil sector. Third, the demand in commercial market for lightweight, rugged, and reliable goods, which is similar to defense requirements. Fourth, the growing gap between worldwide levels of spending for commercial and defense purpose makes it difficult for defense to drive the technology to be used commercially. Implementation of CMI is not without problems, however. The different degrees of complexity between integrated weapon systems and commercial goods makes it difficult to use a common workforce to perform many production functions for military goods. The tortuous change within government acquisition procedure and reluctance of the market to respond to small but highly demanded military requirements are among factors that hamper CMI.

An example of CMI's success in the United States is the mine resistant ambush protected (MRAP) vehicle production to meet critical military needs for ongoing military operations in Iraq and Afghanistan. These operations have dramatically increased demand for MRAP vehicles. The U.S. Department of Defense (DoD) and industry have had to speed up production dramatically from fewer than 100 to over 1,200 vehicles per month in less than one year. This spectacular performance is enabled because of two issues. First, MRAP vehicles were designed primarily with components from the commercial heavy truck industry. Second, DoD and industry work together to eliminate production bottlenecks for specialized items like armor steel and military specification tires.

COMMERCIAL OFF THE SHELF (COTS)

The term *commercial off the shelf* is applied to products, components, and technologies that can meet or be incorporated into equipment that fulfills military requirements, even though they were not developed with this in mind and may not fully meet important military equipment specifications. COTS equipment, components, and technologies have become more attractive in light of spiraling developmental and production costs, and their exploitation features prominently in many initiatives intended to reduce procurement costs and to shorten developmental timeframes. This is true of developed as well as developing states, but COTS items are particularly important in the latter due to their relatively less well-developed industrial capabilities, particularly in terms of research and development (R&D). The disadvantage of this approach stems from the differences between equipment developed for the defense and commercial markets. COTS equipment is often designed to less demanding standards, particularly in terms of ruggedness and survivability. This means that procurement authorities may either be forced to lower their requirements or devote the time and resources necessary to militarize COTS items, which detracts from their attractiveness. The term *non-developmental item* (NDI) is applied by some states to civil-grade equipment or components that are capable of fulfilling military requirements.

COMMERCIAL SALE

A commercial sale is a form of interstate arms transfer where the government of the exporting state does not serve as a middleman, though it still plays an important role in approving the transfer as this will still be subject to export controls. This type of arms transfer also is referred to as a direct sale, direct commercial sale (DCS), or company-country agreement. Commercial sales have an important advantage in that they are generally much easier to negotiate; however, they expose both the vendor and the customer to a higher degree of risk should the product fail to meet required specifications or the customer fail to make a full or timely payment. For this reason, authorities in developing states may prefer to procure arms through the official arms export agencies maintained by some governments or through channels such as that provided by the foreign military sales (FMS) process in the United States, where one of the military services handles the sale, and firms may prefer to export through these mechanisms. Despite this, commercial sales continue to account for the majority of international arms transfers.

CONVERSION

Conversion refers to efforts to reconfigure defense industries to meet commercial requirements. It often is associated with the privatization of government-owned production facilities, where this occurs. Though industrial conversion is a common post-conflict phenomenon, this issue attracted particular attention following the end of the cold war when defense-industrial overcapacity and the contracted defense market in many states encouraged political authorities to consider how they might best avoid serious economic dislocation and substantial job losses. The conversion of defense industries is a complex issue due to the need to determine which defense-industrial research and development (R&D) and production capabilities are crucial, and how these can effectively be maintained in the changed procurement environment. National conversion initiatives can take various forms, but often involve support for the updating of industrial plants in an effort to render enterprises more commercially competitive, and support for commercially oriented R&D and marketing efforts. Interest in placing enterprises on a sounder commercial base also can encourage support for mergers with or acquisition by foreign firms, which may have been resisted prior to this by political authorities intent on maintaining the integrity of the national defense-industrial base.

COPRODUCTION

Coproduction involves the partial production under license of arms developed elsewhere, with the significant and ongoing assistance of the developer of the arms. This is a common feature of arms production in developing states due to local industrial capabilities that are often limited, where it is often approached as a means of defense-industrial and even general industrial development. Coproduction can involve varying levels of local input, ranging from the mere assembly of imported components to the production of significant portions of the equipment in question, but often features local assembly with local production of the less technologically advanced components involved. As a defense-industrial strategy, coproduction offers very limited advantages. While it can help to develop local defense-industrial capabilities and provide a useful general industrial stimulus, it often does little to advance the technological level of local industry and does not provide any significant degree of national autonomy, which is one of the key objectives of defense-industrial development in many states. Where coproduction does serve to promote the objective of national defense-industrial autonomy, it involves a growing local contribution in both qualitative and quantitative terms as experience is gained and local industry develops. Despite its limitations, the coproduction of arms remains widespread, as it is the only viable option for many developing states.

COUNTER-TRADE

This is the practice of paying for arms imports through means other than money, while supporting the local economy. This can involve the supply of manufactured goods (including arms), or commodities such as agricultural goods or minerals. Counter-trade is resorted to by states that lack the necessary financial resources, and thus constitutes an important mechanism for some developing states to meet their arms requirements. Counter-trade for arms is most common during economic downturns or in cases where pressing security concerns generate arms requirements that cannot be met in a timely manner by any other means. This is not a favored type of arrangement from the perspective of arms suppliers due to the requirement for them to then sell the item with which they have been paid, but some firms and even governments are prepared to provide arms on this basis, recognizing that this may be the only way to secure a sale.

CRITICAL TECHNOLOGY

The term *critical technology* refers to defense-related technologies that are regarded as crucial. The determination as to which technologies are critical varies greatly between states, and is includes factors such as the organization and doctrine of the defense establishment, the sophistication of its arms requirements, and the state of local industrial capabilities. Authorities may approach critical technology in terms of the capabilities of arms (particularly advanced arms), the production of arms, or both. The common feature of considerations of critical technology is their impact on defense-industrial policy. Policy in many states reflects efforts to encourage and support the development of local capabilities in critical technological areas. There is particular attention to the capacity to develop and apply critical technologies independently of other states. This *technological sovereignty* is often even pursued in terms of states that are not politico-military rivals. Similarly, national technology control efforts are generally influenced by considerations of which technologies are critical, with these serving as the focus of the most stringent national controls. The issue of how best to promote and protect critical technology is being complicated by recent industrial trends, which are seeing a deepening transnational integration of processes of technological development and application, and accelerated transnational technological diffusion. This potentially encourages political authorities in different states to approach the issue collaboratively, but national security concerns continue to impede this.

DEMONSTRATION PROGRAM

Demonstration programs go by various titles, but generally feature mechanisms for showing that an equipment item is producible, affordable, and that the risks involved in its development have been reduced to the point where *full-scale development* can be initiated with minimal risk. Demonstration programs often constitute a distinct stage in the procurement process, and constitute an important oversight mechanism. One form is the *demonstration and validation program* (dem/val, DEMVAL, D&V), which constitutes a key phase of the American acquisition process. Dem/val programs provide for the production and trialing of developmental models of equipment. Often it is the case that rival firms or industry teams participate in these programs, so that they also serve as an important means of selecting between competing designs for further development. As well as producing equipment under contract for demonstration programs, many firms produce *demonstrators* on their own initiative to demonstrate capabilities to prospective customers.

DE-RATED EQUIPMENT

The term *de-rated equipment* is applied to equipment of deliberately downgraded performance for the export market. The term *sanitization* is also applied in this context. The de-rating of equipment is undertaken in some cases to meet the less demanding needs of some export customers, but more often reflects a desire to control the diffusion of advanced technologies and to help maintain the qualitative edge of the armed forces of the supplier state. Developing a sanitized export version may be required as a condition of export approval. Often it is only particular parts of an equipment item that are subject to de-rating, such as aircraft avionics or engines. This approach surfaced as a deliberate strategy during the cold war, and was practiced by both the United States and the Soviet Union, but is less common now due to the fact that many customers are more discriminating in their requirements and wish to avoid the stigma associated with purchasing de-rated equipment models. The potential impact of this was demonstrated of the failure of the de-rated but still very capable F-16/79 export version of the Fighting Falcon to secure even a single order.

DE-RISKING

De-risking refers to efforts to minimize the degree of risk involved in developing and applying advanced technologies. This risk has increased as technological frontiers have advanced and the resources and time required to bring technologies to the point where they can be fielded have increased. De-risking strategies vary greatly, but generally involve some manner of determining relatively early in a program whether or not technologies are likely to prove viable, and prove affordable in terms of their development and application. De-risking strategies may involve measures such as *technology demonstrations, risk-reduction studies,* or *demonstration and validation programs,* which provide the basis for efforts to address identified aspects of risk in a program. It is important to note that de-risking activities may be undertaken by industry on its own initiative, as well as by procurement authorities in the context of defense research and development (R&D) programs.

DESIGN AUTHORITY

The design authority is the firm or the facility that is considered the overall authority for a particular equipment design. Design authorities are officially responsible for designing hardware changes and developing any necessary production procedures. This role is generally played by the firm that launched the development of the item in question, but may be delegated to a subsidiary, which may be based abroad, particularly once the equipment has been in production for some time. The design authority for a particular equipment item may even be sold on once the original authority sees no further value in continuing to develop or support the design. The globalization of high-technology industry has seen considerable devolution of responsibility for research and development (R&D) to foreign subsidiaries and offshore *capability partners,* with the result that design authority may no longer lie in an industrial actor that is under the effective control of the government under which the design originated. This represents a problem for political authorities intent on maintaining the integrity of the national defense-industrial base and ensuring that key R&D and production capabilities remain under sovereign control. It is important to note that design changes may be and often are undertaken by firms other than the design authority, particularly where an equipment item has been in service for some time and is widely disseminated as a result. In cases where this does not involve the support of the design authority, however, this may come at considerable cost in terms of the effectiveness or even the safety of the resulting equipment model.

DESIGN HOUSE

This is a relatively recent phenomenon in the defense-industrial landscape. A design house is a firm that specializes in undertaking research and development (R&D) in its particular area of expertise under contract to other firms or to government entities, and that itself possesses no production facilities and has no interest in undertaking production. The importance of design houses has increased as technological frontiers have advanced and even large firms may experience difficulties in undertaking specialized R&D. The outsourcing of R&D to design houses is one way in which firms have sought to offset spiraling developmental costs, and this enables them to concentrate their resources on their core areas of expertise. While design houses occupy an importance niche in the defense-industrial market, they raise concerns from the perspective of authorities intent on maintaining the integrity of their national defense-industrial bases, and constitute a major issue in terms of national technology controls.

DUAL/MULTIPLE SOURCING

Dual or multiple sourcing is an approach employed in an effort to ensure the continuity of supply of crucial equipment items, protecting against potential supply disruptions. By expanding the production capacity through providing for multiple suppliers, governments reduce their dependence on individual firms and help to insulate themselves from industrial developments such as firms going out of business or deciding to exit particular product areas. The interfirm competition that this encourages also provides a useful means of leveraging favorable procurement terms and enhances the basis for a *production surge* in periods of conflict or tension. At the same time, however, it tends to be more difficult to manage procurement processes involving dual or multiple sources. Because of its disadvantages of being more complex and slower to implement, this approach is generally not employed in cases where time is an issue. Dual and multiple sourcing tend to be very unpopular with industry due to its profit implications.

DUAL-USE TECHNOLOGY

This also is referred to as *dual-application technology.* This term is applied to technologies that have important civil and military applications, and entered usage during the cold war, when it was recognized just how much scope there was for technologies to meet important defense and commercial requirements. The overlapping nature of technological development in the defense and civil spheres, and the potential military applications of many technologies developed with commercial requirements in mind, means that this term remains important, if redundant. Dual-use technology may provide opportunities or challenges to political authorities. It can be a great benefit due to its potential to save governments from having to support and pay for the development of desired defense technologies. This is the case for developed as well as developing states, but is particularly important in the case of the latter due to their generally greater difficulties in mustering the financial and other resources required for technological development. At the same time, however, the potential for dual-use technologies to contribute to foreign defense-industrial programs generates heightened technology control requirements. This is particularly true of the developed industrial states, which tend to be most concerned over technological diffusion and its implications. These requirements are growing in concert with deepening transnational industrial integration, which is generating growing support for multilateral technology control mechanisms such as the Wassenaar Arrangement.

END-USE/END-USER AGREEMENT

An end-use/end-user agreement is an agreement signed between a supplier and a recipient state under which the latter guarantees that an equipment item it intends to procure is in fact for its own use. This also often commits the recipient to forego transferring the equipment at any point in the future without the approval of the supplier. End-use/end-user agreements can apply to key components such as engines as well as to complete systems. Many arms exporters require end-use/end-user agreements, but they are most vigorously promoted and policed by the United States. The diligence with which U.S. authorities apply this requirement in arms sales leads some offshore arms producers to avoid using U.S.-sourced or U.S.-designed components in the arms they develop and produce for export, in order to increase their potential customer base. Though it has long been recognized that the end-use/end-user agreement system is open to abuse as a result of corruption and a lack of adherence by recipients following changes of government, this remains an important arms and technology control mechanism.

EXPORT RELEASE

Export release refers to the point where an equipment item is made available for supply to export customers. Many arms producers are prepared to export even advanced arms as soon as possible, but political authorities in some states intervene to delay this in order to ensure that their armed services maintain a substantial technological lead. This also is referred to as *export clearance.* Export release may be highly selective, in which case its timing in particular cases generally reflects the closeness of political ties between the supplier and recipient and the importance attached on the part of the former to transferring the equipment in question.

FULL-RATE PRODUCTION (FRP)

Full-rate production (FRP) is the stage where production of an equipment item is accelerated to the rate considered economically viable and operationally desirable in terms of the maturity of the design and the capacity of the operating service to field the item. Waiting until design maturity has been attained is a useful way of ensuring that equipment is operationally ready, and provides important leverage in dealing with industry as FRP is generally not approved until after the equipment is cleared for full operational service. This point may now be reached well after the introduction into service of the equipment item, however, due to a desire to determine an appropriate production-ready standard while getting the equipment into the hands of the user as quickly as possible, and due to the costs involved in full-rate production. This also is referred to as *full-scale production* (FSP), *full-scale series production, serial production,* and series production.

FULL-SCALE DEVELOPMENT (FSD)

The term full-scale development (FSD) applies to the point where the relevant authorities are confident enough in a general design and its affordability, and with the set of requirements it is designed to meet, that they are prepared to commit themselves fully to the developmental process. It often remains the case, however, that there is provision for target milestones and formal progress reviews to ensure that development remains on track and on cost, particularly given the increasing tendency of equipment requirements to evolve while development is underway. FSD increasingly overlaps with production due to the changing nature of defense-related research and development (R&D), which now often involves continually evolving equipment specifications and efforts to incorporate newly emerging technologies in order to ensure that designs are not already dated when they enter production. Full-scale development plans may even provide for the manufacture of preproduction or early-operational examples of equipment. The U.S.'s system development and demonstration (SDD) phase of the procurement process is basically similar to this.

GENERATIONS OF FIGHTER AIRCRAFT

There is no single definition of generations of fighter aircrafts, but approaches toward this issue have involved differentiating stages of design, performance capabilities, and technology innovation. *Fighter aircraft* refers to an aircraft that was designated primarily for, although is not limited to, air-to-air combat. During World War I, *fighter* referred to a two-seater aircraft that can carry guns. In World War II, *fighter* referred to a piston-engine powered aircraft; some of these aircraft were fitted with radar, capable of performing as bombers to provide air support. In time, fighter aircraft were developed into more specific categories according to their primary duty, namely interceptor, fighter bomber, or air superiority. Modern fighters are now able to perform *multi-missions* duty.

Late in World War II, the first jet engine–powered fighter was created. First-generation jet fighters, therefore, generally referred to turbojet engine–powered aircraft. Their primary weapons were machine guns, cannon, dumb bombs, and later air-to-air missiles. Some variants were capable of cruising beyond the speed of sound (supersonic), and some were equipped with radar to be able to operate at night (interceptor). An example from this generation is the U.S. F-86 Sabre, which was highly praised with regard to its air superiority during the Korean War, against the Soviet MiG-15. However, the first generation fighter did not have good endurance and could not sustain a supersonic flight level.

Second-generation fighter referred to a more powerful jet aircraft that was capable of maintaining supersonic speed in level flight. With the invention of the guided missile, air-to-air missile became its primary weapon, replacing the old cannon and machine gun. Innovation in technology enabled this type of aircraft to be fitted with onboard radar, making it possible to track down enemy beyond visual range. As a consequence, emphasis was no longer put on dogfight capability, but on the bigger payload of missile and better radar. An example of this generation of fighter is the Mig-21, which was used extensively in Vietnam and Middle East conflict.

The third generation of fighters was marked with the production of the multi-mission role jet aircraft, which was capable of conducting both ground attack and air defense. New technologies like vertical/ short take-off and landing (V/STOL) and thrust vectoring (the ability of the aircraft to direct the thrust from its main engines in a direction other than parallel to the vehicle's longitudinal axis) were tested and fitted into aircraft, enabling them to use shorter runways and perform better maneuver. Improved ground attack capability was supported by the air-to-surface missile and laser-guided bomb. An example from this generation is the McDonnell F-4 Phantom, a multirole aircraft that could perform as interceptor and bomber as well as fighter for air combat.

Fourth-generation fighters were those designed for *network-centric battlefield*s and performed multi-mission tasks. They emphasized maneuverability rather than speed, which proved to be more effective in winning a dogfight. This type of aircraft was fitted with multimode avionics that can change from air to ground modes, making it easier to perform both ground attack and air superiority tasks. Stealth coating technology, which can absorb radar, was beginning to be introduced, for example in the Boeing F-117 Nighthawk and the General Dynamics F-16 Fighting Falcon.

The term *fourth-and-a-half generation fighter* was coined as a reference to aircraft with more advanced technology compared to those of fourth generation fighters, but that cannot be designated as fifth generation. Some fighters were made of lighter composite material with stealth coating, having high-altitude supercruise ability, and were fitted with digital avionics and more sophisticated weapons like beyond visual range air-to-air missile, global positioning system (GPS)-guided missile, and helmet-mounted display. Examples of this generation are the Eurofighter Typhoon and Dassault Rafale.

The term *fifth-generation fighter* referred to aircraft fitted with advanced very low observable (VLO) stealth, integrated information and sensor fusion, along with air-to-air and air-to-ground capabilities, thus resulting in new fighting agility, reliability, maintainability, and deployability. This kind of fighter equipped pilots with 360 degrees of situational awareness and network-centric capability. Currently, there are only two kinds or fifth-generation fighters being produced: the F-35 Lightening II and the F-22 Raptor, both made by the United States. However, Russia is now trying to develop the MiG MFI and the Sukhoi Su-47 as competitors in this generation.

GLOBALIZATION OF DEFENSE INDUSTRIES

Globalization generally refers to a free flow of goods, services, and ideas, as a result of the increasing integration among countries worldwide. Defense, like public goods, cannot escape from this trend. Globalization in arms production is a shift away from traditional, single country patterns of weapons manufacturing in favor of 'internationalizing' the development, production, and marketing of arms. This also marks the shift from techno-nationalism to techno-globalism, which is manifested in the increasing amount of arms collaboration and the emergence of transnational defense-industrial and military technology bases. There are at least seven types of globalization of arms production: licensed production, coproduction, codevelopment, families of weapons, international strategic alliances, joint ventures, and transnational mergers and acquisitions (M&As).

Globalization in arms production has taken place as a result of several factors: first, the end of cold war, which forced countries to change the way they conduct business with industries. Countries want to retain control over national production of some strategic weapons (self-sufficiency) for modernization purposes, while needing to scale down defense industries' excessive capacity and the steep increase of weapons production costs. International collaborations and mergers are also seen as an alternative strategy to ensure that a particular defense program survives. Joint ventures are created among western European defense industries, as well as with Russia and developing countries like India. Second, the adoption of commercial best practices (lean manufacturing processes) in the defense sector aims to increase cost efficiency. This is manifested in the defense supply chain, within which the need to incorporate leading-edge commercial technology into defense systems stimulates the internationalization process. Commercial off-the-shelf (COTS) procurement is seen as an alternative to reducing development time and the cost of production of major defense systems.

The benefits of globalization for defense industries are mainly considered from an economic perspective. First, globalization permit research and development costs and risks to be shared, hence reducing the military burden on the state's budget. Second, through globalization, defense industries can exploit access to new technology, financial resources, and bigger economies of scale.

GOLDEN SHARE

This is referred to in some countries as a *special share.* A golden share is where the government retains an interest in a private sector firm in order to support its defense-industrial requirements, often in a manner that gives the government extra voting rights or enables it to retain special powers over a firm, such as in enabling it to exercise a veto over production issues and forcing foreign owners to divest if their shareholding exceeds certain levels. Golden shares serve to safeguard key firms from becoming foreign owned or from being subject to unacceptable foreign influence. This approach is being driven by post–cold war industrial trends that are seeing increasing numbers of key high-technology firms entering into industrial alliances with offshore capability partners or experiencing significantly increased foreign control in an effort to remain viable. This practice is most evident on the part of European states such as France and the United Kingdom.

GOVERNMENT-FURNISHED EQUIPMENT (GFE)

Government-furnished equipment involves components that are supplied by a government to industry for incorporation into arms being produced for that government. This may involve components that are sourced from government-operated production facilities or that are taken from equipment already in government service, such as earlier models of the equipment item in question. The provision of government-furnished equipment is stipulated by contract where this occurs. This is one approach to offsetting rising procurement costs, but may require the operator to withdraw equipment from service in advance of the availability of its replacement in order to fulfill the contract.

HOT PRODUCTION LINE

A hot production line is available to produce arms, even if it is not currently doing so. This also is referred to as keeping a production line warm. This term can be applied to production facilities that are geared to civil requirements, or can refer to production lines maintained in a standby mode in order to ensure their ready availability in times of conflict or tension when there is a need for increased arms production. This consideration is growing in importance as the lead times for many advanced components increase, and has been compounded by the contracted post–cold war defense-industrial base in many states. A production line can be kept warm by adjusting production rates so as to spread production out until there is a need to produce the next generation of equipment.

HOT TRANSFER

A hot transfer refers to the supply of arms directly from the inventory of one state to another. Often, this is done in order to meet a pressing requirement on the part of the recipient, particularly in a conflict situation, when standard arms transfer arrangements are far too cumbersome and slow. Arms also can be hot transferred in order to minimize the period during which they are in storage. This is an important consideration in cases where equipment is being taken out of service by the supplier and the longer that it is inactive the more likely it is to degrade or require refurbishment before it can enter service with an export customer. This is an important consideration where strictly commercial considerations underlie arms transfers and the increased costs resulting from their being placed in storage may render the equipment difficult to sell at all.

INCREMENTAL ACQUISITION/INCREMENTAL MODERNIZATION

Incremental acquisition/incremental modernization involves adding or retrofitting components and capabilities that are unavailable or unaffordable at the onset of the procurement program or when the equipment is initially fielded. Recognition of the accelerating pace of technological progress and the desire to incorporate technological developments as seamlessly as possible are encouraging procurement authorities to plan for incremental acquisition and modernization from an early stage in developmental processes, including through preplanned product improvements (P3I) and incremental technology insertion and upgrades. In some states, these are referred to as spiral upgrades. Equipment designed with this in mind from the outset is more readily and more economically modernized, potentially extending its service life. At the same time, however, it complicates the task of procurement authorities by forcing them to carefully consider which capabilities to include and when. It can also result in a situation where there is never any single standard of an equipment model, with resulting logistical and training difficulties.

INDUSTRIAL ALLIANCE

An industrial alliance is a short- or long-term interfirm arrangement where the partners rely on each other for significant research and development (R&D), production, or marketing capabilities. This approach is increasingly popular among high-technology firms due to the difficulties involved in meeting all of their requirements through their own resources as a result of the increasing cost and complexity of technological development and application. Industrial alliances can take a wide variety of forms, such as joint development, technology exchanges, cross-licensing agreements, testing agreements, cross-servicing arrangements, and standards coordination. Industrial alliances constitute a major issue of concern to national authorities where offshore capability partners are involved, due to the defense-industrial base and technology control implications, but are difficult to deal with in practice, particularly where the arrangements involved are recognized as crucial for the long-term economic viability of key firms.

INDUSTRIAL COOPERATION AGREEMENT/INDUSTRIAL PARTICIPATION AGREEMENT (IPA)

This type of agreement is signed by states for the development or production of arms. Industrial cooperation/participation agreements typically set out the terms of collaboration, including work-share arrangements, cost sharing, and any restrictions on the application and diffusion of technologies provided by partner states. Agreements of this nature are crucial to the success of interstate arms development and production programs, particularly where these involve advanced technologies with the potential to support the long-term development and success of offshore commercial rivals.

INITIAL OPERATING/OPERATIONAL CAPABILITY (IOC)

Initial operating/operational capability refers to the point where a type or model of equipment is considered to be fully in service. This may involve a series of stages or milestones as experience with the equipment item is gained, its operational capabilities are established, and the numbers of the type available to the operator increase. The point at which IOC is attained is increasingly blurred as efforts are made to introduce equipment into service as soon as possible, such as through *agile acquisition* processes, and as processes of development and production overlap. Despite this, the scheduled IOC serves as an important procurement planning device in many countries and constitutes the point at which equipment is considered generally available for use.

INTEGRATED LOGISTICS SUPPORT (ILS)

Integrated logistics support, according to the U.S. Army, is the process that facilitates development and integration of all the logistics support elements to acquire, test, field, and support army systems. According to U.K. Ministry of Defence (MoD), integrated logistic support is a group of practices, processes, and standards that ensure supportability is considered early in the acquisition lifecycle, with the aim of optimizing the whole life cost (WLC). The U.S. Army coined the term in its effort to ensure that, from the earliest stage possible, the supportability of an equipment item is considered. The technique was then adopted by the U.K. MoD in 1993. Now, ILS has been integrated widely into acquisition strategy. For example, recent U.K. procurement of Singapore's Bronco all-terrain vehicles requires the supplier countries to provide integrated logistic support of the platforms.

The purpose of ILS is to introduce and sustain fully supportable materiel systems in current and projected environments that meet operational and system readiness objectives (SROs) at minimum life cycle cost, right-size demand for logistics, reduce life cycle cost and cycle times, and reduce the duplication of efforts. It addresses three aspects of supportability during the acquisition and whole lifecycle of the equipment: first, influence on design, within which the supportability aspect (maintenance and routine servicing) has been considered from the design process; second, design of the support solution, which ensures that the solution considers and integrates the elements of ILS; third, initial support package, which includes calculation of requirements for spares, special tools, and documentation for a specific period of time.

There are 10 elements of ILS: maintenance planning; manpower and personnel; supply support; support equipment; technical data; training and training support; computer resources support; facilities; packaging, handling, storage and transportation (PHST); and design influence/interface. All ILS elements have to be developed as part of integral system engineering practice. Not all of the elements need to be fulfilled, as the system allows trade-offs to take place when affordability, operability, supportability, sustainability, transportability, and environmental soundness are being considered within the limits of resources.

INTEGRATED PRODUCT TEAM (IPT)

The integrated product team is an initiative employed in the United States that seeks to improve the management of procurement programs. Increasing numbers of U.S. defense procurement programs are led by IPTs. They involve personnel from the interested stakeholders, and by removing what are regarded as redundant layers of program oversight, IPTs allow more decisions to be made in a timely manner at the working level. This can significantly speed up the developmental process and facilitates efforts to efficiently address issues that arise.

INTEGRATED PROJECT TEAM (IPT)

This is a U.K. approach designed to improve procurement processes by rendering them more efficient and by providing for input from industry into decision making at a much earlier point in the developmental process. IPTs are responsible for particular procurement programs, and are also intended to improve the support of the equipment developed under this process. A number of IPTs have been established to address the maintenance of equipment that is already in service. British IPTs include industry partners, officials of the appropriate arm of service, and procurement officials from the Ministry of Defence. This is proving a popular approach to meeting important defense-industrial objectives.

INTEROPERABILITY

This is one of the considerations that may influence equipment development. Interoperability can be applied in an interstate or interservice context within a particular state. Interoperability is a desirable objective because it facilitates multiservice and multinational military operations and is often valued by export customers. Interoperability can apply to a wide range of equipment design parameters. This potentially encourages the design of equipment around common technical standards, such as those promoted by NATO. Efforts to promote interoperability are facilitated by interest within industry in developing products that meet generally accepted technical standards, though in some cases there are drawn-out disputes over what these standards should be.

JOINT VENTURE

A joint venture is a long-term commitment by two or more parties to conduct joint economic activity through the creation of a new entity. These parties contribute funds, facilities, and services and share revenues, expenses, and control of the enterprise. Companies have various motives to create joint ventures, such as gaining access to new technologies and customers, strengthening a company's power, exploiting the larger economies of scale and size that joint venture offers, and gaining access to new technology, financial resources, and customers, as well as good managerial practices. The durations of joint ventures vary; a joint venture can be entered into either for a specific project or a perpetual business relationship. Joint ventures can materialize in a number of forms, such as corporations, limited liability companies, and other legal institutions.

In defense, the joint venture has become a defense globalization trend. It is an international subsidiary owned and operated by defense firms in two or more countries for the purposes of codeveloping or to study future possible coproduction or codevelopment. Some joint ventures, like Matra-BAE Dynamics, in which the missile production of British Aerospace and Matra are combined, has managed to create the largest missile production venture in Europe. Within many of European joint ventures, the companies agree to retain their original weapon production and to cooperate only for developing future weapons. Other examples of joint ventures are Eurocopter (France's Aerospatiale and Germany's DASA), Matra Marconi Space (Anglo-French subsidiary of Matra and the space system division of GEC Marconi), BrahMos (Defense Research and Development Organization of India and NPO Mashinostroyenia of Russia). A 50–50 joint venture plan has been signed between Germany EADS and Russian Irkut to convert Airbus A320 passenger planes into freighters, starting from 2010. Under the terms of the agreement, Airbus, EFW, and Irkut would design and manufacture the conversion kits, perform the conversion of single-aisle passenger aircraft into cargo aircraft, and market and sell conversion services.

Joint venture has become a popular choice for European countries, Russia, and other developing countries. Throughout 1986–1995, the majority of joint venture took place among western European countries, and only around one-fourth took place in the form of transatlantic joint venture. The reason for this trend is the overcapacity of western European defense industries and the increasing unit production cost of weapon systems, which makes national industry too expensive; hence, it needs to be supplemented by a regional defense-industrial base. This trend has been seen as the reflection of a regionalized arms production system in Europe.

LADDER OF PRODUCTION

Ladder of production is basically a tool to explain the evolutionary road of what are called the new arms producing countries, in their effort to change their status from being dependent on foreign suppliers to becoming self sufficient in weapons provision. It explains the linear steps that every country needs to take in order to have full-fledged defense-industrial base. The steps are defined by the level of industrial capability (maintenance, assembly, production, research and development [R&D], etc.) and independence of production. Although there is no agreement as to what this ladder consists of, it has generally been agreed that this process reflects a defense industrialization evolution that cannot be bypassed. Also, it is not easy to move to a higher step on ladder once a country kick-starts its defense industry.

Political scientist Keith Krause's ladder of production basically tries to explain the evolution and growth of third-tier arms production as an internally driven process that leads from being an arms importer to a fully indigenous and autonomous arms producer. The term *third-tier arms producer* refers to countries that are capable of producing one or two weapon systems of which the sophistication is still below that of the technological frontier, and that are still dependent on critical subsystems and transfer of technology to go beyond copying or reproduction. The third-tier arms ladder of production consists of eleven steps: (1) simple maintenance performance capability; (2) overhaul, refurbishment, and rudimentary modification capabilities; (3) assembly of imported components, simple licensed production; (4) local production of components or raw materials; (5) final assembly of less sophisticated weapons, some local components production; (6) coproduction or complete licensed production of less sophisticated weapons; (7) limited research and development (R&D) improvement for local license-produced arms; (8) limited independent production of less sophisticated weapons, and limited production of more sophisticated weapons; (9) independent R&D and production of less sophisticated weapons; (10) independent R&D

and production of more sophisticated weapons; (11) completely independent R&D and production. Krause used this ladder of production to assess the level of sophistication of the third-tier arms industries. He concluded that the highest stage ever reached by third-tier arms producer was between stage eight and nine of the ladder. The biggest problem that he could identify was limited R&D, which mostly takes place in the first-tier countries, namely the United States and Russia.[1]

Bitzinger, calling the group that Krause referred to *second-tier arms producers,* concluded that most of these countries start on the ladder by assembling weapon systems from imported parts (knock-down kits), then license produce the complete systems with a gradual increase in using local components. Countries begin to climb the ladder by developing limited indigenous weapons with simple technology like small arms or patrol boats, followed by partnering with advanced foreign producers to develop a more sophisticated weapon. With the development of indigenous R&D, countries will try to indigenously develop more complex systems such as armored vehicles or training aircraft. Soon after they reach a sufficient level of R&D capacity, these countries will be able to develop their own advanced weapon systems like fighter aircraft and submarines.[2]

LEGACY EQUIPMENT

The term *legacy equipment* applies to equipment of an earlier generation that remains in service. This term is finding wide acceptance as a method of referring to equipment that, while not necessarily obsolescent or obsolete, is likely to be significantly less capable than is currently required. There is particular attention within the defense-industrial policy of many states over legacy models of equipment and how they can be affordably upgraded or replaced. The requirements of dealing with legacy equipment often constitute a serious drain on national resources. The term *block obsolescence* is often associated with legacy equipment. Block obsolescence applies to a situation where it is recognized that a substantial quantity of equipment has reached the point where it requires upgrading or replacement. This can constitute a major problem, as it may be necessary to replace a large quantity of equipment within as short a time frame as possible. This is referred to as *block aging* in some states.

LETTER OF INTENT (LOI)

A letter of intent is a type of document that is often drafted during arms sales. An LOI is signed by the customer and the firm or government supplying the arms it intends to purchase. Letters of intent are most commonly encountered in export sales. A document of this type precedes and paves the way for the formal placing of an order. While an LOI only indicates a customer's intention to place an order, these documents are important as they provide a basis for the manufacturer to proceed with the long-lead activities required to fulfill the contract. This is an important consideration, as it helps to speed up the acquisition process in cases where the formalities of export approval may take some time. A *letter of interest* or *declaration of intent* (DoI) fulfills a similar purpose to a letter of intent.

LICENSED PRODUCTION

Licensed production refers to the local production under license of arms developed elsewhere. This is a common feature of the defense-industrial landscape, and is found in developed and developing states alike. This is particularly important to the latter, which often approach licensed arms production as a vehicle for industrial development as well as a method of meeting the material requirements of their military establishments. While the licensed production of arms can provide an important stimulus for the developmental and production capacity of local defense industries in developing states, it often fails to achieve this due to the continued reliance on foreign support. Licensed production in many cases fails to rise above *coproduction.* Nonetheless, it remains an important vehicle for arms transfers.

LIFE-EXTENSION PROGRAM

This is referred to in some cases as a *life extension and capability improvement program, life-of-type extension, service life extension program* (SLEP), or *capability life extension.* Life-extension programs are undertaken in order to maintain the operational viability of equipment that has been in service for some time, until it can be replaced. Programs of this nature are assuming greater importance as the costs of high-technology arms increase and procurement authorities turn to this as a more affordable alternative. Such efforts are being facilitated by the potential for *incremental acquisition* and *incremental modernization,* which includes the prospect for less complex upgrading where this has been built into equipment designs from the outset. A related concept is the *mid-life update* or *mid-life upgrade* (MLU), which refers to a program to update an item of equipment when it is well into its service life, with the intention of keeping it viable for some time to come. This often involves the replacement of key systems or components or their upgrading through technology insertions. The terms *mid-life improvement, mid-life modernization,* and *mid-term modernization* also apply to this activity. While not necessarily undertaken at the midpoint of the planned service life of an equipment item, MLUs are generally approached in terms of a significant, one-time-only upgrading of the capabilities of the item. For this reason, the growing popularity of *incremental acquisition* and *incremental modernization* programs potentially comes at the expense of this approach.

LONG-LEAD ITEM

Long-lead items are components that need to be ordered well in advance of the production of the arms into which they are incorporated. These are typically components involving advanced technologies that cannot be provided by the prime contractor and systems integrator, but that must be ordered from specialist firms. These also are referred to as *long–lead time items, long-lead material* (LLM), and *long-lead supplies.* The need to incorporate long-lead items greatly complicates production programs, and makes it particularly difficult to introduce a *production surge* in times of conflict or heightened tension. This encourages procurement authorities to develop *multiyear procurement* programs for key equipment items.

LOW-RATE INITIAL PRODUCTION (LRIP)

The low-rate initial production of arms may be undertaken in order to speed up the introduction of arms into service, enabling the early attainment of initial operational capability, and precedes full-rate production. This term can be applied to the delivery of equipment that has gone through an upgrade or conversion program as well. This approach has best been developed by the United States, where operational requirements encourage the fielding of newer models and generations of equipment as early as possible, even if the quantities concerned are relatively modest.

MILITARY OFF THE SHELF (MOTS)

The term *military off the shelf* refers to components or equipment that have been designed to military requirements and that are available without further development. The advantage of buying MOTS items is that they are already technologically mature and generally can be obtained much more quickly and much more affordably than arms that are still being developed or that require further work to adapt them to local requirements. This approach can involve equipment procured from industry or that is available from another operator. This often is referred to as an *off the shelf* purchase. While it has many benefits, this approach may have implications for the economic viability and sustainability of the progress of the national defense-industrial base, as too great a reliance on MOTS may erode the capacity of defense firms to undertake advanced research and development (R&D).

MODULAR SHIPBUILDING

Modular shipbuilding is a process of building ships in which a complete ship is designed using a computer-aided design (CAD) program, allowing the ship to be built in several huge blocks, to be assembled in a dry dock during the final construction before it is eventually launched into the water. This process is different from the traditional way of making ships, where the complete hull had to be made before the technicians could install all the equipment necessary for the cabin such as engines, electronics, miles of cables, and the armory. The modular technique requires the standardization of cabins, and therefore has some advantages. First, it can speed up the shipbuilding process because different parts of the ship can be made at the same time at different places. Second, it reduces the cost because it uses assembly line methods. Third, it creates safer working conditions for the engineers.

The technique of *inverted modular construction* was developed during World War II, referring to the process in which entire sections of the ship would be built to be assembled and installed on land prior to completing the hull. The technique was then adopted by the Ingalls shipyard in the late 1960s; the USS *Ramage* was one of the first U.S. warships constructed using the modular technique in the 1970s. The ship was built in three separate hull and superstructure modules. Piping, duct work, and electrical cabling, as well as machinery and propulsion equipment, had been installed earlier in each of hulls, which were then assembled into a complete hull. The superstructure or deckhouse was fitted into the mid-body module. Despite the advantages, a modular shipbuilding technique is not easy to adopt. It requires considerable space, and creating new workshops is costly. The technique also necessitates a huge crane to help mate the different superblocks.

Later on, modular shipbuilding started to make use of CAD and laser trackers. Through the use of laser trackers, these modules can be held to high tolerances of quality in production, avoiding the removal of traditional excess material, and thus helping to achieve a consistently higher and more uniform level of finish. During the assembly process, the use of multiple robotic total stations can track the real time of the module and speed up the alignment to the existing structure. Today, modular shipbuilding has been used widely in the world.

MULTIYEAR PROCUREMENT

This is a procurement approach involving contracting for the delivery of equipment over an extended period of time. Multiyear procurement contracts are beneficial to industry through their effect of providing considerable stability, and often benefit the customer by enabling it to obtain equipment at the lower unit price that can result from economies of scale. Multiyear procurement also features as a policy response to the requirement for *long-lead items,* which encourages procurement authorities to contract for these well in advance. This also facilitates planning by the operating military service, as the yearly numbers of an equipment item to be received are known well in advance.

OFFSETS

Offsets refers to economic or other concessions that are granted to foreign governments as part of their purchase of military equipment. This is where a portion of the agreed purchase price is offset by some form of economic activity on the part of the purchasing state. Offsets are usually specified as a condition of the sale, and commonly are expressed in terms of a percentage of the value of the cost of the purchase. They are intended to provide economic benefits while reducing the net balance of payment costs of purchases. There are both direct and indirect offsets. *Direct offsets* are those benefits received by a customer that are directly related to the equipment being purchased, particularly the purchase or the production in the purchasing country of components, subcomponents, and services to be incorporated into or provided for the equipment item as it is being produced or after it enters service, either for itself or for another purchaser of the equipment. The *coproduction* of the arms being purchased is a common form of direct offset. *Indirect offsets* are those benefits received by a customer as conditions of a sale that are not directly related to the product purchased. This may involve the purchase by the supplier of goods, services, or supplies. These may benefit local industrial and technological development, such as technology transfers, by involving industry in research and development (R&D), or establishing an unrelated production facility in the purchasing country. Arms suppliers can use offsets to advance their own interests, such as by establishing foreign subsidiaries for R&D or production.

OPERATIONAL EVALUATION (OPEVAL, OPEVAL)

Operational evaluations (or *field evaluations, operational assessments,* or *operational demonstrations*) are conducted on new equipment times prior to their service entry in many states. It is often the case that operational evaluations involve pre- or early production equipment examples, and it may be the case that *full-rate production* will not be approved until operations have been successfully concluded and it has been confirmed that the equipment is likely to meet operational requirements. Operational evaluations are also often undertaken to ensure that production-standard equipment is fit for service, at which point it can be declared fully operational.

ORIGINAL EQUIPMENT MANUFACTURER (OEM)

There is no single definition of *original equipment manufacturer* (OEM). The term can be used to refer to: first, a company that supplies equipment/products to another firm to be resold or merged into the second firm's product, which then will be sold under the reseller's brand name. In other words, OEM refers to the supplier of components. Second, OEM can refer to a company that accepts other companies' components/products and incorporate or resell them under its own brand name. The second definition refers to the reseller firm, and this is the most common definition of OEM at the moment. Other terminology with similar definition to OEM is *value-added reseller* (VAR). OEM is commonly used in the electronics and computer industries. In defense, forced by the need to be cost effective, a company can subcontract parts of its weapons production to other defense companies or civilian sector firms. Some small defense firms fill the niche in the very competitive sector as value-added resellers. For example, Singapore's ST Engineering imports the Indonesian Pentad's ammunitions to be repackaged and resold at a higher quality, thus resulting in a different price.

PRIVATE FINANCE INITIATIVE (PFI)

The private finance initiative is an innovative approach employed by some governments to procure equipment where there is insufficient funding for traditional procurement processes, and emerged in the 1990s. Some, if not all of the funding required is provided by private sector partners. This can take a variety of forms, including leasing or having equipment operated by private firms, and can run for an extended period of time. This approach has been best developed in the United Kingdom, but is found elsewhere as well. A *public-private partnership* (PPP) is broadly similar. This involves collaboration between a government entity and the private sector in the development or production of arms. Public-private partnerships are employed in a number of countries as a means of developing local defense-industrial capabilities. In many of the countries where this approach is found, the private sector participant is the subordinate partner. This constitutes a means of allowing the government to retain overall control of the program, which is an important consideration in cases where political authorities are reluctant to depend too heavily on the private sector. A *public-private initiative* (PPI) involves a similar concept.

PRODUCTION GAP

The term *production gap* refers to a situation that arises when there is a significant break between the end of the production of one equipment item and the entry into production of another. This is an important issue in terms of the sustainability of the national production base, both because of the economic viability of industry, and because of the need to maintain a critical mass of expertise. The latter concern is particularly acute in high-technology industrial sectors. Concern over production gaps in some cases leads procurement authorities to stretch out production programs so as to cover any potential gap. Concerns over production gaps and maintaining a *hot production line* capability are thus highly complementary.

PRODUCTIONIZATION

Productionization involves adapting an equipment design so that it is suitable for volume production. While this can be factored into equipment designs from the outset, in many cases productionization is undertaken at a relatively late stage of equipment development. This potentially results in increased costs and delayed service entry. The importance attached to this is growing as concern increases over the capacity to initiate a *production surge.* This is encouraging attention to the issue of productionization at much earlier stages of the development cycle in many states.

PRODUCTION SURGE

The term *production surge* refers to the capacity to increase production rates on relatively short notice. This capacity is highly desirable in times of conflict or heightened interstate tension. Accelerating arms production in this manner is complicated by the requirement for *long-lead items,* particularly for more technology-intensive advanced arms, and by deepening transnational industrial integration, which in many cases is leading to the offshore migration of important sections of the defense-industrial base. This encourages efforts to maintain *hot production lines* in some countries, and in some cases forces procurement authorities to carefully consider the composition of the domestic defense-industrial landscape, including in terms of mergers and acquisitions involving foreign firms.

REQUEST FOR INFORMATION (RFI)

This is a relatively informal mechanism employed in procurement programs. A request for information is issued to industry by a prospective customer in advance of a procurement program in order to ascertain what equipment might be available to meet its requirements and what firms are potentially interested in bidding. In some cases, RfIs are issued generally; they can also be issued to selected firms. Sometimes, requests for information are issued to a foreign government, where this is a more efficient approach to dealing with its national defense industry. This can also be used to help define equipment requirements and to identify promising technologies that can be incorporated into this or future equipment items. RfIs generally outline potential equipment requirements and solicit feedback on the potential capacity of firms to meet the requirement, including in terms of candidate systems and the timeframe in which they can supply them. Procurement authorities in many states use the responses from requests for information to inform their *requests for proposals,* enabling them to target particular firms in issuing these.

REQUEST FOR PROPOSALS (RFP)

An RfP is more formal than a *request for information,* and invites firms to bid to meet a procurement requirement by submitting details of their products. In some cases, these bids serve as the basis for a contract award, and sometimes this constitutes an intermediate stage where the field of potential bidders is narrowed. The *request for quotes or quotations* (RfQ) and the *request for tenders* (RfT) used by some states to solicit bids from industry are broadly similar.

SMART ACQUISITION/PROCUREMENT

Smart acquisition/procurement is an approach that can include increased competition for contracts, public-private partnerships, *private finance initiatives,* and other strategies to support greater synergy between the private and public sectors. This objective is to ensure that procurement programs are on time and on budget, as well as to reduce through-life support costs. In the case of the United Kingdom, this includes greater efforts early in a procurement program to ensure that projects will proceed smoothly. A closely related term is *rapid acquisition.* This applies to initiatives designed to shorten the time involved in developing arms, particularly where pressing operational requirements are involved. Rapid acquisition strategies often involve efforts to bypass normal acquisition processes. Examples include the Rapid Fielding Initiative (RFI) of the United States and the *urgent operation requirement* (UOR) process used by procurement authorities in the United Kingdom to quickly deploy new or upgraded equipment in order to meet pressing operational needs. The importance attached to smart acquisition and procurement has increased as developmental costs and timeframes have increased and governments have found themselves hard pressed to meet their procurement objectives. In a number of cases, this is driving renewed attention to collaborative arms development and production with other states, and is encouraging procurement authorities to redefine their approach to dealing with industry.

SPECIAL ACCESS PROGRAM (SAP)

The term *special access program* is applied to programs in the United States that are not subject to the usual level of Department of Defense (DoD) and congressional oversight because of their sensitivity. These are commonly referred to as *black programs,* though this label is only relevant in cases of unacknowledged SAPs that are considered so sensitive that even their existence is not made public. SAPs are referred to by unclassified nicknames. Details of SAPs are provided to DoD and Congress by means that involve as few individuals and bodies as possible. The form of SAP that is of interest here is the *acquisition SAP* (AQ-SAP), which concerns the development and procurement of equipment. Procurement programs can be converted into SAPs, including through the stage of a *prospective SAP,* while they are being formally considered for this status, and SAPs can be fully or partially declassified after development is complete or in order to make some of the technologies available to other procurement programs. This approach provides an enhanced level of security for important research and development (R&D) and production programs, but comes at some cost in terms of the cross-fertilization of research efforts. This approach particularly restricts the scope for multinational collaboration in R&D, though in selected cases trusted foreign partners such as the United Kingdom have been involved in such programs.[3]

STRATEGIC ALLIANCE

A strategic alliance is a form of relationship between two or more independent firms to coordinate their resources for a specific business project, without having to merge into or create a new single entity. It is somewhere between conducting the companies' own business and merging their operations. Different from a joint venture, the relationship among parties being involved in strategic alliances is non-equity, less formal, and formed through a written contract with a termination period. A strategic alliance can materialize in many forms, like a technology transfer agreement, joint development of product, marketing and promotional collaboration, and so on. The alliance can be for a one-off activity, or concentrate on one issue in business, or to develop a new product jointly. The basic reason for creating a strategic alliance is to acquire a competitive advantage for the firms. Even competing firms would create a strategic alliance to gain the benefit it offers. One company can have several strategic alliances with different firms.

In defense, international strategic alliance can be defined as a loose industrial arrangement between defense firms in two or more countries to share information or to study future possible coproduction or codevelopment. The example of strategic alliance is a strategic alliance between Britain's BAE Systems and France's Dassault on a joint defense study for a future attack aircraft. In 1996, the U.K. and French governments inked a memorandum of understanding, in which the two parties agreed to a $58 million joint feasibility study of a future offensive air system. This alliance is preceded by competition between the U.K.-German-Italian-Spanish Eurofighter 2000 and French Rafale, which undermined the export potential of both aircrafts. The competition brings new consciousness that Europe needs a single aircraft collaboration for the future attack aircraft because it cannot afford to continue to have two or more competing fighter programs.

SUPPLIER TIERS

Supplier tiers represent a widely used approach to conceptualizing the structure of the global defense industry. States are categorized on the basis of their capabilities in relation to the development and production of arms and their capacity to supply these to other states. This structure often is expressed in terms of *first-tier suppliers,* which, as well as having comprehensive production capabilities, are a site of advanced innovation; *second-tier suppliers,* which can produce advanced arms, but are limited to adapting designs to their own requirements; and *third-tier suppliers,* which have much more limited production capabilities, and do not engage in innovation. This is a relatively crude mechanism for examining defense industrialization and analyzing arms transfer trends, but has considerable utility given the need to analyze important differences in the manner in which different states contribute to the global defense-industrial landscape.[4]

TECHNOLOGY DEMONSTRATION (OR DEMONSTRATOR) (TD)

A technology demonstration is a demonstration of new technological capabilities in support of a procurement program. Procurement authorities in many states use technology demonstrations as means of helping to determine equipment requirements, particularly in terms of advanced arms, and as a means of reducing the risks associated with developing these arms. The equipment models in question, which are referred to as *technology demonstrators,* are subjected to extensive testing to test capabilities and to indicate areas for further development. In some cases, technology demonstrations are employed as a vehicle for selecting among competing designs for further development. Many firms also use technology demonstrations as a means of demonstrating their capabilities to prospective customers, including export customers. Many firms fund company demonstrators for this reason.

TECHNOLOGY SAFEGUARDS

Sometimes referred to as a *Chinese Wall,* technology safeguards are designed to prevent the onward, uncontrolled diffusion of technology that is made available to a collaborative industrial partner. This issue has increased in importance as interfirm industrial linkages have expanded and firms have sought to collaborate with offshore capability partners in developing and producing advanced arms through *industrial alliances.* Technology safeguards can take the form of restricting access to technologies provided under collaborative agreements, including restricting physical access to the facilities where these technologies are used and requiring firms to implement internal firewalls that limit the scope for different facilities and subsidiaries to work with each other.

TECHNO-NATIONALISM

Technological nationalism, or *techno-nationalism,* refers to the idea that state should retain, control, and support strategic technology industries through a set of policies, namely government procurement policies, that prioritize products with a high content of local technology, import restriction, subsidized export, research and development (R&D), provision of credits, protection of intellectual property rights, control of foreign direct investments, and so on. On behalf of this ideology, government gives excessive supports to domestic enterprises that are considered strategic to develop and strengthen the infant strategic enterprises' competitiveness before they face the fierce competition of the global market independently.

Techno-nationalism has been incorporated into a state's industrial development policy, usually a developing country that aims to be self-sufficient. It serves as a function of national pride and as a promised method of transforming a country into a more sophisticated, high-technology society or to achieve the same technological sophistication as advanced countries. Techno-nationalism is the impetus to kick-start the incorporation of high technology and boost one country's competitiveness. However, as ideology, techno-nationalism has been criticized as rhetorical and misleading. In addition, techno-nationalism serves as an ideology that justifies the use of massive resources in the strategic sector, which does not always serve the interest of the majority of people in the country.

In defense, techno-nationalism has been the main ideology for developing countries that wish to be self-sufficient in weapons provision. With the increasing phenomenon of defense globalization, however, it is very difficult for the state to retain control over the technology. *Techno-globalism,* which is defined as the idea that all nations should join hands and cooperate to develop crucial technology, is eroding techno-nationalism. Nowadays, another term has been coined to provide a third way to deal with this problem: *neo-techno-nationalism.* This refers to the idea of expanding the state's commitment to promoting local technological innovation through engaging private and foreign institutions and support for international coordination.

THROUGH-LIFE SUPPORT

Also known as *through-life customer support* and *whole-life support,* this is a comprehensive approach to the support of in-service equipment. It considers support requirements over the long term, including what is sometimes termed the *lifecycle cost* that encompasses future modifications and upgrades and the expected cost of maintenance over the service life of the equipment, as well as the procurement cost of the equipment. This provides a more realistic, though still necessarily tentative basis for estimating costs, and encourages procurement authorities and equipment operators to consider the long-term requirements of successfully operating equipment. This approach is being encouraged by rising procurement costs, which means that states are generally retaining equipment in service longer than was previously the case, and in many cases far longer than the original design life of equipment.

TURNKEY PROJECT

A turnkey project involves the establishment of a production facility on behalf of a state that can then operate it. This is largely a feature of international arms transfers to less well-developed states, and represents one of the means by which they seek to develop their defense-industrial capabilities. While this can provide a relatively rapid manner of acquiring defense-industrial capabilities, this often comes at the expense of long-term sustainability, as the facilities are sourced from external suppliers, and often lack a sufficient domestic-industrial basis to support them in the absence of foreign support. As a result, such facilities may obsolesce rapidly or cease operations entirely without continued external support, and do little to prevent foreign governments from exerting leverage through arms transfers.

USER COMMUNITY GROUP

User community groups are formed by states that operate a particular equipment type. These groups provide a cooperative forum for discussing common operational and technical interests, disseminating operational experiences, and suggesting ways in which they can better support or modify the equipment. This is recognized as a valuable means of supporting equipment. An example of this approach is the Gripen user's group, which include Hungary, South Africa, and Sweden, all of which operate the Swedish-produced Gripen fighter. As well as supporting the Gripen in service, the Gripen user's group is intended to encourage feedback from the operators of this aircraft that will be useful to the manufacturer.

WEAPONIZATION

The process by which commercial-pattern equipment is adapted to the requirements of defense operators. Weaponization might involve measures ranging from ruggedizing equipment to withstand the stresses of deployment under field conditions to installing armor and military-standard communications systems. Weaponization is often necessary to successfully exploit the potential of *commercial off-the-shelf* (COTS) equipment, and is a process that can be undertaken by governments with this in mind, or by firms themselves as they seek to develop products that meet the needs of potential customers.

NOTES

1. Keith Krause, *Arms and the State: Pattern of Military Production and Trade* (Cambridge: Cambridge University Press, 1995).
2. Richard A. Bitzinger, "Towards a Brave New Arms Industry?" Adelphi paper 356 (IISS, 2003).
3. Bill Sweetman, "In Search of the Pentagon's Billion Dollar Hidden Budgets," *Jane's International Defence Review* 33, no. 1 (2000): 24–32.
4. Krause, *Arms and the State,* 27–32.

APPENDIX II

Organizations, Associations, Legislation, and Initiatives Relating to the Defense Industry and the Arms Trade

Curie Maharani

AEROSPACE AND DEFENSE INDUSTRIES ASSOCIATION OF EUROPE (ASD)

The Aerospace and Defense Industries Association of Europe (ASD) was created in 2004 as the result of a merger between the Europe Association of Aerospace Industries (AECMA), the European Defense Industries Group (EDIG), and EUROSPACE (Organization of Emerging Space Industry). The organization represents the leading aeronautical, space, defense, and security industries in Europe in all matters of common interest, with the aim to promote and support the competitive development of the aerospace sector. The ASD pursues joint industry actions that need to be dealt with on a European level or that related to issues of an agreed transnational nature, and generates common industry positions. The ASD Secretariat is based in Brussels.

Members of the organization are 30 national trade associations in 20 countries across Europe, representing over 2,000 companies with an additional 80,000 small and medium-sized suppliers. In terms of value and significance, the organization represents more than 600,000 employees in an industry that generated a €132.2 billion (US$175 billion) turnover in 2007.

The ASD has at least four roles: representing the European industry's interests; offering a single point of contact between industry and relevant stakeholder; facilitating the development of competitive supply chain; coordinating activities at the European level, such as research and technology (R&T), environment, standardization, training, airworthiness, and so on; and promoting international cooperation. The role of the organization is not only limited to civil aerospace, but is also relevant to defense aerospace. For example, ASD supports the European Defense Agency's code of conduct on defense procurement and encourage European countries to create more contracts for defense industries.

The ASD organizational structure comprises the general assembly, the council, and the board. The general assembly is a joint meeting of the council and board. The council consists of the presidents/CEOs of major member companies, including Airbus SAS, BAE Systems, EADS, Thales, and Saab. The board comprises the presidents of the national association. While the council's responsibility is to set general policy, the board is responsible for the administration of the organization. A secretary general, supported by five directors, runs the organization. The ASD has eight commissions on external affairs, equipment/small and medium-size enterprises, air transport, operation, R&T, security, defense, and space. These commissions are supported by several working groups.

The ASD manages a wide range of programs, including civil aviation (international programs), R&T (Advisory Council for Aeronautics Research in Europe, or ACARE), air transport (Clean Sky), and security (Security Network for Technological Research in Europe, SETRAS, and Security Transition Strategy for Critical Infrastructure Networks, SeNTRE). The ASD's outreach programs are civil aviation projects between the European Commission and aerospace industries and other countries and regions like China, India, South Asia, and Southeast Asia, in which ASD is responsible to the European Commission for the management and implementation of the project. With the Aerospace Industries Association (AIA) in the United States, the ASD maintains communication on important issues like export control modernization, aircraft certification issues, and so on.

One of ASD's programs is participation in the Clean Sky Joint Technology Initiative, agreed on by the Europe Parliament in 2007. It is by far the largest European joint research project, and has cost €1.6 billion (US$2.3 billion) over a seven-year period. The project aims to develop cleaner and quieter aircraft, with fewer emissions and a green product lifecycle. The budget, equally contributed to by European Commission and industry, will be used to create a technological breakthrough for next-generation aircraft. The program is managed under the R&T and air transport commissions of the ASD.

Web site: http:// www.asd-europe.org

AEROSPACE INDUSTRIES ASSOCIATION (AIA)

The U.S.-based Aerospace Industries Association (AIA) was founded in 1919 as THE Aeronautical Chamber of Commerce (ACCA). In 1956, the organization changed its name to the Aerospace Industries Association (AIA). The AIA is the leading representative of the U.S. aerospace, defense, and homeland security industry, representing the country's major manufacturers and suppliers of civil, military, and business aircraft, helicopters, unmanned aerial vehicles (UAVs), space systems, aircraft engines, missiles, materiel, and related components, equipment, services, and information technology (IT). Its mission is to shape public policy that ensures that the U.S. aerospace, defense, and homeland security industry remains preeminent and that its members are successful and profitable in a changing global market.

Headquartered in Arlington, Virginia, the AIA has more than 100 major aerospace and defense companies as members, including major companies such as Boeing, Lockheed Martin, Northrop Grumman, and Raytheon, and even foreign aerospace and defense firms with U.S. subsidiaries, such as Dassault, Embraer, and Rolls-Royce. In addition, the organization has more than 170 associate members, consisting of small and medium-sized suppliers taking part in aerospace production. The AIA's organizational structure consists of a board of governors and an executive committee. The board of governors is the highest authoritative body and consists of senior representatives of member companies, meeting twice a year. The organization has eight departments, including acquisition policy, civil aviation, and space systems.

Web site: http://www.aia-aerospace.org

EUROPEAN DEFENSE AGENCY (EDA)

The European Defense Agency (EDA) is one of the European Union's agencies, and was established under a joint action of the EU Council of Ministers on July 12, 2004. The agency was created to support the member states of the European Union and the European Council in their effort to improve European defense capabilities in the field of crisis management and to sustain the European Security and Defense Policy. The EDA's headquarters are in Brussels, and as of 2009 the agency had 27 participating member countries.

The EDA is under the direction and authority of the European Council and therefore should report to it. However, the highest authoritative body in the EDA is the Steering Board, in which all of the defense ministers from participating member countries sit together and meet at least twice a year to produce detailed guidance for the agency. In addition, the Steering Board also has other meetings at the level of national armaments directors, national research directors, national capability planners, and policy directors. Under the Steering Board, there is a chief executive supported by two deputy chiefs (strategy and operations) and four directorates: capabilities, armaments, research and technology, industry and market, and corporate and service. The organization has two support units: the media and communications unit, and the planning and policy unit.

The agency's tasks include defining and fulfilling the capability needs of the European Security and Defense Policy (ESDP); promoting European defense-relevant research and technology (R&T) through collaboration; promoting European cooperation on defense equipment; and working on preparing an internationally competitive market for defense equipment in Europe. During the short span of its existence, the EDA has achieved some significant outcomes in policy and actions, and as a consequence received significant increase in its annual budget from €22 million (US$31.4 million) in 2007 to €32 million (US$45.6 million) in 2008.

One of the greatest achievements of the EDA is the Intergovernmental Regime in Defense Procurement and its associated code of conduct on defense procurement, which came into force on July 1, 2006, with the support of the Code of Best Practices in the Supply Chain. According to the code, member states must provide fair and equal opportunities for all suppliers by setting from the outset transparent and objective criteria for selecting bidders and awarding contracts, and by publicizing any procurement contract opportunities worth one million euros (US$1.4 million) or more through a new accessible electronic bulletin board. Other EDA achievements are a study of roadmaps of UAVs to address the challenge of enabling them to operate alongside conventional air traffic. The latest accomplishment of the EDA is the voluntary Code of Conduct on Offsets, agreed on by the end of 2008.

The EDA is also used for joint European R&T effort, such as Joint Investment Program on Force Protection (JIP-FP). This is a collaboration program involving 20 European countries, with a budget of €54.93 million (US$78 million), focusing on technology to protect European Union (EU) armed forces against conventional threats such as snipers, booby traps, and improvised bombs. The newest R&T program is a joint research initiative on emerging technologies that might have a disruptive effect on the battlefield. The two-year program involves 11 member countries, and budget of €15.58 million (US$22.7 million).

Web site: http://www.eda.europa.eu

EUROPEAN SPACE AGENCY (ESA)

The European Space Agency (ESA) was formed in 1975, as the result of a merger between the European Launch Development Organisation (ELDO) and the European Space Research Organisation (ESRO). With headquarters in Paris, the ESA serves as Europe's gateway to space. However, ESA is not a European Union agency, and has no organizational link to the EU. Its mission is to shape the development of Europe's space capability and ensure that investment in space continues to deliver benefits to the citizens of Europe and the world.

Starting with 10 members, the ESA now has 18 member states including Germany, France, the United Kingdom, and Spain; the Czech Republic was the latest state to join, in November 2008. In 2008, the ESA received budget of as much as €3.028 billion (US$4.3 billion), and employed 2,043 staff members. The ESA's mandatory activities (space science program and the general budget) are funded by a financial contribution from the agency's member states, calculated in accordance with each country's gross national product. In addition, the ESA conducts a number of optional programs, in which every member can choose to participate and determine its amount of financial contribution.

The agency's governing body is the council, consisting of high-level representative of ESA member states; it is responsible for creating the European Space Plan and ensuring long-term funding. Each member country has one vote in the council, represented by a delegate from the country's minister responsible for space activities. The council meetings are held every three months at the delegate level, and every two to three years at the ministerial level. The ESA has nine directorates, including earth observation programs, sciences programs, and EU and industrial programs. The ESA has several liaison offices in Brussels (especially to deal with the EU), the United States, and Russia, as well as a launch base in French Guiana and ground/tracking stations across the globe. The agency has various offices in Germany, Spain, Italy, and the Netherlands, each managing different aspects of the space program such as astronauts, astronomy, space operations, earth observation, and R&T.

Since its establishment, the ESA has successfully launched various space projects such as Cos-B (satellite monitoring gamma-ray emissions in the universe) in 1975. In 2005, the ESA's Huygens mission to Saturn's largest moon was the first to land on a moon in the outer solar system. The ESA has also cooperated with NASA, for example in launching the IUE (the world's first high-orbit telescope), SOHO, Ulysses, and Hubble Space Telescope. The ESA is now at the forefront of commercial space launches, with various successful projects like Ariane series of launch rockets.

One of the ESA's latest achievements is the endorsement of the European Space Policy in 2007, which marked the new unified approach of the ESA with individual EU member states. The policy addresses the importance of ensuring sustainable funding for space programs, and recognizes space as a strategic sector. It is considered the cornerstone to the European Space Program, in which the ESA will become significant partner for the EU.

Web site: http://www.esa.int/esaCP/index.html

EUROPEAN UNION CODE OF CONDUCT ON ARMS EXPORTS

The European Union (EU) Code of Conduct on Arms Exports was adopted in 1998, as a result of a longstanding effort by several European nongovernmental organizations (NGOs) and the European Union. The code was built on the adoption of common criteria in 1992, the establishment of a group of experts called COARM (Committee Armaments), and the adoption of a Common Foreign and Security Policy (CFSP). Instead of providing the basis for harmonization of arms exports licensing policy, the criteria were interpreted differently by EU member countries, resulting in undercutting practice and disharmony in arms exports. After intensive lobbying by NGOs and the U.K. in the EU, COARM eventually came out with an agreeable draft of code, adopted as a non–legally binding council declaration.

The code aims to "set a high common standard that should be regarded as the minimum for the management of, and restraint in, conventional arms transfer by the entire EU member states." In June 2000, the member countries adopted a common list of military equipment to be covered by the code based on the munitions list of the Wassenaar Arrangement. The code consists of three parts: a preamble, criteria of export license issuance or denial, and operative provision. The preamble recognizes the responsibility of arms exporting states for the effect of arms transfer to armed conflict, human rights, and development, while at the same time recognizing the right of member states to maintain a defense industry as part its defense-industrial base.

Conditions for export license issuing or denial are as follows: First, an export license should be denied in respect to international commitments of the EU, such as sanction by the UN Security Council or the European Community, agreements on proliferation, arms control regimes, and so on. Second, member countries should assess the human rights conditions in importing countries, including the possibility of misuse of the weapons for internal repression or diversion from the recipient country to other end-users for internal repression. Third, an export license should be denied if it would prolong armed conflict or heighten tension in the importing country. Fourth, an export license should not be issued if there is the risk that the item would be used against another country of territorial claim by the recipient country. Fifth, member states should take into account the risk of exporting items for their own, friendly states, and allied countries' security interest without undermining the consideration of human rights and regional peace. Sixth, member states should take into account the behavior of the buyer country toward the international community, humanitarian law, arms control, and disarmament agreements, as well as terrorism and international organized crime. Seventh, member states should assess the technical capability, legitimate use of the exported items, and effects of export controls on the recipient country. Eighth, member states should assess the compatibility between arms and the technical and economic capability of the recipient country, making sure that the import is legitimate and would not hamper the sustainable development of the recipient country.

Based on these provisions, member countries circulate, in confidence, an annual report containing information on national arms exports and implementation of the code. Member countries should report whenever they have issued an arms export license denial, and another member country that receives a similar proposal to the one that had been denied within a three year-period should consult with the first country before making any decisions to issue or deny a new export license. Should an undercut take place, the issuing country is requested to inform the country that denied the request previously of the rationale behind its decision.

Web site: http://ec.europa.eu/external_relations/cfsp/sanctions/codeofconduct.pdf

EXCESS DEFENSE ARTICLES (EDA)

The definition of *excess defense articles* (EDA), as explained in the Foreign Assistance Act of 1961 is

> the quantity of defense articles (other than construction equipment, including tractors, scrapers, loaders, graders, bulldozers, dump trucks, generators, and compressors) owned by the United States Government, and not procured in anticipation of military assistance or sales requirements, or pursuant to a military assistance or sales order, which is in excess of the Approved Force Acquisition Objective and Approved Force retention Stock of all department of Defense Components at the time such articles are dropped from inventory by the supplying agency for delivery to countries or international organizations under this Act. (U.S. Foreign Assistance Act of 1961, as amended, section 644(g), taken from the U.S. Defense Cooperation Security Agency Web site, http://www.dsca.mil/programs/eda/progdef.htm)

EDA can be found in the Military Departments and Defense Reutilization and Marketing Service (DRMS). The Military Departments determine excess articles, survey the requirements of potential recipient countries, and give recommendations for the allocation of excess articles to the EDA Coordinating Committee. The coordinating committee is co-chaired by the Defense Security Cooperation Agency and the Department of State/PM-RSAT, with representatives from the Department of Commerce and regional and functional policy offices in the Department of Defense. The committee is authorized to allocate excess articles.

EDA is offered either at reduced or no cost to eligible foreign recipients on an "as is, where is" basis. Foreign recipients are mostly responsible for the costs of packing, handling, and transportation, as well as any restorative work and follow-on support, which may be purchased from the Department of Defense (DoD) through the foreign military sales (FMS) program. Section 516 of the Foreign Assistance Act of 1961, as amended, authorizes granting transfers of lethal and nonlethal EDA to countries; the receipt of such articles must be justified to Congress for the fiscal year in which the transfer is authorized. EDA may also be sold to foreign countries under the normal FMS system authorized by the Arms Export Control Act (AECA). When EDA are sold, the price is a percentage of the original acquisition value, based on age and condition, and ranges between 5 percent and 50 percent of the original acquisition. These transfers are reported under section 525 of the annual Foreign Operation and Appropriation Act and are shown as section 546 transfers in the system.

FOREIGN COMPARATIVE TEST PROGRAM (FCT)

The Foreign Comparative Test Program (FCT) enables the United States to test items and technologies from its allies and other friendly nations that have a high technology readiness level (TRL) in order to satisfy valid defense requirements more quickly and economically. The program was established by the 1990 DoD Authorization Act, which consolidated the 1970s' individual military component programs for the testing of foreign weapons, the Foreign Weapons Evaluation (FWE) program of the 1980s, and the NATO Comparative Testing (NCT) Program. The objective of the FCT program is to improve the U.S. warfighters' capabilities and reduce expenditures through rapidly fielding quality military equipment; eliminating the unnecessary duplication of research, development, testing, and evaluation; reducing lifecycle or procurement costs; enhancing standardization and interoperability; promoting competition by qualifying alternative sources; and improving the U.S. military-industrial base.

FCT has been managed by the Comparative Testing Office (CTO) in the Office of the Under Secretary of Defense (Acquisition, Technology, and Logistics); this office also funds the testing and evaluation of foreign items. A sponsoring organization in the DoD Government Program Office nominates a foreign item to be tested to determine whether the item meets U.S. military requirements. If the item passes the test, procurement will be carried out by the services. The majority of the foreign items come from the United Kingdom, Germany, and France, as well as from smaller countries like Israel.

The U.S. government has reaped some benefits from the FCT program. The first is that from 1980 to 2007, the FCT program has helped to foster reciprocal spending on defense items between the United States and its allies. A total of 567 projects have been funded, of which 266 successfully met the sponsor's requirement. Around 70 percent of these successful projects (189) resulted in procurement programs valued at over $8.17 billion. Second, the program has generated substantial savings by avoiding research and development (R&D) costs, lowering procurement costs, reducing risk for major acquisition programs, and accelerating the fielding of equipment critical to the readiness and safety of U.S. operating forces. Since its inception in 1980, the program has achieved an estimated research, development, test, and evaluation (RDT&E) cost avoidance of $7 billion.

FOREIGN MILITARY SALES (FMS)/DIRECT COMMERCIAL SALES (DCS)

The foreign military sales (FMS) program is a U.S. government program for transferring defense articles, services, and training to other sovereign nations and international organizations. There are various alternative ways of paying for FMS; they can be funded by foreign countries' national funds, by the U.S. government through assistance program, or by the U.S. government as a grant. There are some benefits of FMS: First, the U.S. government stresses the total package approach to its contracts. This means that a normal FMS buy for a major system includes training, spare parts, and other support needed to sustain a system through the first few years of operation. Direct commercial sales (DCS) contracts may or may not include this in the initial pricing. Second, an FMS sale usually benefits from economies of scale and the U.S. government's experience with a system. Third, entering into a major FMS program also represents the beginning of a long-term relationship with the U.S. military which includes access to joint training and doctrine, as well as increasing possibility of interoperability for future joint operations abroad.

There are two ways of procuring though FMS: the first is through the government and the second is through direct commercial sales (DSC). Under the first scheme, the U.S. government procures defense articles on behalf of the foreign customer. The U.S. president will choose countries and international organizations that are eligible to receive FMS. The Department of State (DoS) will make recommendations and grant approval for individual programs on a case-by-case basis. The Defense Security Cooperation Agency (DCSA) administers the FMS program for the Department of Defense (DoD). The DoD procures defense articles and services for the foreign customer using the same acquisition process used to procure for its own military needs. Recent policy changes in defense federal acquisition regulations have opened the door to allowing foreign governments to participate as appropriate in FMS contract negotiations. In general, these government-to-government purchase agreements tend to ensure standardization with U.S. forces; provide contract administrative services that may not be available through the private sector; and help lower unit costs by consolidating purchases for FMS customers with those of the DoD.

Under the DCS scheme, foreign countries are allowed to enter directly into a contract with U.S. companies. DCS allows the foreign customer to have more direct involvement during contract negotiation, may allow firm-fixed pricing, and may be better suited to fulfilling nonstandard requirements. DCS is subject to the approval of the Department of State, the U.S. Congress, and applicable U.S. exports laws and regulations. Foreign military financing (FMF) may be used to fund DCSs, when approved on a case-by-case basis by the Defense Security Cooperation Agency (DSCA), for the purchase of defense articles, defense services, and design and construction services. The financing of DCSs comes under the review and scrutiny of the General Accounting Office, the DoD inspector general, the Department of Justice, and Congress. The Security Assistance Management Manual (SAMM), DoD 5105.38-M, and its guidelines explain the DoD's policies and procedures for the use of FMF of DCSs between U.S. industry and foreign countries.

MISSILE TECHNOLOGY CONTROL REGIME (MTCR)

The Missile Technology Control Regime (MTCR) was created in 1987 to deter the proliferation of nuclear capable delivery system. It is an informal and voluntary association of countries, with the aim of restricting the proliferation of missiles, complete rocket systems, unmanned aerial vehicles, and related technology for those systems capable of carrying a 500-kilogram (1,100 pound) payload at least 300 kilometers (186 miles), as well as systems intended for the delivery of weapons of mass destruction (WMD), which is to be carried out through coordinated national export licensing efforts. Starting with 7 members (Canada, France, Germany, Italy, Japan, the United Kingdom, and the United States), the MTCR now has 34 partner countries including Russia, Ukraine, the Republic of Korea, and Argentina.

The MTCR has no secretariat, but it holds an annual meeting on a rotational basis and monthly intersessional consultations in Paris, the latter held through the Point of Contact (POC), which is the French ministry of foreign affairs. Other meetings, involving technical experts, information exchanges, and enforcement expert meetings, are held on an ad hoc basis. Since its establishment, the MTCR has implemented several outreach programs with non-partner countries to employ a regional approach to the nonproliferation of missiles, such as through the ballistic-missile free zone and the missile flight test ban. One of the greatest achievements is The Hague Code of Conduct (launched in 2002), the first multilateral arrangement aiming to promote global missile nonproliferation. The code is an open voluntary arrangement with 110 subscribing countries, and serves to complement the MTCR.

The MTCR works on the basis that all partner countries should adapt common export policy guidelines, which apply to a common list of items. The guidelines are the MTCR guidelines and the Equipment, Software and Technology Annex. While the guidelines "define the purpose of the MTCR and provide the overall structure and rules to guide the member countries and those adhering unilaterally to the Guidelines," they are not intended to hamper space programs that do not contribute to the delivery of WMD. Like in other export control mechanism regimes, the final decision to issue or deny an export license is left to each member state, and reviewed on a case-by-case basis.

In 1994, the regime adopted a no undercut policy on license denials, meaning that no partner country can issue an export license for an item whose license had been denied by other member.

The MTCR annex provides the definition of terms being used in it, such as *software, technology,* assistance, and so on. The annex consists of two categories: category I and category II. Category I refers to both equipment and technology with the greatest sensitivity, that is, complete rocket systems or unmanned aerial vehicle (UAV) systems capable of delivering at least a 500-kilogram (1,100 pound) payload to a range at least 300 kilometers (186 miles). The transfer for an item in this category is prohibited; however, it can be approved on rare occasions if the exporting and recipient countries can provide a sufficient guarantee that the item will only be used by the recipient for acceptable purposes and will not be retransferred. Category II includes equipment and technology that could contribute to the creation of missiles or a system capable of delivering WMD, such as propulsion components and equipment, propellant, chemical and propellant production, avionics, launch systems, and so on. Transfers of equipment and technology in this category is reviewed on case-by-case basis, and could be denied if there is indication that such an item will be used to deliver WMD.

Web site: http://www.mtcr.info/english/index.html

NATO CONFERENCE OF NATIONAL ARMAMENTS DIRECTORS (CNAD)

The Conference of National Armaments Directors (CNAD) is a committee of national armaments directors with responsibility for intra-alliance cooperation, material standardization, and defense procurement in NATO. The CNAD was established in May 1966, with the aim to "develop a common approach toward the development and procurement of equipment for NATO, by considering the political, economic and technical aspect, through the cooperative armaments projects that equip NATO with cutting-edge capability." For this purpose, the CNAD formulates a management plan that is annually updated to translate NATO's strategic objectives into guidance for armament cooperation.

The CNAD reports to the North Atlantic Council, NATO's principal decision making body. In undertaking its work, the CNAD is supported by the Defense Investment Division. The NATO assistant secretary general for defense investment chairs all CNAD meeting, and oversees and guides the work of the CNAD subordinate structure. Nevertheless, decision making in the CNAD is based on consensus among its member states. The CNAD has two kinds of meeting that engage the permanent delegation of member countries, of which some sessions are made open to partner countries. The first is held twice a year at the level of national armaments directors (NADREPs). The second is held regularly at the level of representatives of NADREPs.

The CNAD has several subordinate committees: the Army, Air Force and Naval Armaments Group; Research and Technology Board; the NATO Industrial Advisory Group (NIAG); and the CNAD Partnerships Group. NIAG provide advice from industry on issues pertaining to cooperation with industry and among industries. However, in early 2006, the CNAD agreed to restructure the subordinate committee into a capability-based organization. This restructure will merge the Army, Air Force and Naval Armaments Group, and give emphasize to different capability areas like effective engagement, information superiority, and deployability of forces.

The CNAD is responsible for cooperative armaments projects in NATO that are considered key capabilities. The ongoing projects include Work for Defense against Terrorism, the Alliance Ground Surveillance (AGS) Program and the Active Layered Theatre Ballistic Missile Defense Program. Work for Defense against Terrorism is basically developing technologies that can prevent the kinds of attacks perpetrated by terrorists, such as suicide attacks with improvised explosive devices (IEDs) and rocket attacks against helicopters. The AGS program is a mix of manned and unmanned airborne radar platforms, which can look down on the ground and relay data to commanders, providing them with "eyes in the sky." The CNAD program is expected to facilitate interoperability and the information exchange of each country's national program, as well as eliminating duplication between the army, navy, and air force armaments of NATO.

Members of CNAD are free to participate in whichever program they like. Member countries need to reinstate their interest first, agreeing to share the cost, before a program memorandum of understanding for national staffing and signature, as well as a charter for the creation of the project's management organization, is prepared.

Web site: http://www.nato.int/issues/cnad/index.html

UNITED NATIONS REGISTER OF CONVENTIONAL ARMS (UNROCA)

The UN Register of Conventional Arms (UNROCA) was established on January 1, 1992, after the General Assembly agreed to adopt resolution 46/36L on transparency in armaments that was sponsored by 40 countries, including the Russian Federation and the United States, and agreed on by 150 member countries; 12 other countries, including China, abstained. The massive arms transfer that went unnoticed to countries like Iraq, which was then destabilizing the region, was one of the reasons behind the issuance of the resolution.

The resolution requested that member countries provide information on the export and import of weapons to the secretary general on an annual basis by April 30 each year, starting from 1992. The objectives of the resolution are to implement new confidence-building measures, reduce arms transfers, address problems of illicit and covert arms trade, reduce the military acquisition burden on a country's economy, and reduce military expenditures. Despite being voluntary, the register has set a standard of reportage that specifies supplying state, recipient state, state of origin, and number of transferred arms per category. There are seven category items included in the resolution: battle tanks, armored combat vehicles, large-caliber artillery systems, combat aircraft, attack helicopters, warships, and missiles and missile systems. Due to African states' criticism that the register did not include small arms and light weapons (SALW) although these are the main violence multipliers in African conflict, the register eventually added SALW to the reporting requirements in 2003.

The register has been criticized for its lack of success and discrepancy between expectations and results, especially if compared to other arms control regimes like the Wassenaar Arrangement and the MTCR. The criticisms targeted the implementation of the register and the compromise in defining what types of weapons should be incorporated in the register. Because the register works on a voluntary basis with no punitive consequences, not all member countries are willing to submit reports. Moreover, the register also does not provide verification mechanisms to check the accuracy of reports that have been submitted. So far, there have been 172 countries reporting to the register, but the number varies from year to year, with the highest number (126) in 2001 and the lowest (85) in 1998. China, African countries, and most Arab countries do not always participate in the register.

UN member countries are still debating which categories should be included in the register. The Arab League suggested that the register should take into account weapon of mass destruction into the reporting system. The register also does not include domestic production arms, and hence fails to portray a comprehensive picture of arms acquisition in countries with a defense-industrial base, which are often involved in regional tensions. Another problem is that the register does not require states to submit a detailed explanation regarding the transferred weapons, such as whether they are new or used weapons. Therefore, it fails to recognize the intention behind the weapons transfer: whether it is for military build-up or for replacement.

There is no clear advantage to participating in the register for countries that seek to import weapon. Although some countries that also participated in other arms control regimes like the Wassenaar Arrangement and the EU Code of Conduct have stated that a country's record of participation in the register will be used in assessing an export license, countries can always seek weapons from various exporting countries that do not participate in the register; this is an important issue.

Web site: http://disarmament.un.org/cab/register.html.

U.S. ARMS EXPORT CONTROL ACT OF 1976

Initially the Foreign Military Sales Act of 1968, the U.S. Arms Export Control Act (AECA) passed on June 30, 1976, and has been amended several times. The act authorizes the sale or lease of U.S. defense equipment, articles, and services through the government-to-government foreign military sales (FMS) program or through the licensed commercial sales process. The act also regulates the general standard of eligibility of a country to receive U.S.

defense articles and sets limited conditions in which using the defense articles is permissible. Furthermore, the act sets out circumstances in which a nation may lose U.S. foreign military financing (FMF), loans, right to purchase, and right to engage in sales agreements related to defense articles or services due to a substantial violation.

The aim of the act is basically to expand congressional authority for arms export control. One of most important issues the act is the separation of power and authority between Congress and the executive. The act obliges the executive to submit a formal notification to Congress of possible arms sales and whether a substantial violation has been committed by the recipient country. The executive has to make formal notification to Congress within 30 calendar days (15 calendar days for NATO member states, Japan, Australia, or New Zealand) before it takes final steps to conclude a government-to-government foreign military sales agreement for equipment worth $14 million or more, defense articles or services worth $850 million or more, or design and construction services worth $200 million or more. Congress, on the other hand, has the authority to pass legislation to block or modify arms sales at any time up to the point of delivery of the articles involved. If Congress does not do anything within the time period, the executive is free to carry on with the sales.

The act states that defense articles and services must be sold to friendly countries solely for internal security, legitimate self-defense, participating in regional collective arrangements or measures consistent with the Charter of the United Nations, participating in collective measures requested by the United Nations for the purpose of maintaining or restoring international peace and security, and enabling foreign military forces in less developed countries to construct public works and to engage in other activities helpful to the economic and social development of these friendly countries. The act, however, does not define the terms by which using the U.S. defense articles may be interpreted as infringement of the act, thus leaving the authority to president or Congress to interpret this and come to a conclusion. In the case of a possible violation, the U.S. government can suspend or cancel any contract or delivery of defense articles. Alternatively, Congress could pass regular legislation that would exempt the particular country from specific sanctions imposed through AECA procedures, although that legislation would be subject to a presidential veto.

Web sites: http://www.brad.ac.uk/acad/sbtwc/btwc/nat_imp/leg_reg/U.S./arms_exp_cont_act.pdf; http://www.fas.org/programs/ssp/asmp/externalresources/bills_and_laws.html

U.S. DEFENSE SCIENCE BOARD (DSB)

The U.S. Defense Science Board (DSB) was established in 1956 as a response to a recommendation of the Hoover Commission. The recommendation stated that "the Assistant Secretary of Defense must appoint a standing committee of outstanding basic and applied scientist to formulate periodically the needs and opportunities arising from new knowledge for new weapons systems." The aim of creating the board was to provide independent advice and recommendations on science, technology, the acquisition process, and other matters of special interest to the Department of Defense. The Under Secretary Of Defense for Acquisition, Technology, and Logistics (USD/AT&L) has the authority to act upon the advice and recommendations of the board. In 1990, the Defense Manufacturing Board merged with the DSB, therefore adding manufacturing issues to its tasks.

According to its charter, the DSB should include approximately 35 members and six senior fellows, with integrity in the field of science, technology, manufacturing, acquisitions, and so on. The chairperson of DSB is appointed by the secretary of defense, while the vice chairperson and other members of the board are appointed by the USD/AT&L. Both the chairperson and vice chairperson of DSB serve for a two-year term that can be extended. Members of the board have come from a wide array of backgrounds: the board includes graduates of prestigious universities, former government officials, members of think tanks, high-level managers of big defense industries, and private consultants.

The DSB has three permanent taskforces and several current taskforces. The permanent taskforces consist of: first, the Nuclear Weapon Surety, which is assigned to asses all aspects of nuclear surety (military, federal, and contractor), continue the work of the former Joint Advisory Committee, and review and recommending methods and strategies to maintain a safe, secure, and viable nuclear deterrent; second, the Advisory Group on Electronic Devices (AGED), which is assigned to provide independent recommendations and advice on matters related to planning and managing an effective and economical research and development program in the field of electronics technology; third, the Advisory Group on Defense Intelligence, which is assigned to provide research support and independent advice to the under secretary of defense for intelligence on a broad range of defense intelligence matters. The current taskforces include Military Application of Synthetic Biology, Department of Defense (DOD) Policies and Procedures for the Acquisition of Information Technology, and Integrating Commercial Systems into DoD.

The DSB has produced a great number of summer study reports, which then become the impetus for new awareness and government active response on particular issues. For example, the board report on Information Architecture on the Battlefield (1994) alerted the government to the vulnerability of the U.S. information system to *digital attack*. As an independent advisory body for the U.S. government, there were times when the board criticized U.S. policy. In October 2004, the DSB taskforce published a report on strategic communication, criticizing the government's lack of diplomatic credibility in the Muslim world; the board suggested that the U.S. government should create a new body to manage strategic communication more effectively.

Web site: http://www.acq.osd.mil/dsb

U.S. DEFENSE SECURITY COOPERATION AGENCY (DSCA)

The U.S. Defense Security Cooperation Agency (DSCA), known prior to 1988 as the Defense Security Assistance Agency, is a defense agency under the U.S. Department of Defense (DoD) that serves as its focal point and clearinghouse for the development and implementation of security assistance plans and programs. It directs, administers, and provides overall policy guidelines for the execution of security cooperation and additional DoD programs. The DSCA receives directives and reports to the under secretary of defense for policy through the assistant secretary of defense (international security affairs).

The DCSA's program provides financial and technical assistance, transfer of defense materiel, training, and services for friendly countries and allies, and promotes military-to-military contact. The DSCA administers the program outlined in the Arms Export Control

Act of 1976 (AECA) and part II of the Foreign Assistance Act of 1961 (FAA) that includes: sales of defense articles, training and services under the foreign military sales (FMF) program; *drawdown* (transfers of weapons, parts, equipment, services, or training that are not considered excess) of defense articles, training, and services; grants and sales of excess defense articles (EDA); leases of defense articles; funding of the foreign military financing (FMF) program and the international military education training (IMET) program; humanitarian assistance; and demining activities.

Under section 36(b) of AECA, the DSCA, in cooperation with the Military Departments (MILDEPs) and Department of State, has to report to Congress on the government's intention to transfer defense equipment, services, or articles. MILDEPs forward the classified information to DSCA, which then coordinates with the Department of State to send a 20-day advance/informal notification of expiry. Once the informal notification expires, a 15/30-day formal notification is delivered to Congress and the information becomes unclassified.

The DSCA also directs and supervises the organization, functions, training, administrative support, and staffing of DoD elements in foreign countries responsible for managing Security Assistance programs furthermore, it supports the development of cooperative programs with industrialized nations. Security Assistance is a group of programs, authorized by law, that allows the transfer of military articles and services to friendly foreign governments via sales, grants, leases, or loans. DCSA has to cooperate with the Bureau of Political and Military Affairs, Department of State, to manage the Security Assistance Funds.

Each year, the DSCA calls for input from the Military Departments (MILDEPs), other defense agencies, and the Unified Combatant Commands (UCC), through the chairman of the Joint Chiefs of Staff, regarding the upcoming year's Security Assistance legislative initiatives. After the initiative is reviewed, DSCA forwards its legislative proposals to the Office of the General Counsel, which then submits the initiative to the Office of Management and Budget (OMB) for approval before submission to Congress. The DCSA has to deal with Congress again, as the agency has to submit a quarterly report to Congress on security assistance surveys authorized during the preceding calendar quarter.

In wartime or under extraordinary circumstances, the DSCA, through implementing agencies, identifies or open FMS orders and cases and the director of DSCA, in consultation with the Joint Chiefs of Staff, reallocates any undelivered materiel among FMS countries. When appropriate, the DSCA works with the Joint Chiefs of Staff and the MILDEPs to establish a project code to help speed up requisitions for foreign partners.

Web site: http://www.dsca.mil

U.S. DEPARTMENT OF STATE'S DIRECTORATE OF DEFENSE TRADE CONTROLS (DDTC)

The Directorate of Defense Control (DDTC), part of the State Department's Bureau of Political-Military Affairs, is in charge of controlling the export and temporary import of defense articles and defense services covered by the United States Munitions List (USML). Its mandate comes from the Arms Export Control Act (AECA) and the International Traffic in Arms Regulations (ITAR). It is led by the deputy assistant secretary for defense trade and regional security, and supported by one managing director and three offices, namely the Office of Defense Trade Controls Compliance (DTCC), the Office of Defense Trade Controls Licensing (DTCL), and the Office of Defense Trade Control Policy (DTCP). The DTCL has five divisions: military vehicles and naval vessels, missiles and spacecraft, military electronics, aircraft, and firearms.

All manufacturers, exporters, and brokers of defense articles, defense services, or related technical data, as defined by the United States Munitions List (part 121 of ITAR), are required to register with DDTC. Registration is primarily a means to provide the U.S. government with necessary information on who is involved in certain manufacturing and exporting activities. Registration does not confer any export rights or privileges, but is a precondition for the issuance of any license or other approval for export. Persons who have been convicted of violating or conspiracy to violate AECA will be subject to *statutory debarment,* which means that they will be prohibited from participating directly or indirectly in the export of defense articles, service, and technical data. Their names will be published in the Federal Register, and debarment will not be lifted until an application for reinstatement of export privilege is granted by the DDTC.

Certain license applications and other export authorization requests must be reported to Congress: 1) any agreement that involves the overseas manufacture of significant military equipment (SME); 2) a license for the export of firearms in the amount of $1 million or more; 3) in the case of proposed exports of major defense equipment, any request with a value equal to or greater than $14 million ($25 million in the case of NATO member states, Japan, Australia, and New Zealand); 4) in the case of any other proposed export of defense articles, defense services, and/or technical data, any request with a value equal to or greater than $50 million ($100 million in the case of NATO member states, Japan, Australia, and New Zealand). This requirement typically adds six to nine weeks to the process for license application review and adjudication.

The DDTC Web site contains information on approved arms export notifications to Congress, as well as arms export policies and embargoes to foreign countries. The DDTC Web site also provide explanations on commodity jurisdiction (CJ), whose purpose is to determine whether an item or service is covered by the USML and therefore subject to export controls administered by the U.S. Department of State.

Web site: http://www.pmddtc.state.gov

WASSENAAR GROUP

The Wassenaar Group was established in Wassenaar, the Netherlands, in 1995, to replace the cold war era organization, COCOM (Coordinating Committee for Multilateral Export Control), as the West's leading multilateral export control regime. The Wassenaar Group seeks to prevent destabilizing accumulations of conventional arms and dual-use equipment and technologies by promoting transparency and greater responsibility in transfers of conventional arms and dual-use goods and technologies, and to develop mechanisms for information sharing among the participating states as a way to harmonize export control practices and policies. There are 34 participating states in the Wassenaar Agreement, including Argentina, Japan, South Africa, the Russian Federation, and the United States. The group's secretariat is located in Vienna, Austria.

Countries participating in Wassenaar have agreed on four issues: to maintain national controls of listed items via national legislation; to follow best practices guidelines or elements; to report on transfers and denials of specified controlled items to destinations outside the arrangement; and to exchange information on sensitive dual-use goods and technologies. Although decisions on export licensing remain under the national control of participating states, each state is obliged to give information on every export license that has been issued or denied. Participating countries have to follow a set of regulations and procedures, such as the Elements for Objective Analysis and Advice Concerning Potentially Destabilizing Accumulations of Conventional Weapons 1998, the Best Practice Guidelines for Exports of Small Arms and Light Weapons (SALW) 2002, the Statement of Understanding on Control of Non-Listed Dual-Use Items 2003, the Best Practices to Prevent Destabilizing Transfers of Small Arms and Light Weapons through Air Transport 2007, and so on.

The Wassenaar Group maintains an extensive set of control lists. The group follows Guidelines and Procedures, Including the Initial Elements, which regulates control lists, the procedure for the information exchange (general, dual-use goods and technology, arms), confidentiality, and administration. Wassenaar has also set up a munitions list, containing 22 main entries on items designed for military use like small arms and light weapons, tanks and other military armed vehicles, combat vessels, armored/ protective equipment, and aircraft and unmanned aerial vehicles (UAVs). Furthermore, the group also set up a list of dual-use goods and technology that extends from common to sensitive and very sensitive. For the information exchange system among participating countries, the group has established a procedure on arms transfer and dual-use goods and technology transfer in the detailed content of the report. For instance, participating states have to report licenses issued or denied for transfers of dual-use goods that are relevant to the purpose of the arrangement to nonparticipating countries, on an aggregated basis, twice a year.

The group's organizational structure consists of both plenary and subsidiary bodies. The plenary acts as the decision-making and governing body. It consists of representatives from all of the participating states and meets once a year. Subsidiary bodies support the plenary in preparing recommendations for plenary decisions. In 2008, there were two subsidiary bodies: the General Working Group (GWG), which deals with policy, and the Expert Group (EG), which deals with issues related to the lists of controlled items. A periodic meeting called Vienna Points of Contact (VPOC) can be held under the plenary chair to facilitate intersessional information flow and communications between/among participating states and the secretariat.

APPENDIX III

Key Defense Companies

Richard A. Bitzinger

BAE SYSTEMS (UNITED KINGDOM)

BAE Systems is the largest defense company in Europe and the third largest worldwide, with global revenues totaling £18.54 billion ($31 billion) in 2008. BAE Systems is a broad-based mega–defense company that designs, manufactures, and supports military aircraft, surface ships, submarines, space systems, radar, avionics, guided weapons, and command, control, communications, computing, intelligence, surveillance, and reconnaissance (C4ISR) systems. Through its purchase of Vickers and Alvis land ordnance companies, BAE Systems also produces the Challenger II main battle tank and the Warrior infantry fighting vehicle (IFV).

BAE Systems has more than 105,000 employees, including employees involved in joint ventures. It has subsidiaries in Australia, Germany, North America, South Africa, and Sweden, and it is partnered in the pan-European MBDA missile joint venture and on the Eurofighter combat aircraft program. BAE also owns a 20 percent share in Saab. It used to hold a 20 percent stake in Airbus but sold this back to Airbus in 2006.

BAE Systems is divided into five business groups—electronics, intelligence, and support; land and armaments; programs and support; international businesses; and headquarters and other businesses—and defines its home markets to be Australia, Saudi Arabia, South Africa, Sweden, the United Kingdom, and the United States. BAE Systems Land and Armaments includes the U.S.-based United Defense Limited, BAE Systems Hägglunds AB (Sweden), Bofors (Sweden), and BAE Systems Land Systems South Africa. The programs and support group is responsible for the design, development, and production of BAE's major military aircraft programs for the British military, including the Eurofighter Typhoon, F-35 Joint Strike Fighter (JSF), and Hawk trainer jet, along with the Type-45 frigate and the Astute nuclear-powered attack submarine for the Royal Navy.

BAE Systems has particularly expanded its North American activities in recent years, and since the late 1990s the company has acquired more than a dozen U.S. defense firms. Most recently, BAE Systems bought United Defense Limited (UDL) and Armor Holdings, on the expectation that it will earn significant revenues servicing, maintaining, and upgrading armored vehicles for the U.S. military. BAE Systems is also the only level one partner in the U.S.-led F-35 program. Consequently, BAE Systems does more business in North America (£6.4 billion [$10.7 billion] worth of sales in 2007) than in the rest of Europe (£2.6 billion [$4.4 billion]), or, indeed, even the United Kingdom (£3.4 billion [$5.7 billion]). North America, in fact, has become the company's single largest market, accounting for 41 percent of all corporate income in 2007 and making BAE Systems the fourth largest contractor to the U.S. Department of Defense (DoD). It was ranked number three in DoD contracts in 2008.

Web site: http://www.baesystems.com

BOEING (UNITED STATES)

Boeing, headquartered in Chicago, Illinois, is typically among the top 10 defense companies in the world. In 2008, it was the second largest contractor to the U.S. Department of Defense (DoD), and ranked second globally in terms of defense sales. Boeing employs about 162,000 people worldwide and had revenues totaling $61 billion in 2008. Defense contracting accounted for 52 percent of Boeing's revenues in 2008.

Boeing is mostly known for its passenger jet business (such as the B-737, B-747, B-777, and B-787 airliners). The company has long been engaged in defense work, however, serving as a key subcontractor on such programs as the B-2 stealth bomber and the F-22 fighter. It also built the B-52 strategic bomber and the KC-135 air-to-air refueling aircraft, as well as the CH-46 and CH-47 heavy lift helicopters.

In 1997, Boeing bought the McDonnell Douglas Corporation (MDC), its leading U.S. rival in the passenger jet business (such as the MD-90 and MD-11 airliners). It eventually shut down all of MDC's commercial airliner work, but retained its large military business, which was reconstituted as Boeing Integrated Defense Systems (Boeing IDS), based in St. Louis, Missouri. Boeing IDS is responsible for the production of all Boeing combat aircraft, including the F/A-18, F-15, and AV-8B fighter jets, the T-45A Goshawk trainer jet, and the AH-64 attack helicopter. This division also builds the C-17 Globemaster III transport aircraft, the V-22 Osprey tilt-rotor aircraft (with Bell Helicopters), and the P-8A Poseidon maritime patrol aircraft, and manufactures the Harpoon, Tomahawk, and Hellfire air-to-surface missiles. Space launch services (the Delta family of space launch vehicles, Sea Launch venture, with Energia of Russia and Aker of Norway, satellite) also make up a small portion of Boeing's overall business.

Around 40 percent of Boeing's business is outside the United States. Of that, roughly three-quarters is derived from commercial aircraft sales and 25 percent from military (Boeing IDS) sales. IDS revenues from the U.S. government accounted for 46 percent of all Boeing sales in 2008.

Web site: http://www.boeing.com

DASSAULT AVIATION (FRANCE)

Dassault Aviation is a subsidiary of Groupe Dassault; The European Aeronautic Defense and Space Company (EADS) owns a 46 percent share in the company. Dassault is France's leading manufacturer of combat aircraft, especially fighter aircraft. The company was founded in 1930 by Marcel Bloch as Société des Avions Marcel Bloch, later changed to Avions Marcel Dassault. Dassault produced France's first jet fighter, the Ouragan, in the early 1950s, followed by the Mystère and Mirage family of combat aircraft. Other aircraft include the AlphaJet trainer, the Étendard fighter-bomber, and the Anglo-French Jaguar ground attack aircraft.

Current key products are the Rafale and Mirage-2000 fighter jets, and the Falcon family of business jets. The Rafale is a multirole fighter being produced for the French air force, and for the French Navy as a carrier-based aircraft. The French forces were expected to order a total of 294 Rafales: 234 for the air force and 60 for the navy. Dassault is also the lead contractor for the Neuron unmanned combat aerial vehicle (UCAV) technology demonstrator project. The company has approximately 12,000 employees. In 2008, it earned €3.75 billion ($5.3 billion) in revenues, of which 31 percent came from sales to the French military, seven percent were exports, and 62 percent came from sales of the Falcon jet.

Web site: http://www.dassault-aviation.com

DCNS (FRANCE)

DCNS (Direction des Constructions Navales Services), with yards in Brest, Cherbourg, Lorient, and Nantes-Indret, is one of Europe's leading shipbuilders. DCNS is a government-run enterprise formed in 2007 with the merger of the Direction des Constructions Navales (DCN) with Thales' French naval business. Thales owns a 25 percent share in DCNS, while the French government maintains a 75 percent share. The new company has 13,000 employees and earned €2.82 billion ($4 billion) in 2007.

DCNS is France's leading naval shipbuilder. It is currently constructing the Horizon class of frigates for the French Navy, and it is partnering with Fincantieri of Italy on the bilateral FREMM Multipurpose Frigate (*Frégate multi-mission*) program, which will be capable of carrying out anti-air, antisubmarine, and antiship warfare, as well as land attack. DCNS will also be the lead contractor for France's future PA2 (Porte-Avions 2) aircraft carrier.

DCNS also constructs submarines, including the Agosta and Scorpène diesel-electric submarines (the latter of which can be outfitted with the MESMA engine for air-independent propulsion, or AIP), the Barracuda nuclear-powered attack submarine (SSN), and the Triomphant nuclear-powered ballistic missile–carrying submarine (SSBN).

DCNS has a considerable export business, and nearly a quarter of the company's 2007 backlog of orders was with foreign customers. It has sold its La Fayette stealth frigate to Saudi Arabia, Singapore, and Taiwan, the FREMM to Greece and Morocco, and the Scorpène submarines to Brazil, Chile, India, and Malaysia.

Web site: http://www.dcnsgroup.com

EMBRAER (BRAZIL)

Embraer (Empresa Brasileira da Aeronautica) was founded in 1969 with less than 600 workers. Today, it is the third-largest aircraft manufacturer in the world, with 2008 sales exceeding $25 billion and a workforce totaling around 24,000 employees. Embraer has developed the very successful Tucano turboprop primary trainer plane, more than 650 of which have been sold to 15 air forces around the world, including those of France and the United Kingdom. Together with Italy, Embraer also codeveloped the AMX attack jet, which was bought by the Brazilian and Italian air forces and also exported to Venezuela. Other locally produced military aircraft include the Bandeirante and Brasilia light transport planes.

Weak sales and heavy losses in the early 1990s forced the company to lay off more than half of its workforce, and after two unsuccessful attempts to privatize the company, Embraer was sold off in December 1994 (the Brazilian government retained a controlling golden share in the company). In 1999, the company sold a 20 percent stake to a consortium of four European defense firms, Thales, Dassault, EADS, and Snecma, who vote their shares as a bloc. The company concentrated most of its post-privatization efforts on the development of a new family of commercial aircraft, centering around the 37-, 44-, and 50-seat ERJ-135, -140, and -145 family of regional jets, which entered production in 1996. By late 2008, Embraer had produced and delivered more than 1,000 ERJs to more than 37 airlines in 24 countries. The ERJ-145 is also assembled under license in China and is used as a platform for airborne early warning (AEW) and ground surveillance.

Building on its success in the regional jet business, Embraer has expanded to produce two new larger passenger jets, the 70-passenger E-170 and the 100-passenger E-190. By late 2008, the company had 876 orders and 810 options for its E-series jets, and nearly 500 E-jets. Embraer has subsequently deemphasized its defense business, and military aircraft production now accounts for less than 15 percent of Embraer's overall revenues. The company's leading military aircraft is the ALX light attack aircraft, based on the Super Tucano trainer plane, which it is currently producing for the Brazilian Air Force (BAF); the ALX can carry both air-to-air and air-to-ground weapons, and will also be qualified for night missions and as an intermediate trainer. The Super Tucano has also been exported to several South American air forces.

Web site: http://www.embraer.com

EUROPEAN AERONAUTIC DEFENSE AND SPACE COMPANY (FRANCE, GERMANY, SPAIN)

The European Aeronautic Defense and Space Company (EADS) was formed in 2000 with the merger of three European defense firms: France's Aerospatiale Matra, Germany's DaimlerChrysler Aerospace (DASA), and Spain's CASA. Approximately 22.5 percent of EADS stock is held by Daimler AG, 25 percent by SOGEADE (a holding company co-owned by the French government and France's Lagardère), and 5.5 percent by the Spanish holding company SEPI; the remainder is traded publicly on six European stock exchanges.

The company has production facilities in all three home countries, plus a large industrial footprint in the United Kingdom, through its ownership of Racal Instruments and its purchase of BAE Systems' share in both Airbus (now Airbus UK) and the European satellite consortium, Astrium. In 2007, EADS generated revenues of €40.7 billion ($58 billion) and employed a workforce of about 118,000—approximately 39 percent in France, 36 percent in Germany, 8 percent in Spain, 13 percent in the United Kingdom, and four percent in North America and elsewhere.

EADS comprises six major business sectors: Airbus (the A320, A330, A350, and A380 family of commercial passenger jets); military transport aircraft (including the A400M transport plane and A310/A330 multirole tanker transport aircraft); Eurocopter (all types of utility commercial and military helicopters, including the Tiger attack helicopter and the NH-90 military transport helicopter); Astrium (satellites and space launch vehicles); defense and security (e.g., the Eurofighter combat aircraft, the Meteor air-to-air missile, and various defense communications systems and electronics); and other business (including EADS's 50 percent stake in the Franco-Italian ATR regional transport aircraft consortium). EADS also controls 46 percent of Dassault (which produces the Rafale fighter jet) and 37.5 percent of MBDA (missile systems).

In 2007, Airbus accounted for 62 percent of all corporate revenues; military transport aircraft, 3 percent; Eurocopter, 10 percent; Astrium; 9 percent; defense and security, 13 percent; and other business, 3 percent. About one-fifth of its 2007 revenues came from all kinds of military work. More than two-thirds of EADS's revenues come from sales outside its three home countries.

Web site: http://www.eads.eu

EADS-CASA (SPAIN)

EADS-CASA, a subsidiary of EADS, employs approximately 8,900, or 8 percent of EADS's total workforce. Military transport aircraft and maritime patrol aircraft (MPA) provide the backbone of the company's work. CASA produces the C-212, CN-235, and C-295 transport aircraft, which have been widely sold around the world. EADS-CASA is also working on the A400M transport aircraft, and it is to be the lead for the power plant (the TP400-D6 turboprop) as well as being responsible for final assembly of the aircraft; 200-plus aircraft are expected to be built under the program. Marine patrol and search-and-rescue aircraft (utilizing the CN-235 and C-295 airframes) represents 15 percent of the company's business, and CASA has won contracts in Ireland, Thailand, and Venezuela, and for the U.S. Coast Guard's Deepwater program. CASA also provides the MPA fully integrated tactical system, which is available for installation on its own aircraft and for P-3C Orion upgrades. CASA is also a partner in the Eurofighter Typhoon; it has a 14-percent work-share in the program and will manufacture the right wing and leading edge slats; the company will also perform final assembly of 87 Eurofighters for the Spanish Air Force.

EADS-CASA is increasingly involved in tanker aircraft work. The company provided the Airbus A310 tankers for the German Air Force, as well as the tanking kit for the United Kingdom's A330 tanker. This area could provide a substantial business for EADS-CASA. Finally, CASA is a partner in Airbus's commercial jetliner work, where it holds about a five percent work-share.

Web site: http://www.casa.eads.net

FINMECCANICA (ITALY)

Finmeccanica is an Italian conglomerate that controls around 80 percent of all Italian defense production. Finmeccanica owns Alenia Aeronautica (fighter aircraft, including partnering in the Eurofighter Typhoon consortium), Aermacchi (trainer aircraft, including the MB-339 and M-346 trainer jets), AgustaWestland (helicopters, such as the EH-101 utility helicopter and A129 attack helicopter), Oto Melara (land ordnance), and Galileo Avionica (defense electronics, airborne radar, and drones). The company also holds a 25-percent stake in MBDA, the pan-European missile joint venture, a 32-percent share in NHIndustries, which is producing the NH-90 medium-life military helicopter, a 33-percent stake in Thales Alenia Space (satellites), and a 50-percent share in ATR, a Franco-Italian regional aircraft manufacturer. It is also part of the international team developing the F-35 Joint Strike Fighter. Finmeccanica's workforce stood at 60,750 employees at the end of 2007, of which 30 percent are employed outside Italy, mostly in the United Kingdom and the United States.

Finmeccanica's total 2007 revenues were €13.4 billion ($19.1 billion), about 65 percent coming from defense work. Around 38 percent of its business came from its fixed- and rotary-wing business, 8 percent from defense systems (missiles and ground systems), 28 percent from defense electronics, 6 percent from space, and the rest from other non-aerospace and nondefense activities, including transportation and energy.

Web site: http://www.finmeccanica.com

GENERAL DYNAMICS (UNITED STATES)

General Dynamics, headquartered in Falls Church, Virginia, is typically among the top 10 defense companies in the world. In 2008, it was the fifth largest contractor to the U.S. Department of Defense (DoD), and ranked sixth globally. In 2008, the company earned $29.3 billion in sales and employed 92,000 people. Approximately 80 percent of corporate revenues are derived from defense work—around 70 percent from selling to the U.S. Defense Department, and another 10 percent from foreign military sales. All international sales, military and commercial, accounted for 17 percent of General Dynamics' sales in 2008.

General Dynamics was formed in 1952 through the combination of the Electric Boat Company, Canadair Limited, and Convair; in 1982, it acquired Chrysler's combat systems division, which manufactured the M1 tank. General Dynamics was the original developer and manufacturer of the F-16 fighter jet, which it sold off to Lockheed in 1993. In addition, the company divested its tactical missile division to Hughes in 1992 and its space systems division to Martin Marietta in 1993.

Afterwards, General Dynamics concentrated mainly on two core businesses of ship construction—acquiring Bath Iron Works and National Steel and Shipbuilding in the late 1990s—and combat vehicles. In the early 2000s, the company bought three armored vehicle manufacturing companies: GM Defense, based in Canada (which in turned owned MOWAG, a Swiss manufacturer of light combat vehicles), Austria's Steyr Daimler Puch Spezialfahrzeug (SSF), and Santa Bárbara Sistemas of Spain. These acquisitions have greatly expanded the company's international footprint. Other recent acquisitions include the

Gulfstream Aerospace Corporation, a business-jet aircraft and aviation support services company, and a number of small companies specializing in information technology products and services.

General Dynamics has four business groups: aerospace, combat systems, marine systems, and information systems and technology. Major products include the Virginia-class nuclear attack submarine, the Arleigh Burke–class Aegis destroyer, the Zumwalt-class (DDG-1000) destroyer, the M1 series Abrams main battle tank, the Stryker armored combat vehicle, the ASCOD armored fighting vehicle, and the MOWAG light armored vehicle (LAV).

Web site: http://www.gd.com

HINDUSTAN AERONAUTICS LIMITED (INDIA)

Hindustan Aeronautics Limited (HAL), based in Bangalore, is India's state-owned monopoly manufacturer of combat aircraft for the Indian armed forces. HAL was founded in 1940 under British rule and passed into Indian government ownership upon independence. It is one of the largest aerospace companies in Asia, with approximately 40,000 employees and sales of $1.6 billion in 2007.

HAL has 19 production units and nine research and design centers at seven locations throughout India. The company has manufactured over 3,500 aircraft, mostly for the Indian Air Force (IAF), including 14 types that were produced under license and 12 locally designed and developed aircraft programs. Key licensed-production programs include the MiG-21, MiG-27, and Jaguar fighter jets; currently, HAL is assembling the Sukhoi Su-30-MKI for the IAF. Indigenous aircraft programs include the HF-24 Marut (developed in the 1960s), the Dhruv advanced light helicopter (ALH), and the Tejas light combat aircraft (LCA). The ALH and LCA are currently in production or development; in particular, the company hopes to sell more than 200 Tejas fighters to the IAF, as well as a naval variant for India's indigenous aircraft carrier program. HAL is also developing an indigenous turbofan engine, the Kaveri, to power the LCA.

Web site: http://www.hal-india.com

ISRAELI AEROSPACE INDUSTRIES (ISRAEL)

State-owned Israeli Aerospace Industries (IAI), formerly Israeli Aircraft Industries, is Israeli's leading aerospace and aviation manufacturer. The company was founded in 1953 as the Bedek Aviation Company, supplying military goods and services to the Israel Defense Forces (IDF). Initially, it was engaged mostly in the maintenance, repair, and overhaul of IDF aviation equipment, along with the licensed production of the French Fouga-Magister trainer jet. In the 1960s and 1970s, it produced the Nesher and Kfir fighter jets, based heavily on the French Mirage 5; these programs were followed by an attempt to develop an indigenous fighter aircraft, the Lavi, which was eventually cancelled in 1987.

Since then, IAI has concentrated on core competencies in military aircraft upgrades, airborne early warning and control (AEW+C) systems, command, control, communications, computing, intelligence, surveillance, and reconnaissance (C4ISR), and electronic warfare systems, advanced radar systems, precision-guided weapons, navigational and electro-optic systems, missiles, and unmanned aerial vehicles (UAVs). Products include the Arrow anti-tactical ballistic missile; the Harpy anti-radiation drone; the Heron, Ranger, Scout, and Searcher UAVs; the Phalcon AEW+C system; the Shavit space launch vehicle; and the EROS, Amos, and Ofeq satellites. Commercial products include the Astra and Galaxy series of small business jets, produced for Gulfstream Aerospace.

IAI currently employs over 16,500 workers. Sales in 2007 totaled $3.3 billion, of which $2.7 billion (82 percent) were from overseas sales.

Web site: http://www.iai.co.il

KOREA AEROSPACE INDUSTRIES (REPUBLIC OF KOREA)

Korea Aerospace Industries (KAI) was formed in late 1999 with the merger of three of South Korea's aircraft companies—Samsung Aerospace, Daewoo Heavy Industries Aerospace Division, and the Hyundai Space and Aircraft Company. KAI currently has 2,800 employees and earned sales in 2008 of approximately $900 million.

KAI is responsible for most of South Korea's key aerospace manufacturing (and particularly military) programs, including the KT-1 turboprop trainer, the F-16 licensed-production line, UAVs, and satellites. It is also producing parts for the F-15K fighter being procured by the Republic of Korea Air Force (ROKAF). Future military projects include the Korean Helicopter Program, to develop and manufacture an indigenous light helicopter for the Korean armed forces. In addition, the company performs a variety of subcontracting work for foreign aerospace companies.

KAI's flagship product is the T-50 Golden Eagle, a supersonic advanced jet trainer (AJT) and the Lead-In Fighter Trainer (the A-50 LIFT), developed jointly with Lockheed Martin. A fighter version (the F/A-50) is also envisioned. The T-50 is being marketed globally as a state-of-the-art trainer jet to prepare pilots to fly next-generation fighters such as the F/A-22, the F-35, the Rafale, and the Eurofighter. KAI expects to export 600 to 800 T-50 variants by 2030 and capture one-quarter of the world's market for this kind of aircraft. So far, the only solids customer has been the ROKAF, for 94 T-50 and A-50 aircraft.

At one time, KAI had expected to become one of the world's top 10 aerospace companies. Its current vision is to be a "total global aerospace solution provider" by 2010, according to its corporate Web site.

Web site: http://www.koreaaero.com

LOCKHEED MARTIN (UNITED STATES)

Lockheed Martin, headquartered in Bethesda, Maryland, has for the past several years been the world's largest defense firm and the number one contractor to the U.S. Department of Defense (DoD). The company was formed in 1995 with the merger of Lockheed with Martin Marietta. It employs about 146,000 people worldwide and reported sales of $42.7 billion in 2008. In 2007, 58 percent of it revenues came from contracting to the U.S. DoD, 27 percent to other U.S. government departments and agencies, and 15 percent from foreign sales. Over 90 percent of Lockheed Martin's revenues come from defense work.

Lockheed Martin is a multifaceted company engaged in a wide variety of defense contracting, including combat aircraft, strategic missile systems, space launch vehicles and satellites, and defense electronics. The company is organized into four broad business areas:

- *Aeronautics* involves the design, development, manufacture, and maintenance of military aircraft. Current aircraft programs include the F-35 Lightning II Joint Strike Fighter (JSF), the F-16 Fighting Falcon, the F-22 Raptor, the F-117 Stealth Fighter, the C-130J Hercules transport aircraft, the C-5 strategic airlifter, and the P-3 maritime patrol aircraft. The company is also involved in the development and production of Japan's F-2 fighter jet and Korea's T-50 Golden Eagle trainer.
- *Electronic Systems* includes missiles and fire control, naval systems, platform integration, simulation, and training. Products include the Hellfire, Javelin, ATACMS tactical missiles, the Patriot PAC-3 and THAAD air-defense missile systems, Paveway laser-guided bombs, and the JASSM (joint air-to-surface standoff missile).
- *Space Systems* includes space launch, commercial satellites, government satellites, and strategic missiles systems. Lockheed Martin is the prime contractor for the U.S. Navy's strategic ballistic missile arsenal (such as the current Trident II D-5 submarine-launched ballistic missile). It is also a key player in the U.S. military's ballistic missile defense programs.
- *Information Systems and Global Services (IS&GS)* includes command, control, communications, computer, and intelligence (C4I) systems, federal services, and government and commercial IT solutions.

Web site: http://www.lockheedmartin.com

MBDA (FRANCE, ITALY, UNITED KINGDOM)

MBDA is Europe's leading missile manufacturer. The company was created in December 2001, after the merger of the main missile producers in France, Italy, and the United Kingdom. The consolidation of Europe's missile sector began in 1996, when parts of Matra Defense and BAe Dynamics (later BAE Systems) merged to form Matra BAe Dynamics (MBD). MBD represented half of Matra Defense's missile business, the other half being Matra Missiles, which became Aérospatiale-Matra Missiles (AMM), when Matra merged with Aérospatiale in 1999, which in 2000 became part of EADS. In 1998, GEC-Marconi Radar and Defense Systems and Alenia Difesa of Italy combined their missile and radar activities to form Alenia Marconi Systems (AMS), which later became part of BAE Systems when GEC was acquired by BAE. Eventually, MBD (including AMM) and the Missile and Missile Systems activities of AMS were merged to form MBDA. In 2006, the German missile manufacturer LFK, owned by EADS, was folded into MBDA. Subsequently, MBDA has three major aeronautical and defense shareholders: BAE Systems (37.5 percent), EADS (37.5 percent) and Finmeccanica (25 percent).

MBDA is a multinational company with over 10,000 employees located in France, the United Kingdom, Italy, and Germany. Major products include the ASRAAM and Meteor air-to-air missiles; the LFK NG surface-to-air missile; the MILAN, PARS 3 LR, ERYX, and Brimstone antitank missiles; the Exocet antiship cruise missile; and the APACHE and Storm

Shadow land-attack cruise missiles. MBDA is also a partner in the Eurosam consortium, which is developing the future surface-to-air family of missiles (FSAF), including the Aster 15 sea-based surface-to-air missile (SAM) and the Aster 30 land-based SAM.

In 2007, the company recorded a turnover of €3 billion ($4.3 billion), produced over 3,000 missiles, and achieved an order book of €13.1 billion ($18.7 billion).

Web site: http://www.mbda-systems.com

MITSUBISHI HEAVY INDUSTRIES (JAPAN)

Mitsubishi Heavy Industries (MHI) is the largest defense contractor in Japan. MHI's aerospace division produces fighter aircraft for the Japan Air Self-Defense Force (ASDF), including the indigenous F-2 fighter (based on the U.S. F-16) and licensed production of the F-15. In the past, MHI has also assembled the U.S.-developed F-4EJ fighter and the UH-60 helicopter. The company also produces several guided weapon systems, including the Patriot air defense missile (built under license), the AAM-3 air-to-air missile, and the Type-88 antiship cruise missile. Other defense products include jet engines, military trucks, and torpedoes.

MHI's shipbuilding division is the lead contractor for the Japan Maritime Self-Defense Force's (MSDF) Atago and Kongō-class guided missile destroyers; these vessels are outfitted with the U.S. Aegis air-defense system, which includes the capability to intercept ballistic missiles. MHI is also one of two shipbuilders in Japan (the other being Kawasaki Shipbuilding) to construct submarines for the MSDF. Past submarines have included the Oyashio and Harushio classes, and currently the company is building the Sōryū-class diesel-electric submarine, which will be equipped with the Stirling engine for air-independent propulsion.

MHI is a highly diversified company that also produces a variety of commercial products, including power systems, wind turbines, air conditioning and refrigeration systems, machine tools, and light rail vehicles. In addition, the company is the prime contractor for Japan's H-IIA space launch vehicle, and it is a partner with Boeing on the B-767, B-777, and B-787 commercial jetliners. MHI as a whole has 63,500 employees and earned about $2.8 billion in defense revenues in 2007, equal to around 10 percent of the company's total sales.

Web site: http://www.mhi.co.jp

NAVANTIA (SPAIN)

Navantia, formerly IZAR, was formed out of the December 2000 merger of Astilleros Españoles S.A. and Empresa Nacional Bazán. Navantia is one of the world's leading naval systems companies, able to undertake new ship construction, lifecycle maintenance, and ship conversion. It has an overall total capacity in the fields of design, development, production, integration and integrated logistic platform support, propulsion, and naval combat systems, as well as the ability to deliver fully operational naval vessels. Navantia's predecessor companies were pioneers in the use of integrated modular construction techniques, which are used in building both surface ships and submarines.

Navantia's current core activities include naval construction, propulsion and energy, ship repairs, and military and civil platform control systems. It operates shipyards in the Ferrol

Estuary (Ferrol and Fene), the Bay of Cadiz (Cadiz, Puerto Real and San Fernando), and Cartagena, and comprises a workforce of approximately 5,600 employees. In 2004, Navantia's enjoyed a turnover of approximately €1.1 billion ($1.3 billion).

Navantia's predecessor companies have produced the *Príncipe de Asturias* aircraft carrier (equipped with the Harrier STOVL jet) and the F-81 frigate; this work expanded in the 1990s to include amphibious landing ships (LPDs), combat support ships, and minehunters. Current Navantia military products are, for the Spanish Navy, the F-100 air-defense frigate, the LHD-type Strategic Projection Ship, and the S-80 diesel-electric submarine, as well as, for export, the F-310 frigate and Scorpène submarines. The F-310 frigate is being built for Norway, while the Scorpène has been sold to Chile and Malaysia; the Scorpène is also capable of being outfitted with air-independent propulsion (AIP) for long-endurance submerged operations. Navantia was also the only company to ever produce an aircraft carrier for export, the *Chakrinaruebet,* to Thailand in the 1990s. It is expected that up to 20 percent of the company's business will be devoted to commercial applications.

Web site: http://www.navantia.es

NORTHROP GRUMMAN (UNITED STATES)

Northrop Grumman, headquartered in Los Angeles, California, is typically among the top 10 defense companies in the world. In 2008, it was the third largest contractor to the U.S. Department of Defense (DoD), and ranked fourth globally. The company has 122,600 employees and earned $32 billion in 2007, of which 90 percent was from sales to the U.S. government. Foreign sales amounted to approximately 5.5 percent of all revenues.

The company was formed by the 1994 merger of Northrop and Grumman. Since then, Northrop Grumman has acquired a number of other defense firms, particularly in the shipbuilding sector; these companies include Westinghouse Electronic Systems Group (radar and other defense electronics), Logicon, Litton Industries (including Litton Ingalls Shipbuilding), Avondale Shipyard, Newport News Shipbuilding and Drydock, and TRW's space business.

Northrop Grumman is organized into five business units:

- *Information and Services,* including information technologies, mission systems (C3I systems), and technical services (logistical support, sustainment, and technical services).
- *Electronics,* such as airborne radar (including the AN/APG-81 active electronically scanned array [AESA], the F-35 Joint Strike Fighter), airborne early warning (AEW) radar, air-to-ground surveillance radar systems, radar jammers, and precision-guided munitions.
- *Aerospace,* including manufacture of the F-35 JSF (in partnership with lead contractor Lockheed Martin), F/A-18 (center and aft fuselage and vertical tail sections), the Global Hawk unmanned high-altitude surveillance aircraft, the Joint STARS ground surveillance, targeting, and battle management aircraft, and the E-2C Hawkeye AEW aircraft.
- *Shipbuilding,* including construction of nuclear-powered aircraft carriers for the U.S. Navy, the Virginia-class submarine, the Arleigh Burke–class Aegis air-defense

destroyers, the LHD-1 helicopter amphibious assault ship, the LPD-17 multipurpose amphibious assault ship, and the National Security Cutter for the U.S. Coast Guard; in addition, Northrop Grumman is part of the team constructing the next-generation Zumwalt-class (DDG 1000) destroyer.

- *Technical Services,* such as base operations and infrastructure support, training and simulation, lifecycle support, and logistics.

Web site: http://www.northropgrumman.com

RAFAEL ARMAMENT DEVELOPMENT AUTHORITY (ISRAEL)

Rafael is an Israeli government-run firm responsible for developing and producing a variety of military equipment for the Israel Defense Forces (IDF) and for the global market. The company was originally a directly owned subsidiary of the Israeli Defense Ministry. Rafael has approximately 5,000 employees and earned $1.3 billion in sales in 2007.

Rafael is Israel's leading missile manufacturer, including the Python 5 and Derby air-to-air missiles, the Popeye air-to-surface missile, the Spike and Matador anti-armor weapons, and the Barak naval air-defense system. In addition, the company has developed passive and reactive armor protection for tanks and armored vehicles, the Litening target pod (which provides combat aircraft with night and adverse-weather ground-attack capabilities utilizing a variety of weapons, such as laser-guided bombs and global positioning system [GPS]-guided weapons), and mine-clearing systems. Many of the company's products have been widely exported around the world; 65 percent of its 2007 revenues were derived from foreign sales, mostly to Europe and to North and South America.

Web site: http://www.rafael.co.il

RAYTHEON (UNITED STATES)

Raytheon, headquartered in Waltham, Massachusetts, is typically among the top 10 defense companies in the world. In 2008, it was the sixth largest contractor to the U.S. Department of Defense (DoD), and ranked sixth globally. In 2008, the company earned $23.2 billion in sales and employed 73,000 people worldwide. Approximately 90 percent of Raytheon's earnings come from defense work, and about 85 percent of its work is for the U.S. government. Raytheon is partnered with Thales of France in Thales-Raytheon Systems, a joint venture that provides surveillance and locating radars, as well as air command and control systems.

Raytheon has four core markets: sensing (such as radar systems); effects (kinetic weapons such as missile systems, offensive information warfare, etc.); command, control, communications, and intelligence systems (C3I); and mission support. In turn, the company is divided into six business divisions:

- *Integrated Defense Systems:* Products include the Patriot air and missile defense system, radar systems, electronic and combat systems, missile defense.
- *Intelligence and Information Systems:* Intelligence-gathering sensors and systems.
- *Missile Systems:* Products include the Sidewinder and AMRAAM air-to-air missiles, the Seasparrow and ESSM sea-based surface-to-air missiles, the advanced cruise

missile (ACM), the joint standoff weapon (JSOW), the TOW anti-armor precision-guided munition, and the Tomahawk cruise missile.

- *Network Centric Systems:* Combat systems, integrated communications systems, and command and control systems; also oversees Thales-Raytheon Systems.
- *Space and Airborne Systems:* Produces radar for combat aircraft (including the APG-63(V)2 active electronically scanned array [AESA] radar for U.S. Air Force F-15C aircraft), other avionics, maritime surveillance radars, terrain following/terrain avoidance radars, and electro-optical and infrared sensors for surveillance, reconnaissance, and targeting mission support.
- *Raytheon Technical Services Company LLC:* Provides specialized technical, scientific, and professional services for defense, federal and commercial customers worldwide, such as counterproliferation and counterterrorism, base and range operations, and customized engineering services.

Web site: http://www.raytheon.com

ROLLS-ROYCE PLC (UNITED KINGDOM)

Rolls-Royce plc is the second-largest aircraft engine producer in the world, behind GE (General Electric) Aviation. Rolls-Royce began as a car manufacturer in the early 20th century, but began building aircraft engines during World War I. It was one of the first companies to design and build gas turbine jet engines, which powered most British fighters during the 1940s, 1950s, and 1960s. Rolls-Royce was nationalized in 1971, but the company's automobile business was split off in 1973. The present Rolls-Royce plc was reprivatized in 1987.

Rolls-Royce operates in four global markets—defense aerospace, civil aerospace, marine, and energy. The company employs 38,000 people, and sales totaled $14.84 billion in 2007, of which defense revenues accounted for about 30 percent. Rolls-Royce has a major subsidiary in North America, through its acquisition of Allison Engines in 1994, and it operates Rolls-Royce Deutschland in Germany, producing the BR700 family of jet engines.

Rolls-Royce is presently a partner in three fighter jet engine programs: the RB-199 (for the Tornado combat aircraft), the Eurojet EJ200 (for the Eurofighter Typhoon), and the F135 (with Pratt and Whitney) and F136 (with GE Engines) engines (for the F-35 Joint Strike Fighter). It also manufactures the Adour engine for the BAE Hawk advanced jet trainer and the Pegasus for the Harrier vertical and/or short take-off and landing (V/STOL) fighter jet. Civil aerospace products include the Trent family of engines for the Airbus A330, A340, A380, and Boeing-777 commercial passenger jets. It is also partner in the International Aero Engines consortium producing the V2500 engine for the Airbus 320 family. Rolls-Royce also manufactures helicopter turboshaft engines and gas turbines for maritime applications.

Web site: http://www.rolls-royce.com

SAAB (SWEDEN)

Saab controls approximately 75 percent of all Swedish arms production, and boasted 13,750 employees in 2008. The company earned 23.8 billion kronor ($3.3 billion) in 2008, of which approximately 82 percent came from defense work. Sixty-eight percent of its revenues came from international sales: 26 percent from Europe, 18 percent from Africa, 14 percent from Asia, 7 percent from the United States, and 3 percent from other markets. Saab has a large industrial footprint in South Africa, through its acquisition of Grintek Technologies and Avitronics, and smaller holdings in Australia, Denmark, and the United States.

Saab was founded in 1937 as Svenska Aeroplan Aktiebolaget, and was responsible for the design, development, and manufacturing of all Swedish fighter aircraft after World War II, including the J-35 Draken, the JA-37 Viggen, and, currently, the JAS-39 Gripen (which has also been sold to the Czech Republic, Hungary, South Africa, and Thailand). The company also manufactures the Erieye airborne early warning and command (AEW+C) aircraft. Beginning in the 1960s, Saab entered the tactical missile business. It currently produces the RBS-15 antiship cruise missile, the BAMSE air-defense system, and the BILL antitank missile; it is also a partner in the international Meteor and IRIS-T air-to-air missile programs and the Taurus land-attack cruise missile. In the late 1990s, Saab acquired Celsius Industries, a partly state-owned holding company that controlled most of Sweden's ordnance, shipbuilding, and defense electronics businesses (the shipbuilding sector was later sold off to HDW of Germany). Nondefense work includes subcontracting to Airbus on parts and components for the A340, A320, and A380 passenger jets and the A400M military transport aircraft, and to Boeing on the 737 and 777 commercial airliners.

Saab comprises three major segments: defense and security solutions (reconnaissance, surveillance, communication, and command and control); systems and products (anti-armor, air-to-air and surface-to-air missiles, torpedoes, electronic warfare systems, radar and sensors, camouflage, and training systems); and aeronautics (Gripen combat aircraft, Erieye AEW+C aircraft). In 2008, these segments represented 36 percent, 35 percent, and 29 percent of corporate sales, respectively.

Web site: http://www.saabgroup.com

SINGAPORE TECHNOLOGIES ENGINEERING (SINGAPORE)

Singapore Technologies Engineering (ST Engineering) is an integrated conglomerate specializing in military aerospace, electronics, land systems, and maritime systems. The company has a global workforce of more than 19,000 employees and earned $5.05 billion in 2007.

ST Engineering is comprised of four main subsidiaries: ST Aerospace (aircraft manufacturing and maintenance), ST Electronics (communications, sensors, software, and combat systems), ST Kinetics (land systems and ordnance), and ST Marine (shipbuilding). Key products include the Bionix armored fighting vehicle, the Terrex armored personnel carrier, the Primus and Pegasus 155 millimeter artillery systems, and the SAR 21 assault rifle. ST Aerospace is mostly engaged in the maintenance, repair, overhaul, and upgrading of military and commercial aircraft; for example, the company upgraded and modernized both F-5 and A-4 combat aircraft for the Republic of Singapore Air Force. ST Aerospace is also a member of the U.S.-led international consortium currently engaged in the development of the F-35 Joint Strike Fighter, and is collaborating with Eurocopter France in manufacturing and marketing the EC-120 light utility helicopter. ST Marine designed and constructed the

Endurance class of amphibious assault ships and produced the French-designed La Fayette frigate under license. The company has also developed considerable expertise in logistics and depot management, the maintenance and overhaul of aircraft engines, and ship repair.

ST Engineering has a major footprint in the United States through its wholly owned subsidiary, Vision Technologies Systems (VT Systems). VT Systems operates the U.S. shipbuilder Halter Marine, and it is also engaged in manufacturing custom truck bodies and trailers, emergency vehicle units, satellite-based broadband, hardened electronic systems, and aircraft maintenance and repair. Additionally, the company holds a 25-percent stake in the Irish company Timoney, which produces suspension systems for armored vehicles.

Web site: http://www.stengg.com

THALES (FRANCE)

Thales (formerly Thomson-CSF), although French-based, is a self-described *multidomestic* firm with production facilities or joint ventures in 12 countries around the world: Australia, Brazil, Germany, Italy, the Netherlands, Portugal, Singapore, South Africa, South Korea, Spain, the United Kingdom, and the United States (Thales-Raytheon Systems, a 50:50 joint venture with Raytheon). Its major business areas include air traffic management, air command and control systems, surveillance and combat systems (such as radar and satellite systems), military communications, avionics, short-range surface-to-air missile systems, surface and underwater naval systems, optronics, information systems and services (such as simulation, training and synthetic environments, information processing systems, computer services, engineering and security), electron tubes, and microelectronics. Thales had 68,000 employees worldwide in 2008, including 34,000 in France 10,000 in the United Kingdom (Thales' second largest country of operation, with around 15 percent of the total company workforce); 3,000 in the United States (including joint ventures); 1,200 in Canada; 3,600 in Australia; and around 16,000 in Europe and the rest of the world.

In 2008, Thales earned revenues totaling €12.7 billion ($18.1 billion). Approximately three-quarters of its income come from defense work. Thales earned 25 percent of its revenues from sales to the French market in 2008; the United Kingdom and the rest of Europe accounted for 38 percent of sales, North America, 9 percent, and the rest of the world, 28 percent.

Thales is organized along three key business areas: aerospace and space (radar, avionics, opto-electronic systems, satellites, and air-traffic control), defense systems (C4ISR and UAVs), and security (electronic and IT security, training and simulation, and facility management). In 2008, defense systems business accounted for 43 percent of corporate revenues; aerospace and space, 33 percent; and security, 24 percent.

Web site: http://www.thalesgroup.com

THYSSENKRUPP MARINE SYSTEMS (GERMANY)

ThyssenKrupp Marine Systems is a German-based multinational company that owns naval shipyards in Germany (Howaldtswerke-Deutsche Werft, or HDW), Sweden (Kockums), and Greece (Hellenic Shipyards Co.). In total, ThyssenKrupp Marine Systems employs approximately 8,500 workers in these three countries. HDW is mostly known for producing diesel-electric submarines, including the Type-209, of which more than 60 versions have been exported to 13 countries. HDW is currently producing the Type-212/214 submarine, which features hydrogen fuel cells for air-independent propulsion (AIP); this class of submarine has been sold to the German, Italian, South Korean, Greek, and Portuguese navies. HDW also produces the F124 Sachsen-class of frigates for the German Navy.

Kockums, based in Malmö, builds both surface ships (including the Visby-class stealth corvette) and submarines, in particular the current Gotland-class family of attack submarines, which is outfitted with the Stirling engine for AIP. Kockums is currently developing the next-generation submarine (NGU) for the Swedish Navy.

Hellenic Shipyards, located near Athens, has built fast-attack boats and frigates, and is currently constructing the Type-214 submarine under license.

Web sites: http://www.thyssenkrupp-marinesystems.com

HDW: http://www.hdw.de

Kockums: http://www.kockums.se

Hellenic Shipyards: http://www.hellenic-shipyards.gr

UNITED TECHNOLOGIES (UNITED STATES)

United Technologies Corporation (UTC) is an American multinational conglomerate engaged in a wide variety of manufacturing and services, including aircraft engines, helicopters, aerospace and space systems, Carrier heating and air conditioning, Otis elevators and escalators, fire and security, and fuel cells. The company has 223,000 employees and earned $58.7 billion in 2008, of which $7.7 billion (13 percent) were from sales to the U.S. government. Approximately 64 percent of UTC's sales were to international clients. UTC is typically among the world's top 10 defense companies, and was the eighth-largest contractor to the U.S. Department of Defense (DoD) in 2008.

UTC's main defense units include Pratt and Whitney engines (13 percent of corporate business) and Sikorsky Aircraft (5.4 percent). Pratt and Whitney employs 38,500 workers, and manufactures the F135 engine for the F-35 Joint Strike Fighter (JSF), the F119 for the F-22, the F100 family of engines for the F-15 and F-16, and the F117 for the C-17 transport aircraft. Pratt and Whitney's Canadian subsidiary produces a wide range of turboprop engines for military and commercial propeller-driven aircraft.

Sikorsky Aircraft was founded in 1925 as an independent company and was acquired by UTC in 1929. Its current military product is the Black Hawk helicopter, which is produced in army (UH-60), naval (SH-60), and commercial (S-70) versions. A larger version is designated the S-92. Sikorsky also owns PZL Mielec, a Polish aircraft manufacturer.

Web sites: http://www.utc.com

Pratt and Whitney: http://www.pw.utc.com

Sikorsky Helicopter: http://www.sikorsky.com

INDEX

ABOUT THE CONTRIBUTORS

Richard A. Bitzinger is a senior fellow with the S. Rajaratnam School of International Studies, Nanyang Technological University, Singapore, where his work focuses on military and defense issues relating to the Asia-Pacific region, including the challenges of defense transformation in the region, regional military modernization activities, and local defense industries, arms production, and weapons proliferation. Mr. Bitzinger is the author of *Towards a Brave New Arms Industry?* (Oxford University Press, 2003), "Come the Revolution: Transforming the Asia-Pacific's Militaries," *Naval War College Review* (Fall 2005), and *Transforming the U.S. Military: Implications for the Asia-Pacific* (Australian Strategic Policy Institute, 2006). He has written several monographs and book chapters, and his articles have appeared in such journals as *International Security, Orbis, China Quarterly,* and *Survival.* Mr. Bitzinger was previously an associate professor with the Asia-Pacific Center for Security Studies (APCSS), Honolulu, Hawaii, and has also worked for the Rand Corporation, the Center for Strategic and Budgetary Affairs, and the U.S. government. In 1999–2000, he was a senior fellow with the Atlantic Council of the United States. He holds a master's degree from the Monterey Institute of International Affairs and has pursued additional postgraduate studies at the University of California, Los Angeles.

J. D. Kenneth Boutin is a lecturer in international relations at Deakin University in Geelong, Australia. He earned a PhD in political science from York University in Toronto, Canada, and worked on arms control issues at the Verification Research, Training and Information Centre in London prior to joining Deakin. His primary research interests are in the area of the political economy of security, including technology policy, defense industrialization, arms transfers, arms control, and economic security, particularly in the context of the United States and the Asia-Pacific region. Dr. Boutin is currently developing a research project examining economic security issues in developed and developing states.

Francis Cevasco is the president of Cevasco International, LLC. His firm provides advice to domestic and international aerospace and defense corporations about strategic positioning, defense acquisition programs, and strategic partnering. His firm also prepares studies for the U.S. Department of Defense and for Washington think tanks regarding transatlantic security, cooperative research, development, and acquisition (RD&A) programs, export control reform, and export sales reform. Prior to entering the private sector he served as assistant deputy under secretary of defense for international development and production programs where he was principal resident advisor to several under secretaries of defense for Acquisition, Technology, and Logistics (AT&L) regarding international program cooperation and international agreements.

Peter Dombrowski is a professor of strategy and chair of the Strategic Research Department at the U.S. Naval War College. He has been affiliated with several other research institutions, including the East-West Centre, the Brookings Institution, the Friedrich Ebert Foundation, and the Watson Institute for International Studies at Brown University. He has written over 35 articles, monographs, book chapters, and government reports.

J. Paul Dunne is Professor of Economics in the Faculty of Humanities, Languages and Social Sciences at the University of the West of England, Bristol. He was previously Research Professor in Economics at Middlesex University and has held posts at Birkbeck College, Warwick University, Department of Applied Economics and Magdalene College, University of Cambridge, and the University of Leeds. He is an applied economist whose main area of research is the economics of military spending. He has undertaken a wide range of research in this area including the economic effects of military spending, industrial restructuring and conversion, employment issues, investment, the economics of the arms trade.

Philip Finnegan is director of corporate analysis at the Teal Group. He has provided strategic and market analysis for clients in commercial aerospace and defense, including major U.S. and European prime contractors. He also writes and edits Teal's *Defense and Aerospace Companies Briefing Book,* which analyzes the performance, outlook, and strategies of 50 aerospace and defense companies in the United States, Europe, Asia, and South America. Before he joined the Teal Group, Mr. Finnegan covered business trends and international security issues for *Defense News,* a leading publication covering the worldwide defense industry. Earlier, he worked for a year covering Central America as a special correspondent for the *U.S. News and World Report,* based in El Salvador, and for two years as a special correspondent for *Time* based in Cairo, Egypt, covering the Middle East. He earned a BA in modern European history from Carleton College, an MA in modern European history from Stanford University, and an MA in economics from the American University in Washington.

Keith Hayward is currently head of research at the Royal Aeronautical Society. He was formerly head of economic and political affairs at the Society of British Aerospace Companies and professor of international relations at Staffordshire University. Professor Hayward has been a consultant to the U.K. House of Commons Trade and Industry Committee, the U.S.

Congress Office of Technology Assessment, the U.K. Ministry of Defence, and the Department of Trade and Industry. He has written extensively on defense and aerospace industry issues, and has published over 50 books and articles on the subject. He is an associate fellow of the Royal United Services Institute and a visiting professor at Staffordshire and Cranfield Universities.

Aaron Karp is lecturer in political science at Old Dominion University in Norfolk, Virginia, and senior consultant to the Small Arms Survey in Geneva, Switzerland. He was previously arms trade project leader at the Stockholm International Peace Research Institute and fellow in economics and security with the Whitehead Center for International Affairs at Harvard University. He is co-editor of the journal *Contemporary Security Policy* and the Routledge book series *Global Security Studies*. His most recent books are *Global Insurgency and the Future of Armed Conflict* (2007), and *Inconspicuous Disarmament* (2009).

Eugene Kogan holds a BA and MA in history from Tel Aviv University. In 1990, he received his PhD in history from Warwick University in the United Kingdom. His thesis examined the evacuation of Soviet military industries from the war zone in 1941–1942. Dr Kogan is a noted expert in the field of defense technologies. He has held a series of research fellowships at some of Europe's most renowned research institutes, including Deutsche Gesellschaft für Auswaertige Politik, Stiftung Wissenschaft und Politik, the Swedish Defense Research Agency, the Swedish National Defense College, and the Institute of History of the Russian Academy of Sciences. In addition to all of this, he has also conducted research at Harvard University. Recently, he was attached as guest researcher to the Center for Pacific Asia Studies (CPAS) at Stockholm University and to the Department of International Relations at Middle East Technical University (METU).

Curie Maharani is currently an associate research fellow with the S. Rajaratnam School of International Studies at Nanyang Technological University in Singapore, and an MPhil student in defense acquisition at Cranfield University, United Kingdom. Prior to that, she had worked as a program consultant for the Geneva Center for the Democratic Control of Armed Forces' Security Sector Reform Project at the Friedrich Ebert Stiftung Office for Indonesia, and was the program manager for Asia at the Center for Security Sector Management, Cranfield University. She has published several articles in newspapers and journals on defense technology and acquisition issues surrounding Indonesia, Singapore, and Thailand. Her particular interest is on acquisition challenges faced by the small defense economies.

Ron Matthews is professor in defense economics and deputy director of the Institute of Defense and Strategic Studies at S. Rajaratnam School of International Studies, Nanyang Technological University, Singapore. He holds the following degrees: BSc in behavioral sciences (Aston University); MSc in financial economics (University of Wales); MBA (Warwick University); and PhD in development economics (Glasgow University). Professor Matthews's research interests focus on defense industrialization (particularly in relation to Asia-Pacific), countertrade, technology transfer, and civil-military integration. He has been awarded research fellowships from NATO and the World Bank, has been a visiting researcher at the Hoover Institute of War, Revolution and Peace (Stanford University), Capetown University, the National University of Singapore, and the Institute of Strategic Studies, Islamabad. He is presently also a visiting professor at Cranfield University, U.K. Defense Academy, at the Institute of Technology, Bandung, Indonesia, and at the Malaysian National Defense University. Professor Matthews has lectured at Harvard University and numerous other universities and institutions in North America, Europe, and the Far East. He has also written and edited several books and numerous articles on defense industrialization. The most recent publication (co-edited with Jack Treddenick) is titled *Managing the Revolution in Military Affairs*. In 2006, Professor Matthews provided evidence to the House of Commons Select Committee on the U.K. defense-industrial strategy.

Stephanie G. Neuman is director of the Comparative Defense Studies Program, a senior research scholar at the Saltzman Institute of War and Peace, and adjunct professor of third world security studies at Columbia University. She has also taught at the Graduate Faculty of the New School for Social Research and at the United States Military Academy (West Point). Dr. Neuman is the recipient of many research grants and fellowships, including a Senior Fulbright Fellowship to Sweden (1995). She has also served as a consultant to several U.S. government agencies and, from 1996 to 2006, was a member of the U.S. Department of State Defense Trade Advisory Group. Dr. Neuman has served on the editorial board of several professional journals. Most recently she was chair of the editorial advisory board of *International Studies Perspectives,* 2003–2008. Dr. Neuman publishes widely in the fields of third world security affairs, defense industries, and the international arms trade. She is currently working on a book, *Security Assistance and Political Influence,* to be published by Columbia University Press. Her publications include: "Defense Industries and Global Dependency," ORBIS, summer 2006; *Warfare and the Third World* (St. Martin's/Palgrave, 2001, co-authored with Robert Harkavy); *International Relations Theory and the Third World,* ed. (St. Martins, 1998).

The Program on Military Expenditure and Arms Production at the Stockholm International Peace Research Institute (SIPRI) monitors, describes, and analyzes trends and developments in military expenditure and arms production worldwide. The SIPRI program on arms production was initiated in 1989 to study developments in the arms industry. The program collects information on the major arms-producing companies and describes and analyses their adjustment to the changed economic and political context and the resulting changes in industrial structures. The SIPRI Program on Military Expenditure and Arms Production is led by Dr. Elisabeth Sköns.

Andrew L. Ross is director of the Center for Science, Technology, and Policy and professor of political science at the University of New Mexico. He has held research fellowships at Cornell, Princeton, Harvard, the University of Illinois, and the U.S. Naval War College. His work on U.S. grand strategy, national security, defense planning, regional security, weapons proliferation, security, and economics and public policy has appeared in numerous journals and books.

Bernard Udis is a professor emeritus of economics at the University of Colorado (Boulder) and currently serves as a visiting research professor at the U.S. Naval Postgraduate School (NPS) in Monterey, California. His work at NPS has dealt with offsets in defense trade, the Joint Strike Fighter partnership, the experiences of several major European firms in penetrating the U.S. defense market, prospects for a Pan-Nordic defense bloc, and U.S. export control policy. His earlier work has focused on the costs of NATO expansion; differences between arms export controls and classic arms control; the possible role of Japan in a military technical revolution; influences on enlistments in the U.S. volunteer force; and the role of industrial policy in aiding a shift to a reduced level of military spending. He has held Rockefeller, National Science Foundation, and NATO research grants and has served as distinguished visiting professor of economics at the U.S. Air Force Academy, and as a William C. Foster fellow at the U.S. Arms Control and Disarmament Agency.

Kathleen A. Walsh is assistant professor of national security affairs at the U.S. Naval War College. In 2007, she served on a national research council study on the future of the National Defense Stockpile. Ms. Walsh is author of numerous articles, studies, briefings, and testimonies, including "National Security Challenges and Competition: Defense and Space R&D in the Chinese Strategic Context," *Technology in Society* (co-author, 2008); "Soaring Eagle, Flying Dragon: Industrial R&D and Innovation in the United States and China," proceedings of the U.S.-China Forum on Science and Technology Policy (VA: George Mason University, 2007); "Civil-Military Dynamics in Chinese Defense Industry and Arms Policy: An Approaching Tipping Point," *Chinese Civil-Military Relations: The Transformation of the People's Liberation Army,* Nan Li, ed. (London: Routledge, 2006); and *Foreign High-Tech R&D in China: Risks, Rewards, and Implications for US-China Relations* (Stimson Center, June 2003). Previously, she was an independent consultant (2004–2005), a senior associate at the Stimson Center (2000–2004), and a senior associate for a Washington defense contracting firm (1997–2000). She holds an MA in international security policy from the School of International and Public Affairs, Columbia University, and a BA in international affairs from the Elliott School of International Affairs, George Washington University.